Medications and Mothers' Milk

1998-1999

Thomas W. Hale, R.Ph., Ph.D.
Associate Professor of Pediatrics
Associate Professor of Pharmacology
Division of Clinical Pharmacology
Texas Tech University School of Medicine
Amarillo, Texas 79106

Medications and Mothers' Milk

1998 Edition

© Copyright 1992-1998

Pharmasoft Medical Publishing

(806)-358-8138
(800)-378-1317

DISCLAIMER

The information contained in this publication is intended to supplement the knowledge of health care professionals regarding drug use during lactation. This information is advisory only and is not intended to replace sound clinical judgement or individualized patient care. The author disclaims all warranties, whether expressed or implied, including any warranty as to the quality, accuracy, safety, or suitability of this information for any particular purpose.

ISBN   0-9636219-0-4

Dr. Hales # for refer.
806-354-5529
Ruth Lawrence Hotline -

Ordering Information

716-275-0088

Pharmasoft Medical Publishing
21 Tascocita Circle
Amarillo, Tx 79124-7301
8:00 AM to 5:00 PM CST

Call......	**806-358-8138**
Sales....	**800-378-1317**
FAX....	**806-356-9480**

Single Copies	**19.95**
Shipping	**3.00**
	————
Total (USA)	**22.95**

(Texas Residents add 8.25% sales tax)
Prices effective until April 1, 1999

Multiple Copies

1-9	Copies............19.95
10-19	Copies............18.95
20-100	Copies............17.95
> 100	Call

Common Abbreviations

AHL=	Adult elimination half-life
M/P	Milk:Plasma Ratio
PK=	Time to peak plasma level
Vd	Volume of Distribution
PB=	Percent of protein binding in maternal circulation
PHL=	Pediatric elimination half-life
Oral=	Oral bioavailability (adult)
μg/L	Microgram per liter
ng/L	Nanogram per liter
mg/L	Milligram per liter
mL	Milliliter. One cc
Fax #	Fax document number. See appendix for description
NSAIDs	Non-steroidal anti-inflammatory
ACEi	Angiotensin converting enzyme inhibitor
MAOI	Monoamine oxidase inhibitors
Vd	Volume of Distribution
MW	Molecular Weight
μCi	Microcurie of Radioactivity
mmol	Millimole of weight
Cmax	Plasma concentration at peak.

Preface

It is now clear that exclusive breastfeeding significantly reduces the incidence of major newborn illnesses. Documented reductions in the incidence of otitis media, SIDS, viral diarrhea, necrotizing enterocolitis, and a reduced morbidity with respiratory syncytial virus (RSV) infections are now indisputable evidence that breastfeeding should be the preferred method for feeding an infant. Pediatric departments and neonatal nurseries are increasingly recommending breastfeeding as medically preferred therapy in all patients, because it is a natural form of self-immunization for the infant. The publication by the American Academy of Pediatrics of recommendations urging longer breastfeeding in newborn infants was tacit approval by a major medical body that breastfeeding is immunologically and nutritionally the best way to feed infants. Provided with evidence by numerous publications that breast fed infants are not only healthier but may also gain in developmental skills as well, the Academy finally felt that the evidence was overwhelming and justified a stronger stance by this large body of pediatricians.

With this added evidence, many mothers are now increasingly resistant to discontinuing breastfeeding just to take a medication, particularly if the interruption is based solely on the recommendation of their physician. Although interrupting breastfeeding may seem safest to the physician, it is not physiologically or psychologically optimal for the infant or the mother. It is currently known, that most medications have few side effects in breastfeeding infants because the dose transferred via milk is almost always too low to be clinically relevant, or it is poorly bioavailable to the infant.

Preface

Certainly, all medications penetrate milk to some degree. With few exceptions, the concentrations of most medications in human milk are exceedingly low, and the dose delivered to the breast fed infant is often subclinical. It is important for practitioners to understand that breastfeeding an infant provides a strong and unique bond between mother and child, and disrupting this bonding for unfounded reasons is unwarranted and certain to cause conflict between the mother and physician. It is important for the clinician to closely review the documentation on drugs and their levels in human breast milk prior to making decisions that have profound effects on nursing infants. Further, it is important that clinicians understand that almost without exception, pharmaceutical manufacturers' inserts discourage breastfeeding solely for fear of litigation, seldom for well founded pharmacologic reasons. Hence, the PDR is not the best source for obtaining accurate breastfeeding information.

The amount of drug excreted into milk depends on a number of factors: 1) the lipid solubility of the drug, 2) the molecular size of the drug, 3) the blood level attained in the maternal circulation, 4) protein binding in the maternal circulation, 5) oral bioavailability in the infant and mother, and 6) the half-life in the maternal and infant's plasma compartments. Although this is somewhat simplistic for a terribly sophisticated and somewhat obscure system, these pharmacokinetic terms provide a reasonably complete system for evaluating drug penetration into milk and the degree of exposure of the infant.

Drugs enter milk primarily by diffusion driven by equilibrium forces between the maternal plasma compartment and maternal milk compartment. They pass from the maternal plasma through capillary walls into the alveolar cell lining the milk buds. Medications must generally pass through both lipid membranes of the alveolar cell to penetrate milk, although early on, they may pass between alveolar cells. During the first 4 to 10 days of life, large gaps between alveolar cells exist. These gaps permit enhanced access for most drugs, many immunoglobulins, and other maternal proteins to the milk. Soon after the first week, the alveolar cells swell under the influence of prolactin, subsequently closing the intracellular gaps and limiting access to the milk. It is generally agreed, that medications penetrate into milk more during the neonatal period than in mature milk. Although not identical, drug entry into human milk is restricted by a tight secretory epithelial system similar to the blood-brain barrier.

In most instances, the most important determinant of drug penetration into milk is the mother's plasma level. Almost without exception, as the level of the medication in the mother's plasma rises, the concentration in milk begins its rise as well. Drugs both enter milk, and in almost all cases, exit milk as a function of the mother's plasma level. As soon as the maternal plasma level of a medication begins to fall, equilibrium forces drive the medication out of the milk compartment back into the maternal plasma. In some instances, drugs become ion trapped in milk, meaning that due to the slightly lower pH of human milk, the physicochemical structure of the drug changes, and prevents its exit back into the maternal circulation. This is important in weakly basic drugs, and iodides such as ^{131}I. In these instances, the drug may concentrate in milk at high milk:plasma ratios.

Of the many factors, perhaps the two most important and useful are the degree of protein binding, and lipid solubility. Drugs that are extremely lipid soluble, penetrate milk in higher concentrations almost without exception. Of particular interest are the drugs that are active in the central nervous system (CNS). CNS-active drugs invariably have the unique characteristic

Preface

requisite to enter milk. Therefore, if a drug is active in the central nervous system, higher drug levels in milk can be expected. Protein binding also plays an important role. Drugs circulate in the maternal plasma either bound to albumin, or freely soluble in the plasma. It is the free component (unbound) that transfers into milk, while the bound fraction stays in the maternal circulation. Therefore, drugs that have high maternal protein binding (warfarin), have a reduced milk level, simply because they are excluded from the milk compartment.

Once a drug has entered the mother's milk and has been ingested by the infant, it must traverse through the infant's GI tract prior to absorption. Some drugs are poorly stable in this environment due to the proteolytic enzymes and acids. In general, the infant's stomach is quite acidic and can denature many drugs. This includes the aminoglycoside family, omeprazole, and large peptide drugs such as heparin or insulin. Other drugs have poor oral absorption kinetics (oral bioavailability) and are poorly absorbed into the infant's blood stream. Oral bioavailability is a useful tool to estimate just how much of the drug will be absorbed by the infant. In addition, many drugs are sequestered in the liver (first pass) and may never actually reach the plasma compartment where they are active. These absorption problems tend ultimately to reduce the overall effect of many drugs. There are certainly exceptions to this rule, and one must always be aware that the action of a drug in the GI tract can also be profound, producing diarrhea, constipation, and sometimes syndromes such as pseudomembranous colitis.

Although there are many exceptions, a good rule of thumb is that less than 1% of the "maternal dose" of a drug will ultimately find its way into the milk and subsequently the infant (although there are wide variations).

General Rules for the Clinician

1. Determine if the drug is absorbed from the GI tract. Many drugs such as the aminoglycosides, vancomycin, cephalosporin antibiotics (third generation), morphine, magnesium salts and other drugs are so poorly absorbed that it is unlikely the infant will absorb significant quantities. At the same time, be observant for GI side effects from the medication trapped in the GI compartment of the infant (diarrhea).

2. Review the monograph provided herein on the drug. Determine if the milk:plasma ratio is high (>1). Determine if the amount absorbed by the infant has been reported to produce side effects. Review the theoretical dose absorbed, and compare that to the pediatric dose if known. Although useful, the milk:plasma ratio has one great weakness, and that is that it is only a ratio. It does not provide a user with information as to the absolute amount of drug transferred to the infant via milk. Even if the drug has a high milk:plasma ratio, if the maternal plasma level of the medication is very small (such as with propranolol), then the absolute amount (dose) of a drug entering milk will still be quite small and often subclinical.

3. Try to choose shorter half-life drugs, as they generally peak rapidly and just as rapidly, dissipate from the maternal plasma thus exposing the milk compartment (and the infant) to reduced levels of medication. Urge the mother not to breastfeed while the drug is at its peak level in the maternal plasma. Determine the time-to-peak interval, as this will indicate how long the mother must wait before feeding. However, you must first determine the dosage form administered. If the tablet formulation is

a prolonged release form, then all prior assumptions about half-life are pointless, and you must assume that the drug has a long half-life (12-24 hrs).

4.   Be cautious of drugs (or their active metabolites) that have long pediatric half-lives, as they can continually build up in the infant's plasma over time.   The barbiturates, benzodiazepines, meperidine, and fluoxetine are classic examples where higher levels in the infant can and do occur.

5.   If you are provided a choice, choose drugs that have higher protein binding, because they are more often sequestered in the maternal circulation and do not transfer as readily to the milk or the infant. Without doubt, the most important parameter that determines drug penetration into milk is protein binding. Choose drugs with high protein binding.

6.   Although not always true, I have generally found that drugs that affect the brain, frequently penetrate milk in higher levels simply due to their chemistry. If the drug in question produces sedation, depression, or other neuroleptic effects in the mother, it is likely to penetrate the milk, with similar, although reduced, effects in the infant. Sedative drugs may contribute to an elevated risk of SIDS, although this is poorly documented.

7.   Be cautious of herbal drugs, many contain chemical substances that may be dangerous to your infant. Numerous poisoning have been reported. Prior to using, contact a lactation consultant or herbalist who is knowledgeable about their use in breastfeeding mothers..

8.   With radioactive compounds, or for any dangerous drug,

wait at least 5 half-lives before re-starting breastfeeding. After 5 half-lives, approximately 98% of a drug or radioisotope is eliminated.

9. Calculate the daily dose received by the infant via breast milk using the information provided herein. The peak milk levels published provide the clinician with enough information to estimate a maximum dose to the infant. This is the most important method for determining risk.

Finally, the critical ingredient required to determine if you must stop breastfeeding is documentation of a real and substantial risk to the infant. It is no longer acceptable for the clinician to interrupt lactation merely because of heightened anxiety on their part. There are few drugs that have well documented and significant toxicity in infants as a result of breastfeeding and we know most of these. On the other hand, both the mother and the clinician should always be cautious when using medications in breastfeeding mothers, and in those instances where they are not necessary, they should be avoided.

The following review of drugs is a compilation of what we currently know, or don't know, about the use of medications during breastfeeding. One of the most useful tools in determining risk to the infant is to simply calculate the daily dose an infant would receive. By using the published concentrations of medication per liter of milk, one can simply calculate the absolute maximal dose an infant would receive via ingestion of his/her mother's milk. The milk levels published herein are primarily the "peak levels" and in general the actual amount transferred would be significantly less.

With this edition, I have added one new field of information called **Alternatives**. This field provides the user

Preface

with information as to other drugs which may be suitable for a breastfeeding patient. Please remember, that some drugs have very specific actions and unique uses. Therefore, the alternate medications listed may not be suitable for that patient. Only the healthcare professional can determine this.

This new edition, in addition to a large number of new drugs and numerous changes to existing drugs, now has a more thorough listing of Canadian, Australian, and United Kingdom trade names which have been provided and reviewed by consultant pharmacists in their respective countries. New tables in the appendix now contain the names of most radiopaque agents and their trade names.

THE AUTHOR MAKES NO RECOMMENDATIONS AS TO THE SAFETY OF THESE MEDICATIONS DURING LACTATION, BUT ONLY REVIEWS WHAT IS CURRENTLY KNOWN IN THE SCIENTIFIC LITERATURE. Individual use of medications must be left up to the judgement of the physician, the patient, and the healthcare consultant.

Because of the numerous health benefits of breastfeeding it has become increasingly important that all healthcare providers strive to support breastfeeding. This is in the best interest of the mother, certainly the infant, and society in general. Far too often, breastfeeding mothers are urged to discontinue breastfeeding because the physician is ill-informed concerning breastfeeding and various medications. Hopefully this work will provide a higher level of comfort for the prescribing physician concerning the medication and its use in breastfeeding mothers.

Thomas W. Hale

How to Use this Book

This section of the book is designed to aid the reader in determining risk to an infant from maternal medications, and in using the pharmacokinetic parameters throughout this reference.

Drug Name and Generic Name.
Each monograph begins with the generic name of the drug. Several of the most common USA trade names are provided under the *Trade:* section.

Can/Aus/UK:
Most, but not all, of the most common trade names used in Canada, Australia, and the United Kingdom are provided.

Uses:
This lists the general use of the medication, such as penicillin antibiotic, or antiemetic, or analgesic, etc. Remember, many drugs have multiple uses in many syndromes. I have only listed the most common use.

Fax # :
The Fax # is the document number for requesting an automated faxed document to be sent to the fax number of your choosing. Each faxed document is specially formatted for automated transmission 24 hours/day. There is a registration fee and small charge for use. See Lactation Fax Hotline.

AAP:
This entry, lists the recommendation provided by the American Academy of Pediatrics as published in their document, *The*

transfer of drugs and other chemicals into human milk *(Pediatrics 93:137-150, 1994).* Drugs are listed in tables according to the following recommendations: *Drugs that are contraindicated during breastfeeding; Drugs of abuse: Contraindicated during breastfeeding; Radioactive compounds that require temporary cessation of breastfeeding; Drugs whose effects on nursing infants is unknown but may be of concern; Drugs that have been associated with significant effects on some nursing infants and should be given to nursing mothers with caution; and Maternal medication usually compatible with breastfeeding.* In this book, the AAP recommendations have be paraphrased to reflect these recommendations. Because the AAP recommendations are somewhat out of date, "Not Reviewed" simply implies that the drug has not yet been reviewed by this committee. The author recommends that each user review these recommendations for further detail.

Drug Monograph
The drug monograph lists what we currently understand about the drug, its ability to enter milk, the concentration in milk at set time intervals, and other parameters that are important to a clinical consultant. I have attempted at great length to report only what the references have documented.

Alternatives:
Drugs listed in this section may be suitable alternate choices for the medication listed above. In many instances, if the patient cannot take the medication, or it is a poor choice due to high milk levels, these alternates may be suitable candidates. **WARNING**: The alternates listed are only suggestions and may not be at all proper for the syndrome in question. Only the clinician can make this judgement. For instance, nifedipine is a calcium channel blocker with good antihypertensive qualities, but poor antiarrhythmic qualities. In this case, verapamil would be a better choice.

Pregnancy Risk Category:

Pregnancy risk categories have been assigned to almost all medications by their manufacturers, and are based on the level of risk the drug poses to the fetus during gestation. They are not useful in assigning risk via breastfeeding. The FDA has provided these five categories to indicate the risk associated with the induction of birth defects. Unfortunately they do not indicate the importance of when during gestation the medication is used, since some drugs are more dangerous during certain trimesters of pregnancy. The definitions provided below are however, a useful tool in determining the possible risks associated with using the medication during pregnancy. Some newer medications may not yet have pregnancy classifications and are therefore not provided herein.

Category A: Controlled studies in women fail to demonstrate a risk to the fetus in the first trimester (and there is no evidence of a risk in later trimesters), and the possibility of fetal harm appears remote.

Category B: Either animal-reproduction studies have not demonstrated a fetal risk, but there are no controlled studies in pregnant women or animal-reproduction studies have shown an adverse effect (other than a decrease in fertility) that was not confirmed in controlled studies in women in the first trimester (and there is no evidence of a risk in later trimesters).

Category C: Either studies in animals have revealed adverse effects on the fetus (teratogenic or embryocidal, or other) and there are no controlled studies in women or studies in women and animals are not available. Drugs should be given only if the potential benefit justifies the potential risk to the fetus.

Category D: There is positive evidence of human fetal risk, but the benefits from use in pregnant women may be acceptable despite the risk (e.g., if the drug is needed in a life-threatening situation or for a serious disease for which safer drugs cannot be used or are ineffective).

Category X: Studies in animals or human beings have demonstrated fetal abnormalities, or there is evidence of fetal risk based on human experience, or both, and the risk of the use of the drug in pregnant women clearly outweighs any possible benefit. The drug is contraindicated in women who are or may become pregnant.

Adult Concerns:
This section lists the most prevalent undesired or bothersome side effects listed for adults. As with most medications, the occurrence of these is often quite rare, generally less than 1-10% of the time. Side effects vary from one patient to another and should not be overemphasized, since most patients do not experience untoward effects.

Pediatric Concerns:
This section lists the side effects noted in the published literature as associated with medications transferred **via human milk**. Pediatric concerns are those effects that were noted by investigators as being associated with drug transfer via milk. They are not the effects that would result from direct administration to the infant. In some sections, I have added comments that may not have been reported in the literature, but are well known attributes of this medication and are useful information to provide the mother so that she can better care for her infant ("Observe for weakness, apnea").

AHL=

This lists the most commonly recorded adult half-life of the medication. It is very important to remember that short half-life drugs are preferred. Use this parameter to determine if the mother can successfully breastfeed around the medication, by nursing the infant... then taking the medication. If the half-life is short enough (1-3 hrs), then the drug level in the maternal plasma will be declining when the infant feeds again. This is ideal. If the half-life is significantly long (12-24 hrs), and if your physician is open to suggestions, then find a similar medication with a shorter half-life (compare ibuprofen with Naproxen). I have provided "Family" tables in the back of this text, so you can compare family members for half-lives and other kinetic parameters.

PHL=

This lists the most commonly recorded pediatric half-life of the medication. Medications with extremely long half-lives in pediatric patients may accumulate to high levels in the infant's plasma if the half-life is exceeding long(>12 hrs.). Pediatric half-lives are difficult to find due to the paucity of studies.

M/P=

This lists the Milk:plasma ratio. This is the ratio of the concentration of drug in the mother's *milk* divided by the concentration in the mother's *plasma*. If high (> 1-5) it is useful as an indicator of drugs that may sequester in milk in high levels. If low (< 1.0) it is a good indicator that only minimal levels of the drug are transferred into milk (this is preferred). Always try to choose drugs with LOW milk:plasma ratios. However it is important to remember, that some drugs with high M:P ratios also have very low maternal plasma levels, hence the absolute amount transferred to the infant is still minimal.

PK=

This lists the time interval from administration of the drug, until it reaches the highest level in the mother's plasma, which we call the *Peak*. The peak is when you do not want the mother to breastfeed her infant, rather, wait until the peak is subsiding or has at least dropped significantly. Remember, drugs enter breast milk as a function of the maternal plasma concentration. The higher the mom's plasma level, the greater the entry of the drug into her milk. If possible, choose drugs that have short peak intervals, and don't let mom breastfeed when it peaks.

PB=

This lists the percentage of maternal protein binding. Most drugs circulate in the blood bound to plasma albumin. If a drug is highly protein bound, it cannot exit the plasma compartment as well. The higher the percentage of binding, the less likely the drug is to enter the maternal milk. Try to choose drugs that have high protein binding, in order to reduce the infants exposure to the medication. Good protein binding is typically greater than 90%.

Oral=

Oral bioavailability refers to the ability of a drug to reach the systemic circulation after oral administration. It is generally a good indication of the amount of medication that is absorbed into the blood stream of the patient. Drugs with low oral bioavailability are generally either poorly absorbed in the gastrointestinal tract, or they are sequestered by the liver prior to entering the plasma compartment. The oral bioavailability listed in this text is the adult value; almost none have been published for children or neonates. Recognizing this, these values are still useful in estimating if a mother or perhaps an infant will actually absorb enough drug to provide clinically significant levels in the plasma compartment of the individual. The value listed estimates the percent of an oral dose that would be found in the plasma compartment of the individual after oral administration. In many cases, the oral bioavailability of some medications is not listed by manufacturers, but instead, terms such as "Complete", "Nil", or "Poor" are used. For lack of better data, I have included these terms when no data is available on the exact amount (percentage) absorbed.

Vd=
The volume of distribution is a useful kinetic term that describes how widely the medication is distributed in the body. Drugs with high volumes of distribution (Vd) are distributed in higher concentrations in remote compartments of the body, and may not stay in the blood. For instance, digoxin enters the blood compartment and then rapidly leaves to enter the heart and skeletal muscle. Most of the drug is sequestered in these remote compartments (100 fold). Therefore, drugs with high volumes of distribution (1-20 liter/kg) generally require much longer to clear from the body than drugs with smaller volumes (0.1 liter/kg). For instance, whereas it may only require a few hours to totally clear gentamycin (Vd=0.28 l/kg) it may require weeks to clear amitriptyline (Vd=10 l/kg) which has a huge volume of distribution. In addition, some drugs may have one half-life for the plasma compartment, but may have a totally different half-life for the peripheral compartment, as half-life is a function of volume of distribution. For a complete description of Vd, please consult a good pharmacology reference. In this text, the units of measure for Vd are liters/kg.

pKa=
The pKa of a drug is the pH at which the drug is equally ionic and nonionic. The more ionic a drug is, the less capable it is of transferring from the milk compartment to the maternal plasma compartment. Hence they become trapped in milk (ion-trapping). This term is useful, because drugs that have a pKa higher than 7.2 may be sequestered to a slightly higher degree than one with a lower pKa. Drugs with higher pKa generally have higher milk:plasma ratios. Hence, choose drugs with a

lower pKa.

Drug Interactions:
Drug interactions generally indicate which medications, when taken together, may produce higher or lower plasma levels of other medications, or they may decrease or increase the effect of another medication. These effects may vary widely from minimal to dangerous. Because some medications have hundreds of interactions, and because I had limited room to provide this information, I have listed only those that may be significant. Therefore please be advised that this section may not be complete. In several references, I have suggested that due to the large number of interactions the reader consult a more complete drug interaction reference.

MW=
The molecular weight of a medication is a significant determinant as to the entry of that medication into human milk. Medications with small molecular weights (< 200) can easily pass into milk by traversing small pores in the cell walls of the mammary epithelium (see ethanol). Drugs with higher molecular weights must traverse the membrane by dissolving in the lipid bilayers, which may significantly reduce milk levels. As such the smaller the molecular weight, the higher the relative transfer of that drug into milk. Protein medications (Heparin, Insulin) which have enormous molecular weights, are virtually excluded from human breast milk. Therefore, when possible, choose drugs with higher molecular weights to reduce their entry into milk.

Acebutolol   Fax #1001

Trade: Sectral, Monitan
Can/Aus/UK: Monitan, Sectral
Uses: Antihypertensive, beta blocker
AAP: Approved by the American Academy of Pediatrics for use in breastfeeding mothers

Acebutolol is predominately a beta-1 blocker, but can block beta-2 receptors at high doses. It is low in lipid solubility, and contains some intrinsic sympathetic activity (partial beta agonist activity). It increases cold sensitivity . Studies indicate that on a weight basis, acebutolol is approximately 10-30% as effective as propranolol. It is 35-50% bioavailable orally. After relatively high doses in animal studies, acebutolol does not appear to be overly teratogenic or harm the fetus. Acebutolol is well tolerated by pregnant hypertensive women. Acebutolol and diacetolol (its major metabolite) appear in breast milk with a milk:plasma ratio of 1.9 to 9.2 (acebutolol) and 2.3 to 24.7 for the metabolite (diacetolol). These levels are considered relatively high and occurred following maternal doses of 400-1200 mg/day. Approximately 3.5% of the maternal dose is secreted into milk. When the metabolite is added, the dose may approach 10% of maternal dose. Neonates appear much more sensitive to acebutolol. Initial Adult Dosage = 200-400 mg/day. It is usually given once to twice daily.

Alternatives: Propranolol, Metoprolol

Pregnancy Risk Category: B

Adult Concerns: Hypotension, bradycardia, and transient tachypnea have been reported. Drowsiness has been reported.

Pediatric Concerns: Hypotension, bradycardia, and transient tachypnea have been reported. Drowsiness has been reported.

Drug Interactions: Decreased effect when used with aluminum salts, barbiturates, calcium salts, cholestyramine, NSAIDs, ampicillin, rifampin, and salicylates. Beta blockers may reduce the effect of oral sulfonylureas (hypoglycemic agents). Increased toxicity/effect when used with other antihypertensives, contraceptives, MAO inhibitors, cimetidine, and numerous other products. See drug interaction reference for complete listing.

AHL = 3-4 hours		M/P	= 7.1-12.2
PHL =		PB	= 26%
PK = 1-4 hours		Oral	= 35-50%
MW = 336		pKa	=
Vd =			

References:
1. Drug Facts and Comparisons. 1995 ed. Facts and Comparisons, St. Louis.
2. Boutroy MJ, et.al. To nurse when receiving acebutolol: Is it dangerous for the neonate? Eur. J. Clin. Pharmacol. 30:737,1986.

Acetaminophen   Fax #1002

Trade: Tempra, Tylenol, Paracetamol
Can/Aus/UK: Apo-Acetaminophen, Tempra, Tylenol Paracetamol, Panadol, Dymadon, Calpol
Uses: Analgesic
AAP: Approved by the American Academy of Pediatrics for use in breastfeeding mothers

Only small amounts are secreted into breast milk, and are considered too small to be hazardous. Breast milk levels of acetaminophen are approximately 10-15 mg/Liter of milk. Milk:plasma ratios of 0.91 to 1.42 have been reported at 1 and 12 hours respectively and a milk half-life of 4.7 hours. Assuming ingestion of 90 ml of milk at 3, 6, and 9 hour intervals, an estimated range of ingestion would be 0.04 to 0.23% of total maternal dose.

Alternatives:

Pregnancy Risk Category: B

Adult Concerns: Few when taken in normal doses. Diarrhea, gastric upset sweating in overdose.
Pediatric Concerns: None reported via milk.

Drug Interactions: Rifampin can interact to reduce the analgesic effect of acetaminophen. Increased acetaminophen hepatotoxicity when used with barbiturates, carbamazepine, hydantoins, sulfinpyrazone, and chronic alcohol abuse.

AHL	= 2 hours	M/P	= 0.91-1.42
PHL	= 1-3 hours	PB	= 25%
PK	= 0.5-2 hours	Oral	= >85%
MW	= 151	pKa	= 9.5
Vd	= 0.8-1.0		

References:
1. Berlin CM, Jaaffee S, Ragni M. Disposition of acetaminophen in milk, saliva and plasma of lactating women. Pediatr Pharmacol 1:135-41, 1980.
2. Bitzen PO, et.al. Excretion of paracetamol in human breast milk. Eur. J. Clin. Pharmacol. 20:123-125, 1981.

Acetazolamide   Fax #1003

Trade: Dazamide, Diamox
Can/Aus/UK: Acetazolam, Apo-Acetazolamide, Diamox
Uses: Diuretic
AAP: Approved by the American Academy of Pediatrics for use in breastfeeding mothers

Acetazolamide is a carbonic anhydrase inhibitor dissimilar to other thiazide diuretics. In general, diuretics may decrease the volume of breast milk although this is rare. In a patient receiving 500 mg of acetazolamide twice daily, acetazolamide concentrations in milk were 1.3 to 2.1 mg/L (0.06 % of maternal dose) while the maternal plasma levels ranged from 5.2-6.4 mg/L. Plasma concentrations in exposed infants were 0.2 to 0.6µg/mL two to 12 hours after breastfeeding.

These amounts are unlikely to cause adverse effects in the infant.

Alternatives:

Pregnancy Risk Category: C

Adult Concerns: Anorexia, diarrhea, metallic taste, polyuria, muscular weakness, potassium loss. Malaise, fatigue, depression, renal failure have been reported.

Pediatric Concerns: None reported via milk.

Drug Interactions: Increases lithium excretion, reducing plasma levels. May increase toxicity of cyclosporine.   Digitalis toxicity may occur if hypokalemia results from acetazolamide therapy.

AHL = 2.4-5.8 hours		**M/P**	= 0.25
PHL =		**PB**	= 70-95%
PK = 1-3 hours		**Oral**	= Complete
MW = 222		**pKa**	= 7.4
Vd = 0.2			

References:
1.   Soderman P, Hartvig, P, Fagerlund C. Acetazolamide excretion into human breast milk. Br.J.Clin.Pharmacol.17:59-60, 1984.

Acyclovir   Fax #1004

Trade: Zovirax
Can/Aus/UK: Zovirax, Avirax, Apo-Acyclovir, Acyclo-V, Zyclir, Aciclovir
Uses: Antiviral, for herpes simplex
AAP: Approved by the American Academy of Pediatrics for use in breastfeeding mothers

Acyclovir is converted by herpes simplex and varicella zoster virus to acyclovir triphosphate which interferes with viral HSV DNA polymerase.   It is currently cleared for use in HSV infections,

Varicella-Zoster, and under certain instances, cytomegalovirus and Epstein-Barr infections. There is virtually no percutaneous absorption following topical application and plasma levels are undetectable. The pharmacokinetics in children are similar to adults. In neonates, the half-life is 3.8-4.1 hours, and in children one year and older it is 1.9-3.6 hours. Acyclovir levels in breast milk are reported to be 0.6 to 4.1 times the maternal plasma levels. Maximum ingested dose was calculated to be 1500 µg/day assuming 750 mL milk intake. This level produced no overt side effects in one infant. In another study, doses of 800 mg five times daily produced milk levels that ranged from 4.16 to 5.81 mg/L (total infant ingestion per day = 0.73 mg/kg/day). Topical therapy on lesions, other than nipple, is probably safe. If applied to nipples, any residual acyclovir cream should be removed prior to feeding. Toxicities associated with acyclovir are few and usually minor. Acyclovir therapy in neonatal units is common and produces few toxicities. Calculated intake by infant would be less than 1 mg/day.

Alternatives:

Pregnancy Risk Category: C

Adult Concerns: Nausea, vomiting, diarrhea, sore throat, edema, and skin rashes.

Pediatric Concerns: None reported via milk in several studies.

Drug Interactions: Increased CNS side effects when used with zidovudine and probenecid.

AHL = 2.4 hours	**M/P**	= 0.6-4.1
PHL = 3.2 hours (neonates)	**PB**	= 9-33%
PK = 1.5 - 2 hours	**Oral**	= 15-30%
MW = 225	**pKa**	=
Vd =		

References:
1. Lau RJ, Emery MG, Galinsky RE. Unexpected accumulation of acyclovir in breast milk with estimation of infant exposure. Obstet Gynecol. 69:468-471, 1987.
2. Meyer LJ, de Miranda P, Sheth N, et.al. Acyclovir in human breast milk. Am J Obstet Gynecol. 158:586-588,1988.

3.   Taddio A, Klein J, Koren G. Acyclovir excretion in human breast milk. Ann. Pharm. 28:585-7, 1994.

Albuterol   Fax #1005

Trade: Proventil, Ventolin
Can/Aus/UK: Novo-Salmol, Ventolin, Asmavent, Respax, Respolin, Asmol, Salbulin, Salbuvent
Uses: Bronchodilator for asthma
AAP: Not reviewed

Albuterol is a very popular beta-2 adrenergic agonist that is typically used to dilate constricted bronchi in asthmatics. It is active orally, but is most commonly used via inhalation. When used orally, significant plasma levels are attained and transfer to breast milk is possible. When used via inhalation, less than 10% is absorbed into maternal plasma. Small amounts are probably secreted into milk although no reports exist. It is very unlikely that pharmacologic doses will be transferred to the infant via milk following inhaler use.   However, when used orally, breast milk levels could be sufficient to produce tremors and agitation in infants. Commonly used via inhalation in treating pediatric asthma.

Alternatives:

Pregnancy Risk Category: C

Adult Concerns: Observe infant for tremors and excitement.

Pediatric Concerns: None reported via milk

Drug Interactions: Albuterol effects are reduce when used with beta blockers. Cardiovascular effects are potentiated when used with MAO inhibitors, tricyclic antidepressants,   amphetamines, and inhaled anesthetics (enflurane).

AHL = 3.8 hours		**M/P** =	
PHL =		**PB** =	
PK = 5-30 min.(inhaled)		**Oral** = 100%	

MW = 239   pKa = 10.3
Vd = 2.2

References:
1.   Pharmaceutical Manufacturer's Package Insert, 1997.

Alendronate Sodium   Fax #1504

Trade: Fosamax
Can/Aus/UK: Fosamax
Uses: Inhibits bone resorption
AAP: Not reviewed

Alendronate is a specific inhibitor of osteoclast-mediated bone resorption, thus reducing bone loss and bone turnover. While incorporated in bone matrix, it is not pharmacologically active. Because concentrations in plasma are too low to be detected (< 5 ng/mL) it is very unlikely that it would be secreted into human milk in clinically relevant concentrations. Concentrations in human milk have not been reported. Because this product has exceedingly poor oral bioavailability, particularly when ingested with milk, it is exceedingly unlikely that alendronate would be orally absorbed by a breastfeeding infant.

Alternatives:

Pregnancy Risk Category: C

Adult Concerns: Abdominal pain, nausea, dyspepsia, constipation, muscle cramps, headache, taste perversion. There are a number of case reports of esophagitis and esophageal ulceration in patients taking Fosamax.

Pediatric Concerns: None reported via milk.

Drug Interactions: Ranitidine will double the absorption of alendronate. Calcium, milk, and other multivalent cation containing foods reduce the bioavailability of alendronate.

AHL	= <3 hours(plasma)	M/P	=
PHL	=	PB	= 78%
PK	=	Oral	= <0.7%
MW	= 325	pKa	=
Vd	= 0.4		

References:
1.   Pharmaceutical Manufacturer's Package Insert, 1997.

Alfentanil   Fax #1007

Trade: Alfenta
Can/Aus/UK: Alfenta, Rapifen
Uses: Narcotic analgesic
AAP: Not reviewed

Alfentanil is secreted into breast milk. Following a dose of 50µg/kg IV, the mean levels of alfentanil in colostrum at 4 hours varied from 0.21 to 1.56 µg/L of milk, levels probably too small to produce overt toxicity in breastfeeding infants. In another study following 50 micrograms or more, breast milk levels were 0.88 µg/Liter at 4 hours and 0.05 µg/Liter at 28 hours. These levels are probably too low to be clinically relevant.

Alternatives: Remifentanil

Pregnancy Risk Category: C

Adult Concerns: Observe for bradycardia, shivering, constipation and sedation.   In neonates observe for severe hypotension.

Pediatric Concerns: None reported via milk.

Drug Interactions: Phenothiazines may antagonize the analgesic effects of opiates.   Dextromethrophan may increase the analgesia of opiate agonists.   Other CNS depressants such as benzodiazepines, barbiturates, tricyclic antidepressants, erythromycin, reserpine and beta blockers may increase the toxicity of this opiate.

AHL = 1-2 hours
PHL = 5-6 hours (neonates)
PK = immediate
MW = 417
Vd = 0.3-1.0

M/P =
PB   = 92%
Oral =
pKa = 6.5

References:
1. Giesecke, AH, Rice, LJ. Lipton, JM. Alfentanil in colostrum. Anesthesiology 63:A284, 1985.
2. Spigset O. Anaesthetic agents and excretion in breast milk. Acta Anaesthesiologica Scandinavica. 38:94-103, 1994.

Allergy Injections   Fax #1008

Trade:

Can/Aus/UK:

Uses: Desensitizing injections

AAP: Not reviewed

Allergy injections consist of protein and carbohydrate substances from plants, animals, and other species. There are no reported untoward effects.

Alternatives:

Pregnancy Risk Category:

Adult Concerns: Allergic pruritus, anaphylaxis, other immune reactions.

Pediatric Concerns: None.

Drug Interactions:

Allopurinol   Fax #1009

Trade: Zyloprim, Lopurin
Can/Aus/UK: Alloprin, Apo-Allopurinol, Novo-Purol, Zyloprim, Allorin, Capurate, Zygout, Aluline, Caplenal, Cosuric, Hamarin, Zyloric
Uses: Reduces uric acid levels
AAP: Approved by the American Academy of Pediatrics for use in breastfeeding mothers

Allopurinol is a potent antagonist of xanthine oxidase, an enzyme involved in the production of uric acid. It is used to reduce uric acid levels in hyperuricemic individuals. In one report of allopurinol use in a nursing mother (300mg/d), the breast milk concentration at 2 and 4 hours was 0.9 and 1.4 µg/mL respectively. The concentration of the metabolite, oxypurinol, was 53.7 and 48.0 µg/mL at 2 and 4 hours respectively. The milk:plasma ratio ranged from 0.9 to 1.4 for allopurinol and 3.9 for its metabolite, oxypurinol. The average daily dose that an infant would receive from milk would be approximately 0.14-0.20 mg/kg of allopurinol and 7.2-8.0 mg/kg of oxypurinol. No adverse effects were noted in the infant after 6 weeks of therapy. AHL= 1-3 hours (allopurinol), 18-30 hours for (oxypurinol). Pediatric dosages for ages 6 and under is generally 10 mg/Kg/24 hours.

Alternatives:

Pregnancy Risk Category: C

Adult Concerns: Itching skin rash, fever, chills, nausea and vomiting, diarrhea, gastritis.

Pediatric Concerns: No adverse effects were noted in one infant after 6 weeks of therapy.

Drug Interactions: Alcohol decreases allopurinol efficacy. Inhibits metabolism of azathioprine and mercaptopurine. Increased incidence of skin rash when used with amoxicillin and ampicillin. Increased risk of kidney stones when used with high doses of vitamin C. Allopurinol prolongs half-life of oral anticoagulants, theophylline, chlorpropamide.

AHL	= 1-3 hours (allopurinol)	M/P	= 0.9-1.4
PHL	=	PB	= 0%
PK	= 2-6 hours	Oral	= 90%
MW	= 136	pKa	=
Vd	= 1.6		

References:
1.   Kamilli I, and Gresser U. Allopurinol and oxypurinol in human breast milk. Clinical Investigator 71:161-164, 1993.

Aloe Vera   Fax #1010

Trade: Aloe Vera, Cape, Zanzibar, Socotrine
Can/Aus/UK:
Uses: Extract from A. Vera
AAP: Not reviewed

There are over 500 species of aloes. The aloe plant yields two important products, Aloe latex derived from the outer skin, and Aloe gel, a clear, gelatinous material derived from the inner tissue of the leaf. The aloe gel is the most commonly used product in cosmetic and health food products.   The gel contains a polysaccharide glucomannan, similar to guar gum, which is responsible for its emollient effect. Aloe also contains tannins, polysaccharides, organic acids, enzymes, and other products. Bradykininase, a protease inhibitor, is believed to relieve pain and decrease swelling and pruritus.   Other components, such as an anti-prostaglandin compound is believed to reduce inflammation. Aloe latex, a bitter yellow product derived from the outer skin, is a drastic cathartic and produces a strong purgative effect on the large intestine due to its anthraquinone barbaloin content. Do not use the latex orally in children. The most common use of the aloe gel is in burn therapy for minor burns and skin irritation.   Thus far, well controlled studies do not provide evidence of a clear advantage over aggressive wound care. Two FDA advisory panels failed to find sufficient evidence to show Aloe Vera is useful in treatment of minor burns, cuts, or vaginal irritation. Recent evidence suggests that A.vera may accelerate wound healing, such as in frostbite, and in patients undergoing dermabrasion, although another study suggests a delay in healing. Numerous studies have suggested accelerated wound healing, reduction in arthritic inflammation, and other inflammatory diseases, although these are in many cases poorly controlled. The toxicity of A.vera gel when applied topically is minimal. Oral use of the latex derived from the outer skin of A. vera is strongly discouraged as they are drastic cathartics. Aloe emodin and other anthraquinones present in A. vera latex may cause severe gastric cramping, and should never be used in pregnant women and children.

Alternatives:

Pregnancy Risk Category:

Adult Concerns: Severe gastric irritation, strong purgative effect and diarrhea when gel used orally.

Pediatric Concerns: No reports of untoward effects following maternal use or via milk ingestion.

Drug Interactions:

References:
1. Review of Natural Products. Ed: Facts and Comparisons, St. Louis, Missouri, 1997.
2. Leung AY. Encyclopedia of Common Natural Ingredients used in Food, Drugs and Cosmetics. New York, NY: J Wiley and Sons, 1980.
3. Fulton JE: The stimulation of postdermabrasion would healing with stabilized aloe vera gel polyethylene oxide dressing. J. Dermatol Surg Oncol 16(5):460, 1990.
4. Schmidt JM, Greenspoon JS. Aloe vera dermal wound gel is associated with a delay in wound healing. Obstet Gynecol 78(1):115, 1991.

Alprazolam   Fax #1011

Trade: Xanax
Can/Aus/UK: Apo-Alpraz, Novo-Alprazol, Xanax, Kalma, Ralozam
Uses: Benzodiazepine antianxiety agent
AAP: Not reviewed

Alprazolam is a prototypical benzodiazepine drug similar to Valium. The manufacturer is apparently aware of "approximately half a dozen" cases of infant exposure via breast milk, most of which reported no severe adverse effects. However, in one patient who withdrew from alprazolam after 9 months of use, the breastfed infant reportedly suffered mild withdrawal symptoms of irritability, crying, and sleep disturbances.

Alternatives: Lorazepam

Pregnancy Risk Category: D

Adult Concerns: Drowsiness, fatigue, insomnia, confusion, dry mouth, constipation, nausea, vomiting.

Pediatric Concerns: Rarely, withdrawal syndrome reported in one breastfed infant. Observe for sedation, poor feeding, irritability, crying, insomnia on withdrawal.

Drug Interactions: Decreased therapeutic effect when used with carbamazepine, disulfiram. Increased toxicity when used with oral contraceptives, CNS depressants, cimetidine and lithium.

AHL = 12-15 hours		**M/P** =	
PHL =		**PB** = 80%	
PK = 1-2 hours		**Oral** = Complete	
MW = 309		**pKa** =	
Vd = 0.9-1.3			

References:
1. Anderson PO, McGuire GG. Neonatal alprazolam withdrawal:

possible effects of breast feeding. DICP Annal Pharmacother. 23:614, 1989.

Amantadine   Fax #1012

Trade: Symmetrel, Symadine
Can/Aus/UK: Symmetrel, Endantadine, Gen-Amantadine, Mantadine
Uses: Anti-viral
AAP: Not reviewed

Amantadine is a unique compound that has both antiviral activity against influenza A and is effective in treating Parkinsonian symptoms. Pediatric indications for prevention of influenza for ages 1-10 are available. Trace amounts are believed to be secreted in milk although no reports are found. Adult plasma levels following doses of 200 mg daily are 400-900 nanograms/mL. Even assuming a theoretical milk:plasma ratio of 1.0, the average daily dose to a breastfeeding infant would be far less than 0.9 mg, a dose that would be clinically irrelevant compared to the 4-8 mg/Kg dose used in 1 year old infants.

Alternatives:

Pregnancy Risk Category: C

Adult Concerns: Urinary retention, vomiting, skin rash in infants. Insomnia, depression, confusion, disorientation, nausea, anorexia, constipation, vomiting.

Pediatric Concerns: None reported via milk.

Drug Interactions: May increase anticholinergic effects when used with anticholinergic or CNS active drugs. Increased toxicity/levels when used with hydrochlorothiazide plus triamterene, or amiloride.

AHL = 1-28 hours	**M/P**	**=**
PHL =	**PB**	**= 67%**
PK = 1-4 hours	**Oral**	**= 86-94%**
MW = 151	**pKa**	**= 10.1**

Vd = 4.4

References:
1. Pharmaceutical Manufacturer's Package Insert, 1997.
2. CDC: Prevention and control of influenza. Recommendations of the Immunization Practices Advisory Committee (ACIP). MMWR 39:1-15, 1990.
3. Cedarbaum JM: Clinical pharmacokinetics of anti-parkinsonian drugs. Clin Pharmacokinetics 13:141-178, 1987.

Amikacin   Fax #1013

Trade: Amikin
Can/Aus/UK: Amikin
Uses: Aminoglycoside antibiotic
AAP: Not reviewed

Amikacin is a typical aminoglycoside antibiotic used for gram negative infections. Other aminoglycoside antibiotics are poorly absorbed from GI tract in infants although they could produce changes in GI flora. Only very small amounts are secreted into breast milk. Following 100 and 200 mg IM doses, only trace amounts have been found in breast milk and then in only 2 of 4 patients studied.

Alternatives:

Pregnancy Risk Category: C

Adult Concerns: Diarrhea, changes in GI flora.

Pediatric Concerns: None reported via milk. Commonly used in neonates.

Drug Interactions: Increased aminoglycoside toxicity when used with indomethacin, amphotericin, loop diuretics, vancomycin, enflurane, methoxyflurane, depolarizing neuromuscular blocking agents.

AHL = 2.3 hours		**M/P** =	
PHL = 4-5 hours		**PB** = 4%	
PK = 0.75-2.0 hours		**Oral** = Poor	

MW = 586   pKa =
Vd = 0.28

References:
1.   Matsuda C, et. al. A study of amikacin in the obstetrics field. Jpn
      J Antibiot 27:633-6,1974.

Aminosalicylic Acid (para)   Fax #1014

Trade: Paser, PAS
Can/Aus/UK: Tubasal, Nemasol
Uses: Antitubercular
AAP: Drugs associated with significant side effects and should be
given with caution

PARA inhibits folic acid synthesis and is selective only for tuberculosis
bacteria. Following a maternal dose of 4.0 gm/day, the peak maternal
plasma level was 70.1 mg/L and occurred at 2 hours. The breast milk
concentration of 5-ASA at 3 hours was 1.1 mg/L. In another study,
the concentration in milk ranged from 0.13 to 0.53 umol/liter.   In a 29
year old mother who received 3 gm/day of 5-ASA for ulcerative colitis,
the estimated intake for an infant receiving 120-200 mL of milk was
0.02 to 0.012 mg of 5-ASA.   The concentrations of 5-ASA and its
metabolite Acetyl-5-ASA present in milk appear too low to produce
overt toxicity in most infants.   Only one report of slight diarrhea in
one infant has been reported.

Alternatives:

Pregnancy Risk Category: C

Adult Concerns: Nausea, vomiting, diarrhea.

Pediatric Concerns: Only one report of slight diarrhea in one infant
has been reported.

Drug Interactions: Reduces levels of digoxin and vitamin B-12.

AHL = 1 hr.		**M/P**	= 0.09-0.17
PHL =		**PB**	= 50-73%
PK = 2 hours		**Oral**	= >90%
MW = 153		**pKa**	=
Vd =			

References:

1. Holdiness, MR. Antituberculosis drugs and breast-feeding. Arch. Int. Med. 144:1888, 1984.
2. Christensen, LA. Disposition of 5-aminosalicylic acid and N-acetyl-5-aminosalicylic acid in fetal and maternal body fluids during treatment with different 5-aminosalicylic acid preparations. Acta.Obstet. Gynecol. Scand 74:399-402, 1994.
3. Klotz U. Negligible excretion of 5-aminosalicylic acid in breast milk. The Lancet 342:618-9, 1993.

Amiodarone   Fax #1015

Trade: Cordarone
Can/Aus/UK: Cordarone, Aratac
Uses: Strong antiarrhythmic agent
AAP: Not reviewed

Amiodarone is a potent and sometimes dangerous antiarrhythmic drug and requires close supervision by clinicians. Although poorly absorbed by the mother (<50%), maximum serum levels are attained after 3-7 hours. This drug has a very large volume of distribution, resulting in accumulation in adipose, liver, spleen and lungs and has a high rate of fetal toxicity (10-17%). It should not be given to pregnant mother unless critically required. Significant amounts are secreted into breast milk at levels higher than the plasma level. In one case 2-3 days postpartum, the milk concentrations of amiodarone and desmethylamiodarone were 0.5-1.8 mg/L and 0.4-0.8 mg/L of milk respectfully. Because amiodarone contains significant iodine, one reported case of hypothyroidism has been reported in an infant following therapy in the mother. Because of the long half-life and high concentrations in various organs, amiodarone could continuously build up to higher levels in the infant. Milk:plasma ratio (dose=200 mg/day) in one group of mothers varied from 0.4 to 13. This product should be used only under the most extraordinary conditions, and the infant should be closely monitored for cardiovascular and thyroid function. Continuing lactation while using this product is probably unwarranted.

Alternatives: Disopyramide, Mexiletine

Pregnancy Risk Category: C

Adult Concerns: Hypothyroidism, myocardial arrhythmias, pulmonary toxicity, serious liver injury, congestive heart failure.

Pediatric Concerns: Hypothyroidism has been reported. Extreme caution is urged.

Drug Interactions: Amiodarone interferes with the metabolism of a number of drugs including: oral anticoagulants, beta blockers, calcium channel blockers, digoxin, flecainide, phenytoin, procainamide, quinidine. Plasma levels of these drugs tend to be increased to hazardous levels.

AHL = 26-107 days	**M/P = 0.4-13**
PHL =	**PB = 99.98%**
PK = 3-7 hours	**Oral = 22-86%**
MW = 643	**pKa = 6.6**
Vd = 18-148	

References:
1. Plomp TA, Vulsma T, and deVijlder JJ. Use of amiodarone during pregnancy. Eur. J. of Obstet. Gyn. and Rep. Biol. 43:201-7, 1992.
2. Strunge, P. et.al. Amiodarone during pregnancy. Eur. Heart J. 9:106-109, 1988.
3. McKenna WJ, Harris L, .et.al. Amiodarone therapy during pregnancy. Am. J. Cardiol. 51:1231-3, 1983.
4. Pitcher D, Leather HM, et.al. Amiodarone in pregnancy. The Lancet 1:597-8,1983.

Amitriptyline   Fax #1016

Trade: Elavil, Endep
Can/Aus/UK: Apo-Amitriptyline, Elavil, Novo-Tryptin Amitrol, Endep, Mutabon D, Tryptanol, Domical, Lentizol
Uses: Tricyclic antidepressant
AAP: Drugs whose effect on nursing infants is unknown but may be of concern

Amitriptyline and its active metabolite, nortriptyline, are secreted into breast milk in small amounts. In one report of a mother taking 100 mg/day of amitriptyline, serum levels were 0.141 mg/L and milk levels 0.151 mg/L, suggesting a milk:plasma ratio of 1.0. From this data, an infant consuming 500 cc of milk daily would consume approximately 0.075 mg/day, a dose that is unlikely to be clinically relevant. In another study following a maternal dosage of 150 mg for 3 weeks, the maternal serum level was 90 ng/mL and 146 ng/mL for nortriptyline. No detectible amount of drug (less than 28 ng/mL) was found in the infant's serum. Therefore, it is estimated that a nursing infant would receive less than 1% of the maternal dose.

Alternatives: Amoxapine, Imipramine

Pregnancy Risk Category: D

Adult Concerns: Anticholinergic side effects, such as drying of secretions, dilated pupil, sedation.

Pediatric Concerns: No untoward effects have been noted in several studies.

Drug Interactions: Phenobarbital may reduce effect of amitriptyline. Amitriptyline blocks the hypotensive effect of guanethidine. May increase toxicity of amitriptyline when used with clonidine. Dangerous when used with MAO inhibitors, other CNS depressants. May increase anticoagulant effect of coumadin, warfarin. SSRIs (Prozac, Zoloft, etc) should not be used with or soon after amitriptyline or other TCAs due to serotonergic crisis.

AHL = 31-46 hours		M/P	= 1.0
PHL =		PB	= 94.8%
PK	= 2-4 hours	Oral	= Complete
MW	= 277	pKa	= 9.4
Vd	= 6-10		

References:

1. Brixen-Rasmussen L, Halgrener J, Jergensen A. Amitriptyline and nortriptyline excretion in human breast milk. Psychopharmacology 76:94-95, 1982.
2. Bader, T. and Newman, K. Amitriptyline in human breast milk and the nursing infant's serum. Am. J. Psychiatry 137:855-856, 1980.
3. Misri S. and Sivertz K. Tricyclic drugs in pregnancy and lactation: A preliminary report. Intl. J. Psych. in Med. 21:157-171, 1991.

Amlodipine Besylate   Fax #1017

Trade: Norvasc
Can/Aus/UK: Norvasc, Istin
Uses: Antihypertensive, calcium channel blocker
AAP: Not reviewed

Amlodipine is a typical calcium channel blocker antihypertensive agent which has greater bioavailability and a longer duration of action. No data are currently available on transfer of amlodipine into breast milk. Because most calcium channel blockers (CCB) readily transfer into milk, we should assume the same for this drug. Use caution if administering to lactating women.

Alternatives: Nifedipine, Nimodipine

Pregnancy Risk Category: C

Adult Concerns: Hypotension, bradycardia, edema, headache, or nausea.

Pediatric Concerns: None reported but observe for bradycardia, hypotension upon prolonged use.

Drug Interactions: Cyclosporine levels may be increased when used with calcium channel blockers. Use with azole antifungals (fluconazole, itraconazole, ketoconazole, etc) may lead to enhanced amlodipine levels. Use with rifampin may significantly reduce plasma levels of calcium channel blockers.

AHL = 30-50 hours		M/P	=
PHL =		PB	= 93%
PK = 6-9 hours		Oral	= 64-65%
MW = 408		pKa	=
Vd = 21			

References:
1.   Pharmaceutical Manufacturer's Package Insert, 1996.

Amoxapine   Fax #1018

Trade: Asendin
Can/Aus/UK: Asendin, Asendis
Uses: Tricyclic antidepressant
AAP: Drugs whose effect on nursing infants is unknown but may be of concern

Amoxapine, and its metabolite are both secreted into breast milk at relatively low levels. Following a dose of 250 mg/day, milk levels of amoxapine were less than 20 µg/L and 113 µg/L of the active metabolite. Milk levels of active metabolite varied from 113 to 168 µg/L in two other milk samples. Maternal serum levels of amoxapine and metabolite at steady state were 97 µg/L and 375 µg/L respectively. Milk levels are generally less than 20% of the maternal plasma level.

Alternatives:

Pregnancy Risk Category: C

Adult Concerns: Dry mouth, constipation, urine retention, drowsiness or sedation, anxiety, emotional disturbances, parkinsonism, tardive dyskinesia, seizures.

Pediatric Concerns: None reported.

Drug Interactions: Decreased effect of clonidine, guanethidine. Amoxapine may increase effect of CNS depressants, adrenergic agents, anticholinergic agents. Increased toxicity with MAO inhibitors.

AHL = 8 hours (parent)		**M/P**	= 0.21
PHL =		**PB**	= 15-25%
PK = 2 hours		**Oral**	= 18-54%
MW = 314		**pKa**	=
Vd = 65.7			

References:
1. Gelenberg AJ. Amoxapine, a new antidepressant, appears in human milk. J. Nerv. Ment. Dis. 167:635-636, 1979.

Amoxicillin   Fax #1019

Trade: Larotid, Amoxil
Can/Aus/UK: Amoxil, Apo-Amoxi, Novamoxin, Alphamox, Moxacin, Cilamox, Betamox
Uses: Penicillin antibiotic
AAP: Approved by the American Academy of Pediatrics for use in breastfeeding mothers

Amoxicillin is a popular oral penicillin used for otitis media and many other pediatric/adult infections. In one group of 6 mothers who received 1 gm oral doses, the concentration of amoxicillin in breast milk ranged from 0.68 to 1.3 mg/L of milk (average = 0.9 mg/L). Peak levels occurred at 4-5 hours. Milk:plasma ratios at 1,2, and 3 hours were 0.014, 0.013, and 0.043. Less than 0.7% of the maternal dose is secreted into milk. No harmful effects have been reported. Also see penicillins.

Alternatives:

Pregnancy Risk Category: B

Adult Concerns: Diarrhea, rashes, and changes in GI flora. Pancytopenia, rarely pseudomembranous colitis.

Pediatric Concerns: None reported. Commonly used in neonates and children.

Drug Interactions: Efficacy of oral contraceptives may be reduced. Disulfiram and probenecid may increase plasma levels of amoxicillin. Allopurinol may increase the risk of amoxicillin skin rash.

AHL = 1.7 hours	M/P = 0.014-0.043
PHL = 4 hours (neonate)	PB = 18%
PK = 1.5 hours	Oral = 89%
MW = 365	pKa =
Vd = 0.3	

References:
1. Kefetzis DA, Siafas CA, Georgakopoulous PA, et.al. Passage of cephalosporins and amoxicillin into the breast milk. Acta Paediatr Scan 70:285-286,1981.

Amoxicillin + Clavulanate   Fax #1020

Trade: Augmentin
Can/Aus/UK: Clavulin, Augmentin
Uses: Penicillin antibiotic, extended spectrum
AAP: Not reviewed

Addition of clavulanate extends spectrum of amoxicillin by inhibiting beta lactamase enzymes. Small amounts of amoxicillin (0.9 mg/L milk) are secreted in breast milk. No harmful effects have been reported. See amoxicillin. Although clavulanic acid is well absorbed and widely distributed, no reports of secretion into human milk exist, but it should be expected (AHL= 1 hr. PB= 45%). May cause changes in GI flora, and possibly fungal (candida) overgrowth.

Alternatives:

Pregnancy Risk Category: B

Adult Concerns: Diarrhea, rash, thrush, or diarrhea.

Pediatric Concerns: None reported but observe for diarrhea, rash.

Drug Interactions: Efficacy of oral contraceptives may be reduced. Disulfiram and probenecid may increase plasma levels of amoxicillin. Allopurinol may increase the risk of amoxicillin skin rash.

AHL = 1.7 hours	M/P = 0.014-0.043
PHL = 4 hours (neonate)	PB = 18%
PK = 1.5 hours	Oral = 89%
MW = 365	pKa =
Vd = 0.3	

References:

1.   Kefetzis DA, Siafas CA, Georgakopoulous PA, et.al. Passage of cephalosporins and amoxicillin into the breast milk.   Acta Paediatr Scan 70:285-286,1981.

Ampicillin   Fax #1021

Trade: Polycillin, Omnipen
Can/Aus/UK: Apo-Ampi, Novo-Ampicillin, NuAmpi, Penbriton, Ampicyn, Austrapen, Amfipen, Britcin, Vidopen
Uses: Penicillin antibiotic
AAP: Not reviewed

Small amounts may transfer into milk (1 mg/L). Low milk:plasma ratios of 0.2 have been reported.   Observe infant for allergies. Ampicillin is one of the most commonly used prophylactic antibiotics in pediatric neonatal nurseries. Neonatal half-life is 2.8 to 4 hours. Possible rash, sensitization, diarrhea, or candidiasis could occur, but unlikely. May alter GI flora.

Alternatives:

Pregnancy Risk Category: B

Adult Concerns: Diarrhea, rash, fungal overgrowth, agranulocytosis, pseudomembranous colitis, anaphylaxis.

Pediatric Concerns: None reported but observe for diarrhea.

Drug Interactions: Efficacy of oral contraceptives may be reduced. Disulfiram and probenecid may increase plasma levels of ampicillin. Allopurinol may increase the risk of ampicillin skin rash.

AHL	= 1.3 hours	M/P	= 0.2
PHL	= 1.7 hours (30 day old)	PB	= 8-20
PK	= 1-2 hours	Oral	= 50%
MW	= 349	pKa	=
Vd	= 0.38		

References:

1.   Kefetzis DA, Siafas CA, Georgakopoulous PA, et.al. Passage of cephalosporins and amoxicillin into the breast milk.   Acta Paediatr Scan 70:285-286,1981.

Ampicillin + Sulbactam   Fax #1022

Trade: Unasyn
Can/Aus/UK: Dicapen
Uses: Penicillin antibiotic with extended spectrum.
AAP: Not reviewed

Small amounts of ampicillin may transfer (1 mg/L). Possible rash, sensitization, diarrhea, or candidiasis could occur, but unlikely. May alter GI flora. There are no reports of sulbactam secretion into human milk, but it is probably low and largely without side effects (AHL= 1 hr. PB= 38%).

Alternatives:

Pregnancy Risk Category: B

Adult Concerns: Diarrhea, rash, fungal overgrowth, agranulocytosis, pseudomembranous colitis, anaphylaxis.

Pediatric Concerns: None reported but observe for diarrhea.

Drug Interactions: Efficacy of oral contraceptives may be reduced. Disulfiram and probenecid may increase plasma levels of amoxicillin. Allopurinol may increase the risk of amoxicillin skin rash.

AHL = 1.3 hours		**M/P**	= 0.01-0.5
PHL = 1.7 hours (15-30 days old)		**PB**	= 28%
PK = 1-2 hours		**Oral**	= 60%
MW = 349		**pKa**	=
Vd = 0.38			

References:
1. Kefetzis DA, Siafas CA, Georgakopoulous PA, et.al. Passage of cephalosporins and amoxicillin into the breast milk. Acta Paediatr Scan 70:285-286,1981.

Antipyrine   Fax #1025

Trade: Antipyrine
Can/Aus/UK:
Uses: Analgesic, antipyretic
AAP: Not reviewed

Insignificant secretion into breast milk. This product is no longer used in the USA due to high incidence of fatal bone marrow toxicity. Contraindicated.

Alternatives: Ibuprofen

Pregnancy Risk Category:

Adult Concerns: Severe bone marrow toxicity.

Pediatric Concerns: None reported but due to better medications, this product should never be used.

Drug Interactions:

AHL	=	M/P	= 1.0
PHL	=	PB	= <1%
PK	= 1-2 hours	Oral	=
MW	= 188	pKa	= 1.4
Vd	= 0.56		

References:

1.   Berlin, C. and Vesell, E. Antipyrine disposition in milk and saliva of lactating women. Clin Pharmacol. Ther 31:38-44, 1982.

Ascorbic Acid   Fax #1429

Trade: Ascorbica, Cecon, Cevi-bid, Ce-vi-sol, Vitamin C
Can/Aus/UK:
Uses: Vitamin C
AAP: Not reviewed

Ascorbic acid is an essential vitamin. Without supplementation, 75 mg/day is excreted in the urine of the average individual due to overabundance.   Renal control of vitamin C is significant, and maintains plasma levels at   0.4 to 1.5 mg/dL regardless of dose. Ascorbic acid is secreted into human milk in well controlled sequence and mature milk contains 5 mg/100 mL.   Excessive Vitamin C intake in the mother does not alter (or increase) the controlled secretion into breast milk.   The RDA for mother is 100 mg/day.   Maternal supplementation is only required in undernourished mothers. Pregnant women should not use excessive ascorbic acid due to metabolic induction in the fetal liver, followed by a metabolic rebound scurvy early postpartum in the neonate. Ascorbic acid should not routinely be administered to breastfed infants unless to treat clinical scurvy.

Alternatives:

Pregnancy Risk Category: A at normal doses
C at doses above RDA

Adult Concerns: Renal calculi with large doses. Faintness, flushing, dizziness, nausea, vomiting, gastritis.

Pediatric Concerns: None reported via breast milk, but excessive use prepartum is strongly discouraged.

Drug Interactions: Ascorbic acid decreases propranolol peak concentrations. Aspirin decreases ascorbate levels and increases aspirin levels. Reduced effect of warfarin when used with ascorbic acid. Urinary acidification results in decreased retention of many basic drugs, including tricyclic antidepressants, amoxapine, amphetamines. Do not use with aluminum antacids. Ascorbic acid reduces renal elimination of aluminum leading to encephalopathy, seizures, coma.

AHL =		M/P	=
PHL =		PB	=
PK	= 2-3 hours	Oral	= Complete
MW	= 176	pKa	=
Vd	=		

References:
1. Sneed SM, et. al. The effects of ascorbic acid, vitamin B6, vitamin B12, and folic acid supplementation on the breast milk and maternal nutritional status of low socioeconomic lactating women. Am J Clin Nutr 34:1338-46, 1981.

Aspartame   Fax #1026

Trade: Nutrasweet
Can/Aus/UK:
Uses: Artificial sweetener
AAP: Not reviewed

Aspartame consists of two linked amino acids, aspartic acid and phenylalanine.   Once in the GI tract, it is rapidly metabolized to phenylalanine and aspartic acid.   Maternal ingestion of 50 mg/kg aspartame will approximately double (2.3 to 4.8 umol/dL) aspartate milk levels. Phenylalanine milk levels similarly increased from 0.5 to 2.3 umol/dL. This dose is 3-4 times the normal dose used, and these milk levels are too low to produce significant side effects in normal infants.   Contraindicated in infants with proven phenylketonuria.

Alternatives:

Pregnancy Risk Category: B

Adult Concerns: Only contraindicated in infants with PKU.

Pediatric Concerns: None reported except contraindicated in infants with documented phenylketonuria.

Drug Interactions:

AHL =		M/P	=
PHL =		PB	=
PK =		Oral	= Complete
MW = 294		pKa	=
Vd =			

References:
1. Levels of free amino acids in lactating women following ingestion of the sweetener aspartame. Nutrition Reviews. 38:183-184, 1980.
2. Stegink LD, Filer LJ, Baker GL. Plasma, erythrocyte and human milk levels of free amino acids in lactating women administered aspartame or lactose, J. Nutr. 109:2173-81, 1979.

Aspirin   Fax #1027

Trade: Ecotrin
Can/Aus/UK: Coryphen, Ecotrin, Novasen, Entrophen, Disprin, Aspro, Cartia
Uses: Salicylate analgesic

AAP: Drugs associated with significant side effects and should be given with caution

Extremely small amounts secreted into breast milk. Few harmful effects have been reported. Following single or multiple doses, peak levels occur at approximately 3 hours and vary from 1.12 to 1.69 mg/L. Extremely high doses in mother could potentially produce slight bleeding in infant. Because aspirin is strongly implicated in Reye's Syndrome in febrile-viral illnesses, it is a poor choice of analgesic to use in breastfeeding mothers. See ibuprofen or acetaminophen as a better choice.

Alternatives: Ibuprofen, Acetaminophen

Pregnancy Risk Category: C

Adult Concerns: GI ulceration, distress, esophagitis, nephropathy, hepatotoxicity, tinnitus, platelet dysfunction.

Pediatric Concerns: None reported via milk, but aspirin use in pediatric patients may increase risk of Reye's syndrome in viral infections.

Drug Interactions: May decrease serum levels of other NSAIDs as well as GI distress. Aspirin may antagonize effect of probenecid. Aspirin may increase methotrexate serum levels, and increase free valproic acid plasma levels and valproate toxicity. May increase anticoagulant effect of warfarin.

AHL = 2.5-7 hours		**M/P**	= 0.03-0.08
PHL =		**PB**	= 88-93%
PK = 1-2 hours		**Oral**	= 80-100%
MW = 180		**pKa**	=
Vd = 0.15			

References:
1. Erickson SH, Oppenheim Gl. Aspirin in breast milk. J Fam Pract. 8:189-190,1979.
2. Findlay JW, DeAngelis RI, Kearney MF, et.al. Analgesic drugs in breast milk and plasma. Clin Pharmacol. Ther. 29:625-633, 1981.

Astemizole   Fax #1028

Trade: Hismanal
Can/Aus/UK: Hismanal
Uses: Antihistamine
AAP: Not reviewed

Astemizole is a second generation antihistamine with little or no sedation or anticholinergic side effects. The manufacturer indicates astemizole is transferred into animal milk and assumes the same for human, although no data on concentrations in human milk is available. In animal studies, milk:plasma ratios as high as 4.6 have been reported for astemizole and its metabolite, desmethylastemizole. Astemizole has a very long half-life in adults, and probably longer in infants. Poor absorption from the adult GI tract suggests that it might be poorly absorbed in infant unless in the preterm or early neonatal period. This compound fails to achieve brain levels in adult, therefore has few CNS side effects. Astemizole has numerous drug-drug interactions and should not be used concomitantly with erythromycin, ketoconazole, itraconazole, fluvoxamine, fluticasone, nefazodone nor many others. A detailed risk assessment would suggest that other antihistamines provide a better safety margin.

Alternatives: Cetirizine, Loratadine

Pregnancy Risk Category: C

Adult Concerns: Liver toxicity, drug interactions, nausea, nervousness, diarrhea.

Pediatric Concerns: None reported via milk but caution is urged due to long half-life and cardiotoxicities.

Drug Interactions: Increased toxicity with CNS depressants. Life-threatening arrhythmias have been reported and include cardiac toxicity with triazole antifungals such as itraconazole, fluconazole, ketoconazole, etc. Increased cardiotoxicity when used with erythromycin and other macrolides, fluvoxamine, fluticasone, or nefazodone.

AHL	= 20 hours	M/P	=
PHL	=	PB	= 96.7%
PK	= 1-2 hours	Oral	= Poor
MW	= 459	pKa	=
Vd	=		

References:
1. Pharmaceutical Manufacturer's Package Insert, 1993, 1994.
2. Paton DM, Webster DR. Clinical pharmacokinetics of H1-receptor antagonists (the antihistamines). Clin. Pharm. 10:477-497, 1985.
3. Richards DM, Brogden RN, Heel RC et al: Astemizole. A review of its pharmacodynamic properties and therapeutic efficacy. Drugs 28:38-61, 1984.

Atenolol   Fax #1029

Trade: Tenoretic, Tenormin
Can/Aus/UK: Apo-Atenolol, Tenormin, Anselol, Noten, Tenlol, Tensig, Antipress
Uses: Antihypertensive beta blocker
AAP: Approved by the American Academy of Pediatrics for use in breastfeeding mothers

Atenolol is a potent cardio-selective beta blocker. Data conflict on the secretion of atenolol into breast milk. One author reports an incident of significant bradycardia, cyanosis, low body temp., and low blood pressure in breastfeeding infant of mother consuming 100 mg atenolol daily, while a number of others have failed to detect plasma levels in the neonate or untoward side effects. Data seem to indicate that atenolol secretion into breast milk is highly variable but may be as high as 10 times greater than for propranolol. In one study, women taking 50-100 mg/day were found to have M:P ratios of 1.5-6.8. However, even with high M:P ratios, the calculated intake per day (at peak levels) for a breastfeeding infant would only be 0.13 mg. In another study, the estimated daily intake for an infant receiving 500 mL milk per day, would be 0.3 mg. In a study by Kulas (1984), the amount of atenolol transferred into milk varied from 0.66 mg/L with a maternal dose of 25 mg, 1.2 mg/L with a maternal dose of 50 mg, and 1.7 mg/L with a maternal dose of 100 mg per day. Although atenolol is approved by the AAP, some caution is recommended due to the milk:plasma ratios and the reported problem with one infant.

Alternatives: Propranolol, Metoprolol

Pregnancy Risk Category: C

Adult Concerns: Persistent bardycardia, hypotension, heart failure, dizziness, fatigue, insomnia, lethargy, confusion, impotence, dyspnea, wheezing in asthmatics.

Pediatric Concerns: One report of bradycardia, cyanosis, low body temperature, and hypotension in a breastfeeding infant of mother consuming 100 mg atenolol daily, but other reports do not suggest clinical effects on breastfed infants.

Drug Interactions: Decreased effect when used with aluminum salts, barbiturates, calcium salts, cholestyramine, NSAIDs, ampicillin, rifampin, and salicylates. Beta blockers may reduce the effect of oral sulfonylureas (hypoglycemic agents). Increased toxicity/effect when used with other antihypertensives, contraceptives, MAO inhibitors, cimetidine, and numerous other products. See drug interaction reference for complete listing.

AHL = 6.1 hours		**M/P**	= 1.5-6.8
PHL = 6.4 hours		**PB**	= 5%
PK = 2-4 hours		**Oral**	= 50-60%
MW = 266		**pKa**	= 9.6
Vd = 1.3			

References:
1. Thorley KJ, McAninsh J. Levels of beta-blockers atenolol and propranolol in the breast milk of women treated for hypertension in pregnancy. Biopharm Drug Dispos. 4:299-301,1983.
2. Schmimmel MS, et.al. Toxic effects of atenolol consumed during breast feeding. J. Pediatrics 114:476, 1989.
3. Liedholm H, Melander A, et.al. Accumulation of atenolol and

metoprolol in human breast milk. Eur. J. Clin. Pharmcol. 20:229-31, 1981.

4. White WB, et.al. Atenolol in human plasma and breast milk. Obj. and Gyn. 63:42S-44S, 1984.

Atorvastatin Calcium   Fax #1545

Trade: Lipitor
Can/Aus/UK: Lipitor
Uses: Cholesterol-lowering agent
AAP: Not reviewed

Atorvastatin is a typical HMG Co-A reductase inhibitor for lowering plasma cholesterol levels. It is known to transfer into animal milk, but human studies are not available. Due to its poor oral absorption, and high protein binding, it is unlikely that clinically relevant amounts would transfer into human milk. Nevertheless, atherosclerosis is a chronic process and discontinuation of lipid-lowering drugs during pregnancy and lactation should have little to no impact on the outcome of long-term therapy of primary hypercholesterolemia. Cholesterol and other products of cholesterol biosynthesis are essential components for fetal and neonatal development and the use of cholesterol-lowering drugs would not be advisable under any circumstances.

Alternatives:

Pregnancy Risk Category: X

Adult Concerns: Liver dysfunction, rhabdomyolysis with acute renal failure.

Pediatric Concerns: None reported, but the use of these products in lactating women is not recommended.

Drug Interactions: Increased risk of myopathy when used with cyclosporin, fibric acid derivatives, niacin, erythromycin, and azole antifungals (Diflucan, etc). Decreased plasma levels of atorvastatin when used with antacids, or colestipol.

AHL	= 14 hours	M/P	=
PHL	=	PB	= 98%
PK	= 1-2 hours	Oral	= 12-30%
MW	= 1209	pKa	=
Vd	= 8		

References:

Atropine   Fax #1030

Trade: Belladonna, Atropine
Can/Aus/UK: Atropine, Minims, Atropisol, Isopto-Atropine, Atropt, Eyesule
Uses: Anticholinergic, drying agent
AAP: Approved by the American Academy of Pediatrics for use in breastfeeding mothers

Atropine is a powerful anticholinergic that is well distributed throughout the body. Only small amounts are believed secreted in milk. Effects may be highly variable. Slight absorption together with enhanced neonatal sensitivity creates hazardous potential. Use caution. Avoid if possible but not definitely contraindicated.

Alternatives:

Pregnancy Risk Category: C

Adult Concerns: Dry, hot skin. Decreased flow of breast milk. Decreased bowel motility, drying of secretions, dilated pupil, and increased heart rate.

Pediatric Concerns: No reports are available, although caution is urged.

Drug Interactions: Phenothiazines, levodopa, antihistamines, may decrease anticholinergic effects of atropine. Increased toxicity when admixed with amantadine and thiazide diuretics.

AHL	= 4.3 hours	M/P	=
PHL	=	PB	= 14-22%
PK	= 1 hr.	Oral	= 90%
MW	= 289	pKa	= 9.8
Vd	= 2.3-3.6		

References:

1. Drug Facts and Comparisons. 1995 ed. Facts and Comparisons, St. Louis.
2. Wilson, J. Drugs in Breast Milk. New York: ADIS Press, 1981.

Azathioprine   Fax #1031

Trade: Imuran
Can/Aus/UK: Imuran, Thioprine
Uses: Immunosuppressive agent
AAP: Not reviewed

Azathioprine is a powerful immunosuppressive agent that is metabolized to 6-mercaptopurine. It should only be used under close observation. Although small amounts are known to be secreted in human milk, no immunosuppressive effects have been noted in infants. Extreme caution is urged. Azathioprine is mutagenic in humans, and may increase the risk of cancer in those exposed.

Alternatives:

Pregnancy Risk Category: D

Adult Concerns: Bone marrow suppression, megaloblastic anemia, infections, skin cancers, lymphoma, nausea, vomiting, hepatotoxicity, pulmonary dysfunction and pancreatitis.

Pediatric Concerns: None reported, but caution is urged.

Drug Interactions: Increased toxicity when used with allopurinol. Reduce azathioprine dose to 1/3 to 1/4 of normal. Use with ACE inhibitors has produced severe leukopenia.

AHL = 0.6 hr.	M/P	=
PHL =	PB	= 30%
PK = 1-2 hours	Oral	= 41-44%
MW = 277	pKa	=
Vd =		

References:
1. Coulam, C. et.al. Breast-feeding after renal transplantation. Trans. Proc. 14:605-609, 1982.

Azithromycin   Fax #1032

Trade: Zithromax
Can/Aus/UK: Zithromax
Uses: Erythromycin-like antibiotic
AAP: Not reviewed

Azithromycin belongs to erythromycin family. Extremely long half-life particularly in tissues. Azithromycin is concentrated for long periods in phagocytes which are known to be present in human milk. In one study of a patient who received 1 gm initially, followed by two 500mg doses at 24 hr intervals, the concentration of azithromycin in breast milk varied from 0.64 mg/L (initially) to 2.8 mg/L on day 3. The predicted dose of azithromycin received by the infant would be approximately 0.482 mg/day (assuming milk volume of 150 mL/day and 37% bioavailability). This would suggest that the level of azithromycin ingested by a breastfeeding infant is not clinically significant. New pediatric formulations of azithromycin have been recently introduced. Pediatric dosing is 10 mg/kg STAT, followed by 5 mg/kg per day for up to 5 days.

Alternatives:

Pregnancy Risk Category: B

Adult Concerns: Diarrhea, loose stools, abdominal pain, vomiting, nausea.

Pediatric Concerns: None reported via breast milk. Pediatric formulations are available.

Drug Interactions: Aluminum and magnesium-containing antacids may slow, but not reduce absorption of azithromycin. Increased effect/toxicity when used with tacrolimus, alfentanil, astemizole, terfenadine, loratadine, carbamazepine, cyclosporine, digoxin, disopyramide, triazolam.

AHL = 48-68 hours		**M/P** =	
PHL =		**PB** = 7-51%	
PK = 3-4 hours		**Oral** = 37%	
MW = 749		**pKa** =	
Vd = 23-31			

References:
1. Pharmaceutical Manufacturer's Package Insert, 1996.
2. Kelsey JJ, Moser LR, Jennings JC, et.al. Presence of azithromycin breast milk concentrations: A case report. Am. J. Obstet. Gynecol. 170:1375-6, 1994.

Aztreonam   Fax #1033

Trade: Azactam
Can/Aus/UK: Azactam
Uses: Antibiotic
AAP: Approved by the American Academy of Pediatrics for use in breastfeeding mothers

Aztreonam is a monobactam antibiotic whose structure is similar but different than the penicillins and is used for documented gram-negative sepsis. Following a single 1 g IV dose, breast milk level was 0.18 mg/L at 2 hours and 0.22 mg/L at 4 hours. An infant ingesting 1 Liter per day of milk, would ingest 0.3 mg or 0.03% of the maternal dose per day. The manufacturer reports that less than 1% of a maternal dose is transferred into milk. Due to poor oral absorption (<1%) no untoward effects would be expected in nursing infants, aside from changes in GI flora. Aztreonam is commonly used in pediatric units.

Alternatives:

Pregnancy Risk Category: B

Adult Concerns: Changes in GI flora, diarrhea, rash, elevations of hepatic function tests.

Pediatric Concerns: None reported via milk.

Drug Interactions: Check hypersensitivity to penicillins and other beta-lactams. Requires dosage adjustment in renal failure.

AHL	= 1.7 hours	M/P	= 0.005
PHL	= 2.6 hours	PB	= 60%
PK	= 0.6-1.3 hours	Oral	= <1%
MW	= 435	pKa	=
Vd	= 0.26-0.36		

References:
1. Fleiss PM, et.al. Aztreonam in human serum and breast milk. Br. J. Clin. Pharmacol. 19(4):509-11, 1985.
2. Pharmaceutical Manufacturer's Package Insert, 1996.

Baclofen   Fax #1035

Trade: Lioresal, Atrofen
Can/Aus/UK: Lioresal, Novo-Baclofen, Apo-Baclofen, Clofen, Lioresal
Uses: Skeletal muscle relaxant
AAP: Approved by the American Academy of Pediatrics for use in breastfeeding mothers

Baclofen inhibits spinal reflexes and is used to reverse spasticity associated with multiple sclerosis or spinal cord lesions. Animal studies indicate baclofen inhibits prolactin release, and may inhibit lactation. Small amounts of baclofen are secreted into milk. In one mother given a 20 mg dose, total consumption by infant over a 26 hr period was estimated to be 22 μg, about 0.1% of the maternal dose. The milk half-life was 5.6 hours. It is quite unlikely that baclofen administered intrathecally would be secreted into milk in significant quantities.

Alternatives:

Pregnancy Risk Category: C

Adult Concerns: Drowsiness, excitement, dry mouth, urinary retention, tremor, rigidity, and wide pupils.

Pediatric Concerns: None reported.

Drug Interactions: Decreased effect when used with lithium. Increased effect of opiate analgesics, CNS depressants, alcohol (sedation), tricyclic antidepressants, clindamycin (neuromuscular blockade), guanabenz, MAO inhibitors.

AHL	= 3-4 hours	M/P	=
PHL	=	PB	= 30%
PK	= 2-3 hours	Oral	= Complete
MW	= 214	pKa	=
Vd	=		

References:
1.   Eriksson G, Swahn CG. Concentrations of baclofen in serum and breast milk from a lactating woman. Scand. J. Clin. Lab. Invest. 41:185, 1981.

Barium   Fax #1036

Trade: Barium
Can/Aus/UK:
Uses: Radiopaque agent
AAP: Not reviewed

Contrast agent used in radiology that is not absorbed orally.   No reported harmful effects.   Maternal absorption limited.

Alternatives:

Pregnancy Risk Category:

Adult Concerns: Nausea, vomiting, constipation.

Pediatric Concerns: None reported, not absorbed.

Drug Interactions:

References:

Beclomethasone   Fax #1037

Trade: Vanceril, Beclovent, Beconase
Can/Aus/UK: Propaderm, Vanceril, Beconase, Becloforte, Aldecin, Becotide, Beclovent
Uses: Intranasal, intrapulmonary steroid
AAP: Not reviewed

Beclomethasone is a potent steroid that is generally used via inhalation in asthma, or via intranasal administration for allergic rhinitis.   Due to its potency only very small doses are generally used, and therefore minimal plasma levels are attained.   Intranasal absorption is generally minimal.   Due to small doses administered, absorption into maternal plasma is extremely small.   Therefore it is unlikely that these doses would produce clinical significance in a breastfeeding infant.   See corticosteroids.

Alternatives:

Pregnancy Risk Category: C

Adult Concerns: When administered intra-nasally or via inhalation, adrenal suppression is very unlikely. Complications include headaches, hoarseness, bronchial irritation, oral candidiasis, cough. When used orally, complications may include adrenal suppression.

Pediatric Concerns: None reported via milk and inhalation or intranasal use.   Oral doses could suppress the adrenal cortex, and induce premature closure of the epiphysis, but would require high doses.

Drug Interactions: Corticosteroids have few drug interactions.

AHL = 15 hours		M/P	=
PHL =		PB	= 87%
PK =		Oral	= 90% (oral)
MW = 409		pKa	=
Vd =			

References:
1. Pharmaceutical Manufacturer's Package Insert, 1996.
2. McEvoy GE(ed):AFHS Drug Information, New York, NY. 1995.

Benazepril HCL   Fax #1038

Trade: Lotensin
Can/Aus/UK: Lotensin
Uses: Antihypertensive, ACE inhibitor
AAP: Not reviewed

Benazepril belongs to the ACE inhibitor family. Oral absorption is rather poor(37%). The active component(benazeprilat) reaches a peak at approximately 2 hours after ingestion. Generally, ACE inhibitors are seldom used during the early neonatal period due to profound neonatal hypotension. However, only minimal amounts are secreted into human milk. A newborn infant ingesting only breast milk would receive less than 0.1% of the mg/kg maternal dose of benazepril and benazeprilat.

Alternatives: Enalapril, Captopril

Pregnancy Risk Category: D

Adult Concerns: Significant fetal and neonatal morbidity, hypotension.

Pediatric Concerns: Neonatal morbidity, severe hypotension after in-utero exposure.

Drug Interactions: Decreased bioavailability with antacids. Reduced hypotensive effect with NSAIDS. Phenothiazines increase hypotensive effect. Allopurinol dramatically increase hypersensitivities (Steven-Johnson Syn.). ACE inhibitors dramatically increase digoxin levels. Lithium levels may be significantly increased with ACE use. Elevated potassium levels with oral potassium supplements.

AHL = 10-11 hours		**M/P** =	
PHL =		**PB** = 96.7%	
PK = 0.5 - 1 hr.		**Oral** = 37%	
MW =		**pKa** =	
Vd =			

References:
1. Pharmaceutical Manufacturer's Package Insert, 1996.

Bendroflumethiazide   Fax #1039

Trade: Naturetin
Can/Aus/UK: Naturetin, Aprinox, Berkozide, Centyl, Urizid
Uses: Thiazide diuretic
AAP: Approved by the American Academy of Pediatrics for use in breastfeeding mothers

Bendroflumethiazide is a thiazide diuretic sometimes used to suppress lactation. In one study, the clinician found this thiazide to effectively inhibit lactation. Use with caution. Not generally recommended in breastfeeding mothers.

Alternatives: Hydrochlorothiazide

Pregnancy Risk Category: D

Adult Concerns: Diuresis, fluid loss, leukopenia, hypotension, dizziness, headache, vertigo, reduced milk production.

Pediatric Concerns: None reported, but may inhibit lactation.

Drug Interactions: Enhanced hyponatremia and hypotension when used with ACE inhibitors. May elevate lithium levels.

AHL = 3-3.9 hours   M/P =
PHL =   PB = 94%
PK = 2-4 hours   Oral = Complete
MW = 421   pKa =
Vd = 1,48

References:
1.   Healy M. Suppressing lactation with oral diuretics. The Lancet, June 17, 1961, p 1353-4.

Benzonatate   Fax #1599

Trade: Tessalon Perles
Can/Aus/UK:
Uses: Antitussive
AAP: Not reviewed

Benzonatate is a nonnarcotic cough suppressant similar to the local anesthetic tetracaine. It anesthetizes stretch receptors in respiratory passages, dampening their activity and reducing the cough reflex. There are little pharmacokinetic data on this product, and no data on transfer into human milk. Because codeine is almost equally effective, and because we know that codeine only marginally transfers into human milk, it is probably a preferred antitussive in breastfeeding mothers.

Alternatives: Codeine

Pregnancy Risk Category: C

Adult Concerns: Sedation, headache, dizziness, constipation, nausea, have been reported.

Pediatric Concerns: None reported via milk.

Drug Interactions:
AHL = < 8 hours   M/P =
PHL =   PB =
PK = 20 minutes   Oral = Good

MW =   pKa   =
Vd =

References:
1.   Drug Facts and Comparisons. 1998. ed. Facts and Comparisons,
       St. Louis.

Bepridil HCL   Fax #1040

Trade: Vascor
Can/Aus/UK:
Uses: Antihypertensive, calcium channel blocker
AAP: Not reviewed

Following therapy with bepridil, milk levels were reported to approach 1/3 of serum levels. As with other calcium channel blockers, this family has been found to produce embryo toxic effects, and should never be used in pregnant women. Long half-life, enhanced oral absorption, and potency of this compound would increase the danger in nursing infant. Caution is recommended if used in nursing mother.

Alternatives: Nifedipine, Nimodipine

Pregnancy Risk Category: C

Adult Concerns: Bradycardia, hypotension.

Pediatric Concerns: None reported, but other calcium channel blockers may be preferred. See nifedipine.

Drug Interactions: H2 blockers may enhance oral absorption of bepridil. Beta blockers may enhance hypotensive effect. Bepridil may increase carbamazepine, cyclosporin, digitalis, quinidine, theophylline levels when used with these products.

AHL = 42 hours	M/P	= 0.33
PHL =	PB	= >99%
PK = 2-3 hours	Oral	= 60%

MW = 367   pKa =
Vd = 8

References:
1. Pharmaceutical Manufacturer's Package Insert, 1996.
2. Drug Facts and Comparisons. 1995 ed. Facts and Comparisons, St. Louis.

Betamethasone   Fax #1041

Trade: Betameth, Celestone
Can/Aus/UK: Beben, Betadermetnesol, Celestone, Diprolene, DIOR, Betnovate, Betnelan, Diprosone
Uses: Synthetic corticosteroid
AAP: Not reviewed

Betamethasone is a potent long-acting steroid. It generally produces less sodium and fluid retention that other steroids.   See prednisone.

Alternatives: Prednisone, Methylprednisolone

Pregnancy Risk Category: C

Adult Concerns: See prednisone.

Pediatric Concerns: None reported, used in pediatric patients.

Drug Interactions:

AHL = 5.6 hours   M/P =
PHL =   PB = 64%
PK = 10-36 minutes.   Oral = Complete
MW = 392   pKa =

References:
1. Drug Facts and Comparisons. 1995 ed. Facts and Comparisons, St. Louis.

Betaxolol   Fax #1042

Trade: Kerlone, Betoptic
Can/Aus/UK: Betoptic, Kerlone
Uses: Beta blocker antihypertensive
AAP: Not reviewed

Betaxolol is a long-acting, cardioselective beta blocker primarily used for glaucoma, but can be used orally for hypertension.   No data are available on betaxolol except one report by manufacturer of side effects which occurred in one nursing infant.   Many in this family readily transfer into human milk (see atenolol, acebutolol). Manufacturer indicates that levels secreted in milk are sufficient to produce pharmacological effects in the infant.   Caution is urged.

Alternatives: Propranolol, Metoprolol

Pregnancy Risk Category: C

Adult Concerns: Hypotension, bradycardia, fatigue.

Pediatric Concerns: No data are available on betaxolol except one report by manufacturer of side effects which occurred in one nursing infant.

Drug Interactions: Decreased effect when used with aluminum salts, barbiturates, calcium salts, cholestyramine, NSAIDs, ampicillin, rifampin, and salicylates. Beta blockers may reduce the effect of oral sulfonylureas (hypoglycemic agents). Increased toxicity/effect when used with other antihypertensives, contraceptives, MAO inhibitors, cimetidine, and numerous other products. See drug interaction reference for complete listing.

AHL = 14-22 hours	**M/P** = 2.5-3.0
PHL =	**PB** = 50%
PK = 3 hours	**Oral** = 89%
MW = 307	**pKa** =
Vd = 4.9	

References:

1.   Pharmaceutical Manufacturer's Package Insert, 1995.

Bethanechol Chloride   Fax #1043

Trade: Urabeth, Urecholine
Can/Aus/UK: Duvoid, Urocarb, Urecholine, Myotonine
Uses: Cholinergic stimulant
AAP: Not reviewed

Bethanechol is a cholinergic stimulant useful for urinary retention. Although poorly absorbed from GI tract, no reports on entry into breast milk are available.   However, it could conceivably cause abdominal cramps, colicky pain , nausea, salivation, bronchial constriction, or diarrhea in infants. There are several reports of discomfort in nursing infants. Use cautiously.

Alternatives:

Pregnancy Risk Category: C

Adult Concerns: Gastric distress such as colicky pain, cramping, nausea, salivation, breathing difficulties, diarrhea, hypotension, heart block, headache, urinary urgency.

Pediatric Concerns: Gi distress, discomfort, diarrhea.

Drug Interactions: Bethanechol when used with ganglionic blockers may lead to significant hypotension. Bethanechol effects may be antagonized by procainamide and quinidine.

AHL = 1-2 hours		**M/P** =	
PHL =		**PB** =	
PK = 60-90 min.(oral)		**Oral** = Poor	
MW = 197		**pKa** =	
Vd =			

References:
1.   Shore MF. Drugs can be dangerous during pregnancy and lactation. Can Pharmaceut J 103:358, 1970.

Bisacodyl   Fax #1044

Trade: Bisacodyl, Dacodyl, Dulcolax
Can/Aus/UK: Bisacolax, Dulcolax, Laxit, Apo-Bisacodyl, Bisalax, Durolax, Paxolax
Uses: Laxative
AAP: Not reviewed

Bisacodyl is a stimulant laxative that selectively stimulates colon contractions and defecation. It has only limited secretion into breast milk due to poor gastric absorption and subsequently minimal systemic levels. Little or no known harmful effects on infants.

Alternatives:

Pregnancy Risk Category: C

Adult Concerns: Diarrhea, GI cramping, rectal irritation.

Pediatric Concerns: None reported via milk.

Drug Interactions: By speeding emptying of GI tract may reduce efficacy of warfarin, and other products by reducing absorption.

AHL =		M/P	=
PHL =		PB	=
PK =		Oral	= < 5%
MW = 361		pKa	=
Vd =			

References:
1. Vorherr, H. Drug excretion in breast milk. Postgrad. Med. 56:97-104, 1974.

Bismuth Subsalicylate   Fax #1045

Trade: Pepto-Bismol
Can/Aus/UK: Bismuth Liquid, Pepto-Bismol
Uses: Antisecretory, antimicrobial salt
AAP: Drugs whose effect on nursing infants is unknown but may be of concern

Bismuth subsalicylate is present in many diarrhea mixtures. Although bismuth salts are poorly absorbed from the maternal GI tract, significant levels of salicylate could be absorbed from these products. As such, these drugs should not be routinely used due to the association of salicylates in Reyes syndrome in children. Some forms (Parepectolin, Infantol Pink) may contain tincture of opium (morphine). See morphine. See aspirin.

Alternatives:

**Pregnancy Risk Category: C in first 2 trimesters
                           D in third trimester**

Adult Concerns: Constipation, salicylate poisoning (tinnitus). May enhance risk of Reyes syndrome in children.

Pediatric Concerns: Risk of Reyes syndrome in neonates, but has not been reported with this product in a breastfed infant.

Drug Interactions: May reduce effects of tetracyclines, and uricosurics. May increase toxicity of aspirin, warfarin, hypoglycemics.

AHL =		**M/P** =	
PHL =		**PB** =	
PK =		**Oral** = Poor	
MW = 362		**pKa** =	
Vd =			

References:
1. Anderson P. Drug use during breast-feeding. Clinical Pharmacy 10:594-624, 1991.
2. Wilson, J. Drugs in Breast Milk. New York: ADIS Press, 1981.

3. Findlay JW, DeAngelis RI, Kearney MF, et.al. Analgesic drugs in breast milk and plasma. Clin Pharmacol. Ther. 29:625-633, 1981.

Bisoprolol   Fax #1046

Trade: Ziac, Zebeta
Can/Aus/UK: Emcor, Monocor
Uses: Beta-adrenergic antihypertensive
AAP: Not reviewed

Bisoprolol is a typical beta blocker used to treat hypertension. The manufacturer states that small amounts (<2%) are secreted into milk of animals. Others in this family are known to produce problems in lactating infants (see atenolol, acebutolol). Ziac is a combination of bisoprolol and hydrochlorothiazide.

Alternatives: Propranolol, Metoprolol

Pregnancy Risk Category: C

Adult Concerns: Bradycardia, hypotension, fatigue, excessive fluid loss.

Pediatric Concerns: None reported with this product, but other beta blockers have produced hypotension, hypoglycemia. See propranolol as alternative.

Drug Interactions: Decreased effect when used with aluminum salts, barbiturates, calcium salts, cholestyramine, NSAIDs, ampicillin, rifampin, and salicylates. Beta blockers may reduce the effect of oral sulfonylureas (hypoglycemic agents). Increased toxicity/effect when used with other antihypertensives, contraceptives, MAO inhibitors, cimetidine, and numerous other products. See drug interaction reference for complete listing.

AHL = 9-12 hours		**M/P** =	
PHL =		**PB** = 30%	
PK = 2 - 3 hours		**Oral** = 80%	

71

MW = 325   pKa =
Vd =

References:
1. Pharmaceutical Manufacturer's Package Insert, 1995.

Blue Cohosh   Fax #1605

Trade: Blue Ginseng, Squaw Root, Papoose Root, Yellow Ginseng
Can/Aus/UK:
Uses: Uterine stimulant
AAP: Not reviewed

Blue Cohosh is also known as blue ginseng, squaw root, papoose root, yellow ginseng. It is primarily used as a uterotonic drug, to stimulate uterine contractions. In one recent paper, an infant born of a mother who ingested Blue Cohosh root for 3 weeks prior to delivery, suffered from severe cardiogenic shock and congestive heart failure. Blue Cohosh root contains a number of chemicals, including the alkaloid methylcytisine, and the glycosides caulosaponin and caulophyllosaponin. Methylcytisine is pharmacologically similar to nicotine, and may result in elevated blood pressure, gastric stimulation, and hyperglycemia. Caulosaponin and caulophyllosaponin are uterine stimulants. They also apparently produce severe ischemia of the myocardium due to intense coronary vasoconstriction. This product should not be used in pregnant women. No data are available as to its transfer into human milk. It is primarily used prior to delivery.

Alternatives: Oxytocin

Pregnancy Risk Category:

Adult Concerns: The leaves and seeds contain alkaloids and glycosides that can cause severe stomach pain when ingested. Poisonings have been reported.

Pediatric Concerns: One case of severe congestive heart failure in newborn.

Drug Interactions:

References:

1. Jones TK, Lawson BM: Profound neonatal congestive heart failure caused by maternal consumption of blue cohosh herbal medication. J. Pediatrics 132(3):550-552, 1998.

Botulism   Fax #1048

Trade: Botox
Can/Aus/UK:
Uses: Botulism poisoning
AAP: Not reviewed

Botulism is a syndrome produced by the deadly toxin secreted by clostridium botulinum. Although the bacteria is wide spread, its colonization in food or the intestine of infants produces a deadly toxin. The syndrome is characterized by GI distress, weakness, malaise, lightheadedness, sore throat and nausea. Dry mouth is almost universal. In most adult poisoning, the bacteria is absent, only the toxin is present. In most pediatric poisoning, the stomach is colonized by the bacterium, often from contaminated honey. In one published report, a woman severely poisoned by botulism toxin continued to breastfeed her infant throughout. Four hours after admission, her milk was free of botulinum toxin and C. botulinum bacteria although she was still severely ill. The infant showed no symptoms of poisoning. It is apparent from this case that botulinum bacteria, nor the toxin may be secreted in breast milk. The product Botox is botulinum toxin type B.

Alternatives:

Pregnancy Risk Category:

Adult Concerns: GI distress, weakness, malaise, lightheadedness, sore throat, nausea, dry mouth.

Pediatric Concerns: None reported in one case.

Drug Interactions:

References:
1.   Middaugh J. Botulism and Breast Milk. N. Engl. J. Med. 298:343, 1978

Bromides   Fax #1049

Trade:
Can/Aus/UK:
Uses: Sedatives
AAP: Approved by the American Academy of Pediatrics for use in breastfeeding mothers

Small amounts are known to be secreted in milk. May cause persistent rash, drowsiness, or weakness in infants. Secretion in milk has been known for many years. Bromide preparations are no longer available in the US. They are poorly effective products and have no place in modern medicine. Contraindicated in nursing mothers.

Alternatives:

Pregnancy Risk Category: D

Adult Concerns: Rash, sedation.

Pediatric Concerns: Rash, drowsiness, weakness.

Drug Interactions:

References:
1.   Vorherr, H. Drug excretion in breast milk. Postgrad. Med. 56:97-104, 1974.
2.   Tyson RM, et. al. Drugs transmitted through breast milk. III. Bromides. J Pediatr 13:91-3, 1938.
3.   Van der Bogert F. Bromine poisoning through mother's milk. Am J Dis Child ;1921;21:167.

Bromocriptine Mesylate   Fax #1050

Trade: Parlodel
Can/Aus/UK: Parlodel, Apo-Bromocriptine, Kripton, Bromolactin
Uses: Inhibits prolactin secretion
AAP: Contraindicated by the American Academy of Pediatrics in Breastfeeding Mothers

Anti-parkinsonian, synthetic ergot alkaloid which inhibits prolactin secretion and hence physiological lactation. Most of the dose is absorbed first-pass by the liver, leaving less than 6% to remain in the plasma. Maternal serum prolactin levels remain suppressed for up to 14 hours after a single dose. The FDA approved indication for lactation suppression has been withdrawn, and it is no longer approved for this purpose due to numerous maternal deaths, seizures, and strokes. Observe for transient hypotension or vomiting. It is sometimes used in hyperprolactinemic patients who have continued to breastfeed, although the incidence of maternal side-effects is significant. Bromocriptine should only be used in lactating women for short periods if at all. In one breastfeeding patient who received 5 mg/day for a pituitary tumor, continued lactation produced no untoward effects in her infant. Profound postpartum hypotension has been reported.

Alternatives: Cabergoline

Pregnancy Risk Category: C

Adult Concerns: Most frequent side effects include nausea (49%), headache (19%), and dizziness (17%), peripheral vasoconstriction. Rarely, significant hypotension, shock, myocardial infarction. Transient hypotension and hair loss. A number of deaths have been associated with this product and it is no longer cleared for postpartum use to inhibit lactation.

Pediatric Concerns: No reports of direct toxicity to infant via milk but use with caution. Inhibits lactation.

Drug Interactions: Amitriptyline, butyrophenones, imipramine, methyldopa, phenothiazines, reserpine, may decrease efficacy of bromocriptine at reducing serum prolactin. May increase toxicity of other ergot alkaloids.

AHL	= 50 hours	**M/P**	=	
PHL	=	**PB**	= 90-96%	
PK	= 1-3 hours	**Oral**	= <28%	
MW	= 654	**pKa**	=	
Vd	= 3.4			

References:

1.   American Academy of Pediatrics, Committee on Drugs. Transfer of drugs and other chemicals into human milk. Pediatrics 93(1):137-150, 1994.
2.   Eickman FM. Recurrent myocardial infarction in a postpartum patient receiving bromocriptine. Clin. Cardiol. 15:781-3, 1992.
3.   Meese MG, et.al. Reassessment of bromocriptine use for lactation suppression. P and T. 17:1003-4, 1992.
4.   Spalding G. Bromocriptine for suppression of lactation. Aust. and NZ J. of Obstet. and Gyn. 31:344-45, 1991.
5.   Canales ES, Garcia IC, et.al. Bromocriptine as prophylactic therapy in prolactinoma during pregnancy. Fertil Steril 36:524-6, 1981.

Brompheniramine   Fax #1051

Trade: Dimetane, Brombay, Dimetapp, Bromfed
Can/Aus/UK: Dimetane, Dimotane
Uses: Antihistamine
AAP: Not reviewed

Brompheniramine is a popular antihistamine sold as Dimetane by itself, or in combination with phenylpropanolamine as Dimetapp, or with d-isoephedrine as Bromfed. Although untoward effects appear limited, some reported side effects from Dimetapp preparations are known. Although only insignificant amounts appear to be secreted into breast milk, there are a number of reported cases of irritability, excessive crying, and sleep disturbances that have been reported in breastfeeding infants. Only modest amounts of phenylpropanolamine (PPA, Propadrine) are believed to be secreted into breast milk. See phenylpropanolamine.

Alternatives: Loratadine, Cetirizine

Pregnancy Risk Category: C

Adult Concerns: Drowsiness, dry mucosa, excessive crying, irritability, sleep disturbances.

Pediatric Concerns: Irritability, excessive crying, and sleep disturbances have been reported.

Drug Interactions: May enhance toxicity of other CNS depressants, MAO inhibitors, alcohol and tricyclic depressants.

AHL = 24.9 hours		**M/P** =	
PHL =		**PB** =	
PK = 3.1 hours		**Oral** = Complete	
MW = 319		**pKa** =	
Vd = 11.7			

References:
1. O'Brien, T. Excretion of drugs in human milk. Am.J. Hosp. Pharm. 31:844-854, 1974.
2. Mortimer EA Jr. Drug toxicity from breast milk? Pediatrics 60:780-781, 1977.
3. Paton DM, Webster DR. Clinical pharmacokinetics of H1-receptor antagonists (the antihistamines). Clin. Pharm. 10:477-497, 1985.

Budesonide   Fax #1524

Trade: Rhinocort
Can/Aus/UK: Entocort, Pulmicort, Rhinocort
Uses: Corticosteroid
AAP: Not reviewed

Budesonide is a new and potent corticosteroid primarily used intra-nasally for allergic rhinitis. As such, the systemic bioavailability is minimal with less than 20% of the intranasal dose ever reaching systemic circulation. Once absorbed systemically budesonide is a weak systemic steroid and should not be used to replace other steroids. In one 5 year study of children aged 2-7 years, no changes in linear growth, weight, and bone age were noted. Adrenal suppression at these doses is extremely remote. Using normal doses, it is unlikely that clinically relevant concentrations of budesonide would ever reach the milk, nor be systemically bioavailable to a breastfed infant.

Alternatives:

Pregnancy Risk Category: C

Adult Concerns: Adverse effects following intranasal use include irritation, pharyngitis, cough, bleeding, candidiasis, dry mouth. No adrenal suppression has been reported.

Pediatric Concerns: None reported via milk. Pediatric use down to age 6 is permitted.

Drug Interactions:

AHL = 2.8 hours	**M/P**	=	
PHL =	**PB**	=	
PK = 2-4 hours (oral)	**Oral**	= 10.7% (oral)	
MW = 430	**pKa**	=	
Vd = 4.3			

References:

1. Volovitz B, Amir J, Malik H et al: Growth and pituitary-adrenal function in children with severe asthma treated with inhaled budesonide. N Engl J Med 329:1703-1708, 1993.
2. Manufacturer's Package Insert, 1997.

Bumetanide   Fax #1493

Trade: Bumex
Can/Aus/UK: Burinex
Uses: Loop diuretic
AAP: Not reviewed

Bumetanide is a potent loop diuretic similar to Lasix. As with all diuretics, some reduction in breast milk production may result but it is rare. It is not known if bumetanide transfers into human milk. If needed furosemide may be a better choice, as the oral bioavailability of furosemide in neonates is minimal.

Alternatives: Furosemide

Pregnancy Risk Category: D

Adult Concerns: Dehydration, hepatic cirrhosis, ototoxicity, potassium loss. See furosemide.

Pediatric Concerns: None reported via milk.

Drug Interactions: Numerous interactions exist, this is a partial list of the most important. NSAIDS may block diuretic effect. Lithium excretion may be reduced. Increased effect with other antihypertensives. May induce hypoglycemia when added to sulfonylurea users. Clofibrate may induce an exaggerated diuresis. Increased ototoxicity with aminoglycoside antibiotics. Increased anticoagulation with anticoagulants.

AHL = 1-1.5		M/P	=
PHL = 2.5 hours (neonate)		PB	= 95%
PK = 1 hour (oral)		Oral	=
MW = 364		pKa	=
Vd =			

References:
1. Drug Facts and Comparisons. 1996 ed. Facts and Comparisons, St. Louis.
2. Pharmaceutical Manufacturer's Package Insert, 1996.

Bupivacaine   Fax #1053

Trade: Marcaine
Can/Aus/UK: Marcaine, Marcain
Uses: Epidural, local anesthetic
AAP: Not reviewed

Bupivacaine is the most commonly employed regional anesthetic used in delivery because it concentrations in the fetus are the least of the local anesthetics. In one study of five patients, levels of bupivacaine in breast milk were below the limits of detection (< 0.02 mg/L) at 2 to 48 hours postpartum. These authors concluded that bupivacaine is a safe drug for perinatal use in mothers who plan to breastfeed.

Alternatives: Lidocaine

Pregnancy Risk Category: C

Adult Concerns: Sedation, bradycardia, respiratory depression.

Pediatric Concerns: None reported via milk.

Drug Interactions: Increases effect of hyaluronidase, beta blockers, MAO inhibitors, tricyclic antidepressants, phenothiazines, and vasopressors.

AHL = 2.7 hours		M/P	=
PHL = 8.1 hours		PB	= 95%
PK = 30-45 min.		Oral	=
MW = 288		pKa	= 8.1
Vd = 0.4-1.0			

References:
1. Naulty JS, Ostheimer G, et.al. Bupivacaine in breast milk following epidural anesthesia for vaginal delivery. Regional Anesthesia 8(1):44-45, 1983.
2. Rosenblatt, DB. et.al. The influence of maternal analgesia on neonatal behavior: II. Epidural Bupivacaine. Brit. J. Obstet. Gyn. 88:407-13, 1981.

Buprenorphine   Fax #1590

Trade: Buprenex
Can/Aus/UK: Temgesic
Uses: Narcotic analgesic
AAP: Not reviewed

Buprenorphine is a potent long-acting narcotic agonist and antagonist, and may be useful as a replacement for methadone treatment in addicts. In one patient who received 4 mg/day for withdrawal off of other opiates, the amount of buprenorphine transferred via milk was only 3.28 micrograms per day, an amount that was clinically insignificant. No symptoms were noted in the breastfed infant.

Alternatives:

Pregnancy Risk Category: C

Adult Concerns: Typical opiate side effects include pruritus, sedation, analgesia, hallucinations, euphoria, dizziness, respiratory depression.

Pediatric Concerns: None reported via milk.

Drug Interactions: May enhance effects of other opiates, benzodiazepines, and barbiturates.

AHL = 3 hours		**M/P** =	
PHL =		**PB** = 96%	
PK = 15-30 minutes		**Oral** = 31%	
MW =		**pKa** =	
Vd = 2,7			

References:
1. Marquet P, Lachatre G et.al. Buprenorphine withdrawal syndrome in a newborn. Clin. Pharmacol. Ther. 62(5):569-71, 1997.

Bupropion   Fax #1054

Trade: Wellbutrin, Zyban
Can/Aus/UK:
Uses: Antidepressant, smoking deterrent
AAP: Not reviewed

Bupropion is an older antidepressant with a structure unrelated to tricyclics. It may be teratogenic in pregnant women. One report in the literature indicates that bupropion probably accumulates in human milk, although the absolute dose transferred appears minimal. A new formulation is currently recommended for smoking cessation therapy and is called Zyban. Following one 100 mg dose in a mother the milk:plasma ratio ranged from 2.51 to 8.58, clearly suggesting a concentrating mechanism for this drug in human milk. However, plasma levels of bupropion (or its metabolites) in the infant were undetectable, indicating that accumulation in infant plasma apparently did not occur under these conditions (infant was fed 7.5 to 9.5 hours after dosing). The peak milk bupropion level (0.189 mg/L) occurred two hours after a 100 mg dose. This milk level would provide 0.019% of the maternal dose, a dose that is likely to be clinically insignificant to a breastfed infant.

Alternatives: Sertraline, Paroxetine

Pregnancy Risk Category: B

Adult Concerns: Seizures, restlessness, agitation, sleep disturbances. Probably contraindicated in patients with seizure disorders.

Pediatric Concerns: None reported in one study, but this infant was breastfed but twice daily.

Drug Interactions: May increase clearance of diazepam, carbamazepine, phenytoin. May increase effects of MAO inhibitors.

AHL = 8-24 hours	M/P = 2.51-8.58
PHL =	PB = 75-88%
PK = 2 hours	Oral =
MW = 240	pKa = 8.0

Vd = 40

References:
1.   Briggs GG, et.al. Excretion of bupropion in breast milk. Annals of Pharmacotherapy 27:431-433, 1993.

Buspirone   Fax #1055

Trade: BuSpar
Can/Aus/UK: BuSpar, Apo-Buspirone, Novo-Buspirone
Uses: Antianxiety medication
AAP: Not reviewed

No data exists on excretion into human milk. It is secreted into animal milk, so would expect the same in human milk. BuSpar is mg for mg equivalent to diazepam (Valium) in its anxiolytic properties, but does not produce significant sedation or addiction as the benzodiazepine family. Its metabolite is partially active, but has a brief half-life (4.8 hours) as well. Compared to the benzodiazepine family, this product would be a better choice for treatment of anxiety in breastfeeding women. But without accurate breast milk levels, it is not known if the product is safe for breastfeeding women or the levels the infant would ingest daily. The rather brief half-life of this product and its metabolite would not likely lead to buildup in the infants plasma.

Alternatives:

Pregnancy Risk Category: B

Adult Concerns: Dizziness, nausea, drowsiness, fatigue, excitement, euphoria.

Pediatric Concerns: None reported.

Drug Interactions: Cimetidine may increase the effect of buspirone. Increased toxicity may occur when used with MAO inhibitors, phenothiazines, CNS depressants, digoxin and haloperidol.

AHL	= 2-3 hours	M/P	=
PHL	=	PB	= 95%
PK	= 60-90 minutes	Oral	= 90%
MW	= 386	pKa	=
Vd	= 5.3		

References:
1. Pharmaceutical Manufacturer's Package Insert, 1996.

Busulfan   Fax #1056

Trade: Myleran
Can/Aus/UK: Myleran
Uses: Antineoplastic, anti-cancer drug.
AAP: Not reviewed

Busulfan is a potent antineoplastic agent that can produce severe bone marrow suppression, anemia, loss of blood cells, and elevated risk of infection. It is not known if busulfan is distributed to human milk. Its use in breastfeeding mothers is probably contraindicated. No data are available concerning breast milk concentrations, but this agent would be extremely toxic to growing infants and continued breastfeeding would not be justified. Use of this drug during breastfeeding is definitely not recommended.

Alternatives:

Pregnancy Risk Category: D

Adult Concerns: Severe bone marrow suppression, anemia, leukopenia, pulmonary fibrosis, cholestatic jaundice.

Pediatric Concerns: Extremely cytotoxic, use is not recommended in nursing women.

Drug Interactions:

AHL	= 2.6 hours.	M/P	=
PHL	=	PB	= 14%
PK	= 0.5-2 hours.	Oral	= Complete

84

MW = 246   pKa =
Vd   = 1.0

References:
1.   McEvoy GE(ed):AHFS Drug Information, New York, NY. 1995.

Butabarbital   Fax #1057

Trade: Butisol, Butalan
Can/Aus/UK:
Uses: Sedative, hypnotic
AAP: Not reviewed

Butabarbital is an intermediate acting barbiturate similar to phenobarbital. Small amounts are secreted in breast milk. No harmful effects have been reported. Watch for drowsiness and sedation.
Alternatives:

Pregnancy Risk Category: D

Adult Concerns: Sedation, weakness.

Pediatric Concerns: None reported but observe for sedation.

Drug Interactions: May have a decreased effect when used with phenothiazines, haloperidol, cyclosporin, tricyclic antidepressants, doxycycline, beta-blockers. May increase effects of benzodiazepines, CNS depressants, valproic acid, methylphenidate, and chloramphenicol.

AHL = 100 hours   M/P   =
PHL =   PB   =
PK   = 3-4 hours.   Oral = Complete
MW = 232   pKa   = 7.9
Vd   =

References:
1.   Tyson RM, Shrader EA, Perlman HH. Drugs transmitted through breast milk. II Barbiturates. J Pediatr. 14:86-90, 1938.
2.   Kaneko S, Sato T, Suzuki K. The levels of anticonvulsants in

breast milk. Br J Clin Pharmacol. 7:624-627,1979.

3.   O'Brien, T. Excretion of drugs in human milk. Am.J. Hosp. Pharm. 31:844-854, 1974.

4.   Vorherr, H. Drug excretion in breast milk. Postgrad. Med. 56:97-104, 1974.

Butalbital Compound   Fax #1058

Trade: Fioricet, Fiorinal, Bancap, Two-dyne
Can/Aus/UK: Tecnal, Fiorinal
Uses: Mild analgesic, sedative
AAP: Not reviewed

Mild analgesic with acetaminophen (325mg) or aspirin, caffeine (40mg), and butalbital (50mg). Butalbital is a mild, short-acting barbiturate that probably transfers into breast milk to a limited degree, although it is unreported. No data are available on the transfer of butalbital to breast milk, but it is likely minimal.

Alternatives:

Pregnancy Risk Category: D

Adult Concerns: Sedation.

Pediatric Concerns: Sedation.

Drug Interactions: Decreased effect when used with phenothiazines, haloperidol, cyclosporin, tricyclic antidepressants, and oral contraceptives.   Increased effect when used with alcohol, benzodiazepines, CNS depressants, valproic acid, methylphenidate.

AHL = 40-140 hours		**M/P** =	
PHL =		**PB** = 26%	
PK = 40-60 min.		**Oral** = Complete	
MW = 224		**pKa** =	
Vd = 0.8			

References:
1.   McEvoy GE(ed):AHFS Drug Information, New York, NY. 1995.

Butorphanol   Fax #1060

Trade: Stadol
Can/Aus/UK: Stadol
Uses: Potent narcotic analgesic
AAP: Approved by the American Academy of Pediatrics for use in breastfeeding mothers

Butorphanol is a potent narcotic analgesic. It is available both by IV, IM, and a nasal spray. Butorphanol passes into breast milk in low to moderate concentrations (estimated 4 µg/L of milk following 2 mg IM 4 times daily). Levels produced in infants are considered very low to insignificant. Butorphanol undergoes first-pass extraction by the liver, hence only 17% of the oral dose reaches the plasma. Butorphanol has been frequently used in labor and delivery in women who subsequently nursed their infants although it has been noted to produce a sinusoidal fetal heart rate pattern, and dysphoric or psychotomimetic responses in postpartum women.

Alternatives:

**Pregnancy Risk Category: B if used in first 2 trimesters
                            D if used at delivery**

Adult Concerns: Sedation, respiratory depression.

Pediatric Concerns: None reported via milk but sedation is possible in newborns.

Drug Interactions: May produce increase toxicity when used with CNS depressants, other opiates, phenothiazines, barbiturates, benzodiazepines, MAO inhibitors.

AHL = 3-4 hours.	M/P =
PHL =	PB = 80%
PK = 1 hour	Oral = 17 %

MW = 327   pKa = 8.6
Vd = 5

References:
1.   Pittman, K. et.al. Human perinatal distribution of butorphanol. Am. J. Obstet. Gynecol. 138:797-800, 1980.
2.   Drug Facts and Comparisons. 1996 ed. Facts and Comparisons, St. Louis.
3.   McEvoy GE(ed):AHFS Drug Information, New York, NY. 1995.

·Cabergoline   Fax #1548

Trade: Dostinex
Can/Aus/UK: Dostinex
Uses: Anti-prolactin
AAP: Not reviewed

Cabergoline is a long-acting synthetic ergot alkaloid derivative which produces a dopamine agonist effect similar but much safer than bromocriptine (Parlodel).   Cabergoline directly inhibits prolactin secretion by the pituitary.   It is primarily indicated for pathological hyperprolactinemia, but in several European studies, it has been used for inhibition of postpartum lactation. In several European countries, cabergoline is indicated for the inhibition or suppression of physiologic lactation.   The dose regimen used for the inhibition of physiologic lactation is cabergoline 1 mg administered as a single dose on the first day postpartum.   For the suppression of established lactation, cabergoline 0.25 mg is taken every 12 hours for 2 days for a total of 1 mg.   Single doses of 1 mg have been found to completely inhibit postpartum lactation. Transfer into human milk is not reported.

Alternatives:

Pregnancy Risk Category: B

Adult Concerns: Headache, dizziness, fatigue, orthostatic hypotension, nose bleed, inhibition of lactation.

Pediatric Concerns: Transfer via milk is unknown. Will completely and irreversibly suppress lactation and should not be used in mothers who are breastfeeding.

Drug Interactions: Do not use with other dopamine antagonists such as the phenothiazines (Thorazine, etc), butyrophenones (Haldol), thioxanthines, and metoclopramide (Reglan).

AHL = 80 hours		M/P	=
PHL =		PB	=
PK = 2-3 hours		Oral	= Complete
MW = 451		pKa	=
Vd =			

References:
1. Caballero-Gordo A, et.al. Oral cabergoline: Single-dose inhibition of puerperal lactation. J. Reprod. Med. 36(10):717-721, 1991.
2. European Multicentre Study Group for Cabergoline in Lactation Inhibition. Single dose cabergoline versus bromocriptine in inhibition of puerperal lactation. Randomized, double blind, multicentre study. BMJ 302(6789):1367-71, 1991.

Caffeine   Fax #1061

Trade: Vivarin, NoDoz, Coffee
Can/Aus/UK:
Uses: CNS stimulant
AAP: Approved by the American Academy of Pediatrics for use in breastfeeding mothers

Only limited amounts are secreted into breast milk. Caffeine levels secreted into breast milk average approximately 1-2 mg per day. Its long half-life in newborns may produce higher blood levels in neonates. The average cup of coffee contains 100-150 mg of caffeine. Peak levels of caffeine are found in breast milk 60 minutes after ingestion. The average daily dose received by infants is estimated to be less than

3 mg/kg/day in light to moderate users and generally averages 0.06 to 0.15% of the caffeine found in breast milk.   These concentrations are well below the doses used in neonatal units for treating neonatal apnea. Irritability and insomnia may occur and have been reported. Occasional use of caffeine is not contraindicated, but persistent, chronic use may lead to high plasma levels in the infant during the neonatal period. PHL= 80 hours (newborn), 97.5 hours (neonate), 2.6 hours (6 month old).

Alternatives:

Pregnancy Risk Category: B

Adult Concerns: Agitation, irritability, poor sleeping patterns.

Pediatric Concerns: Rarely, irritability and insomnia.

Drug Interactions: Reduces vasodilation of adenosine.   Reduces bioavailability of alendronate by 60%.   Cimetidine reduces caffeine clearance by 50%. Fluoroquinolone antibiotics increases half-life of caffeine by 5 to 8 hours.

AHL = 4.9 hours		**M/P**	= 0.52 - 0.76
PHL = 80-97.5 hours		**PB**	= 36%
PK = 60 min.		**Oral**	= 100%
MW = 194		**pKa**	= 0.8
Vd = 0.4-0.6			

References:
1.   Berlin CM Jr. Excretion of the methylxanthines in human milk. Semin Perinatol 5:389-94, 1981.
2.   Hill RM, et. al. Utilization of over-the-counter drugs during pregnancy. Clin Obstet Gynecol 20:381-94, 1977.
3.   Nehlig A, Debry G. Consequences on the newborn of chronic maternal consumption of coffee during gestation and lactation: A review. J. Am. Coll. Nutrit. 13:6-21, 1994.

Calcitonin   Fax #1560

Trade: Calcimar, Salmonine, Osteocalcin, Miacalcin
Can/Aus/UK: Caltine, Calcimar, Calcitare, Calsynar, Miacalcic
Uses: Calcium metabolism
AAP: Not reviewed

Calcitonin is a large polypeptide hormone (32 amino acids) secreted by the parafollicular cells of the thyroid that inhibits osteoclastic bone resorption thus maintaining calcium homeostasis in mammals. It is used for control of postmenopausal osteoporosis and other calcium metabolic diseases. Calcitonin is destroyed by gastric acids, requiring parenteral (SC, IM) or intranasal dosing. Calcitonin is unlikely to pentrate human milk due to its large molecular weight. Further, its oral bioavailability is nil, due to destruction in the GI tract. It has been reported to inhibit lactation in animals, although this has not been reported in humans.

Alternatives:

Pregnancy Risk Category: C

Adult Concerns: Nausea, facial flushing, shivering, edema, metallic taste, and increased urinary frequency.

Pediatric Concerns: None reported via milk. Unlikely to enter milk. Calcitonins have been reported to inhibit lactation in animals.

Drug Interactions: It is reported that ketoprofen inhibits the calciuric and uricosuric effect of porcine calcitonin. May have additive effect with plicamycin.

AHL = 1 hour		M/P =	
PHL =		PB =	
PK = 2 hours		Oral = None	
MW =		pKa =	
Vd =			

References:
1.   Pharmaceutical manufacturer's package insert, Armour. 1997.

2.   Fiore CE, Petralito A, Mazzarino MC et al: Effects of ketoprofen on the calciuric and uricosuric activities of calcitonin in man. J Endocrinol Invest 4:81-83, 1981.

Calendula   Fax #1535

Trade: Calendula, Marigold, Garden Marigold, Holligold, Gold Bloom, Marybud
Can/Aus/UK:
Uses: Herbal wound healing
AAP: Not reviewed

Calendula, grown worldwide, has been used topically to promote wound healing, and to alleviate conjunctivitis and other ocular inflammations. It consists of a number of flavonol glycosides and saponins, but the active ingredients are unknown. Despite these claims, there are almost no studies regarding its efficacy in any of these disorders. Further, there are no suggestions of overt toxicity, with exception of allergies. Although it may have some uses externally, its internal use as an antiphlogistic and spasmolytic is largely obsolete.

Alternatives:

Pregnancy Risk Category:

Adult Concerns: Allergies, anaphylactoid shock.

Pediatric Concerns: None reported via milk.

Drug Interactions:

References:
1.   Bissett NG.   In: Herbal Drugs and Phytopharmaceuticals. Medpharm Scientific Publishers, CRC Press, Boca Raton, 1994.

Cannabis   Fax #1063

Trade: Marijuana
Can/Aus/UK:
Uses: Sedative, hallucinogen
AAP: Contraindicated by the American Academy of Pediatrics in Breastfeeding Mothers

Commonly called marijuana, the active component is delta-9-THC is rapidly distributed to the brain and adipose tissue. It is stored in fat tissues for long periods (weeks to months). Small to moderate secretion into breast milk has been documented. Analysis of breast milk in chronic heavy user revealed an eightfold accumulation in breast milk compared to plasma although the dose received is insufficient to produce significant side effects in the infant. Studies have shown significant absorption and metabolism in infants, although long term sequelae have not been shown. Marijuana could produce sedation and growth delay, but it is highly dose dependent. In one study of 27 women who smoked marijuana during breastfeeding, no differences were noted in outcomes on growth, mental, and motor development. Studies in animals suggests that marijuana inhibits prolactin production and could inhibit lactation. Contraindicated in nursing mothers. Infants exposed to marijuana via breast milk will test positive in urine screens for long periods (2-3 weeks).

Alternatives:

Pregnancy Risk Category: C

Adult Concerns: Sedation, weakness, poor feeding patterns. Possible decreased milk production.

Pediatric Concerns: Sedation.

Drug Interactions:

AHL = 25-57 hours	**M/P**	**= 8**
PHL =	**PB**	**= 99.9%.**
PK =	**Oral**	**= Complete**
MW =	**pKa**	**=**

Vd   = High

References:
1.   Perez-Reyes M, Wall ME. Presence of tetrahydrocannabinol in human milk. N Engl J Med. 307:819-820, 1982.
2.   Tennes K, et.al. Marijuana: prenatal and postnatal exposure in the human. Natl. Inst. Drug Abuse Res. Monogr. Ser. 59:48-60, 1985.

Capsaicin   Fax #1489

Trade: Zostrix, Axsain, Capsin, Capzasin-P, No-Pain
Can/Aus/UK: Zostrix, Axsain
Uses: Analgesic, topical
AAP: Not reviewed

Capsaicin is an alkaloid derived from peppers from the Solanaceae family.   After topical absorption it increases,   depletes, and then suppresses substance P release from sensory neurons, thus preventing pain sensation.   Substance P is the principal chemical mediator of pain from the periphery to the CNS.   After repeated application (days to weeks), it depletes substance P and prevents re-accumulation in the neuron.   Very little or nothing is known about the kinetics of this product. It is approved for use in children > 2 years of age.   No data are available on transfer into human milk.

Alternatives:

Pregnancy Risk Category: C

Adult Concerns: Local irritation, burning, stinging, erythema. Cough and infrequently neurotoxicity. Avoid use near eyes.

Pediatric Concerns: None reported.   Avoid transfer to eye and other sensitive surfaces via hand contact.

Drug Interactions: May increase risk of cough with ACE inhibitors.

AHL = Several hours   M/P   =

PHL	=	PB	=
PK	=	Oral	=
MW	= 305	pKa	=
Vd	=		

References:
1. Bernstein JE: Capsaicin in dermatologic disease. Semin Dermatol 7:304-309, 1988.
2. Bernstein JE: Capsaicin in the treatment of dermatologic disease. Cutis 39:352-353, 1987.
3. Watson CPN, et.al. : The post-mastectomy pain syndrome and the effect of topical capsaicin. Pain 38:177-186, 1989.
4. Watson CPN: Postherpetic neuralgia. Neurologic Clin N Amer 7:231-248, 1989.

Captopril   Fax #1064

Trade: Capoten
Can/Aus/UK: Capoten, Apo-Capto, Novo-Captopril, Acenorm, Enzace, Acepril
Uses: Antihypertensive drug (ACE inhibitor)
AAP: Approved by the American Academy of Pediatrics for use in breastfeeding mothers

Captopril is a typical angiotensin converting enzyme inhibitor (ACE) used to reduce hypertension. Small amounts are secreted (4.7 µg/L milk). In one report of 12 women treated with 100 mg three times daily, maternal serum levels averaged 713 µg/L, while breast milk levels averaged 4.7 µg/L at 3.8 hours after administration. Data from this study suggest that an infant would ingest approximately 0.002% of the free captopril consumed by its mother (300mg) on a daily basis. No adverse effects have been reported in this study. Use only if determined to be important to mother's health.

Alternatives: Enalapril

Pregnancy Risk Category: D

Adult Concerns: Hypotension, bradycardia, decreased urine output and possible seizures. A decrease in taste acuity or metallic taste.

Pediatric Concerns: None reported but observe for hypotension.

Drug Interactions: Probenecid increases plasma levels of captopril. Captopril and diuretics have additive hypotensive effects. Antacids reduce bioavailability of ACE inhibitors. NSAIDS reduce hypotension of ACE inhibitors. Phenothiazines increase effects of ACE inhibitors. Allopurinol may increase risk of Steven-Johnson's syndrome with admixed with captopril. ACE inhibitors increase digoxin and lithium plasma levels. May elevate potassium levels when potassium supplementation is added.

AHL = 2.2 hours		**M/P**	= 0.012
PHL =		**PB**	= 30%
PK = 1 hr.		**Oral**	= 60-75%
MW = 217		**pKa**	= 3.7, 9.8
Vd = 0.7			

References:
1. Devlin RG, Fleiss PM. Selective resistance to the passage of captopril into human milk. Clin Pharmacol Ther 27:250, 1980.
2. Devlin RG, Fleiss PM. Captopril in human blood and breast milk. J Clin Pharmacol 21:110-3,1981.

Carbamazepine   Fax #1065

Trade: Tegretol, Epitol
Can/Aus/UK: Apo-Carbamazepine, Mazepine, Teril, Tegretol
Uses: Anticonvulsant
AAP: Approved by the American Academy of Pediatrics for use in breastfeeding mothers

Carbamazepine is a unique anticonvulsant commonly used for grand mal, clonic-tonic, simple and complex seizures. It is also used in manic depression and a number of other neurologic syndromes. It is one of the most commonly used anticonvulsants in pediatric patients. Normal pediatric peak plasma levels should be between 4 to 12 µg/mL. Small amounts are secreted in breast milk. Other studies generally show a range of breast milk concentration from 1.3 to 3.6 mg/L of milk following maternal doses from 200-800 mg/day. Plasma levels in breastfeeding infants are generally found to be less than 1 µg/mL and have not been found to produce toxicity in infant. Accumulation does not seem to occur.

Alternatives:

Pregnancy Risk Category: C

Adult Concerns: Sedation, nausea, respiratory depression, tachycardia, vomiting, diarrhea, blood dyscrasia.

Pediatric Concerns: None reported via milk.

Drug Interactions: Carbamazepine may induce the metabolism of warfarin, cyclosporin, doxycycline, oral contraceptives, phenytoin, theophylline, benzodiazepines, ethosuximide, valproic acid, corticosteroids, and thyroid hormones. Macrolide antibiotics, isoniazid, verapamil, danazol, diltiazem may inhibit metabolism of carbamazepine and increase plasma levels.

AHL = 18-54 hours.	**M/P** = 0.69
PHL = 8-28 hours.	**PB** = 74%
PK = 4-5 hours.	**Oral** = 100%
MW = 236	**pKa** = 7.0
Vd = 0.8-1.8	

References:
1. Niebyl JR, Blake DA, Freeman JM, et.al. Carbamazepine levels in pregnancy and lactation. Obstet Gynecol. 53:139-140,1979.
2. Nau H, et.al. Anticonvulsants during pregnancy and lactation. Clin. Pharmacokinetics 7:508-543, 1982.

Carbamide Peroxide   Fax #1498

Trade: Gly-Oxide, Debrox, Auro Otic
Can/Aus/UK: Exterol
Uses: Antibacterial, whitening agent
AAP: Not reviewed

Carbamide peroxide is stable while immersed in glycerin, but upon contact with moisture, releases hydrogen peroxide and nascent oxygen, both strong oxidizing agents. It is used to disinfect infected lesions and for whitening of teeth and dental appliances. Hydrogen peroxide is rapidly metabolized by hydroperoxidases, peroxidases and catalase present in all tissues, plasma, and saliva. Its transfer to the plasma is minimal if at all. It would be all but impossible for any to reach breast milk unless under extreme overdose.

Alternatives:

Pregnancy Risk Category: C

Adult Concerns: Dermal irritation, mucous membrane irritation, inflammation. Overgrowth of candida and other opportunistic infections.

Pediatric Concerns: Toxic in major overdose. Exposure to small amounts may lead to inflamed membranes.

Drug Interactions:

References:

Carbenicillin   Fax #1066

Trade: Geopen, Geocillin, Carindacillin
Can/Aus/UK: Geopen
Uses: Extended spectrum penicillin antibiotic
AAP: Not reviewed

Carbenicillin is an extended spectrum penicillin antibiotic. Only limited levels are secreted into breast milk (0.26 mg/liter or about 0.001% of adult dose). Due to its poor oral absorption (< 10%) the amount absorbed by a nursing infant would be minimal. Not considered harmful to infant unless infant is extremely hypersensitive to penicillins.

Alternatives:

Pregnancy Risk Category: B

Adult Concerns: Rash, thrush, or diarrhea. Headache, rash, hyperthermia.

Pediatric Concerns: None reported via milk.

Drug Interactions: Co-administration of aminoglycosides (within 1 hour) may inactivate both drugs. Increased half-life with probenecid.

AHL = 1 hour	**M/P = 0.02**
PHL = 0.8-1.8 hours	**PB = 26-60%**
PK = 1-3 hours	**Oral = <10-30%**
MW = 378	**pKa =**
Vd =	

References:
1.   Pharmaceutical Manufacturer's Package Insert, 1996.

Carbidopa   Fax #1067

Trade: Lodosyn
Can/Aus/UK: Sinemet, Kinson, Sinacarb
Uses: Inhibits levodopa metabolism
AAP: Not reviewed

Carbidopa inhibits the metabolism of levodopa in parkinsonian patients therefore extending the half-life of levodopa.   Its effect on lactation is largely unknown, but skeletal malformations have occurred in pregnant rabbits. Use discretion in administering to pregnant or lactating women.

Alternatives:

Pregnancy Risk Category: C

Adult Concerns: GI distress, nausea, vomiting, diarrhea.

Pediatric Concerns:

Drug Interactions: May interact with tricyclic antidepressants leading to hypertensive reactions.

AHL = 1-2 hours.		**M/P** =	
PHL =		**PB** = 36%	
PK =		**Oral** = 40-70%	
MW = 244		**pKa** =	
Vd =			

References:
1. Pharmaceutical Manufacturer's Package Insert, 1996.
2. McEvoy GE(ed):AHFS Drug Information, New York, NY. 1995.

Carbimazole   Fax #1557

Trade:
Can/Aus/UK: Neo-Mercazole
Uses: Thyroid inhibitor
AAP: Not reviewed

Carbimazole is a pro-drug of methimazole and is rapidly and completely converted to the active methimazole in the plasma. Only methimazole is detected in plasma, urine and thyroid tissue. See breastfeeding specifics for methimazole. Data from Rylance (1987) suggests that subclinical levels of methimazole enter milk subsequent to administration of 30 mg/day carbimazole. Free methimazole measured on 10 occasions averaged 43 nanogram/mL. Plasma methimazole in twins was 45 to 52 nanograms/mL. Thyroid suppression is believed to occur only when plasma levels exceed 50-100 ng/mL. No thyroid suppression was noted in these two twins. Peak transfer into milk occurred at 2-4 hours, and the lowest at 6 hours after the dose. The authors suggest that breastfeeding is permissible if the maternal dose is less than 30 mg/day. See propylthiouracil as alternative.

Alternatives: Propylthiouracil

Pregnancy Risk Category: D

Adult Concerns: Hypothyroidism, hepatic dysfunction, bleeding, drowsiness, skin rash, nausea, vomiting, fever.

Pediatric Concerns: None reported via milk, but propylthiouracil is generally preferred in breastfeeding women.

Drug Interactions: Use with iodinated glycerol, lithium, and potassium iodide may increase toxicity.

AHL = 6-13 hours		M/P	= 0.3-0.7
PHL =		PB	= 0%
PK = 4 hours		Oral	= Complete
MW = 186		pKa	=
Vd =			

References:
1. Rylance GW, Woods CG, Donnelly MC et al: Carbimazole and breastfeeding (letter). Lancet 1987; 1:928

Carisoprodol   Fax #1069

Trade: Soma Compound, Solol
Can/Aus/UK: Soma, Carisoma
Uses: Muscle relaxant, CNS depressant
AAP: Not reviewed

Carisoprodol is a commonly used skeletal muscle relaxant that is a CNS depressant. As Soma Compound it also contains 325 mg of aspirin.

It is transferred into human milk at 2-4 times the maternal plasma level. Although it may produce infant drowsiness and GI upset, long term maternal use has not produced toxicity in infants.

Alternatives:

Pregnancy Risk Category: C

Adult Concerns: Nausea, vomiting, hiccups, sedation, weakness, mild withdrawal symptoms after chronic use.

Pediatric Concerns: None reported, but observe for sedation.

Drug Interactions: Increased toxicity when added to alcohol, CNS depressants, MAO inhibitors.

AHL = 8 hours		**M/P**	= 2-4
PHL =		**PB**	=
PK =		**Oral**	= Complete
MW = 260		**pKa**	=
Vd =			

References:
1.   McEvoy GE(ed):AHFS Drug Information, New York, NY. 1995.

Carteolol   Fax #1070

Trade: Cartrol
Can/Aus/UK: Teoptic
Uses: Beta-adrenergic antihypertensive
AAP: Not reviewed

Carteolol is a typical beta blocker used for hypertension. Carteolol is reported to be excreted in breast milk of lactating animals. No data available on human milk.

Alternatives: Propranolol, Metoprolol

Pregnancy Risk Category: C

Adult Concerns: Hypotension, bradycardia, lethargy, and sedation.

Pediatric Concerns: None reported but observe for hypoglycemia, hypotension, bradycardia, lethargy.

Drug Interactions: Decreased effect when used with aluminum salts, barbiturates, calcium salts, cholestyramine, NSAIDs, ampicillin, rifampin, and salicylates. Beta blockers may reduce the effect of oral sulfonylureas (hypoglycemic agents). Increased toxicity/effect when used with other antihypertensives, contraceptives, MAO inhibitors, cimetidine, and numerous other products. See drug interaction reference for complete listing.

AHL = 6 hours	M/P	=
PHL =	PB	= 23-30%
PK =	Oral	= 80%
MW = 292	pKa	=
Vd =		

References:
1.   Pharmaceutical Manufacturer's Package Insert, 1996.

Carvedilol   Fax #1568

Trade: Coreg
Can/Aus/UK: Coreg, Eucardic
Uses: Antihypertensive
AAP: Not reviewed

Carvedilol is a nonselective beta-adrenergic blocking agent (and partial alpha-1 blocking activity) with high lipid solubility and no intrinsic sympathomimetic activity. There are no data available on the transfer of this drug into human milk. However, due to its high volume of distribution and high lipid solubility, some may transfer. Caution is recommended.

Alternatives: Propranolol, metoprolol.

Pregnancy Risk Category: C

Adult Concerns: Postural hypotension, fatigue, dizziness, lightheadedness, bradycardia, bronchospasm. Use with caution in asthmatics.

Pediatric Concerns: None reported via milk. Observe for hypotension, bradycardia, hypoglycemia.

Drug Interactions: Severe bradycardia may result when used with amiodarone. Digoxin may prolong AV conduction time. Severe hypotension when added with calcium channel blockers. Severe hypertension, bradycardia when used with epinephrine.

AHL = 6-10 hours		M/P	=
PHL =		PB	=
PK = 1-1.5 hours		Oral	= 25-35%
MW =		pKa	=
Vd = 1.88			

References:
1. Pharmaceutical Manufacturer's Package Insert, 1998.

Cascara Sagrada   Fax #1071

Trade: Cascara Sagrada
Can/Aus/UK: Cascara Sagrada
Uses: Laxative
AAP: Approved by the American Academy of Pediatrics for use in breastfeeding mothers

Trace amounts appear to be secreted into breast milk. No exact estimates have been published. May cause loose stools and diarrhea in neonates.

Alternatives:

Pregnancy Risk Category: C

Adult Concerns: Diarrhea, GI cramping.

Pediatric Concerns: May loosen stools in infants.

Drug Interactions: Decreased effect of oral anticoagulants.

References:
1.	O'Brien, T. Excretion of drugs in human milk. Am.J. Hosp. Pharm. 31:844-854, 1974.
2.	Vorherr, H. Drug excretion in breast milk. Postgrad. Med. 56:97-104, 1974.

Castor Oil   Fax #1072

Trade: Alphamul, Neoloid, Emulsoil
Can/Aus/UK: Castrol Oil, Seda-rash, Exzem Oil
Uses: Laxative
AAP: Not reviewed

Castor oil is converted to ricinoleic acid in the gut. Its transfer into milk is unknown. Caution should be used. Excess amounts could produce diarrhea, insomnia and tremors in exposed infants.

Alternatives:

Pregnancy Risk Category: X

Adult Concerns: Insomnia, tremors, diarrhea.

Pediatric Concerns: Observe for diarrhea, insomnia, tremors in infants.

Drug Interactions:

AHL =		M/P =	
PHL =		PB =	
PK = 2-3 hours.		Oral = Unknown	
MW = 932		pKa =	
Vd =			

References:

Cefaclor   Fax #1073

Trade: Ceclor
Can/Aus/UK: Ceclor, Apo-Cefaclor, Keflor, Distaclor
Uses: Cephalosporin antibiotic
AAP: Not reviewed

Cefaclor is a commonly used pediatric cephalosporin antibiotic. Small amounts are known to be secreted into human milk. Following a 500 mg oral dose, milk levels averaged 0.16 to 0.21 mg/L.

Alternatives:

Pregnancy Risk Category: B

Adult Concerns: Diarrhea, GI irritation, rash, penicillin allergy, delayed serum sickness at 14 days.

Pediatric Concerns: None reported via milk.

Drug Interactions: Probenecid may increase levels of cephalosporins by reducing renal clearance.

AHL = 0.5-1 hr.	M/P =
PHL =	PB = 25%
PK = 0.5-1 hr.	Oral = 100%
MW = 386	pKa =
Vd =	

References:
1. Takase Z. Clinical and laboratory studies of cefaclor in the field of obstetrics and gynecology. Chemotherapy 27:(Suppl)668, 1979.

Cefadroxil   Fax #1074

Trade: Ultracef, Duricef
Can/Aus/UK: Duricef, Baxan
Uses: Cephalosporin antibiotic
AAP: Approved by the American Academy of Pediatrics for use in breastfeeding mothers

Cefadroxil is a typical first-generation cephalosporin antibiotic. Small amounts are known to be secreted into milk. Milk concentrations following a 1000 mg oral dose were 0.10 mg/L at 1 hour and 1.24 mg/L at 5 hours. Milk:serum ratios were 0.009 at 1 hour and 0.019 at 3 hours.

Alternatives:

Pregnancy Risk Category: B

Adult Concerns: Diarrhea, allergic rash.

Pediatric Concerns: None reported via milk. Observe for GI symptoms such as diarrhea.

Drug Interactions: Probenecid may decrease clearance. Furosemide, aminoglycosides may enhance renal toxicity.

AHL = 1.5 hours		**M/P** = 0.009-0.019	
PHL =		**PB** = 20%	
PK = 1-2 hours		**Oral** = 100%	
MW = 381		**pKa** =	
Vd =			

References:
1.   Kafetzi D, Siafas C, et.al. Passage of cephalosporins and amoxicillin into the breast milk. Acta. Paediatr. Scand. 70:285-8, 1981.

Cefazolin   Fax #1075

Trade: Ancef, Kefzol
Can/Aus/UK: Ancef, Kefzol, Cefamezin
Uses: Cephalosporin antibiotic
AAP: Approved by the American Academy of Pediatrics for use in breastfeeding mothers

Cefazolin is a typical first-generation cephalosporin antibiotic that has adult and pediatric indications. It is only used IM or IV, never orally. In 20 patients who received a 2 gm STAT dose over 20 minutes, the average concentration of cefazolin in milk 2, 3, and 4 hours post-dose was 1.25, 1.51, and 1.16 mg/L, respectively. A very small milk:plasma ratio (0.023) indicates insignificant transfer into milk. Cefazolin is poorly absorbed orally, therefore the infant would absorb a minimal amount. Plasma levels in infants are reported to be too small to be detected.

Alternatives:

Pregnancy Risk Category: B

Adult Concerns: Allergic rash, thrush, diarrhea.

Pediatric Concerns: None reported via milk. Observe for GI symptoms such as diarrhea.

Drug Interactions: Probenecid may decrease clearance. Furosemide, aminoglycosides may enhance renal toxicity.

AHL = 1.2-2.2 hours	M/P	= 0.023
PHL =	PB	= 89%
PK = 1-2 hours	Oral	= Poor
MW = 455	pKa	=
Vd =		

References:
1.   von Kobyletzki D, et. al. Pharmacokinetic studies with cefazolin in obstetrics and gynecology. Infection 2(Suppl):60-7,1974.

Cefepime   Fax #1563

Trade: Maxipime
Can/Aus/UK: Maxipime
Uses: Cephalosporin antibiotic
AAP: Not reviewed

Cefepime is a new 'fourth-generation' parenteral cephalosporin. Cefepime is secreted in human milk in small amount averaging 0.5 µg/mL. A nursing infant consuming one liter of milk daily would receive about 0.5 mg of cefepime or about 0.0005 % of the maternal dose.

Alternatives:

Pregnancy Risk Category: B

Adult Concerns: Headache, blurred vision, dyspepsia, diarrhea, transient elevation of liver enzymes.

Pediatric Concerns: None reported via milk.

Drug Interactions: May produce additive nephrotoxic effects when used with aminoglycosides.

AHL = 2 hours	M/P	= 0.8
PHL =	PB	= 16-19%
PK = 0.5-1.5 hours	Oral	= Poor
MW =	pKa	=
Vd = 0.3		

References:
1. Pharmaceutical Manufacturer's Package Insert, 1997.
2. Sanders CC: Cefepime: the next generation? Clin Infect Dis 17:369-379, 1993.

Cefixime   Fax #1076

Trade: Suprax
Can/Aus/UK: Suprax
Uses: Cephalosporin antibiotic
AAP: Not reviewed

Cefixime is an oral third-generation cephalosporin used in treating infections. It is poorly absorbed (30-50%) by the oral route. It is secreted to a limited degree in the milk, although in one study of a mother receiving 100 mg, it was undetected in the milk from 1-6 hours after the dose.

Alternatives:

Pregnancy Risk Category: B

Adult Concerns: Allergic rash, diarrhea, thrush.

Pediatric Concerns: None reported. Observe for GI symptoms such as diarrhea.

Drug Interactions: Probenecid may decrease clearance. Furosemide, aminoglycosides may enhance renal toxicity.

AHL = 7 hours		M/P	=
PHL =		PB	= 70%
PK = 2-6 hours		Oral	= 30-50%
MW = 453		pKa	=
Vd =			

References:
1.   Pharmaceutical Manufacturer's Package Insert, 1996.
2.   McEvoy GE(ed):AHFS Drug Information, New York, NY. 1995.

Cefoperazone Sodium   Fax #1077

Trade: Cefobid
Can/Aus/UK: Cefobid
Uses: Cephalosporin antibiotic
AAP: Not reviewed

Cefoperazone is a broad spectrum third-generation cephalosporin antibiotic. It is poorly absorbed from GI tract and is only available via IV and IM injection. Cefoperazone is extremely labile in acid environments which would account both for its destruction and its lack of absorption via the GI tract. Following an IV dose of 1000 mg, milk levels ranged from 0.4 to 0.9 mg/L. Cefoperazone is extremely acid labile and would be destroyed in the GI tract of an infant. It is unlikely that significant absorption would occur. Cefoperazone is sometimes administered for neonatal sepsis. Daily ingestion by infant from breastfeeding is estimated to be less than 0.9% of maternal dose.

Alternatives:

Pregnancy Risk Category: B

Adult Concerns: Diarrhea, allergic rash, thrush.

Pediatric Concerns: None reported. Observe for GI symptoms such as diarrhea.

Drug Interactions: Probenecid may decrease clearance. Furosemide, aminoglycosides may enhance renal toxicity.

AHL = 2 hours		**M/P** =	
PHL = 6-10 hours (neonatal)		**PB** = 82-93%	
PK = 73-153 min.(IV)		**Oral** = Poor	
MW = 645		**pKa** =	
Vd =			

References:
1.   Personal Communication. Pfizer/Roerig Laboratories . 1996.

Cefotaxime   Fax #1078

Trade: Claforan
Can/Aus/UK: Claforan
Uses: Cephalosporin antibiotic
AAP: Approved by the American Academy of Pediatrics for use in breastfeeding mothers

Cefotaxime is poorly absorbed orally and is only used via IV or IM administration. Milk levels following a 1000 mg IV maternal dose were 0.26 mg/L at 1 hour, 0.32 mg/L at 2 hours, and 0.30 mg/L at 3 hours. No effect on infant or lactation were noted. Milk:serum ratio at 3 hours was 0.160.

Alternatives:

Pregnancy Risk Category: B

Adult Concerns: Diarrhea, allergic rash, thrush.

Pediatric Concerns: None reported. Observe for GI symptoms such as diarrhea.

Drug Interactions: Probenecid may decrease clearance. Furosemide, aminoglycosides may enhance renal toxicity.

AHL	= < 0.68 hr.	M/P	= 0.027 - 0.17
PHL	= 2-3.5 hours	PB	= 40%
PK	= 30 min.	Oral	= Poor
MW	= 455	pKa	=
Vd	=		

References:
1. Kafetzis DA, et.al. Transfer of cefotaxime in human milk and from mother to foetus. J. Antimicrob. Chemother. 6:135-41(Suppl), 1980.

Cefotetan   Fax #1079

Trade: Cefotan
Can/Aus/UK: Cefotan, Apatef
Uses: Cephalosporin antibiotic
AAP: Not reviewed

Cefotetan is a third generation cephalosporin that is poorly absorbed orally and is only available via IM and IV injection. The drug is distributed into human milk in low concentrations. Following a maternal dose of 1000mg IV, breast milk concentrations averaged 0.22, 0.34, and 0.28 mg/L at 1, 4, and 6 hours, respectively.

Alternatives:

Pregnancy Risk Category: B

Adult Concerns: Diarrhea, allergic rash, thrush.

Pediatric Concerns: None reported. Observe for GI symptoms such as diarrhea.

Drug Interactions: Probenecid may decrease clearance. Furosemide, aminoglycosides may enhance renal toxicity.

AHL = 3-4.6 hours		**M/P** =	
PHL =		**PB** = 76-91%	
PK = 1.5-3 hours.		**Oral** = Poor	
MW = 576		**pKa** =	
Vd =			

References:
1. Cho N, Fukunaga K, Kunii K. Fundamental and clinical studies on cefotetan in the field of obstetrics and gynecology. Chemotherapy 30:(Supp. 1) 832-42, 1982.
2. Novelli A. et.al. The penetration of intramuscular cefotetan disodium into human extra-vascular fluid and maternal milk secretion. Chemoterapia II(5): 337-342,1983.

Cefoxitin   Fax #1080

Trade: Mefoxin
Can/Aus/UK: Mefoxin
Uses: Cephalosporin antibiotic
AAP: Approved by the American Academy of Pediatrics for use in breastfeeding mothers

Cefoxitin is a cephalosporin antibiotic with a spectrum similar to the second generation family. It is transferred into human milk in very low levels. In a study of 18 women receiving 2000-4000 mg doses, only one breast milk sample contained cefoxitin (0.9 mg/L), all the rest were too low to be detected.

Alternatives:

Pregnancy Risk Category: B

Adult Concerns: Diarrhea, allergic rash, thrush.

Pediatric Concerns: None reported. Observe for GI symptoms such as diarrhea.

Drug Interactions: Probenecid may decrease clearance. Furosemide, aminoglycosides may enhance renal toxicity.

AHL = 0.7-1.1 hr.		M/P	=
PHL =		PB	= 85-99%
PK = 20-30 min.(IM)		Oral	= Poor
MW = 427		pKa	=
Vd =			

References:
1. Kefetzis DA, Siafas CA, Georgakopoulous PA, et.al. Passage of cephalosporins and amoxicillin into the breast milk. Acta Paediatr Scan 70:285-286,1981.
2. Roex AJM, van Loenen AC, et.al. Secretion of cefoxitin in breast milk following short-term prophylactic administration in caesarean section. Eur. J. Obstet. Gynecol. Reprod. Biol. 25:299-301, 1987.

Cefpodoxime Proxetil   Fax #1081

Trade: Vantin
Can/Aus/UK: Orelox
Uses: Cephalosporin antibiotic
AAP: Not reviewed

Cefpodoxime is a cephalosporin antibiotic that is subsequently metabolized to an active metabolite. Only 50% is orally absorbed. In a study of 3 lactating women, levels of cefpodoxime in human milk were 0%, 2%, and 6% of maternal serum levels at 4 hours following a 200 mg oral dose. At 6 hours post-dosing, levels were 0%, 9%, and 16% of concomitant maternal serum levels. Pediatric indications down to 6 months of age are available.

Alternatives:

Pregnancy Risk Category: B

Adult Concerns: Diarrhea, allergic rash, thrush.

Pediatric Concerns: None reported. Observe for GI symptoms such as diarrhea.

Drug Interactions: Probenecid may decrease clearance. Furosemide, aminoglycosides may enhance renal toxicity. Antacids and H2 blockers reduce GI absorption of cefpodoxime.

AHL = 2.09-2.84 hours		**M/P**	= 0-0.16
PHL =		**PB**	= 22-33%
PK = 2-3 hours		**Oral**	= 50%
MW = 558		**pKa**	=
Vd =			

References:
1.   Pharmaceutical Manufacturer's Package Insert, 1996.

Cefprozil   Fax #1082

Trade: Cefzil
Can/Aus/UK:
Uses: Oral cephalosporin antibiotic
AAP: Approved by the American Academy of Pediatrics for use in breastfeeding mothers

Cefprozil is a typical second-generation cephalosporin antibiotic. Following an oral dose of 1000 mg, the breast milk concentrations were 0.7, 2.5, and 3.4 mg/L at 2, 4, and 6 hours post-dose respectively. The peak milk concentration occurred at 6 hours, and was lower thereafter. Milk:plasma ratios varied from 0.05 at 2 hours to 5.67 at 12 hours. However, the milk concentration at 12 hours was small (1.3 μg/ml). Using the highest concentration found in breast milk (3.5 mg/L) an infant consuming 800 ml of milk daily would ingest about 2.8 mg of cefprozil daily or less than 0.3% of the maternal dose. Because the dose used in this study is approximately twice that normally used, it is reasonable to assume that an infant would ingest less than 1.7 mg per day, an amount clinically insignificant. Pediatric indications for infants 6 months and older are available.

Alternatives:

Pregnancy Risk Category: C

Adult Concerns: Diarrhea, allergic rash, and thrush.

Pediatric Concerns: None reported. Observe for GI symptoms such as diarrhea.

Drug Interactions: Probenecid may decrease clearance. Furosemide, aminoglycosides may enhance renal toxicity.

AHL = 78 minutes		**M/P**	= 0.05 - 5.67
PHL =		**PB**	= 36 %
PK = 1.5 hours		**Oral**	= Complete
MW =		**pKa**	=
Vd =			

References:
1.   Shyu WC, et.al. Excretion of cefprozil into human breast milk. Antimic. Agents & Chemo. 36(5):938-41,1992

Ceftazidime   Fax #1083

Trade: Ceftazidime, Fortaz, Tazidime
Can/Aus/UK: Fortaz, Ceptaz, Fortum
Uses: Cephalosporin antibiotic
AAP: Approved by the American Academy of Pediatrics for use in breastfeeding mothers

Ceftazidime is a broad spectrum third-generation cephalosporin antibiotic. Is has poor oral absorption (<10%). In lactating women who received 2000 mg (IV) every 8 hours, concentrations of Ceftazidime in milk averaged 3.8 mg/L before the dose and 5.2 mg/L at 1 hour post-dose (neonatal dose is 30-50 mg/kg every 12 hours).

Alternatives:

Pregnancy Risk Category: B

Adult Concerns: Diarrhea, allergic rash, thrush.

Pediatric Concerns: None reported. Observe for GI symptoms such as diarrhea.

Drug Interactions: Probenecid may decrease clearance. Furosemide, aminoglycosides may enhance renal toxicity.

AHL = 1.4-2 hours		M/P	=
PHL = 2.2-4.7 hours (neonates)		PB	= 5-24%
PK = 69-90 min.		Oral	= < 10%
MW = 547		pKa	=
Vd =			

References:
1.   Blanco JD et.al. Ceftazidime levels in human breast milk. Antimicro. Agents and Chemotherapy 23:479-480, 1983.

Ceftibuten   Fax #1440

Trade: Cedax
Can/Aus/UK:
Uses: Cephalosporin antibiotic
AAP: Not reviewed

Ceftibuten is a broad spectrum third generation oral cephalosporin antibiotic. No data yet available on penetration into human breast milk. Small to moderate amounts may penetrate into milk, but ceftibuten is cleared for pediatric use. Its strength is in activity against gram negative species. Its weakness is in staphylococci, and strep. pneumonia coverage (which causes many inner ear infections).

Alternatives:

Pregnancy Risk Category: B

Adult Concerns: Diarrhea, vomiting, loose stools, abdominal pain.

Pediatric Concerns: None reported. Observe for GI symptoms such as diarrhea.

Drug Interactions: Probenecid may decrease clearance. Furosemide, aminoglycosides may enhance renal toxicity.

AHL = 2.4 hours.	M/P	=	
PHL = 2-3 hours.	PB	= 65%	
PK = 2.6 hours.	Oral	= High	
MW = 410	pKa	=	
Vd =			

References:
1. Pharmaceutical manufactures package insert, 1996.
2. The Medical Letter on Drugs and Therapeutics. 38(970):21-23, 1996.
3. Barr WH, et.al. Pharmacokinetics of ceftibuten in children. Pediatr. Infect. Dis. J. 14:S93-101, 1995.

Ceftriaxone   Fax #1084

Trade: Rocephin
Can/Aus/UK: Rocephin
Uses: Cephalosporin antibiotic
AAP: Approved by the American Academy of Pediatrics for use in breastfeeding mothers

Ceftriaxone is a very popular third-generation broad spectrum cephalosporin antibiotic. Small amounts are transferred into milk (3-4% of maternal serum level). Following a 1 gm IM dose, breast milk levels were approximately 0.6 mg/L at between 4-8 hours. Another source indicates that at steady state, approximately 4.4 % of dose penetrates into milk. In this study, the maximum breast milk concentration was 7.89 mg/L after prolonged therapy (7days). Poor oral absorption of ceftriaxone would limit systemic absorption by the infant. Half-life of ceftriaxone in human milk varies from 12.8 to 17.3 hours (longer than maternal serum). Ceftriaxone levels in breast milk are probably too low to be clinically relevant, except for changes in GI flora. Ceftriaxone is commonly used in neonates.

Alternatives:

Pregnancy Risk Category: B

Adult Concerns: Diarrhea, allergic rash, pseudomembranous colitis, thrush.

Pediatric Concerns: None reported. Observe for GI symptoms such as diarrhea.

Drug Interactions: Probenecid may decrease clearance. Furosemide, aminoglycosides may enhance renal toxicity.

AHL = 7.3 hours		**M/P**	= 0.03
PHL =		**PB**	= 95%
PK = 1 hour		**Oral**	= Poor
MW = 555		**pKa**	=
Vd =			

References:

1.   Kefetzis DA, Siafas CA, Georgakopoulous PA, et.al. Passage of cephalosporins and amoxicillin into the breast milk. Acta Paediatr Scan 70:285-286,1981.
2.   Kafetzis DA, Brater DC, Fanourgakis JE, et.al. Ceftriaxone distribution between maternal blood and fetal blood and tissues at parturition and between blood and milk postpartum. Antimicrob Agents Chemother. 23:870-873,1983.
3.   Bourget P, et.al. Ceftriaxone distribution and protein binding between maternal blood and milk postpartum. Annals of Pharmaco. 27:294-7, 1993.

Cefuroxime   Fax #1471

Trade: Ceftin, Zinacef, Kefurox
Can/Aus/UK: Zinacef, Ceftin, Zinnat
Uses: Cephalosporin antibiotic
AAP: Not reviewed

Cefuroxime is a broad spectrum second generation cephalosporin antibiotic that is available orally and IV. The manufacturer states that it is secreted into human milk in small amounts, but the levels are not available. Thus far, no untoward effects in infants have been reported. Cefuroxime has a very bitter taste. The IV salt form, cefuroxime sodium is very poorly absorbed orally. Only the axetil salt form is orally bioavailable.

Alternatives:

Pregnancy Risk Category: B

Adult Concerns: Nausea, vomiting, diarrhea, GI distress, skin rash, allergies.

Pediatric Concerns: None reported. Observe for GI symptoms such as diarrhea.

Drug Interactions: Probenecid may decrease clearance. Furosemide, aminoglycosides may enhance renal toxicity.

AHL = 1.4 hours		**M/P** =	
PHL =		**PB** = 33-50%	
PK =		**Oral** = 30-50%	
MW = 424		**pKa** =	
Vd =			

References:
1.   Pharmaceutical Manufacturer's Package Insert, 1995.

Cephalexin   Fax #1085

Trade: Keflex
Can/Aus/UK: Apo-Cephalex, Ceporex, Novo-Lexin, Ibilex, Keflex
Uses: Cephalosporin antibiotic
AAP: Not reviewed

Cephalexin is a typical first-generation cephalosporin antibiotic. Only minimal concentrations are secreted into human milk. Following a 1000 mg maternal oral dose, milk levels at 1, 2, 3, 4, and 5 hours ranged from 0.20, 0.28, 0.39, 0.50, and 0.47 mg/L respectively. Milk:serum ratios varied from 0.008 at 1 hour, to 0.140 at 3 hours. These levels are probably too low to be clinically relevant.

Alternatives:

Pregnancy Risk Category: B

Adult Concerns: Diarrhea, allergic rash, thrush.

Pediatric Concerns: None reported. Observe for diarrhea.

Drug Interactions: Probenecid may decrease clearance. Furosemide, aminoglycosides may enhance renal toxicity.

AHL = 50-80 minutes	**M/P**	= 0.008-0.14
PHL =	**PB**	= 10%

PK = 1 hour	Oral = Complete
MW = 347	pKa =
Vd =	

References:

1. Kefetzis DA, Siafas CA, Georgakopoulous PA, et.al. Passage of cephalosporins and amoxicillin into the breast milk. Acta Paediatr Scan 70:285-286,1981.

Cephalothin   Fax #1087

Trade: Keflin

Can/Aus/UK: Ceporacin, Keflin

Uses: Cephalosporin antibiotic

AAP: Not reviewed

Cephalothin is a first-generation cephalosporin antibiotic for use by IM or IV administration. Following a 1000 mg IV maternal dose, milk levels varied from 0.27, 0.41, 0.47, 0.36, and 0.28 mg/L at 0.5, 1, 2, 3, and 4 hours respectively. Milk:serum ratios varied from 0.06 at 1 hour to 0.51 at 3 hours.

Alternatives:

Pregnancy Risk Category: B

Adult Concerns: Diarrhea, allergic rash, thrush.

Pediatric Concerns: None reported. Observe for diarrhea.

Drug Interactions: Probenecid may decrease clearance. Furosemide, aminoglycosides may enhance renal toxicity.

AHL = 30-50 minutes	M/P = 0.06-0.5 1
PHL =	PB = 70%
PK = 1-2 hours	Oral = Poor
MW = 396	pKa =
Vd =	

References:

1. Kefetzis DA, Siafas CA, Georgakopoulous PA, et.al. Passage of cephalosporins and amoxicillin into the breast milk. Acta Paediatr Scan 70:285-286,1981.

Cephapirin   Fax #1088

Trade: Cefadyl
Can/Aus/UK:
Uses: Cephalosporin antibiotic
AAP: Not reviewed

Cephapirin is a typical first-generation cephalosporin antibiotic for IM or IV administration. Following a 1000 mg IV maternal dose, milk levels varied from 0.26, 0.41, 0.43, 0.33, and 0.27 mg/L at 0.5, 1, 2, 3, and 4 hours respectively. These are too low to be clinically relevant. Milk:serum ratios varied from 0.068 at 1 hour to 0.48 at 3 hours.

Alternatives:

Pregnancy Risk Category: B

Adult Concerns: Diarrhea, allergic rash, thrush.

Pediatric Concerns: None reported. Observe for GI symptoms such as diarrhea.

Drug Interactions: Probenecid may decrease clearance. Furosemide, aminoglycosides may enhance renal toxicity.

AHL = 24-36 minutes		M/P	= 0.068-0.48
PHL =		PB	= 54%
PK = 1-2 hours		Oral	= Poor
MW = 445		pKa	=
Vd =			

References:
1. Kefetzis DA, Siafas CA, Georgakopoulous PA, et.al. Passage of cephalosporins and amoxicillin into the breast milk. Acta Paediatr Scan 70:285-286,1981.

Cephradine   Fax #1089

Trade: Velosef
Can/Aus/UK: Velosef
Uses: Cephalosporin antibiotic
AAP: Not reviewed

Cephradine is typical first-generation cephalosporin antibiotic. In a group of 6 lactating women receiving 500 mg orally every 6 hours for 2 days, milk levels averaged about 0.6 mg/L. These levels are too low to be clinically relevant.

Alternatives:

Pregnancy Risk Category: B

Adult Concerns: Diarrhea, allergic rash, thrush, liver dysfunction.

Pediatric Concerns: None reported. Observe for GI symptoms such as diarrhea.

Drug Interactions: Probenecid may decrease clearance. Furosemide, aminoglycosides may enhance renal toxicity.

AHL = 0.7-2 hours.	M/P	= 0.2
PHL =	PB	= 8-17%
PK = 1 hour	Oral	= Complete
MW = 349	pKa	=
Vd =		

References:
1. Mischier TW, et.al. Cephradine and epicillin in body fluids of lactating and pregnant women. J. Reprod. Med. 21:130-6, 1978.

Cetirizine   Fax #1457

Trade: Zyrtec
Can/Aus/UK: Reactine, Zyrtec
Uses: Antihistamine
AAP: Not reviewed

Cetirizine is a popular new antihistamine useful for seasonal allergic rhinitis. It is a metabolite of hydroxyzine, and is one of the most potent of the antihistamines. It is rapidly and extensively absorbed orally, and due to a rather long half-life is used only once daily. It penetrates the CNS poorly and therefore produces minimal sedation. Compared to other new antihistamines, cetirizine is not very toxic in overdose, and produces few cardiovascular changes at higher doses. Further, as with many other antihistamines, cetirizine has very few drug interactions, alcohol being the main one. Studies in dogs suggests that only 3% of the dose is transferred into milk.

Alternatives:

Pregnancy Risk Category: B

Adult Concerns: Sedation, fatigue, dry mouth.

Pediatric Concerns: None reported but observe for sedation.

Drug Interactions: Increased sedation with other CNS sedatives, alcohol.

AHL = 8.3 hours	**M/P** =
PHL = 6.2 hours	**PB** = 93%
PK = 1.7 hour	**Oral** = 70%
MW = 389	**pKa** =
Vd =	

References:
1. Pharmaceutical Manufacturer's Package Insert, 1996.
2. Pharmaceutical Manufacturer. Personal Communication, 1996.

Chloral Hydrate   Fax #1090

Trade: Aquachloral, Noctec
Can/Aus/UK: Nortec, Novo-Chlorhydrate
Uses: Sedative, hypnotic
AAP: Approved by the American Academy of Pediatrics for use in breastfeeding mothers

Chloral Hydrate is a sedative hypnotic.   Small to moderate amounts are known to be secreted into milk. Mild drowsiness was reported in one infant following administration of dichloraphenazone (1300 mg/d), which is metabolized to the same active metabolite as chloral hydrate. Infant growth and development were reported to be normal. In a study of 50 postpartum women using a 1.3 gm rectal suppository, the average milk concentration of chloral hydrate at 1 hour was 3.2 mg/L. The maximum level found in this study was 15 mg/L in one patient. The oral pediatric sedative dose of chloral hydrate is generally 5-15 mg/kg/dose every 8 hours.

Alternatives: Alprazolam, Midazolam

Pregnancy Risk Category: C

Adult Concerns: Irritating to mucous membrane, laryngospasm, GI irritation, paradoxical excitement, delirium, hypotension, respiratory depression and sedation.

Pediatric Concerns: None reported via milk, but observe for sedation.

Drug Interactions: May potentiate effects of warfarin,   CNS depressants such as alcohol, etc. Use with furosemide (IV) may induce flushing, hypotension.

AHL = 7-10 hours.		M/P	=
PHL =		PB	= 35-41%
PK = 30-60 min.		Oral	= Complete
MW = 165		pKa	= 10.0
Vd = 0.6			

References:

1.	Bernstine JB, et. al. Maternal blood and breast milk estimation following the administration of chloral hydrate during the puerperium. J Obstet Gynecol Br Emp 63:228-31, 1956.
2.	Lacey JH. Dichloralphenazone and breast milk. Br.Med.J. 4:684,1971.
3.	Johnson KB, ed. The Harriet Lane Handbook, Thirteenth Edition, Mosby, 1993, p. 407.

Chlorambucil   Fax #1091

Trade: Leukeran
Can/Aus/UK: Leukeran
Uses: Antineoplastic compound
AAP: Not reviewed

Chlorambucil is an antineoplastic, anti-cancer agent. No data are available on concentrations secreted into human milk. This product would be extremely dangerous to growing infants and is probably contraindicated in nursing mothers.

Alternatives:

Pregnancy Risk Category: D

Adult Concerns: Hepatotoxicity with jaundice. Pulmonary fibrosis, seizures, pneumonia.

Pediatric Concerns: None reported via milk, but due to overt toxicity, breastfeeding is discouraged.

Drug Interactions:

AHL = 1.3 hours		M/P	=
PHL =		PB	= 99%
PK = 1 hour.		Oral	= 80%
MW = 304		pKa	=
Vd = 0.14-0.24			

References:
1.   Drug Facts and Comparisons. 1995 ed. Facts and Comparisons, St. Louis.

Chloramphenicol   Fax #1092

Trade: Chloromycetin
Can/Aus/UK: Ak-Chlor, Chloromycetin, Chloroptic, Sopamycetin, Chlorsig, Biocetin
Uses: Antibiotic
AAP: Drugs whose effect on nursing infants is unknown but may be of concern

Chloramphenicol is a broad spectrum antibiotic.   In one study of 5 women receiving 250 mg PO four times daily, the concentration of chloramphenicol in milk ranged from 0.54 to 2.84 mg/L.   In another group receiving 500 mg four times daily, the concentration of chloramphenicol in milk ranged from 1.75 to 6.10 mg/L.   Safety in infants is highly controversial. Milk levels are too low to produce overt toxicity in infants, but could produce allergic sensitization to subsequent exposures. Generally considered contraindicated in nursing mothers, although chloramphenicol is occasionally used in infants. Pediatric half-life = 22 hours (neonates), 12 hours (at 17 days). This antibiotic can be extremely toxic, particularly in newborns, and should not be used for trivial infections. Blood levels should be constantly monitored and kept below 20 µg/mL.

Alternatives:

Pregnancy Risk Category: C

Adult Concerns: Numerous blood dyscrasia, aplastic anemia, fever, skin rashes.

Pediatric Concerns: None reported via milk.

Drug Interactions: Phenobarbital and rifampin may reduce plasma levels of chloramphenicol.   Chloramphenicol inhibits metabolism of chlorpropamide, phenytoin, and oral anticoagulants.

AHL	= 4 hours	**M/P**	= 0.5-0.6
PHL	= 22 hours (neonates)	**PB**	= 53%
PK	= 1 hour.	**Oral**	= Complete
MW	= 323	**pKa**	= 5.5
Vd	= 0.57		

References:
1. Havelka J. et.al. Excretion of chloramphenicol in human milk. Chemotherapy 13:204-211, 1968.
2. Nouws JFM, Ziv G. Pharmacological aspects of chloramphenicol administration by the intramammary route to lactating dairy cows. Vet Q. 4:23-31, 1982.

Chlordiazepoxide   Fax #1094

Trade: Librium, Libritabs, Solium
Can/Aus/UK: Apo-Chlordiazepoxide, Librium, Medilium
Uses: Antianxiety, benzodiazepine sedative
AAP: Not reviewed

Chlordiazepoxide is an older benzodiazepine that belongs to Valium family. It is secreted in breast milk in moderate but unreported levels. See Diazepam.

Alternatives: Alprazolam

Pregnancy Risk Category: D

Adult Concerns: Sedation.

Pediatric Concerns: Observe for sedation.

Drug Interactions: Increased CNS sedation when used with other sedative-hypnotics. May increase risk when used with anticoagulants, alcohol, tricyclic antidepressants, MAO inhibitors.

AHL = 5-30 hours
PHL =
PK   = 1-4 hours
MW = 300
Vd   = 0.3-0.5

M/P   =
PB   = 90-98%
Oral = Complete
pKa   = 4.8

References:
1.   Pharmaceutical Manufacturer's Package Insert, 1996.

Chlorhexidine   Fax #1095

Trade: Peridex, Bactoshield, Betasept, Dyna-hex, Hibiclens
Can/Aus/UK: Peridex, Hibitane, Hexol, Savlon, Bactigras
Uses: Lozenge antimicrobial
AAP: Not reviewed

Chlorhexidine is a topical antimicrobial used in oral lozenges.   It is poorly absorbed in humans and is not likely to cause untoward effects in nursing infant due to poor oral absorption by mother and infant as well.

Alternatives:

Pregnancy Risk Category: B

Adult Concerns: Staining of teeth and dentures. Keep out of eyes. Changes in taste, increased plaque, staining of tongue.

Pediatric Concerns: None reported via milk.

Drug Interactions:

AHL = < 4 hours
PHL =
PK   =
MW = 505
Vd   =

M/P   =
PB   =
Oral = Poor
pKa   =

References:

1.   Lacy C. et.al. Drug information handbook. Lexi-Comp Inc.
      Cleveland OH 1996.

Chloroquine   Fax #1096

Trade: Aralen, Novo-chloroquine
Can/Aus/UK: Aralen, Chlorquin, Avloclor
Uses: Antimalarial
AAP: Approved by the American Academy of Pediatrics for use in
breastfeeding mothers

Chloroquine is an antimalarial drug. Following 5mg/kg IM injection
in lactating mothers 17 days postpartum, milk levels averaged 0.227
mg/L. Based on these levels, the infant would consume approximately
113.5 μg/day, an amount considered safe. Other studies have shown
absorption to vary from 2.2 to 4.2% of maternal dose. The breast milk
concentration of chloroquine in this study averaged 0.58 mg/L
following a single dose of 600 mg. Current recommended pediatric
dose for patients exposed to malaria is 8.3 mg/Kg per week. Pediatric
patients are exceedingly sensitive to chloroquine. If used children
should be closely monitored.

Alternatives:

Pregnancy Risk Category: C

Adult Concerns: Ocular disturbances including blindness, skin lesions,
headache, fatigue, nervousness, hypotension, neutropenia, aplastic
anemia.

Pediatric Concerns: None reported but close observation is required.
Observe for diarrhea, GI distress, hypotension.

Drug Interactions: Decreased oral absorption if used with kaolin and
magnesium trisilicate. Increased toxicity if used with cimetidine.

AHL = 72-120 hours	**M/P** = 0.358
PHL =	**PB** = 61%
PK = 1-2 hours.	**Oral** = Complete
MW = 320	**pKa** = 8.4, 10.8

Vd   = 116-285

References:
1.   Clyde, D. and Shute, G. Transfer of pyrimethamine in human milk. J. Trop. Med. Hyg. 59:277-284, 1956.
2.   Akintonwa A, et.al. Placental and milk transfer of chloroquine in humans. Ther. Drug. Mon. 10:147-149, 1988.
3.   Edstein MD, Veenendaal JR, Newman K. et.al. Excretion of chloroquine, dapsone and pyrimethamine in human milk. Br. J. Clin. Pharmacol. 22:733-735, 1986.

Chlorothiazide   Fax #1097

Trade: Hydrodiuril
Can/Aus/UK: Chlotride, Saluric
Uses: Diuretic
AAP: Approved by the American Academy of Pediatrics for use in breastfeeding mothers

Chlorothiazide is a typical thiazide diuretic.   In one study of 11 lactating women,   each receiving 500 mg of chlorothiazide,   the concentrations in milk samples taken one, two, and three hours after the dose were all less than 1 mg/L with a milk:plasma ratio of 0.05. Although thiazide diuretics are reported to produce thrombocytopenia in nursing infants, it is remote and unsubstantiated.   Most thiazide diuretics are considered compatible with breastfeeding if doses are kept low and milk production is unaffected.

Alternatives:

Pregnancy Risk Category: D

Adult Concerns: Fluid loss, dehydration, lethargy.

Pediatric Concerns: None reported but observe for reduced milk production.

Drug Interactions: NSAIDs may reduce hypotensive effect of chlorothiazide. Cholestyramine resins may reduce absorption of chlorothiazide. Diuretics reduce efficacy of oral hypoglycemics. May reduce lithium clearance leading to high levels. May elevate digoxin levels.

AHL = 1.5 hours		**M/P** = 0.05	
PHL =		**PB** = 95%.	
PK = 1 hour.		**Oral** = 20%	
MW = 296		**pKa** = 6.7, 9.5	
Vd =			

References:
1.   Werthman MW, Krees SV. Excretion of chlorothiazide in human breast milk. J. Pediatr. 81:781-3,1972.

Chlorpheniramine   Fax #1098

Trade: Aller Chlor, Chlor-Tripolon, Chlor-Trimeton
Can/Aus/UK: Chlor-Tripolon, Demazin, Alunex, Piridon
Uses: Antihistamine
AAP: Not reviewed

Chlorpheniramine is a commonly used antihistamine. Although no data are available on secretion into breast milk, it has not been reported to produce side effects. Sedation is the only likely side effect.

Alternatives: Cetirizine, Loratadine

Pregnancy Risk Category: B

Adult Concerns: Sedation, dry mouth.

Pediatric Concerns: None reported but observe for sedation.

Drug Interactions: May increase sedation when used with other CNS depressants such as opiates, tricyclic antidepressants, MAO inhibitors.

AHL = 12-43 hours.	**M/P** =	
PHL = 9.5-13 hours	**PB** = 70%	
PK = 2-6 hours	**Oral** = 25-45%	

MW = 275   pKa = 9.2
Vd = 5.9

References:
1.   Paton DM, Webster DR. Clinical pharmacokinetics of H1-
      receptor antagonists (the antihistamines). Clin. Pharm. 10:477-
      497, 1985.

Chlorpromazine   Fax #1099

Trade: Thorazine, Ormazine
Can/Aus/UK: Chlorpromanyl, Largactil, Novo-Chlorpromazine
Chloractil
Uses: Tranquilizer
AAP: Drugs whose effect on nursing infants is unknown but may be
of concern

Chlorpromazine is a powerful CNS tranquilizer. Small amounts are
known to be secreted into milk. Following a 1200 mg oral dose,
samples were taken at 60, 120, and 180 minutes. Breast milk
concentrations were highest at 120 minutes and were 0.29 mg/L at that
time. The milk:plasma ratio was less than 0.5. Ayd (1964) suggests
that in one group of 16 women who took chlorpromazine during and
after pregnancy while breastfeeding, the side effects were minimal and
infant development was normal.   There are controversial suggestions
that phenothiazines may increase the risk of SIDS.

Alternatives:

Pregnancy Risk Category: C

Adult Concerns: Sedation, lethargy, extrapyramidal jerking motion.

Pediatric Concerns: None reported via milk, but caution is urged due
to increased risk of SIDS.

Drug Interactions: Additive effects when used with other CNS
depressants. May increase valproic acid plasma levels.

AHL	= 30 hours	M/P	= <0.5
PHL	=	PB	= 95%
PK	= 1-2 hours.	Oral	= Complete
MW	= 319	pKa	= 9.3
Vd	= 10-35		

References:

1. Blacker KH, Weinstein BJ, et.al. Mothers milk and chlorpromazine. Am. J. Psychol. 114:178-9, 1962.
2. Ayd FJ. Excretion of psychotropic drugs in breast milk. In : International Drug Therapy Newsletter. Ayd Medical Communications. November-December 1973. Vol. 8.
3. Ayd FJ. Clin. Med 71:1758, 1964.

Chlorpropamide   Fax #1100

Trade: Diabinese
Can/Aus/UK: Apo-Chlorpropamide, Diabinese, Novopropamide, Melitase
Uses: Oral hypoglycemic
AAP: Not reviewed

Chlorpropamide stimulates the secretion of insulin in some patients. Following one 500 mg dose, the concentration of chlorpropamide in milk after 5 hours was approximately 5 mg/L of milk. May cause hypoglycemia in infant although effects are largely unknown and unreported.

Alternatives:

Pregnancy Risk Category: D

Adult Concerns: Hypoglycemia, diarrhea, edema.

Pediatric Concerns: None actually reported, but observe for hypoglycemia although unlikely.

Drug Interactions: Thiazides and hydantoins reduce hypoglycemic effect of chlorpropamide. Chlorpropamide may increase disulfiram effects when used with alcohol. Increases anticoagulant effect when used with warfarin. Sulfonamides may decrease chlorpropamide clearance.

AHL = 33 hours		**M/P** =	
PHL =		**PB** = 96%	
PK = 3-6 hours		**Oral** = Complete	
MW = 277		**pKa** = 4.8	
Vd = 0.1-0.3			

References:
1.   Pharmaceutical Manufacturer's Package Insert, 1986.

Chlorprothixene   Fax #1101

Trade: Taractan
Can/Aus/UK:
Uses: Sedative, tranquilizer
AAP: Not reviewed

Sedative commonly used in psychotic or disturbed   patients. Chlorprothixene is poorly absorbed orally (<40%) and has been found to increase serum prolactin levels in mothers.   Although the milk:plasma ratios are relatively high,   only modest levels of chlorprothixene are actually secreted into human milk. In one patient taking 200 mg/day, maximum milk concentrations of the parent and metabolite were 19 µg/L and 28.5 µg/L   respectively. If an infant ingested 800 mL of milk per day, the estimated ingestion of chlorprothixene would be < 15 µg/day. This is approximately 0.1% of the maternal dose.

Alternatives:

Pregnancy Risk Category: C

Adult Concerns: Sedation, hypotension, pseudo-parkinsonian jerking, constipation.

Pediatric Concerns: None reported, but observe for sedation.

Drug Interactions: May reduce effect of guanethidine. May increase effects of alcohol and other CNS sedatives.

AHL = 8-12 hours		**M/P**	= 1.2-2.6
PHL =		**PB**	=
PK = 4.25 hours		**Oral**	= < 40%
MW = 316		**pKa**	= 8.8
Vd = 11-23			

References:
1. Matheson I, Evang A, Fredricson OK, et.al. Presence of chlorprothixene and its metabolites in breast milk. Eur. J. Clin. Pharm. 27:611, 1984.

Chlorthalidone   Fax #1102

Trade: Hygroton
Can/Aus/UK: Apo-Chlorthalidone, Hygroton, Novo-Thalidone
Uses: Diuretic
AAP: Approved by the American Academy of Pediatrics for use in breastfeeding mothers

See hydrochlorothiazide. Avoid if possible. May reduce milk production.

Alternatives:

Pregnancy Risk Category: D

Adult Concerns: Thrombocytopenia, hypotension, reduction of milk supply.

Pediatric Concerns: None reported via milk, but may reduce milk supply.

Drug Interactions: Reduces hypoglycemic effect of oral sulfonylureas used in diabetics. Increases digoxin related arrhythmias. May increase lithium levels.

AHL = 54 hours		**M/P** =	
PHL =		**PB** = 75%	
PK =		**Oral** = Complete	
MW = 339		**pKa** =	
Vd =			

References:
1. McEvoy GE(ed):AHFS Drug Information, New York, NY. 1995.

Cholera Vaccine   Fax #1103

Trade: Cholera Vaccine
Can/Aus/UK:
Uses: Cholera vaccination
AAP: Not reviewed

Cholera vaccine is a sterile solution containing equal parts of phenol inactivated Ogawa and Inaba serotypes of Vibrio cholerae bacteria. Maternal immunization with cholera vaccine significantly increases levels of anti-cholera antibodies (IgA, IgG) in their milk.   It is not contraindicated in nursing mothers.   Breastfed infants are generally protected from cholera transmission.   Immunization is approved from the age of 6 months and older.

Alternatives:

Pregnancy Risk Category: C

Adult Concerns: Malaise, fever, headache, pain at injection site.

Pediatric Concerns: None reported.

Drug Interactions: Decreased effect when used with yellow fever vaccine. Wait at least 3 weeks between.

References:
1.   Merson MH, et. al. Maternal cholera immunization and secretory IgA in breast milk. Lancet 1:931-2, 1980.

Cholestyramine   Fax #1104

Trade: Questran, Cholybar
Can/Aus/UK: Questran, Novo-Cholamine
Uses: Cholesterol binding resin
AAP: Not reviewed

Cholestyramine is a bile salt chelating resin. Used orally in adults, it binds bile salts and prevents reabsorption of bile salts in the gut, thus reducing cholesterol plasma levels. This resin is not absorbed from the maternal GI tract.   Therefore, it is not secreted into breast milk.

Alternatives:

Pregnancy Risk Category: C

Adult Concerns: Constipation, skin rash, nausea, vomiting, malabsorption, intestinal obstruction.

Pediatric Concerns: None reported via milk.

Drug Interactions: Decreases oral absorption of digoxin, warfarin, thyroid hormones, thiazide diuretics, propranolol, phenobarbital, amiodarone, methotrexate, NSAIDs, and many other drugs.

References:
1.   Pharmaceutical Manufacturer's Package Insert, 1995.

Chondroitin Sulfate   Fax #1607

Trade: Viscoat
Can/Aus/UK:
Uses: Biologic polymer used for arthritis
AAP: Not reviewed

Chondroitin is a biological polymer that acts as a flexible connecting matrix between the protein filaments in cartilage. It is derived largely from natural sources such as shark or bovine cartilage and chemically is composed of a high-viscosity mucopolysaccharide (glycosaminoglycan) polymer found in most mammalian cartilaginous tissues. Thus far, chondroitin has been found to be nontoxic. Its molecular weight averages 50,000 daltons which is far too large to permit its entry into human milk. Combined with a poor oral bioavailability and large molecular weight, it is unlikely to pose a problem for a breastfed infant.

Alternatives:

Pregnancy Risk Category:

Adult Concerns: Virtually nontoxic and poorly absorbed orally.

Pediatric Concerns: None reported via milk.

Drug Interactions:

AHL =		M/P	=
PHL =		PB	=
PK =		Oral	= 0-13%
MW = 50,000		pKa	=
Vd =			

References:
1.   Review of Natural Products. Facts and Comparisons, St. Louis, Mo. 1996.

Chorionic Gonadotropin   Fax #1531

Trade: A.P.L., Chorex-5, Profasi, Gonic, Pregnyl
Can/Aus/UK: Humegon, Pregnyl, Profasi HP, Profasik, APL
Uses: Placental hormone
AAP: Not reviewed

Human chorionic gonadotropin (HCG) is a large polypeptide hormone produced by the human placenta with functions similar to luteinizing hormone (LH). Its function is to stimulate the corpus luteum of the ovary to produce progesterone, thus sustaining pregnancy. During pregnancy, HCG secreted by the placenta, maintains the corpus luteum, supporting estrogen and progesterone secretion and preventing menstruation. It is used for multiple purposes including pediatric cryptorchidism, male hypogonadism, and ovulatory failure. HCG has no known effect on fat mobilization, appetite, sense of hunger or body fat distribution. HCG has NOT been found to be effective in treatment of obesity. Due to the large molecular weight (47,000) of HCG, it would be extremely unlikely penetrate into human milk. Further, it would not be orally bioavailable, due to destruction in the GI tract.

Alternatives:

Pregnancy Risk Category: X

Adult Concerns: Headache, irritability, restlessness, depression, fatigue, edema, gynecomastia, pain at injection site.

Pediatric Concerns: None reported via milk. Absorption unlikely due to gastric digestion and poor penetration into milk.

Drug Interactions:

AHL = 5.6 hours		M/P	=
PHL =		PB	=
PK = 6 hours		Oral	= 0%
MW = 47,000		pKa	=
Vd =			

References:
1.   Drug Facts and Comparisons. 1996. ed. Facts and Comparisons, St. Louis.
2.   Pharmaceutical Manufacturer's Package Insert, 1997.

Chromium   Fax #1105

Trade: Chromium Picrolinate, Chromium-51
Can/Aus/UK:
Uses: Metal supplement
AAP: Not reviewed

Trace metal, required in glucose metabolism. Less than 1% is absorbed following oral administration.   Chromium levels are depleted in multiparous women. Chromium levels in neonate are approximately 2.5 times that of mother, due to concentrating mechanism during gestation. Because chromium is difficult to measure, levels reported vary widely. One article reports that breast milk levels are less than 2% of the estimated safe and adequate daily intake of 10 µg (which is probably excessive and needs review). Most importantly, breast milk levels are independent of dietary intake in mother, and do not apparently increase with increased maternal intake.   Chromium is apparently secreted into breast milk by a well controlled pumping mechanism. Hence, breast milk levels of chromium are independent of maternal plasma levels, so increased maternal plasma levels may not alter milk chromium levels.   Radioactive chromium-51, sometimes used for various tests, has a radioactive half-life of 27.7 days.

Alternatives:

Pregnancy Risk Category: C

Adult Concerns: Chromium poisoning if used in excess.

Pediatric Concerns: None reported.

Drug Interactions:

AHL	=		M/P	=
PHL	=		PB	=
PK	=		Oral	= < 1%
MW	= 52		pKa	=
Vd	=			

References:

1. Anderson RA, et.al. Breast milk chromium and its association with chromium intake, chromium excretion, and serum chromium. Am. J. Clin. Nutr. 57:519-23,1993.

Ciclopirox Olamine   Fax #1586

Trade: Loprox
Can/Aus/UK: Loprox
Uses: Antifungal
AAP: Not reviewed

Ciclopirox is a broad spectrum antifungal and is active again numerous species including tinea, candida albicans, and trichophyton rubrum. An average of 1.3% ciclopirox is absorbed when applied topically. Topical application produces minimal systemic absorption; it is unlikely that topical use would expose the nursing infant to significant risks. The risk to a breastfeeding infant associated with application directly on the nipple is not known; only small amounts should be used. Ciclopirox and miconazole are comparable in treatment of vaginal candida.

Alternatives: Fluconazole, Miconazole.

Pregnancy Risk Category: B

Adult Concerns: Pruritus and burning following topical therapy.

Pediatric Concerns: None via milk.

Drug Interactions:

AHL	= 1,7 hours	**M/P**	=	
PHL	=	**PB**	= 98%	
PK	= 6 hours	**Oral**	=	
MW	=	**pKa**	=	
Vd	=			

References:
1.   Pharmaceutical manufacturer's package insert, 1998.

Cimetidine   Fax #1106

Trade: Tagamet
Can/Aus/UK: Apo-Cimetidine,   Novo-Cimetine,   Peptol,
Tagamet, Magicul, Sigmetadine, Peptimax, Zita
Uses: Reduces gastric acid production
AAP: Approved by the American Academy of Pediatrics for use in
breastfeeding mothers

Cimetidine is an antisecretory, histamine-2 antagonist that reduces
stomach acid secretion. Cimetidine is secreted into breast milk.   A
relatively high milk:plasma ratio varies depending on dose from 4.6 to
11.76. Such levels could potentially reduce infant gastric acidity, and
drug metabolizing ability although these effects have not been reported
and seem unlikely due to the minimal dose transferred to the infant. The
potential dose from lactation would be approximately 6 mg/L of milk,
which is quite small.   The pediatric dose administered IV for
therapeutic treatment of pediatric gastroesophageal reflux averages 8-
20 mg/kg/24 hours   Other choices for breastfeeding mothers should
preclude the use of this drug. See famotidine, nizatidine. Short term
use (days) would not be incompatible with breastfeeding.

Alternatives: Famotidine, Nizatidine

Pregnancy Risk Category: B

Adult Concerns: Headache, dizziness, somnolence.

Pediatric Concerns: None reported via milk. Frequently used in pediatric patients.

Drug Interactions: Cimetidine inhibits the metabolism of many drugs and may potentially increase their plasma levels. Such drugs include: lidocaine, theophylline, phenytoin, metronidazole, triamterene, procainamide, quinidine, propranolol, warfarin, tricyclic antidepressants, diazepam, cyclosporin.

AHL = 2 hours		M/P	= 4.6-11.76
PHL = 3.6 hours (neonate)		PB	= 19%
PK = 0.75-1.5 hours		Oral	= 60-70%
MW = 252		pKa	=
Vd =			

References:
1. Somogyi A, Gugler R. Cimetidine excretion into breast milk. Br J Clin Pharmacol. 7:627-9,1979.

Ciprofloxacin   Fax #1107

Trade: Cipro
Can/Aus/UK: Cipro, Ciloxan, Ciproxin
Uses: Fluoroquinolone antibiotic
AAP: Not reviewed

Ciprofloxacin has in the past been implicated in arthropathy in newborn animals. Levels secreted into breast milk (2.26 to 3.79 mg/L) are somewhat conflicting, and vary from the low to moderate range to levels that are higher than maternal serum up to 12 hours after a dose. In one study of 10 women who received 750 mg every 12 hours , milk levels of ciprofloxacin ranged from 3.79 mg/L at 2 hours post-dose to 0.02 mg/L at 24 hours. In another study of a single patient receiving one 500 mg tablet daily at bedtime, the concentrations in maternal serum, breast milk, and infant's serum were 0.21 μg/mL, 0.98 μg/mL and undetectable (< 0.03 μg/mL), respectively. Dose to the 4 month old infant was estimated to be 0.92 mg/day or 0.15 mg/Kg/day. No adverse effects were noted in this infant. There has been one reported case of severe pseudomembranous colitis in an infant of a mother who self-medicated with ciprofloxacin for 6 days. If used in lactating mothers, observe the infant closely for GI symptoms. Current studies seem to suggest that the amount of ciprofloxacin present in milk is quite low and the use of this family of antibiotics in breastfeeding mothers requires a risk-vs-benefit assessment. The use of fluoroquinolone antibiotics in adolescent children has been associated with arthropathy, or swollen joints. These were following several weeks of normal oral doses, not breast milk.

Alternatives: Norfloxacin, Ofloxacin, Trovafloxacin

Pregnancy Risk Category: C

Adult Concerns: Nausea, vomiting, diarrhea, abdominal cramps, GI bleeding. Several cases of tendon rupture have been noted.

Pediatric Concerns: Pseudomembranous colitis in one infant. Ciprofloxacin has been associated with erosions of the cartilage in weight-bearing joints and other arthropathies in immature animals although this does not appear to occur in humans. Observe for diarrhea. Tooth discoloration in several infants reported.

Drug Interactions: Decreased absorption with antacids. Quinolones cause increased levels of caffeine, warfarin, cyclosporine, theophylline. Cimetidine, probenecid, azlocillin increase ciprofloxacin levels. Increased risk of seizures when used with foscarnet.

AHL = 4.1 hours	**M/P**	**= > 1**
PHL = 2.5 hours	**PB**	**= 40%**
PK = 0.5-2.3 hours	**Oral**	**= 50-85%**
MW = 331	**pKa**	**= 7.1**
Vd = 1.4		

References:

1. Cover DL, Mueller BA. Ciprofloxacin penetration into human breast milk: a case report. DICP 24:703-704,1990.
2. Harmon T, Burkhart G, and Applebaum H. Perforated pseudomembranous colitis in the breast-fed infant. J. Ped. Surg. 27:744-6,1992.

3.   Giamarellou H, Kolokythas E, Petrikkos G, et.al. Pharmacokinetics of three newer quinolones in pregnant and lactating women. Amer. Jour. of Med. 87:5A-49S-51S, 1989.
4.   Gardner DK, Gabbe SG, Harter C. Simultaneous concentrations of ciprofloxacin in breast milk and in serum in mother and breast-fed infant. Clin. Pharmacy 11(4):352-354, 1992.

Cisapride   Fax #1108

Trade: Propulsid
Can/Aus/UK: Propulsid, Prepulsid
Uses: Gastrointestinal tract stimulant
AAP: Approved by the American Academy of Pediatrics for use in breastfeeding mothers

Cisapride is a gastrointestinal stimulant used to increase lower esophageal sphincter pressure, and increase the rate of gastric emptying. It is frequently used in gastroesophageal reflux. It is often preferred over metoclopramide (Reglan) due to the lack of CNS side effects. CNS concentrations are generally 2-3 fold less than the serum levels. It is frequently used in pediatric patients and neonates. Breast milk levels following a maternal dose of 60 mg/day for 4 days averaged 6.2 µg/L while maternal plasma levels averaged 137 µg/L. The dose of cisapride absorbed in breastfeeding infants would be expected to be 600-800 times lower than the usual therapeutic dose. Manufacturer's internal data suggest that breast milk levels are less than 5% of maternal plasma levels (approximately 2.2 to 3.0 µg/L).

Alternatives:

Pregnancy Risk Category: C

Adult Concerns: Diarrhea, abdominal pain, cramping. Note many drug-drug interactions.

Pediatric Concerns: None reported via milk.

Drug Interactions: Increased effect of atropine and digoxin. Increased toxicity when used with warfarin, diazepam levels may be increased, cimetidine, ranitidine, CNS depressants. Cisapride levels may rise when used with azole antifungals such as ketoconazole, fluconazole, or the erythromycin family.

AHL = 7-10 hours		M/P	= 0.045
PHL =		PB	= 98%
PK = 1-2 hours		Oral	= 35-40%
MW = 466		pKa	=
Vd =			

References:
1. McCallum RW, Prakash C, et.al. Cisapride: a preliminary review of its pharmacodynamic and pharmacokinetic properties, and therapeutic use as a prokinetic agent in gastrointestinal motility disorders. Drugs, 36(6):652-81, 1988.
2. Hofmeyr GJ, Sonnendecker WW. Secretion of the gastrokinetic agent cisapride in human milk. Eur. J. Clin. Pharmacol. 30:735-6,1986.
3. Janssen Pharmaceuticals, personal communication, 1996.

Cisplatin   Fax #1109

Trade: Platinol
Can/Aus/UK: Abiplatin, Platinol, Platinol-AQ, Cisplatin Platosin
Uses: Anti-cancer drug
AAP: Approved by the American Academy of Pediatrics for use in breastfeeding mothers

Cisplatin is a potent and very toxic anti-cancer medication. Plasma and breast milk samples were collected from a 24 year old woman treated for three prior days with cisplatin (30mg/meter). On the third day, 30 minutes prior to chemotherapy, platinum levels in milk were 0.9 mg/L and plasma levels were 0.8 mg/L. In another study, no cisplatin was found in breast milk following a dose of 100 mg/meter. Other studies suggest that milk levels are 10 fold lower than serum levels in an older lactating woman. Cisplatin has multiple half-lives with the terminal half-life equal to greater than 24 to 73 hours. These studies generally support the recommendation that mothers should not breastfeed while undergoing cisplatin therapy.

Alternatives:

Pregnancy Risk Category: D

Adult Concerns: Nausea, vomiting, tinnitus, ototoxicity, renal toxicity, leukopenia, peripheral neuropathy, etc.

Pediatric Concerns: None reported via milk, but due to enormous toxicity, do not use in breastfeeding women.

Drug Interactions: Increased toxicity when used with ethacrynic acid (ototoxicity). Delayed bleomycin metabolism. Sodium thiosulfate inactivates cisplatin.

AHL = 24-73 hours		**M/P**	= > 1
PHL =		**PB**	= 90%
PK = < 1 hour.		**Oral**	=
MW = 300		**pKa**	=
Vd =			

References:
1. deVries EGE, et.al. Excretion of platinum into breast milk [letter]. Lancet 1(8636):497,1989.
2. Egan PC, et. al. Doxorubicin and cisplatin excretion into human milk. Cancer Treat Rep 69:1387-9, 1985.

Clarithromycin   Fax #1110

Trade: Biaxin
Can/Aus/UK: Biaxin, Klacid, Klaricid
Uses: Antibiotic
AAP: Not reviewed

Antibiotic that belongs to erythromycin family. Clarithromycin is known to transfer into animal milk, although no studies have been done on humans. This drug is a weak base and could concentrate in human milk by ion trapping. However, it is a commonly used pediatric antibiotic and pediatric indications down to 6 months of age are available. See azithromycin as alternative.

Alternatives:

Pregnancy Risk Category: C

Adult Concerns: Diarrhea, nausea, dyspepsia, abdominal pain, metallic taste.

Pediatric Concerns: None reported via milk. Pediatric indications are available.

Drug Interactions: Clarithromycin increases serum theophylline by as much as 20%. Increases plasma levels of carbamazepine, cyclosporin, digoxin, ergot alkaloids, tacrolimus, triazolam, zidovudine, terfenadine, astemizole, cisapride (serious arrhythmias). Fluconazole increases clarithromycin serum levels by 25%. Numerous other drug-drug interactions are unreported, but probably occur.

AHL	= 5-7 hours	M/P	= >1
PHL	=	PB	= 40-70%
PK	= 1.7 hours	Oral	= 50%
MW	= 748	pKa	=
Vd	=		

References:
1. Drug Facts and Comparisons. 1995 ed. Facts and Comparisons, St. Louis.
2. Pharmaceutical Manufacturer's Package Insert, 1996.

Clemastine   Fax #1111

Trade: Tavist
Can/Aus/UK: Tavist, Tavegyl
Uses: Antihistamine
AAP: Drugs associated with significant side effects and should be given with caution

Clemastine is a long-acting antihistamine. Following a maternal dose of 1 mg twice daily a 10 week old breastfeeding infant developed drowsiness, irritability, refusal to feed, and neck stiffness. Levels in milk and plasma (20 hours post dose) were 5-10 µg/L(milk) and 20 µg/L (plasma) respectively.

Alternatives: Cetirizine, Loratadine

Pregnancy Risk Category: C

Adult Concerns: Drowsiness, headache, fatigue, nervousness, appetite increase, depression.

Pediatric Concerns: Drowsiness, irritability, refusal to feed, and neck stiffness in one infant. Increased risk of seizures.

Drug Interactions: Increased toxicity when mixed with CNS depressants, anticholinergics, MAO inhibitors, tricyclic antidepressants, phenothiazines.

AHL = 10-12 hours.		**M/P**	= 0.25-0.5
PHL =		**PB**	=
PK = 2-5 hours.		**Oral**	= 100%
MW = 344		**pKa**	=
Vd =			

References:
1. Kok THHG, Taitz LS, Bennett MJ, et.al. Drowsiness due to clemastine transmitted in breast milk. Lancet 1:914-915,1982.

Clindamycin   Fax #1112

Trade: Cleocin

Can/Aus/UK: Clindatech, Dalacin, Cleocin

Uses: Antibiotic

AAP: Approved by the American Academy of Pediatrics for use in breastfeeding mothers

Clindamycin is a broad spectrum antibiotic frequently used for anaerobic infections. In one study of two nursing mothers and following doses of 600 mg IV every 6 hours, the concentration of clindamycin in breast milk was 3.1 to 3.8 mg/L at 0.2 to 0.5 hours after dosing. Following oral doses of 300 mg every 6 hours, the breast milk levels averaged 1.0 to 1.7 mg/L at 1.5 to 7 hours after dosing. An alteration of GI flora is possible, even though the dose is low. One case of bloody stools (pseudomembranous colitis) has been associated with clindamycin and gentamycin therapy on day 5 postpartum, but this is considered rare. In this case, the mother of a newborn infant was given 600 mg IV every 6 hours. In rare cases, pseudomembranous colitis can appear several weeks later. There are a number of pediatric clinical uses of clindamycin (anaerobic infections, bacterial endocarditis, pelvic inflammatory disease, and bacterial vaginosis). The current pediatric dosage recommendation is 10-40 mg/kg/day divided every 6-8 hours.

Alternatives:

Pregnancy Risk Category: B

Adult Concerns: Diarrhea, rash, pseudomembranous colitis, nausea, vomiting, GI cramps.

Pediatric Concerns: One case of pseudomembranous colitis has been reported. But this is rare. It is unlikely the levels in breast milk would be clinically relevant. Commonly used in pediatric infections. Observe for diarrhea.

Drug Interactions: Increased duration of muscle blockade when administered with neuromuscular blockers such as tubocurarine and pancuronium.

AHL = 2.9 hours.		**M/P** =	
PHL = 3.6 hours (term).		**PB** = 94%	
PK = 45-60 minutes.		**Oral** = 90%	
MW = 425		**pKa** =	
Vd =			

References:
1.　Smith JA, Morgan JR, et.al. Clindamycin in human breast milk. Can. Med. Assn. J. 112:806, 1975.
2.　Mann CF. Clindamycin and breast-feeding. Pediatrics 66:1030-1031, 1980.
3.　Johnson KB. The Harriet Lane Handbook. Thirteenth Edition. Mosby Publishing.

Clindamycin Vaginal　　　　　Fax #1113

Trade: Cleocin Vaginal
Can/Aus/UK: Dalacin Vaginal Cream, Dalacin T
Uses: Antibiotic
AAP: Approved by the American Academy of Pediatrics for use in breastfeeding mothers

Clindamycin when administered by IV has been found in breast milk (see clindamycin). One case of bloody stools (pseudomembranous colitis) has been associated with oral clindamycin. However, only about 5% of Clindamycin Vaginal (100 mg/dose) is absorbed into the maternal circulation, which would be approximately 5 mg clindamycin/day. It is unlikely that clindamycin when administered via a vaginal gel would produce any significant danger to a breastfeeding infant.

Alternatives:

Pregnancy Risk Category: B

Adult Concerns: Diarrhea, rash, GI cramps, colitis, rarely bloody diarrhea.

Pediatric Concerns:

Drug Interactions:

AHL = 2.9 hours		M/P	=
PHL =		PB	= 94%
PK =		Oral	= 90%
MW = 425		pKa	=
Vd =			

References:
1. Pharmaceutical Manufacturer's Package Insert, 1996.

Clobazam   Fax #1452

Trade: Frisium
Can/Aus/UK: Frisium
Uses: Benzodiazepine anxiolytic
AAP: Not reviewed

Clobazam (Frisium) is a typical benzodiazepine very similar to Valium. It is primarily an anxiolytic, but it is sometimes used to treat refractory seizures. The median half-life for tolerance is only 3.5 months, so it would not be suitable for long term therapy of seizures. It has a rather long half-life averaging 17-31 hours for the parent drug in young adults and 11-77 hours for the active metabolite desmethylclobazam. As with Valium, it would probably reach relatively high levels in a breastfeeding infant. No data are available on breast milk concentrations.

Alternatives: Alprazolam

Pregnancy Risk Category:

Adult Concerns: Sedation, drowsiness, hangover, weakness, insomnia.

Pediatric Concerns: Typical benzodiazepine, use caution. See Diazepam.

Drug Interactions: May increase effects of opiates, CNS depressants. Macrolide (erythromycin) antibiotics may increase levels of clobazam. Clobazam may increase levels of carbamazepine.

AHL = 17-31 hours		**M/P** =	
PHL =		**PB** = 90%	
PK = 1-2 hours.		**Oral** = 87%	
MW = 301		**pKa** =	
Vd = 0.87-1.8			

References:
1. Pharmaceutical Manufacturer's Package Insert, 1995.

Clofazimine   Fax #1598

Trade: Lamprene
Can/Aus/UK: Lamprene
Uses: Antimicrobial for leprosy
AAP: Not reviewed

Clofazimine exerts a slow bacteriocidal effect on M. Leprae. In a study of 8 female leprosy patients on clofazimine (50 mg/day or 100 mg on alternate days) for 1-18 months, blood samples were take at 4-6 hours after the dose. Average plasma and milk levels were 0.9 μg/mL and 1.33 μg/mL (1.33 mg/Liter) respectively. The milk:plasma ratio varied from 1.0 to 1.7 with a mean of 1.48. A red tint and pigmentation has been reported in breastfed infants (2,3).

Alternatives:

Pregnancy Risk Category: C

Adult Concerns: Reversible red-brown discoloration of skin and eyes. Gastrointestinal effects include nausea, abdominal cramps and pain, nausea and vomiting. Splenic infarction, crystalline deposits of clofazimine in multiple organs and tissues.

Pediatric Concerns: Reddish discoloration of milk and infant.

Drug Interactions:

AHL	= 70 days	M/P	= 1,7
PHL	=	PB	=
PK	=	Oral	= 45-70%
MW	= 473	pKa	=
Vd	=		

References:

1. Venkatesan L, Girdhar BL. et.al. Excretion of clofazimine in human milk in leprosy patients. Lepr Rev 68(3):242-6, 1997.
2. Farb H et al: Clofazimine in pregnancy complicated by leprosy. Obstet Gynecol 59:122-123, 1982.
3. Freerksen E and Seydel JK: Critical comments on the treatment of leprosy and other mycobacterial infections with clofazimine. Arzneim-Forsch Drug Res 42:1243-1245,1992.

Clomiphene   Fax #1114

Trade: Clomid, Serophene, Milophene
Can/Aus/UK: Clomid, Serophene
Uses: Ovulation stimulator for ovulatory failure
AAP: Not reviewed

Clomiphene appears to stimulate the release of the pituitary gonadotropins, follicle-stimulating hormone (FSH) and luteinizing hormone (LH), which result in development and maturation of the ovarian follicle, ovulation, and subsequent development and function of the corpus luteum. It has both estrogenic and anti-estrogenic effects. LH and FSH peak at 5-9 days after completing clomiphene therapy. In a study of 60 postpartum women (1-4 days postpartum), clomiphene was effective in totally inhibiting unestablished lactation, and in suppressing established lactation (day 4). Only 7 of 40 women receiving clomiphene to inhibit lactation had signs of congestion or discomfort. In the 20 women who received clomiphene to suppress established lactation(on day 4), a rapid amelioration of breast engorgement and discomfort was produced. After 5 days of treatment no signs of lactation were present. Clomiphene appears to be very effective in suppressing lactation when used up to 4 days postpartum. However, its efficacy in reducing milk production in women months after lactation has been established is unknown, but believed to be minimal.

Alternatives:

Pregnancy Risk Category: X

Adult Concerns: Dizziness, insomnia, lightheadedness, hot flashes, ovarian enlargement, depression, headache, alopecia. May inhibit lactation early postpartum.

Pediatric Concerns: Transfer and effect on infant is unreported, but may suppress early lactation.

Drug Interactions:

AHL	= 5-7 days	M/P	=
PHL	=	PB	=
PK	=	Oral	= Complete
MW	= 406	pKa	=
Vd	=		

References:
1. Masala, A. Clomiphene and puerperal lactation. Panminerva. Med. 20: 161-163, 1978.
2. Zuckerman, H. and Carmel, S. The inhibition of lactation by clomiphene. J. Obstet. and Gynecology of Brit. Common. 80:822-23, 1973.

Clomipramine   Fax #1115

Trade: Anafranil
Can/Aus/UK: Anafranil, Apo-Clomipramine, Placil
Uses: Anti-obsessional, antidepressant drug
AAP: Approved by the American Academy of Pediatrics for use in

breastfeeding mothers

Clomipramine is a tricyclic antidepressant frequently used for obsessive-compulsive disorder. In one patient taking 125 mg/day, on the 4th and 6th day postpartum, milk levels were 342.7 and 215.8 μg/L respectively. Maternal plasma levels were 211 and 208.4 μg/L at day 4 and 6 respectively. Milk:plasma ratio varies from 1.62 to 1.04 on day 4 to 6 respectively. Neonatal plasma levels continued to drop from a high of 266.6 ng/mL at birth to 127.6 ng/mL at day 4, to 94.8 ng/mL at day 6, to 9.8 ng/mL at 35 days. In a study of four breastfeeding women who received doses of 75 to 125 mg/day, plasma levels of clomipramine in the breastfed infants were below the limit of detection, suggesting minimal transfer to the infant via milk. No untoward effects were noted in any of the infants.

Alternatives:

Pregnancy Risk Category: C

Adult Concerns: Drowsiness, fatigue, dry mouth, seizures, constipation, sweating, reduced appetite.

Pediatric Concerns: None reported in several studies.

Drug Interactions: Decreased effect when used with barbiturates, carbamazepine and phenytoin. Increased sedation when used with alcohol, CNS depressants (hypnotics). Increased dangers when used with MAO inhibitors. Additive anticholinergic effects when used with other anticholinergics.

AHL = 19-37 hours		M/P	= 0.84- 1.62
PHL = 92.8 hours		PB	= 96%
PK =		Oral	= Complete
MW = 315		pKa	= 9.5
Vd = 17			

References:
1. Pharmaceutical Manufacturer's Package Insert, 1996.
2. Schimmell MS, et.al. Toxic neonatal effects following maternal clomipramine therapy. J. Toxicol. Clin. Toxicol. 29:479-84, 1991.

3.   Wisner KL, Perel JM, Foglia JP.   Serum clomipramine and
      metabolite levels in four nursing mother-infant pairs.

Clonazepam   Fax #1116

Trade: Klonopin
Can/Aus/UK: Rivotril, Apo-Clonazepam, PMS-Clonazepam,
Paxam
Uses: Benzodiazepine anticonvulsant
AAP: Not reviewed

Clonazepam is a typical benzodiazepine sedative, anticonvulsant. In
one case report, milk levels varied between 11 and 13 µg/L (the
maternal dose was omitted).   Maternal Milk:serum ratio was
approximately 0.33.   In this report, the infant's serum level of
clonazepam dropped from 4.4 µg/L at birth to 1.0 µg/L at 14 days
while continuing to breastfeed.

Alternatives:

Pregnancy Risk Category: C

Adult Concerns: Apnea, sedation, ataxia, hypotonia. Behavioral
disturbances(in children) include aggressiveness, irritability, agitation.

Pediatric Concerns: None reported via milk. Observe for sedation.

Drug Interactions: Phenytoin and barbiturates may increase clearance
of clonazepam. CNS depressants may increase sedation.

AHL = 18-50 hours		**M/P**	= 0.33
PHL =		**PB**	= 50-86%
PK = 1-4 hours		**Oral**	= Complete
MW = 316		**pKa**	= 1.5, 10.5
Vd = 1.5-4.4			

References:
1.   Fisher JB, Edgren BE, et.al. Neonatal apnea associated with
      maternal clonazepam therapy: a case report. Obstet. Gynecol.

66:34S(Suppl), 1985.

Clonidine   Fax #1117

Trade: Catapres
Can/Aus/UK: Catapres, Dixarit, Apo-Clonidine, Novo-Clonidine
Uses: Antihypertensive
AAP: Not reviewed

Clonidine is an antihypertensive that reduces sympathetic nerve activity from the brain. Clonidine is excreted in human milk. In a study of 9 nursing women receiving between 241.7 and 391.7 µg/day of clonidine, milk levels varied from approximately 1.8 µg/L to as high as 2.8 µg/L on postpartum day 10-14. In another report following a maternal dose of 37.5 µg twice daily, maternal plasma was determined to be 0.33 ng/mL and milk level was 0.60 µg/L. The dose an infant would receive is estimated to be approximately 6.8 % of maternal dose (90 ng/kg/d vs 1320 ng/kg/d in adults). Clinical symptoms of neonatal toxicity are unreported and are unlikely in normal full term infants. Clonidine may reduce maternal blood pressure and hence milk production. Clonidine may also reduce prolactin secretion, reducing milk production.

Alternatives:

Pregnancy Risk Category: C

Adult Concerns: Drowsiness, dry mouth, hypotension, constipation, dizziness.

Pediatric Concerns: None reported, but may induce hypotension in infant. May reduce milk production by reducing prolactin secretion.

Drug Interactions: Tricyclic antidepressants inhibit hypotensive effect of clonidine. Beta blockers may potentiate slow heart rate when administered with clonidine. Discontinue beta blockers several days to week prior to using clonidine.

AHL = 20-24 hours	M/P = 2
PHL =	PB = 20-40 %
PK = 3-5 hours.	Oral = Complete
MW = 230	pKa = 8.3
Vd = 3.2-5.6	

References:
1. Hartikainen-Sorri AL, Heikkinen JE, Koivisto M. Pharmacokinetics of clonidine during pregnancy and nursing. Obstet Gynecol. 69:598-600,1987.
2. Bunjes R, Schaefer C, and Holzinger D. Clonidine and breast-feeding. Clinical Pharmacy 12:178, 1993.

Clotrimazole   Fax #1118

Trade: Gyne-Lotrimin, Mycelex, Lotrimin, Femcare
Can/Aus/UK: Canesten, Clotrimaderm, Myclo, Clonea, Hiderm
Uses: Antifungal
AAP: Not reviewed

Clotrimazole is a broad spectrum antifungal agent. It is generally used for candidiasis, and various tinea species (athletes foot, ring worm). Clotrimazole is available in oral lozenges, topical creams, intravaginal tablets and creams. No data are available on penetration into breast milk. However, after intravaginal administration only 3-10% of the drug is absorbed (peak serum level= 0.01 to 0.03 µg/mL), and even less by oral lozenge. Hence, from vaginal administration it seems very unlikely that levels absorbed by a breastfeeding infant would be high enough to produce untoward effects. Approximately 15% of patients receiving oral lozenges have elevated (minimally) liver enzymes. Safety of clotrimazole lozenges in children younger than 3 years of age has not been established.

Alternatives: Fluconazole, Miconazole

Pregnancy Risk Category: B

Adult Concerns: Nausea, vomiting from oral administration. Itching, burning, and stinging following topical application. Elevated liver enzymes in > 10% of treated.

Pediatric Concerns: None reported via milk. Limited oral absorption probably limits clinical relevance in breastfed infants.

Drug Interactions: May inhibit amphotericin activity. Clotrimazole is reported to increase cyclosporin plasma levels. May enhance hypoglycemic effect of oral hypoglycemic agents. Clotrimazole inhibits cytochrome P450 III A and may inhibit metabolism of any number of other medications.

AHL = 3.5-5 hours		**M/P** =	
PHL =		**PB** =	
PK = 3 hours (oral)		**Oral** = Poor	
MW = 345		**pKa** =	
Vd =			

References:
1. McEvoy GE(ed):AFHS Drug Information, New York, NY. 1995, pp 417-26.

Cloxacillin   Fax #1119

Trade: Tegopen, Cloxapen
Can/Aus/UK: Apo-Cloxi, Novo-Cloxin, Orbenin, Alclox, Kloxerate-DC
Uses: Penicillin antibiotic
AAP: Not reviewed

Cloxacillin is an oral penicillinase-resistant penicillin frequently used for peripheral (non-CNS) Staphylococcus aureus and S. epidermidis infections, particularly mastitis. Following a single 500 mg oral dose of cloxacillin in lactating women, milk concentrations of the drug were zero to 0.2 mg/L one and two hours after the dose respectively, and 0.2 to 0.4 mg/L after 6 hours. Usual dose for adults is 250-500 mg four times daily for at least 10-14 days. As with most penicillins, it is unlikely these levels would be clinically relevant.

Alternatives:

Pregnancy Risk Category: B

Adult Concerns: Rash, diarrhea, nephrotoxicity, fever, shaking, chills.

Pediatric Concerns: None reported but observe for GI symptoms such as diarrhea.

Drug Interactions: Efficacy of oral contraceptives may be reduced. Disulfiram, probenecid may increase cloxacillin levels. Increased effect of oral anticoagulants.

AHL = 0.7-3 hours		**M/P** =	
PHL = 0.8-1.5 hours		**PB** = 90-96%	
PK = 0.5-2 hours		**Oral** = 37-60%	
MW = 436		**pKa** =	
Vd = 6.6-10.8			

References:
1. Matsuda S. Transfer of antibiotics into maternal milk. Biol Res Pregnancy Perinatol 5:57-60, 1984.
2. McEvoy GE(ed):AHFS Drug Information, New York, NY. 1995.

Clozapine   Fax #1120

Trade: Clozaril
Can/Aus/UK: Clozaril
Uses: Antipsychotic, sedative
AAP: Not reviewed

Clozapine is an atypical antipsychotic, sedative drug somewhat similar to the phenothiazine family. Studies with animals suggest that an unknown amount may transfer into breast milk. No levels are available.

Alternatives:

Pregnancy Risk Category: C

Adult Concerns: Drowsiness, salivation, constipation, dizziness, tachycardia, nausea, GI distress, agranulocytosis.

Pediatric Concerns: None reported via milk but caution is urged with this family.

Drug Interactions: Decreased effect of epinephrine, phenytoin. Increased sedation with CNS depressants. Increased effect with guanabenz, anticholinergics. Increased toxicity with cimetidine, MAO inhibitors, tricyclic antidepressants.

AHL = 8-12 hours		M/P	=
PHL =		PB	= 95%
PK = 2.5 hours		Oral	= 90%
MW = 327		pKa	=
Vd = 5			

References:
1. Pharmaceutical Manufacturer's Package Insert, 1993, 1994.

Co-Trimoxazole   Fax #1513

Trade: TMP-SMZ, Bactrim, Cotrim, Septra
Can/Aus/UK: Novo-Trimel, Septrin, Bactrim, Trimogal
Uses: Sulfonamide antibiotic
AAP: Approved by the American Academy of Pediatrics for use in breastfeeding mothers

Co-Trimoxazole is the mixture of trimethoprim and sulfamethoxazole. See individual monographs for each of these products.

Cocaine   Fax #1121

Trade: Crack
Can/Aus/UK:
Uses: Powerful CNS stimulant, local anesthetic
AAP: Contraindicated by the American Academy of Pediatrics in Breastfeeding Mothers

Cocaine is a local anesthetic and a powerful central nervous system stimulant. It is well absorbed from all locations including the stomach, nasal passages, intrapulmonary tissues via inhalation, and even via ophthalmic instillation. Adverse effects include agitation, nervousness, restlessness, euphoria, hallucinations, tremors, tonic-clonic seizures, and myocardial arrhythmias. Although the pharmacological effects of Cocaine are relatively brief (20-30 min.) due to redistribution out of the brain, cocaine is slowly metabolized and excreted over a prolonged period. Urine samples can be positive for cocaine metabolites for up to 7 days or longer in adults. Breastfeeding infants will likewise become urine positive for cocaine for even longer periods. Even after the clinical effects of cocaine have subsided, the breast milk will still probably contain significant quantities of benzoylecgonine, the inactive metabolite of cocaine. The infant could still test positive for urine cocaine metabolites for long periods (days).   The ingestion of small amounts of cocaine by infants via inhalation of smoke (environmental) is likely. Studies of exact estimates of cocaine transmission to breast milk have not been reported. Significant secretion into breast milk is suspected with a probable high milk:plasma ratio. A number of case reports in the literature clearly indicate the transmission of maternal cocaine to the infant via milk with significant agitation in the breastfeeding infant resulting.   In one case study, a woman who applied topical cocaine to her nipples and breastfed her infant, produced extreme toxicity in the infant. Topical application to nipples is EXTREMELY dangerous and is definitely contraindicated. Oral, intranasal, and smoking of crack cocaine is dangerous and definitely contraindicated.

Alternatives:

Pregnancy Risk Category: C
                            X if abused near term

Adult Concerns: Nausea, vomiting, CNS excitement, hypertension, tachycardia, arrhythmias.

Pediatric Concerns: Choking, vomiting, diarrhea, tremulousness, hyperactive startle reflex, gasping, agitation, irritability, hypertension, tachycardia. Extreme danger.

Drug Interactions: Increased toxicity when used with MAO inhibitors.

AHL = 0.8 hr.		M/P	=
PHL =		PB	= 91%
PK = 15 min.		Oral	= Complete
MW = 303		pKa	= 8.6
Vd = 1.6-2-7			

References:
1.   Chaney NE, Franke J, and Wadington WB. Cocaine convulsions in a breast-feeding baby. J. Pediatr. 112:134-135, 1988.
2.   Chasnoff IJ, Lewis DE, Squires L. Cocaine intoxication in a breast-fed infant. Pediatrics 80:836-838, 1987.

Codeine   Fax #1122

Trade: Empirin #3 # 4, Tylenol # 3 # 4
Can/Aus/UK: Paveral, Penntuss, Actacode, Codalgin, Codral, Panadeine, Veganin, Kaodene, Teropin
Uses: Analgesic
AAP: Approved by the American Academy of Pediatrics for use in breastfeeding mothers

Codeine is considered a mild opiate analgesic whose action is probably due to its metabolism to small amounts of morphine. The amount of codeine secreted into milk is low and dose dependent.   Infant response is higher during neonatal period (first or second week). Four cases of neonatal apnea have been reported following administration of 60 mg codeine every 4-6 hours to breastfeeding mothers although codeine was not detected in serum of the infants tested. Apnea resolved after discontinuation of maternal codeine. Number # 3 tablets contain 30 mg and #4 tablets contain 60 mg of codeine. In another study, following a dose of 60 mg, milk concentrations averaged 140 μg/L of milk with a peak of 455 μg/L at 1 hour. Following 12 doses in 48 hours, the estimated dose of codeine in milk (2000 mL milk) was 0.7 mg which is approximately 0.1% of the maternal dose. There are few reported side effects following doses of 30 mg, and it is believed to produce only minimal side effects in newborns.

Alternatives:

Pregnancy Risk Category: C

Adult Concerns: Sedation, respiratory depression, constipation.

Pediatric Concerns: Several rare cases of neonatal apnea have been reported, but at higher doses. Codeine analgesics are so commonly used postpartum, that side effects are extremely rare and seldom reported. Observe for sedation, apnea in premature or weakened infants.

Drug Interactions: Cigarette smoking increases effect of codeine. Increased toxicity/sedation when used with CNS depressants, phenothiazines, tricyclic antidepressants, other opiates, guanabenz, MAO inhibitors, neuromuscular blockers.

AHL	**= 2.9 hours**	**M/P**	**= 1.3-2.5**
PHL	**=**	**PB**	**= 7%**
PK	**= 0.5-1 hr.**	**Oral**	**= Complete**
MW	**= 299**	**pKa**	**= 8.2**
Vd	**= 3.5**		

References:
1.	Horning MG, Identification and quantification of drugs and drug metabolites in human milk using GC-MS-COM methods. Mod Probl Paediatr 15:73-9,1975.
2.	Kwit NT, Hatcher RA. Excretion of drugs in milk. Am J Dis Child 49:900-4,1935.
3.	Davis JM and Bhutani VK. Neonatal apnea and maternal codeine

use. Ped.Res. 19(4):170A abstract.

4.   Anderson PO. Medication use while breast feeding a neonate. Neonatal Pharmacology Quarterly 2:3-12,1993.
5.   Findlay JW, DeAngelis RI, Kearney MF, et.al. Analgesic drugs in breast milk and plasma. Clin Pharmacol. Ther. 29:625-633, 1981.

Colchicine   Fax #1123

Trade: Colchicine

Can/Aus/UK: Colchicine, Colgout

Uses: Analgesic in gouty arthritis

AAP: Approved by the American Academy of Pediatrics for use in breastfeeding mothers

Colchicine is an old product primarily used to reduce pain associated with inflammatory gout. Although it reduces the pain, it is not a true analgesic, but simply reduces the inflammation associated with uric acid crystals by inhibiting leukocyte and other cellular migration into the region. However, it is quite toxic, and routine CBCs should be done while under treatment.   Blood dyscrasia, hepatomegaly, and bone marrow depression are all possible, particularly in infants.   Although the plasma half-life is only 20 minutes, it deposits in blood leukocytes and many other tissues, thereby extending the elimination half-life to over 60 hours. Little or no consistent data on breast milk levels are available. In the one study published, even the authors questioned the percent recovery in the breast milk, so the data must be considered questionable. Nevertheless, the milk concentration varied from 1.2 to 2.5 µg/L (16-19 days postpartum) in one patient receiving 0.6 mg of colchicine twice daily.

Alternatives:

Pregnancy Risk Category: D

Adult Concerns: Nausea, vomiting, diarrhea, myopathy, leukopenia, bone marrow suppression.

Pediatric Concerns: None reported in one case reviewed.

Drug Interactions: Colchicine reduces vitamin B-12 absorption. Avoid alcohol.

AHL = 12-30 minutes		M/P	=
PHL =		PB	= 10-31%
PK = 1-2 hours.		Oral	= Complete
MW = 399		pKa	= 1.7, 12.4
Vd = 10-12			

References:
1. Milunsky JM, and Milunsky A. Breast-feeding during colchicine therapy for familial Mediterranean fever. J. Pediatr. 119: 164, 1991.

Comfrey   Fax #1534

Trade: Russian Comfrey, Knitbone, Bruisewort, Blackwort, Slippery Root
Can/Aus/UK:
Uses: Herbal poultice
AAP: Not reviewed

Comfrey has been claimed to heal gastric ulcers, hemorrhoids and suppress bronchial congestion and inflammation.   The product contains allantoin, tannin, and a group of dangerous pyrrolizidine alkaloids. Ointments containing comfrey have been found to be anti-inflammatory, probably due to the allantoin content. However, when administered orally to animals, most members of this family (Boraginaceae) have been noted to induce severe liver toxicity including elevated liver enzymes and liver tumors (hepatocellular adenomas). Bladder tumors were noted at low concentrations. Russian comfrey has been found to induce liver damage and pancreatic islet cell tumors. A number of significant human toxicities have been reported including several deaths, all associated with the ingestion of comfrey teas, or yerba mate tea.   Even when applied to the skin, pyrrolizidine alkaloids were noted in the urine of rodents.   Lactating rats excreted pyrrolizidine alkaloids into breast milk. Comfrey and members of this family are exceedingly dangerous and should not be used topically, ingested orally, or used in any form in breastfeeding mothers.

Alternatives:

Pregnancy Risk Category:

Adult Concerns: Liver toxicity, hepatic carcinoma, hepatocellular adenomas.

Pediatric Concerns: Passes into animal milk. Too dangerous for breastfeeding mothers and infants.

Drug Interactions:

References:
1.   Review of Natural Products. Facts and Comparisons, St. Louis, Mo. 1996.
2.   Hirono et.al. Carcinogenic activity of symphytum officinale. J. Nat. Cancer Inst 61:865, 1978.
3.   Yeong ML. Hepatocyte membrane injury and bleb formation following low dose comfrey toxicity in rats. Inter J of Exp Pathol 74:211, 1993.
4.   Yeong ML.   The effects of comfrey derived pyrrolizidine alkaloid on rat liver. Path 23:35, 1991.
5.   McGee J. et.al. A case of veno-occlusive disease of the liver in Britain associated with herbal tea consumption. J. Clin. Pathol. 29:788, 1976.
6.   Bissett NG.   In: Herbal Drugs and Phytopharmaceuticals. Medpharm Scientific Publishers, CRC Press, Boca Raton, 1994.

Copper-64   Fax #1124

Trade: Copper-64
Can/Aus/UK:
Uses: Radioisotope

AAP: Radioactive compound that requires temporary cessation of breastfeeding.

Copper-64 is a radioactive compound. Radioactivity is present in milk after 50 hours. Pump and discard until radioactivity has decayed (approximately 5-6 half-lives = 64 hours). Radioactive half-life is 12.7 hours.

AHL = 12.7 hours.		**M/P**	**=**
PHL =		**PB**	**=**
PK **=**		**Oral**	**=**
MW **= 64**		**pKa**	**=**
Vd **= 2.0**			

References:

Corticosteroids   Fax #1125

Trade: ACTH
Can/Aus/UK:
Uses: Steroid, corticosteroid
AAP: Not reviewed

Small amounts of most corticosteroids are secreted into breast milk. Following a 10 mg oral dose of prednisone, 2 hr milk levels of prednisolone and prednisone were 1.6 µg/L and 26.7 µg/L respectively. Doses of 80 mg/day in mothers produce insignificant absorption in infant (< 0.1% of dose).   In small doses, most steroids are not contraindicated in nursing mothers. Whenever possible use low-dose alternatives such as aerosols or inhalers. Following administration, wait at least 4 hours if possible prior to feeding infant to reduce exposure. With high doses, particularly for longer periods, steroids may inhibit epiphyseal bone growth, weaken bones, and may induce gastric ulcerations in children. Brief applications of high dose steroids are probably not contraindicated, but this will require a risk-benefit assessment.

Alternatives:

Pregnancy Risk Category: C

Adult Concerns: Gastric distress, gastric ulceration, glaucoma, thinning skin.

Pediatric Concerns: None reported via milk. Limit degree and duration of exposure if possible. Use inhaled or intranasal steroids to reduce exposure.

Drug Interactions: Decreased effect when used with barbiturates, phenytoin, rifampin.

AHL = 24+ hours		M/P	= 0.25
PHL =		PB	= 75%
PK = 1 hr.(milk)		Oral	= Complete
MW = 346		pKa	=
Vd =			

References:
1. Berlin CM, Kaiser DG, Demmers L. Excretion of prednisone and prednisolone in human milk. Pharmacologist 21:264, 1979.
2. Ost L, Wettrell G. Bjorkhem I, et.al. Prednisolone excretion in human milk. J Pediatr. 106:1008-1011,1985.
3. Wilson, J. Drugs in Breast Milk. New York: ADIS Press, 1981.
4. Katz FH, Duncan BR. Entry of prednisone into human milk. N Engl J Med 293:1154, 1975.
5. Ost L, et. al. Prednisolone excretion in human milk. J Pediatr 106:1008-11, 1985.
6. Greenberger PA, et.al. Pharmacokinetics of prednisolone transfer to breast milk. Clinical Pharmacology and Therapeutics 53:324-328, 1993.

Corticotropin   Fax #1126

Trade: Act, Acthar, ACTH
Can/Aus/UK: Acthar
Uses: Stimulates cortisol release

AAP: Not reviewed

ACTH is secreted by the anterior pituitary in the brain and stimulates the adrenal cortex to produce and secrete adrenocortical hormones (cortisol, hydrocortisone). As a peptide product, ACTH is easily destroyed in the infants' GI tract. None would be absorbed by the infant. ACTH stimulates the endogenous production of cortisol which theoretically can transfer to the breastfed infant. However, the use of ACTH in breastfeeding mothers largely depends on the dose and duration of exposure, and the risks to the infant. Brief exposures are probably not contraindicated.

Alternatives:

Pregnancy Risk Category: C

Adult Concerns: Hypersensitivity reactions, increased risk of infection, embryocidal effects, other symptoms of hypercorticalism.

Pediatric Concerns: None reported via milk.

Drug Interactions:

AHL = 15 minutes.	**M/P** =
PHL =	**PB** =
PK =	**Oral** = 0%
MW =	**pKa** =
Vd =	

References:

Cromolyn Sodium   Fax #1128

Trade: Nasalcrom, Gastrocrom, Intal
Can/Aus/UK: Intral, Nalcrom, Opticrom, Vistacrom, Cromese, Rynacrom, Intal
Uses: Antiasthmatic, antiallergic
AAP: Not reviewed

Cromolyn is an extremely safe drug that is used clinically as an antiasthmatic, antiallergic, and to suppress mast cell degranulation and allergic symptoms. No data on penetration into human breast milk is available, but it has an extremely low pKa, and minimal levels would be expected. Less than 0.001% of a dose is distributed into milk of the monkey. No harmful effects have been reported on breastfeeding infants. Less than 1% of this drug is absorbed from the maternal (and probably the infant's) GI tract, so it is unlikely to produce untoward effects in nursing infants. This product is frequently used in pediatric patients.

Alternatives:

Pregnancy Risk Category: B

Adult Concerns: Headache, itching, nausea, diarrhea, allergic reactions, hoarseness, coughing.

Pediatric Concerns: None reported via milk.

Drug Interactions:

AHL = 80-90 minutes		M/P	=
PHL =		PB	=
PK = < 15 minutes		Oral	= < 1%
MW = 468		pKa	= Low
Vd =			

References:
1. McEvoy GE(ed):AHFS Drug Information, New York, NY. 1995.

Cyclizine   Fax #1129

Trade: Marezine
Can/Aus/UK: Marzine, Migral, Diconal, Valoid
Uses: Anti-histamine, antiemetic
AAP: Not reviewed

Cyclizine is an antihistamine frequently used as an antiemetic, and for motion sickness. In past years, this drug was frequently used for nausea and vomiting of pregnancy, although it is no longer used for this purpose. No reports concerning its secretion into human milk are available.

Alternatives:

Pregnancy Risk Category: B

Adult Concerns: Sedation, dry mouth.

Pediatric Concerns: None reported via milk.

Drug Interactions: Increased sedation with CNS depressants such as alcohol, barbiturates.

AHL =		M/P =	
PHL =		PB =	
PK =		Oral =	
MW = 266		pKa = 7.7	
Vd =			

References:

Cyclobenzaprine   Fax #1450

Trade: Flexeril, Cycoflex
Can/Aus/UK: Flexeril, Novo-Cycloprine
Uses: Muscle relaxant, CNS depressant
AAP: Not reviewed

Cyclobenzaprine is a centrally acting skeletal muscle relaxant that is structurally and pharmacologically similar to the tricyclic antidepressants. Cyclobenzaprine is used as an adjunct to rest and physical therapy for the relief of acute, painful musculoskeletal conditions. Studies have not conclusively shown whether the skeletal muscle relaxation properties are due to the sedation or placebo effects. At least one study has found it no more effective than placebo. It is not known if cyclobenzaprine is secreted in milk, but one must assume that its secretion would be similar to the tricyclics (see amitriptyline, desipramine). There are no pediatric indications for this product.

Alternatives:

Pregnancy Risk Category: B

Adult Concerns: Drowsiness, dry mouth, dizziness, nausea, vomiting, unpleasant taste sensation. Tachycardia, hypotension, arrhythmias.

Pediatric Concerns: None reported, but caution is urged.

Drug Interactions: Do not use with 14 days of MAO inhibitor. Additive effect with tricyclic antidepressants. Enhances effect of alcohol, barbiturates, and other CNS depressants.

AHL = 24-72 hours.		M/P	=
PHL =		PB	= 93%
PK = 3-8 hours		Oral	= Complete
MW = 275		pKa	=
Vd = High			

References:
1.   McEvoy GE(ed):AHFS Drug Information, New York, NY. 1995.

Cyclophosphamide   Fax #1130

Trade: Neosar, Cytoxan
Can/Aus/UK: Cytoxan, Procytox, Cycloblastin, Endoxana
Uses: Antineoplastic
AAP: Contraindicated by the American Academy of Pediatrics in Breastfeeding Mothers

Cyclophosphamide is a powerful and toxic antineoplastic drug. A number of reports in the literature indicate that cyclophosphamide can transfer into human milk as evidenced by the production of leukopenia and bone marrow suppression in at least 3 breastfed infants. Thus far, no reports have provided quantitative estimates of cyclophosphamide in milk.   This agent should not be used in breastfeeding mothers.

Alternatives:

Pregnancy Risk Category: D

Adult Concerns: Leukopenia, infections, anemia, GI distress, nausea, vomiting, diarrhea, hemorrhagic colitis.

Pediatric Concerns: Leukopenia and bone marrow suppression in at least 3 breastfed infants.

Drug Interactions: Cyclophosphamide may reduce digoxin serum levels. Increased bone marrow suppression when used with allopurinol, and cardiotoxicity when used with doxorubicin. May prolong effect of neuromuscular blocking agents.   Chloramphenicol increases half-life of cyclophosphamide. Numerous others, see complete review.

AHL = 7.5 hours		M/P	=
PHL =		PB	= 13%
PK = 2-3 hours.		Oral	= 75%
MW = 261		pKa	=
Vd =			

References:
1.   Amato D, Niblett JS. Neutropenia from cyclophosphamide in breast milk. Med. J. Australia 1:383-4, 1977.
2.   Durodola JL. Administration of cyclophosphamide during late pregnancy and early lactation: a case report. J.Nat.Med.Assoc. 71:165-6,1979.

Cycloserine   Fax #1131

Trade: Seromycin
Can/Aus/UK: Closina, Cycloserine
Uses: Anti-tuberculosis drug
AAP: Approved by the American Academy of Pediatrics for use in breastfeeding mothers

Cycloserine is an antibiotic primarily used for treating tuberculosis. It is also effective against various Staphylococcal infections. It is a small molecule with a structure similar to an amino acid, D-alanine. Following 250 mg oral dose given four times daily to mothers, milk levels ranged from 6 to 19 mg/L, an average of 72% of maternal serum levels. Vorherr estimates the percent of maternal daily dose excreted in milk to be 0.6%.

Alternatives:

Pregnancy Risk Category: C

Adult Concerns: Drowsiness, CNS confusion, dizziness, headache, lethargy, depression, seizures. Precautions urged in epilepsy, depression, severe anxiety.

Pediatric Concerns: None reported.

Drug Interactions: Increased toxicity with alcohol, isoniazid. Phenytoin levels may be elevated due to inhibition of metabolism.

AHL = 12+ hours		**M/P** = 0.72	
PHL =		**PB** =	
PK = 3-4 hours		**Oral** = 70-90%	
MW = 102		**pKa** =	
Vd =			

References:
1. Morton RF, et.al. Studies on the absorption, diffusion, and excretion of cycloserine. Antibiot. Ann. 3:169-72, 1955.
2. Snider DE, Powell KE. Should women taking antituberculosis drugs breast-feed? Arch Inter Med. 144:589-590, 1984.
3. Vorherr, H. Drug excretion in breast milk. Postgrad. Med. 56:97-104, 1974.

Cyclosporine   Fax #1132

Trade: Sandimmune, Neoral
Can/Aus/UK: Sandimmune, Neoral
Uses: Immunosuppressant
AAP: Not reviewed

Cyclosporine is an immunosuppressant used to reduce organ rejection following transplant and in autoimmune syndromes such as arthritis, etc. In one report, cyclosporine was secreted into breast milk with a milk:plasma ratio of 0.4. In another, following a dose of 320 mg, the milk level at 22 hours post dose was 16 µg/L and the milk:plasma ratio was 0.28. In another report (personal communication) of a mother receiving 250 mg twice daily, the maternal plasma level of cyclosporine was measured at 187 µg/L, the breast milk level was 167 µg/L. None was detected in the plasma of the infant. Use during lactation is subject to risk, and close observation of a breastfeeding infant is mandatory.

Alternatives:

Pregnancy Risk Category: C

Adult Concerns: Kidney toxicity, edema, tremor, seizures, elevated liver enzymes, hypertension, hirsutism. Use during pregnancy does not pose a major risk. Infections and possible lymphomas may result.

Pediatric Concerns: None reported, but caution is urged.

Drug Interactions: Rifampin, phenytoin, phenobarbital decrease plasma concentrations of cyclosporine. Ketoconazole, fluconazole, and itraconazole increase plasma concentrations of cyclosporine.

AHL = 5.6 hours	**M/P**	= 0.28-0.4
PHL =	**PB**	= 93%
PK = 3.5 hours.	**Oral**	= 28% pediatric
MW =	**pKa**	=
Vd = 3.1-4.3		

References:
1. Flechner SM, Katz AR, Rogers AJ, et.al. The presence of cyclosporine in body tissue and fluids during pregnancy. Am J Kidney Dis. 5:60-63,1985.
2. Lowenstein, BR. et.al. Successful pregnancy and vaginal delivery after heart transplantation. Am. J. Obstet. Gynecol 158:589-590, 1988.
3. Thiagarajan, KD. (personal communication), 1997.

Cyproheptadine   Fax #1529

Trade: Periactin
Can/Aus/UK: Periactin, PMS-Cyproheptadine
Uses: Antihistamine
AAP: Not reviewed

Cyproheptadine is a serotonin and histamine antagonist with anticholinergic and sedative effects.   It has been used as an appetite stimulant in children, and for rashes and pruritus (itching).   No data are available on its transfer to human milk.

Alternatives: Hydroxyzine

Pregnancy Risk Category: B

Adult Concerns: Sedation, nausea, vomiting, diarrhea.

Pediatric Concerns: None reported. Observe for sedation.

Drug Interactions: Additive sedation when used with other antihistamines and CNS depressants. Increased toxicity (hallucinations) when used with MAO inhibitors.

AHL = 16 hours	**M/P** =
PHL =	**PB** =
PK =	**Oral** =
MW = 287	**pKa** = 9.3
Vd =	

References:

Cytarabine   Fax #1133

Trade: Cytosar
Can/Aus/UK: Alexan, Cytosar
Uses: Antineoplastic
AAP: Not reviewed

Cytarabine is converted intra-cellularly to a nucleotide that interrupts DNA synthesis. No data has been reported on transfer into breast milk. The compound is poorly absorbed orally and is therefore used IM or IV only. This drug would be extremely toxic to an infant and is generally contraindicated in breastfeeding mothers.

Alternatives:

Pregnancy Risk Category: D

Adult Concerns: Anemia, bone marrow suppression, nausea, vomiting, diarrhea, GI hemorrhage, elevated liver enzymes.

Pediatric Concerns: None reported via milk. But due to toxicity, this product should never be used in a breastfeeding mother.

Drug Interactions: Decreases effect of gentamycin flucytosine, digoxin. Increases toxicity of alkylating agents, radiation, purine analogs, methotrexate.

AHL = 1-3 hours.	**M/P**	=
PHL =	**PB**	= 13%.
PK =	**Oral**	= <20%
MW = 243	**pKa**	=
Vd =		

References:
1. Drug Facts and Comparisons. 1995 ed. Facts and Comparisons, St. Louis.

Cytomegalovirus　　　　Fax #1458

Trade: Human Cytomegalovirus, CMV
Can/Aus/UK:
Uses: Viral infection
AAP: Not reviewed

Cytomegalovirus is one of the family of herpes viruses. CMV is rather ubiquitous, many infants having been exposed in utero, and later in day care centers. Maternal cervical infection is very common. CMV is found in breast milk of virtually all CMV positive women using the newer PCR techniques. The timing of maternal infection is important. If the mother seroconverts early in gestation, the infant is likely to be affected. Symptoms include: small for gestational age, jaundice, microcephaly, petechia, hepatosplenomegaly, hearing loss. If the mother seroconverts late in gestation, the infant is less likely to be severely affected. In most infants from seropositive mothers, the CMV found in breast milk is not overtly dangerous, and these mothers can breastfeed successfully. However, infants who are not provided with maternal antibodies to CMV may be exceedingly susceptible to CMV in breast milk. Breast milk from CMV positive mothers should never be fed to unprotected infants.

Alternatives:

Pregnancy Risk Category:

Adult Concerns: Asymptomatic to Hepatosplenomegaly. Fever, mild hepatitis.

Pediatric Concerns: CMV transfer into breast milk is known but of low risk to infants born of CMV positive mothers. Breast milk from CMV positive mothers should never be fed to unprotected non-immune infants.

References:
1. Dworsky M et.al. Cytomegalovirus infection of breast milk and transmission in infancy. Pediatrics 72:295, 1983.
2. Lawrence RA. Breastfeeding, A guide for the medical profession.

Mosby, St. Louis, 1994.

3. Hotsubo T, Nagata N, et.al. Detection of human cytomegalovirus DNA in breast milk by means of polymerase chain reaction. Microbiol. Immunol. 38(10):809-811,1994.

Dactinomycin   Fax #1134

Trade: Cosmegen
Can/Aus/UK: Cosmegen
Uses: Antibiotic used in cancer chemotherapy
AAP: Not reviewed

Dactinomycin is an antineoplastic antibiotic that inhibits DNA and RNA synthesis. It is extremely dangerous and very toxic. Transfer into breast milk is unreported. Although its oral absorption is very poor, it is extremely irritating to tissues and must be administered IV only. Definitely contraindicated in nursing mothers.

Alternatives:

Pregnancy Risk Category: C

Adult Concerns: Anemia, bone marrow suppression, skin lesions and rashes, alopecia, malaise, fatigue, fever, liver toxicity.

Pediatric Concerns: None reported, but could be extremely toxic. Caution urged.

Drug Interactions: Dactinomycin potentiates the toxicity of radiation therapy.

AHL = 36 hours		M/P =	
PHL =		PB =	
PK =		Oral = Poor	
MW = 1255		pKa =	
Vd =			

References:
1. Drug Facts and Comparisons. 1995 ed. Facts and Comparisons, St. Louis.

Dalteparin Sodium   Fax #1566

Trade: Fragmin, Low Molecular Weight Heparin
Can/Aus/UK: Fragmin
Uses: Anticoagulant
AAP: Not reviewed

Dalteparin is a low molecular weight fraction of heparin used clinically as an anticoagulant. There are no data available on the transfer of this peptide into human milk, but it is extremely unlikely. Because it is a polysaccharide fragment of heparin, its molecular weight is large and varies from 2000-9000 daltons, which would largely preclude its entry into human milk. Due to minimal oral bioavailability, any present in milk would not be orally absorbed by the infant.

Alternatives: Enoxaparin.

Pregnancy Risk Category: B

Adult Concerns: Anticoagulant effects in adults when administered subcutaneously.

Pediatric Concerns: None reported via milk. Molecular weight is too large to produce clinically relevant milk levels.

Drug Interactions:

AHL = 2.3 hours		M/P	=
PHL =		PB	=
PK = 2-4 hours (SC)		Oral	= None
MW = 9000		pKa	=
Vd = 0.06			

References:

Danazol   Fax #1135

Trade: Danocrine
Can/Aus/UK: Cyclomen, Azol, Danocrine, Danol
Uses: Synthetic androgen, antigonadotropic agent
AAP: Not reviewed

Danazol suppresses the pituitary-ovarian axis by inhibiting output of pituitary and hypothalamic hormones. It also appears to inhibit the synthesis of sex steroids and provides anti-estrogenic effects.   It is primarily used for treating endometriosis. Due to its effect on pituitary hormones and its androgenic effects, it is likely to reduce the rate of breast milk production, although this has not been documented. No data on its transfer to human milk is available.

Alternatives:

Pregnancy Risk Category: X

Adult Concerns: Breast size reduction. Androgenic effects, hirsutism, acne, weight gain, edema, testicular atrophy,   thrombocytopenia, thrombocytosis, hot flashes, break through menstrual bleeding.

Pediatric Concerns: None reported, but caution is urged.

Drug Interactions: Decreased insulin requirements.   May increase anticoagulation with warfarin therapy.

AHL = 4.5 hours		**M/P** =	
PHL =		**PB** =	
PK = 2 hours		**Oral** = Complete	
MW = 337		**pKa** =	
Vd =			

References:
1.   White, G. and White, M. Breastfeeding and drugs in human milk. Vet. and Human Tox. 26:supplement 1, 1984.

Dantrolene   Fax #1507

Trade: Dantrium
Can/Aus/UK: Dantrium
Uses: Skeletal muscle relaxant
AAP: Not reviewed

Dantrolene produces a direct skeletal muscle relaxation and is indicated for spasticity resulting from upper motor neuron disorders such as multiple sclerosis, cerebral palsy, etc. It is not indicated for rheumatic disorders, or musculoskeletal trauma. No data on transfer into human milk are available.

Alternatives:

Pregnancy Risk Category: C

Adult Concerns: Adverse effects are quite common and include weakness, dizziness, diarrhea, slurred speech, drooling, and nausea. Significant risk for hepatotoxicity. Visual and auditory hallucinations.

Pediatric Concerns: None reported, but caution is urged.

Drug Interactions: Increased toxicity with estrogens, CNS sedatives, MAO inhibitors, phenothiazines, calcium channel blockers, warfarin, and tolbutamide.

AHL = 8.7 hours		M/P =	
PHL = 7.3 hours		PB =	
PK = 5 hours		Oral = 35%	
MW = 314		pKa =	
Vd =			

References:
1. Pharmaceutical Manufacturer's Package Insert, 1997.

Desipramine   Fax #1136

Trade: Pertofrane, Norpramin
Can/Aus/UK: Norpramin, Pertofrane, Novo-Desipramine Pertofran
Uses: Tricyclic antidepressant
AAP: Drugs whose effect on nursing infants is unknown but may be of concern

Desipramine is a prototypical tricyclic antidepressant. In one case report, a mother taking 200 mg of desipramine at bedtime had milk:plasma ratios of 0.4 to 0.9 with milk levels ranging between 17-35 µg/L. Desipramine was not found in the infant's blood, although these levels are probably too low to measure. In another study of a mother consuming 300 mg of desipramine daily, the milk levels were 30% higher than the maternal serum. The milk concentrations of desipramine were reported to be 316 to 328 µg/L, with peak concentrations occurring at 4 hours post-dose. Assuming an average milk concentration of 280 ng/ml, a 4 Kg infant would receive approximately 72 µg/Kg. This dose is approximately 1/100th the maternal dose. No untoward effects have been reported.

Alternatives: Amoxapine, Imipramine

Pregnancy Risk Category: C

Adult Concerns: Anticholinergic side effects, such as drying of secretions, dilated pupil, sedation, constipation, fatigue, peculiar taste.

Pediatric Concerns: None reported in many studies.

Drug Interactions: Do not use with MAO inhibitors or within two weeks of therapy. Increased effects occur following use with stimulants, and benzodiazepines. Decreased effects occur with barbiturates, carbamazepine, and phenytoin use.

AHL = 7-60 hours	**M/P**	= 0.4-0.9
PHL =	**PB**	= 82%
PK = 4-6 hours	**Oral**	= 90%

MW = 266   pKa   = 9.5
Vd = 22-59

References:
1.   Erickson, S. et.al. Tricyclics and breast feeding. Am.J.Psychiatry
     136: 1483-1484, 1979.
2.   Sovner R, Orsulak PJ. Excretion of imipramine and desipramine
     in human breast milk. Am J Psychiatry 136:451-2, 1979.
3.   Stancer HC, Reed KL. Desipramine and 2-Hydroxydesipramine
     in human breast milk and the nursing infant's serum. Am. J. Psy.
     143:1597-1600, 1986.

Desmopressin Acetate   Fax #1434

Trade: DDAVP, Stimate
Can/Aus/UK: DDAVP, Rhinyle, Minirin, Desmospray
Uses: Synthetic antidiuretic hormone
AAP: Not reviewed

Desmopressin (DDAVP) is a small synthetic octapeptide antidiuretic
hormone.   Desmopressin increases reabsorption of water by the
collecting ducts in the kidneys resulting in decreased urinary flow
(ADH effect).   Generally used in patients who lack pituitary
vasopressin, it is primarily used intra-nasally or intravenous.   Unlike
natural vasopressin, desmopressin has no effect on growth hormone,
prolactin, or luteinizing hormone. Following intranasal administration,
less than 10-20% is absorbed through the nasal mucosa. This peptide
has been used in lactating women without effect on nursing infants.
Although it is believed to be secreted to some degree in human milk,
it is easily destroyed in the GI tract by trypsin and is not absorbed
orally.

Alternatives:

Pregnancy Risk Category: B

Adult Concerns: Reduced urine production, edema, fluid retention.

Pediatric Concerns: None reported.

Drug Interactions: Lithium, demeclocycline may decrease ADH effect. Chlorpropamide, fludrocortisone may increase ADH effect.

AHL = 75.5 minutes.		M/P	=
PHL =		PB	=
PK = 1-5 hours.		Oral	= None
MW = 1069		pKa	=
Vd =			

References:
1.   McEvoy GE(ed):AFHS Drug Information, New York, NY. 1992, pp 417-26.
2.   Hime MC, Richardson JA. Diabetes insipidus and pregnancy. Obstet. Gynecol. Surv. 33:375-379, 1978.
3.   Hadi HA et.al. Diabetes insipidus during pregnancy complicated by preeclampsia. A Case Report. J. Reprod. Med. 30:206, 1985.

Dexfenfluramine   Fax #1497

Trade: Redux
Can/Aus/UK: Adifax
Uses: Anorexigenic, diet pill
AAP: Not reviewed

Dexfenfluramine is the dextro stereoisomer of fenfluramine (Pondimin) and is used for its anorexiant effect in weight reduction. It is both a serotonin reuptake inhibitor and releasing agent. It is metabolized to d-norfenfluramine (active) which has a half-life of 32 hours. Its transfer to human milk has not been reported although it is secreted in animal milk. Due to the low molecular weight, and high CNS penetration, it is likely that this product may attain moderate levels in breast milk. Further, its long half-life and active metabolite could possibly induce higher steady state plasma levels in the neonate with corresponding anorexia and weight loss after prolonged therapy. Risk assessment with this product may not justify exposure of a breastfeeding infant.

Alternatives:

Pregnancy Risk Category: C

Adult Concerns: Adverse effects include diarrhea, drowsiness, dizziness, mood disorders, sleep disorders, tiredness, dry mouth, nausea, constipation, polyuria, suicide ideations, impaired concentration and memory(18%), pulmonary hypertension (1 per 22-44,000).

Pediatric Concerns: None reported, but caution urged.

Drug Interactions: Increased risk of serotonin syndrome when used with sumatriptan, dihydroergotamine, and tricyclic antidepressants. Increased toxicity when used with MAO inhibitors. Allow at least 14 days after MAOI use. May cause false positive results on urine drug screens.

AHL = 17-20 hours	**M/P** =	
PHL =	**PB** = 36%	
PK = 2 hours	**Oral** = 68%	
MW = 231	**pKa** =	
Vd = 10		

References:
1. Drug Facts and Comparisons. 1996. ed. Facts and Comparisons, St. Louis.
2. Pharmaceutical Manufacturer's Package Insert, 1997.

Dextroamphetamine   Fax #1137

Trade: Dexedrine, Amphetamine, Oxydess
Can/Aus/UK: Dexedrine, Dexten
Uses: Powerful CNS stimulant
AAP: Contraindicated by the American Academy of Pediatrics in Breastfeeding Mothers

Amphetamines are concentrated in breast milk. Following a 20 mg daily dose milk levels in breast milk varied from 55-138 µg/L. These levels were 2.8-7.5 times higher than maternal plasma levels. Even though significant levels are found, several studies of exposed infants do not report many side effects. May produce insomnia, irritability, anorexia, or poor sleeping patterns in infants.

Alternatives:

Pregnancy Risk Category: C

Adult Concerns: Nervousness, insomnia, anorexia, hyperexcitability.

Pediatric Concerns: Possible insomnia, irritability, anorexia, or poor sleeping patterns in infants.

Drug Interactions: May precipitate hypertensive crisis in patients on MAO inhibitors and arrhythmias in patients receiving general anesthetics. Increased effect/toxicity with tricyclic antidepressants, phenytoin, phenobarbital, norepinephrine, meperidine.

AHL = 6-8 hours		M/P	= 2.8-7.5
PHL =		PB	= 16-20%
PK	= 1-2 hours	Oral	= Complete
MW	= 368	pKa	=
Vd	=		

References:
1.   Steiner E, Hallberg V. Amphetamine secretion in breast milk. Eur J Clin Pharmacol. 27:123-124, 1959.

Dextromethorphan   Fax #1514

Trade: DM, Benylin, Delsym, Pertussin, Robitussin DM
Can/Aus/UK: Balminil-DM, Delsym, Benylin DM, Cosylan
Uses: Antitussive, Cough preparation
AAP: Not reviewed

Dextromethorphan is a weak antitussive commonly used in infants and adults. It is a congener of codeine and appears to elevate the cough threshold in the brain. It does not have addictive, analgesic, or sedative actions, and it does not produce respiratory depression at normal doses. It is the safest of the antitussives and is routinely used in children and infants. No data on its transfer to human milk are available. It is very unlikely that enough would transfer via milk to provide clinically significant levels in a breastfed infant.

Alternatives: Codeine

Pregnancy Risk Category: C

Adult Concerns: Drowsiness, fatigue, dizziness, hyperpyrexia.

Pediatric Concerns: None reported.

Drug Interactions: May interact with MAO inhibitors producing hypotension, hyperpyrexia, nausea, coma.

AHL = <4 hours		**M/P** =	
PHL =		**PB** =	
PK = 1-2 hours		**Oral** = Complete	
MW = 271		**pKa** = 8.3	
Vd =			

References:
1. Pender ES, Parks BR: Toxicity with dextromethorphan-containing preparations: a literature review and report of two additional cases. Pediatr Emerg Care 7:163-165, 1991.

Diazepam   Fax #1139

Trade: Valium
Can/Aus/UK: Apo-Diazepam, Meval, Novo-Dipam, Vivol Antenex, Ducene, Valium, Sedapam
Uses: Sedative, anxiolytic drug
AAP: Drugs whose effect on nursing infants is unknown but may be

of concern

Diazepam is a powerful CNS depressant and anticonvulsant. Published data on milk and plasma levels are highly variable and many are poor studies. In 3 mothers receiving 10 mg three times daily for up to 6 days, the maternal plasma levels of diazepam averaged 491 ng/mL (day 4) and 601 ng/mL (day 6). Corresponding milk levels were 51 ng/mL (day 4) and 78 ng/mL (day6). The milk:plasma ratio was approximately 0.1. Other reports suggest slightly higher values. Taken together, most results suggest that the dose of diazepam and its metabolite, desmethyldiazepam, to a suckling infant will be on average 5% and at a maximum 12% of the weight-adjusted maternal dose of diazepam. The active metabolite, desmethyldiazepam, in general has a much longer half-life in adults and pediatric patients and may tend to accumulate on longer therapy. Some reports of lethargy, sedation, poor suckling have been found. PHL= 20-50 hours (full-term neonate), 40-400 hours (premature). Sustained long-term therapy may prove troublesome. Single or occasional doses may be less problematic. Newer, shorter half-life benzodiazepines should be preferred.

Alternatives: Lorazepam, Midazolam

Pregnancy Risk Category: D

Adult Concerns: Poor suckling, sedation, lethargy, constipation.

Pediatric Concerns: Some reports of lethargy, sedation, poor suckling have been found.

Drug Interactions: May increase sedation when used with CNS depressants such as alcohol, barbiturates, opioids. Cimetidine may decrease metabolism and clearance of diazepam. Cisapride can dramatically increase plasma levels of diazepam. Valproic may displace diazepam from binding sites, thus increasing sedative effects. SSRIs (fluoxetine, sertraline, paroxetine) can dramatically increase diazepam levels by altering clearance, thus leading to sedation .

AHL = 43 hours		M/P	= 0.2-2.7
PHL = 20-50 hours (full-term neo)		PB	= 99%
PK = 1-2 hours		Oral	= Complete

MW = 285   pKa   = 3.4
Vd   = 0.7-2.6

References:
1.   Erkkola R. Kanto J. Diazepam and breastfeeding. The Lancet,
      1:1235-1236, 1972.
2.   Wesson DR, Camber S, Harkey M et.al. Diazepam and
      desmethyldiazepam in breast milk. J Psychoactive Drugs 17:55-
      56, 1985.
3.   Spigset O. Anaesthetic agents and excretion in breast milk. Acta
      Anaesthesiologica Scandinavica. 38:94-103, 1994.

Dibucaine   Fax #1443

Trade: Nupercainal
Can/Aus/UK: Nupercainal, Cinchocaine, Nupercaine,
Ultraproct, Dermacaine
Uses: Local anesthetic
AAP: Not reviewed

Dibucaine is a long-acting local anesthetic generally used topically. It
is primarily used topically in creams and ointments, and due to toxicity,
has been banned in the USA for IV or IM injections.   No data are
available on transfer to breast milk.   Dibucaine is effective for
sunburn, topical burns, rash, rectal hemorrhoids, and other skin
irritations. Long-term use and use over large areas of the body are
discouraged. Although somewhat minimal, some dibucaine can be
absorbed from irritated skin.

Alternatives:

Pregnancy Risk Category: C

Adult Concerns: Rash or allergic symptoms.

Pediatric Concerns: None reported via milk.

Drug Interactions:

AHL =		M/P =	
PHL =		PB =	
PK =		Oral =	
MW = 379		pKa =	
Vd =			

References:
1.   Pharmaceutical Manufacturer's Package Insert, 1995.

Diclofenac   Fax #1140

Trade: Cataflam, Voltaren
Can/Aus/UK: Voltaren, Apo-Diclo, Novo-Difenac, Fenac
Uses: NSAID analgesic for arthritis
AAP: Not reviewed

Diclofenac is a typical nonsteroidal analgesic (NSAID). Voltaren is a sustained release product whereas Cataflam is an immediate release product. Time to peak for Voltaren is 2.0 hours In one study of six postpartum mothers receiving 100 mg of Voltaren daily, the levels of diclofenac in breast milk were undetectable (limit of detection < 19 ng/mL). The amount an infant would consume would therefore be less than 2.5 µg/Kg, an amount that is not clinically relevant.

Alternatives: Ibuprofen

Pregnancy Risk Category: B

Adult Concerns: GI distress, diarrhea, nausea, vomiting.

Pediatric Concerns: None reported via milk.

Drug Interactions: May prolong prothrombin time when used with warfarin. Antihypertensive effects of ACEi family may be blunted or completely abolished by NSAIDs. Some NSAIDs may block antihypertensive effect of beta blockers, diuretics. Used with cyclosporin, may dramatically increase renal toxicity. May increase digoxin, phenytoin, lithium levels. May increase toxicity of methotrexate. May increase bioavailability of penicillamine. Probenecid may increase NSAID levels.

AHL = 1.1 hours		**M/P** =	
PHL =		**PB** = 99.7%	
PK = 1 hr. (Cataflam)		**Oral** = Complete	
MW = 318		**pKa** = 4.0	
Vd = 0.55			

References:
1. Sioufi A, Stierlin H. et.al. Recent findings concerning clinically relevant pharmacokinetics of diclofenac sodium. In: Kass(ed), Voltaren-new findings. pp19-30, Hans Huber Publishers, Bern 1982.

Dicloxacillin   Fax #1141

Trade: Pathocil, Dycill, Dynapen
Can/Aus/UK: Diclocil
Uses: Penicillin antibiotic
AAP: Not reviewed

Dicloxacillin is an oral penicillinase-resistant penicillin frequently used for peripheral (non CNS) infections caused by Staph. aureus and Staph. epidermidis infections, particularly mastitis. Following oral administration of a 250 mg dose, milk concentrations of the drug were 0.1, and 0.3 mg/L at 2 and 4 hours after the dose, respectively. Levels were undetectable after 6 hours. Usual dose for adults is 250-500 mg four times daily for at least 10-14 days.

Alternatives:

Pregnancy Risk Category: B

Adult Concerns: Elimination is delayed in neonates. Rash, diarrhea.

Pediatric Concerns: None reported via milk.

Drug Interactions: May increase effect of oral anticoagulants.

Disulfiram, probenecid may increase levels of penicillin. May reduce efficacy of oral contraceptives.

AHL	= 0.6-0.8 hr.	M/P	=
PHL	= 1.9 hours.	PB	= 96%
PK	= 0.5-2 hours.	Oral	= 35-76%
MW	= 470	pKa	=
Vd	=		

References:
1. McEvoy GE(ed):AHFS Drug Information, New York, NY. 1995.

Dicyclomine   Fax #1451

Trade: Bentyl, Antispas, Spasmoject
Can/Aus/UK: Bentylol, Formulex, Lomine, Merbentyl
Uses: Anticholinergic, drying agent
AAP: Not reviewed

Dicyclomine is a tertiary amine antispasmodic. It belongs to the family of anticholinergics such as atropine and the belladonna alkaloids. It was previously used for infant colic, but due to overdoses and reported apnea, it is seldom recommended for this use. Infants are exceeding sensitive to anticholinergics, particularly in the neonatal period. Following a dose of 20 mg in a lactating woman, a 12 day old infant reported severe apnea. The manufacturer reports milk levels of 131 μg/L with corresponding maternal serum levels of 59 μg/L. The reported milk:plasma level was 2.22.

Alternatives:

Pregnancy Risk Category: B

Adult Concerns: Apnea, dry secretions, urinary hesitancy, dilated pupils.

Pediatric Concerns: Severe apnea in one 12 day old infant. Observe for anticholinergic symptoms, drying, constipation, rapid heart rate.

Drug Interactions: Decreased effect with antacids, phenothiazines, haloperidol. Increased toxicity when used with other anticholinergics, amantadine, opiates, antiarrhythmics, antihistamines, tricyclic antidepressants.

AHL	= 9-10 hours.		**M/P**	=
PHL	=		**PB**	=
PK	= 1-1.5 hours.		**Oral**	= 67%
MW	= 345		**pKa**	=
Vd	=			

References:
1. Pharmaceutical Manufacturer's Package Insert, 1995.

Diethyl Ether   Fax #1143

Trade: Diethyl Ether, Ether
Can/Aus/UK:
Uses: Anesthetic
AAP: Not reviewed

Ether is seldom used today. Although some would be transferred into human milk, it would rapidly redistribute back to the blood and be eliminated, particularly if the mother were to withhold breast milk for at least 12 or more hours after administration.

Alternatives:

Pregnancy Risk Category:

Adult Concerns: GI distress, unique ether odor.

Pediatric Concerns:

Drug Interactions:

AHL =		**M/P**	=
PHL =		**PB**	=

PK	= 10-20 min.		Oral	=
MW	=		pKa	=
Vd	=			

References:

Diethylpropion   Fax #1144

Trade: Tepanil, Tenuate
Can/Aus/UK: Tenuate Dospan, Tenuate
Uses: Anorexiant
AAP: Not reviewed

Diethylpropion belongs to the amphetamine family and is typically used to reduce food intake. No data available other than manufacturer states this medication is secreted into breast milk. Diethylpropion's structure is similar to amphetamines. Upon withdrawal, significant withdrawal symptoms have been reported in adults. Such symptoms could be observed in breastfeeding infants of mothers using this product. The use of this medication during lactation is simply unrealistic and not justified.

Alternatives:

Pregnancy Risk Category: B

Adult Concerns: Overstimulation, insomnia, anorexia, jitteriness, rapid heart rate, elevated blood pressure.

Pediatric Concerns: None reported, but observe for anorexia, agitation, insomnia.

Drug Interactions: Increased toxicity with MAO inhibitors, CNS depressants, general anesthetics (arrhythmias), other adrenergics.

AHL	= 8 hours.		**M/P**	=
PHL	=		**PB**	=
PK	= 2 hours.		**Oral**	= 70%
MW	= 205		**pKa**	=

Vd =

References:
1.   Pharmaceutical Manufacturer's Package Insert, 1995.

Diethylstilbestrol   Fax #1145

Trade:
Can/Aus/UK: Honvol, Honvan, Fosfestrol, Apstil
Uses: Synthetic estrogen
AAP: Not reviewed

Diethylstilbestrol is a synthetic estrogen that is seldom used today. It
is known to produce a high risk of cervical cancer in female infants
exposed during pregnancy.   It has been shown to cause anatomical
abnormalities in males and females, neoplasia, reduced fertility and
immunologic changes.   Its effect in the breastfeeding infant is
unknown but should be absolutely avoided.   DES would probably
inhibit milk production. Strongly suggest using other estrogens during
breastfeeding if absolutely mandatory.   Contraindicated.

Alternatives:

Pregnancy Risk Category: X

Adult Concerns: Decreased breast milk production.

Pediatric Concerns: None reported via milk, but this product is too
dangerous for use in breastfeeding mothers.

Drug Interactions:

AHL =	M/P	=
PHL =	PB	=
PK =	Oral	= Complete
MW = 268	pKa	=
Vd =		

References:

1. O'Brien, T. Excretion of drugs in human milk. Am.J. Hosp. Pharm. 31:844-854, 1974.
2. Shapiro S, Sloan D. The effects of exogenous female sex hormones on the fetus. Epidemiol Rev I:110, 1979.

Diflunisal   Fax #1146

Trade: Dolobid
Can/Aus/UK: Apo-Diflunisal, Dolobid, Novo-Diflunisal
Uses: Nonsteroidal anti-inflammatory analgesic
AAP: Not reviewed

Diflunisal is a derivative of salicylic acid. Diflunisal is excreted into human milk in concentrations 2-7% of the maternal plasma levels. No reports of side-effects have been located. This product is potentially a higher risk NSAID and other less toxic compounds should be used. Because it is a derivative of salicylic acid, an increased risk of Reyes syndrome cannot be excluded.

Alternatives: Ibuprofen

**Pregnancy Risk Category: C if used in first, second trimester
                          D if used in third trimester**

Adult Concerns: Prolonged bleeding time, headache, GI distress, diarrhea, GI cramping, fluid retention. Ulcer complications. Worsening hypertension.

Pediatric Concerns: None reported but alternatives advised.

Drug Interactions: Antacids reduce effect. Increased toxicity of digoxin, methotrexate, anticoagulants, phenytoin, sulfonylureas, lithium, acetaminophen.

AHL = 8-12 hours		**M/P** =	
PHL =		**PB** = 99%	
PK = 2-3 hours		**Oral** = Complete	
MW = 250		**pKa** =	
Vd = 0.1-0.2			

References:
1. Pharmaceutical Manufacturer's Package Insert, 1995.

Digitoxin   Fax #1147

Trade: Crystodigin
Can/Aus/UK: Digitaline
Uses: Cardiac stimulant
AAP: Not reviewed

No data are available on digitoxin and its transfer to human milk. Occasionally given to infants. High lipid solubility and good oral bioavailability would suggest some transfer into breast milk. See digoxin.

Alternatives: Digoxin

Pregnancy Risk Category: C

Adult Concerns: Nausea, vomiting, anorexia, cardiac arrhythmias.

Pediatric Concerns: None reported thus far.

Drug Interactions: Reduced plasma levels when used with antacids, penicillamine, bran fiber, sucralfate, cholestyramine, rifampin, etc. Increased toxicity when used with diltiazem, ibuprofen, cimetidine, omeprazole, etc.

AHL = 6.7 days	**M/P** =
PHL =	**PB** = 97%
PK = 4 hours	**Oral** = 90-100%
MW = 765	**pKa** =
Vd = 7 (variable)	

References:
1. Levy, M. et.al. Excretion of drugs in human milk, New Engl. J. Med. 297:789, 1977.

Digoxin   Fax #1148

Trade: Lanoxin, Lanoxicaps
Can/Aus/UK: Lanoxin, Novo-Digoxin
Uses: Cardiac stimulant
AAP: Approved by the American Academy of Pediatrics for use in breastfeeding mothers

Digoxin is a cardiac stimulant used primarily to strengthen the contractile process. In one mother receiving 0.25 mg digoxin daily, the amount found in breast milk ranged from 0.96 to 0.61 µg/L at 4 and 6 hours post-dose respectively. Mean peak breast milk levels varied from 0.78 µg/L in one patient to 0.41 µg/L in another. Plasma levels in the infants were undetectable. In another study of 5 women receiving digoxin therapy, the average breast milk concentration was 0.64 µg/L. From these studies, it is apparent that a breastfeeding infant would receive less than 1 µg/day of digoxin, too low to be clinically relevant. The small amounts secreted into breast milk have not produced problems in nursing infants. Poor and erratic GI absorption could theoretically reduce absorption in nursing infant. Frequently used in infancy.

Alternatives:

Pregnancy Risk Category: C

Adult Concerns: Nausea, vomiting, bradycardia, arrhythmias.

Pediatric Concerns: None reported in several studies.

Drug Interactions: Too numerous to list all. Decreased digoxin effect when used with antacids, bran fiber, sucralfate, sulfasalazine, diuretics, phenytoin, cholestyramine, aminoglutethimide. Increase digoxin effects may result when used with diltiazem, ibuprofen, cimetidine, omeprazole, bepridil, reserpine, amphotericin B, erythromycin, quinine, tetracycline, cyclosporine, etc.

AHL = 39 hours	M/P	= <0.9
PHL = 20-180 hours	PB	= 25%
PK = 1.5-3 hours	Oral	= 65-85%

MW = 781   pKa =
Vd = 5.1-7.4

References:
1. Loughnan PM. Digoxin excretion in human breast milk. J. Pediatr. 92:1019-1020,1978.
2. Levy, M. et.al. Excretion of drugs in human milk, New Engl. J. Med. 297:789, 1977.

Diltiazem HCL   Fax #1149

Trade: Cardizem Sr, Dilacor-XR, Diltiazem, Cardizem CD
Can/Aus/UK: Cardizem, Apo-Diltiazem, Apo-Diltiaz, Cardcal, Coras, Dilzem, Adizem, Britiazim, Tildiem
Uses: Antihypertensive, calcium channel blocker
AAP: Approved by the American Academy of Pediatrics for use in breastfeeding mothers

Diltiazem is an typical calcium channel blocker antihypertensive. One report indicates levels in milk parallel those of serum (Milk:plasma ratio is approximately 1.0). Peak level in milk (and plasma) was slightly higher than 200 µg/L and occurred at 8 hours. Remember, many formulations are extended release preparations (12-24 hours ..SR,XR,CD) and it would be difficult to breastfeed between the peak levels. Best choice of CCB may be nifedipine (< 5% of dose transferred). Authors recommend against using diltiazem in breastfeeding mothers.

Alternatives: Nifedipine, Nimodipine, Verapamil

Pregnancy Risk Category: C

Adult Concerns: Hypotension, bradycardia.

Pediatric Concerns: Hypotension, bradycardia is possible. See nifedipine.

Drug Interactions: H-2 blockers may increase bioavailability of diltiazem. Beta blockers may increase cardio depressant effect. May increase cyclosporine, and carbamazepine levels. Fentanyl may increase hypotension.

AHL	= 3.5-6 hours	M/P	= 1.0
PHL	=	PB	= 78%
PK	= 2-3 hours	Oral	= 40-60%
MW	= 433	pKa	=
Vd	= 1.7		

References:
1.   Pharmaceutical Manufacturer's Package Insert, 1995.
2.   Okada M, Inoue H, Nakamura Y, et.al. Excretion of diltiazem in human milk. N. Eng. J. Med. 312:992,1985.

Dimenhydrinate   Fax #1150

Trade: Marmine, Dramamine
Can/Aus/UK: Gravol, Traveltabs, Andrumin, Travacalm
Uses: Antihistamine for vertigo and motion sickness
AAP: Not reviewed

Consists of 55% diphenhydramine and 45% of 8-chlorotheophylline. Diphenhydramine (Benadryl) is considered to be the active ingredient. See Benadryl.

Alternatives: Hydroxyzine

Pregnancy Risk Category: B

Adult Concerns: Sedation, dry secretions.

Pediatric Concerns:

Drug Interactions: May enhance CNS depressants, anticholinergics, tricyclic antidepressants, and MAO exhibitors. Increased toxicity of antibiotics, especially aminoglycosides "ototoxicity".

AHL = 8.5 hours		**M/P** =	
PHL =		**PB** = 78%	
PK = 1-2 hours		**Oral** =	
MW = 470		**pKa** =	
Vd =			

References:
1. Pharmaceutical Manufacturer's Package Insert, 1995.

Diphenhydramine   Fax #1152

Trade: Benadryl, Cheracol
Can/Aus/UK: Allerdryl, Benadryl, Insomnal, Nytol, Delixir, Paedamin
Uses: Antihistamine, antitussive
AAP: Not reviewed

Small but unreported levels are thought to be secreted into breast milk. In rodents, milk:plasma ratio has been reported to be 3.85-9.54, although the total transfer was minimal. Only probable side effect would be slight drowsiness in infant.

Alternatives: Cetirizine, Hydroxyzine, Loratadine

Pregnancy Risk Category: C

Adult Concerns: Sedation, drowsiness.

Pediatric Concerns: None reported, but observe for sedation.

Drug Interactions: Increased sedation when used with other CNS depressants. MAO inhibitors may increase anticholinergic side effects.

AHL = 4.3 hours	**M/P** =	
PHL =	**PB** = 78%	
PK = 2-3 hours	**Oral** = 43-61%	
MW = 255	**pKa** = 8.3	
Vd = 3-4		

References:

1. O'Brien, T. Excretion of drugs in human milk. Am.J. Hosp. Pharm. 31:844-854, 1974.
2. Paton DM, Webster DR. Clinical pharmacokinetics of H1-receptor antagonists (the antihistamines). Clin. Pharm. 10:477-497, 1985.

Diphenoxylate   Fax #1153

Trade: Lomotil, Lofene
Can/Aus/UK: Lofenoxal, Lomotil
Uses: Antidiarrheal
AAP: Not reviewed

Lomotil is a combination product of diphenoxylate and atropine. Diphenoxylate belongs to the opiate family(meperidine) and acts on the intestinal tract inhibiting GI motility and excessive GI propulsion. The drug has no analgesic activity.   Although no reports are available, it is probably secreted in breast milk but in very small quantities. Some authors consider diphenoxylate to be contraindicated.

Alternatives:

Pregnancy Risk Category: C

Adult Concerns: Anticholinergic effects, such as drying, constipation, and sedation.

Pediatric Concerns: None reported, but observe for dryness, constipation, sedation.

Drug Interactions: Increased toxicity when used with MAO inhibitors, CNS depressants, anticholinergics.

AHL = 2.5 hours	M/P =
PHL =	PB =
PK = 2 hours	Oral = 90%
MW = 453	pKa = 7.1
Vd = 3.8	

References:
1.   Drug Facts and Comparisons. 1994 ed. Facts and Comparisons, St. Louis.
2.   Stewart JJ. Gastrointestinal drugs. In Wilson JT, ed. Drugs in Breast Milk. Balgowlah, Australia;ADIS Press, 71, 1981.

Diphtheria And Tetanus Toxoid   Fax #1155

Trade: DT, TD
Can/Aus/UK: ADT, CDT, Triple Antigen
Uses: Vaccine
AAP: Not reviewed

Diphtheria and tetanus toxoid contains large molecular weight protein toxoids.   It is extremely unlikely proteins of this size would be secreted in breast milk. No reported harmful effects.

Alternatives:

Pregnancy Risk Category: C

Adult Concerns: Swelling, fretfulness, drowsiness, anorexia, vomiting.

Pediatric Concerns: None reported via breast milk exposure.

Drug Interactions:

Diphtheria-Tetanus-Pertussis Vaccine   Fax #1154

Trade: DTAP, Acel-Imune, Tripedia, Tetramune, DPT
Can/Aus/UK:
Uses: Vaccine
AAP: Not reviewed

DTP injections come in two forms, one including acellular pertussis (Acel-Imune, Tripedia), and one including whole-cell pertussis, and Haemophilus Influenzae Type B Conjugate (Tetramune). Both are inactivated bacterial vaccines or toxoids. The use of pertussis vaccinations in individuals over 7 years of age is generally contraindicated. Hence there is no indication for administering this vaccine to adult mothers. Because these are inactivated bacterial products, there is no specific contraindication in breastfeeding following injection with these vaccines.

Alternatives:

Pregnancy Risk Category: B

Adult Concerns: Pain, fever, swelling

Pediatric Concerns: None reported via breast milk.

Drug Interactions: Immunosuppressive agents, high dose corticosteroids, may reduce immunogenicity.

References:
1. Pharmaceutical Manufacturer's Package Insert, 1996.

Dipyridamole   Fax #1156

Trade: Persantine
Can/Aus/UK: Apo-Dipyridamole, Novo-Dipiradol, Persantin
Uses: Vasodilator, antiplatelet agent
AAP: Not reviewed

According to the manufacturer, only small amounts are believed to be secreted in human milk. No untoward effects have been reported.

Alternatives:

Pregnancy Risk Category: C

Adult Concerns: Headache, dizziness, GI distress, nausea, vomiting, diarrhea, flushing.

Pediatric Concerns: No untoward effects have been reported.

Drug Interactions: When used with Heparin, may increase anticoagulation. Theophylline may reduce the hypotensive effect of dipyridamole.

AHL = 10-12 hours	**M/P** =	
PHL =	**PB** = 91-99%	
PK = 45-150 min.	**Oral** = Poor	
MW = 505	**pKa** =	
Vd = 2-3		

References:
1. Pharmaceutical Manufacturer's Package Insert, 1995.
2. Briggs GG, Freeman R, Yaffe S. Drugs in Pregnancy and Lactation, 4th ed. Baltimore, Williams and Wilkins 1994.

Dirithromycin   Fax #1558

Trade: Dynabac
Can/Aus/UK:
Uses: Macrolide antibiotic
AAP: Not reviewed

Dirithromycin is a macrolide antibiotic similar to the erythromycins, but is characterized by low serum levels and high tissue levels. Dirithromycin is metabolized to erythromycyclamine which is the active component. No data on the transfer of erythromycyclamine into human milk is available, but it is known to transfer into animal milk. Due to the kinetics of dirithromycin and its distribution largely to tissues, it is unlikely that major levels in milk will result. Suitable alternatives include erythromycin and azithromycin.

Alternatives: Azithromycin

Pregnancy Risk Category: C

Adult Concerns: GI distress, abdominal pain, diarrhea, nausea, vomiting, skin rash, headache and dizziness. Changes in liver function have been reported.

Pediatric Concerns: None reported via milk. Suitable alternatives are erythromycin and azithromycin.

Drug Interactions: Increased anticoagulant effect when used with warfarin, dicoumarol, phenindione, and anisindione. Dirithromycin may increase the level of astemizole significantly. May increase digoxin levels. Acute and dangerous toxicity have resulted following use of dirithromycin with ergot alkaloids. Increased serum levels of pimozide and triazolam may result.

AHL = 20-50 hours		**M/P** =	
PHL =		**PB** = 15-30%	
PK = 3.9 hours		**Oral** = 6-14%	
MW =		**pKa** =	
Vd = 11			

References:
1. Pharmaceutical Manufacturer's Package Insert, 1998.

Disopyramide   Fax #1157

Trade: Norpace, Napamide
Can/Aus/UK: Norpace, Rythmodan, Rythmodan, Isomide, Rhythmodan
Uses: Antiarrhythmic
AAP: Approved by the American Academy of Pediatrics for use in breastfeeding mothers

Disopyramide is used for treating cardiac arrhythmias similar to quinidine and procainamide. Small levels are secreted into milk. Following a maternal dose of 450 mg every 8 hours for two weeks, the milk:plasma ratio was approximately 1.06 for disopyramide, and 6.24 for its active metabolite. Although no disopyramide was measurable in the infant's plasma, the milk levels were 2.6-4.4 mg/L (disopyramide), and 9.6-12.3 mg/L (metabolite). Infant urine collected over an 8 hour period contained 3.3 mg/L of disopyramide. Such levels are probably too small to affect infant. No reported side effects. In another study, in a woman receiving 100 mg five times daily, the maternal serum level was 10.3 umol/L and the breast milk level was 4.0 umol/L, giving a milk:serum ratio of 0.4. From these levels, an infant ingesting 1 liter of milk would receive only 1.5 mg per day. Lowest milk levels are at 6-8 hours post-dose.

Alternatives:

Pregnancy Risk Category: C

Adult Concerns: Dry mouth, constipation, edema, hypotension, nausea, vomiting, diarrhea.

Pediatric Concerns: None reported.

Drug Interactions: Increased side effects with drugs such as phenytoin, phenobarbital, rifampin. Increased effects/toxicity with rifamycin. Increased plasma levels of digoxin.

AHL = 8.3-11.65 hours	**M/P** = 0.4-1.06
PHL =	**PB** = 50%
PK = 2.3 hours	**Oral** = 60-83%
MW = 339	**pKa** = 8.4
Vd = 0.6-1.3	

References:
1. MacKintosh D, Buchanan N. Excretion of disopyramide in human breast milk. Br J Clin Pharmacol 19:856-7, 1985.
2. Ellsworth AJ, et.al. Disopyramide and N-monodesalkyl disopyramide in serum and breast milk. DICP 23(1):56-7,1989.

Docusate   Fax #1151

Trade: Colace, Docusate, Softgels, Dialose, Surfak
Can/Aus/UK: Albert, Docusate, Colax-C, Colace, Surfak Coloxyl, Rectalad, Waxsol, Audinorm, Diocytl-Medo
Uses: Laxative, stool softener
AAP: Not reviewed

Although some drug is absorbed by mother via her GI tract (generally very small) transfer into breast milk is unknown but probably very minimal. Watch for loose stools in infant. Probably compatible with breastfeeding.

Alternatives:

Pregnancy Risk Category: C

Adult Concerns: Nausea, diarrhea.

Pediatric Concerns: None reported.

Drug Interactions: Decreased effect of Coumadin with high doses of docusate. Increased toxicity with mineral oil, phenolphthalein.

AHL =	M/P =
PHL =	PB =
PK =	Oral = Poor
MW = 444	pKa =
Vd =	

References:

Domperidone   Fax #1158

Trade: Motilium
Can/Aus/UK: Motilium, Motilidone
Uses: Nausea and vomiting, stimulates lactation
AAP: Approved by the American Academy of Pediatrics for use in

213

breastfeeding mothers

Domperidone (Motilium) is a peripheral dopamine antagonist (similar to Reglan) generally used for controlling nausea and vomiting, dyspepsia, and gastric reflux. It is an investigational drug in the USA, and available only for compassionate use. It blocks peripheral dopamine receptors in the GI wall and in the chemoreceptor trigger zone (nausea center) in the brain stem and is currently used in Canada as an antiemetic. Unlike Reglan, it does not enter the brain compartment and it has few CNS effects such as depression. It is also known to produce significant increases in prolactin levels and has proven useful as a galactagogue. Concentrations of domperidone reported in milk vary according to dose but following a dose of 10 mg three times daily, the average concentration in milk was 2.6 μg/L. The usual oral dose for controlling GI distress is 20-40 mg three to four times daily. The galactagogue dose is suggested to be 10 orally 3-4 times daily. At present, this product is unavailable in the USA.

Alternatives: Metoclopramide, Cisapride

Pregnancy Risk Category:

Adult Concerns: Dry mouth, skin rash, itching, headache, thirst, abdominal cramps, diarrhea, drowsiness. Seizures have occurred rarely.

Pediatric Concerns: None reported.

Drug Interactions: Cimetidine, famotidine, nizatidine, ranitidine (H-2 blockers) reduce absorption of domperidone. Prior use of bicarbonate reduces absorption of domperidone.

AHL = 7-14 hours (oral)		**M/P** = 0.25
PHL =		**PB** = 93%
PK = 30 min.		**Oral** = 13-17%
MW = 426		**pKa** =
Vd =			

References:

1. Drug Facts and Comparisons. 1994 ed. Facts and Comparisons, St. Louis.

2.   Michiels M, Hendriks R & Heykants J: On the pharmacokinetics of domperidone in animals and man. II. Tissue distribution, placental and milk transfer of domperidone in the Wistar rat. Eur J Drug Metab Pharmacokinetics 6:37, 1981.

3.   Hofmeyr GJ and van Iddekinge B. Domperidone and lactation. Lanet i, 647, 1983.

4.   Hofmeyr GJ, et.al. Domperidone: secretion in breast milk and effect on puerperal prolactin levels. Brit. J. Obs. and Gyn. 92:141-144, 1985.

Dopamine-Dobutamine   Fax #1453

Trade: Intropin
Can/Aus/UK: Intropin, Revimine-Dobutrex, Inotropin
Uses: Adrenergic stimulants
AAP: Not reviewed

Dopamine and dobutamine are catecholamine pressor agents used in shock and severe hypotension. They are rapidly destroyed in the GI tract and are only used IV. It is not known if they transfer into human milk, but the half-life is so short they would not last long. Dopamine, while in the plasma, significantly (> 60%) inhibits prolactin secretion and would likely inhibit lactation while being used.

Alternatives:

Pregnancy Risk Category: C

Adult Concerns: Stimulation, agitation, tachycardia.

Pediatric Concerns: None reported. No GI absorption.

Drug Interactions: Increased effect when used with monoamine oxidase inhibitors MAO, alpha and beta adrenergic blockers, general anesthetics, and phenytoin.

AHL = 2 minutes	M/P	=
PHL = 7 minutes	PB	=

PK	= 5 minutes.	Oral	= Poor
MW	= 153	pKa	=
Vd	=		

References:
1.   McEvoy GE(ed):AHFS Drug Information, New York, NY. 1995.

Dornase   Fax #1467

Trade: Pulmozyme
Can/Aus/UK: Pulmozyme
Uses: Mucolytic enzyme
AAP: Not reviewed

Dornase is mucolytic enzyme used in the treatment of cystic fibrosis. It is a large molecular weight peptide (260 amino acids, 37,000 daltons) that selectively digests DNA.   It is poorly absorbed by the pulmonary tissues.   Serum levels are undetectable.   Even if it were to reach the milk, it would be unabsorbed by the infant.

Alternatives:

Pregnancy Risk Category: B

Adult Concerns: In adults: hoarseness, sore throat, facial edema.

Pediatric Concerns: None reported.

Drug Interactions:

AHL =		M/P	=
PHL =		PB	=
PK	=	Oral	= None
MW	=	pKa	=
Vd	=		

References:
1.   Pharmaceutical Manufacturer's Package Insert, 1995.

Dorzolamide   Fax #1578

Trade: Trusopt
Can/Aus/UK: Trusopt
Uses: Glaucoma treatment
AAP: Not reviewed

Dorzolamide is a carbonic anhydrase-II inhibitor used for treatment increased intraocular pressure in glaucoma patients and reduces intraocular pressure by reducing the production of aqueous humor. Some systemic absorption of dorzolamide is known and is primarily associated with red blood cell carbonic anhydrase. It produces sustained inhibition of erythrocyte carbonic anhydrase (T1/2 = 147 days). No data are available on levels in milk. This is an incredibly potent and long-lasting inhibitor of carbonic anhydrase. Transfer of small amounts into breast milk over a sustained period could prove detrimental to breastfed infants. Exercise caution when using with breastfeeding mothers.

Alternatives:

Pregnancy Risk Category: C

Adult Concerns: Headache, vertigo, taste disorders, renal stones, burning, stinging, conjunctivitis.

Pediatric Concerns: None reported via milk. Exercise caution.

Drug Interactions:

References:
1.   Pharmaceutical Manufacturer's package insert, 1997.

Dothiepin   Fax #1159

Trade: Prothiaden
Can/Aus/UK: Dothep, Prothiaden
Uses: Tricyclic antidepressant
AAP: Drugs whose effect on nursing infants is unknown but may be of concern

New analog of the older tricyclic antidepressant amitriptyline. Dothiepin appears in breast milk in a concentration of 11 µg/L following a dose of 75 mg/day, while the maternal plasma level was 33 µg/L. If the infant ingests 150 ml/kg/day of milk, the total daily dose of dothiepin ingested by the infant in this case would be approximately 1.65 µg/kg/day, approximately 1/650th of the adult dose. No reports of adverse effects have been found. In an outcome study of 15 mother/infant pairs 3-5 years postpartum, no overall cognitive differences were noted in dothiepin treated mothers/infants, suggesting that this medication did not alter cognitive abilities in breastfed infants.

Alternatives:

Pregnancy Risk Category: D

Adult Concerns: Anticholinergic side effects, such as drying of secretions, dilated pupil, sedation, dizziness, drowsiness, urinary retention.

Pediatric Concerns: None reported.

Drug Interactions: Phenobarbital may reduce effect of dothiepin. Dothiepin blocks the hypotensive effect of guanethidine. May increase toxicity of dothiepin when used with clonidine. Dangerous when used with MAO inhibitors, other CNS depressants. May increase anticoagulant effect of coumadin, warfarin. SSRIs (Prozac, Zoloft, etc) should not be used with or soon after dothiepin or other TCAs due to serotonergic crisis.

AHL	= 14.4-23.9 hours.	M/P	= 0.3
PHL	=	PB	=
PK	= 3 hours.	Oral	= 30%
MW	= 295	pKa	=
Vd	= 20-92		

References:
1. Rees JA, Glass RC, Sporne GA. Serum and breast milk concentrations of dotheipin. Practitioner 217:686, 1976.
2. Buist A, Janson H. Effect of exposure to dothiepin and northiaden in breast milk on child development. Brit. J. Psy. 167:370-373, 1995.

Doxazosin Mesylate — Fax #1160

Trade: Cardura
Can/Aus/UK: Cardura, Carduran
Uses: Antiadrenergic antihypertensive
AAP: Not reviewed

Studies in lactating animals indicate milk levels that are 20 times that of maternal plasma levels, suggesting a concentrating mechanism in breast milk. It is not known if this occurs in human milk. Extreme caution recommended.

Alternatives: Propranolol, Metoprolol

Pregnancy Risk Category: B

Adult Concerns: Low blood pressure, malaise, and edema.

Pediatric Concerns: None reported, but extreme caution is recommended.

Drug Interactions: Decreased antihypertensive effect with NSAIDs. Increased effect with other diuretics, antihypertensive medications particularly beta blockers.

AHL = 9-22 hours		**M/P**	= 20
PHL =		**PB**	= 98%
PK = 2 hours		**Oral**	= 62-69%
MW = 451		**pKa**	=
Vd =			

References:
1.   Pharmaceutical Manufacturer's Package Insert, 1995.

Doxepin   Fax #1161

Trade: Adapin, Sinequan
Can/Aus/UK: Sinequan, Triadapin, Novo-Doxepin, Deptran
Uses: Antidepressant
AAP: Drugs whose effect on nursing infants is unknown but may be of concern

Small but significant amounts are secreted in milk. Two published reports indicate absorption by infant varying from significant to modest. One report of dangerous sedation and respiratory arrest in one infant. Doxepin has an active metabolite with long half-life (37 hours). In one study, peak milk doxepin levels were 27 and 29 µg/L four-five hours after a dose of 25 mg, and the level of metabolite was 9 µg/L. In this infant, the metabolite was believed responsible for the severe depression. Although the milk concentrations were low, the infant's plasma level of metabolite was similar to the maternal plasma level. It is apparent, that the active metabolite of doxepin can concentrate in nursing infants and may be hazardous.

Alternatives: Sertraline, Paroxetine

Pregnancy Risk Category: C

Adult Concerns: Respiratory arrest, sedation, dry mouth.

Pediatric Concerns: One report of dangerous sedation and respiratory arrest in one infant.

Drug Interactions: Decreased effect of Doxepin when use with bretylium, guanethidine, clonidine, levodopa, ascorbic acid and cholestyramine. Increased toxicity when used with carbamazepine, amphetamines, thyroid preparations. Increased toxicity with fluoxetine, thyroid preparations, MAO inhibitors, albuterol, CNS depressants such as benzodiazepines and opiate analgesics, anticholinergics, cimetidine.

AHL = 8-24 hours	**M/P** = 1.08-1.66
PHL =	**PB** = 80-85%
PK = 2 hours	**Oral** = Complete
MW = 279	**pKa** = 8.0
Vd = 9-33	

References:
1. Kemp J, et. al. Excretion of doxepin and N-desmethyldoxepin in human milk. Br J Clin Pharmacol 20:497-9, 1985.
2. Matheson I, et. al. Respiratory depression caused by N-desmethyldoxepin in breast milk. Lancet 2:1124, 1985.

Doxepin Cream   Fax #1162

Trade: Zonalon Cream
Can/Aus/UK: Zonalon
Uses: Anti-itch cream
AAP: Drugs whose effect on nursing infants is unknown but may be of concern

Doxepin cream is an antihistamine-like cream used to treat severe itching. In one study of 19 women, plasma levels ranged from zero to 47 ng/mL following transcutaneous absorption. Target therapeutic ranges in doxepin antidepressant therapy is 30-150 ng/mL. Small but significant amounts are secreted in milk. Two published reports indicate absorption by infant varying from significant to modest, but only in mother consuming oral doses. See doxepin.

Alternatives:

Pregnancy Risk Category: B

Adult Concerns: Respiratory arrest, sedation, dry mouth.

Pediatric Concerns: Sedation, respiratory arrest have been reported following oral administration.

Drug Interactions: Decreased effect of Doxepin when use with bretylium, guanethidine, clonidine, levodopa, ascorbic acid and cholestyramine. Increased toxicity when used with carbamazepine, amphetamines, thyroid preparations. Increased toxicity with fluoxetine, thyroid preparations, MAO inhibitors, albuterol, CNS depressants such as benzodiazepines and opiate analgesics, anticholinergics, cimetidine.

AHL	= 28-52 hours	M/P	= 1.08, 1.66
PHL	=	PB	= 80-85%
PK	= 2 hours	Oral	= Complete
MW	= 279	pKa	=
Vd	=		

References:
1. Drug Facts and Comparisons. 1994 ed. Facts and Comparisons, St. Louis.
2. Kemp J, et. al. Excretion of doxepin and N-desmethyldoxepin in human milk. Br J Clin Pharmacol 20:497-9, 1985.
3. Matheson I, et. al. Respiratory depression caused by N-desmethyldoxepin in breast milk. Lancet 2:1124, 1985.

Doxorubicin   Fax #1163

Trade: Adriamycin
Can/Aus/UK: Adriamycin
Uses: Anti-cancer drug
AAP: Contraindicated by the American Academy of Pediatrics in Breastfeeding Mothers

Doxorubicin and its metabolite are secreted in significant amounts in breast milk. Following a dose of 70 mg/meter sq., peak milk levels of doxorubicin and metabolite occurred at 24 hours and were 128 and 111 µg/L respectively. The highest milk:plasma ratio was 4.43 at 24 hours Due to the extraordinary toxicity of this compound, breastfeeding is not recommended.

Alternatives:

Pregnancy Risk Category: D

Adult Concerns: Bone marrow suppression, cardiac toxicity, arrhythmias, nausea, vomiting, stomatitis, liver toxicity.

Pediatric Concerns: This product could be extremely toxic to a breastfeeding infant and is not recommended.

Drug Interactions: Doxorubicin may decrease digoxin plasma levels and renal excretion. Allopurinol, and verapamil may increase cytotoxicity of doxorubicin.

AHL = 17-30 hours	**M/P**	= 4.43
PHL =	**PB**	= 85%
PK = 24 hours	**Oral**	= Poor
MW = 544	**pKa**	=
Vd = 25		

References:
1. Egan PC, et. al. Doxorubicin and cisplatin excretion into human milk. Cancer Treat Rep 69:1387-9, 1985.

Doxycycline   Fax #1164

Trade: Doxychel, Vibramycin
Can/Aus/UK: Apo-Doxy, Doxycin, Vibramycin, Vibra-Tabs, Doryx, Doxylin, Vibra-Tabs, Doxylar
Uses: Tetracycline antibiotic
AAP: Not reviewed

Doxycycline is a long half-life tetracycline antibiotic. In a study of 15 subjects, the average doxycycline level in milk was 0.77 mg/L following a 200 mg oral dose.   One oral dose of 100 mg was administered 24 hours later, and the breast milk levels were 0.380 mg/L.   Tetracyclines administered orally to infants are known to bind in teeth producing discoloration and inhibit bone growth. Although most tetracyclines secreted into milk are generally bound to calcium, thus inhibiting their absorption, doxycycline is the least bound (20%), and may provide more absorption by a breastfeeding infant than the base tetracyclines. Prolonged use could potentially alter GI flora, stain teeth, and reduce bone growth.   Short term use is not necessarily contraindicated.   No harmful effects have yet been reported in breastfeeding infants.

Alternatives:

Pregnancy Risk Category: D

Adult Concerns: Nausea, vomiting, diarrhea, photosensitivity.

Pediatric Concerns: None reported, but prolonged exposure may lead to dental staining, and decreased bone growth.

Drug Interactions: Reduced absorption with aluminum, calcium, or magnesium salts, iron or bismuth subsalicylate. Reduced doxycycline half-life when used with barbiturates, phenytoin, and carbamazepine.

AHL = 15-25 hours	M/P = 0.3-0.4
PHL =	PB = 90%
PK = 1.5-4 hours	Oral = 90-100%
MW = 462	pKa =
Vd =	

References:
1.   Morganti G, et. al. Comparative concentrations of a tetracycline antibiotic in serum and maternal milk. Antibiotica 6:216-23, 1968.

Doxylamine   Fax #1454

Trade: Unisom Nighttime
Can/Aus/UK: Dozile, Mersyndol, Panalgesic, Syndol
Uses: Antihistamine, sedative
AAP: Not reviewed

Doxylamine is an antihistamine similar in structure to Benadryl. Because it has significant sedative properties, it is primarily used in over-the-counter sleep aids. Like other antihistamines, it should not be used in infants, and particularly in premature or full-term neonates due to paradoxical effects such as CNS stimulation, or even sedation. Levels in breast milk are not known.

Alternatives:

Pregnancy Risk Category: B

Adult Concerns: Sedation, paradoxical CNS stimulation, agitation.

Pediatric Concerns: None reported via milk, but observe for sedation and paradoxical CNS stimulation. Do not use in infants with apnea.

Drug Interactions: Increased CNS sedation when added to other antihistamines and CNS sedative-hypnotics.

AHL = 10.1 hours.		M/P =	
PHL =		PB =	
PK = 2.4 hours.		Oral = Complete	
MW = 270		pKa = 9.2	
Vd = 2.7			

References:
1. Friedman H, Greenblatt DJ, Scavone JM et al: Clearance of the antihistamine doxylamine reduced in elderly men but not in elderly women. Clin Pharmacokinet 16:312-316, 1989.
2. Friedman H & Greenblatt DJ: The Pharmacokinetics of doxylamine: use of automated gas chromatography with nitrogen-phosphorus detection. J Clin Pharmacol 25:448-451, 1985..

Droperidol   Fax #1165

Trade: Inapsine
Can/Aus/UK: Inapsine, Droleptan
Uses: Tranquilizer, antiemetic
AAP: Not reviewed

Droperidol is a powerful tranquilizer. It is sometimes used as preanesthetic medication in labor and delivery because of fewer respiratory effects in neonates. In pediatric patients 2-12 years of age, it is sometimes used as an antiemetic (20-75 micrograms/kg IM, IV). It apparently crosses the placenta only very slowly. There are no data available on secretion into breast milk. Due to the potent sedative properties of this medication, caution is urged.

Alternatives: Haloperidol

Pregnancy Risk Category: C

Adult Concerns: Sedation, hypotension, dizziness, chills, shivering, unusual ocular movements.

Pediatric Concerns: None reported via milk, but observe for sedation, hypotension.

Drug Interactions: Can cause peripheral vasodilation and hypotension when used with certain anesthesia medications. Can potentiate effects of other CNS depressants and antidepressants such as barbiturates.

AHL = 2.2 hours		M/P	=
PHL =		PB	= High
PK = 10-30 min.(IM)		Oral	=
MW = 379		pKa	=
Vd = 2.0			

References:
1. McEvoy GE(ed):AFHS Drug Information, New York, NY. 1992, pp 417-26.
2. Pharmaceutical Manufacturer's package insert, 1995.

Dyphylline   Fax #1166

Trade: Dilor, Lufyllin, Dyphylline
Can/Aus/UK: Silbephylline
Uses: Anti-asthmatic drug
AAP: Approved by the American Academy of Pediatrics for use in breastfeeding mothers

Dyphylline is a methylzanthine bronchodilator similar to theophylline. It is apparently secreted into milk in small quantities. Following a 5 mg/kg dose IM, the milk:plasma ratio was 2.08. and the estimated maximum milk concentration was 72 μg/mL. No reported untoward effects. Observe infant for irritability, insomnia, elevated heart rate.

Alternatives: Theophylline

Pregnancy Risk Category: C

Adult Concerns: Irritability, insomnia, tachycardia, arrhythmias, GI distress, headache, seizures, hyperglycemia.

Pediatric Concerns: None reported via milk, but observe for irritability, insomnia, tachycardia.

Drug Interactions: Probenecid significantly increases half-life of dyphylline and increases plasma levels.

AHL = 3-12.8 hours	**M/P** = 2.08
PHL =	**PB** = 56%
PK = 1-2 hours (oral)	**Oral** = Complete
MW = 254	**pKa** =
Vd = 0.6-1.1	

References:
1. Jarboe CH, et. al. Dyphylline elimination kinetics in lactating women: blood to milk transfer. J Clin Pharmacol 21:405-10, 1981.

Echinacea   Fax #1533

Trade: Echinacea Angustifolia, Echinacea Purpurea, American Cone Flower, Black Susans, Snakeroot
Can/Aus/UK:
Uses: Herbal immunostimulant
AAP: Not reviewed

Echinacea is a popular herbal remedy in the central US and has been traditionally used topically to stimulate wound healing, and internally to stimulate the immune system. The plant contains a complex mixture of compounds and thus far, no single component appears responsible for its immunostimulant properties. A number of in vitro and animal studies have documented the activation of immunologic properties although most of these are via intraperitoneal injections, not orally. The activity of orally administered extracts is unknown. Echinacea extracts appear to stimulate phagocytosis of macrophages, increase cellular respiration, and increase the mobility of phagocytic leukocytes. Extracts of E. Purpurea are highly effective in activating macrophages to engulf tumor cells, to produce tumor necrosis factor, interleukin-1, and interferon beta-2. One study suggests a radioprotective effect (antioxidant) of Echinacea. Another study in humans (Coeugniet 1987) suggests that while single doses may stimulate the immune system, repeated daily doses may actually suppress the immune response. Thus far, little is known about the toxicity of this plant although its use has been widespread for many years. Apparently, purified Echinacea extract is relatively non-toxic even at high doses. No data are available on its transfer into human milk, or its effect on lactation.

Alternatives:

Pregnancy Risk Category:

Adult Concerns: None reported.

Pediatric Concerns: None reported via milk.

References:

1. Steinmuller C. et.al. Polysaccharides isolated from plant cell cultures of Echinacea purpurea enhance the resistance of immunosuppressed mice against systemic infections with Candida albicans and Listeria monocytogenes. Int J. Immunopharmacol 15(5):605, 1993.
2. Coeugniet EG, Elek E. Immunomodulation with Viscum album and Echinacea purpurea extracts. Onkologie 10(supp 3):27, 1987.
3. Review of Natural Products. Facts and Comparisons, St. Louis, Mo. 1996.
4. Bissett NG. In: Herbal Drugs and Phytopharmaceuticals. Medpharm Scientific Publishers, CRC Press, Boca Raton, 1994.

Enalapril Maleate   Fax #1167

Trade: Vasotec

Can/Aus/UK: Vasotec, Amprace, Renitec, Innovace

Uses: Antihypertensive, ACE inhibitor

AAP: Approved by the American Academy of Pediatrics for use in breastfeeding mothers

Enalapril maleate is an ACE inhibitor used as an antihypertensive. Upon absorption, it is rapidly metabolized by the adult liver to enalaprilat, the biologically active metabolite. In one study of 5 lactating mothers who received a single 20 mg dose, the maximum concentration of enalapril and enalaprilat were 5.9 µg/L and 2.3 µg/L, respectively. The author suggests that in an infant consuming 150 mL of milk/kg/day, the infant would consume 885 ng/kg/day of enalapril and 345 ng/kg/day of enalaprilat. This represents only 0.27% of the weight adjusted maternal dose of enalapril. However, this was only a single dose and the levels transferred into milk at steady state may be slightly higher. Exercise caution when administering to lactating women, although the data thus far indicates the levels secreted into milk are clinically insignificant.

Alternatives: Captopril, Benazepril

Pregnancy Risk Category: D

Adult Concerns: Hypotension, bradycardia, headache, fatigue, diarrhea, rash, cough.

Pediatric Concerns: None reported via milk, but observe for hypotension.

Drug Interactions: Bioavailability of ACE inhibitors may be decreased when used with antacids. Capsaicin may exacerbate coughing associated with ACE inhibitor treatment. Pharmacologic effects of ACE inhibitors may be increased. Increased plasma levels of digoxin may result. Increased serum lithium levels may result when used with ACE inhibitors.

AHL	= 35 hours (metabolite)	M/P	=
PHL	=	PB	= 60%
PK	= 0.5-1.5 hours	Oral	= 60%
MW	= 492	pKa	=
Vd	=		

References:
1. Redman CG, Kelly JG, Cooper WD. The excretion of enalapril and enalaprilat in human breast milk. Eur. J. Clin. Pharmacol 38:99, 1990.
2. Rush JE, et.al. Comment on Huttunen K. et.al. 1989. Enalapril treatment of a nursing mother with slightly impaired renal function. Clin Nephrol 31:278.

Encainide   Fax #1455

Trade: Enkaid
Can/Aus/UK:
Uses: Antiarrhythmic agent
AAP: Not reviewed

Encainide is a local anesthetic-type antiarrhythmic agent. It was voluntarily removed from the market in 1991, but is available on a limited basis for certain patients with life-threatening arrhythmias. The plasma kinetics are highly variable depending on the metabolic capabilities of the maternal liver. The oral bioavailability is extremely variable, and varies from 25-65% in extensive metabolizers to 80-90% in poor metabolizers. Half-lives are variable as well according to the metabolic capacity of the individual's liver. However, encainide and its 3 active metabolites are excreted into human milk. Milk concentrations of encainide and o-demethyl encainide are 200-400 µg/L and 100-200 µg/L respectively. These concentrations are similar to the maternal serum levels.

Alternatives:

Pregnancy Risk Category: B

Adult Concerns: Arrhythmias, chest pain, congestive heart failure, abdominal pain.

Pediatric Concerns: None reported, but extreme caution is recommended.

Drug Interactions: Use caution when encainide is used with any other drug that effects cardiac conduction. Cimetidine increases plasma concentrations of encainide.

AHL = 2-36 hours.		**M/P** = 1	
PHL =		**PB** = 70.5-78%	
PK = 1.7 hours.		**Oral** = Variable	
MW = 352		**pKa** =	
Vd = 2.7-4.3			

References:
1. Pharmaceutical Manufactures Product Information, 1992.

Enoxacin   Fax #1553

Trade: Penetrex
Can/Aus/UK: Enoxin, Comprecin
Uses: Antibiotic
AAP: Not reviewed

Enoxacin is a typical fluoroquinolone antibiotic similar to ciprofloxacin, norfloxacin, and others. At present the fluoroquinolones are not cleared for use in pediatric patients due to arthropathy in young animals. No data on the transfer of enoxacin into human milk are available. See ofloxacin and norfloxacin as alternatives.

Alternatives: Ofloxacine, Norfloxacine, Trovafloxacin

Pregnancy Risk Category: C

Adult Concerns: Nausea, vomiting, diarrhea, abdominal cramps, GI bleeding, increased intracranial pressure, tremor, restlessness, other CNS reactions. Photosensitivity.

Pediatric Concerns: None reported via milk, but caution urged. See norfloxacin.

Drug Interactions: Decreased absorption with antacids. Quinolones cause increased levels of caffeine, warfarin, cyclosporine, theophylline. Cimetidine, probenecid, azlocillin increase ciprofloxacin levels. Increased risk of seizures when used with foscarnet.

AHL = 3-6 hours		**M/P** =	
PHL =		**PB** = 40%	
PK =		**Oral** = 90%	
MW =		**pKa** =	
Vd = 2.5			

References:

Enoxaparin   Fax #1565

Trade: Lovenox, Low Molecular Weight Heparin
Can/Aus/UK: Lovenox, Clexane
Uses: Anticoagulant
AAP: Not reviewed

Enoxaparin is a low molecular weight fraction of heparin used clinically as an anticoagulant. There are no data available on the transfer of this peptide into human milk, but it is extremely unlikely. Because it is a peptide fragment of heparin, its molecular weight is large and varies from 2000-8000 daltons, which would largely preclude its entry into human milk. Due to minimal oral bioavailability, any present in milk would not be orally absorbed by the infant.

Alternatives: Dalteparin

Pregnancy Risk Category: B

Adult Concerns: Anticoagulant effects in adults when administered subcutaneously.

Pediatric Concerns: None reported via milk. Molecular weight is too large to produce clinically relevant milk levels.

Drug Interactions: Anticoagulants and platelet inhibitors. NSAIDS may increase risk of bleeding.

AHL = 4.5 hours		**M/P** =	
PHL =		**PB** =	
PK = 3-5 hours		**Oral** = None	
MW = 8000		**pKa** =	
Vd = 0.1			

References:

Ephedrine   Fax #1168

Trade: Vatronol Nose Drops
Can/Aus/UK: Anestan, Anodesyn, CAM
Uses: Adrenergic stimulant, anti-asthmatic
AAP: Not reviewed

Ephedrine is a mild stimulant that belongs to the adrenergic family and functions similar to the amphetamines. Small amounts of d-isoephedrine, a close congener of ephedrine, is believed to be secreted into milk, although no data are available on ephedrine itself. This is an old product that has been replaced by far more selective adrenergics and has few legitimate uses today.

Alternatives:

Pregnancy Risk Category: C

Adult Concerns: Anorexia, tachycardia, arrhythmias, agitation, insomnia, hyperstimulation.

Pediatric Concerns: None reported, but observe for anorexia, irritability, crying, disturbed sleeping patterns, excitement.

Drug Interactions: May increase toxicity and cardiac stimulation when used with theophylline. MAO inhibitors or atropine may increase blood pressure.

AHL = 3-5 hours		**M/P** =	
PHL =		**PB** =	
PK = 15-60 min.		**Oral** = 85%	
MW = 165		**pKa** = 9.6	
Vd =			

References:
1. Mortimer EA J. Drug toxicity from breast milk? Pediatrics 60:780-1, 1977.

Epinephrine   Fax #1169

Trade: Adrenalin, Sus-Phrine, Medihaler, Primatene
Can/Aus/UK: Adrenalin, Bronkaid, Epi-Pen, Adrenutol, Eppy, Simplene
Uses: Stimulant
AAP: Not reviewed

Epinephrine is a powerful adrenergic stimulant. Although likely to be secreted in milk, it is rapidly destroyed in the GI tract. It is unlikely that any would be absorbed by the infant unless in the early neonatal period or premature.

Alternatives:

Pregnancy Risk Category: C

Adult Concerns: Nervousness, tremors, agitation, tachycardia.

Pediatric Concerns: None reported, but observe for brief stimulation.

Drug Interactions: Increase cardiac irritability when used with halogenated inhaled anesthetics, alpha blocking agents. Do not use with MAO inhibitors.

AHL = 1 hr.(inhalation)		M/P	=
PHL =		PB	=
PK = <1-10 min.		Oral	= Poor
MW = 183		pKa	=
Vd =			

References:
1.   Wilson, J. Drugs in Breast Milk. New York: ADIS Press, 1981.

Epstein-Barr Virus   Fax #1588

Trade: Mononucleosis, EBV
Can/Aus/UK:
Uses: Herpesvirus infection (EBV)
AAP: Not reviewed

Infectious mononucleosis is caused by the Epstein-Barr virus, which belongs to the herpesvirus family. Symptoms include fever, exudative pharyngitis, lymphadenopathy, hepatosplenomegaly, and atypical lymphocytosis. Close personal contact is generally required for transmission and it is not known if EBV is secreted into human milk, although it is likely. Studies by Kusuhara(1997) indicate that the seroprevelance of EBV at 12-23 months was the same in bottle-fed, and in breastfed infants. This data suggests that breast milk is not a significant source of early EBV infections.

Alternatives:

Pregnancy Risk Category:

Adult Concerns:

Pediatric Concerns:

Drug Interactions:

References:
1. Kushhara K, Takabayashi A, et.al. Breast milk is not a significant source for early Epstein-Barr virus or human herpesvirus 6 infection in infants: a Seroepidemiologic study in 2 endemic areas of human T-Cell lymphotropic virus Type 1 in Japan. Microbiol. Immunol. 41(4):309-312, 1997.

Ergonovine Maleate   Fax #1170

Trade: Ergotrate, Ergometrine
Can/Aus/UK: Ergotrate, Ergometrine, Syntometrine
Uses: Postpartum uterine bleeding
AAP: Not reviewed

Ergonovine and its close congener, methylergonovine maleate, directly stimulate uterine and vascular smooth muscle contractions. They are primarily used to prevent/treat postpartum hemorrhage. Although pharmacologically similar, many clinicians prefer methylergonovine because it produces less hypertension than ergonovine. In addition, one study clearly indicates that methylergonovine does not alter postpartum maternal prolactin levels, while another study indicates a significant inhibition of prolactin production by ergonovine. Ergonovine use in lactating women would undoubtedly suppress lactation, whereas methylergonovine may not. When used at doses of 0.2mg up to 3-4 times daily, only small quantities of ergonovine are found in milk. Short-term (1 week) low-dose regimens of these agents do not apparently pose problems in nursing mothers or their infants. Methylergonovine is preferred because it does not inhibit lactation and levels in milk are minimal. The prolonged use of ergot alkaloids should be avoided and can lead to severe gangrenous manifestations.

Alternatives: Methylergonovine

Pregnancy Risk Category: X

Adult Concerns: Hypertension, seizures, vomiting, diarrhea, cold extremities.

Pediatric Concerns: None reported, but long term exposure is not recommended. Methyl-ergonovine is commonly recommended early postpartum for breastfeeding mothers to reduce uterine bleeding.

Drug Interactions:

AHL = 0.5-2 hours		**M/P** =	
PHL =		**PB** =	
PK = 30- 180 min.		**Oral** = >60%	

MW = 441   pKa =
Vd =

References:
1. Erkkola R, et.al. Excretion of methylergometrine (methylergonovine) into the human breast milk. Int. J. Clin. Pharmacol. 16:579-80,1978.
2. Del Pozo E, Brun del Rey R, Hinselmann M. Lack of effect of methyl-ergonovine on postpartum lactation. Am. J. Obstet. Gynecol. 123:845-6,1975.
3. Canales ES, Facog JT et.al. Effect of ergonovine on prolactin secretion and milk Let-Down. Obstet. Gynecol. 48:2228-9, 1976.

Ergotamine Tartrate   Fax #1171

Trade: Wigraine, Cafergot, Ergostat, Ergomar, DHE-45
Can/Aus/UK: Ergomar, Gynergen, Cafergot, Ergodryl, Migral, Lingraine
Uses: Anti-migraine, inhibits prolactin
AAP: Contraindicated by the American Academy of Pediatrics in Breastfeeding Mothers

Ergotamine is a potent vasoconstrictor, generally used in acute phases of migraine headache. It is never used chronically for prophylaxis of migraine. Although early reports suggest ergotamine compounds are secreted in breast milk and cause symptoms of ergotism (vomiting, and diarrhea) in infants, other authors (White & White, 1980) suggest that the short term use of ergotamine (0.2 mg postpartum) generally presents no problem to a nursing infant. This is likely, due to the fact that less than 5% of ergotamine is orally absorbed in adults. However, excessive dosing and prolonged administration may inhibit prolactin secretion and hence lactation. Although the initial plasma half-life is only 2 hours, ergotamine is stored for long periods in various tissues producing long-lasting effects (terminal half-life = 21 hours). Use during lactation should be strongly discouraged.

Alternatives: Propranolol, Sumatriptan

Pregnancy Risk Category: X

Adult Concerns: Ergotism, peripheral artery insufficiency, nausea, vomiting, paresthesia, cold skin temperatures, headache.

Pediatric Concerns: One case of ergotism reported and included symptoms such as vomiting and diarrhea. Long term exposure is contraindicated.

Drug Interactions: Rifamycin and other macrolide antibiotics may enhance ergot toxicity.

AHL = 21 hours (terminal)	**M/P**	=	
PHL =	**PB**	=	
PK = 0.5-3 hours	**Oral**	= < 5%	
MW = 581	**pKa**	=	
Vd =			

References:
1. Fomina PI. Untersuchungen uber den Ubergang des aktiven agens des Muttrkorns in die milch stillender Mutter. Arch Gynecol 157:275, 1934.
2. White GJ & White MK: Breast feeding and drugs in human milk. Vet Hum Toxicol 1980; 22(Suppl 1):18.

Erythromycin   Fax #1172

Trade: E-Mycin, Ery-tab, ERYC, Ilosone
Can/Aus/UK: E-Mycin, ERYC, Erythromid, Novo-Rythro, PCE, Ilotyc, EMU-V, Ilosone, EES, Erythrocin, Ceplac, Erycen
Uses: Macrolide antibiotic
AAP: Approved by the American Academy of Pediatrics for use in breastfeeding mothers

Erythromycin is an older narrow spectrum antibiotic. Milk levels ranged from 0.4 to 1.5 mg/L following a maternal dose of 400 mg every 8 hours in one study. There is one report of hypertrophic pyloric stenosis apparently linked to erythromycin administration in one patient.

Alternatives: Azithromycin

Pregnancy Risk Category: B

Adult Concerns: Abdominal cramping, nausea, vomiting, hepatitis, ototoxicity, and hypersensitivity.

Pediatric Concerns: One case of pyloric stenosis reported, but this is extremely rare. Erythromycin is commonly used in children.

Drug Interactions: Erythromycin may decrease clearance of carbamazepine, cyclosporin, triazolam. Erythromycin may decrease theophylline clearance by as much as 60%. May increase terfenadine plasma levels and increase Q/T intervals. May potentiate anticoagulant effect of warfarin.

AHL = 1.5-2 hours		**M/P** =	
PHL =		**PB** = 84%	
PK = 2-4 hours		**Oral** = Variable	
MW = 734		**pKa** =	
Vd =			

References:
1. O'Brien, T. Excretion of drugs in human milk. Am.J. Hosp. Pharm. 31:844-854, 1974.
2. Knowles JA. Drugs in milk. Pediatr Currents 1:28-32, 1972.
3. Stang H: Pyloric stenosis associated with erythromycin ingested through breast milk. Minn Med 69:669-682, 1986.

Esmolol   Fax #1444

Trade: Brevibloc
Can/Aus/UK: Brevibloc
Uses: Beta blocker antiarrhythmic
AAP: Not reviewed

Esmolol is an ultra short-acting beta blocker agent with low lipid solubility. It is of the same family as propranolol. It is primarily used for treatment of supraventricular tachycardia. It is only used IV and has an extremely short half-life. It is almost completely hydrolyzed in 30 minutes. No data on breast milk levels are available.

Alternatives: Propranolol, metoprolol

Pregnancy Risk Category: C

Adult Concerns: Hypotension, bradycardia, dizziness, somnolence.

Pediatric Concerns: None reported.

Drug Interactions: Beta blockers may decrease the effect of sulfonylureas. Increased effect with calcium channel blockers, contraceptives, ciprofloxacin, MAO inhibitors, thyroid hormones, haloperidol, and numerous other medications.

AHL = 9 minutes	M/P =
PHL = 4.5 min.	PB = 55%
PK = 15 min.	Oral = Poor
MW = 295	pKa =

References:
1.   McEvoy GE(ed):AHFS Drug Information, New York, NY. 1995.
2.   Lacy C. et.al. Drug information handbook. Lexi-Comp, Hudson(Cleveland), Oh. 1996.

Estazolam   Fax #1173

Trade: PROSOM
Can/Aus/UK:
Uses: Benzodiazepine sedative
AAP: Not reviewed

Estazolam is a benzodiazepine sedative hypnotic that belongs to the Valium family. Estazolam, like other benzodiazepines, is secreted into rodent milk, although the levels are unpublished. No data are available on human milk levels. It is likely that some is secreted into human milk as well.

Alternatives: Lorazepam, Midazolam, Alprazolam

Pregnancy Risk Category: X

Adult Concerns: Sedation.

Pediatric Concerns: None reported via milk, but observe for sedation, apnea.

Drug Interactions: Certain enzyme inducers such as barbiturates may increase the metabolism of estazolam. CNS depressants may increase adverse effects of estazolam. Cimetidine may decrease metabolism of estazolam.

AHL = 10-24 hours		M/P	=
PHL =		PB	= 93%
PK = 0.5-3 hours		Oral	= Complete
MW = 295		pKa	=
Vd =			

References:
1. Pharmaceutical Manufacturer's Package Insert, 1995.
2. Drug Facts and Comparisons. 1995 ed. Facts and Comparisons, St. Louis.

Estrogen-Estradiol   Fax #1174

Trade: Estratab, Premarin, Menest
Can/Aus/UK: Estrace, Estraderm, Delestrogen, Estinyl, Estring Evorel
Uses: Estrogen hormone
AAP: Approved by the American Academy of Pediatrics for use in breastfeeding mothers

Although small amounts may pass into breast milk, the effects of estrogens on the infant appear minimal. Early postpartum use of estrogens may reduce volume of milk produced and the protein content, but it is variable and depends on dose and the individual. Breastfeeding mothers should attempt to wait until lactation is firmly established (6-8 weeks) prior to use of estrogen-containing oral contraceptives. In one study of six lactating women who received 50 or 100 mg vaginal suppositories of estradiol, the plasma levels peaked at 3 hours. These doses are extremely large and are not used clinically. In this study of 11 women, the mean concentration of estradiol in breast milk was found to be 113 picograms/mL. This is very close to that seen when the woman begins ovulating during lactation. If oral contraceptives are used during lactation, the transfer of estradiol to human milk will be low and will not exceed the transfer during physiologic conditions when the mother has resumed ovulation. See oral contraceptives.

Alternatives: Norethindrone

Pregnancy Risk Category: X

Adult Concerns: Estrogen use has been associated with breast tenderness, increased risk of thromboembolic disorders, headache, nausea, vomiting, etc.

Pediatric Concerns: None reported. Infantile feminization is unlikely at normal dosages.

Drug Interactions: Rifampin reduces the serum levels of estrogen. Exogenous estrogens increase toxicity of hydrocortisone, and thromboembolic events with anticoagulants such as warfarin.

AHL = 60 minutes		**M/P** = 0.08	
PHL =		**PB** = 98%	
PK = Rapid		**Oral** = Complete	
MW = 272		**pKa** =	
Vd =			

References:
1. Booker DE, Pahyl IR. Control of postpartum breast engorgement with oral contraceptives. Am J Obstet Gynecol 98:1099-1101, 1967.
2. Laukaran VH. The effects of contraceptive use on the initiation and duration of lactation. Int J Gynecol Obstet. 25(suppl)129-

142, 1987.

3. Nilsson S, et.al. Transfer of estradiol to human milk. Am. J. Obstet. Gynecol. 132:653-7, 1978.

Ethacrynic Acid   Fax #1175

Trade: Edecrin
Can/Aus/UK: Edecrin, Edecril
Uses: Powerful loop diuretic
AAP: Not reviewed

Ethacrynic acid is a potent short acting loop diuretic similar to Lasix. It is listed by the manufacturer as contraindicated in nursing women. A significant decrease in maternal blood pressure, or blood volume may reduce milk production. No data on transfer into human milk is available.

Alternatives: Furosemide

Pregnancy Risk Category: B

Adult Concerns: Diuresis, hypotension, diarrhea.

Pediatric Concerns: None reported.

Drug Interactions: Increased toxicity when used with antihypertensives, other diuretics, aminoglycosides. Increased risk of arrhythmias when used with digoxin. Probenecid reduces diuresis of this product.

AHL = 2-4 hours.	**M/P** =
PHL =	**PB** = 90%
PK = 2 hours (oral)	**Oral** = 100%
MW = 303	**pKa** =
Vd =	

References:
1. Pharmaceutical Manufacturer's Package Insert, 1996.
2. Lacy C. et.al. Drug information handbook. Lexi-Comp, Hudson(Cleveland), Oh. 1996.

Ethambutol   Fax #1176

Trade: Ethambutol, Myambutol
Can/Aus/UK: Etibi, Myambutol
Uses: Antitubercular drug
AAP: Approved by the American Academy of Pediatrics for use in breastfeeding mothers

Ethambutol is an antimicrobial used for tuberculosis. Small amounts are secreted in milk, although no studies are available which clearly document levels. In one unpublished study, the mother had an ethambutol plasma level of 1.5 mg/L three hours after a dose of 15 mg/Kg. Following a similar dose, the concentration in milk was 1.4 mg/L. In another patient, the plasma level was 4.62 mg/L and the corresponding milk concentration was 4.6 mg/L (no dose available).

Alternatives:

Pregnancy Risk Category: B

Adult Concerns: Optic neuritis, dizziness, confusion, nausea, vomiting, anorexia.

Pediatric Concerns: None reported, but caution is recommended.

Drug Interactions: Aluminum salts may decrease oral absorption.

AHL = 3.1 hours	M/P = 1.0
PHL =	PB = 8-22%
PK = 2-4 hours	Oral = 80%
MW = 204	pKa =
Vd =	

References:
1. Snider DE, Powell KE. Should women taking antituberculosis drugs breast-feed? Arch Inter Med. 144:589-590, 1984.
2. Chaplin S, Sanders GL & Smith JM: Drug excretion in human breast milk. Adv Drug React Ac Pois Rev 1:255-287, 1982.

Ethanol   Fax #1006

Trade: Alcohol
Can/Aus/UK:
Uses: Depressant
AAP: Approved by the American Academy of Pediatrics for use in breastfeeding mothers

Significant amounts of alcohol are secreted into breast milk, although it not considered harmful to the infant if the amount and duration are limited. The amount of alcohol transferred to milk is generally low. One recent report suggests a 23% reduction (156 to 120 mL) in breast milk production following ingestion of beer, and an increase in milk odor. Excess levels may lead to drowsiness, deep sleep, weakness, and decreased linear growth in infant. Maternal blood alcohol levels must attain 300 mg/dL before significant side effects are reported in the infant. Reduction of letdown is apparently dose-dependent and requires alcohol consumption of 1.5 to 1.9 gm/Kg body weight. Other studies have suggested psychomotor delay in infants of moderate drinkers (2+ drinks daily). Avoid breastfeeding during and for 2-3 hours after drinking alcohol. Adult metabolism of alcohol is approximately 1 oz in 3 hours

Alternatives:

Pregnancy Risk Category: D

Adult Concerns: Sedation, decreased milk supply, altered milk taste.

Pediatric Concerns: Sedation, irritability, weak sucking, decreased milk supply, increased milk odor.

Drug Interactions: Increased CNS depression when used with barbiturates, benzodiazepines, chloral hydrate, and other CNS depressants. A disulfiram-like reaction (flushing, weakness, sweating, tachycardia, etc) may occur when used with cephalosporins, chlorpropamide, disulfiram, furazolidone, metronidazole, procarbazine. Increased hypoglycemia when used with sulfonylureas and other hypoglycemic agents. Intolerance of bromocriptine.

AHL = 0.24 hours   M/P = 1.0
PHL =   PB   = 0%
PK = 30-90 min.(oral)   Oral = 100%
MW = 46   pKa =
Vd = 0.53

References:
1. Cobo E. Effect of different doses of ethanol on the milk ejecting reflex in lactating women. Am J obstet Gynecol. 115:817-821, 1973.
2. Mennella, J.A. Effects of Beer on Breast-fed infants. Letter to Editor. JAMA 269:1637, 1993.
3. Mennella JA and Beauchamp, GK. The transfer of alcohol to human milk. Effects on flavor and the infant's behavior. NEJM 325:981-985, 1991.

Ethosuximide   Fax #1177

Trade: Zarontin
Can/Aus/UK: Zarontin
Uses: Anticonvulsant used in epilepsy
AAP: Approved by the American Academy of Pediatrics for use in breastfeeding mothers

Ethosuximide is an anticonvulsant used in epilepsy. Rane's (1981) data suggest that although significant levels of ethosuximide are transferred into human milk, the plasma level in the infant is quite low. A peak milk concentration of approximately 55 mg/L was reported at 1 month postpartum. Milk:plasma ratios were reported to be 1.03 on day 3 postpartum, and 0.8 during the first three months of therapy. The infant's plasma reached a peak (2.9 mg/dL) at approximately 1.5 months postpartum and then declined significantly over the next 3 months suggesting increased clearance by the infant. Although these levels are considered sub-therapeutic, it is suggested that the infant's plasma levels be occasionally tested.

Alternatives:

Pregnancy Risk Category: C

Adult Concerns: Drowsiness, ataxia, nausea, vomiting, anorexia, rash.

Pediatric Concerns: After 5 months of maternal therapy with ethosuximide, no untoward effects were noted in breastfed infant.

Drug Interactions: Decreased efficacy of ethosuximide when used with phenytoin, carbamazepine, primidone, phenobarbital (may reduce plasma levels). Elevated levels of ethosuximide may result when used with isoniazid.

AHL	= 31-60 hours	M/P	= 1.0
PHL	= 25-60 hours	PB	= 0%
PK	= 4 hours	Oral	= Complete
MW	= 141	pKa	= 9.3
Vd	= 0.72		

References:
1. Rane, A and Tunnell, R. Ethosuximide in human milk and in plasma of a mother and her nursed infant. Br. J. Clin. Pharmacol. 12:855-58, 1981.
2. Kaneko S, et. al. The levels of anticonvulsants in breast milk. Br J Clin Pharmacol 7:624-6, 1979.

Ethotoin   Fax #1178

Trade: Peganone
Can/Aus/UK:
Uses: Anticonvulsant
AAP: Not reviewed

Ethotoin is a typical phenytoin-like anticonvulsant. Although no data are available on concentrations in breast milk, it's similarity to phenytoin would suggest that some is secreted via breast milk. No data are available in the literature. See phenytoin.

Alternatives:

Pregnancy Risk Category: D

Adult Concerns: Drowsiness, dizziness, insomnia, headache, blood dyscrasia.

Pediatric Concerns: None reported, but see phenytoin.

Drug Interactions: See phenytoin.

AHL = 3-9 hours		**M/P** =	
PHL =		**PB** = Low-41%	
PK = 1-2 hours		**Oral** = Complete	
MW = 204		**pKa** =	
Vd =			

References:
1.   McEvoy GE(ed):AHFS Drug Information, New York, NY. 1995.

Etidronate   Fax #1540

Trade: Didronel
Can/Aus/UK: Didronel
Uses: Slows bone turnover
AAP: Not reviewed

Etidronate is a bisphosphonate that slows the dissolution of hydroxyapatite crystals in the bone, thus reducing bone calcium loss in certain syndromes such as Paget's syndrome. Etidronate also reduces the remineralization of bone and can result in osteomalacia over time. It is not known how the administration of this product during active lactation would effect the maternal bone porosity. It is possible that milk calcium levels could be reduced, although this has not been reported. Etidronate is poorly absorbed orally (1%) and must be administered in between meals on an empty stomach. Its penetration into milk is possible due to its small molecular weight, but it has not yet been reported. However, due to the presence of fat and calcium in

Medications and Mothers' Milk, 1998

milk, its oral bioavailability in infants would be exceedingly low. Whereas the plasma half-life is approximately 6 hours, the terminal elimination half-life (from bone) is > 90 days.

Alternatives:

Pregnancy Risk Category: B

Adult Concerns: Untoward effects include loss of taste, nephrotoxicity, risk of fractures, and focal osteomalacia after prolonged use. Fever, convulsions, bone pain.

Pediatric Concerns: None reported via milk. Although unreported, it could result in reduced milk calcium levels. Oral absorption in infant would be minimal.

Drug Interactions: IV Ranitidine doubles the oral absorption of alendronate (similar to etidronate). Oral products containing calcium or magnesium will significantly reduce oral bioavailability. Take on empty stomach.

AHL = 6 hours(plasma)	**M/P** =	
PHL =	**PB** =	
PK = 2 hours	**Oral** = 1-2.5%	
MW = 206	**pKa** =	
Vd = 1.37		

References:
1.   Drug Facts and Comparisons. 1996. ed. Facts and Comparisons, St. Louis.

Etodolac   Fax #1179

Trade: Etodolac, Lodine
Can/Aus/UK: Lodine, Ultradol
Uses: Non-steroidal analgesic, antipyretic
AAP: Not reviewed

Etodolac is a prototypical nonsteroidal anti-inflammatory agent (NSAID) with analgesic, antipyretic, and anti-inflammatory properties. No data was found on its secretion into human breast milk.

Alternatives: Ibuprofen

Pregnancy Risk Category: C

Adult Concerns: Dyspepsia, nausea, diarrhea, indigestion, heartburn, abdominal pain, and gastrointestinal bleeding.

Pediatric Concerns: None reported via milk, but observe for nausea, diarrhea, indigestion. Ibuprofen probably preferred at this time.

Drug Interactions: May prolong prothrombin time when used with warfarin. Antihypertensive effects of ACEi family may be blunted or completely abolished by NSAIDs. Some NSAIDs may block antihypertensive effect of beta blockers, diuretics. Used with cyclosporin, may dramatically increase renal toxicity. May increase digoxin, phenytoin, lithium levels. May increase toxicity of methotrexate. May increase bioavailability of penicillamine. Probenecid may increase NSAID levels.

AHL = 7.3 hours		**M/P** =	
PHL =		**PB** = 95-99%	
PK = 1-2 hours		**Oral** = 80-100%	
MW = 287		**pKa** = 4.7	
Vd = 0.4			

References:
1. Pharmaceutical Manufacturer's Package Insert, 1995.

Etretinate   Fax #1180

Trade: Tegison
Can/Aus/UK: Tigason
Uses: Antipsoriatic
AAP: Not reviewed

Etretinate is an oral Vitamin A derivative primarily used for psoriasis and sometimes acne. It is teratogenic and should not be administered to pregnant women or women about to become pregnant. Etretinate is known to transfer into animal milk although no data are available on human milk. Etretinate is still detectible in human serum up to 2.9 years after administration has ceased due to storage at high concentrations in adipose tissue. Mothers who wish to breastfeed following therapy with this compound should be informed of its long half-life in the human. The manufacturer considers this drug to be contraindicated in breastfeeding mothers due to the potential for serious adverse effects.

Alternatives:

Pregnancy Risk Category: X

Adult Concerns: Dry nose, chapped lips, nose bleeds, hair loss, peeling of skin on soles, palms, sunburns, and headaches. Elevated liver enzymes, lipids. Fatigue, headache, fever.

Pediatric Concerns: None reported but great caution is urged. Premature epiphyseal closure has been reported in children treated with this product.

Drug Interactions: Milk increases absorption of oral etretinate. Exogenous vitamin A increases toxicity.

AHL = 120 days (terminal)	M/P	=	
PHL =	PB	= >99%	
PK = 2-6 hours	Oral	= Complete	
MW = 354	pKa	=	
Vd = High			

References:
1. Pharmaceutical Manufacturer's Package Insert, 1995.
2. Lacy C. et.al. Drug information handbook. Lexi-Comp, Hudson(Cleveland), Oh. 1996.

Evening Primrose Oil   Fax #1543

Trade: EPO
Can/Aus/UK: Efamol
Uses: Nutritional supplement
AAP: Not reviewed

Evening primrose oil is a rich source of essential polyunsaturated fatty acids (EFA) particularly gamma linoleic acid (GLA). Human milk is generally rich in 6-desaturated essential fatty acids including arachidonic, GLA, and dihomoj-GLA (DGLA), which may play an important role in development of the infants brain. The brain contains about 20% of 6-desaturated EFAs. Supplementation in pregnant women has been found to significantly increase EFA content in human breast milk. Although there is some evidence that GLA may be beneficial in syndromes such as cardiovascular disease, rheumatoid arthritis, multiple sclerosis, atopic dermatitis, many of these studies were sponsored by the manufacturer and need independent confirmation. Overt toxicity of this product appears quite low. A number of studies in adults using GLA at rather high doses have not been found to produce significant toxicity.

Alternatives:

Pregnancy Risk Category:

Adult Concerns: Major untoward effects are largely unreported, although some patients have quit various studies for unspecified reasons.

Pediatric Concerns: None reported.

Drug Interactions:

References:
1.	Cant A, Shay J, Horrobin DF. The effect of maternal supplementation with linoleic and gamma-linolenic acids on the fat composition and content of human milk: a placebo-controlled trial. J.Nutr. Sci Vitaminol 37(6):573-9, 1991.
2.	Horrobin DF Manku MS. How do polyunsaturated fatty acids

lower plasma cholesterol levels? Lipids 18:558-62, 1983.
3. Review of Natural Products. Facts and Comparisons, St. Louis, Mo. 1996.

Famciclovir   Fax #1181

Trade: Famvir
Can/Aus/UK: Famvir
Uses: Antiviral for Herpes Zoster
AAP: Not reviewed

Famciclovir is an antiviral use in the treatment of uncomplicated herpes zoster infection (shingles) and genital herpes. It is rapidly metabolized to the active metabolite, penciclovir. Although similar to Acyclovir, no data are available on levels in human milk. Oral bioavailability of famciclovir (77%) is much better than acyclovir (15-30%). Studies with rodents suggest that the milk:plasma ratio is greater than 1.0. Because famciclovir provides few advantages over acyclovir, at this point acyclovir would probably be preferred in a nursing mother although the side-effect profile is still minimal with this product.

Alternatives: Acyclovir

Pregnancy Risk Category: B

Adult Concerns: Headache, dizziness, nausea, diarrhea, fever, anorexia.

Pediatric Concerns: None reported.

Drug Interactions: Cimetidine increases plasma levels of the active metabolite penciclovir. Famciclovir increases digoxin plasma levels by 19%. Probenecid significantly increase penciclovir plasma levels.

AHL = 2-3 hours	**M/P** = >1
PHL =	**PB** = 20%
PK = 0.9 hours	**Oral** = 77%
MW =	**pKa** =
Vd = 1,08	

References:
1. Drug Facts and Comparisons. 1994 ed. Facts and Comparisons, St. Louis.
2. Pharmaceutical Manufacturer's Package Insert, 1995.

Famotidine   Fax #1182

Trade: Pepcid, Axid-AR, Pepcid-AC
Can/Aus/UK: Pepcid, Apo-Famotidine, Novo-Famotidine Amfamox, Pepcidine
Uses: Reduces gastric acid secretion
AAP: Not reviewed

Famotidine is a typical Histamine-2 antagonist that reduces stomach acid secretion. In one study of 8 lactating women receiving a 40 mg/day dose, the peak concentration in breast milk was 72 µg/L and occurred at 6 hours post-dose. The milk:plasma ratios were 0.41, 1.78, and 1.33 at 2, 6, and 24 hours respectively. These levels are apparently much lower than other histamine H-2 antagonists (ranitidine, cimetidine) and make it a preferred choice.

Alternatives: Nizatidine

Pregnancy Risk Category: B

Adult Concerns: Headache, constipation, increased liver enzymes.

Pediatric Concerns: None reported. Pediatric indications are available.

Drug Interactions: Famotidine reduces bioavailability of ketoconazole, itraconazole due to reduced oral absorption of these two products.

AHL = 2.5-3.5 hours	M/P = 0.41-1.78
PHL =	PB = 17%
PK = 1-3.5 hours	Oral = 50%
MW = 337	pKa =
Vd =	

References:
1.   Courtney TP, Shaw RW, et.al. Excretion of famotidine in breast milk. Br.J.Clin.Pharmacol. 26:639, 1988.
2.   Echizen H & Ishizaki T: Clinical pharmacokinetics of famotidine. Clin Pharmacokinet 1991; 21:178-194.

Felbamate   Fax #1478

Trade: Felbatol
Can/Aus/UK:
Uses: Anticonvulsant
AAP: Not reviewed

Felbamate is an oral antiepileptic agent for partial seizures and Lennox-Gastaut syndrome. Felbamate is known to be secreted in rodent milk, and was detrimental to their offspring. No data are available on human milk.

Alternatives:

Pregnancy Risk Category: C

Adult Concerns: Aplastic anemia, weight gain, flu-like symptoms, tachycardia, nausea, vomiting, headache, insomnia.

Pediatric Concerns: None reported, but caution is urged.

Drug Interactions: Felbamate causes an increase in phenytoin plasma levels.   Phenytoin produces a 45% decrease in felbamate levels. Carbamazepine levels may be decreased, whereas felbamate levels may drop by 40%. Valproic acid plasma levels may be increased.

AHL = 20-23 hours		**M/P** =	
PHL =		**PB** = 25%	
PK = 1-4 hours		**Oral** = 90%	
MW =		**pKa** =	
Vd = 0.7-1.0			

References:
1.   Pharmaceutical Manufacturer's Package Insert, 1995.

Felodipine   Fax #1183

Trade: Plendil
Can/Aus/UK: Plendil, Renedil, Agon SR, Plendil-ER
Uses: Calcium channel blocker, antihypertensive
AAP: Not reviewed

Felodipine is a calcium channel antagonist structurally related to
nifedipine. It may produce significant digital anomalies in an exposed
fetus.   Administration of many calcium channel blockers during
lactation is not generally recommended, but few reports are available.

Alternatives: Nifedipine, Nimodipine, Verapamil

Pregnancy Risk Category: C

Adult Concerns: Headache, dizziness, edema, flushing, hypotension,
constipation, cardiac arrhythmias.

Pediatric Concerns: None reported via milk,   but caution is
recommended.

Drug Interactions: Barbiturates may reduce bioavailability of calcium
channel blockers (CCB). Calcium salts may reduce hypotensive effect.
Dantrolene may increase risk of hyperkalemia and myocardial
depression. H2 blockers may increase bioavailability of certain CCBs.
Hydantoins may reduce plasma levels. Quinidine increases risk of
hypotension, bradycardia, tachycardia. Rifampin may reduce effects of
CCBs. Vitamin D may reduce efficacy of CCBs.   CCBs may increase
carbamazepine, cyclosporin, encainide, prazosin levels.

AHL = 11-16 hours	**M/P** =	
PHL =	**PB** = >99%	
PK = 2.5-5 hours	**Oral** = 20%	
MW = 384	**pKa** =	
Vd =		

References:
1.   Pharmaceutical Manufacturer's Package Insert, 1996.

Fenfluramine   Fax #1522

Trade: Pondimin
Can/Aus/UK: Ponderal, Ponderax, Gastromiro, Niopam
Uses: Appetite suppressant
AAP: Not reviewed

Fenfluramine is an appetite suppressant with a structure similar to amphetamine although its effects are somewhat different. No data are available on its transfer to human milk. But due to the small molecular weight (231), its high lipid solubility, its long half-life, and its rapid transfer into the CNS, it is likely that significant quantities may be secreted into milk. Such transfer could lead to neonatal depression, anorexia, insomnia, etc. The use of this product in breastfeeding mothers would be difficult to justify and is not advised.

Alternatives:

Pregnancy Risk Category: C

Adult Concerns: Primary pulmonary hypertension, palpitations, insomnia, hallucinations, drowsiness, CNS depression, hemolytic anemia, diarrhea, dry mouth, constipation. May exacerbate glaucoma.

Pediatric Concerns: None reported, but use (PO) in pediatric patients is generally contraindicated.

Drug Interactions: Fatal cardiac arrest when used with halothane anesthesia, withdraw one week prior to surgery. Fenfluramine may raise plasma levels of desipramine significantly.

AHL = 20 hours		M/P	=
PHL =		PB	=
PK = 2-4 hours		Oral	= Complete
MW = 231		pKa	=

Vd =

References:
1. Lacy C. et.al. Drug information handbook. Lexi-Comp, Hudson(Cleveland), Oh. 1996.
2. Drug Facts and Comparisons. 1996. ed. Facts and Comparisons, St. Louis.
3. Pharmaceutical Manufacturer's Package Insert, 1997.

Fenoprofen   Fax #1184

Trade: Nalfon
Can/Aus/UK: Nalfon, Fenopron, Progesic
Uses: NSAID, nonsteroidal analgesic
AAP: Not reviewed

Fenoprofen is a typical nonsteroidal anti-inflammatory and analgesic. Following 600 mg four times daily for 4 days postpartum, the milk:plasma ratio was approximately 0.017 and fenoprofen levels in milk were too low to be accurately detected and was estimated to be approximately 1/60 th of the maternal plasma level. Fenoprofen was undetectable in cord blood, amniotic fluid, saliva or washed red blood cells after multiple doses.

Alternatives: Ibuprofen

Pregnancy Risk Category: B in first two trimesters
D if used in third trimester

Adult Concerns: GI distress and bleeding, dyspepsia, nausea, constipation, ulcers, hepatotoxicity, rash, tinnitus.

Pediatric Concerns: None reported.

Drug Interactions: May prolong prothrombin time when used with warfarin. Antihypertensive effects of ACEi family may be blunted or completely abolished by NSAIDs. Some NSAIDs may block antihypertensive effect of beta blockers, diuretics. Used with cyclosporin, may dramatically increase renal toxicity. May increase digoxin, phenytoin, lithium levels. May increase toxicity of methotrexate. May increase bioavailability of penicillamine. Probenecid may increase NSAID levels.

AHL = 2.5 hours		**M/P**	= 0.017
PHL =		**PB**	= 99%
PK = 1-2 hours		**Oral**	= 80%
MW = 242		**pKa**	= 4.5
Vd = 0.08-0.10			

References:
1. Rubin A, et. al. A profile of the physiological disposition and gastrointestinal effects of fenoprofen in man. Curr Med Res Opin 2:529-44, 1974.

Fentanyl   Fax #1185

Trade: Sublimaze
Can/Aus/UK: Sublimaze, Duragesic
Uses: Opiate analgesic
AAP: Approved by the American Academy of Pediatrics for use in breastfeeding mothers

Fentanyl is a potent narcotic analgesic used (IV, IM, transdermally) during labor and delivery. When used parenterally, its half-life is exceedingly short. The transfer of fentanyl into human milk has been documented, but is low. In a group of ten women receiving a total dose of 50 to 400 µg fentanyl IV during labor (Leuschen 1990), the concentration of fentanyl in milk was exceedingly low, generally below the level of detection (<0.05 ng/mL). In a few samples, the levels were between 0.05 and 0.15 ng/mL. Using this data, an infant would ingest less than 3% of the weight-adjusted maternal dose per day. The relatively low level of fentanyl found in human milk is presumably a result of the short maternal half-life, and the rather rapid redistribution out of the maternal plasma compartment. It is apparent that fentanyl transfer to milk under most clinical conditions is poor and is probably clinically unimportant.

Alternatives:

Pregnancy Risk Category: B

Adult Concerns: Apnea, respiratory depression, muscle rigidity, hypotension, bradycardia.

Pediatric Concerns: No adverse effects reported via milk.

Drug Interactions: Increased toxicity when used with other CNS depressants, phenothiazines, tricyclic antidepressants.

AHL = 2-4 hours.		**M/P** =	
PHL = 3-13 hours (neonates)		**PB** = 80-86%	
PK = 7-8 min.(IV)		**Oral** = 25-75%	
MW = 336		**pKa** = 8.4	
Vd = 3-8			

References:
1. Madej TH, Strunin L. Comparison of epidural fentanyl with sufentanil. Anaesthesia 42:1156-1161, 1987.
2. Spigset O. Anaesthetic agents and excretion in breast milk. Acta Anaesthesiologica Scandinavica. 38:94-103, 1994.
3. Leuschen MP, Wolf LJ, Rayburn WF: Fentanyl excretion in breast milk. Clin Pharm 1990; 9:336-337.

Fenugreek   Fax #1525

Trade: Fenugreek
Can/Aus/UK:
Uses: Herbal spice
AAP: Not reviewed

Fenugreek is commonly sold as the dried ripe seed and extracts are used as an artificial flavor for maple syrup. The seeds contain from 0.1 to 0.9% diosgenin. Several coumarin compounds have been noted in the seed as well as a number of alkaloids such as trigonelline, gentianine, and carpaine. The seeds also contain approximately 8% of a foul-smelling oil. Fenugreek has been noted to reduce plasma cholesterol in animals when 50% of their diet contained fenugreek seeds. The high fiber content may have accounted for this change although it may be due to the steroid saponins. A hypoglycemic effect has also been noted. When added to the diet of diabetic dogs, a decrease in insulin dose and hyperglycemia was noted. It is not known if these changes are due to the fiber content of the seeds or a chemical component. When dosed in moderation, fenugreek has limited toxicity and is listed in the US as a GRAS herbal (Generally Regarded As Safe). A maple syrup odor via urine and sweat is commonly reported. Higher doses may produce hypoglycemia. A stimulant effect on the isolated uterus (guinea pig) has been reported and its use in late pregnancy may not be advisable. Fenugreek's reputation as a galactagogue is widespread but undocumented. The dose commonly employed is variable but is approximately 2-3 capsules taken three times daily. The transfer of fenugreek into milk is unknown, but untoward effects have not been reported.

Alternatives: Metoclopramide, domperidone

Pregnancy Risk Category:

Adult Concerns: Maple syrup odor in urine and sweat. Diarrhea, hypoglycemia, dyspnea (exaggeration of asthmatic symptoms). Two cases of fenugreek allergy have been reported.

Pediatric Concerns: None reported via milk.

Drug Interactions:

References:
1. Review of Natural Products. Facts and Comparisons, St. Louis, Mo. 1996.
2. Sauvaire Y, Baccou JC. Extraction of diosgenine, (25R)-spirost-5-ene-3beta-ol; problems of the hydrolysis of the saponins. Lloydia 41:247, 1978.
3. Valette G. et.al. Hypocholesterolaemic effect of fenugreek seeds in dogs. Atherosclerosis 50(1):105, 1984.
4. Ribes G, et.al. Effects of fenugreek seeds on endocrine pancreatic secretions in dogs. Ann Nutr Metab 28(1): 37, 1984.

5.   Dugue P, Bel J, Figueredo M. Fenugreek causing a new type of occupational asthma. Presse Medicale 22(19):922, 1993.
6.   Patil SP, Niphadkar Pv, Bapat MM. Allergy to fenugreek. Annals of Allergy, Asthma, and Immunology 78(3):297-300, 1997.

Fexofenadine   Fax #1495

Trade: Allegra
Can/Aus/UK: Allegra
Uses: Antihistamine
AAP: Not reviewed

Fexofenadine is a non-sedating histamine-1 receptor antagonist and is the active metabolite of terfenadine (Seldane).   It is indicated for symptoms of allergic rhinitis and other allergies.   Unlike Seldane, no cardiotoxicity has been reported with this product.   No data are available on its transfer into human milk.

Alternatives:

Pregnancy Risk Category: C

Adult Concerns: Drowsiness, fatigue, leukopenia, nausea, dyspepsia, dry mouth, headache and throat irritation have been reported. Thus far, no cardiotoxicity has been reported .

Pediatric Concerns: None reported.

Drug Interactions: Erythromycin and ketoconazole (and potentially other azole antifungals and macrolide antibiotics) may elevate the plasma level of fexofenadine(82%) significantly.

AHL = 14.4 hours		M/P	=
PHL =		PB	= 60-70%
PK = 2.6 hours		Oral	= Complete
MW = 538		pKa	=
Vd =			

References:
1.   Pharmaceutical Manufacturer's Package Insert, 1997.

Flavoxate   Fax #1575

Trade: Urispas
Can/Aus/UK: Urispas
Uses: Urinary tract antispasmodic
AAP: Not reviewed

Flavoxate is use as an antispasmodic to provide relief of painful urination, urgency, nocturia, urinary frequency, or incontinence. It exerts a direct smooth muscle relaxation on the bladder wall and has been used in children for enuresis. No data are available on its transfer into human milk.

Alternatives:

Pregnancy Risk Category: B

Adult Concerns: Drowsiness, dry mouth and throat, nervousness, headache, confusion, nausea, vomiting, blurred vision. Do not use with pyloric or duodenal obstruction, GI hemorrhage, or obstructive uropathies.

Pediatric Concerns: None reported via milk.

Drug Interactions:

AHL = < 10 hours	M/P =
PHL =	PB =
PK = 2 hours	Oral = Complete
MW = 391	pKa =
Vd =	

References:
1.   Pharmaceutical Manufacturer's package insert, 1997.

Fluconazole   Fax #1186

Trade: Diflucan
Can/Aus/UK: Diflucan
Uses: Antifungal, particularly candida infections
AAP: Not reviewed

Fluconazole is a synthetic triazole antifungal agent and is frequently used for vaginal, oropharyngeal and esophageal candidiasis. Many of the triazole antifungals (itraconazole, terconazole,) have similar mechanisms of action and are considered fungistatic in action. In vivo studies have found fluconazole to have fungistatic activity against a variety of fungal strains including C. albicans, C. tropicalis, T. glabrata, and C. neoformans. The pharmacokinetics are similar following both oral and IV administration. The drug is almost completely absorbed orally (> 90%). Peak plasma levels occur in 1-2 hours after oral administration. Unlike ketoconazole and itraconazole, fluconazole absorption is unaffected by gastric pH and does not require an acid pH to be absorbed. Steady state plasma levels are only attained after 5-10 days of therapy, but can be achieved on day two with a loading dose (twice the daily dose) on the first day. Average plasma levels are 4.12 to 8.1 µg/mL. Fluconazole is widely and evenly distributed in most tissues and fluids and is distributed in total body water. Concentrations in skin and urine may be 10 fold higher than plasma levels. CSF concentrations are 50-94% of the plasma levels. Plasma protein binding is minimal at about 11%. Fluconazole is primarily excreted by the kidneys.   Oral fluconazole is currently cleared for pediatric candidiasis for infants 6 months and older, and has an FDA Safety Profile for neonates 1 day and older. Clinical cure rate for oropharyngeal candidiasis in pediatric patients is reported at 86% with fluconazole (2-3 mg/kg/day) compared to 46% of nystatin treated patients. Fluconazole is transferred into human milk with a milk:plasma ratio of approximately 0.85. Following a single 150 mg dose, the following milk levels have been reported:

Fluconazole Milk Levels [2]

	2 hrs	5 hrs	24 hrs	48 hrs
Milk Level (mg/L)	2.93	2.66	1.76	0.98
Plasma(mg/L)	6.4	2.79	2.52	1.19
Milk:Plasma Ratio	0.46	0.85	0.85	0.83

From these data, an infant consuming 450 cc of milk daily would receive less than 1.1 mg of fluconazole daily, only 1% of the maternal dose and less than 5% of the recommended pediatric dose. At this rate, it is not reasonable to assume that the infant will receive enough fluconazole via breast milk to affect therapy for the infant. The infant will require separate therapy with oral fluconazole or nystatin.

Side effects: Of the antifungals, fluconazole is very well tolerated. Adverse effects have only been reported in about 5-30% of patients, and in these, only 1-2.8% of patients have required discontinuation of the medication. Although adverse hepatic effects have been reported, they are very rare, and many occur coincident with the administration of other medications in AIDS patients. The most common complications include vomiting, diarrhea, abdominal pain, and skin rashes.

Dosage Recommendations: The recommended oral adult dose of fluconazole for oropharyngeal candidiasis depends on the severity of the infection, but is usually 200 mg STAT followed by 100 mg daily (see table above). Because symptoms of candidiasis are sometimes slow to resolve, many clinicians now recommend up to two weeks of therapy. Patients with esophageal candidiasis should be treated for a minimum of 3 weeks and for at least 2 weeks following resolution of symptoms (Manufacturer's Package Insert, 1994). Fluconazole has been used prophylactically in immunocompromised patients at a dose of 150 mg weekly to prevent recurrence (Leen, 1990, Winston, 1993) and this may be suitable for deep ductal candidiasis that is difficult to resolve. For treatment of vaginal candidiasis, 150 mg in one single dose is the current FDA recommendation. This therapy is not sufficient for ductal candidiasis in lactating women. For the treatment of systemic candidiasis (ductal), 400 mg STAT followed by 200 mg daily for periods up to 4 weeks is generally recommended by many clinicians. The recommended pediatric dosing for oral candidiasis is 6 mg/kg STAT followed by 3 mg/kg/day. For systemic candidiasis, 6-12 mg/kg/day is generally recommended. These current recommendations are for infants 6 months and older. The manufacturer states that a number of infants 1 day old and older have been safely treated. One study of premature infants suggests that the dose in very low birth weight infants should be 6 mg/Kg every 2 to 3 days (Saxen 1993).

Fluconazole Dosage [4]

Indication	Day 1	Daily Therapy	Minimum Duration of Therapy
Oropharyngeal candidiasis	200 mg	100 mg	14 d
Esophageal candidiasis	200 mg	100 mg	21 d
Systemic candidiasis	400 mg	200 mg	28 d
Cryptococcal meningitis acute	400 mg	200 mg	10-12 wk after CSF culture becomes negative
relapse	200 mg	200 mg	

Availability: 50, 100, 200 mg tablets. Oral suspensions = 10 mg/mL and 40 mg/mL

Alternatives: Itraconazole, Nystatin

Pregnancy Risk Category: C

Adult Concerns: Side effects are minimal and usually include GI symptoms such as vomiting, diarrhea, abdominal pain. Skin rashes, liver toxicity, elevated bilirubin in neonates may occur.

Pediatric Concerns: Pediatric complications from oral ingestion include GI symptoms such as vomiting, nausea, diarrhea, abdominal pain. Nephrotoxicity has not been reported. No complications from exposure to breast milk have been found.

Drug Interactions: Decreased hepatic clearance of fluconazole results from use with cyclosporin, zidovudine, rifabutin, theophylline, oral hypoglycemics (glipizide and tolbutamide), warfarin, phenytoin, and terfenadine. Decreased plasma levels of fluconazole have resulted following administration with rifampin, and cimetidine.

AHL = 30 hours	**M/P**	= 0.46-0.85	
PHL = 88.6 hours (neonate)	**PB**	= 15%.	
PK = 1-2 hours	**Oral**	= >90%	
MW = 306	**pKa**	=	
Vd =			

References:
1. Saxen H. et.al. Pharmacokinetics of fluconazole in very low birth weight infants during the first two weeks of life. Clin. Pharmax. and Ther. 54:269, 1993.
2. Force RW. Fluconazole concentrations in breast milk. Pedi. Infectious Dis. 14(3):235-236, 1995.
3. Andriole V, Bodey GP. In: Systemic Antifungal Therapy. Scientific Therapeutics Information, 1994.
4. Pharmaceutical Manufacturer's Package Insert, 1996.
5. Winston DJ, Chandrasekar PH, Lazarus HM et al: Fluconazole prophylaxis of fungal infections in patients with acute leukemia. Ann Intern Med 118:495-503, 1993.
6. Leen CLS, et.al. Once-weekly fluconazole to prevent recurrence of oropharyngeal candidiasis... J. Infection 21:55-60, 1990.
7. Paap C. Update on fluconazole. Pharmacology Forum. Infectious Diseases in Children. p. 19-21, April 1996.

Fludeoxyglucose F 18   Fax #1479

Trade: Fludeoxyglucose F-18
Can/Aus/UK:
Uses: PET Scanning pharmaceutical
AAP: Not reviewed

Fludeoxyglucose F 18 is a positron-emitting radiopharmaceutical used in conjunction with positron emission tomography (PET Scanning) to detect alterations in tissue glucose metabolism, and is useful in detecting brain tumors, certain malignancies, chronic coronary artery disease, partial epilepsy and Alzheimer's disease. Fludeoxyglucose F 18 is rapidly distributed to all parts of the body that have significant glucose metabolism, including the breast. No levels in breast milk have been reported, but it probably penetrates milk to some degree. The half-life of the F-18 is short, only 110 minutes. Due to concentration in some tissues, such as the bladder, radiation exposure could be a problem and emptying of the breast at routine intervals would reduce radiation exposure to breast tissue. The USPDI (1994) recommends interruption of breastfeeding for 12-24 hours. At 9 hours, 97% of the radioisotope would be decayed away. It is likely that after 12 hours, almost all radioisotope would be decayed to almost background levels. Recommend pumping and dumping of breast milk after the procedure for at least 12-24 hours.

Alternatives:

Pregnancy Risk Category:

Adult Concerns: No untoward effects have been reported for this product.

Pediatric Concerns: None reported, but possible radiation exposure if breastfed prior to 12-24 hours after dose.

Drug Interactions:

AHL = 110 minutes		M/P	=
PHL =		PB	= Minimal

PK	= 30 minutes	Oral	= Complete
MW	=	pKa	=
Vd	=		

References:
1. Jamieson D, Alavi A, Jolles P et al: Positron emission tomography in the investigation of central nervous system disorders. Radiol Clin North Am 26:1075-1088, 1988.
2. Jones SC, Alavi A, Christman D et al: The radiation dosimetry of 2-(F-18) fluoro-2-deoxy-d-glucose in man. Nucl Med 23:613-617, 1982.
3. Som P, Atkins HL, Bandoypadhyay D, Fowler JS et al: A fluorinated glucose analog, 2-fluoro-2-deoxy-d-glucose (F-18): nontoxic tracer for rapid tumor detection. J Nucl Med 21:670-675, 1980.
4. Jones SC, Alavi A, Christman D et al: The radiation dosimetry of 2-(F-18)fluoro-2-deoxy-d-glucose in man. J Nucl Med 23:613-617, 1982.

Flunarizine   Fax #1584

Trade: Sibelium
Can/Aus/UK: Sibelium, Novo-Flunarizine
Uses: Antihypertensive
AAP: Not reviewed

Flunarizine is a calcium channel blocker primarily indicated for use in migraine headache prophylaxis, and peripheral vascular disease. It has a very long half-life, and a huge volume of distribution, which contributes to the long half-life. No data are available on the transfer of this product into human milk. However, due to its incredibly long half-life, and high volume of distribution, it is possible that this product over time could build up and concentrate in a breastfed infant. Other calcium channel blockers may be preferred. Use with extreme caution.

Alternatives: Nifedipine, Nimodipine, Verapamil

Pregnancy Risk Category:

Adult Concerns: Extrapyramidal symptoms in elderly patients, depression, porphyria, thrombophlebitis, drowsiness, headache, dizziness.

Pediatric Concerns: None reported via milk, but caution is advised.

Drug Interactions: Prolonged bradycardia with adenosine. Sinus arrest when used with amiodarone. Hypotension and bradycardia when used with beta blockers. Increase of carbamazepine and cyclosporin plasma levels when used with flunarizine.

AHL = 19 days		M/P	=
PHL = 23 days		PB	= 99%
PK = 2-4 hours		Oral	= Complete
MW =		pKa	=
Vd = 43.2			

References:
1. Pharmaceutical Manufacturer's package insert, 1998.

Flunisolide   Fax #1187

Trade: Nasalide, Aerobid
Can/Aus/UK: Bronalide, Rhinalar, PMS-Flunisolide, Syntaris
Uses: Inhaled and intranasal steroid
AAP: Not reviewed

Flunisolide is a potent corticosteroid used to reduce airway hyperreactivity in asthmatics. It is also available as Nasalide for intranasal use for allergic rhinitis. Generally, only small levels of flunisolide are absorbed systemically (about 40%), thereby reducing systemic effects and presumably breast milk levels as well. After inhalation of 1 mg flunisolide, systemic availability was only 40% and plasma level was 0.4-1 nanogram/mL. Adrenal suppression in children has not been documented even after therapy of 2 months with 1600 µg/day. Once absorbed flunisolide is rapidly removed from the plasma compartment by first-pass uptake in the liver. Although no data on breast milk levels are yet available, it is unlikely that the level secreted in milk is clinically relevant.

Alternatives:

Pregnancy Risk Category: C

Adult Concerns: Most common side effect is irritation, due to vehicle not drug itself. Loss of taste, nasal irritation, flu-like symptoms, sore throat, headache.

Pediatric Concerns: None reported. Can be used in children down to age 6.

Drug Interactions:

AHL	= 1.8 hours	M/P	=
PHL	=	PB	=
PK	= 30 min.	Oral	= 21% (oral)
MW	= 435	pKa	=
Vd	= 1.8		

References:
1. Pharmaceutical Manufacturer's Package Insert, 1995.
2. Drug Facts and Comparisons. 1995 ed. Facts and Comparisons, St. Louis.

Flunitrazepam   Fax #1491

Trade: Rohypnol
Can/Aus/UK: Rohypnol, Hypnodor, Raohypnol
Uses: Benzodiazepine sedative
AAP: Not reviewed

Flunitrazepam is a prototypical benzodiazepine. Frequently called the "Date Rape Pill", it induces rapid sedation and significant amnesia, particularly when admixed with alcohol. Effects last about 8 hours. It is recommended for adult insomnia, and for pediatric preanesthetic sedation.

Alternatives: Lorazepam, Alprazolam

Pregnancy Risk Category:

Adult Concerns: Drowsiness, sedation, ataxia, headache, memory impairment, tremors.

Pediatric Concerns: None reported via milk, but observe for sedation.

Drug Interactions: Clarithromycin and other macrolide antibiotics may increase plasma levels for benzodiazepines by inhibiting metabolism. May have enhanced effect when added to fentanyl, ketamine, nitrous oxide. Addition of even small amounts of alcohol may produce profound sedation, psychomotor impairment, and amnesia. Theophylline may reduce the sedative effects of benzodiazepines.

AHL = 20-30 hours		**M/P** =	
PHL =		**PB** = 80%	
PK = 2 hours		**Oral** = 80-90%	
MW = 313		**pKa** =	
Vd = 3.6			

References:
1.   Kanto J, Erkkola R, Kangas L et al: Placental transfer of flunitrazepam following intramuscular administration during labour. Br J Clin Pharmacol 23:491-494, 1987.
2.   Kanto J, Kangas L, Leppanen T: A comparative study of the clinical effects of oral flunitrazepam, medazepam, and placebo. Int J Clin Pharmacol Ther Toxicol 20:431-433, 1982.

Fluoride   Fax #1188

Trade: Pediaflor, Flura
Can/Aus/UK: Fluor-A-Day, Fluotic, Fluor-A-Day, Fluorigard
Uses: Hardening enamel of teeth

AAP: Reported as having no effect on breastfeeding.

Fluoride is an essential element required for bone and teeth development. It is available as salts of sodium, and stannis (tin). Excessive levels are known to stain teeth irreversibly. One study shows breast milk levels of 0.024 - 0.172 ppm in milk of a population exposed to fluoridated water (0.7ppm). Fluoride probably forms calcium fluoride salts in milk which may limit the oral bioavailability of the fluoride provided by human milk. Maternal supplementation is unnecessary and not recommended in areas with high fluoride content (> 0.7 ppm) in water. Allergy to fluoride has been reported in one infant. Younger children (2-6 yrs) should be instructed to use minimal quantities of toothpaste and to not swallow large amounts. The American Academy of Pediatrics no longer recommends supplementing of breastfed infants with oral fluoride.

Fluoride Ion

Fluoride Content of Drinking Water	Daily Dose, Oral (mg) In Non-Breastfed Infants
<0.3 ppm Birth - 2 y	0.25
2-3 y	0.5
3-12 y	1
0.3-0.7 ppm Birth - 2 y	0
2-3 y	0.25
3-12 y	0.5

Alternatives:

Pregnancy Risk Category: C

Adult Concerns: Stained enamel, allergic rash.

Pediatric Concerns: Allergy to fluoride has been reported in one infant. Do not use maternal doses > 0.7 ppm.

Drug Interactions: Decreased absorption when used with magnesium, aluminum, and calcium containing products.

AHL = 6 hours		**M/P** =	
PHL =		**PB** =	
PK =		**Oral** = 90% (Na)	
MW = 19		**pKa** =	
Vd = 0.5-0.7			

References:
1. Green JC. Fluoride supplementation of the breast-fed infant. JAMA 263:2179, 1990.
2. Spak CJ, Hardell LI, deChateau P. Fluoride in human milk. Acta Paediatr Scand. 72:699-701, 1983.
3. Shea, J. et.al. Allergy to fluoride. Ann. Allergy 25:388, 1967.
4. Latifah R and Razak IA. Fluoride levels in mother's milk. J. Pedodontics 13:149, 1989.
5. McEvoy GE(ed):AHFS Drug Information, New York, NY. 1995.

Fluorouracil   Fax #1189

Trade: 5 FU, Adrucil, Efudex, Fluoroplex
Can/Aus/UK: Adrucil, Efudex, Fluoroplex, Efudix, Fluoroplex
Uses: Anti-cancer drug, actinic keratosis
AAP: Not reviewed

Fluorouracil is a potent antineoplastic agent generally used topically for various skin cancers, and IV for various carcinomas. No data are available on its transfer into breast milk. 5FU is an extremely toxic and dangerous compound, and is probably contraindicated in breastfeeding women following IV therapy. It is rapidly cleared by the liver and two long-half-life metabolites (FdUMP, FUTP) are formed. The clinical effect and half-life of these metabolites is unknown. 5FU is commonly used topically as a cream for actinic or solar keratosis. The topical absorption of 5FU is minimal, reported to be less than 6%. Although it is unlikely that significant quantities of 5FU would be transferred to a breastfed infant following topical application to small areas, caution is urged.

Alternatives:

Pregnancy Risk Category: **D via injection**
                                               X topical

Adult Concerns: Nausea, vomiting, anorexia, blood dyscrasia, bone marrow suppression, myocardial toxicity, dyspnea, cardiogenic shock, rashes.

Pediatric Concerns: None reported but caution is urged.

Drug Interactions: Drug interactions are numerous and include allopurinol, cimetidine, methotrexate, leukovorin and others.

AHL = 8-22 minutes		**M/P** =	
PHL =		**PB** = 8-12%	
PK = Immediate(IV)		**Oral** = 0-80%	
MW = 130		**pKa** =	
Vd = 0.12			

References:
1.   McEvoy GE(ed):AHFS Drug Information, New York, NY. 1995.

Fluoxetine   Fax #1190

Trade: Prozac
Can/Aus/UK: Prozac, Apo-Fluoxetine, Novo-Fluoxetine, Lovan, Zactin
Uses: Antidepressant
AAP: Drugs whose effect on nursing infants is unknown but may be of concern

Fluoxetine is a very popular serotonin reuptake inhibitor (SSRI) currently used for depression and a host of other syndromes. Fluoxetine absorption is rapid and complete and the parent compound is rapidly metabolized to norfluoxetine, which is an active, long half-life metabolite. Both fluoxetine and norfluoxetine appear to permeate breast milk to levels approximately 1/5 to 1/4 of maternal plasma. In one patient at steady-state (dose=20mg/day), plasma levels of fluoxetine were 100.5 µg/L and levels of norfluoxetine were 194.5 µg/L (Isenberg, 1990). Fluoxetine levels in milk were 28.8 µg/L and norfluoxetine levels were 41.6 µg/L. Milk:plasma ratios were 0.286 for fluoxetine, and 0.21 for norfluoxetine. In another patient receiving 20 mg daily at bedtime, the milk concentration of fluoxetine was 67 µg/L and norfluoxetine 52 µg/L at four hours. At 8 hours post-dose, the concentration of fluoxetine was 17 µg/L and norfluoxetine was 13 µg/L. Using this data, the authors estimated that the total daily dose was only 15-20 µg/Kg per day which represents a low exposure. In another study of 10 breastfeeding women receiving 0.39 mg/kg/day of fluoxetine, the average breast milk levels for fluoxetine and norfluoxetine ranged from 24.4-181.1 µg/L and 37.4-199.1 µg/L respectively. Peak milk concentrations occurred within 6 hours. The milk:plasma ratios for fluoxetine and norfluoxetine were 0.88 and 0.72, respectively. Fluoxetine plasma levels in one infant were undetectable (< 1 ng/mL). Using this data, an infant consuming 150 mL/kg/day would consume approximately 11-51 µg/kg/day total fluoxetine (and metabolite), which represents 5-9% of the maternal dose. No adverse effects were noted in the infants in this study. Severe colic, fussiness, and crying have been reported in one case report (Lester 1993). The mother was receiving a dose of 20 mg fluoxetine per day. Concentrations of fluoxetine and norfluoxetine in breast milk were 69 µg/L and 90 µg/L respectively. The plasma levels in the infant for fluoxetine and norfluoxetine were 340 ng/mL and 208 ng/mL respectively which is almost twice that of normal maternal ranges. The author does not report the maternal plasma levels but suggests they were similar to Isenberg's adult levels (100.5 ng/mL and 194.5 ng/mL for fluoxetine and norfluoxetine). In this infant, the plasma levels would approach those of a mother receiving twice the above 20 mg dose per day (40 mg/day). The symptoms resolved upon discontinuation of fluoxetine by the mother. It is not known if these reported side effects (colic, fussiness, crying) are common, although this author has received 3 other personal communications similar to this. However, current data on Sertraline and Paroxetine which suggest these medications have difficulty entering milk, and more importantly, the infant, may suggest that they are preferred agents over fluoxetine for therapy of depression in breastfeeding mothers.

Alternatives: Sertraline, Paroxetine

Pregnancy Risk Category: B

Adult Concerns: Nausea, tachycardia, hypotension, headache, anxiety, nervousness, insomnia, dry mouth, anorexia and visual disturbances.

Pediatric Concerns: Severe colic, fussiness, and crying have been reported in one case study.

Drug Interactions: Cimetidine may increase plasma levels 50%. Hallucinations have occurred when used with dextromethorphan. Serious fatal reactions have occurred when used after MAO inhibitors. Phenytoin may reduce plasma levels of fluoxetine by 50%. CNS toxicity may result if used with L-tryptophan. Fluoxetine may increase plasma levels of tricyclic antidepressants. Significant increase in propranolol levels have been reported. Effects of buspirone may be decreased. Serum carbamazepine levels may be increased resulting in toxicity. Bradycardia has been reported when used with diltiazem. Use with digoxin reduces digoxin levels by 15%. Lithium levels may be increased by fluoxetine with possible neurotoxicity. Sertraline did not effect lithium levels. Methadone levels have been significantly increased with SSRIs. Clearance of theophylline may be decreased by three fold. When used with warfarin, a significant increase in bleeding time has been reported.

AHL	= 2-3 days(fluoxetine)	**M/P**	= 0.286
PHL	=	**PB**	= 94.5%
PK	= 1.5 - 12 hours	**Oral**	= 100%
MW	= 309	**pKa**	=
Vd	= 2.6		

References:

1. Isenberg KE. Excretion of fluoxetine in human breast milk. J Clin Psychiatry 51:169, 1990.
2. Burch KJ, and Well BG. Fluoxetine/Norfluoxetine concentrations in human milk. Pediatrics 89:676, 1992.
3. Taddio A, Ito S, Koren G. Excretion of fluoxetine and its metabolite in human breast milk. Pediatric Res 35(4, part 2): 149a, 1994. Abstract.
4. Wisner KL, Perel JM, Findling RL: Antidepressant treatment during breast-feeding. Am J Psychiatry 153(9): 1132-1137, 1996.
5. Lester, BM et.al. Possible association between fluoxetine hydrochloride and colic in an infant. J. Am. Acad. Child. Adolesc. Psychiatry 32(6): 1253-1255, 1993.

Fluphenazine   Fax #1191

Trade: Prolixin, Permitil
Can/Aus/UK: Apo-Fluphenazine, Moditen, Modecate, Anatensol
Uses: Psychotherapeutic agent
AAP: Not reviewed

Fluphenazine is a phenothiazine tranquilizer and presently has the highest milligram potency of this family. Fluphenazine decanoate injections (IM) provide extremely long plasma levels with half-lives approaching 14.3 days at steady state. Members of this family generally have milk:plasma ratios ranging from 0.5 to 0.7. No specific reports on fluphenazine breast milk levels have been located.

Alternatives:

Pregnancy Risk Category: C

Adult Concerns: Depression, seizures, appetite stimulation, blood dyscrasia, weight gain, hepatic toxicity, sedation.

Pediatric Concerns: None reported, but observe for sedation.

Drug Interactions: Increased toxicity when administered with ethanol. CNS effects may be increased when used with lithium. May stimulate the effects of narcotics including respiratory depression.

AHL = 10-20 hours	M/P =
PHL =	PB = 91-99%
PK = 1.5 - 2 hours	Oral = Complete
MW = 438	pKa = 3.9, 8.1
Vd = 220	

References:
1. Ayd FJ. Excretion of psychotropic drugs in breast milk. In : International Drug Therapy Newsletter. Ayd Medical Communications. November-December 1973. Vol. 8.

Flurazepam   Fax #1192

Trade: Dalmane
Can/Aus/UK: Apo-Flurazepam, Dalmane, Novo-Flupam
Uses: Sedative, hypnotic
AAP: Not reviewed

Flurazepam is a sedative, hypnotic generally used as an aid for sleep. It belongs to the benzodiazepine (Valium) family. It is rapidly and completely metabolized to several long half-life active metabolites. Because most benzodiazepines are secreted into human milk, flurazepam entry into milk should be expected. However, no specific data on flurazepam breast milk levels are available. .

Alternatives: Lorazepam, Alprazolam

Pregnancy Risk Category: X

Adult Concerns: Sedation, tachycardia, jaundice, apnea.

Pediatric Concerns: None reported, but caution is recommended.

Observe for sedation.

Drug Interactions: Decreased effect when used with enzyme inducers such as barbiturates. Increased toxicity when used with other CNS depressants and cimetidine.

AHL = 47-100 hours		M/P	=
PHL =		PB	= 97%
PK = 0.5-1 hours		Oral	= Complete
MW = 388		pKa	= 1.9, 8.2
Vd = 3.4-5.5			

References:
1.   Drug Facts and Comparisons. 1995 ed. Facts and Comparisons, St. Louis.

Flurbiprofen   Fax #1193

Trade: Ansaid, Froben, Ocufen
Can/Aus/UK: Ansaid, Froben, Ocufen
Uses: Analgesic
AAP: Not reviewed

Flurbiprofen is a nonsteroidal analgesic similar in structure to ibuprofen, but used both as an ophthalmic preparation (in eyes) and orally.   In one study of 12 women and following nine oral doses (50mg/dose, 3-5 days postpartum) the concentration of flurbiprofen in two women ranged from 0.05 to 0.07 mg/L of milk, but was < 0.05 mg/L in 10 of the 12 women.   Concentrations in breast milk and plasma of nursing mothers suggest that a nursing infant would receive less than 0.1 mg flurbiprofen per day, a level considered exceedingly low. In another study of 10 nursing mothers following a single 100 mg dose, the average peak concentration of flurbiprofen in breast milk was 0.09 mg/L, or about 0.05% of the maternal dose.   Both of these studies suggest that the amount of flurbiprofen transferred in human milk would be clinically insignificant to the infant.

Alternatives: Ibuprofen

Pregnancy Risk Category: B/C

Adult Concerns: GI distress, diarrhea, constipation, cramping, may worsen jaundice.

Pediatric Concerns: None reported.

Drug Interactions: May prolong prothrombin time when used with warfarin. Antihypertensive effects of ACEi family may be blunted or completely abolished by NSAIDs. Some NSAIDs may block antihypertensive effect of beta blockers, diuretics. Used with cyclosporin, may dramatically increase renal toxicity. May increase digoxin, phenytoin, lithium levels. May increase toxicity of methotrexate. May increase bioavailability of penicillamine. Probenecid may increase NSAID levels.

AHL = 3.8-5.7 hours		**M/P**	= 0.008 - 0.013
PHL = 2.71 hours (children)		**PB**	= 99%
PK = 1.5 hours		**Oral**	= Complete
MW = 244		**pKa**	= 4.2
Vd = 0.1			

References:
1. Pharmaceutical Manufacturer's Package Insert, 1995.
2. Smith IJ, et.al. Flurbiprofen in postpartum women: plasma and breast milk disposition. J. Clin. Pharmacol. 29(2):174-84,1989.
3. Cox SR, Forbes KK, Excretion of flurbiprofen into breast milk. Pharmacother. 7:211-215, 1987.

Fluticasone   Fax #1474

Trade: Flonase, Flovent, Cutivate
Can/Aus/UK: Flovent, Flonase, Flixotide, Flixonase
Uses: Intranasal, inhaled steroid
AAP: Not reviewed

Fluticasone is a typical steroid primarily used intra-nasally for allergic rhinitis, and intrapulmonary for asthma. Intranasal form is called Flonase, inhaled form is Flovent. When instilled intra-nasally, the absolute bioavailability is less than 2%, so virtually none of the dose instilled is absorbed systemically. Oral absorption following inhaled fluticasone is approximately 30%, although almost instant first-pass absorption virtually eliminates plasma levels of fluticasone. Peak plasma levels following inhalation of 880 μg is only 0.1 to 1.0 nanogram/mL. Adrenocortical suppression following oral, or even systemic absorption at normal doses is extremely rare due to limited plasma levels. Plasma levels are not detectible when using suggested doses. Although fluticasone is secreted into milk of rodents, the dose used was many times higher than found under normal conditions. With the above oral and systemic bioavailability, and rapid first-pass uptake by the liver, it is not likely that milk levels will be clinically relevant, even with rather high doses.

Alternatives:

Pregnancy Risk Category: C

Adult Concerns: Intranasal: pruritus, headache (1-3%), burning (3-6%), epistaxis. Adverse effects associated with inhaled fluticasone include headache, nasal congestion, and oral candidiasis.

Pediatric Concerns: When used topically on large surface areas, some adrenal suppression has been noted. No effects have been reported in breastfeeding infants. In children receiving up to 5 times the normal inhaled dose (1000 μg/day), some growth suppression was noted.

Drug Interactions:

AHL = 7.8 hours.	**M/P** =	
PHL =	**PB** =	
PK = 15-60 minutes	**Oral** = Inhaled(30%)	
MW = 500	**pKa** =	
Vd = 3.7		

References:
1.   Pharmaceutical Manufacturer's Package Insert, 1996.

2.   Harding SM: The human pharmacology of fluticasone propionate. Respir Med 84(Suppl A):25-29, 1990.
3.   Todd G, Dunlop K, McNaboe J et al: Growth and adrenal suppression in asthmatic children treated with high-dose fluticasone propionate. Lancet 348:27-29, 1996.

Fluvastatin   Fax #1194

Trade: Lescol
Can/Aus/UK: Lescol, Vastin
Uses: Reduces blood cholesterol levels
AAP: Not reviewed

Fluvastatin is an inhibitor of cholesterol synthesis in the liver. Fluvastatin levels in human milk are reported to be 2 fold that of serum levels.   Effect on infant is unknown but could reduce cholesterol synthesis in infant.   Atherosclerosis is a chronic process and discontinuation of lipid-lowering drugs during pregnancy and lactation should have little to no impact on the outcome of long-term therapy of primary hypercholesterolemia.   Cholesterol and other products of cholesterol biosynthesis are essential components for fetal and neonatal development and the use of cholesterol-lowering drugs would not be advisable under any circumstances.

Alternatives:

Pregnancy Risk Category: X

Adult Concerns: Headache, insomnia, dyspepsia, diarrhea, gas, elevated liver enzymes.

Pediatric Concerns: None reported, but reduced plasma cholesterol levels could occur.

Drug Interactions: Anticoagulant effect of warfarin may be increased.

AHL = 1.2 hours	**M/P**	**= 2.0**
PHL =	**PB**	**= > 98%**
PK = < 1 hr.	**Oral**	**= 20-30%**

MW =   pKa =
Vd =

References:
1.   Drug Facts and Comparisons. 1994 ed. Facts and Comparisons, St. Louis.
2.   Pharmaceutical Manufacturer's Package Insert, 1995.

Fluvoxamine   Fax #1480

Trade: Luvox
Can/Aus/UK: Luvox, Apo-Fluvoxamine, Alti-Fluvoxamine, Faverin, Floxyfral, Myroxim
Uses: Antidepressant
AAP: Not reviewed

Although structurally dissimilar to the other serotonin reuptake inhibitors, fluvoxamine provides increased synaptic serotonin levels in the brain. It has several hepatic metabolites which are not active. Its primary indications are for the treatment of obsessive-compulsive disorders (OCD) although it also functions as an antidepressant. There are a number of significant drug-drug interactions with this product. In a case report of one 23 year old mother and following a dose of 100 mg twice daily for 2 weeks, the maternal plasma level of fluvoxamine base was 0.31 mg/Liter and the milk concentration was 0.09 mg/Liter. The authors reported a theoretical dose to infant of 0.0104 mg/kg/day of fluvoxamine, which is only 0.5% of the maternal dose. According to the authors, the infant suffered no side effects as a result of this intake and that this dose poses little risk to a nursing infant.

Alternatives: Sertraline, Paroxetine

Pregnancy Risk Category: C

Adult Concerns: Somnolence, insomnia, nervousness, nausea.

Pediatric Concerns: None reported in one study.

Drug Interactions: Increased toxicity may be result when used with terfenadine and astemizole. Sometimes serious fatal reactions have occurred close following the use of MAO inhibitors. Smokers have a 25% increase in the metabolism of fluvoxamine. Enhanced CNS toxicity when used with L-tryptophan. Plasma tricyclic antidepressant levels may be increased when used with fluvoxamine. Plasma levels of propranolol have been increased by five fold when used with fluvoxamine. Bradycardia has resulted when used with diltiazem. Lithium levels may be increased by fluvoxamine with possible neurotoxicity. Increased bleeding time may result when used with warfarin.

AHL	= 15.6 hours	M/P	= 0.29
PHL	=	PB	= 80%
PK	= 3-8 hours	Oral	= 53%
MW	= 318	pKa	=
Vd	=		

References:
1. Wright S, Dawling S et.al. Excretion of fluvoxamine in breast milk (letter). Br. J. Clin. Pharmacol. 31:209, 1991.

Folic Acid   Fax #1195

Trade: Folacin, Wellcovorin
Can/Aus/UK: Apo-Folic, Folvite, Novo-Folacid, Accomin, Bioglan, Daily, Megafol
Uses: Vitamin
AAP: Approved by the American Academy of Pediatrics for use in breastfeeding mothers

Folic acid is an essential vitamin. Individuals most susceptible to folic acid deficiency are the pregnant patient, and those receiving anticonvulsants or birth control medications. Folic acid supplementation is now strongly recommended in women prior to becoming pregnant due to a documented reduction of spinal cord malformations. Folic acid is actively secreted into breast milk even if mother is deficient. If maternal diet is adequate, folic acid is not generally required. The infant receives all required from a normal milk supply. Cooperman (1982) determined milk folic acid content to be 15.2 ng/mL in colostrum, 16.3 ng/mL in transitional, and 33.4 ng/mL in mature milk. In one study of 11 breastfeeding mothers receiving 0.8-1 mg/day of folic acid, the folic acid secreted into human milk averaged 45.6 µg/L. Excessive doses (> 1 mg/day) are not generally recommended.

Alternatives:

Pregnancy Risk Category: A if dose = RDA
C if dose exceeds RDA

Adult Concerns: Allergies, rash, nausea, anorexia, bitter taste.

Pediatric Concerns: None reported.

Drug Interactions: May increase phenytoin metabolism and reduce levels. Phenytoin, primidone, sulfasalazine, and para-aminosalicylic acid may decrease serum folate concentrations and cause deficiency. Oral contraceptives also impair folate metabolism producing depletion.

AHL =		M/P	=
PHL =		PB	=
PK = 30-60 min.		Oral	= 76-93%
MW = 441		pKa	=
Vd =			

References:
1. Cooperman JM, et. al. The folate in human milk. Am J Clin Nutr 36:576-80, 1982.
2. Tamura T, et. al. Human milk folate and folate status in lactating mothers and their infants. Am J Clin Nutr 33:193-7, 1980.
3. Smith AM, et.al. Folate supplementation during lactation: maternal folate status, human milk folate content, and their relationship to infant folate status. J.Pediatr. Gastroenterol.Nutrit. 2:622-628, 1983.

Formaldehyde   Fax #1506

Trade: Formaldehyde, Formalin, Methyl Aldehyde
Can/Aus/UK:
Uses: Preservative
AAP: Not reviewed

Formaldehyde exposure in laboratory or embalming environments is strictly controlled by federal regulations to a permissible level of 2 ppm. At room temperature it is a colorless gas with a pungent, irritating odor detectible at 0.5 ppm. At exposure to 1-4 ppm, formaldehyde is a strong mucous membrane irritant, producing burning and lacrimation. Formaldehyde is rapidly destroyed by plasma and tissue enzymes and it is very unlikely than any would enter human milk following environmental exposures. However, acute intoxications following high oral or inhaled doses could lead to significant levels of maternal plasma formic acid which could enter milk. There are no data suggesting untoward side effects in nursing infants as a result of mild to minimal environmental exposure of the mother.

Alternatives:

Pregnancy Risk Category: X

Adult Concerns: Cough, mucous membrane irritation, chest pain, dyspnea, and wheezing occur in individuals exposed to 5-30 ppm.

Pediatric Concerns: None reported via milk.

Drug Interactions:

AHL =	M/P =
PHL =	PB =
PK =	Oral =
MW = 30	pKa =
Vd =	

References:
1.   Ellenhorn MJ, Barceloux DG. In: Medical Toxicology, Elsevier, New York, USA, 1988.

Foscarnet Sodium   Fax #1196

Trade: Foscavir
Can/Aus/UK: Foscavir
Uses: Antiviral for herpes, CMV infections
AAP: Not reviewed

Foscarnet is an antiviral used to treat mucocutaneous herpes simplex manifestations, and cytomegalovirus retinal infections in patients with AIDS. It is not known if foscarnet is secreted into human milk, but studies in animals indicate levels in milk were three times higher than serum levels (suggesting a Milk:plasma ratio of 3.0). Foscarnet is a potent and potentially dangerous drug including significant renal toxicity, seizures, and deposition in bone and teeth.

Alternatives:

Pregnancy Risk Category: C

Adult Concerns: Fever, nausea, diarrhea, vomiting, tremor, headache, fatigue, kidney toxicity, anemia due to bone marrow suppression.

Pediatric Concerns: None reported but caution is urged.

Drug Interactions: Increased hypocalcemia with pentamidine, and increased seizures with ciprofloxacin.

AHL = 3 hours	M/P	= 3.0
PHL =	PB	= 14-17%
PK = Immediate(IV)	Oral	= 12-21%
MW = 192	pKa	=
Vd =		

References:
1. Pharmaceutical Manufacturer's Package Insert, 1995.
2. Sjovall J, et al. Pharmacokinetics and absorption of foscarnet after intravenous and oral administration to patients with human immunodeficiency virus. Clin Pharmacol Ther 44:65-73, 1988.

Fosfomycin Trometamol — Fax #1595

Trade: Monuril
Can/Aus/UK: Monuril
Uses: Urinary antibiotic
AAP: Not reviewed

Fosfomycin is a broad-spectrum antibiotic used primarily for uncomplicated urinary tract infections. It is believed safe for use in pregnancy and has been used in children less than 1 year of age. Fosfomycin absorption is largely dependent on the salt form, trometamol salts are modestly absorbed (34-58%), and calcium salts are poorly absorbed (< 12%). Fosfomycin secreted into human milk would likely be in the calcium form and is unlikely to be absorbed as secreted in human milk. Foods and the acidic milieu of the stomach both significantly reduce oral absorption. Levels secreted into human milk have been reported to be about 10% of the maternal plasma level (4). Generally, a single 3 gm oral dose is effective treatment for many urinary tract infections in women. It is not likely that the levels present in breast milk would produce untoward effects in a breastfeeding infant.

Alternatives:

Pregnancy Risk Category:

Adult Concerns: GI symptoms include nausea, vomiting, diarrhea, epigastric discomfort, anorexia. Skin rashes and pruritus have been reported.

Pediatric Concerns: None reported via milk.

Drug Interactions: Antacids, calcium salts and foods will reduce absorption. Metoclopramide reduces serum concentration, by reducing oral bioavailability.

AHL = 4-8 hours	**M/P = 0.1**
PHL = 5-7 hours	**PB = < 3%**
PK = 1.5-3 hours	**Oral = 34-58%**
MW = 138	**pKa =**
Vd = 0.22	

References:

1. Bergan T: Degree of absorption, pharmacokinetics of fosfomycin trometamol and duration of antibacterial activity. Infection 8(suppl 2):S65-S69, 1990.
2. Bergan T: Pharmacokinetic comparison between fosfomycin and other phosphonic acid derivatives. Chemotherapy 36(suppl 1):10-18, 1990.
3. Segre G, Bianchi E, Cataldi A et al: Pharmacokinetic profile of fosfomycin trometamol (Monuril). Eur Urol 13(suppl 1):56-63,1987.
4. Kirby WMM. Pharmacokinetics of fosfomycin. Chemotherapy 23, suppl 1: 141-151,1977.

Fosinopril   Fax #1197

Trade: Monopril
Can/Aus/UK: Monopril, Staril
Uses: Antihypertensive, ACE inhibitor
AAP: Not reviewed

Fosinopril is a pro-drug that is metabolized by the gut and liver upon absorption to fosinoprilat, which is an ACE inhibitor used as an antihypertensive. The manufacturer reports that the ingestion of 20 mg daily for three days resulted in detectible levels in human milk, although no values are provided. See enalapril, benazepril, captopril as alternatives.

Alternatives: Enalapril, Benazepril, Captopril

Pregnancy Risk Category: D

Adult Concerns: Anemia, dry cough, headache, dizziness, diarrhea, fatigue, nausea, vomiting, hypotension.

Pediatric Concerns: None reported.

Drug Interactions: Bioavailability of ACEi may be decreased when used with antacids. Capsaicin may exacerbate coughing associated with

ACEi treatment. Pharmacologic effects of ACE inhibitors may be increased. Increased plasma levels of digoxin may result. Increased serum lithium levels may result when used with ACE inhibitors.

AHL	= 11-35 hours	M/P	=
PHL	=	PB	= 95 %
PK	= 3 hours	Oral	= 30-36%
MW	= 564	pKa	=
Vd	=		

References:
1. Drug Facts and Comparisons. 1995 ed. Facts and Comparisons, St. Louis.
2. Pharmaceutical Manufacturer's Package Insert, 1995.

Furazolidone   Fax #1437

Trade: Furoxone
Can/Aus/UK: Furoxone
Uses: Antibiotic
AAP: Not reviewed

Furazolidone belongs to the nitrofurantoin family of antibiotics (see nitrofurantoin). It has a broad spectrum of activity against gram-positive and gram-negative enteric organisms including cholera, but is generally used for giardiasis. Following an oral dose, furazolidone is poorly absorbed (< 5%) and is largely inactivated in the gut. Concentrations transferred to milk are unreported, but the total amounts would be exceedingly low due to the low maternal plasma levels attained by this product. Due to poor oral absorption, systemic absorption in a breastfeeding infant would likely be minimal. Caution should be observed in newborns.

Alternatives:

Pregnancy Risk Category: C

Adult Concerns: Hemolytic anemia in newborns, nausea, vomiting, diarrhea, abdominal pain.   Dark yellow to brown discoloration of urine.

Pediatric Concerns: Caution is urged in neonates < 1 month due to possibility of hemolytic anemia.

Drug Interactions: Increased effect when used with sympathomimetic amines, tricyclic antidepressants, MAO inhibitors, meperidine, dextromethorphan, fluoxetine, paroxetine, sertraline, trazodone.

AHL =		M/P	=
PHL =		PB	=
PK =		Oral	= < 5%
MW = 225		pKa	=
Vd =			

References:
1.McEvoy GE(ed):AHFS Drug Information, New York, NY. 1995.

Furosemide   Fax #1198

Trade: Lasix
Can/Aus/UK: Apo-Furosemide, Novo-Semide, Lasix, Frusemide, Uremide, Frusid
Uses: Loop diuretic
AAP: Not reviewed

Furosemide is a potent loop diuretic with a rather short duration of action. Furosemide has been found in breast milk although the levels are unreported. Diuretics, by reducing blood volume, could potentially reduce breast milk production, although this is largely theoretical. Furosemide is frequently used in neonates in pediatric units, so pediatric use is common.   The oral bioavailability of furosemide in newborns is exceedingly poor and very high oral doses are required (1-4mg/Kg BID).   It is very unlikely the amount transferred into human milk would produce any effects in a nursing infant, although its maternal use could suppress lactation.

Alternatives:

Pregnancy Risk Category: C

Adult Concerns: Hypotension, fluid loss, potassium loss.

Pediatric Concerns: None reported.

Drug Interactions: Furosemide interferes with hypoglycemic effect of antidiabetic agents. NSAIDS may reduce diuretic effect of furosemide. Effects of antihypertensive agents may be increased. Renal clearance of lithium is decreased. Increases ototoxicity of aminoglycosides.

AHL = 92 minutes		M/P	=
PHL =		PB	= >98%
PK = 1-2 hours		Oral	= 60-70%
MW = 331		pKa	=
Vd =			

References:
1. Healy M. Suppressing lactation with oral diuretics. Lancet 1:1353-1354, 1961.
2. Pharmaceutical Manufacturer's Package Insert, 1995.

Gabapentin   Fax #1477

Trade: Neurontin
Can/Aus/UK: Neurontin
Uses: Anticonvulsant
AAP: Not reviewed

Gabapentin is a newer anticonvulsant used primarily for partial (focal) seizures with or without secondary generalization. Unlike many anticonvulsants, gabapentin is excreted by the kidneys without metabolism, it does not induce hepatic enzymes, and is remarkably well tolerated. No reports are available on its transfer into human milk.

Alternatives:

Pregnancy Risk Category: C

Adult Concerns: Dizziness, somnolence, weight gain, vomiting, tremor, and CNS depression. Abrupt withdrawal may induce severe seizures.

Pediatric Concerns: None reported. Cleared for children > 12 yrs.

Drug Interactions: Antacids reduce gabapentin absorption by 20%. Cimetidine may decrease clearance of gabapentin. No interaction has been reported with other anticonvulsants. Antacids may reduce oral absorption by 20%.

AHL = 5-7 hours		**M/P** =	
PHL =		**PB** = < 3%	
PK = 1-3 hours		**Oral** = 50-60%	
MW =		**pKa** =	
Vd = 0.8			

References:
1. Goa KL & Sorkin EM: Gabapentin: a review of its pharmacological properties and clinical potential in epilepsy. Drugs 46:409-427, 1993.
2. Ramsay RE: Clinical efficacy and safety of gabapentin. Neurology 44(Suppl 5):S23-S30, 1994.
3. Dichter MA & Brodie MJ: New antiepileptic drugs. J Med 334:1583-1590, 1996.

Gadopentetate   Fax #1199

Trade: Magnevist, Gadolinium
Can/Aus/UK: Magnevist
Uses: Radiopaque agent (MRI)
AAP: Not reviewed

Sometimes called gadolinium, gadopentetate is a radiopaque agent used in magnetic resonance imaging of the kidney. It is nonionic, non-iodinated and has low osmolarity and contains a gadolinium ion as the radiopaque entity. Following a dose of 7 mmol, the amount of gadopentetate secreted in breast milk was 3.09, 2.8, 1.08, and 0.5 umol/L at 2, 11, 17, and 24 hours respectively. The cumulative amount excreted from both breasts in 24 hours was only 0.023% of the administered dose. Oral absorption is minimal, only 0.8% of gadopentetate is absorbed. These authors suggest that only 0.013 mmol of a gadolinium-containing compound would be absorbed by the infant in 24 hours, which is incredibly low. They further suggest that 24 hours of pumping would eliminate risks, although this seems rather extreme in view of the short (1 hr) half-life, poor oral bioavailability, and limited milk levels.

Alternatives:

Pregnancy Risk Category: C

Adult Concerns: Headache, rash, nausea, dry mouth, altered taste.

Pediatric Concerns: Virtually none enters milk. No reported side-effects via milk.

Drug Interactions:

AHL = < 1-2 hours		**M/P** =	
PHL =		**PB** =	
PK = Immediate((V)		**Oral** = 0.8%	
MW = 547		**pKa** =	
Vd =			

References:
1. Rofsky NM, et.al. Quantitative analysis of gadopentetate dimeglumine secreted in breast milk. J. Magnetic Resonance Imaging. 3:131, 1993.

Gadoteridol   Fax #1591

Trade: ProHance, Gadoteridol, Gadolinium
Can/Aus/UK: ProHance
Uses: Radiopaque agent for MRI
AAP: Not reviewed

Gadoteridol is a nonionic, non-iodinated gadolinium chelate complex used as a radiopaque agent in MRI scans. The metabolism of gadoteridol is unknown, but a similar gadolinium salt (gadopentetate) is not metabolized at all. The half-life is brief (1.6 hours) and the volume of distribution is very small, suggesting that gadoteridol does not penetrate tissues well, and is unlikely to penetrate milk in significant quantities. A similar compound, gadopentetate, is barely detectible in breast milk. Although not reported, the oral bioavailability is probably similar to gadopenetate, which is minimal to none. No data are available on the transfer of gadoteridol into human milk, although it is probably minimal. A brief interruption of breastfeeding for 12-24 hours should remove risk.

Alternatives: Gadopentetate

Pregnancy Risk Category: C

Adult Concerns: Nausea, bad taste, headache, rash, urticaria, chest pain rarely.

Pediatric Concerns: None reported via milk.

Drug Interactions:

AHL = 1.6 hours		M/P	=
PHL =		PB	=
PK =		Oral	= Poor
MW =		pKa	=
Vd = 0.2			

References:
1. Pharmaceutical Manufacturer's package insert, 1997.

Gallium-67 Citrate   Fax #1200

Trade: Gallium-67 Citrate
Can/Aus/UK:
Uses: Radioactive isotope

AAP: Radioactive compound that require temporary cessation of breastfeeding.

Gallium-67 Citrate is a radioactive substance used for bone scanning. In one breastfeeding mother who received 3 mCi, the radioactive content in breast milk was 0.15, 0.045, and 0.01 µCi/mL at 3, 7, and 14 days respectively. If the infant ingested milk, the whole body exposure would have been very significant, 1.4-2.0 rad/mCi. This is significantly more than the mother's exposure of only 0.26 rad/mCi. Therefore, a significant radioactive hazard exists. Whole body scans showed intense radiation in the breast tissue of the mother. With a 14 day waiting period, the theoretical whole body dose to the infant would be 0.04 rads and 0.07 rads to the skeleton. Radioactive half-life of Gallium-67 is 78.3 hours, while the biological half-life of the gallium ion is 9 days. These approximations suggest that breastfeeding should be interrupted for a minimum of 14 days following Gallium-67 scanning in the mother.

Alternatives:

Pregnancy Risk Category:

Adult Concerns:

Pediatric Concerns: Significant radiation exposure. Remove from breast for 14 days.

Drug Interactions:

AHL = 78.3 hours	**M/P**	=
PHL =	**PB**	=
PK =	**Oral**	=
MW =	**pKa**	=
Vd =		

References:
1. Tobin, R. and Schneider, P. Uptake of 67-Ga in the lactating breast and its persistence in milk: a case report.. J. Nucl. Med. 17: 1055-56, 1976.

Garlic   Fax #1536

Trade: Allium, Stinkin Rose, Rustic Treacle, Camphor Of The Poor
Can/Aus/UK:
Uses: Herbal antioxidant
AAP: Not reviewed

Garlic contains a number of sulfur-containing compounds, which when ground, are metabolized to allicin, which is responsible for the pungent odor of garlic, and the pharmacologic effects attributed to garlic. Garlic has been reported to increase the levels of important plasma antioxidants, glutathione and catalase, probably due to the allicin content. Five sulfur containing compounds have been isolated which produce profound inhibition of lipid peroxidation in liver cells. A number of studies have found hypolipidemic effects of garlic oil, reducing plasma cholesterol, triglyceride levels and elevating HDL levels significantly. Garlic oil also inhibits platelet aggregation, thus reducing risk of thrombosis. Taken together, there is significant evidence to suggest that garlic oil may reduce the risks of cardiovascular disease, reducing plasma lipids, and reducing the risk of clot formation. Garlic is known to be modestly antimicrobial, having about 1% of the antimicrobial potency of penicillin. Interestingly, the hypolipidemic and antimicrobial properties appear to reside in the odiferous constituents, and may not be present in the "deodorized" oils. Although garlic oil is commonly used, the safety for long term use is still unresolved. The extract has caused a reduction in liver and kidney protein in animal studies, and a potential interaction with other anticoagulants (warfarin) should be expected. Transfer into human milk is probable but not reported.

Alternatives:

Pregnancy Risk Category:

Adult Concerns: Few reported, but observe for excessive bleeding.

Pediatric Concerns: None reported.

Drug Interactions: May enhance anticoagulant effects of warfarin.

References:
1.   Bissett NG. In: Herbal Drugs and Phytopharmaceuticals. Medpharm Scientific Publishers, CRC Press, Boca Raton, 1994.
2.   Review of Natural Products. Facts and Comparisons, St. Louis, Mo. 1996.

Gentamicin   Fax #1201

Trade: Garamycin
Can/Aus/UK: Alocomicin, Cidomycin, Garamycin, Garatec, Palacos, Septopal
Uses: Aminoglycoside antibiotic
AAP: Not reviewed

Gentamicin is a narrow spectrum antibiotic generally used for gram negative infections. The oral absorption of gentamicin (<1%) is generally nil with exception of premature neonates where small amounts may be absorbed. In one study of 10 women given 80 mg three times daily IM for 5 days postpartum, milk levels were measured on day 4. Gentamicin levels in milk were 0.42, 0.48, 0.49, and 0.41 mg/L at 1, 3, 5, and 7 hours respectively. The milk:plasma ratios were 0.11 at one hour and 0.44 at 7 hours. Plasma gentamicin levels in neonates were small, were found in only 5 of the 10 neonates, and averaged 0.41 µg/ml. The authors estimate that daily ingestion via breast milk would be 307 µg for a 3.6 Kg neonate (normal neonatal dose = 2.5 mg/Kg every 12 hours). These amounts would be clinically irrelevant in most infants.

Alternatives:

Pregnancy Risk Category: C

Adult Concerns: Changes in GI flora, diarrhea, kidney damage, etc.

Pediatric Concerns: None reported.

Drug Interactions: Increased toxicity when used with certain penicillins, cephalosporins, amphotericin B, loop diuretics, and neuromuscular blocking agents.

AHL = 2-3 hours	M/P = 0.11-0.44
PHL = 3-5.5 hours (neonates)	PB = <10-30 %.
PK = 30-90 min.(IM)	Oral = < 1%
MW =	pKa = 8.2
Vd = 0.28(adult)	

References:

1. McCracken, G and Nelson, J. The Current status of gentamicin for the neonate and young infant. Am. J. Dis. Child. 124:13-14, 1972.
2. Celiloglu M, Celiker S, Guven H, et.al. Gentamicin excretion and uptake from breast milk by nursing infants. Obstet. Gynecol. 84(2):263-5, 1994.

Gentian Violet   Fax #1466

Trade: Crystal Violet, Methylrosaniline Chloride, Gentian Violet
Can/Aus/UK:
Uses: Antifungal, antimicrobial
AAP: Not reviewed

Gentian violet is an older product that when used topically and orally is an exceptionally effective antifungal and antimicrobial. It is a strong purple dye that is difficult to remove. Gentian violet has been found to be equivalent to ketoconazole and far superior to nystatin in treating oral (not esophageal) candidiasis in patients with advanced AIDS. Oral solutions used for pediatric patients should be 0.25% to 0.5% and in aqueous (non-alcoholic) solutions. Higher concentrations are known to be very irritating, leading to oral ulceration and necrotic skin reactions in children. If used, a small swab should be soaked in the solution, and then have the baby suck on the swab, or apply it directly to the affected areas in the mouth no more than once or twice daily for no more than 3 days. Direct application to the nipple has been reported and is indicated for candidiasis of the nipple.

Alternatives:

Pregnancy Risk Category: C

Adult Concerns: Oral ulceration, stomatitis, staining of skin and clothing, nausea, vomiting, diarrhea.

Pediatric Concerns: Irritation leading to buccal ulcerations and necrotic skin reactions if used excessively and in higher concentrations. Nausea, vomiting, diarrhea.

Drug Interactions:

References:
1. McEvoy GE(ed): AHFS Drug information, New York, NY. 1995.
2. Newman J. Personal communication, 1997.

Ginkgo Biloba   Fax #1593

Trade: Ginkgo
Can/Aus/UK:
Uses: Herbal antioxidant
AAP: Not reviewed

Ginkgo Biloba is the world's oldest living tree. Extracts of the leaves (GBE) contain numerous chemical compounds including dimeric flavones and their glycosides, amino acids such as 6-hydroxyknurenic acid, and numerous other compounds. The seeds contain ginkgotoxin, which is particularly toxic, and should not be consumed. Numerous studies reviewing gingko have been reported, including treatments for cerebral insufficiency, asthma, dementia and circulatory disorders. Gingko appears particularly efficient at increasing cerebral blood flow, with increases varying from 20-70%, Older patients were more responsive. This supports the clinical use of GBE to treat cognitive impairment in the elderly. The anxiolytic properties of GBE have been reported to be due to MAO inhibition in animal studies. Ginkgolides inhibit platelet-activating factor and is believed responsible for the anti-allergic and anti-asthmatic properties of this extract. No data are available on the transfer of GBE into human milk. Thus far, with exception of the seeds, GBE appears relatively non-toxic.

Alternatives:

Pregnancy Risk Category:

Adult Concerns: Headache, dizziness, heart palpitations, GI symptoms, dermatologic reactions.

Pediatric Concerns: None reported via human milk.

Drug Interactions:

References:
1. Review of Natural Products. Facts and Comparisons, St. Louis, Mo. 1998.
2. Newall CA, Anderson LA, Phillipson JD. In: Herbal Medicines, A guide for the Health-care Professionals, The Pharmaceutical Press, London, 1996.

Ginseng   Fax #1537

Trade: Panax
Can/Aus/UK: Minomycin, Red Kooga
Uses: Herbal tonic
AAP: Not reviewed

Ginseng is perhaps the most popular and widely recognized product in the herbal remedy market. It is available in many forms, but the most common is the American root called Panax quinquefolium L. The root primarily contains steroid-like saponin glycosides (ginsenosides), of which there are at least two dozen and vary as a function of species, age, location, and season when harvested. Early claims have suggested that ginseng provided "strengthening" effects, and included increased mental capacity for work. Animal studies have suggested that ginseng can increase swimming time, prevent stress-induced ulcers, stimulate certain immune cells, etc. A number of studies, mostly small and poorly controlled, have been reported and many suggest beneficial effects of ingesting ginseng, with minimal side effects. Reported toxicities have included estrogen-like effects including diffuse mammary nodularity, vaginal bleeding, etc. The most commonly reported event is nervousness, excitation, morning diarrhea, and inability to concentrate. No data are available concerning transfer into human milk.

Alternatives:

Pregnancy Risk Category:

Adult Concerns: Excitement, nervousness, inability to concentrate, diarrhea, skin eruptions, hypertension, hypoglycemia, mammary nodularity. Ginseng products sometimes contain germanium, which can induce a state of severe loop-diuretic resistance.

Pediatric Concerns: None reported, but caution is urged.

Drug Interactions:

References:
1. Review of Natural Products. Facts and Comparisons, St. Louis, Mo. 1996.
2. Bissett NG. In: Herbal Drugs and Phytopharmaceuticals. Medpharm Scientific Publishers, CRC Press, Boca Raton, 1994.

Glimepiride   Fax #1550

Trade: Amaryl
Can/Aus/UK:
Uses: Lowers plasma glucose
AAP: Not reviewed

Glimepiride is a second-generation sulfonylurea used to lower plasma glucose in patients with non-insulin dependent diabetes mellitus. No data are available on the transfer of this product into human milk. However, rodent studies demonstrated significant transfer and plasma levels in pups. Caution is urged if used in breastfeeding humans. Observe for hypoglycemia.

Alternatives:

Pregnancy Risk Category: C

Adult Concerns: Hypoglycemia, nausea, hyponatremia, dizziness, headache, elevated liver enzymes, blurred vision.

Pediatric Concerns: None reported via milk. Observe for hypoglycemia.

Drug Interactions: The hypoglycemic effect of sulfonylureas may be increased by non-steroidal analgesics, salicylates, sulfonamides, coumarins, probenecid, and other drugs with high protein binding. Numerous other interactions exist, see product information.

AHL = 9 hours		M/P	=
PHL =		PB	= 99%
PK = 2-3 hours		Oral	= 100%
MW = 490		pKa	=
Vd = 37			

References:
1. Pharmaceutical manufactures package insert, 1998.
2. Bressler R & Johnson DG: Pharmacological regulation blood glucose levels in non-insulin-dependent diabetes mellitus. Arch Intern Med 157:836-848, 1997.

Glipizide   Fax #1202

Trade: Glucotrol XL, Glucotrol
Can/Aus/UK: Melizide, Minidiab, Glibenese, Minodiab
Uses: Prolonged release hypoglycemic agent
AAP: Not reviewed

Glipizide is a potent hypoglycemic agent that belongs to sulfonylurea family. It is formulated in regular and extended release formulations and it is used only for non insulin-dependent (Type II) diabetes. Thus the half-life and time-to-peak depends on the formulation used. It reduces glucose levels by stimulating insulin secretion from the pancreas. No reports on transfer into human milk were found. Other sulfonylureas (tolbutamide, chlorpropamide) are known to pass into milk in low concentrations. Although hypoglycemia in infants is a potential problem, no reports of such have been published. AHL= 2-5 hours (Glucotrol), 24 hours (Glucotrol-XL).

Alternatives:

Pregnancy Risk Category: C

Adult Concerns: Hypoglycemia, jaundice, nausea, vomiting, diarrhea, constipation.

Pediatric Concerns: None reported, but observe for hypoglycemia.

Drug Interactions: The hypoglycemic effect may be enhanced by : anticoagulants, chloramphenicol, clofibrate, fenfluramine, fluconazole, H2 antagonists, magnesium salts, methyldopa, MAO inhibitors, probenecid, salicylates, TCAs, sulfonamides. The hypoglycemic effect may be reduced by: beta blockers, cholestyramine, diazoxide, phenytoin, rifampin, thiazide diuretics.

AHL = 1.1-3.7 hours.		M/P	=
PHL =		PB	= 92-99 %
PK = 6-12 hours (XL)		Oral	= 80-100%
MW = 446		pKa	=
Vd =			

References:
1.   Pharmaceutical Manufacturer's Package Insert, 1996.

Glucosamine   Fax #1581

Trade: Glucosamine
Can/Aus/UK:
Uses: Antiarthritic
AAP: Not reviewed

Glucosamine is an endogenous amino monosaccharide that has been reported effective in resolving symptoms of osteoarthritis. Administered in large doses, most is sequestered in the liver with only minimal amounts reaching other tissues, thus oral bioavailability is low. Most of the oral dose is metabolized in the liver and subsequently incorporated into other plasma proteins. No data are available on transfer into human milk. Because glucosamine is primarily sequestered and metabolized in the liver, and because the plasma levels are almost undetectable, it is unlikely that much would enter human milk. Further, the fact it is so poorly bioavailable, it is unlikely that an infant would receive clinically relevant amounts.

Alternatives:

Pregnancy Risk Category:

Adult Concerns: Minimal but include nausea, dyspepsia, vomiting, drowsiness, headache and skin rash. Peripheral edema and tachycardia have been reported.

Pediatric Concerns: None reported via milk.

Drug Interactions:

AHL = 0.3 hours	M/P	=
PHL =	PB	= 0%
PK =	Oral	= < 26%
MW = 179	pKa	=

Vd = 0.035

References:
1.   Setnikar I, Palumbo R, Canali S et al: Pharmacokinetics of glucosamine in man. Arzneimittelforschung 43:1109-1113, 1993.

Glyburide   Fax #1203

Trade: Micronase, Diabeta, Glynase
Can/Aus/UK: Diabeta, Euglucon, Gen-Glybe, Daonil
Uses: Hypoglycemic, antidiabetic agent
AAP: Not reviewed

Glyburide is a "second generation" sulfonylurea agent useful in the treatment of non insulin-dependent (Type II) diabetes mellitus. It belongs to the sulfonylurea family (tolbutamide, glipizide) of hypoglycemic agents of which glyburide is one of the most potent. Glyburide apparently stimulates insulin secretion, thus reducing plasma glucose. Although no data exist on the secretion of glyburide into breast milk, others in this family are secreted in low levels, and it is likely that this product may attain even lower levels than the first generation family. Glyburide apparently does not even cross the placenta. Although we do not have reports of breast milk levels, it is likely (theoretical) that breast milk levels will be very low as well.

Alternatives:

Pregnancy Risk Category: B

Adult Concerns: Hypoglycemia, headache, anorexia, nausea, heartburn, allergic skin rashes.

Pediatric Concerns: None reported but observe for hypoglycemia, weakness.

Drug Interactions: Thiazide diuretics and beta blockers may decrease efficacy of glyburide. Increased toxicity may result from use with phenylbutazone, oral anticoagulants, hydantoins, salicylates, NSAIDS, sulfonamides. Alcohol increases disulfiram effect.

AHL	= 4-13.7 hours	**M/P**	=
PHL	=	**PB**	= 99%
PK	= 2-3 hours	**Oral**	= Complete
MW	= 494	**pKa**	=
Vd	= 0.73		

References:
1. Pharmaceutical Manufacturer's Package Insert, 1998.
2. McEvoy GE(ed):AHFS Drug Information, New York, NY. 1995.

Glycopyrrolate   Fax #1541

Trade: Robinul
Can/Aus/UK: Robinul
Uses: Anticholinergic
AAP: Not reviewed

Glycopyrrolate is a quaternary ammonium anticholinergic used prior to surgery to dry secretions. After administration, its plasma half-life is exceedingly short (< 5 min.) with most of the product being distribution out of the plasma compartment rapidly. No data on transfer into human milk are available, but due to its short plasma half-life, and its quaternary structure, it is very unlikely that significant quantities would penetrate milk. Further, along with the poor oral bioavailability of this product, it is very remote that glycopyrrolate would pose a significant risk to a breastfeeding infant.

Alternatives:

Pregnancy Risk Category: B

Adult Concerns: Blurred vision, dry mouth, tachycardia.

Pediatric Concerns: None reported via milk.

Drug Interactions: May reduce effect of levodopa. Increased toxicity when used with amantadine and cyclopropane.

AHL = 1.7 hours	M/P	=
PHL =	PB	=
PK = 5 hours(oral)	Oral	= 10-25%
MW = 398	pKa	=
Vd = 0.64		

References:
1. Lacy C. et.al. Drug information handbook. Lexi-Comp, Hudson(Cleveland), Oh. 1996.
2. Drug Facts and Comparisons. 1996. ed. Facts and Comparisons, St. Louis.

Gold Compounds   Fax #1204

Trade: Ridaura, Myochrysine, Solganal
Can/Aus/UK: Myochrysine, Ridaura, Myocrisin
Uses: Antiarthritic
AAP: Approved by the American Academy of Pediatrics for use in breastfeeding mothers

Gold salts are potent and toxic, anti-inflammatory agents used to treat rheumatoid arthritis. Two injectable forms exist, gold sodium thiomalate (Myochrysine) and sodium aurothioglucose (Solganal). One oral form exists, auranofin (Ridaura). The plasma kinetics of the gold salts are highly variable and are difficult to report, but in general, their half-lives are very extended and increase as duration of treatment continues. Auranofin is the only orally available salt form and is approximately 20-25% bioavailable. They are all probably secreted into breast milk in small quantities. In one study of a patient receiving Myochrysine, 50 mg/week for 7 weeks, the concentration of gold sodium thiomalate varied from 0.022 to 0.04 mg/L at 66 hours and 7 days post-dose respectively. Although the infant showed no signs or symptoms of toxicity at this time, the authors noted that 3 months after treatment the infant developed transient facial edema of unexplained origin. Approximately 10% or more of the concentration of gold measured in maternal serum appears in breast milk. Gold is retained in the human body for long periods of time (months). For this reason prolonged exposure of a nursing infant may not be justified.

Alternatives:

Pregnancy Risk Category: C

Adult Concerns: GI distress, diarrhea, nausea, vomiting, exfoliative dermatitis, nephrotoxicity, proteinuria, and blood dyscrasia.

Pediatric Concerns: Possible facial edema 3 months after therapy. Relationship is questionable.

Drug Interactions: Decreased gold effects with penicillamine and acetylcysteine.

AHL	= 3-26 days	M/P	= 0.02-0.3
PHL	=	PB	= 95%
PK	= 3-6 hours (IM)	Oral	= 20-25%(auranofin)
MW	=	pKa	=
Vd	= 0.1		

References:

1. Blau SP. Metabolism of gold during lactation. Arthritis Rheum 16:777-778,1973.
2. Bell RAF, and Dale IM. Gold Secretion in maternal milk. Arth. Rheum. 19:1374, `1976.
3. Ostensen M, et.al. Excretion of gold into human breast milk. Eur. J. Clin. Pharmcol. 31:251-2, 1986.

Gonadorelin Acetate   Fax #1532

Trade: Lutrepulse
Can/Aus/UK: Lutrepulse, Wyeth-Ayerst HRF, Fertiral
Uses: Gonadotropin-releasing hormone
AAP: Not reviewed

Gonadorelin is used for the induction of ovulation in anovulatory women with primary hypothalamic amenorrhea. Gonadorelin is a small decapeptide identical to the physiologic GnRH secreted by the hypothalamus which stimulates the pituitary release of luteinizing hormone(LH) and to a lesser degree follicle stimulating hormone (FSH). LH and FSH subsequently stimulate the ovary to produce follicles. Gonadorelin plasma half-life is very brief (< 2-4 minutes) and it is primarily distributed to the plasma only. Gonadorelin has been detected in human breast milk at concentrations of 0.1 to 3 nanograms/mL (adult dose = 20-100 micrograms), although its oral bioavailability in the infant would be minimal to none.

Alternatives:

Pregnancy Risk Category: B

Adult Concerns: Ovarian hyperstimulation, bronchospasm, tachycardia, flushing, urticaria, induration at injection site.

Pediatric Concerns: None reported via milk.

Drug Interactions:

AHL = 2-4 minutes	**M/P** =
PHL =	**PB** =
PK =	**Oral** = None
MW =	**pKa** =
Vd = 0.14	

References:
1. Reynolds JEF (Ed): Martindale: The Extra Pharmacopoeia (electronic version). Micromedex, Inc, Denver, CO, 1990.
2. Drug Facts and Comparisons. 1996. ed. Facts and Comparisons, St. Louis.

Grepafloxacin   Fax #1569

Trade: Raxar
Can/Aus/UK:
Uses: Fluoroquinolone antibiotic
AAP: Not reviewed

Grepafloxacin is a typical fluoroquinolone antibiotic similar to Ciprofloxacin. The manufacturer suggests that grepafloxacin is detectible in human milk after a 400 mg dose, but does not provide the exact levels. Studies in rodents suggest a concentrating mechanism of about 16 times that of the plasma compartment. Because this fluoroquinolone has a rather long half-life, high volume of distribution, the ability to enter many body compartments, and is concentrated in rodent milk, it is probably advisable to use this product with extreme caution, if at all, in breastfeeding women.

Alternatives: Norfloxacin, Ofloxacin, Trovafloxacin

Pregnancy Risk Category: C

Adult Concerns: Nausea, taste perversion, dizziness, headache, diarrhea, abdominal pain.

Pediatric Concerns: None reported with this product, but diarrhea and pseudomembranous colitis has been reported with ciprofloxacin. Arthropathy has been reported following pediatric use of fluoroquinolones.

Drug Interactions: Decreased absorption with antacids. Quinolones cause increased levels of caffeine, warfarin, cyclosporine, theophylline. Cimetidine, probenecid, azlocillin increase ciprofloxacin levels. Increased risk of seizures when used with foscarnet.

AHL = 15.7 hours		**M/P** =	
PHL =		**PB** = 50%	
PK = 2-3 hours		**Oral** = 72%	
MW = 422		**pKa** =	
Vd = 5.07			

References:
1.   Pharmaceutical Manufacturer's Package Insert, 1998.

Griseofulvin   Fax #1205

Trade: Fulvicin, Gris-peg
Can/Aus/UK: Fulvicin, Grisovin-FP, Fulcin, Griseostatin, Grisovin, Fulcin
Uses: Antifungal
AAP: Not reviewed

Griseofulvin is an older class antifungal. Much better safety profiles with the newer families of antifungals have reduced the use of griseofulvin. The drug is primarily effective against tinea species and not candida albicans. There are no data available for humans. In one study in cows following a dose of 10mg/kg/day for 5 days (human dose => 5 mg/kg/day) milk concentrations were 0.16 mg/L. Although these data cannot be directly extrapolated to humans, they indicate transfer to milk in some species. Oral use in adults is associated with low risk of hepatic cancer. Griseofulvin is still commonly used in pediatric tinea capitis (ringworm) where it is a preferred medication.

Alternatives: Fluconazole

Pregnancy Risk Category: C

Adult Concerns: Headache, depression, hepatotoxicity, skin rashes, hallucinations. Symptoms of overdose include lethargy, vertigo, blurred vision, nausea, vomiting, and diarrhea.

Pediatric Concerns: None reported from breast milk.

Drug Interactions: Barbiturates may reduce plasma levels. May inhibit warfarin activity. May reduce effectiveness of oral contraceptives. May produce increased toxicity and tachycardia when used with alcohol.

AHL = 9-24 hours	**M/P** =
PHL =	**PB** =
PK = 4-8 hours	**Oral** = Poor to 50%
MW = 353	**pKa** =
Vd =	

References:
1.   McEvoy GE(ed):AHFS Drug Information, New York, NY. 1995.
2.   Hiddeston WA: Antifungal activity of penicillium griseofulvin mycelium. Vet Rec 86:75-76, 1970.

Guaifenesin   Fax #1206

Trade: GG, Robitussin
Can/Aus/UK: Balminil, Resyl, Robitussin, Benylin-E Orthoxicol, Respenyl
Uses: Expectorant, loosens respiratory tract secretions
AAP: Not reviewed

Guaifenesin is an expectorant used to irritate the gastric mucosa and stimulate respiratory tract secretions in order to reduce phlegm viscosity. It does not suppress coughing and should not be used in persistent cough such as with smokers. No data are available on transfer into human breast milk.   In general, clinical studies documenting the efficacy of guaifenesin are lacking, and the usefulness of this product as an expectorant is highly questionable. Poor efficacy of these drugs (expectorants in general) would suggest that they do not provide enough justification for use in lactating mothers. But untoward effects have not been reported. Pediatric dose: < 2 years = 12 mg/Kg/day in 6 divided doses; 2-5 years = 50-100 mg every 4 hours; 6-11 years = 100-200 mg every 4 hours; Children > 12 years and adults = 200-400 mg every 4 hours for a maximum of 2.4 gm/day. Always dose with large volumes of fluids.

Alternatives:

Pregnancy Risk Category: C

Adult Concerns: Vomiting, diarrhea, nausea, sedation, skin rash, GI dyspepsia.

Pediatric Concerns: None reported.

Drug Interactions:

AHL	= < 7 hours.	**M/P**	=
PHL	=	**PB**	=
PK	=	**Oral**	= Complete
MW	= 198	**pKa**	=
Vd	= 1.0		

References:
1. Lacy C. et.al. Drug information handbook. Lexi-Comp, Hudson(Cleveland), Oh. 1996.

Guanfacine   Fax #1207

Trade: Tenex
Can/Aus/UK:
Uses: Antihypertensive
AAP: Not reviewed

Guanfacine is a centrally acting antihypertensive that stimulates alpha-2 adrenergic receptors (similar to Clonidine). Studies in animals indicate that guanfacine is secreted into milk (M:P ratio = 0.75), but human studies are lacking. Because this product has a low molecular weight (246), a high volume of distribution 6.3 L/kg), and penetrates the CNS at high levels, it is likely to penetrate milk at significant levels. Caution is urged.

Alternatives:

Pregnancy Risk Category: B

Adult Concerns: Bradycardia, hypotension, dry mouth, sedation, weakness, constipation.

Pediatric Concerns: None reported but observe for hypotension, sedation, weakness.

Drug Interactions: Decreased hypotensive effect when used with tricyclic antidepressants. Increased effect when used with other antihypertensive agents.

AHL	= 17 hours	M/P	=
PHL	=	PB	= 20-30%
PK	= 2.6 hours	Oral	= 81-100%
MW	= 246	pKa	=
Vd	= 6.3		

References:
1. Pharmaceutical Manufacturer's Package Insert, 1995.
2. Lacy C. et.al. Drug information handbook. Lexi-Comp, Hudson(Cleveland), Oh. 1996.

Haemophilus B Conjugate Vaccine.   Fax #1208

Trade: Hibtiter, Haemophilus B Vaccine
Can/Aus/UK: Act-HIB, PedvaxHIB, HibTiter
Uses: H. influenza Vaccine
AAP: Not reviewed

Hib Vaccine is a purified capsular polysaccharide vaccine made from haemophilus influenza bacteria. It is non-infective. It is currently recommended for initial immunizations in children at 2 months, and at 2 month intervals, for a total of 3 injections. A booster is recommended at 12-15 months. Although there are no reasons for administering to adult mothers, it would not be contraindicated in breastfeeding mothers.

Alternatives:

Pregnancy Risk Category: C

Adult Concerns: Itching, skin rash, injection site reaction, vomiting, fever. Few anaphylactoid-type reaction.

Pediatric Concerns: Itching, skin rash, injection site reaction, vomiting, fever. Few anaphylactoid-type reaction.

Drug Interactions: Decreased immunogenicity when used with immunosuppressive agents. Immunoglobulins with 1 month may decrease antibody production.

References:
1.   Pharmaceutical Manufacturer's Package Insert, 1996.

Halazepam   Fax #1209

Trade: Paxipam
Can/Aus/UK:
Uses: Benzodiazepine antianxiety drug
AAP: Not reviewed

Halazepam is a benzodiazepine (Valium family) used to treat anxiety disorders. Halazepam is metabolized to desmethyldiazepam, which has an elimination half-life of 50-100 hours. Although no information is available on halazepam levels in human milk, it should be similar to diazepam. See diazepam.

Alternatives: Alprazolam, Lorazepam

Pregnancy Risk Category: D

Adult Concerns: Sedation, bradycardia, euphoria, disorientation, confusion, nausea, constipation, hypotension.

Pediatric Concerns: None reported, but see diazepam.

Drug Interactions:

AHL = 14 hours.	M/P	=
PHL =	PB	= High
PK = 1-3 hours	Oral	= Complete
MW = 353	pKa	=
Vd = 1.0		

References:
1.   Drug Facts and Comparisons. 1995 ed. Facts and Comparisons, St. Louis.

Haloperidol   Fax #1210

Trade: Haldol
Can/Aus/UK: Apo-Haloperidol, Haldol, Novo-Peridol, Peridol, Serenace
Uses: Antipsychotic
AAP: Drugs whose effect on nursing infants is unknown but may be of concern

Haloperidol is a potent antipsychotic agent than is reported to increase prolactin levels in some patients. In one study of a woman treated for puerperal hypomania and receiving 5 mg twice daily, the concentration of haloperidol in milk was 0.0, 23.5, 18.0, and 3.25 µg/L on day 1, 6, 7 and 21 respectively. The corresponding maternal plasma levels were 0, 40, 26, and 4 µg/L at day 1, 6, 7, and 21 respectively. The milk:plasma ratios were 0.58, 0.69, and 0.81 on days 6, 7, and 21 respectively. After 4 weeks of therapy the infant showed no symptoms of sedation and was feeding well. In another study after a mean daily dose of 29.2 mg, the concentration of haloperidol in breast milk was 5 µg/L 11 hours post-dose.

Alternatives:

Pregnancy Risk Category: C

Adult Concerns: Extrapyramidal symptoms, sedation, anemia, tachycardia, hypotension.

Pediatric Concerns: None reported via milk, but caution is recommended. Observe for sedation, weakness.

Drug Interactions: Carbamazepine may increase metabolism and decrease effectiveness of haloperidol. CNS depressants may increase adverse effects. Epinephrine may cause hypotension. Concurrent use with lithium has caused acute encephalopathy syndromes.

AHL = 12-38 hours	M/P	= 0.58-0.81
PHL =	PB	= 92%
PK = 2-6 hours	Oral	= 60%

MW = 376   pKa = 8.3
Vd = 18-30

References:
1.   Whalley LJ, et. al. Haloperidol secreted in breast milk. Br Med J 282:1746-7, 1981.
2.   Stewart RB, et. al. Haloperidol excretion in human milk. Am J Psychiatry 137:849-50, 1980.

Halothane   Fax #1211

Trade: Fluothane
Can/Aus/UK: Fluothane
Uses: Anesthetic gas
AAP: Approved by the American Academy of Pediatrics for use in breastfeeding mothers

Halothane is an anesthetic gas similar to enflurane, methoxyflurane, and isoflurane. Approximately 60-80% is rapidly eliminated by exhalation the first 24 hours postoperative, and only 15% is actually metabolized by the liver. Cote (1976) reviewed the secretion of halothane in breast milk. After a 3 hour surgery, only 2 ppm was detected in milk. At another exposure in one week, only 0.83 and 1.9 ppm were found. The authors assessed the exposure to the infant as negligible. Halothane is probably stored in the adipose tissue and eliminated for several days. There is no available information on the oral bioavailability of halothane.   Pumping and dumping milk the first 24 hours postoperatively is generally recommended, but is probably unnecessary.

Alternatives:

Pregnancy Risk Category:

Adult Concerns: Nausea, vomiting, sedation, transient hepatotoxicity.

Pediatric Concerns: None reported.

Drug Interactions: When used with rifampin, or phenytoin, may have increased risk of hepatotoxicity.

AHL	=	M/P	=
PHL	=	PB	=
PK	= 10-20 min.	Oral	=
MW	= 197	pKa	=
Vd	= 1		

References:

HCTZ +Triamterene   Fax #1544

Trade: Dyrenium, Maxzide
Can/Aus/UK: Dyazide, Novo-Triamzide, Hydrene
Uses: Diuretic
AAP: Not reviewed

Numerous diuretic products contain varying combinations of hydrochlorothiazide (HCTZ) and triamterene. For specifics on HCTZ, see the monograph on hydrochlorothiazide.   Triamterene is a potassium sparing diuretic. Following a dose of 100-200 mg, it attains plasma levels in adults of 26-30 ng/mL.   It is secreted in small amounts in cow's milk but no human data are available. Assuming a high milk:plasma ratio of one, an infant ingesting 125 ml/Kg/day would theoretically ingest less than 4 µg/Kg/day, an amount unlikely to provide clinical problems.

Alternatives:

Pregnancy Risk Category: B

Adult Concerns: Diarrhea, nausea, vomiting, hepatitis, leukopenia, hyperkalemia.

Pediatric Concerns: None reported. Hyperkalemia.

Drug Interactions: Increased risk of hyperkalemia when given with amiloride, spironolactone, and ACE inhibitors.   Increased risk of toxicity with amantadine.

AHL	= 1.5-2.5 hours	M/P	=
PHL	=	PB	= 55%
PK	= 1.5-3 hours	Oral	= 30-70%
MW	= 253	pKa	= 6.2
Vd	=		

References:
1. Pharmaceutical Manufacturer's Package Insert, 1998.

Heparin   Fax #1212

Trade: Heparin
Can/Aus/UK: Hepalean, Canusal, Heplok, Pularin
Uses: Anticoagulant
AAP: Not reviewed

Heparin is a large protein molecule. It is used SC, IM and IV because it is not absorbed orally in mother or infant. Due to its high molecular weight (40,000 Daltons), it is unlikely any would transfer into breast milk. Any that did enter the milk would be rapidly destroyed in the gastric contents of the infant.

Alternatives:

Pregnancy Risk Category: C

Adult Concerns: Hemorrhage.

Pediatric Concerns: None reported via milk.

Drug Interactions: Increased toxicity with NSAIDS, aspirin, dipyridamole, hydroxychloroquine.

AHL	= 1-2 hours	M/P	=
PHL	=	PB	=
PK	= 20 min.	Oral	= None
MW	= 30000	pKa	=
Vd	=		

References:
1.   McEvoy GE(ed):AHFS Drug Information, New York, NY. 1995.

Hepatitis B Infection   Fax #1214

Trade: Hepatitis B Infection
Can/Aus/UK:
Uses: Hepatitis B exposure
AAP: Not reviewed

Hepatitis B virus (HBV) causes a wide spectrum of infections, ranging from a mild asymptomatic form to a fulminant fatal hepatitis.   Mild asymptomatic illness is most common in pediatric patients, although the chronic infectious state occurs in as many as 90% of infants who become infected by perinatal transmission. Chronically infected individuals are at increased risk for chronic liver diseases and liver cancer in later life. HBV is transmitted through blood or body fluids. Hepatitis B antigen has been detected in breast milk. Infants of mothers who are HBV positive (HBsAg) should be given Hepatitis immune globulin (HBIG) (preferably within 1 hour of birth) and a Hepatitis B vaccination AT BIRTH which is believed to effectively reduce the risk of post-natal transmission, particularly via breast milk.   Inject in different sites. Thus far, several older studies have indicated that breastfeeding poses no additional risk of transmission, and thus far no cases of horizontal transmission of Hepatitis B via breast milk have been reported.

Alternatives:

Pregnancy Risk Category:

Adult Concerns: Hepatitis, increased risk of liver cancer.

Pediatric Concerns: None reported if immunized with HBIG and HB vaccination.

Drug Interactions:

References:

1. Boxall EH, Flewett TH, Dane DS et.al. Hepatitis-B surface antigen in breast milk. Lancet 2:1007-8, 1974.
2. Beasley RP, Shiao I-S, Stevens CE et.al. Evidence against breast-feeding as a mechanism for vertical transmission of hepatitis B. Lancet 2:740-1, 1975.
3. Woo D, Cummins M, et.al. Vertical transmission of hepatitis B surface antigen in carrier mothers, in two west London hospitals. Arch Dis. Child 54:670-5, 1979.
4. American Academy of Pediatrics. Committee on Infectious Diseases. Red Book 1994.
5. Stevens CE, Beasley PR, et.al. Vertical transmission of hepatitis B antigen in Taiwan. N.Engl. J. Med. 292:771, 1975.

Hepatitis A Infection   Fax #1213

Trade:

Can/Aus/UK:

Uses: Hepatitis A infection

AAP: Approved by the American Academy of Pediatrics for use in breastfeeding mothers

Hepatitis A is an acute viral infection characterized by jaundice, fever, anorexia, and malaise. In infants, the syndrome is either asymptomatic or causes only mild nonspecific symptoms. Current therapy recommended following exposure to Hepatitis A is an injection of gamma globulin. A majority of the population is immune to Hepatitis A due to prior exposure. Fulminant hepatitis A infection is rare in children and a carrier state is unknown. It is spread through fecal-oral contact and can be spread in day care centers. Viral shedding continues from onset up to 3 weeks. Unless the mother is jaundiced and acutely ill, breastfeeding can continue without interruption. Proper hygiene should be stressed. Protect infant with IM gamma globulin.

Alternatives:

Pregnancy Risk Category:

Adult Concerns: Jaundice, fever, malaise.

Pediatric Concerns: None reported. Protect with gamma globulin injection.

Drug Interactions:

References:
1. American Academy of Pediatrics. Committee on Infectious Diseases. Red Book 1997.
2. Gartner L (personal communication) 1997.

Hepatitis A Vaccine — Fax #1602

Trade: Havrix
Can/Aus/UK: Havrix, Vaqta
Uses: Vaccine
AAP: Not reviewed

Hepatitis A vaccine is an inactivated, noninfectious viral vaccination for Hepatitis A. Although there are no specific data on the use of Hepatitis A vaccine in breastfeeding women, Hepatitis A vaccine can be used in pregnant women after 14 weeks, and in infants. There is little likelihood that Hepatitis A vaccinations in breastfeeding women would cause untoward effects in breast fed infants.

Alternatives:

Pregnancy Risk Category: C

Adult Concerns: Lymphadenopathy, headache, insomnia, vertigo, fatigue and malaise, fever, anorexia and nausea, photophobia, injection-site soreness.

Pediatric Concerns: None reported via milk.

Drug Interactions:

References:

1. Drug Facts and Comparisons. 1997. ed. Facts and Comparisons, St. Louis.
2. Pharmaceutical Manufacturer's Package Insert, 1997.

Hepatitis B Immune Globulin   Fax #1456

Trade: H-BIG, Hep-B-Gammagee, HyperHep
Can/Aus/UK:
Uses: Anti-Hepatitis B Immune globulins
AAP: Not reviewed

HBIG is a sterile solution of immunoglobulin (10-18% protein) containing a high titer of antibody to hepatitis B surface antigen. It is most commonly used as prophylaxis therapy for infants born to hepatitis B surface antigen positive mothers. The carrier state can be prevented in about 75% of such infections in newborns given HBIG immediately after birth. HBIG is generally administered to infants from HBsAg positive mothers who wish to breastfeed. The prophylactic dose for newborns is 0.5 mL IM (thigh) as soon after birth as possible, preferably with 1 hour. The infant should also be immunized with Hepatitis B vaccine (0.5 mL IM) within 12 hours of birth (use separate site), and again at 1 and 6 months.

Alternatives:

Pregnancy Risk Category: C

Adult Concerns: Pain at injection site, erythema, rash, dizziness, malaise.

Pediatric Concerns: Pain at injection site, erythema, rash.

Drug Interactions:

AHL =		M/P	=
PHL =		PB	=
PK	= 1-6 days	Oral	= None

MW =   pKa =
Vd =

References:
1.   Pharmaceutical Manufacturer's Package Insert, 1995.
2.   Lawrence RA. Breastfeeding, A guide for the medical profession. Mosby, St. Louis, 1994.
3.   Johnson KB. In: The Harriet Lane Handbook. Mosby, 1993.

Hepatitis B Vaccine   Fax #1216

Trade: Heptavax-b, Engerix-B, Recombivax HB
Can/Aus/UK:
Uses: Hepatitis B vaccination
AAP: Not reviewed

Hepatitis B vaccine is an inactivated non-infectious hepatitis B surface antigen vaccine. It can be used in pediatric patients at birth. No data are available on its use in breastfeeding mothers, but it is unlikely to produce untoward effects on a breastfeeding infant.   Hepatitis B vaccination is approximately 80-95% effective in preventing acute hepatitis B infections.   It requires at least 3 immunizations and the immunity lasts about 5-7 years.   In infants born of HB surface antigen positive mothers, the American Academy of Pediatrics recommends hepatitis B vaccine (along with HBIG) should be administered to the infant within 1-12 hours of birth (0.5 mL IM) and again at 1 and 6 months. If so administered, breastfeeding poses no additional risk for acquisition of HBV by the infant.

Alternatives:

Pregnancy Risk Category: C

Adult Concerns: Pain at injection site, swelling, erythema, fever.

Pediatric Concerns: Fever, malaise, fatigue when directly injected. None reported via breast milk.

Drug Interactions: Immunosuppressive agents would decrease effect.

References:
1.   Pharmaceutical Manufacturer's Package Insert, 1996.
2.   American Academy of Pediatrics. Committee on Infectious Diseases. Red Book 1997.

Hepatitis C Infection   Fax #1215

Trade: Hepatitis C Infection
Can/Aus/UK:
Uses: Hepatitis exposure
AAP: Not reviewed

Hepatitis C (HCV) is characterized by a mild or asymptomatic infection with jaundice and malaise. On average, 50% of patients develop chronic liver disease, including cirrhosis, and liver cancer in later life. HCV infection can be spread by blood-blood transmission, although most are not associated with blood transfusions and may be transmitted by other unknown methods. Although perinatal transmission can occur, its incidence is known to be very low. The average incubation period is 7-9 weeks.   Mothers infected with HCV should be advised that transmission of HCV by breastfeeding is possible but has not been documented. It is not known with certainty if the virus is shed in breast milk, although several studies so suggest. In one study of 17 HCV positive mothers (Grayson, 1995), 11 of the 17 had HCV antibody present in milk, but zero of 17 had HCV-RNA in milk after birth, suggesting that the virus itself was not detected in milk. Although it is possible that during episodes of direct exposure to blood, such as from bleeding nipples, or following initial infection and viremia, that transmission could occur, this does not appear to be certain at this time.   Currently a number of other studies have yet to document vertical transmission of HCV by breast milk. Available data seem to suggest an elevated risk of vertical transmission to the infant occurs in HIV infected women and women with elevated titers of HCV RNA. The risk of transmission of HCV via breast milk is unknown at this time. HCV-infected women should be counseled that transmission of HCV by breastfeeding is theoretically possible, but has not yet been documented (AAP). The Center for Disease Control (CDC) does not consider chronic hepatitis C infection in the mother as a contraindication to breastfeeding. The decision to breastfeed should be based largely on informed discussion between the mother and her health care provider.

References:
1. Paccagnini S, et.al. Perinatala transmission and manifestations of hepatitis C virus infection in a high risk population. Ped. Infect. Dis J. 14:195-9, 1995.
2. Nagata I, Shiraki K, et.al. Mother to infant transmission of hepatitis C virus. J. Pediatrics 120:432-4, 1992.
3. Grayson ML, Braniff KM, et.al. Breastfeeding and the risk of virtical transmission of hepatitis C virus. Med. J. Australia 163:107, 1995.
4. Ruff AJ. Breast milk, Breastfeeding, and Transmission of Viruses to the Neonate. Sem. In Perinatol. 18:510-516, 1994.
5. American Academy of Pediatrics. Committee on Infectious Diseases. Red Book 1997.
6. Lawrence RA. Breastfeeding, A guide for the medical profession. Mosby, St. Louis, 1994.

Herbal Teas   Fax #1217

Trade: Herbal Teas
Can/Aus/UK:
Uses: Herbal teas, tablets, powders, antioxidants
AAP: Not reviewed

Herbal teas should be used with great caution, if at all. A number of reports in the literature indicate potential toxicity in pregnant women from some herbal teas which contain pyrrolizidine alkaloids (PA). Such alkaloids have been associated with feticide, birth defects and liver toxicity. Other reports of severe hepatotoxicity requiring liver transplant have occurred with an herbal antioxidant called "Chaparral". A Chinese herbal product called "Jin Bu Huan" has been implicated in clinically recognized hepatitis in 7 patients. Other hepatotoxic remedies include germander, comfrey, mistletoe and skullcap, margosa oil, mate tea, Gordolobo yerba tea, and pennyroyal (squawmint) oil . A recent report of seven poisonings with anticholinergic symptoms following ingestion of "Paraguay Tea" was published and was an apparent adulteration. A recent report on Blue Cohosh suggests it may be cardiotoxic when used late in pregnancy. Because exact ingredients are seldom listed on many teas, this author strongly suggests that lactating mothers limit exposure to these substances as much as possible. Never consume herbal remedies of unknown composition. Remember, breastfeeding infants are much more susceptible to such toxicants than are adults.

Alternatives:

Pregnancy Risk Category:

Adult Concerns: Severe toxicity including hepatotoxicity, anticholinergic poisoning, etc.

Pediatric Concerns: None reported via breast milk, but caution is recommended. Agents listed above would be contraindicated.

Drug Interactions:

References:
1. Anonymous. Drug Therapy 16:64, 1993.
2. Ellenhorn, MJ. and Barceloux, DG. Medical Toxicology. Elsevier Publishing Co. 1988. p. 1292-1299.
3. Gordon DW, Rosenthal G, Hart J, et.al. Chaparral Ingestion. JAMA, 273:(6),489-502, 1995.
4. Hsu CK, et.al. Anticholinergic poisoning associated with heabal tea. Arch. Intern. Med. 155:2245-48, 1995.
5. Siegel, RK. Herbal Intoxication. JAMA 236:473-477, 1976.
6. Rosti L. et.al. Toxic effects of a herbal tea mixture in two newborns. Acta. Pediatr 83:683, 1994.

Heroin   Fax #1218

Trade:
Can/Aus/UK:
Uses: Narcotic analgesic
AAP: Contraindicated by the American Academy of Pediatrics in Breastfeeding Mothers

Heroin is diacetyl-morphine (diamorphine), a pro-drug that is rapidly converted by plasma cholinesterases to 6-acetyl morphine and more slowly to morphine. With oral use, rapid and complete first-pass metabolism occurs in the liver. The half-life of diamorphine is only 3 minutes, with the large majority of the pro-drug converted to morphine. Peak levels of morphine occur in about 30 minutes following oral doses. Heroin, as is morphine, is known to transfer into breast milk. See morphine for kinetics. Detoxify mother prior to nursing.

Alternatives:

Pregnancy Risk Category: B

Adult Concerns: Sedation, hypotension, euphoria, nausea, vomiting, dry mouth, respiratory depression, constipation.

Pediatric Concerns:

Drug Interactions:

AHL = 1.5-2 hours	**M/P** = 2.45
PHL =	**PB** = 35%
PK = 0.5-1 hours	**Oral** = Poor
MW = 369	**pKa** = 7.6
Vd = 25	

References:
1. Feilberg VL, Rosenborg D, Broen Christensen C, et.al. Excretion of morphine in human breast milk. Acta Anaesthiol Scan. 33:426-428, 1989.
2. Wittels Bk, Scott DT, Sinatra RS. Exogenous opioids in human

breast milk and acute neonatal neurobehavior: a preliminary study. Anesthesiology 73:864-869, 1990.

Herpes Simplex Infections   Fax #1219

Trade:

Can/Aus/UK:

Uses: Herpes simplex type I, II

AAP: Breastfeeding is acceptable if no lesions are on the breast or are adequately covered

HSV-1 and HSV-2 have been isolated from human milk, even in the absence of vesicular lesions or drainage. Transmission after birth can occur and herpetic infections during the neonatal period are often severe and fatal.   Exposure to the virus from skin lesions of caregivers, including lesions of the breast, have been described.   On average however, perinatal infection is generally believed to occur during delivery rather than through breast milk. Breast milk does not appear to be a common mode of transmission, although women with active lesions around the breast and nipple should refrain from breastfeeding until the lesions are adequately covered. Lesions directly on the nipple generally preclude breastfeeding.   A number of cases of herpes simplex transmission via breast milk have been reported (Dunkle, 1979, Quinn 1978).   Women with active lesions should be extremely meticulous in handwashing to prevent spread of the disease from other active lesions. Lawrence (1994) provides a good review of the risks.

Alternatives:

Pregnancy Risk Category:

Adult Concerns: Skin eruptions, CNS changes, gingivostomatitis, skin lesions, fever.

Pediatric Concerns: Transfer of virus to infants has been reported, but may be from exposure to lesions. Cover lesions on breast.

Drug Interactions:

References:

1. Light IJ. Postnatal acquisition of herpes simpollex virus by the newborn infant: a review of the literature. Pediatrics 63:480-2, 1979.

2. Sullivan-Bolyai JZ, Fife KH et.al. Disseminated neonatal herpes simplex virus type-1 from a maternal breast lesion. Pediatrics 71:455-7, 1983.

3. Whitley RJ, et.al. The natural history of herpes simples virus infection of mother and newborn. Pediatrics 66:489, 1980.

4. Dunkle LM, Schmidt RR, O'Connor DM. Neonatal herpes simplex infection possibly acquired via maternal breast milk. Pediatrics 63:250, 1979.

5. Quinn PT, Lofberg JV. Maternal herpetic breast infection: another hazard of neonatal herpes simplex. Med. J. Aust. 2:411, 1978.

6. Lawrence RA. Breastfeeding, A guide for the medical profession. Mosby, St. Louis, 1994.

Hexachlorophene   Fax #1220

Trade: Septisol, Phisohex, Septi-soft
Can/Aus/UK: pHisoHex, Sapoderm, Dermalex
Uses: Antiseptic scrub
AAP: Not reviewed

Hexachlorophene is an antibacterial which is an effective inhibitor of gram positive organisms. It is generally used topically as a surgical scrub and sometimes vaginally in mothers. Due to its lipophilic structure, it is well absorbed through intact and denuded skin producing significant levels in plasma, brain, fat and other tissues in both adults and infants. It has been implicated in causing brain lesions (spongioform myelinopathy), blindness and respiratory failure in both animals and humans. Although there are no studies reporting concentrations of this compound in breast milk, it is probably transferred in significant levels. Transfer into breast milk is known to occur in rodents. Topical use in infants is absolutely discouraged due to the high absorption of hexachlorophene through an infant's skin and proven toxicity.

Alternatives:

Pregnancy Risk Category: C

Adult Concerns: Seizures, respiratory failure, hypotension, brain lesions, blindness in overdose.

Pediatric Concerns: Following direct application, CNS injury, seizures, irritability have been reported in neonates. Toxicity via breast milk has not been reported.

Drug Interactions:

AHL =		M/P	=
PHL = 6.1-44.2 hours		PB	=
PK =		Oral	= Complete
MW = 407		pKa	=
Vd =			

References:
1. Pharmaceutical Manufacturer's Package Insert, 1996.
2. Tyrala EE, Hillman RE and Dodson WE. Clinical pharmacology of hexachlorophene in newborn infants. J Pediatr 91:481-6, 1977.

HIV Infection   Fax #1221

Trade: AIDS
Can/Aus/UK:
Uses: HIV infections
AAP: Advise not to breastfeed

The AIDS (HIV) virus has been isolated from human milk. In addition, recent reports from throughout the world have documented the transmission of HIV through human milk. At least 9 or more cases in the literature currently suggest that HIV-1 is secreted and can be transmitted horizontally to the infant via breast milk. Although these studies clearly indicate a risk, currently no studies clearly show the exact risk associated with breastfeeding in HIV infected women. However, women who develop a primary HIV infection while breastfeeding may shed especially high concentrations of HIV viruses and pose a high risk of transmission to their infants. In some studies, the risk of transmission during primary infection was 29%. In various African populations, recent reports suggest the incremental risk of transmitting HIV via breastfeeding ranges from 3-12%. Because the risk is now well documented, HIV infected mothers in the USA and others countries with safe alternative sources of feeding should be advised to not breastfeed their infants (AAP, 1994). Mothers at-risk for HIV should be screened and counseled prior to initiating breastfeeding.

Alternatives:

Pregnancy Risk Category:

Adult Concerns:

Pediatric Concerns: HIV transmission has been documented. HIV infected women are advised not to breastfeed.

Drug Interactions:

References:

1.   Committee on Pediatric AIDS. Human milk, breastfeeding, and transmission of human immunodeficiency virus in the United States. Pediatrics 96:977-9, 1995.
2.   Oxtoby MJ. Human immunodeficiency virus and other viruses in human milk: placing the issues in broader perspective. Pediatr. Infect. Dis. 7:825-835, 1988.
3.   Goldfarb J. Breastfeeding: Aids and other infectious diseases. Clin. Perinatol 20:225-243, 1993.
4.   Van de Perre P. et.al. Infective and anti-infective properties of breastmil from HIV-1-infected women. Lancet 341:914-18, 1993.
5.   Dunn DT, et.al. Risk of human immunodeficiency virus type I

transmission through breastfeeding. Lancet 340:585-588, 1992.

6. St.Louis ME. et.al. The timing of HIV-1 transmission in an African setting. Presented at the First National Conference on Human Retroviruses and Related Infections. December 12-16, 1993; Washington DC.

7. Martino M. Human immunodeficiency virus type 1 infection and breast milk. Acta. Paediatr. Suppl. 400:51-8, 1994.

8. Report of the Committee on Infectious Diseases. American Academy of Pediatrics, 1994.

Hydralazine   Fax #1222

Trade: Apresoline
Can/Aus/UK: Apresoline, Novo-Hylazin, Apo-Hydralazine, Alphapress
Uses: Antihypertensive
AAP: Approved by the American Academy of Pediatrics for use in breastfeeding mothers

Hydralazine is a popular antihypertensive used for severe pre-eclampsia and gestational and postpartum hypertension. In a study of one breastfeeding mother receiving 50 mg three times daily, the concentrations of hydralazine in breast milk at 0.5 and 2 hours after administration was 762, and 792 nmol/L respectively. The respective maternal serum levels were 1525, and 580 nmol/L at the aforementioned times. From these data, an infant consuming 1000 cc of milk would consume only 0.17 mg of hydralazine, an amount too small to be clinically relevant. The published pediatric dose for hydralazine is 0.75 to 1 mg/kg/day.

Alternatives:

Pregnancy Risk Category: C

Adult Concerns: Hypotension, tachycardia, renal failure, liver toxicity, paresthesias.

Pediatric Concerns: None reported but observe for hypotension, sedation, weakness.

Drug Interactions: Increased effect with other antihypertensives, MAO inhibitors. Decreased effect when used with indomethacin.

AHL	= 1.5-8 hours.	M/P	= 0.49-1.36
PHL	=	PB	= 87%
PK	= 2 hours	Oral	= 30-50%
MW	= 160	pKa	= 7.1
Vd	= 1.6		

References:

1. Liedholm H, et. al. Transplacental passage and breast milk concentrations of hydralazine, Eur J Clin Pharmacol 21:417-9,1982.

Hydrochlorothiazide   Fax #1223

Trade: Hydrodiuril, Esidrix, Oretic
Can/Aus/UK: Apo-Hydro, Diuchlor H, Hydrodiuril, Novo-Hydrazide, Amizide, Dyazide, Modizide, Direma, Esidrex
Uses: Thiazide diuretic
AAP: Approved by the American Academy of Pediatrics for use in breastfeeding mothers

Hydrochlorothiazide (HCTZ) is a typical thiazide diuretic.   In one study of a mother receiving a 50 mg dose each morning,   milk levels were almost 25% of maternal plasma levels.   The dose ingested (assuming milk intake of 600 ml) would be approximately 50 μg/day, a clinically insignificant amount. The concentration of HCTZ in the infant's serum was undetectable(< 20 ng/ml).   Some authors suggest that HCTZ can produce thrombocytopenia in nursing infant, although this is remote and unsubstantiated. Thiazide diuretics could potentially reduce milk production by depleting maternal blood volume, although it is seldom observed.   Most thiazide diuretics are considered compatible with breastfeeding if doses are kept low.

Alternatives:

Pregnancy Risk Category: D

Adult Concerns: Fluid loss, hypotension. May reduce milk supply.

Pediatric Concerns: None reported via milk, but may reduce milk supply in mother.

Drug Interactions: May increase hypoglycemia with antidiabetic drugs. May increase hypotension associated with other antihypertensives. May increase digoxin associated arrhythmias. May increase lithium levels.

AHL = 5.6-14.8 hours	M/P = 0.25
PHL =	PB = 58%
PK = 2 hours	Oral = 72%
MW = 297	pKa = 7.9, 9.2
Vd = 3	

References:
1. Miller ME, Cohn RD, and Burghart PH. Hydrochlorothiazide disposition in a mother and her breast-fed infant. J. Pediatr. 101:789-91, 1982.

Hydrocodone   Fax #1224

Trade: Lortab, Vicodin
Can/Aus/UK: Hycodan, Robidone, Hycomine
Uses: Analgesic for pain
AAP: Not reviewed

Hydrocodone is a narcotic analgesic and antitussive structurally related to codeine although somewhat more potent. One author suggests that doses of 5 mg every 4 hours or more has a minimal effect on nursing infants, particularly older infants. Attempt to feed infant prior to medicating. Neonates may be more sensitive to this product. Lortab and Vicodin also contain acetaminophen. See codeine.

Alternatives: Codeine

Pregnancy Risk Category: B

Adult Concerns: Sedation, dizziness, apnea, bradycardia, nausea, or constipation.

Pediatric Concerns: None reported via milk, but observe closely for sedation, apnea, constipation.

Drug Interactions: May reduce analgesia when used with phenothiazines. May increase toxicity associated with CNS depressants and tricyclic antidepressants.

AHL = 3.8 hours.		M/P =	
PHL =		PB =	
PK = 1.3 hours		Oral = Complete	
MW = 299		pKa = 8.9	
Vd = 3.3-4.7			

References:
1. Horning MG, Identification and quantification of drugs and drug metabolites in human milk using GC-MS-COM methods. Mod Probl Paediatr 15:73-9,1975.
2. Kwit NT, Hatcher RA. Excretion of drugs in milk. Am J Dis Child 49:900-4,1935.
3. Anderson PO. Medication use while breast feeding a neonate. Neonatal Pharmacology Quarterly 2:3-12,1993.

Hydrocortisone Topical   Fax #1587

Trade: Westcort
Can/Aus/UK: Cortate, Cortone, Emo-Cort, Aquacort, Dermaid, Egocort, Hycor, Cortef, Dermacort
Uses: Corticosteroid
AAP: Not reviewed

Hydrocortisone is a typical corticosteroid with glucocorticoid and mineralocorticoid activity. When applied topically it suppresses inflammation and enhances healing. Initial onset of activity when applied topically is slow and may require several days for response. Absorption topically is dependent on placement; percutaneous absorption is 1% from the forearm, 2% from rectum, 4% from the scalp, 7% from the forehead, and 36% from the scrotal area. The amount transferred into human milk has not been reported, but as with most steroids, is believed minimal. Topical application to the nipple is generally approved by most authorities if amounts applied, and duration of use are minimized. Only small amounts should be applied and then only after feeding; larger quantities should be removed prior to breastfeeding. 0.5 to 1 % ointments, rather than creams, are generally preferred.

Alternatives:

Pregnancy Risk Category: C

Adult Concerns: Local irritation.

Pediatric Concerns: None reported via milk.

Drug Interactions:

AHL = 1-2 hours		**M/P** =	
PHL =		**PB** = 90%	
PK =		**Oral** = 96%	
MW = 362		**pKa** =	
Vd = 0.48			

References:
1. Derendorf H, Mollmann H, Barth J et al: Pharmacokinetics and oral bioavailability of hydrocortisone. J Clin Pharmacol 31:473-476, 1991.

Hydromorphone   Fax #1559

Trade: Dilaudid
Can/Aus/UK: Dilaudid, Hydromorph, Contin
Uses: Opiate analgesic
AAP: Not reviewed

Hydromorphone is a potent synthetic narcotic analgesic used to alleviate moderate to severe pain. No data are available on its transfer to human milk.

Alternatives: Codeine, Hydrocodone

Pregnancy Risk Category:

Adult Concerns: Dihydromorphone is highly addictive. Adverse effects include dizziness, sedation, agitation, hypotension, respiratory depression, nausea, and vomiting.

Pediatric Concerns:

Drug Interactions:

AHL = 2.5 hours	**M/P**	=
PHL =	**PB**	=
PK =	**Oral**	=
MW =	**pKa**	=
Vd =		

References:

Hydroxychloroquine   Fax #1225

Trade: Plaquenil
Can/Aus/UK: Plaquenil
Uses: Antimalarial, Antirheumatic, Lupus
AAP: Approved by the American Academy of Pediatrics for use in breastfeeding mothers

Hydroxychloroquine (HCQ) is effective in the treatment of malaria, but is also used in immune syndromes such as rheumatoid arthritis and Lupus erythematosus. HCQ is known to produce significant retinal damage and blindness if used over a prolonged period, and this could occur (theoretically) in breastfed infants. Patients on this product should see an ophthalmologist routinely. In one study of a mother receiving 400 mg HCQ daily, the concentrations of HCQ in breast milk were 1.46, 1.09, and 1.09 mg/L at 2, 9.5, and 14 hours after the dose. The average milk concentration was 1.1 mg/L. The milk:plasma ratio was approximately 5.5. Assuming a daily intake of 1 Liter of milk, an infant would ingest approximately 1.1 mg. This dose is 0.35% of the daily maternal dose of 310 mg. On a body weight basis, the infant's dose would be 2% of the maternal dose. HCQ is mostly metabolized to chloroquine and has an incredibly long half-life. The pediatric dose for malaria prophylaxis is 5 mg/kg/week.

Alternatives: Chloroquine

Pregnancy Risk Category: C

Adult Concerns: Blood dyscrasia, nausea, vomiting, diarrhea, retinopathy, rash, aplastic anemia, psychosis, porphyria, psoriasis, corneal deposits.

Pediatric Concerns: None reported, but observe for retinal damage, blood dyscrasia.

Drug Interactions: Increased risk of blood dyscrasia when used with aurothioglucose. May increase serum digoxin levels.

AHL = >40 days		**M/P**	= 5.5
PHL =		**PB**	= 63%
PK = 1-2 hours		**Oral**	= 74%
MW = 336		**pKa**	=
Vd =			

References:
1. Nation RL, Hackett LP, Dusci LJ. Excretion of hydroxychloroquine in human milk. Br. J. Clin. Pharm. 17:368-9, 1984.

Hydroxyurea   Fax #1476

Trade: Hydrea
Can/Aus/UK: Hydrea
Uses: Antineoplastic agent
AAP: Not reviewed

Hydroxyurea is an antineoplastic agent used to treat melanoma, leukemia, and other neoplasms. It is well absorbed orally and rapidly metabolized to urea by the liver. In one study following a dose of 500 mg three times daily for 7 days, milk samples were collected two hours after the last dose. The concentration of hydroxyurea in breast milk averaged 6.1 mg/L (range 3.8 to 8.4 mg/L). Hydroxyurea is rapidly cleared from the plasma compartment and appears to leave no residuals or metabolites. Approximately 80% of the dose is excreted by the kidneys within 12 hours.

Alternatives:

Pregnancy Risk Category: D

Adult Concerns: Bone marrow suppression, drowsiness, convulsion, hallucinations, fever, nausea, vomiting, diarrhea, constipation.

Pediatric Concerns: None reported via milk, but extreme caution is recommended due to overt toxicity of this product.

Drug Interactions: May have increased toxicity and neurotoxicity when used with fluorouracil.

AHL = 2-3 hours	**M/P** =	
PHL =	**PB** =	
PK = 2 hours	**Oral** = Complete	
MW = 76	**pKa** =	
Vd =		

References:
1. Sylvester RK, Lobell M, Teresi ME et al. Excretion of hydroxyurea into milk. Cancer 60:2177-2178, 1987.

Hydroxyzine   Fax #1226

Trade: Atarax, Vistaril
Can/Aus/UK: Apo-Hydroxyzine, Novo-Hydroxyzin, Atarax
Uses: Antihistamine, antiemetic
AAP: Not reviewed

Hydroxyzine is an antihistamine structurally similar to cyclizine and meclizine. It produces significant CNS depression, anticholinergic side effects (drying), and antiemetic side effects. Hydroxyzine is largely metabolized to cetirizine (Zyrtec). No data are available on secretion into breast milk.

Alternatives: Cetirizine, Loratadine

Pregnancy Risk Category: C

Adult Concerns: Sedation, hypotension, dry mouth.

Pediatric Concerns: None reported via milk, but observe for sedation, tachycardia, dry mouth.

Drug Interactions: May reduce epinephrine vasopressor response. Increased sedation when used with CNS depressants. Increased anticholinergic side effects when admixed with other anticholinergics.

AHL = 3-7 hours.	M/P =
PHL = 7.1 hours	PB =
PK = 2 hours	Oral = Complete
MW = 375	pKa = 2.1, 7.1
Vd = 13-31	

References:
1. Paton DM, Webster DR. Clinical pharmacokinetics of H1-receptor antagonists (the antihistamines). Clin. Pharm. 10:477-497, 1985.

Hyoscyamine   Fax #1227

Trade: Anaspaz, Levsin
Can/Aus/UK: Buscopan, Levsin, Hyoscine
Uses: Anticholinergic, antisecretory agent
AAP: Not reviewed

Hyoscyamine is an anticholinergic, antisecretory agent that belongs to the belladonna alkaloid family. Its typical effects are to dry secretions, produce constipation, dilate pupils, blurred vision, and may produce urinary retention. Although no exact amounts are listed, hyoscyamine is known to be secreted into breast milk in trace amounts. Thus far, no untoward effects from breastfeeding while using hyoscyamine have been found. Levsin (hyoscyamine) drops have in the past been used directly in infants for colic, although it is no longer recommended for this use. As with atropine, infants and children are especially sensitive to anticholinergics and their use is discouraged. Atropine is composed of two isomers of hyoscyamine. See atropine. Use with caution.

Alternatives:

Pregnancy Risk Category: C

Adult Concerns: Tachycardia, dry mouth, blurred vision, constipation, urinary retention.

Pediatric Concerns: Decreased heart rate, anticholinergic effects from direct use, but none reported from breast milk ingestion. Never use directly in infants with projectile vomiting, or in infants with bilious (green) vomitus.

Drug Interactions: Decreased effect with antacids. Increased toxicity with amantadine, antimuscarinics, haloperidol, phenothiazines, tricyclic antidepressants, MAO inhibitors.

AHL = 3.5 hours	**M/P**	=
PHL =	**PB**	= 50%
PK = 40-90 min.(oral)	**Oral**	= 81%
MW = 289	**pKa**	=
Vd =		

References:
1. Drug Facts and Comparisons. 1995 ed. Facts and Comparisons, St. Louis.
2. Pharmaceutical Manufacturer's Package Insert, 1995.
3. Wilson, J. Drugs in Breast Milk. New York: ADIS Press, 1981.

I-125 I-131 I-123   Fax #1228

Trade:
Can/Aus/UK:
Uses: Radioactive iodine
AAP: Radioactive compound that requires temporary cessation of breastfeeding

Radioactive Iodine concentrates in the thyroid gland, as well as in breast milk, and if ingested by an infant, may suppress its thyroid function, or increase the risk of future thyroid carcinomas . High levels may be transferred to infant producing thyroid destruction. Radioactive iodine is clinically used to ablate or destroy the thyroid (dose= 355 MBq), or in much smaller doses (7.4 MBq) , to scan the thyroid for malignancies. Following ingestion, radioactive iodine concentrates in the thyroid and lactating tissues, and it is estimated 27.9% of total radioactivity is secreted via breast milk(6). Two potential half-lives exist for radioactive iodine. One is the radioactive half-life which is solely dependent on radioactive decay of the molecule. And two, the biological half-life which is often briefer, and is the half-life of the chemical itself in the human being. This half-life is influenced most by elimination via the kidneys and other routes.   Previously published data have suggested that Iodine-125 is present in milk for at least 12 days and Iodine-131 is present for 2-14 days, but these studies may be in error as they ignored the second component of the biexponential breast milk disappearance curve. The radioactive half-life of I-131 is 8.1 days. The half-life of I-125 is 60.2 days and the half-life of I-123 is 13.2 hours. The biological half-life may be shorter due to excretion in urine, feces, and milk. A well done study by Dydek (1988) reviewed the transfer of both tracer, and ablation doses of I-131 into human milk. If the tracer doses are kept minimal (0.1 uCi or 3.7 kBq) breastfeeding could resume as early as the eighth day. However, if larger tracer doses (8.6 uCi or 0.317 MBq) are used, nursing could not resume until 46 days following therapy. Doses used for ablation of the maternal thyroid (111 MBq) would require an interruption of breastfeeding for a minimum of 106 days or more. However, an acceptable dose to an infant as a result of ingestion of radioiodine is a matter for debate, although an effective dose of < 1 mSv has been suggested(8).Suggest to mothers that they pump and store milk PRIOR to exposure to radioactive iodides. Most authors conclude that radioiodine ablation therapy should not be performed in mothers who wish to continue breastfeeding. Another study of I-131 use in a mother was followed for 32 days. These authors recommend discontinuing breastfeeding for up to 50-52 days, to ensure safety of the infant thyroid. Thyroid scans use either radioactive iodine or technetium-99m pertechnetate. Technetium has a very short half-life and should be preferred in breastfeeding mothers for thyroid scanning (Dydek, 1988). Another alternative is I-123, a newer isotope that is increasing in popularity. I-123 has a short half-life of only 13.2 hours and is radiologically ideal for thyroid and other scans. If radioactive iodine compounds are mandatory for various scanning procedures, I-123 should be preferred, followed by pumping and dumping for 6-26 days depending on the dose. However, the return to breastfeeding following I-123 therapy is dependent on the purity of this product. During manufacture of I-123, I-124 and I-125 are created. If using I-123, breastfeeding should be temporarily interrupted (see table in appendices). I-123 is not used for ablation of the thyroid. Due to the fact that significant concentrations of I-131 are concentrated in breast milk, women should discontinue breastfeeding prior to treatment, as the cumulative exposure to breast tissues could be excessively high. It is generally recommended that women discontinue breastfeeding several days to weeks before undergoing therapy, or that they pump and discard milk for several weeks after exposure to iodine to reduce the overall radioactive exposure to breast tissues. The estimated dose of radioactivity to the breasts would give a "theoretical" probability of induction of breast cancer of 0.32%. In addition, holding the infant close to the breast or thyroid gland for long periods may expose the infant to gamma irradiation and is not recommended. Patients should consult with the radiologist concerning exposure of the infant.

Alternatives: Technetium-99M

Pregnancy Risk Category:

Adult Concerns: Ablation of thyroid function. Theoretical risk of breast cancer if used in lactating women.

Pediatric Concerns: None reported, but damage to thyroid is probable if the infant is breastfed while I-131 levels are high.

Drug Interactions:

AHL =	M/P =
PHL =	PB =
PK =	Oral = Complete
MW =	pKa =
Vd =	

References:

1. American Academy of Pediatrics, Committee on Drugs. Transfer of drugs and other chemicals into human milk. Pediatrics 93(1):137-150, 1994.
2. Palmer, KE. Excretion of 125-I in breast milk following administration of labeled fibrinogen. Br. J. Radiol. 52:672, 1979.
3. Karjalainen, P, et.al. The amount and form of radioactivity in human milk after lung scanning, renography and placental localization by 131-I labeled tracers. Acta Obstet Gynecol Scand 50:357, 1971.
4. Hedrick WR. et.al. Radiation dosimetry from breast milk excretion of radioiodine and pertechnetate. J. Nucl. Med. 27:1569, 1986.
5. Romney B, Nickoloff EL, Esser PD. Excretion of radioiodine in breast milk. J. Nucl. Med. 30:124-6,1989.
6. Robinson PS, Barker P, Campbell A, et.al. Iodine-131 in breast milk following therapy for thyroid carcinoma. J. Nuci. Med. 35:1797-1801, 1994.
7. Saha GB. In: Fundamentals of Nuclear Pharmacy. Third Edition. Springer, 1992.

8.   International Commission on Radiological Protection. 1990 Recommendation of the ICRP. ICRP Publication 60. Annals of the ICRP, Volume 21, no. 1-3, Oxford: Pergamon Press, 1991.

Ibuprofen   Fax #1229

Trade: Advil, Nuprin, Motrin, Pediaprofen
Can/Aus/UK: Actiprofen, Advil, Amersol, Motrin, ACT-3, Brufen, Nurofen, Rafen
Uses: Analgesic, antipyretic
AAP: Approved by the American Academy of Pediatrics for use in breastfeeding mothers

Ibuprofen is a nonsteroidal anti-inflammatory analgesic. It is frequently used for fever in infants. Ibuprofen enters milk only in very low levels (less than 0.6% of maternal dose). Even large doses produce very small milk levels. In one patient receiving 400 mg twice daily, milk levels were less than 0.5 mg/L. In another study of twelve women who received 400 mg doses every 6 hours for a total of 5 doses, all breast milk levels of ibuprofen were less than 1.0 mg/L, the lower limit of the assay. Data in these studies document that no measurable concentrations of ibuprofen are detected in breast milk following the above doses. Ibuprofen is presently popular for therapy of fever in infants. Current recommended dose is 5-10 mg/Kg every 6 hours.

Alternatives: Acetaminophen

Pregnancy Risk Category: **B if used first 2 trimesters**
                              D if used in third trimester

Adult Concerns: Nausea, epigastric pain, dizziness, edema, GI bleeding.

Pediatric Concerns: None reported from breastfeeding.

Drug Interactions: Aspirin may decrease serum ibuprofen levels. May prolong prothrombin time when used with warfarin. Antihypertensive effects of ACEi family may be blunted or completely abolished by

NSAIDs. Some NSAIDs may block antihypertensive effect of beta blockers, diuretics. Used with cyclosporin, may dramatically increase renal toxicity. May increase digoxin, phenytoin, lithium levels. May increase toxicity of methotrexate. May increase bioavailability of penicillamine. Probenecid may increase NSAID levels.

AHL = 1.8-2.5 hours		**M/P** =	
PHL =		**PB** = >99%	
PK = 1-2 hours		**Oral** = 80%	
MW = 206		**pKa** = 4.4	
Vd = 0.14			

References:
1. Weibert RT, Townsend RJ, Kaiser DG, et.al. Lack of ibuprofen secretion into human milk. Clin Pharm 1:457-458,1982.
2. Townsend RJ, et. al. Excretion of ibuprofen into breast milk. Am J Obstet Gynecol 149:184-6, 1984.

Imipenem-Cilastatin   Fax #1230

Trade: Primaxin
Can/Aus/UK: Primaxin
Uses: Antibiotic
AAP: Not reviewed

Imipenem is structurally similar to penicillins and acts similarly. Cilastatin is added to extend the half-life of imipenem. Both imipenem and cilastatin are poorly absorbed orally and must be administered IM or IV. Imipenem is destroyed by gastric acidity. Transfer into breast milk is probably minimal. Changes in GI flora could occur but is probably remote.

Alternatives:

Pregnancy Risk Category: C

Adult Concerns: Nausea, diarrhea, vomiting, abdominal pain, decreased white blood cells, decreased hemoglobin, seizures.

Pediatric Concerns:

Drug Interactions: May have increased toxicity when used with other beta lactam antibiotics. Probenecid may increase toxic potential.

AHL = 0.85-1.3 hr.		M/P	=
PHL = 1.5-2.6 hours (neonate)		PB	= 20-35%
PK = Immediate(IV)		Oral	= Poor
MW = 317		pKa	=
Vd =			

References:
1. Pharmaceutical Manufacturer's Package Insert, 1995.
2. McEvoy GE(ed):AHFS Drug Information, New York, NY. 1995.

Imipramine   Fax #1231

Trade: Tofranil, Janimine
Can/Aus/UK: Apo-Imipramine, Impril, Novo-Pramine, Melipramine, Tofranil, Tofanil
Uses: Tricyclic antidepressant
AAP: Drugs whose effect on nursing infants is unknown but may be of concern

Imipramine is a classic tricyclic antidepressant. Imipramine is metabolized to desipramine, the active metabolite. Milk levels approximate those of maternal serum. In a patient receiving 200 mg daily at bedtime, the milk levels at 1, 9, 10, and 23 hours were 29, 24, 12, and 18 µg/L respectively. The calculated dose per day to this infant was approximately 20 µg. However, in this previous study the mother was not in a therapeutic range. In a mother with full therapeutic levels, it is suggested that an infant would ingest approximately 0.2 mg/day/Liter of milk. This represents a dose of only 0.04 mg/kg, far less than the 1.5 mg/kg dose recommended for older children. The long half-life of this medication in infants could, under certain conditions, lead to high plasma levels, although they have not been reported. Although no untoward effects have been reported, the infant should be monitored closely. Therapeutic plasma levels in children 6-12 yrs are 200-225 ng/ml.

Alternatives: Amoxapine

Pregnancy Risk Category: D

Adult Concerns: Dry mouth, sedation, hypotension, arrhythmias, confusion, agitation, seizures.

Pediatric Concerns: None reported, but observe for sedation, dry mouth.

Drug Interactions: Barbiturates may lower serum levels of TCAs. Central and respiratory depressant effects may be additive. Cimetidine has increased serum TCA concentrations. Anticholinergic symptoms may be exacerbated. Use with clonidine may produce dangerous elevation in blood pressure and hypertensive crisis. Dicumarol anticoagulant capacity may be increased when used with TCAs. Co-use with fluoxetine may increase the toxic levels and effects of TCAs. Symptoms may persist for several weeks after discontinuation of fluoxetine. Haloperidol may increase serum concentrations of TCAs. MAO inhibitors should never be given immediately after or with tricyclic antidepressants. Oral contraceptives may inhibit the metabolism of tricyclic antidepressants and may increase their plasma levels.

AHL = 8-16 hours		**M/P**	= 0.5-1.5
PHL =		**PB**	= 90%
PK = 1-2 hours		**Oral**	= 90%
MW = 280		**pKa**	= 9.5
Vd = 20-40			

References:
1. Sovner R, Orsulak PJ. Excretion of imipramine and desipramine in human breast milk. Am J Psychiatry 136:451-2, 1979.
2. Erickson SH, et. al. Tricyclics and breast feeding. Am J Psychiatry 136:1483, 1979.
3. Buist A, Norman T, and Dennerstein L. Breastfeeding and the use of psychotropic medication: a review. J. Affective Disorders 19:197-206,1990.

4.   Wisner KL, Perel JM, Findling RL: Antidepressant treatment during breast-feeding.   Am J Psychiatry 153(9): 1132-1137, 1996.

Indapamide   Fax #1232

Trade: Lozol
Can/Aus/UK: Lozide, Gen-Indapamide, Apo-Indapamide, Dapa-Tabs, Nadide, Napamide, Natrilix
Uses: Antihypertensive diuretic
AAP: Not reviewed

Indapamide is the first of a new class of indoline diuretics used to treat hypertension. No data exists on transfer into human milk. Some diuretics may reduce the production of breast milk.   See hydrochlorothiazide as alternative.

Alternatives:

Pregnancy Risk Category: D

Adult Concerns: Sodium and potassium loss, hypotension, dizziness, nausea, vomiting, constipation.

Pediatric Concerns: None reported, but observe for reduction in milk supply, and volume depletion.

Drug Interactions: May reduce effect of oral hypoglycemics. Cholestyramine may reduce absorption of indapamide. May increase the effect of furosemide and other diuretics. May increased toxicity and levels of lithium.

AHL = 14 hours		M/P	=
PHL =		PB	= 71%
PK = 0.5-2 hours		Oral	= Complete
MW = 366		pKa	=
Vd =			

References:
1.   Pharmaceutical Manufacturer's Package Insert, 1996.

Indium - 111m   Fax #1233

Trade:

Can/Aus/UK:

Uses: Radioactive diagnostic agent

AAP: Radioactive compound that requires temporary cessation of breastfeeding

Indium-111 is a radioactive material used for imaging neuroendocrine tumors. While the plasma half-life is extremely short (<10 minutes), with the majority of this product leaving the plasma compartment and distributing to tissue sites, the radioactive half-life is 2.8 days.   In one patient receiving 12 MBq (0.32 mCi), the concentration in milk at 6 and 20 hours was   0.09 Bq/ml and 0.20 Bq/ml per MBq injected. These data indicate that breastfeeding may be safe if this radiopharmaceutical is used. Assuming an ingestion of 500 cc daily, the infant would receive approximately 100 Bq per MBq given to the mother (approximately 0.1 uCi).   Although the authors do not recommend a waiting period, a brief wait of 24-48 hours would probably reduce radiation risk to an absolute minimum.

Alternatives:

Pregnancy Risk Category:

Adult Concerns: Nausea, dizziness, headache, flushing, hypotension.

Pediatric Concerns: None reported, but slight risk of radiation exposure.

Drug Interactions:

AHL = 2.8 days	M/P =
PHL =	PB =
PK = Immediate(IV)	Oral =
MW = 358	pKa =

Vd =

References:
1. American Academy of Pediatrics, Committee on Drugs. Transfer of drugs and other chemicals into human milk. Pediatrics 93(1):137-150, 1994.
2. Pullar M. and Hartkamp, A. Excretion of radioactivity in breast milk following administration of an 113- Indium labeled chelate complex. Br. J. Radial 50:846, 1977.

Indomethacin   Fax #1234

Trade: Indocin

Can/Aus/UK: Apo-Indomethacin, Indocid, Novo-Methacin, Arthrexin, Hicin, Indoptol

Uses: Non-steroidal anti-inflammatory

AAP: Approved by the American Academy of Pediatrics for use in breastfeeding mothers

Indomethacin is a potent nonsteroidal anti-inflammatory agent frequently used in arthritis. It is also used in newborns in neonatal units to close a patent ductus arteriosus. There is one reported case of convulsions in an infant of a breastfeeding mother early postpartum (day 7). Another report of 7 women indicates an average milk:plasma ratio of 0.37. Total infant dose, assuming daily milk intake of 150 ml/kg, ranged from 0.07% to 0.98% of the weight adjusted maternal dose. In six of seven infants, indomethacin levels were below detection. In one infant the plasma level was 47 µg/L. No adverse affects were noted in this study.

Alternatives: Ibuprofen

**Pregnancy Risk Category: B if used first 2 trimesters
                             D if used in third trimester**

Adult Concerns: Renal dysfunction, GI distress, gastric bleeding, diarrhea, clotting dysfunction.

Pediatric Concerns: One case of seizures in neonate. Additional report suggests no untoward effects. Frequently used in neonatal nurseries for patent ductus.

Drug Interactions: May prolong prothrombin time when used with warfarin. Antihypertensive effects of ACEi family may be blunted or completely abolished by NSAIDs. Some NSAIDs may block antihypertensive effect of beta blockers, diuretics. Used with cyclosporin, may dramatically increase renal toxicity. May increase digoxin, phenytoin, lithium levels. May increase toxicity of methotrexate. May increase bioavailability of penicillamine. Probenecid may increase NSAID levels.

AHL = 4.5 hours		**M/P** = 0.37	
PHL = 30 hours (premature)		**PB** = >90%	
PK = 1-2 :2-4(SR) hours		**Oral** = 90%	
MW = 357		**pKa** = 4.5	
Vd = 0.33-0.40			

References:
1. Eeg-Olofsson O, et. al. Convulsions in a breast-fed infant after maternal indomethacin. Lancet 1978;2:215.
2. Lebedevs TH, et.al. Excretion of indomethacin in breast milk. Brit. J. Clin. Pharmacol. 32(6):751-4,1991.

Influenza Virus Vaccine   Fax #1235

Trade: Vaccine- Influenza, Flu-Imune, Fluogen, Fluzone
Can/Aus/UK: Fluviral, Fluzone
Uses: Vaccine
AAP: Not reviewed

Influenza vaccine is prepared from inactivated, non-viable influenza viruses and infection of the neonate via milk would not be expected. There are no reported side effects, nor published contraindications for using influenza virus vaccine during lactation.

Alternatives:

Pregnancy Risk Category: C

Adult Concerns: Fever, myalgia.

Pediatric Concerns: None reported in breastfeeding mothers.

Drug Interactions: Do not administer within seven days after DTP immunizations. Decreased effect with immunosuppressants.

References:
1.   Kilbourne ED. Questions and answers. Artificial influenza immunization of nursing mothers not harmful. JAMA 226:87, 1973.
2.   Pharmaceutical manufacturer package insert, 1996.

Insect Stings   Fax #1236

Trade: Insect Stings, Spider Stings, Bee Stings
Can/Aus/UK:
Uses: Insect stings
AAP: Not reviewed

Insect stings are primarily composed of small peptides, enzymes such as hyaluronidase, and other factors such as histamine. Because the total amount injected is so small, most reactions are local. In cases of systemic reactions, the secondary release of maternal reactants produces the allergic response in the injected individual. Nevertheless, the amount of injection is exceeding small. In the case of black widow spiders, the venom is so large in molecular weight, it would not likely penetrate milk. In addition, most of the venoms and allergens would be destroyed in the acidic milieu of the infant's stomach. The sting of the Loxosceles spider (brown recluse, fiddle back) is primarily a local necrosis without systemic effects. No reports of toxicity to nursing infants has been reported from insect stings.

Alternatives:

Pregnancy Risk Category:

Adult Concerns: Nausea, vomiting.

Pediatric Concerns: None reported via milk.

Drug Interactions:

References:

Insulin   Fax #1237

Trade: Humulin
Can/Aus/UK: Novolin, Humulin, Humalog, Iletin, Mixtard, Protaphane, Monotard
Uses: Human insulin
AAP: Not reviewed

Insulin is a large peptide that is not secreted into milk. Even if secreted, it would be destroyed in the infant's GI tract leading to minimal or no absorption.

Alternatives:

Pregnancy Risk Category: B

Adult Concerns: Hypoglycemia.

Pediatric Concerns: None reported via milk.

Drug Interactions: A decreased hypoglycemic effect may result when used with oral contraceptives, corticosteroids, diltiazem, epinephrine, thiazide diuretics, thyroid hormones and niacin. Increased hypoglycemic effects may result when used with alcohol, beta blockers, fenfluramine, MAO inhibitors, salicylates, tetracyclines.

AHL =		M/P =	
PHL =		PB =	
PK =		Oral = 0%	

MW = >6000   **pKa** =
Vd = 0.37

References:

Interferon Alpha-n3   Fax #1564

Trade: Alferon N, Interferon Alpha
Can/Aus/UK:
Uses: Immune modulator, antiviral
AAP: Not reviewed

Interferon alpha is a pure clone of a single interferon subspecies with antiviral, anti-proliferative, and immunomodulatory activity . The alpha-interferons are active against various malignancies and viral syndromes, such as hairy cell leukemia, melanoma, AIDS-related Kaposi's sarcoma, condyloma acuminata, and chronic hepatitis B and C infection. Very little is known about the secretion of interferons in human milk, although some interferons are known to be secreted normally and may contribute to the antiviral properties of human milk. However, interferons are large in molecular weight (16-28,000 daltons) which would limit their transfer into human milk. Following treatment with a massive dose of 30 million units IV in one breastfeeding patient, the amount of interferon alpha transferred into human milk was 894, 1004, 1551, 1507, 788, 721 at 0 (baseline), 2, 4, 8, 12, and 24 hours respectively (Kumar and Hale, 1998). Hence, even following a massive dose, no change in breast milk levels were noted. One thousand international units is roughly equivalent to 500 nanograms of interferon. The oral absorption of interferons is controversial, and is believed to be minimal. Interferons are relatively nontoxic unless extraordinarily large doses are administered parenterally. Interferons are sometimes used in infants and children to treat idiopathic thromboplastinemia (ITP) in huge doses.

Alternatives:

Pregnancy Risk Category: C

Adult Concerns: Thrombocytopenia and neutropenia. Flu-like syndrome which occurs 30 minutes after administration and persists for several hours. Fatigue, hyperglycemia, nausea and vomiting.

Pediatric Concerns: None reported via milk.

Drug Interactions: Hematologic abnormalities (granulocytopenia, thrombocytopenia) may occur when used with ACE inhibitors.

AHL = 5-7 hours		**M/P** =	
PHL =		**PB** =	
PK = Immediate		**Oral** = Low	
MW = 28,000		**pKa** =	
Vd = 0.44			

References:
1. Kumar, A. and Hale, T. Excretion of human interferon alpha-n3 into human milk. In press. 1998.
2. Pharmaceutical Manufacturer's Package Insert, 1997.

Interferon Beta-1b   Fax #1542

Trade: Betaseron
Can/Aus/UK: Betaseron, Betaferon
Uses: Antiviral, immunomodulator
AAP: Not reviewed

Interferon Beta-1B is a glycoprotein with antiviral, antiproliferative, and immunomodulatory activity presently used for treatment of multiple sclerosis. Very little is known about the secretion of interferons in human milk, although some interferons are known to be secreted and may contribute to the antiviral properties of human milk. However, interferons are large in molecular weight, generally containing 165 amino acids, which would limit their transfer into human milk. Their oral absorption is controversial, but is believed to be minimal. However, interferons are relatively nontoxic unless extraordinarily large doses are administered parenterally. Interferons are sometimes used in infants and children to treat idiopathic thromboplastinemia (ITP) in huge doses. See Interferon Alpha.

Alternatives:

Pregnancy Risk Category: C

Adult Concerns: Headache, myalgia, nausea, diarrhea, dyspepsia, fever, chills, malaise, sweating, depression, flu-like symptoms. These effects generally follow huge doses.

Pediatric Concerns: None reported.

Drug Interactions: Hematologic abnormalities (granulocytopenia, thrombocytopenia) may occur when added to ACE inhibitors.

AHL = 4.3 hours		M/P	=
PHL =		PB	=
PK = 3-15 hours (IM)		Oral	= Poor
MW =		pKa	=
Vd = 2.9			

References:
1. Chiang J, Gloff CA, et.al. Pharmacokinetics of recombinant human interferon-Bser in healthy volunteers and its effect on serum neopterin. Pharm. Res. 10:567-72, 1993.
2. Wills RJ. Clinical pharmacokinetics of interferons. Clin. Pharmacokinet. 19:390-399, 1990.

Iodinated Glycerol   Fax #1238

Trade: Organidin, Iophen, R-gen
Can/Aus/UK: Organidin
Uses: Expectorant
AAP: Not reviewed

This product contains 50% organically bound iodine. High levels of iodine are known to be secreted in milk. Milk:plasma ratios as high as 26 have been reported. Following absorption by the infant, high levels of iodine could lead to severe thyroid depression in infants.

Normal iodine levels in breast milk are already four times higher that RDA for infant. Expectorants, including iodine, work very poorly. Recently, many iodine containing products have been replaced with guaifenesin, which is considered safer. High levels of iodine-containing drugs should not be used in lactating mothers.

Alternatives:

Pregnancy Risk Category: X

Adult Concerns: Depressed thyroid function. Diarrhea, nausea, vomiting. Acne, dermatitis. Metallic taste.

Pediatric Concerns: Iodine concentrates in milk and should not be administered to breastfeeding mothers. Infantile thyroid suppression is likely.

Drug Interactions: Increased toxicity with disulfiram, metronidazole, procarbazine, MAO inhibitors, CNS depressants, lithium.

AHL =		M/P	=
PHL =		PB	=
PK =		Oral	= Complete
MW = 258		pKa	=
Vd =			

References:
1. Delange F, Chanoine JP, Abrassart C, et.al. Topical iodine, breastfeeding, and neonatal hypothyroidism. Arch Dis Child. 63: 106-107, 1988.
2. Postellon DC, Aronow R. Iodine in mother's milk. JAMA 247:463, 1982.

Iohexol   Fax #1573

Trade: Omnipaque
Can/Aus/UK: Omnipaque
Uses: Radiopaque agent
AAP: Not reviewed

Iohexol is a nonionic radiopaque agent. Radiopaque agents (except barium) are iodinated compounds used to visualize various organs during X-ray, CAT scans, and other radiological procedures. These compounds are highly iodinated benzoic acid derivatives. Although under usual circumstances, iodine products are contraindicated in nursing mothers (due to ion trapping in milk), these products are unique in that they are extremely inert and are largely cleared without metabolism. In a study of 4 women who received 0.755 g/kg (350 mg iodine/mL) of iohexol IV, the mean peak level of iohexol in milk was 35 mg/L at 3 hours post-injection. The average concentration in milk was only 11.4 mg/L over 24 hours. Assuming a daily milk intake of 150 mL/Kg body weight, the amount of iohexol transferred to an infant during the first 24 hours would be 3.7 mg/Kg which corresponds to 0.5 % of the maternal dose. As a group, these radiopaque agents are virtually unabsorbed after oral administration (< 0.1%). Iohexol has a brief half-life of just 2 hours and the estimated dose ingested by the infant is only 0.2 % of the radiopaque dose used clinically for various scanning procedures in infants. Although most company package inserts suggest that an infant be removed from the breast for 24 hours, no untoward effects have been reported with these products in breastfed infants. Because the amount of iohexol transferred into milk is so small, the authors conclude that breastfeeding is acceptable after intravenously administered iohexol.

Alternatives:

Pregnancy Risk Category: B

Adult Concerns: Hypersensitivity to iodine. Arrhythmias, renal failure. Volume expansion.

Pediatric Concerns: None reported via milk in one study.

Drug Interactions: Lower seizure threshold when used with amitriptyline, other tricyclics, CNS stimulants, MAO inhibitors, . Should not be used in patients on metformin therapy.

AHL = 2 hours		M/P	=
PHL =		PB	=
PK = 3-10 minutes		Oral	= Nil

MW = pKa =
Vd = 0.55

References:
1.   Nielsen ST et.al. Excretion of iohexol and metrizoate in human breast milk. Acta. Radiol. 28:523-26, 1987.

Iopamidol   Fax #1523

Trade: Isovue-128
Can/Aus/UK: Ascorbef
Uses: Radiopaque agent
AAP: Not reviewed

Iopamidol is a nonionic radiopaque agent used for numerous radiological procedures.   Although it contains significant iodine content, the iodine is covalently bound to the parent molecule and the bioavailability of the iodine molecule is minuscule. As with other ionic and nonionic radiopaque agents, it is primarily extracellular and intravascular, its does not pass the blood-brain barrier, and it would be extremely unlikely that it would penetrate into human milk. However, no data are available on its transfer into human milk.   As with most of these products, it is virtually nonabsorbable from the GI tract and rapidly excreted from the maternal circulation due to a extremely short half-life.

Alternatives:

Pregnancy Risk Category:

Adult Concerns: Infrequently seizures, deformed and dehydrated red blood cells. Hot flashes, angina, flushing.

Pediatric Concerns: None reported.

Drug Interactions:

AHL = < 2 hours.	**M/P** =
PHL =	**PB** = < 2 hours

PK	= Immediate	Oral	= None
MW	= 777	pKa	=
Vd	= 0.35		

References:
1.   Pharmaceutical Manufacturer's Package Insert, 1997.

Ipratropium Bromide   Fax #1239

Trade: Atrovent
Can/Aus/UK: Atrovnet, Atrovent, Apo-Ipravent
Uses: Bronchodilator in asthmatics
AAP: Not reviewed

Ipratropium is an anticholinergic drug that is used via inhalation for dilating the bronchi of asthmatics.   Ipratropium is a quaternary ammonium compound, and although no data exists, it probably penetrates into breast milk in exceedingly small levels due to its structure.   It is unlikely that the infant would absorb any due to the poor tissue distribution and oral absorption of this family of drugs.

Alternatives:

Pregnancy Risk Category: B

Adult Concerns: Nervousness, dizziness, nausea, GI distress, bitter taste.

Pediatric Concerns: None reported.   Commonly used in pediatric patients.

Drug Interactions: Albuterol may increase effect of ipratropium. May have increased toxicity when used with other anticholinergics.

AHL	= 2 hours.	M/P	=
PHL	=	PB	=
PK	= 1-2 hours	Oral	= 0-2%
MW	= 412	pKa	=
Vd	=		

References:
1.   Pharmaceutical Manufacturer's Package Insert, 1996.

Iron   Fax #1240

Trade: Fer-in-sol
Can/Aus/UK: Infufer, Jectofer, Slow-Fe, Feospan
Uses: Metal supplement
AAP: Not reviewed

Secretion into breast milk appears to be very low although bioavailability of that present in milk is high.   One recent study suggests that supplementation is not generally required until the 4th month postpartum when some breastfed infants may become iron deficient, although these assumptions are controversial. Premature infants are more susceptible to iron deficiencies, because they do not have the same hepatic stores available as full term infants.   These authors recommend iron supplementation, particularly in exclusively breastfed infants, beginning at 4th month.   Supplementation in pre-term infants should probably be initiated earlier.   Again, avoid excessively high doses.

Alternatives:

Pregnancy Risk Category:

Adult Concerns: Constipation, GI distress.

Pediatric Concerns: None reported via milk.

Drug Interactions: Decreased iron absorption when used with antacids, cimetidine, levodopa, penicillamine, quinolones, tetracyclines. Slightly increased absorption with ascorbic acid.

AHL =	M/P =
PHL =	PB =
PK =	Oral = <30%
MW = 56	pKa =

Vd   =

References:
1.   O'Brien, T. Excretion of drugs in human milk. Am.J. Hosp. Pharm. 31:844-854, 1974.
2.   Calvo EB, Galindo AC, and Aspres NB. Iron status in exclusively breast-fed infants. Pediatrics 90:375-9,1992.

Isoetharine   Fax #1241

Trade: Bronkosol, Bronkometer
Can/Aus/UK: Numotac
Uses: Bronchodilator
AAP: Not reviewed

Isoetharine is a selective beta-2 adrenergic bronchodilator for asthmatics. There are no reports on its secretion into human milk. However, plasma levels following inhalation are exceedingly low, and breast milk levels would similarly be low. Isoetharine is rapidly metabolized in the GI tract, so oral absorption by the infant would likely be minimal.

Alternatives:

Pregnancy Risk Category: C

Adult Concerns: Tremors and excitement, hypertension, anxiety, insomnia.

Pediatric Concerns: None reported.

Drug Interactions: May have decreased effect with beta blockers and increased toxicity with other adrenergic stimulants such as epinephrine.

AHL = 1-3 hours		**M/P** =
PHL =		**PB** =
PK = 5-15 min.(inhaled)		**Oral** =
MW = 239		**pKa** =
Vd =		

References:
1. Drug Facts and Comparisons. 1995. ed. Facts and Comparisons, St. Louis.

Isometheptene Mucate   Fax #1439

Trade: Midrin
Can/Aus/UK: Midrin
Uses: For tension and migraine headache
AAP: Not reviewed

Isometheptene is a mild stimulate (sympathomimetic) that apparently acts by constricting dilated cranial and cerebral arterioles, thus reducing vascular headaches. It is listed as "possibly" effective by the FDA and is probably only marginally effective. Midrin also contains acetaminophen and a mild sedative dichloralphenazone, of which little is known. No data are available on transfer into human milk. Due to its size and molecular composition, it is likely to attain low to moderate levels in breast milk. Because better drugs exist for migraine therapy, this product is probably not a good choice for breastfeeding mothers. See sumatriptan, amitriptyline, or propranolol as alternatives.

Alternatives: Sumatriptan, amitriptyline, propranolol

Pregnancy Risk Category:

Adult Concerns: Dizziness, skin rash, hypertension, sedation.

Pediatric Concerns: None reported. Observe for stimulation.

Drug Interactions:

AHL =	M/P	=
PHL =	PB	=
PK =	Oral	=
MW =	pKa	=
Vd =		

References:

1. Drug Facts and Comparisons. 1995. ed. Facts and Comparisons, St. Louis.

Isoniazid   Fax #1242

Trade: INH, Laniazid
Can/Aus/UK: Isotamine, PMS Isoniazid, Pycazide
Uses: Antituberculosis agent
AAP: Approved by the American Academy of Pediatrics for use in breastfeeding mothers

Isoniazid (INH) is an antimicrobial agent primarily used to treat tuberculosis. It is secreted into milk in quantities ranging from 0.75 to 2.3% of the maternal dose. Following doses of 5 and 10 mg/kg, one report measured peak milk levels at 6 mg/L and 9 mg/L respectively. Isoniazid was not measurable in the infant's serum, but was detected in the urine of several infants. In another study, following a maternal dose of 300 mg of isoniazid, the concentration of isoniazid in milk peaked at 3 hours at 16.6 mg/L while the acetyl derivative (AcINH) was 3.76 mg/L. The 24 hour excretion of INH in milk was estimated at 7 mg. The authors felt this dose was potentially hazardous to a breastfed infant. Caution and close monitoring of infant for liver toxicity and neuritis are recommended. Peripheral neuropathies, common in INH therapy, can be treated with 10-50 mg/day pyridoxine in adults. PHL= 8-20 hours (neonate), 2-5 hours (1.5-15 yrs).

Alternatives:

Pregnancy Risk Category: C

Adult Concerns: Mild hepatic dysfunction, peripheral neuritis, nausea, vomiting, dizziness.

Pediatric Concerns: None reported, but the infant should be closely monitored for toxicity including hepatitis, vision changes. Observe for fatigue, weakness, malaise, anorexia, nausea, vomiting.

Drug Interactions: Decreased effect/plasma levels of isoniazid with aluminum products. Increased toxicity/levels of oral anticoagulants, carbamazepine, cycloserine, phenytoin, certain benzodiazepines. Disulfiram reactions.

AHL = 1.1 - 3.1 hours		M/P =	
PHL = 8-20 hours (neonate)		PB = 10-15%	
PK = 1-2 hours (oral)		Oral = Complete	
MW = 137		pKa = 1.9, 3.5,	
Vd = 0.6			

References:
1. Snider DE, Powell KE. Should women taking antituberculosis drugs breast-feed? Arch Inter Med. 144:589-590, 1984.
2. Berlin CM, Lee C. Isoniazid and acetylisoniazid disposition in human milk, saliva and plasma. Fed. Proc. 38:426, 1979.

Isoproterenol   Fax #1243

Trade: Medihaler-Iso, Isuprel
Can/Aus/UK: Isuprel, Medihaler-Iso, Isoprenaline, Saventrine
Uses: Bronchodilator
AAP: Not reviewed

Isoproterenol is an old class adrenergic bronchodilator. Currently it is seldom used for this purpose. There are no data available on breast milk levels. It is probably secreted into milk in extremely small levels. Isoproterenol is rapidly metabolized in the gut, and it is unlikely a breastfeeding infant would absorb clinically significant levels.

Alternatives: Albuterol

Pregnancy Risk Category: C

Adult Concerns: Insomnia, excitement, agitation, tachycardia.

Pediatric Concerns: None reported.

Drug Interactions: Increased toxicity when used with other adrenergic stimulants and elevation of blood pressure. When used with isoproterenol, general anesthetics may cause arrhythmias.

AHL = 1-2 hours		**M/P** =	
PHL =		**PB** =	
PK = 10 min.(Inhaled)		**Oral** = Poor	
MW = 211		**pKa** = 8.6	
Vd = 0.5			

References:
1. Drug Facts and Comparisons. 1995 ed. Facts and Comparisons, St. Louis.

Isotretinoin   Fax #1244

Trade: Accutane
Can/Aus/UK: Accutane, Accure, Isotrex, Roaccutane
Uses: Vitamin A derivative used for acne
AAP: Not reviewed

Isotretinoin is a synthetic derivative of the Vitamin A family called retinoids. Isotretinoin is known to be incredibly teratogenic producing profound birth defects in exposed fetuses. It is primarily used for cystic acne where it is extremely effective if used by skilled physicians. While only 25% reaches the plasma, the remaining is either metabolized in the GI tract or removed first-pass by the liver. It is distributed to the liver, adrenals, ovaries, and lacrimal glands. Unlike vitamin A, isotretinoin is not stored in the liver. Secretion into milk is unknown, but is likely as with other retinoids. Isotretinoin is extremely lipid soluble, and concentrations in milk may be significant. The manufacturer strongly recommends against using isotretinoin in a breastfeeding mother.

Alternatives:

Pregnancy Risk Category: X

Adult Concerns: Cheilitis(inflammation of the lips), dry nose, pruritus, elevated serum triglycerides, arthralgia, altered CBC, fatigue, headache, anorexia, nausea, vomiting, abnormal liver function tests, birth defects.

Pediatric Concerns: None reported, but this product poses too many risks to use in a lactating woman.

Drug Interactions: May increased clearance of carbamazepine. Avoid use of other vitamin A products.

AHL	= >20 hours	M/P	=
PHL	=	PB	= 99.9%
PK	= 3.2 hours	Oral	= 25%
MW	= 300	pKa	=
Vd	=		

References:
1. Zbinden G. Investigation on the toxicity of tretinoin administered systemically to animals. Acta Derm Verereol Suppl(Stockh) 74:36-40,1975.

Isradipine   Fax #1245

Trade: DynaCirc
Can/Aus/UK: Prescal
Uses: Calcium channel blocker, antihypertensive
AAP: Not reviewed

It is not known if isradipine is secreted into milk but it should be expected. Such drugs have proven dangerous during pregnancy. Exercise extreme caution if used during lactation. Observe for lethargy, low blood pressure, and headache. See nifedipine as alternative.

Alternatives: Nifedipine, Verapamil, Nimodipine

Pregnancy Risk Category: C

Adult Concerns: Hypotension, headache, dizziness, fatigue, bradycardia, nausea, dyspnea.

Pediatric Concerns: None reported, but observe for hypotension, fatigue, bradycardia, apnea.

Drug Interactions: H2 blockers may increased oral absorption of isradipine. Carbamazepine levels may be increased. Cyclosporine levels may be increased. May increase hypotension associated with fentanyl use. Digitalis levels may be increased. May increase quinidine levels including bradycardia, arrhythmias, and hypotension.

AHL = 8 hours		**M/P** =	
PHL =		**PB** = 95%	
PK = 1.5 hours		**Oral** = 17%	
MW = 371		**pKa** =	
Vd =			

References:
1. Pharmaceutical Manufacturer's Package Insert, 1996.

Itraconazole   Fax #1246

Trade: Sporanox
Can/Aus/UK: Sporanox
Uses: Antifungal
AAP: Not reviewed

Itraconazole is an antifungal agent active against a variety of fungal strains. It is extensively metabolized to hydroxyitraconazole, an active metabolite. Itraconazole has an enormous volume of distribution, and large quantities (20 fold compared to plasma) concentrate in fatty tissues, liver, kidney and skin. Although the levels are unreported, itraconazole penetration into milk is known to occur, and leakage from fat tissues into milk over prolonged periods (weeks) should be expected. Nevertheless, itraconazole oral absorption in an infant is somewhat unlikely as it requires an acidic milieu for absorption, which is unlikely in a diet high in milk. Never use with terfenadine or astemizole. Itraconazole has also been reported to induce significant bone defects in newborn animals, and it is not cleared for pediatric use. Until further studies are done, fluconazole is probably a preferred choice in breastfeeding mothers.

Alternatives: Fluconazole

Pregnancy Risk Category: C

Adult Concerns: Nausea, vomiting, diarrhea, epigastric pain, dizziness, rash, hypertension, abnormal liver enzymes.

Pediatric Concerns: None reported via breast milk. Absorption via milk is unlikely.

Drug Interactions: Decreased serum levels with isoniazid, rifampin and phenytoin. Decreased absorption under alkaline conditions. Agents which increase stomach pH such as H-2 blockers (cimetidine, famotidine, nizatidine, ranitidine), omeprazole, sucralfate, and milk significantly reduce absorption. Cyclosporin levels are significantly increased by 50%. May increase phenytoin levels, inhibit warfarin metabolism, and increase digoxin levels. Significantly increases terfenadine, astemizole plasma levels.

AHL = 64 hours		M/P	=
PHL =		PB	= 99.8%
PK = 4 hours		Oral	= 55%
MW = 706		pKa	=
Vd = 10			

References:
1. Drug Facts and Comparisons. 1994 ed. Facts and Comparisons, St. Louis.
2. Pharmaceutical Manufacturer's Package Insert, 1996.

Ivermectin   Fax #1247

Trade: Mectizan
Can/Aus/UK:
Uses: Antiparasitic

AAP: Not reviewed

Ivermectin is now widely used to treat human onchocerciasis and lymphatic filariasis, other worms and parasites such as head lice. In a study of 4 women given 150 µg/Kg orally, the maximum breast milk concentration averaged 14.13 µg/L. Milk:plasma ratios ranged from 0.39 to 0.57 with a mean of 0.51. Highest breast milk concentration was at 4-6 hours Average daily ingestion of ivermectin was calculated at 2.75 µg/Kg (assuming 778 ml milk consumption daily), which is 10 fold less than the adult dose. No adverse effects were reported.

Alternatives:

Pregnancy Risk Category:

Adult Concerns: Headaches, pruritus, transient hypotension.

Pediatric Concerns: None reported.

Drug Interactions:

AHL = 28 hours	M/P	= 0.39-0.57
PHL =	PB	=
PK = 4 hours	Oral	= Variable
MW =	pKa	=
Vd =		

References:
1. Ogbuokiri JE, Ozumba BC, Okonkwo PO. Ivermectin levels in human breast milk. Eur. J. Clin. Pharm. 46:89-90, 1994.

Kanamycin   Fax #1248

Trade: Kebecil, Kantrex
Can/Aus/UK: Kannasyn
Uses: Antibiotic
AAP: Approved by the American Academy of Pediatrics for use in breastfeeding mothers

Kanamycin is an aminoglycoside antibiotic primarily used for gram negative infections. It is secreted into breast milk in small amounts. Following a 1 g dose (IM), milk levels were 12 mg/L at 30 minutes and 18.4 mg/L one hour post dose. Poor oral absorption (only 1%) in infant would limit amount absorbed. Could potentially alter GI flora in infant.

Alternatives:

Pregnancy Risk Category: D

Adult Concerns: Diarrhea, ototoxicity, nephrotoxicity.

Pediatric Concerns: None reported, but observe for diarrhea.

Drug Interactions: May have increased toxicity when used with penicillins, cephalosporins, amphotericin B, and diuretics. May increase neuromuscular blockade when used with neuromuscular blocking agents.

AHL = 2.1 hours	M/P = <0.4
PHL = 4-18 hours	PB = 0%.
PK = 1 hr.	Oral = 1%
MW =	pKa = 7.2
Vd = 0.2-0.3	

References:
1. O'Brien, T. Excretion of drugs in human milk. Am.J. Hosp. Pharm. 31:844-854, 1974.
2. Wilson, J. Drugs in Breast Milk. New York: ADIS Press, 1981.

Kaolin - Pectin   Fax #1249

Trade: Kaolin, Kaopectate
Can/Aus/UK: Donnagel-MB, Kao-Con, Kaopectate
Uses: Antidiarrheal
AAP: Not reviewed

Kaolin and pectin (attapulgite) are used as antidiarrheal agents. Kaolin is a natural hydrated aluminum silicate. Pectin is a purified polymerized carbohydrate obtained from citrus fruits. Kaolin and pectin are not absorbed following oral use. Some preparations may contain opiate compounds and atropine-like substances. Observe bottle for ingredients. Never use in children less than 3 years of age.

Alternatives:

Pregnancy Risk Category: C

Adult Concerns: Constipation, fecal impaction, reduce drug absorption.

Pediatric Concerns: None reported via milk.

Drug Interactions: Decreases oral absorption of clindamycin, tetracyclines, penicillamine, digoxin.

AHL =		M/P =	
PHL =		PB =	
PK =		Oral = 0%	
MW =		pKa =	
Vd =			

References:

Ketoconazole   Fax #1250

Trade: Nizoral Shampoo, Nizoral
Can/Aus/UK: Nizoral
Uses: Antifungal, anti-dandruff
AAP: Not reviewed

Ketoconazole is an antifungal similar in structure to miconazole and clotrimazole.   It is used orally, topically, and via shampoo. Ketoconazole is not detected in plasma after chronic shampooing. Ketoconazole levels in milk following oral use as systemic antifungal have not been reported but it is probably secreted to some degree. The absorption of ketoconazole is highly variable, and could be reduced in infants due to the alkaline condition induced by milk ingestion. Ketoconazole requires acidic conditions to be absorbed, and its absorption and distribution in children is not known. A number of clinical studies show fluconazole to be superior for oral and vaginal candidiasis and achieve higher tissue and salivary fluid levels. See fluconazole as alternative.

Alternatives: Fluconazole

Pregnancy Risk Category: C

Adult Concerns: Itching, dizziness, fever, chills, hypertension, hepatotoxicity.

Pediatric Concerns: None reported.

Drug Interactions: Decreased ketoconazole levels occur with rifampin, isoniazid and phenytoin use. Theophylline levels may be reduced. Absorption requires acid pH, so anything increasing gastric pH will significantly reduce absorption. This includes cimetidine, ranitidine, famotidine, omeprazole, sucralfate, antacids, etc. Do not co-administer with cisapride or terfenadine (very dangerous). May increase cyclosporin levels by 50%, inhibits warfarin metabolism and prolongs coagulation.

AHL = 2-8 hours		**M/P**	**=**
PHL =		**PB**	**= 99%**
PK = 1-2 hours		**Oral**	**= Variable (75%)**
MW = 531		**pKa**	**=**
Vd =			

References:
1. Pharmaceutical Manufacturer's Package Insert, 1996.
2. Force RW, Nahata MC. Salivary concentrations of ketoconazole and fluconazole: implications for drug efficacy in oropharyngeal and esophageal candidiasis. Ann Pharmacother 29:10-15, 1995.

Ketoprofen   Fax #1251

Trade: Orudis, Oruvail
Can/Aus/UK: Apo-Keto, Orudis, Rhodis, Oruvail, Rhovail
Uses: NSAID analgesic
AAP: Not reviewed

Ketoprofen is a typical nonsteroidal analgesic. It is structurally similar to ibuprofen. Due to tablet formulation (Oruvail), maternal absorption is prolonged during the day, requiring 6-7 hours to peak levels. Studies in animals indicate the milk concentration to be 4-5% of maternal plasma levels. There is no information available on levels produced in human breast milk. See ibuprofen as alternative.

Alternatives: Ibuprofen

Pregnancy Risk Category: B

Adult Concerns: GI distress, diarrhea, vomiting, gastric bleeding.

Pediatric Concerns: None reported, but observe for GI symptoms including diarrhea, cramping.

Drug Interactions: May prolong prothrombin time when used with warfarin. Antihypertensive effects of ACEi family may be blunted or completely abolished by NSAIDs. Some NSAIDs may block antihypertensive effect of beta blockers, diuretics. Used with cyclosporin, may dramatically increase renal toxicity. May increase digoxin, phenytoin, lithium levels. May increase toxicity of methotrexate. May increase bioavailability of penicillamine. Probenecid may increase NSAID levels.

AHL = 2-4 hours	**M/P** =	
PHL =	**PB** = >99%	
PK = 1.2	**Oral** = 90%	
MW = 254	**pKa** = 4.0	
Vd = 0.1-0.5		

References:
1.   Pharmaceutical Manufacturer's Package Insert, 1996.

Ketorolac   Fax #1252

Trade: Toradol, Acular
Can/Aus/UK: Acular, Toradol
Uses: Non-steroidal anti-inflammatory, analgesic
AAP: Approved by the American Academy of Pediatrics for use in breastfeeding mothers

Ketorolac is a popular nonsteroidal analgesic. Although previously used in labor and delivery, its use has subsequently been contraindicated because it is believed to adversely effect fetal circulation and inhibit uterine contractions, thus increasing the risk of hemorrhage. In a study of 10 lactating women who received 10 mg orally four times daily, milk levels of ketorolac were not detectible in 4 of the subjects. In the 6 remaining, the concentration of ketorolac in milk 2 hours after a dose ranged from 5.2 to 7.3 μg/L on day 1 and 5.9 to 7.9 μg/L on day 2. In most patients, the breast milk level was never above 5 μg/L. The maximum daily dose an infant could absorb (maternal dose = 40 mg/day) would range from 3.16 to 7.9 μg/day assuming a milk volume of 400 ml or 1000 ml. An infant would therefore receive less than 0.4% of the daily maternal dose (Please note, the original paper contained a misprint on the daily intake of ketorolac (mg instead of μg).

Alternatives: Ibuprofen

Pregnancy Risk Category: B during first 2 trimesters
                            D during third trimester

Adult Concerns: GI irritability, dry mouth, nausea, vomiting, edema, or rash.

Pediatric Concerns: None reported.

Drug Interactions: May prolong prothrombin time when used with warfarin. Antihypertensive effects of ACEi family may be blunted or completely abolished by NSAIDs. Some NSAIDs may block antihypertensive effect of beta blockers, diuretics. Used with cyclosporin, may dramatically increase renal toxicity. May increase digoxin, phenytoin, lithium levels.   May increase toxicity of methotrexate. May increase bioavailability of penicillamine. Probenecid may increase NSAID levels.

AHL = 2.4-8.6 hours		**M/P**	= 0.015-0.037
PHL =		**PB**	= 99%
PK = 0.5 - 1 hr.		**Oral**	= >81%
MW = 255		**pKa**	= 3.5
Vd = 0.15-0.33			

References:
1.   Wischnik A, Manth SM, Lloyd J. The excretion of ketorolac tromethamine into breast milk after multiple oral dosing. Eur. J. Clin. Pharm. 36:521-524, 1989.

Kombucha Tea   Fax #1472

Trade:
Can/Aus/UK:
Uses: Herbal tea
AAP: Not reviewed

Kombucha tea is a popular health beverage made by incubating the Kombucha mushroom in sweet black tea.   During 1995, several reported cases of toxicity and one fatality were reported to the CDC. Based on these reports, the Iowa Department of Health has recommended that persons refrain from drinking Kombucha tea until the role of the tea in these cases has been resolved.

Alternatives:

Pregnancy Risk Category:

Adult Concerns: Shortness of breath, respiratory distress, fatigue, metabolic acidosis, disseminated intravascular coagulopathy.

Pediatric Concerns:

Drug Interactions:

References:
1. Anonymous. Unexplained severe illness possibly associated with consumption of Kombucha Tea - Iowa, 1995. MMWR 44:892-900, December 1995.

Labetalol   Fax #1253

Trade: Trandate, Normodyne
Can/Aus/UK: Trandate, Presolol, Labrocol
Uses: Antihypertensive, beta blocker
AAP: Approved by the American Academy of Pediatrics for use in breastfeeding mothers

Labetalol is a selective beta blocker with moderate lipid solubility that is used as an antihypertensive and for treating angina. In one study of 3 women receiving 600 mg, 600 mg, or 1200 mg/day, the peak concentration of labetalol in breast milk was 129, 223, and 662 µg/L respectively. In only one infant were measurable plasma levels found, 18 µg/L following a maternal dose of 600 mg. Therefore, only small amounts are secreted into human milk (0.004% of maternal dose). Others report 0.05 to 0.07% of maternal dose. Peak levels in milk occurred between 2-3 hours.

Alternatives: Propranolol, Metoprolol

Pregnancy Risk Category: C

Adult Concerns: Bradycardia, hypotension, dizziness, nausea, aggravation of asthma, lethargy.

Pediatric Concerns: None reported, but observe for hypotension, apnea.

Drug Interactions: Decreased effect when used with aluminum salts, barbiturates, calcium salts, cholestyramine, NSAIDs, ampicillin, rifampin, and salicylates. Beta blockers may reduce the effect of oral sulfonylureas (hypoglycemic agents). Increased toxicity/effect when used with other antihypertensives, contraceptives, MAO inhibitors, cimetidine, and numerous other products. See drug interaction reference for complete listing.

AHL	= 6-8 hours	**M/P**	= 0.8-2.6
PHL	=	**PB**	= 50%
PK	= 1-2 hours (oral)	**Oral**	= 30-40%
MW	= 328	**pKa**	= A7.4, B8.7
Vd	= 10		

References:
1. Anderson PO. Medication use while breast feeding a neonate. Neonatal Pharmacology Quarterly 2:3-12,1993.
3. Lunnell NO, Kulas J. Rane A. Transfer of labetalol into amniotic fluid and breast milk in lactating women. Eur. J. Clin. Pharmacol. 28:597-9, 1985

Lamotrigine   Fax #1486

Trade: Lamictal
Can/Aus/UK: Lamictal
Uses: Anticonvulsant
AAP: Not reviewed

Lamotrigine is a new anticonvulsant primarily indicated for treatment of simple and complex partial seizures. No data are available on its transfer into human milk. Due to its lipid solubility, its ability to penetrate the CNS, and its large volume of distribution, it is likely that some penetrates milk. If one were to assume a Milk:plasma ratio of 1 which is probably high, and using the normal plasma level of 1-4 µg/mL, then an infant consuming 500 cc of milk would ingest at most approximately 2 mg lamotrigine daily (theoretical), a dose that is far less than the 75-700 mg daily adult dose. Dose in children is 2-15 mg/Kg/day.

Alternatives:

Pregnancy Risk Category: C

Adult Concerns: Rash, fatigue, ataxia, dizziness, ataxia, somnolence, and headache. Breast pain has been infrequently reported. Taper over at least 2 weeks.

Pediatric Concerns: Not indicated for children less than 16 years of age, but has been studied safely in patients down to 5 years of age.

Drug Interactions: Acetaminophen reduces lamotrigine half-life by 15-20% and may require increased doses. Carbamazepine, phenytoin, phenobarbital, and other anticonvulsants may reduce plasma levels of lamotrigine by increasing clearance, but this is highly variable.

AHL	= 24 hours	**M/P**	=
PHL	=	**PB**	= 55%
PK	= 1-4 hours	**Oral**	= 98%
MW	= 256	**pKa**	=
Vd	= 0.9-1.3 L/Kg		

References:
1. Peck AW: Clinical pharmacology of lamotrigine. Epilepsia 32(suppl 2):S9-S12, 1991.
2. Cohen AF, Land GS, Breimer DD et al: Lamotrigine, a new anticonvulsant: pharmacokinetics in normal humans. Clin Pharmacol Ther 42:535-541, 1987.
3. Cohen AF, Land GS, Breimer DD et al: Lamotrigine, a new anticonvulsant: pharmacokinetics in normal humans. Clin Pharm Ther 42:535:541, 1987

Lansoprazole   Fax #1445

Trade: Prevacid
Can/Aus/UK: Prevacid, Zoton
Uses: Reduces stomach acid secretion
AAP: Not reviewed

Lansoprazole is a new proton pump inhibitor that suppresses the release of acid protons from the parietal cells in the stomach, effectively raising the pH of the stomach. Similar to omeprazole, it is very acid labile and to some degree is probably denatured by the acid pH of the infants stomach. Therefore, its absorption is likely to be somewhat reduced. Lansoprazole is secreted in animal milk, although no data is available on the amount secreted in human milk. It is a weak base (pKa = 8.9) which might produce some trapping in milk. The only likely untoward effects would be a reduced stomach acidity. Currently omeprazole and the Histamine-2 blockers (Zantac, Pepcid) are used for gastroesophageal reflux in many infants without undue problems. This product has no current pediatric indications.

Alternatives: Omeprazole, famotidine

Pregnancy Risk Category: B

Adult Concerns: Reduced stomach acidity. Diarrhea, nausea, elevated liver enzymes.

Pediatric Concerns: None reported via milk.

Drug Interactions: Decreased absorption of ketoconazole, itraconazole, and other drugs dependent on acid for absorption. Theophylline clearance is increased slightly. Reduced lansoprazole absorption when used with sucralfate (30%).

AHL = 1.5 hours	M/P =
PHL =	PB = 97%
PK = 1.7 hours	Oral = 80%(Enteric only)
MW =	pKa =
Vd =	

References:
1.   Pharmaceutical Manufacturer's Package Insert, 1996.

Latanoprost   Fax #1583

Trade: Xalatan
Can/Aus/UK: Xalatan
Uses: Prostaglandin for glaucoma
AAP: Not reviewed

Latanoprost is a prostaglandin F2-alpha analogue used for the treatment of ocular hypertension and glaucoma. One drop used daily is usually effective. No data are available on the transfer of this product into human milk but it is unlikely. Prostaglandins are by nature, rapidly metabolized. Plasma levels are barely detectible, and then only for 1 hour after use. Combined with the short half-life, and minimal plasma levels, poor oral bioavailability, untoward effects via milk are unlikely.

Alternatives:

Pregnancy Risk Category: C

Adult Concerns: Ocular irritation, headache, rash, muscle aches, joint pain.

Pediatric Concerns: None reported via milk.

Drug Interactions:

AHL	= < 30 minutes	M/P	=
PHL	=	PB	=
PK	= < 1 hour	Oral	= Nil
MW	=	pKa	=
Vd	= 0.16		

References:
1.   Pharmaceutical Manufacturer's package insert, 1998.

Lead   Fax #1254

Trade:
Can/Aus/UK:
Uses: Environmental pollutant
AAP: Not reviewed

Lead is an environmental pollutant. It serves no useful purpose in the body and tends to accumulate in the body's bony structures based on their exposure. Due to the rapid development of the nervous system, children are particularly sensitive to elevated levels. Lead transfers into human milk at a rate proportional to maternal blood levels, but the absolute transfer is controversial. One study evaluated lead transfer into human milk in population of women with an average blood lead of 45 µg/dL (considered very high). The average lead level in milk was 2.47 µg/dL. Using these parameters, the average intake in an infant would be 8.1 µg/kg/d. The daily permissible level by WHO is 5.0 µg/kg/d. Using these parameters, mothers contaminated with lead should not breastfeed their infants. However, in another study of two lactating women whose blood lead levels were 29 and 33 mcg/dL, the breast milk levels were < 0.005 µg/mL and < 0.010 µg/mL respectively. Although both infants had high lead levels (38 µg/dL and 44 µg/dL), it was probably derived from the environment or in-utero. Using this data, breastfeeding would appear to be safe. In the last decade, the permissible blood level (according to CDC) in children has dropped from 25 to less than 10 µg/dL. Lead poisoning is known to significantly alter IQ, and neurodevelopment, particularly in infants. Therefore, infants receiving breast milk from mothers with high lead levels should be closely monitored. Mothers undergoing chelation therapy to remove lead may mobilize significant quantities of lead and should not breastfeed during the treatment period.

Alternatives:

Pregnancy Risk Category:

Adult Concerns: Constipation, abdominal pain, anemia, anorexia, vomiting, lethargy.

Pediatric Concerns: Pediatric lead poisoning, but appears unlikely via milk. More likely environmental.

Drug Interactions:

AHL = 20-30 years(bone)	M/P	=
PHL =	PB	=
PK =	Oral	= 5-10%
MW = 207	pKa	=
Vd =		

References:

1. Namihira D. et.al. Lead in human blood and milk from nursing women living near a smelter in Mexico City. J. Toxicol. Envir. Health 38(3):225-32,1993.
2. Baum C, Shannon M. Lead-Poisoned lactating women have insignificant lead in breast milk. Abstract # 144 J. Clin. Toxicol. 33(5):540-1, 1995.

Leuprolide Acetate   Fax #1501

Trade: Lupron
Can/Aus/UK: Lupron, Prostap
Uses: Gonadotropin-Releasing Hormone Analog
AAP: Not reviewed

Leuprolide is a synthetic nonapeptide analog of naturally occurring gonadotropin-releasing hormone with greater potency than the naturally occurring hormone. After initial stimulation, it inhibits gonadotropin release from the pituitary and after sustained use, suppresses ovarian and testicular hormone synthesis(2-4 weeks).   Almost complete suppression of estrogen, progesterone, and testosterone result. Although Lupron is contraindicated in pregnant women, no reported birth defects have been reported in humans. It is commonly used prior to fertilization, but should never be used during pregnancy.   It is not known whether Leuprolide transfers into human milk, but due to its nonapeptide structure, it is not likely that its transfer would be extensive. In addition, animal studies have found that it has zero oral bioavailability, therefore it is unlikely it would be orally bioavailable in the human infant if ingested via milk.   Its effect on lactation is unknown, but it could suppress lactation particularly early postpartum (4). Lupron would reduce estrogen and progestin levels to menopausal ranges, which may or may not suppress lactation, depending on the duration of lactation. Interestingly, several studies show no change in prolactin levels, although these were not in lactating women. One study of a hyperprolactinemic patient showed significant suppression of prolactin.

Alternatives:

Pregnancy Risk Category: X

Adult Concerns: Vasomotor hot flashes, gynecomastia, edema, bone pain, thrombosis, and GI disturbances. Body odor, fever, headache.

Pediatric Concerns: May suppress lactation, particularly early in lactation.

Drug Interactions:

AHL	= 3.6 hours	M/P	=
PHL	=	PB	= 43-49%
PK	= 4-6 hours	Oral	= None
MW	= 1400	pKa	=
Vd	= 0.52		

References:

1. Sennello LT, Finley RA, et.al. Single-dose pharmacokinetics of leuprolide in humans following intravenous and subcutaneous administration. J. Pharm Sci 75(2):158-160, 1986.
2. Chantilis SJ, et.al. The effect of gonadotropin-releasing hormone agonist on thyroid-stimulating hormone and prolactin secretion in adult premenopausal women. Fertil Steril 64:698-702, 1995.
3. Pharmaceutical Manufacturer's Package Insert, 1997.
4. Frazier, SH. Personal Communication, 1997.

Levobunolol   Fax #1481

Trade: Bunolol
Can/Aus/UK: Betagan, Ophtho-Bunolol
Uses: Beta blocker for glaucoma
AAP: Not reviewed

Levobunolol is a typical beta blocker used intra-ophthalmic for treatment of glaucoma. Some absorption has been reported, with resultant bradycardia in patients. No data on transfer to human milk are available.

Alternatives:

Pregnancy Risk Category:

Adult Concerns: Bradycardia, hypotension, headache, dizziness, fatigue, lethargy.

Pediatric Concerns: None reported via milk, but transfer of some beta blockers is reported. Observe for lethargy, hypotension, bradycardia, apnea.

Drug Interactions: May have increased toxicity when used with other systemic beta adrenergic blocking agents. May produce bradycardia following use with quinidine and verapamil.

AHL = 6.1 hours	M/P	=
PHL =	PB	=
PK = 3 hours	Oral	= Complete
MW = 291	pKa	=
Vd = 5.5		

References:
1. Pharmaceutical Manufacturer's Package Insert, 1997.

Levocabastine   Fax #1255

Trade: Livostin
Can/Aus/UK: Livostin
Uses: Ophthalmic antihistamine for itching
AAP: Not reviewed

Levocabastine is an antihistamine primarily used via nasal spray and eye drops. It is used for allergic rhinitis and ophthalmic allergies. After application to eye or nose, very low levels are attained in the systemic circulation (<1 ng/mL). In one nursing mother, it was calculated that the daily dose of levocabastine in the infant was about 0.5 µg, far too low to be clinically relevant.

Alternatives:

Pregnancy Risk Category: C

Adult Concerns: Sedation, dry mouth, fatigue, eye and nasal irritation.

Pediatric Concerns: None reported via milk.

Drug Interactions:

AHL = 33-40 hours.		**M/P** =	
PHL =		**PB** =	
PK = 1-2 hours		**Oral** = 100%	
MW =		**pKa** =	
Vd =			

References:
1. Pharmaceutical Manufacturer's Package Insert, 1996.

Levodopa   Fax #1256

Trade: Dopar, Larodopa
Can/Aus/UK: Sinemet, Prolopa, Endo Levodopa/Carbidopa, Kinson, Madopar, Brocadopa, Eldopa, Weldopa
Uses: Antiparkinsonian
AAP: Not reviewed

Levodopa is a pro-drug of dopamine used primarily for parkinsonian symptoms. Its use during pregnancy is extremely dangerous. In one group of 30 patients, levodopa significantly reduced prolactin plasma levels. It would likely reduce milk production as well.

Alternatives:

Pregnancy Risk Category: C

Adult Concerns: Nausea, vomiting, anorexia, orthostatic hypotension. Reduces prolactin levels and may reduce milk production. Do not use in glaucoma patients with MAO inhibitors, asthmatics, peptic ulcer disease, or parkinsonian disease.

Pediatric Concerns: None reported.

Drug Interactions: MAO inhibitors may predispose to hypertensive reactions. Decreased effect when administered with phenytoin, pyridoxine, phenothiazines.

AHL = 1-3 hours.		**M/P** =	
PHL =		**PB** = <36%	
PK = 1-2 hours.		**Oral** = 41%-70%	
MW = 197		**pKa** =	
Vd =			

References:
1. Barbieri C, Ferrari C, et al. Growth hormone secretion in hypertensive patients: evidence for a derangement in central adrenergic function. Clin Sci 58:135-8, 1980.

Levofloxacin   Fax #1561

Trade: Levaquin
Can/Aus/UK: Levaquin
Uses: Antibiotic
AAP: Not reviewed

Levofloxacin is a derivative of the fluoroquinolone Ofloxacin and its kinetics including milk levels should be identical. See ofloxacin for specifics.

Alternatives: Norfloxacin, Ofloxacin, Trovafloxacin

Pregnancy Risk Category: C

Adult Concerns: Nausea, vomiting, diarrhea, abdominal cramps, GI bleeding.

Pediatric Concerns: None reported, see ofloxacin.

Drug Interactions: Decreased absorption with antacids. Quinolones cause increased levels of caffeine, warfarin, cyclosporine, theophylline.

Cimetidine, probenecid, azlocillin may increase ofloxacin levels. Increased risk of seizures when used with foscarnet.

AHL	= 6-8 hours	M/P	=
PHL	=	PB	= 24-38%
PK	= 1-1.8 hours	Oral	= 99%
MW	=	pKa	=
Vd	= 1.25		

References:
1. Pharmaceutical Manufacturer's Package Insert, 1998.
2. McEvoy GE(ed):AHFS Drug Information, New York, NY. 1997.

Levonorgestrel   Fax #1257

Trade: Norplant
Can/Aus/UK: Norplant, Triquilar, Levelen, Microlut, Microval, Norgeston
Uses: Implant contraceptive
AAP: Approved by the American Academy of Pediatrics for use in breastfeeding mothers

Levonorgestrel is the active progestin in Norplant. From several studies, it appears to produce limited if any effect on milk volume or quality. One report of 120 women with implants at 5-6 weeks postpartum showed no change in lactation. The level of progestin in the infant is approximately 10% that of maternal circulation. Thus far, long term effects on infant appear minimal, if any.

Alternatives:

Pregnancy Risk Category: X

Adult Concerns: Interruption of the menstrual cycle and spotting, with headache, weight gain, and occasional depression.

Pediatric Concerns: None reported.

Drug Interactions: Reduced effect of carbamazepine and phenytoin.

AHL = 11-45 hours		M/P	=
PHL =		PB	=
PK =		Oral	= Complete
MW = 312		pKa	=
Vd =			

References:
1. Shaaban MM, Salem HT, Abdullah KA. Influence of levonorgestrel contraceptive implants, Norplant, initiated early postpartum upon lactation and infant growth. Contraception 32:623-635, 1985.
2. Shaaban MM. Contraception with progestogens and progesterone during lactation. J. Steroid Biochem. & Mole. Biol. 40:705-10, 1991.
3. Pharmaceutical Manufactures Package Insert, 1996.

Levothyroxine   Fax #1406

Trade: Synthroid, Levothroid, Thyroid, Levo-T, Levoxyl
Can/Aus/UK: Eltroxin, Synthroid, Thyroxine, Oroxine
Uses: Thyroid supplements
AAP: Not reviewed

Levothyroxine is also called T4. Most studies indicate that minimal levels of maternal thyroid are transferred into human milk, and further, that the amount secreted is extremely low and insufficient to protect a hypothyroid infant even while nursing. The amount secreted after supplementing a breastfeeding mother is highly controversial and numerous reports conflict. Anderson indicates that levothyroxine is not detectible in breast milk, while others using sophisticated assay methods have shown extremely low levels (4 ng/ml). It is generally recognized that some thyroxine will transfer, and that if a mother takes thyroid supplements, the infant may need to be periodically evaluated for thyroid function. Liothyronine (T3) appears to transfer into milk in higher concentrations than levothyroxine (T4), but Liothyronine is seldom used in clinical medicine due to its short half-life (<1 day). If the mother is supplemented with thyroid products, periodic monitoring of the infant may be indicated.

Alternatives:

Pregnancy Risk Category: A

Adult Concerns: Nervousness, tremor, agitation, weight loss.

Pediatric Concerns: None reported via milk.

Drug Interactions: Phenytoin may decrease levothyroxine levels. Cholestyramine may decreased absorption of levothyroxine. May increase oral hypoglycemic requirements and doses. May increase effects of oral anticoagulants. Use with tricyclic antidepressants may increase toxicity.

AHL = 6-7 days.		**M/P** =	
PHL =		**PB** = 99%	
PK = 2-4 hours.		**Oral** = 50-80%	
MW = 798		**pKa** =	
Vd =			

References:

1. Mizuta H, Amino N, Ichihara K et al: Thyroid hormones in human milk and their influence on thyroid function of breast-fed babies. Pediatr Res 17:468-471, 1983.
2. Oberkotter LV, Hahn HB. Thyroid function and human breast milk. Am .J Dis Child. 137:1131, 1983
3. Sack J. et. al. Thyroxine concentration in human milk. J Clin Endocrinol Metab 45:171-3, 1977.
4. Anderson PO. Drugs and breast feeding - a review. Drug Intell Clin Pharm 11:208, 1977.
5. Varma SK, et.al. Thyroxine, triiodothyronine, and reverse triiodothyronine concentrations in human milk. J. Pediatr. 93:803-6, 1978.

Lidocaine   Fax #1258

Trade: Xylocaine
Can/Aus/UK: Xylocard, Xylocaine, Lignocaine, EMLA
Uses: Local anesthetic
AAP: Approved by the American Academy of Pediatrics for use in breastfeeding mothers

Lidocaine is an antiarrhythmic and a local anesthetic. In one study of a breastfeeding mother who received IV lidocaine for ventricular arrhythmias, the mother received approximately 965 mg over 7 hours including the bolus starting doses. At seven hours, breast milk samples were drawn and the concentration of lidocaine was 0.8 mg/L, or 40% of the maternal plasma level (2.0 mg/L). Assuming that the mothers' plasma was maintained at 5 μg/mL (therapeutic = 1.5-5 μg/mL), an infant consuming 1 L per day of milk would ingest approximately 2 mg/day. This amount is exceeding low in view of the fact that the oral bioavailability of lidocaine is very poor (35%). The lidocaine dose recommended for pediatric arrhythmias is 1 mg/kg given as a bolus. Once absorbed by the liver, lidocaine is rapidly metabolized. These authors suggest that a mother could continue to breastfeed while on parenteral lidocaine. Recommended doses are as follows: Caudal blockade, <300 mg; Epidural blockade, < 300 mg; Dental nerve block , < 100 mg. When administered as a local anesthetic for dental and other surgical procedures, only small quantities are used, generally less than 40 mg. Because most of these solutions contain adrenergics to slow absorption, the maternal plasma levels would be exceedingly low. It is not likely the concentrations secreted in milk would even approach the levels mentioned above.

Alternatives:

Pregnancy Risk Category: C

Adult Concerns: Bradycardia, confusion, cardiac arrest, drowsiness, seizures, bronchospasm.

Pediatric Concerns: None reported via milk.

Drug Interactions: Use of local anesthetics with sulfonamides may reduce antibacterial efficacy.

AHL = 1.8 hours		**M/P** = 0.4	
PHL = 3 hours (neonate)		**PB** = 70%	
PK = Immediate(IM, IV)		**Oral** = <35%	
MW = 234		**pKa** = 7.9	
Vd = 1.3			

References:
1. Rothermel P, Faber M. Drugs in breast milk: a consumer's guide. Birth and Family J 2:76-78, 1975.
2. Zeisler JA, Gaarder TD, De Mesquita SA. Lidocaine excretion in breast milk. Drug Intell. Clin. Pharm. 20:691-3, 1986.

Lincomycin   Fax #1259

Trade: Lincocin
Can/Aus/UK: Lincocin
Uses: Antibiotic
AAP: Not reviewed

Lincomycin is an effective antimicrobial used for gram positive and anaerobic infections. It is secreted into breast milk in small but detectible levels. In a group of 9 mothers who received 500 mg every 6 hours for 3 days, breast milk concentrations ranged from 0.5 to 2.4 mg/L (mean = 1.28). In this same group, the maternal plasma levels averaged 1.37 mg/L. Although effects on infant are unlikely, some modification of gut flora or diarrhea is possible.

Alternatives: Clindamycin

Pregnancy Risk Category: B

Adult Concerns: Diarrhea, changes in GI flora, colitis, blood dyscrasia, jaundice.

Pediatric Concerns: None reported via milk, but observe for GI symptoms such as diarrhea.

Drug Interactions: GI absorption of lincomycin is decreased when used with kaolin-pectin antidiarrheals. The actions of neuromuscular blockers may be enhanced when used with lincomycin.

AHL = 4.4-6.4 hours		M/P = 0.9	
PHL =		PB = 72%	
PK = 2-4 hours		Oral = <30%	
MW = 407		pKa =	
Vd =			

References:
1.   Medina A, Fiske N, Hjelt-Harvey I, Brown CD, Prigot A. Absorption, diffusion, and excretion of a new antibiotic, lincomycin. Antimicrob. Agents Chemother. 3:189-96, 1963.

Lindane   Fax #1494

Trade: Kwell, G-Well, Scabene
Can/Aus/UK: Hexit, Kwellada, PMS-Lindane
Uses: Pediculicide, scabicide
AAP: Not reviewed

Lindane is an older pesticide also called gamma benzene hexachloride. It is primarily indicated for treatment of Pediculus capitis (head lice) and less so for scabies (crab lice). Because of its lipophilic nature, it is significantly absorbed through the skin of neonates (up to 13%) and has produced elevated liver enzymes, seizures disorders and hypersensitivity. It is not recommended for use in neonates or young children.   Lindane is transferred into human milk although the exact amounts are unpublished.   Estimates by the manufacturer indicate a total daily dose of an infant ingesting 1 Liter of milk daily (30 ng/mL), would be approximately 30 µg/day, an amount that would probably be clinically insignificant. If used in children, lindane should not be left on the skin for more than 6 hours before being wash off, as peak plasma levels in occur in children at about 6 hours after application. Although there are reports of some resistance, head lice and scabies should generally be treated with permethrin products (NIX, Elimite) which are much safer in pediatric patients. See permethrin.

Alternatives:

Pregnancy Risk Category: B

Adult Concerns: Dermatitis, seizures (excess dose), nervousness, irritability, anxiety, insomnia, dizziness, aplastic anemia, thrombocytopenia, neutropenia.

Pediatric Concerns: Lindane is not recommended for children. Potential CNS toxicity includes lethargy, disorientation, restlessness, and tonic-clonic seizures.

Drug Interactions: Oil based hair dressings may enhance skin absorption.

AHL = 18-21 hours		**M/P** =	
PHL = 17-22 hours		**PB** =	
PK = 6 hours		**Oral** =	
MW = 290		**pKa** =	
Vd =			

References:
1. Pharmaceutical Manufacturer's Package Insert, 1996.
2. Drug Facts and Comparisons. 1996. ed. Facts and Comparisons, St. Louis.

Liothyronine   Fax #1459

Trade: Cytomel
Can/Aus/UK: Cytomel, Tertroxin
Uses: Thyroid supplement
AAP: Not reviewed

Liothyronine is also called T3. It is seldom used for thyroid replacement therapy due to its short half-life. It is generally recognized that only minimal levels of thyroid hormones are secreted in human milk, although several studies have shown that hypothyroid conditions only became apparent when breastfeeding was discontinued. Although some studies indicate that breastfeeding may briefly protect hypothyroid infants, it is apparent that the levels of T4 and T3 are too low to provide long-term protection from hypothyroid disease. Levels of T3 reported in milk vary, but in general are around 238 ng/dL and considerably higher than T4 levels. The maximum amount of T3 ingested daily by an infant would be 2.1 to 2.6 µg/day, or approximately 1/10 the minimum requirement. From these studies, it is apparent that only exceedingly low levels of T3 are secreted into human milk and are insufficient to protect an infant from hypothyroidism.

Alternatives:

Pregnancy Risk Category: A

Adult Concerns: Tachycardia, tremor, agitation, hyperthyroidism.

Pediatric Concerns: None reported via milk.

Drug Interactions: Cholestyramine and colestipol may reduce absorption of thyroid hormones. Estrogens may decrease effectiveness of thyroid hormones. The anticoagulant effect of certain medications is increased. Serum digitalis levels are reduced in hyperthyroidism or when the hyperthyroid patient is converted to the euthyroid state. Therapeutic effects of digitalis glycosides may be reduced. A decrease in theophylline clearance can be expected.

AHL = 25 hours.		M/P	=
PHL =		PB	= Low
PK = 1-2 hours		Oral	= 95 %
MW = 651		pKa	=
Vd =			

References:
1. Bode HH, et.al. Mitigation of cretinism by breast-feeding. Pediatrics 62:13-6, 1978.
2. Rovet, F. Does breastfeeding protect the hypothyroid infant whose condition is diagnosed by newborn screening. AJDC 144:319-323, 1990.

3.	Varma SK, et.al. Thyroxine, triiodothyronine, and reverse triiodothyronine concentrations in human milk. J. Pediatr. 93:803-6, 1978.
4.	Hahn HB, et.al. Thyroid function tests in neonates fed human milk. Am. J. Dis. Child. 137:220-222, 1983.
5.	Letarte J. et.al. Lack of protective effect of breastfeeding in congenital hypothyroidism: report of 12 cases. Pediatrics 65:703-5, 1980.
6.	Franklin R. et.al. Neonatal thyroid function: comparison between breast-fed and bottle-fed infants. J. Pediatr. 106: 124-6, 1985.

Lisinopril   Fax #1260

Trade: Prinivil, Zestril
Can/Aus/UK: Prinivil, Zestril, Apo-Lisinopril, Prinvil, Carace
Uses: Antihypertensive, ACE inhibitor
AAP: Not reviewed

Lisinopril is a typical long-acting ACE inhibitor used as an antihypertensive. No breastfeeding data are available on this product. Use caution. Infants are exceedingly sensitive to ACE inhibitors. See enalapril, benazepril, captopril as alternatives.

Alternatives: Captopril, Enalapril

Pregnancy Risk Category: D

Adult Concerns: Hypotension, headache, cough, GI upset, diarrhea, nausea.

Pediatric Concerns: None reported, but observe for hypotension, weakness.

Drug Interactions: Probenecid increases plasma levels of ACEi. ACEi and diuretics have additive hypotensive effects. Antacids reduce bioavailability of ACE inhibitors. NSAIDS reduce hypotension of ACE inhibitors. Phenothiazines increase effects of ACEi.   ACEi increase digoxin and lithium plasma levels. May elevate potassium levels when potassium supplementation is added.

AHL = 12 hours		**M/P** =	
PHL =		**PB** = Low	
PK = 7 hours		**Oral** = 29%	
MW = 442		**pKa** =	
Vd =			

References:
1.   McEvoy GE(ed):AHFS Drug Information, New York, NY. 1995.

Lithium Carbonate   Fax #1261

Trade: Lithobid, Eskalith
Can/Aus/UK: Carbolith, Duralith, Lithane, Lithicarb, Camcolit, Liskonum, Phasal
Uses: Antimanic drug in bipolar disorders
AAP: Contraindicated by the American Academy of Pediatrics in Breastfeeding Mothers

Lithium is a potent antimanic drug used in bipolar disorder. Its use in the first trimester of pregnancy is associated with a number of birth anomalies, particularly cardiovascular. If used during pregnancy, the dose required is generally elevated due to the increased renal clearance during pregnancy. Soon after delivery, maternal lithium levels should be closely monitored as the mother's renal clearance drops to normal in the next several days.   Several cases have been reported of lithium toxicity in newborns. There have been several reports of side effects in breastfeeding infants, including cyanosis, T-wave abnormalities, and decreased muscle tone.   In one study, the milk concentration was approximately 40-60% of the maternal serum levels 3-4 weeks postpartum. The infant's serum levels were approximately 10% of the maternal serum levels.   In another study, the milk concentration (0.3 mmol/L) was approximately 33% of the maternal plasma level at 7 days postpartum.   In another lactating mother receiving 300 mg three times daily throughout the newborn period, the maternal serum lithium levels were 0.62 mmol/L while the infant's serum levels were 0.31

mmol/L at 14 days postpartum. No untoward effects were reported. In another case report of a mother receiving 300 mg three times daily, and breastfeeding her infant at two weeks postpartum, the mother and infant's lithium levels were 0.62 and 0.31 mmol/L respectively. The infant's neuro behavioral development and thyroid function were reported normal (5).From these studies it is apparent that lithium can permeate milk and is absorbed by the breastfed infant. If the infant continues to breastfeed, it is strongly suggested that the infant be closely monitored for serum lithium levels. Lithium does not reach steady state levels for approximately 10 days. Clinicians may wish to wait at least this long prior to evaluating the infant's serum lithium level, or sooner if symptoms occur. In addition, lithium is known to reduce thyroxine production, and periodic thyroid evaluation should be considered. A number of studies of lithium suggest that lithium administration is not an absolute contraindication to breastfeeding, if the physician monitors the infant closely for elevated plasma lithium. Current studies, as well as unpublished experience, suggest that the infants' plasma levels rise to about 30-40% of the maternal level, most often without untoward effects in the infant.

Alternatives:

Pregnancy Risk Category: D

Adult Concerns: Nausea, vomiting, diarrhea, frequent urination, tremor, drowsiness.

Pediatric Concerns: In one study cyanosis, T-wave abnormalities, and decreased muscle tone were reported. Other studies report no side effects. Evaluate infant lithium levels along with mothers.

Drug Interactions: Decreased lithium effect with theophylline and caffeine. Increased toxicity with alfentanil. Thiazide diuretics reduce clearance and increase toxicity. NSAIDS, haloperidol, phenothiazines, fluoxetine and ACE inhibitors may increase toxicity.

AHL = 17-24 hours		**M/P**	= 0.24-0.66
PHL = 17.9 hours.		**PB**	= 0%
PK = 2-4 hours		**Oral**	= Complete
MW = 74		**pKa**	=

Vd = 0.7-1.0

References:

1. Schou M. Lithium treatment during pregnancy, delivery, and lactation: an update. J Clin Psychiatry 51:410-413, 1990.
2. Sykes PA, Quarrie J, Alexander FW. Lithium carbonate and breast-feeding. Br Med J. 2:1299, 1976.
3. Tunnessen WW, Hertz CG. Toxic effects of lithium in newborn infants: a commentary. J. Pediatr 81:804-7, 1972.
4. Fries H. Lithium in pregnancy. Lancet 1:1233, 1970.
5. Montgomery A., Use of lithium for treatment of bipolar disorder during pregnancy and lactation. Academy of breastfeeding Medicine News and Views 3 (1): 4-5, 1997.

Lomefloxacin   Fax #1262

Trade: Maxaquin
Can/Aus/UK:
Uses: Fluoroquinolone antibiotic
AAP: Not reviewed

Lomefloxacin belongs the fluoroquinolone family of antibiotics. The use of fluoroquinolone antibiotics in adolescent children has been associated with arthropathy, or swollen joints. These were following several weeks of normal oral doses, not breast milk. In addition, the FDA is reviewing several pediatric indications for this group. At least one case of bloody colitis (pseudomembranous colitis) has been reported in a breastfeeding infant whose mother ingested ciprofloxacin. It is reported that lomefloxacin is excreted in the milk of lactating animals, although levels are low.

Alternatives: Norfloxacin, Ofloxacin, Trovafloxacin

Pregnancy Risk Category: C

Adult Concerns: GI distress, diarrhea, colitis, headaches, photo toxicity.

Pediatric Concerns: None reported with this drug.   Colitis has been reported with another member of this family. Observe closely for bloody diarrhea.

Drug Interactions: Antacids, iron salts, sucralfate, and zinc salts may interfere with the GI absorption of the fluoroquinolones resulting in decreased serum levels. Cimetidine may interfere with the elimination of the fluoroquinolones.   Nitrofurantoin may interfere with the antibacterial properties of the fluoroquinolone family. Probenecid may reduce renal clearance as much as 50%. Nephrotoxic side effects of cyclosporine may be significantly increased when used with fluoroquinolones. Phenytoin serum levels may be reduced producing a decrease in therapeutic effects.   Anticoagulant effects may be increased when used with fluoroquinolones. Decreased clearance and increased plasma levels and toxicity of theophylline have been reported with the use of the fluoroquinolones.

AHL	= 8 hours	M/P	=
PHL	=	PB	= 20.6 %
PK	= 0.7-2.0 hours	Oral	= 92%
MW	= 351	pKa	=
Vd	= 2		

References:
1.   Pharmaceutical Manufacturer's Package Insert, 1996.

Loperamide   Fax #1263

Trade: Imodium, Pepto Diarrhea, Control, Maalox Anti-diarrheal Caplets, Kaopectate II Caplets
Can/Aus/UK: Imodium, Novo-Loperamide, Gastro-Stop
Uses: Antidiarrheal drug
AAP: Approved by the American Academy of Pediatrics for use in breastfeeding mothers

Loperamide is an antidiarrheal drug. Because it is only minimally absorbed orally (0.3%), only extremely small amounts are secreted into breast milk. Following a 4 mg oral dose, milk levels 6 hours after the second dose were 0.27 µg/L. A breastfeeding infant consuming 165 mL/kg/day of milk would ingest 2000 times less than the recommended daily dose. Loperamide (as with any antidiarrheal) is not generally recommended in children. One case of mild delirium has been reported in a 4 year old infant.

Alternatives:

Pregnancy Risk Category: B

Adult Concerns: Fatigue, dry mouth, respiratory depression, dry mouth, and constipation.

Pediatric Concerns: One case of mild delirium has been reported in a 4 year old infant.

Drug Interactions: CNS depressants, phenothiazines, and TCA antidepressants may potentiate adverse effects.

AHL = 10.8 hours	**M/P** = 0.37
PHL =	**PB** =
PK = 4-5 hours (capsules)	**Oral** = 0.3%
MW = 477	**pKa** =
Vd =	

References:
1. Nikodem VC, and Hofmeyr GJ. Secretion of the antidiarrhoeal agent loperamide oxide in breast milk. Eur.J.Clin.Pharmacol. 42:695-6, 1992.

Loracarbef   Fax #1463

Trade: Lorabid
Can/Aus/UK:
Uses: Synthetic penicillin-like antibiotic
AAP: Not reviewed

Loracarbef is a synthetic beta-lactam antibiotic. It is structurally similar to the cephalosporin family. It is used for gram negative and gram positive infections. Pediatric indications are available for infants 6 months and children to 12 years of age. No data are available on levels in breast milk.

Alternatives:

Pregnancy Risk Category: B

Adult Concerns: Nausea, vomiting, diarrhea, allergic rashes.

Pediatric Concerns: None reported. Observe for GI changes such as diarrhea.

Drug Interactions: Probenecid may increase levels of cephalosporins by reducing renal clearance.

AHL = 1 hour		**M/P** =	
PHL =		**PB** = 25%	
PK = 1.2 hours		**Oral** = 90%	
MW =		**pKa** =	
Vd =			

References:
1. Pharmaceutical Manufacturer's Package Insert, 1995.

Loratadine   Fax #1264

Trade: Claritin
Can/Aus/UK: Claritin, Claratyne, Clarityn
Uses: Long-acting antihistamine
AAP: Not reviewed

Loratadine is a long-acting antihistamine with minimal sedative properties. Milk:plasma ratios for loratadine and its active metabolite are 1.17 and 0.85 respectively. Following a single oral dose of 40 mg a small amount of loratadine and metabolite were transferred into human milk (approximately 0.029% over 48 hours). Loratadine does not transfer into the CNS of adults. The half-life in neonates is not known although it is likely quite long. Pediatric formulations are available. AHL= 8.4 hours (loratadine), 28 hours (metabolite).

Alternatives: Cetirizine

Pregnancy Risk Category: B

Adult Concerns: Sedation, dry mouth, fatigue, nausea, tachycardia, palpitations.

Pediatric Concerns: None reported, but observe for sedation, dry mouth, tachycardia.

Drug Interactions: Increased plasma levels of loratadine may result when used with ketaconazole, the macrolide antibiotics, and other products.

AHL	= 8.4-28 hours	M/P	= 1.17
PHL	=	PB	= 97%
PK	= 1.5 hours	Oral	= Complete
MW	= 383	pKa	=
Vd	=		

References:
1.   Pharmaceutical Manufacturer's Package Insert, 1996.
2.   Hilbert J, Radwanski E, Affrime MB et al.   Excretion of loratadine in human breast milk. J Clin Pharmacol 28:234-9, 1988.

Lorazepam   Fax #1265

Trade: Ativan
Can/Aus/UK: Apo-Lorazepam, Ativan, Novo-Lorazepam, Almazine
Uses: Antianxiety, sedative drug
AAP: Drugs whose effect on nursing infants is unknown but may be

of concern

Lorazepam is a typical benzodiazepine from the Valium family of drugs. It is frequently used prenatally and pre-surgically as a sedative agent. In one prenatal study, it has been found to produce a high rate of depressed respiration, hypothermia, and feeding problems in newborns. Newborns were found to secrete lorazepam for up to 11 days postpartum. In McBrides's (1979) study, the infants were unaffected following the prenatal use of 2.5 mg IV prior to delivery. Plasma levels of lorazepam in infants were equivalent to those of the mothers. The rate of metabolism in mother and infant appears slow, but equal following delivery. In this study there were no untoward effects noted in any of the infants. In one patient receiving 2.5 mg twice daily for 5 days postpartum, the breast milk levels were 12 µg/L. In another patient four hours after an oral dose of 3.5 mg, milk levels averaged 8.5 µg/L. Summerfield (1985) reports an average concentration in milk of 9 µg/L and an average milk:plasma ratio of 0.22. It would appear from these studies that the amount of lorazepam secreted into milk would be clinically insignificant under most conditions.

Alternatives: Midazolam

Pregnancy Risk Category: D

Adult Concerns: Sedation, agitation, respiratory depression, withdrawal syndrome.

Pediatric Concerns: None reported via milk, but observe for sedation.

Drug Interactions: Increased sedation when used with morphine, alcohol, CNS depressants, MAO inhibitors, loxapine, and tricyclic antidepressants.

AHL = 12 hours		**M/P**	= 0.15-0.26
PHL =		**PB**	= 85%
PK = 2 hours		**Oral**	= 90%
MW = 321		**pKa**	= 1.3, 11.5
Vd = 0.9-1.3			

References:

1.   Johnstone M. Effect of maternal lorazepam on the neonate. Br

Med J 282:1973, 1981.

2. Summerfield RJ, Nielson MS. Excretion of lorazepam into breast milk. Br.J. Anaesth. 57:1042-43, 1985

3. Spigset O. Anaesthetic agents and excretion in breast milk. Acta Anaesthesiologica Scandinavica. 38:94-103, 1994.

4. McBride RJ, et.al. A study of the plasma concentrations of lorazepam in mother and neonate. Br J Anaesth 51(10):971-8, 1979.

Losartan   Fax #1499

Trade: Cozaar, Hyzaar
Can/Aus/UK: Cozaar
Uses: ACE-like antihypertensive
AAP: Not reviewed

Losartan is a new ACE-like antihypertensive. Rather than inhibiting the enzyme that makes angiotensin such as the ACE inhibitor family, this medication selectively blocks the ACE receptor site preventing attachment of angiotensin II. No data are available on its transfer to human milk. Although it penetrates the CNS significantly, its rather high protein binding would probably reduce its ability to enter milk. This product is only intended for those few individuals who cannot take ACE inhibitors. No data on transfer into human milk is available. The trade name Hyzaar contains losartan plus hydrochlorothiazide.

Alternatives: Captopril, Enalapril

Pregnancy Risk Category: C if used during first trimester
                                              D if used during second trimester

Adult Concerns: Dizziness, insomnia, hypotension, anxiety, ataxia, confusion, depression. Cough, nor angioedema, commonly associated with ACE inhibitors does not apparently occur with losartan.

Pediatric Concerns: None reported.

Drug Interactions: Decreased effect when used with phenobarbital, ketoconazole, troleandomycin, sulfaphenazole. Increased effect when used with cimetidine, moxonidine.

AHL	= 4-9 hours(metabolite)	M/P	=
PHL	=	PB	= 99.8%
PK	= 1 hour	Oral	= 25-33%
MW	=	pKa	=
Vd	= 12		

References:
1. Lacy C. et.al. Drug information handbook. Lexi-Comp, Hudson(Cleveland), OH. 1996.
2. Pharmaceutical Manufacturer's Package Insert, 1997.

Lovastatin   Fax #1266

Trade: Mevacor
Can/Aus/UK: Mevacor, Apo-Lovastatin
Uses: Lowers cholesterol
AAP: Not reviewed

Lovastatin is an effective inhibitor of hepatic cholesterol synthesis. It is primarily used for hypercholesterolemia. Pregnancy normally elevates maternal cholesterol and triglyceride levels. Following delivery, lipid levels gradually decline to pre-pregnancy levels within about 9 months. Small but unpublished levels are known to be secreted into human breast milk. Less then 5% of a dose reaches the maternal circulation due to extensive first-pass removal by the liver. The effect on the infant is unknown but it could reduce hepatic cholesterol synthesis. There is little justification for using such a drug during lactation, but due to the extremely small maternal plasma levels, it is unlikely that the amount in breast milk would be clinically active. Others in this same family of drugs include simvastatin, pravachol, atorvastatin and fluvastatin. Atherosclerosis is a chronic process and discontinuation of lipid-lowering drugs during pregnancy and lactation should have little to no impact on the outcome of long-term therapy of primary hypercholesterolemia. Cholesterol and other products of cholesterol biosynthesis are essential components for fetal and neonatal development and the use of cholesterol-lowering drugs would not be advisable under any circumstances.

Alternatives:

Pregnancy Risk Category: X

Adult Concerns: Diarrhea, dyspepsia, flatulence, constipation, headache.

Pediatric Concerns: None reported.

Drug Interactions: Increased toxicity when added to gemfibrozil (myopathy, myalgia, etc), clofibrate, niacin (myopathy), erythromycin, cyclosporine, oral anticoagulants (elevated bleeding time).

AHL = 1.1-1.7		M/P	=
PHL =		PB	= >95%
PK = 2-4 hours		Oral	= 5-30%
MW = 405		pKa	=
Vd =			

References:
1. Drug Facts and Comparisons. 1996 ed. Facts and Comparisons, St. Louis.
2. Whittaker P. Cholesterol levels and the breastfeeding mom. JAMA 261(7):1064, 1989.
3. Darmody JM, Postle AD. Lipid metabolism in pregnancy. Brit. J. Obstet. Gynecol. 89:211-215, 1982.

Loxapine   Fax #1460

Trade: Loxitane
Can/Aus/UK: Loxapac, PMS-Loxapine
Uses: CNS tranquilizer
AAP: Not reviewed

Loxapine produces pharmacologic effects similar to the phenothiazines and haloperidol family.   The drug does not appear to have antidepressant effects and may lower the seizure threshold. It is a powerful tranquilizer and has been found to be secreted into the milk of animals, but no human data are available. This is a potent tranquilizer than could produce significant sequella in breastfeeding infants. Caution is urged.

Alternatives: Haloperidol

Pregnancy Risk Category: C

Adult Concerns: Drowsiness, tremor, rigidity, extrapyramidal symptoms.

Pediatric Concerns: None reported, but extreme caution is recommended.

Drug Interactions: Increased toxicity when used with CNS depressants, metrizamide, and MAO inhibitors.

AHL = 19 hours		**M/P** =	
PHL =		**PB** =	
PK = 1-2 hours		**Oral** = 33%	
MW = 328		**pKa** = 6.6	
Vd =			

References:
1.   McEvoy GE(ed):AHFS Drug Information, New York, NY. 1995.

LSD   Fax #1267

Trade:
Can/Aus/UK:
Uses: Hallucinogen
AAP: Not reviewed

LSD is a power hallucinogenic drug. No data are available on transfer into breast milk. However, due to its extreme potency and its ability to pass the blood-brain-barrier, LSD is likely to penetrate milk and produce hallucinogenic effects in the infant. This drug is definitely CONTRAINDICATED. Maternal urine may be positive for LSD for 34-120 hours post ingestion.

Alternatives:

Pregnancy Risk Category:

Adult Concerns: Hallucinations, dilated pupil, salivation, nausea.

Pediatric Concerns: None reported via milk, but due to potency, hallucinations are likely. Contraindicated.

Drug Interactions:

AHL = 3 hours	M/P	=
PHL =	PB	=
PK = 30-60 min.(oral)	Oral	= Complete
MW = 268	pKa	=
Vd =		

References:
1. Ellenhorn MJ and Barceloux DG. In: Medical Toxicology. Elsevier, New York, NY. 1988.

Lyme Disease   Fax #1511

Trade: Lyme Disease, Borrelia
Can/Aus/UK:
Uses: Borrelia Burgdorferi infections
AAP: Not reviewed

Lyme disease is caused by infection with the spirochete, borrelia burgdorferi. This spirochete is transferred in-utero to the fetus, and is secreted into human milk and can cause infection in breastfed infants. If diagnosed postpartum or in a breastfeeding mother, the mother and infant should be treated immediately. In children (> 7 yrs) and adults, preferred therapy is doxycycline (100 mg PO twice daily for 14-21 days), or, Amoxicillin (500 mg three times daily for 21 days). In breastfeeding patients, amoxicillin therapy is probably preferred. In the infant, amoxicillin (40 mg/kg/day (max 3 gm) with probenecid (25 mg/kg/day) divided in three doses/day for a duration of 21 days. Alternative therapy for adults includes clarithromycin (500 mg PO twice daily for 21 days), or azithromycin (500 mg PO daily for 14-21 days), or cefuroxime axetil (500 mg PO twice daily for 21 days. Although doxycycline therapy is not definitely contraindicated in breastfeeding mothers, alternates such as amoxicillin, cefuroxime, clarithromycin or azithromycin should be preferred.

Alternatives: Azithromycin, Amoxicillin, Cefuroxime

Pregnancy Risk Category:

Adult Concerns:

Pediatric Concerns:

Drug Interactions:

References:
1. Stiernstedt G: Lyme borreliosis during pregnancy. Scan. J. Infect. Dis. Suppl 71:99, 1990.
2. Bartlett JG. In: Pocket Book of Infectious Disease Therapy. Williams and Wilkins, Baltimore, USA. 1996.
3. Nelson JD. In: Pocket Book of Pediatric Antimicrobial Therapy. Williams and Wilkins, Baltimore, USA. 1995.

Magnesium Hydroxide   Fax #1268

Trade: Milk Of Magnesia
Can/Aus/UK: Citro-Mag, Phillips' Milk of Magnesia, Mylanta, Gastrobrom
Uses: Laxative, antacid
AAP: Not reviewed

Poorly absorbed from maternal GI tract. Only about 15-30 % of an orally ingested magnesium product is absorbed. Magnesium rapidly deposits in bone (> 50%) and is significantly distributed to tissue sites. See magnesium sulfate.

Alternatives:

Pregnancy Risk Category: C/A

Adult Concerns: Hypotension, diarrhea, nausea.

Pediatric Concerns: None reported.

Drug Interactions: Decreased absorption of tetracyclines, digoxin, indomethacin, and iron salts.

AHL =		M/P	=
PHL =		PB	= 33%
PK =		Oral	= 15-30%
MW = 58		pKa	=
Vd =			

References:

Magnesium Sulfate　　　　Fax #1269

Trade: Epsom Salt
Can/Aus/UK: Magnoplasm, Salvital, Zinvit, Epsom Salts
Uses: Saline laxative and anticonvulsant (IV,IM)
AAP: Approved by the American Academy of Pediatrics for use in breastfeeding mothers

Magnesium is a normal plasma electrolyte. It is used pre and postnatally as an effective anticonvulsant in preeclamptic patients. In one study of 10 preeclamptic patients who received a 4 gm IV loading dose followed by 1 gm per hour IV for more than 24 hours, the average milk magnesium levels in treated subjects was 6.4 mg/dL, only slightly higher than controls (untreated) which were 4.77 mg/dL. On day 2, the average milk magnesium levels in treated groups was 3.83 mg/dL which was not significantly different from untreated controls, 3.19 mg/dL. By day 3, the treated and control groups breast milk levels were identical (3.54 vs 3.52 mg/dL). The mean maternal serum magnesium level on day 1 in treated groups was 3.55 mg/dL, which was significantly higher than control untreated, 1.82 mg/dL. In both treated and control subjects, levels of milk magnesium were approximately twice those of maternal serum magnesium levels, with the milk-to-serum ratio being 1.9 in treated subjects, and 2.1 in control subjects. This study clearly indicates a normal concentrating mechanism for magnesium in human milk. It is well known that oral magnesium absorption is very poor, averaging only 4-30%. Further, this study indicates that in treated groups, infants would only receive about 1.5 mg of oral magnesium more than the untreated controls. It is very unlikely that the amount of magnesium in breast milk would be clinically relevant.

Alternatives:

Pregnancy Risk Category: B

Adult Concerns: IV-hypotension, sedation, muscle weakness.

Pediatric Concerns: None reported via milk. Sedation, hypotonia following in-utero exposure.

Drug Interactions: May decrease the hypertensive effect of nifedepine. May increase the depression associated with other CNS depressants, neuromuscular blocking agents, and the cardiotoxicity associated with ritodrine.

AHL = < 3 hours		**M/P** = 1.9	
PHL =		**PB** = 0%	
PK = Immediate(IV)		**Oral** = 4-30%	
MW = 120		**pKa** =	
Vd =			

References:

1. Cruikshank DP, Varner MW, Pitkin RM. Breast milk magnesium and calcium concentrations following magnesium sulfate treatment. AM J Obstet Gynecol. 143:685-688, 1982.

Mebendazole   Fax #1436

Trade: Vermox
Can/Aus/UK: Vermox, Sqworm
Uses: Anthelmintic
AAP: Not reviewed

Mebendazole is an anthelmintic used primarily for pin worms, although it is active against round worms, hookworms, and a number of other nematodes. Mebendazole is poorly absorbed orally. Following oral administration of multiple doses in two adults, mean peak plasma levels were only 0.08 µg/mL after 2 hours. In children following multiple oral doses, the mean peak plasma levels were less than 0.03 µg/mL. No data are available on its penetration into human milk. Considering the poor oral absorption and high protein binding, it is unlikely to be transmitted to the infant in clinically relevant concentrations. However, in one patient after two days therapy with mebendazole, it was reported to significantly reduce production of breast milk to the point that milk production ceased after one week. This is the only report which has noted this side effect.

Alternatives: Pyrantel

Pregnancy Risk Category: C

Adult Concerns: Diarrhea, abdominal pain, nausea, vomiting, headache. Observe mother for reduced production of breast milk.

Pediatric Concerns: None reported via milk. May inhibit milk production.

Drug Interactions: Carbamazepine and phenytoin may increase metabolism of mebendazole.

AHL = 2.8-9 hours.	M/P =
PHL =	PB = High
PK = 0.5-7.0 hours.	Oral = 2-10%
MW = 295	pKa =
Vd =	

References:
1.   Rao TS, Does mebendazole inhibit lactation? NZ Medical J. 96:589-590, 1983

Meclizine   Fax #1270

Trade: Antivert, Bonine
Can/Aus/UK: Bonamine
Uses: Antiemetic, antivertigo, motion sickness
AAP: Not reviewed

Meclizine is an antihistamine frequently used for nausea, vertigo, and motion sickness, although it is inferior to scopolamine. Meclizine was previously used for nausea and vomiting of pregnancy. No data are available on its secretion into breast milk. There are no pediatric indications for this product.

Alternatives: Hydroxyzine, Cetirizine

Pregnancy Risk Category: B

Adult Concerns: Drowsiness, sedation, dry mouth, blurred vision.

Pediatric Concerns: None reported.

Drug Interactions: May have increased sedation when used with CNS depressants and other neuroleptics and anticholinergics.

AHL = 6 hours		**M/P** =	
PHL =		**PB** =	
PK = 1-2 hours		**Oral** = Complete	
MW = 391		**pKa** =	
Vd =			

References:
1.   Vorherr, H. Drug excretion in breast milk. Postgrad. Med. 56:97-104, 1974.

Medroxyprogesterone   Fax #1271

Trade: Provera, Depo-Provera, Cycrin
Can/Aus/UK: Depo-Provera, Provera, Alti-MPA, Gen-Medroxy, Farlutal, Provelle, Divina, Ralovera
Uses: Injectable progestational agent
AAP: Approved by the American Academy of Pediatrics for use in breastfeeding mothers

Medroxyprogesterone (DMPA) is a synthetic progestin compound. It is used orally for amenorrhea, dysmenorrhea, uterine bleeding, and infertility. It is used IM primarily for contraception. The calculated average oral dosage of injected medroxyprogesterone ingested by a breastfeeding infant would be approximately 0.3-10 µg/day, too low to be clinically relevant. In a series of huge studies, the World Health Organization reviewed the developmental skills of children and their weight gain following exposure to progestin-only contraceptives during lactation. These studies documented that no adverse effects on overall development, or rate of growth, were notable. Further, they suggested there is no apparent reason to deny lactating women the use of progestin-only contraceptives, preferably after 6 weeks postpartum. There have been consistent and controversial studies suggesting that males exposed to early postnatal progestins have higher feminine scores. Ehrhardt's studies have provided convincing data that males exposed to early progestins were no different than controls. A number of other short and long-term studies available on development of children have found no differences with control groups. Much more research is required, however, to establish a clear picture of these effects. The use of Depo-Provera in breastfeeding women is common. It is reported, but unsubstantiated, that some women may experience a decline in milk volume following injection. At present there is no published data to support this, nor the relative incidence of this untoward effect, although it is probably rare. Therefore, in some instances, it might be advisable to recommend treatment with oral progestational-only contraceptives, so that women who experience reduced milk supply could easily withdraw from the medication without significant loss of breast milk supply.

Alternatives:

Pregnancy Risk Category: D

Adult Concerns: Fluid retention, GI distress, menstrual disorders, breakthrough bleeding, weight gain.

Pediatric Concerns: None reported via milk, although unsubstantiated reports of depressed milk supply have been made.

Drug Interactions: Aminoglutethimide may increase the hepatic clearance of medroxyprogesterone, reducing its efficacy.

AHL = 14.5 hours.		**M/P** =	
PHL =		**PB** =	
PK =		**Oral** = Complete	
MW = 344		**pKa** =	
Vd =			

References:

1. Guiloff E, et. al. Effect of contraception on lactation. Am J Obstet Gynecol 118:42-5, 1974.
2. Schwallie PC. The effect of depo-medroxyprogesterone acetate on the fetus and nursing infant: a review. Contraception 23:375-86, 1981.
3. Pardthaison T, Yenchit C, Gray R. The long-term growth and development of children exposed to Depo-Provera during pregnancy or lactation. Contraception 45:313-24,1992.
4. WHO Task Force for Epidemiological Research on Reproductive Health. Progestogen-only contraceptives during lactation: I. Infant Growth. Contraception 50:35-53, 1994.
5. WHO Task Force for Epidemiological Research on Reproductive Health. Progestogen-only contraceptives during lactation: II. Infant development. Contraception 50:55-68, 1994.
6. Ehrhardt AA. et.al. Prenatal exposure to medroxyprogesterone acetate (MPA) in girls. Psycho-neuroendocrinol 2:391, 1977.
7. Meyer-Bahlberg HFL, Ehrhardt AA. Effects of prenatal hormone treatment on mental abilities. In: Progress in sexology. (eds R. Gemme, CC Wheeler). Plenum Press, New York, 1977.
8. Diaz S, Croxatto HB. Contraception in lactating women. Current

Opinion in Obstetrics and Gynecology 5:815-822, 1993.

Mefloquine   Fax #1461

Trade: Lariam
Can/Aus/UK: Lariam
Uses: Antimalarial
AAP: Not reviewed

Mefloquine is an antimalarial and a structural analog of quinine. It is concentrated in red cells and therefore has a long half-life. Following a single 250 mg dose in two women, the milk:plasma ratio was only 0.13 to 0.16 the first 4 days of therapy. The concentration of mefloquine in milk ranged from 32 to 53 µg/L. The estimated ingestion by an infant consuming 1 L of milk daily would be 0.08 mg/day. Unfortunately, these studies were not carried out after steady state conditions, which would probably increase to some degree the amount transferred to the infant. According to the manufacturer, mefloquine is secreted in small concentrations approximating 3% of the maternal dose. Assuming a daily intake of 1 liter of milk, an infant would ingest approximately 0.14 mg/kg/day of mefloquine which in not sufficient to protect the infant from malaria. The therapeutic dose for malaria prophylaxis is 62 mg in a 15-19 kg infant. Thus far, no untoward effects have been reported.

Alternatives:

Pregnancy Risk Category: C

Adult Concerns: GI upset, dizziness, elevated liver enzymes, possible retinopathy.

Pediatric Concerns: None reported but discontinue lactation if neuropsychiatric disturbances occur.

Drug Interactions: Decreases effect of valproic acid. Increased toxicity of beta blockers, chloroquine, quinine, quinidine.

AHL = 10-21 days.   M/P = 0.13-0.27
PHL =   PB   = 98%
PK   = 1-2 hours.   Oral = 85%
MW = 414   pKa =
Vd   = 19

References:
1.   Edstein MD, Veenendaal JR & Hyslop R: Excretion of mefloquine in human breast milk. Chemotherapy 34:165-9, 1988.
2.   Pharmaceutical Manufacturer's Package Insert, 1995.

Melatonin   Fax #1488

Trade:
Can/Aus/UK:
Uses: Hormone
AAP: Not reviewed

Melatonin (N-acetyl-5-methoxytryptamine) is a normal hormone secreted by the pineal gland in the human brain. It is circadian in rhythm, with nighttime values considerably higher than daytime levels. It is postulated to induce a sleep-like pattern in humans. It is known to be passed into human milk, and is believed responsible for entraining the newborn brain to phase shift its circadian clock to that of the mother by communicating the time of day information to the newborn. On the average, the amount of melatonin in human milk is about 35% of the maternal plasma level, but can range to as high as 80%. Post-feeding milk levels appear to more closely reflect the maternal plasma level than pre-feeding values, suggesting that melatonin may be transported into milk at night, during the feeding, rather than being stored in foremilk. In neonates, melatonin levels are low and progressively increase up to the age of 3 months when the characteristic diurnal rhythm is detectible. Night-time melatonin levels reach a maximum at the age of 1-3 years and thereafter decline to adult values. While night-time maternal serum levels average 280 pmol/L, milk levels averaged 99 pmol/L in a group of ten breastfeeding mothers. The effect of orally administered melatonin on newborns is unknown, but melatonin has thus far not been associated with significant untoward effects.

Alternatives:

Pregnancy Risk Category:

Adult Concerns: Headache and confusion, drowsiness, fatigue, hypothermia, and dysphoria in depressed patients.

Pediatric Concerns: None reported.

Drug Interactions:

AHL = 30-50 minutes		**M/P**	= 0.35-0.8
PHL =		**PB**	=
PK = 0.5-2 hours		**Oral**	= Complete
MW = 232		**pKa**	=
Vd =			

References:
1. Illnerova H, Buresova M, Presl J. : Melatonin rhythm in human milk. J. Clin. Endocrin. and Metab. 77(3):838-841, 1993.
2. Aldhous M, Franey C, Wright J et al: Plasma concentrations of melatonin in man following oral absorption of different preparations. Br J Clin Pharmacol 19:517-521, 1985.
3. Davis FC, Mannion J. Entrainment of hamster pup circadian rhythms by prenatal melatonin injections. Am. J. Physiol 255:R439-R48, 1988.
4. Hartman L et.al. Plasma and urinary melatonin in male infants during the first 12 months of life. Clin. Chim. Acta. 121:37-42, 1982.
5. Attanasio A. et.al. Ontogeny of circadian rhythmicity for melatonin, serotonin and N-acetylserotonin in humans. J. Pineal Res 3:251-256, 1986.
6. Dollins AB, Lunch HJ, Wurtman RJ et al: Effect of pharmacological daytime doses of melatonin on human mood and performance. Psychopharmacology 112:490-496, 1993.
7. Dollins AB, Zhdanova IV, et al: Effect of inducing nocturnal serum melatonin concentrations in daytime on sleep, mood, body

temperature, and performance. Proc Natl Acad Sci 91:1824-1828, 1994.

Menotropins   Fax #1530

Trade: Pergonal, Humegon
Can/Aus/UK: Pergonal, Humegon
Uses: Produces follicle growth
AAP: Not reviewed

Menotropins is a purified preparation of gonadotropins hormones extracted from the urine of postmenopausal women. It is a biologically standardized form containing equal activity of follicle stimulating hormone(FSH) and luteinizing hormone (LH). It is primarily used to stimulate follicle growth in women and sperm production in men. FSH and LH are large molecular weight peptides and would not likely penetrate into human milk. Further, they are unstable in the GI tract and their oral bioavailability would be minimal to zero even in an infant.

Alternatives:

Pregnancy Risk Category: X

Adult Concerns: Ovarian enlargement, cysts, hemoperitoneum, fever, chills, aches, joint pains, nausea, vomiting, abdominal pain, diarrhea, bloating, rash, dizziness.

Pediatric Concerns: None reported via milk.

Drug Interactions:

AHL = 3.9 and 70.4 hours		**M/P** =	
PHL =		**PB** =	
PK = 6 hours		**Oral** = 0%	
MW = 34,000		**pKa** =	
Vd = 1.08			

References:

1. Sharma V, Riddle A, et al: Studies on folliculogenesis and in vitro fertilization outcome after the administration of follicle-stimulating hormone at different times during the menstrual cycle. Fertil Steril 51:298-303, 1989.
2. Kjeld JM, Harsoulis P, et al: Infusions of hFSH and hLH in normal men: kinetics of human follicle stimulating hormone. Acta Endocrinologica 81:225-233, 1976.
3. Yen SSC, Llerena LA, Pearson OH et al: Disappearance rates of endogenous follicle-stimulating hormone in serum following surgical hypophysectomy in man. J Clin Endocrinol 30:325-329, 1970.

Meperidine   Fax #1272

Trade: Demerol
Can/Aus/UK: Demerol, Pethidine
Uses: Narcotic analgesic
AAP: Not reviewed

Meperidine is a potent opiate analgesic. It is rapidly and completely metabolized by the adult and neonatal liver to an active form, normeperidine. Significant but small amounts of meperidine are secreted into breast milk. In a study of 9 nursing mothers two hours after a 50 mg IM injection, the concentration of meperidine in breast milk was 0.13 mg/L. In another study of two nursing mothers, the concentration of meperidine 8-12 hours following a dose of 150 or 75 mg was 0.209 and 0.275 mg/L respectively. This study clearly shows a much longer half-life for the active metabolite. Normeperidine levels were detected after 56 hours post-administration in human milk (8.1 ng/mL) following a single 50 mg dose. The milk:plasma ratios varied from 0.84 to 1.59 depending on dose and timing of sampling. Published neonatal half-lives for meperidine (13 hours) and normeperidine (63 hours) are long and with time could concentrate in the plasma of a neonate. Wittels (1990) studies clearly indicate that infants from mothers treated with meperidine (PCA post-cesarian) were neurobehaviorally depressed. Infants from similar groups treated with morphine were not affected.

Alternatives: Morphine, Fentanyl, Hydrocodone

Pregnancy Risk Category: B

Adult Concerns: Sedation, respiratory depression.

Pediatric Concerns: Sedation, poor suckling reflex, neurobehavioral delay.

Drug Interactions: Phenytoin may decrease analgesic effect. Meperidine may aggravate adverse effects of isoniazid. MAO inhibitors, Fluoxetine and other SSRIs, and tricyclic antidepressants may greatly potentiate the effects of meperidine.

AHL = 3.2 hours	M/P = 0.84-1.59
PHL = 6-32 hours (neonates)	PB = 65-80 %
PK = 30-50 min.(IM)	Oral = <50%
MW = 247	pKa = 8.6
Vd = 3.7-4.2	

References:
1. Cobrinik RW, Hood RT, Chusid E. The effect of maternal narcotic addiction on the newborn infant: review of literature and report of 22 cases. Pediatrics 24:288-304, 1959.
2. Wittels Bk, Scott DT, Sinatra RS. Exogenous opioids in human breast milk and acute neonatal neurobehavior: a preliminary study. Anesthesiology 73:864-869, 1990.
3. Peiker G, et. al. Excretion of pethidine in mother's milk. Zentralbl Gynaekol 102:537-41, 1980.
4. Spigset O. Anaesthetic agents and excretion in breast milk. Acta Anaesthesiologica Scandinavica. 38:94-103, 1994.
5. Quinn PG, Kuhner BR, Kaine CJ, and Syracuse CD. Measurement of meperidine and normeperidine in human breast milk by selected ion monitoring. Biomed. & Environ. Mass Spec. 13(3):133:5, 1986.

Mepivacaine   Fax #1556

Trade: Carbocaine, Polocaine
Can/Aus/UK: Carbocaine, Polocaine
Uses: Local anesthetic
AAP: Not reviewed

Mepivacaine is a long acting local anesthetic similar to bupivacaine.
Mepivacaine is used for infiltration, peripheral nerve blocks, and central
nerve blocks (epidural or caudal anesthesia). No data are available on
the transfer of mepivacaine into human milk, however its structure is
practically identical to bupivacaine and one would expect its entry into
human milk is similar and low. Bupivacaine enters milk in exceedingly
low levels (see bupivacaine). Due to higher fetal levels, and reported
toxicities, mepivacaine is never used antenatally. For use in
breastfeeding patients, bupivacaine is preferred.

Alternatives:

Pregnancy Risk Category:

Adult Concerns: Sedation, bradycardia, respiratory sedation, transient
burning, anaphylaxis.

Pediatric Concerns: None reported via milk. Neonatal depression and
convulsive seizures occurred in 7 neonates 6 hours after delivery.

Drug Interactions: Increases effect of hyaluronidase, beta blockers,
MAO inhibitors, tricyclic antidepressants, phenothiazines, and
vasopressors.

AHL = 1.9-3.2 hours		M/P	=
PHL = 8.7-9 hours		PB	= 60-85%
PK = 30 minutes		Oral	=
MW =		pKa	= 7.6
Vd =			

References:
1. Pharmaceutical Manufacturer's information, 1997.
2. Hillman LS, Hillman RE & Dodson WE: Diagnosis, treatment,

and follow-up of neonatal mepivacaine intoxication secondary to paracervical and pudendal blocks during labor. Pediatrics 95:472-477, 1979.

3. Teramo K and Rajamaki A: Foetal and maternal plasma levels of mepivacaine and foetal acid-base balance and heart rate after paracervical block during labour. Br J Anesth 43:300-312, 1971.

Meprobamate   Fax #1273

Trade: Equanil, Miltown
Can/Aus/UK: Equanil, Novo-Mepro, Apo-Meprobamate, Meprate
Uses: Antianxiety drug
AAP: Not reviewed

Meprobamate is an older antianxiety drug. It is secreted into milk at levels 2-4 times that of the maternal plasma level. It could produce some sedation in a breastfeeding infant.

Alternatives: Lorazepam, Alprazolam

Pregnancy Risk Category: D

Adult Concerns: Blood dyscrasia, sedation, hypotension, withdrawal reactions.

Pediatric Concerns: None reported, but observe for sedation.

Drug Interactions: May have increased CNS depression when used with other neuroleptic depressants.

AHL = 6-17 hours	**M/P**	= 2-4
PHL =	**PB**	= 15%
PK = 1-3 hours	**Oral**	= Complete
MW = 218	**pKa**	=
Vd = 0.7		

References:
1. Pharmaceutical Manufacturer's Package Insert, 1993, 1994.

2.   Wilson JT, et. al. Drug excretion in human breast milk: principles, pharmacokinetics and projected consequences. Clin Pharmacokinet 5:1-66, 1980.

Mercaptopurine   Fax #1274

Trade: Purinethol
Can/Aus/UK: Purinethol, Puri-Nethol
Uses: Antimetabolite
AAP: Not reviewed

Mercaptopurine is an anti-cancer drug that acts intra-cellularly as an purine antagonist, ultimately inhibiting DNA and RNA synthesis. It is an extremely toxic drug producing significant bone marrow suppression. Because it has a pKa of 7.6, it would likely penetrate milk, although no data are available. Mercaptopurine is probably too dangerous and toxic to expose a breastfeeding infant. Toxic risks probably outweigh benefits of breastfeeding.

Alternatives:

Pregnancy Risk Category: D

Adult Concerns: Bone marrow suppression, liver toxicity, nausea, vomiting, diarrhea.

Pediatric Concerns: None reported, but this product is probably too dangerous to continue breastfeeding.

Drug Interactions: When used with allopurinol, reduced mercaptopurine to 1/3 to 1/4 the usual dose. When used with trimethoprim sulfamethoxazole, may enhance bone marrow suppression.

AHL = 0.9 hr.		M/P	=
PHL =		PB	= 19%
PK = 2 hours		Oral	= 50%
MW = 152		pKa	= 7.6
Vd =			

References:
1.   Pharmaceutical Manufacturer's Package Insert, 1995.

Mercury   Fax #1275

Trade:
Can/Aus/UK:
Uses: Environmental contaminate
AAP: Not reviewed

Mercury is an environmental contaminate that is available in multiple salt forms. Elemental mercury, or the form in thermometers, is poorly absorbed orally (0.01%), but completely absorbed via inhalation (> 80%). Inorganic mercury causes most forms of mercury poisoning and is available in mercury disk batteries (7-15% orally bioavailable). Organic mercury (methylmercury fungicides, phenyl mercury) is readily absorbed (90% orally).   Mercury poisoning produces encephalopathy, acute renal failure, severe GI necrosis, and numerous other systemic toxicities.   Mercury transfers into human milk with a milk:plasma ratio that varies according to the mercury form. Pitkin (1976) reports that in the USA that 100 non-exposed women had 0.9 µg/L total mercury in their milk. Concentrations of mercury in human milk are generally much higher in populations that ingest large quantities of fish.   Mothers known to be contaminated with mercury should not breastfeed.

Alternatives:

Pregnancy Risk Category:

Adult Concerns: Brain damage, acute renal failure, severe GI necrosis, and numerous other systemic toxicities.

Pediatric Concerns: Mercury transfer into milk is reported. Risks are too high to continue exposure of the infant if mother is contaminated.

Drug Interactions:

AHL	= 70 days	M/P	=
PHL	=	PB	=
PK	=	Oral	= Variable
MW	= 201	pKa	=
Vd	=		

References:

1. Wofff MS. Occupationally derived chemicals in breast milk. Amer. J. Indust. Med. 4:359-281, 1983.

Mesalamine   Fax #1276

Trade: Asacol, Pentasa, Rowasa
Can/Aus/UK: Salofalk, Mesasal, Quintasa, Mesalazine, Asacol
Uses: Anti-inflammatory in ulcerative colitis
AAP: Should be given with caution

Mesalamine is an anti-inflammatory agent used in ulcerative colitis. Although it contains 5-aminosalicylic acid, the mechanism of action is unknown. Some 5-aminosalicylic acid (5-ASA) can be converted into salicylic acid and absorbed, but the amount is very small. Acetyl-5-aminosalicylic (Acetyl-5-ASA) acid is the common metabolite and has been found in breast milk. The effect of mesalamine is primarily local on the mucosa of the colon itself. Mesalamine is poorly absorbed from the GI tract. Only 5-35% of a dose is absorbed. Oral tablets are enteric coated for delayed absorption. Rectal mesalamine is generally retained for 3.5-12 hours. Mesalamine rectal suppositories are generally retained for 1-3 hours. In one patient receiving 500 mg mesalamine orally three times daily, the concentration of 5-ASA in breast milk was 0.11 mg/L, and the Acetyl-5-ASA metabolite was 12.4 mg/L. The milk:plasma ratio for 5-ASA was 0.27, and for Acetyl-5-ASA was 5.1.Mesalamine is useful in patients allergic to sulfasalazine, or salicylazosulfapyridine. Estimates of total daily intake in an infant (1000ml milk volume) would be 12.4 mg AC-5-ASA or about 1% of the maternal dose. At least one report of a watery diarrhea in an infant whose mother was using rectal 5-ASA has been reported.

Alternatives:

Pregnancy Risk Category: B

Adult Concerns: Watery diarrhea, abdominal pain, cramps, flatulence, nausea, headache.

Pediatric Concerns: Watery diarrhea in one breastfed patient, although this appears rare.

Drug Interactions: May significantly reduce bioavailability of digoxin.

AHL	= 5-10 hours (metabolite)	M/P	= 0.27, 5.1
PHL	=	PB	= 55%
PK	= 4-12 hours	Oral	= 15-35%
MW	= 153	pKa	=
Vd	=		

References:
1. Nelis GF. Diarrhoea due to 5-aminosalicyclic acid in breast milk. Lancet 1:383, 1989.
2. Jenss H, Weber P, Hartman F. 5-Aminosalicyclic acid and its metabolite in breast milk during lactation. Am. J. Gastroenterol. 85:331, 1990.

Mesoridazine   Fax #1549

Trade: Serentil
Can/Aus/UK: Serentil
Uses: Phenothiazine antipsychotic
AAP: Not reviewed

Mesoridazine is a typical phenothiazine antipsychotic used for treatment of schizophrenia. No data on transfer into human milk are available. However, the use of the phenothiazine family in breastfeeding mothers is risky and may increase the risk of SIDS.

Alternatives:

Pregnancy Risk Category: C

Adult Concerns: Adverse effects include leukopenia, eosinophilia, thrombocytopenia, anemia, aplastic anemia, hypotension, drowsiness, agitation, dystonic reactions, seizures, galactorrhea, gynecomastia, dry mouth, nausea, vomiting, constipation, priapism, incontinence, and photo toxicity.

Pediatric Concerns: None reported via milk, but use in breastfeeding mothers is discouraged due to possible sedation in infant and elevated risk of SIDS.

Drug Interactions: Decreased effect with anticonvulsants, anticholinergics. Increased toxicity when used with CNS depressants, metrizamide(increased seizures) and propranolol.

AHL = 24-48 hours		M/P	=
PHL =		PB	= 91%
PK = 4 hours		Oral	= Erratic
MW =		pKa	=
Vd =			

References:
1.   Ayd FJ. Excretion of psychotropic drugs in breast milk. In : International Drug Therapy Newsletter.   Ayd Medical Comminications. November-December 1973. Vol. 8.
2.   Ayd FJ. Clin. Med 71:1758, 1964.
3.   Pharmaceutical Manufacturer's Package Insert, 1998.

Metaxalone   Fax #1277

Trade: Skelaxin
Can/Aus/UK:
Uses: Sedative, skeletal muscle relaxant
AAP: Not reviewed

Metaxalone is a centrally acting sedative used primarily as a muscle relaxant.   Its ability to relax skeletal muscle is weak and is probably due to its sedative properties. Hypersensitivity reactions in adults (allergic) have occurred as well as liver toxicity. No data are available on its transfer into breast milk.

Alternatives:

Pregnancy Risk Category:

Adult Concerns: Sedation, nausea, vomiting, GI upset, hemolytic anemia, abnormal liver function.

Pediatric Concerns: None reported. No data available.

Drug Interactions:

AHL = 2-3 hours		**M/P** =	
PHL =		**PB** =	
PK = 2 hours		**Oral** =	
MW = 221		**pKa** =	
Vd =			

References:
1.   McEvoy GE(ed):AHFS Drug Information, New York, NY. 1995.

Metformin   Fax #1278

Trade: Glucophage
Can/Aus/UK: Glucophage, Gen-Metformin, Glycon, Diabex, Diaformin, Diguanil
Uses: Oral hypoglycemic agent for diabetes
AAP: Not reviewed

Metformin belongs to the biguanide family and is used to reduce glucose levels in non-insulin dependent diabetics. Oral bioavailability is only 50%. Whereas plasma half-life is 6.2 hours, whole blood half-life is 17.6 hours Studies in animals suggest a milk:plasma ratio of 1.0 with milk levels comparable to the maternal plasma. No data from human studies were found. Due to low protein binding, and the low molecular weight (165) of this product,   other oral hypoglycemics would be preferred.

Alternatives:

Pregnancy Risk Category: B

Adult Concerns: Diarrhea, nausea, vomiting, bloating, lactic acidosis, hypoglycemia.

Pediatric Concerns: None reported, but observe for hypoglycemia.

Drug Interactions: Alcohol potentiates the effect of metformin on lactic metabolism.   Cimetidine produces a 60% increase in peak metformin plasma levels. Furosemide may increase metformin plasma levels by 22%. Use of iodinated contrast material in patients receiving metformin has produced acute renal failure and been associated with lactic acidosis. Use of nifedepine increases oral bioavailability of metformin by 20%.

AHL = 6.2 hours (plasma)	**M/P** = 1.0
PHL =	**PB** = Minimal
PK = 2.75 hours	**Oral** = 50%
MW = 129	**pKa** = 11.5
Vd = 3.7	

References:
1.   Pharmaceutical Manufacturer's Package Insert, 1995.

Methadone   Fax #1280

Trade: Dolophine
Can/Aus/UK: Physeptone
Uses: Narcotic analgesic
AAP: Approved by the American Academy of Pediatrics for use in breastfeeding mothers

Methadone is a potent and very long-acting opiate analgesic. It is primarily used to prevent withdrawal in opiate addiction. In one study of 10 women receiving methadone 10-80 mg/day, the average milk:plasma ratio was 0.83. Due to the variable doses used, the milk concentrations ranged from 0.05 mg/L in one patient receiving 10 mg/day to 0.57 mg/L in a patient receiving 80 mg/day. Depending on the maternal dose, the amount in breast milk could be quite significant. One infant death has been reported in a breastfeeding mother receiving maintenance methadone therapy. The AAP approves breastfeeding in patients undergoing methadone therapy if the dose is less than 20 mg/24 hours. Please note, withdrawal symptoms in newborns of addicted mothers, may be slow in onset, and require as much as 2-6 weeks.

Alternatives:

Pregnancy Risk Category: B

Adult Concerns: Nausea, vomiting, constipation, respiratory depression, sedation, withdrawal syndrome.

Pediatric Concerns: One death has been reported. Observe for sedation, respiratory depression, addiction, withdrawal syndrome. Infant withdrawal may be slow in onset (> 3 weeks).

Drug Interactions: Phenytoin, pentazocine, and rifampin may increase metabolism of methadone and produce withdrawal syndrome. CNS depressants, phenothiazines, tricyclic antidepressants, and MAO inhibitors may increase adverse effects of methadone.

AHL = 13-55 hours.	**M/P** = 1.5
PHL =	**PB** = 89%
PK = 0.5-1 hours.	**Oral** = 50%
MW = 346	**pKa** = 8.6
Vd = 4-5	

References:
1. Cobrinik RW, Hood RT, Chusid E. The effect of maternal narcotic addiction on the newborn infant: review of literature and report of 22 cases. Pediatrics 24:288-304, 1959.
2. Smialek JE, et. al. Methadone deaths in children-a continuing problem. JAMA 238:2516-7, 1977.
3. Blinick G, et. al. Methadone assays in pregnant women and progeny. Am J Obstet Gynecol 121:617-21, 1975.

Methicillin   Fax #1281

Trade: Staphcillin
Can/Aus/UK: Celbenin
Uses: Penicillin antibiotic
AAP: Not reviewed

Methicillin is a penicillin antibiotic only available by IM and IV formulations. It is extremely unstable at acid pH (stomach), hence it would have only limited oral absorption. No data available on transfer into breast milk, although it would appear to be similar to other penicillins.

Alternatives:

Pregnancy Risk Category: B

Adult Concerns: Allergic rash, thrush, diarrhea, drug fever, changes in GI flora, renal toxicity, pseudomembranous colitis.

Pediatric Concerns: None reported via milk.

Drug Interactions: The effect of oral contraceptives may be reduced. Disulfiram and probenecid may significantly increase penicillin levels. Methicillin may increase the effect of anticoagulants.

AHL = 1-2 hours	**M/P**	=
PHL = 1.4-2.4 hours (neonates)	**PB**	= 40%
PK = 30-60 min.	**Oral**	= Poor
MW = 402	**pKa**	=
Vd =		

References:
1. Drug Facts and Comparisons. 1994 ed. Facts and Comparisons, St. Louis.

Methimazole   Fax #1282

Trade: Tapazole
Can/Aus/UK: Tapazole
Uses: Antithyroid agent
AAP: Approved by the American Academy of Pediatrics for use in breastfeeding mothers

Methimazole, carbimazole, and propylthiouracil are used to inhibit the secretion of thyroxine. Significant amounts of methimazole have been found to be secreted into breast milk. Levels depend on maternal dose. There are three reports of over 10 women in which methimazole or carbimazole excretion in breast milk was examined. All three studies show that methimazole freely enters breast milk with a milk:plasma ratio of 1.0. Calculations indicate that an infant may receive as much as 70 µg after a 40 mg dose of methimazole, an amount that could be toxic to an infant's thyroid. However, studies by Lamberg (1984) in 12 women who were treated with the methimazole derivative carbimazole (5-15 mg daily, equal to 3.3 -10 mg methimazole), found all 12 infants had normal thyroid function following maternal treatments. Thus, in small maternal doses, methimazole may also be safe for the nursing mother. In another study of 12 women who received methimazole both during pregnancy and early postpartum, and a second group who received methimazole 2-8 months postpartum, thyroid function was normal in the totally breastfed infants. These patients received doses varying from 5-10 mg/day for periods up to 6 months. All infants had normal thyroid function. However, clinicians should use caution in nursing mothers. Propylthiouracil is still the preferred drug of choice for treating hyperthyroidism in lactating mothers.

Alternatives: Propylthiouracil

Pregnancy Risk Category: D

Adult Concerns: Hypothyroidism, hepatic dysfunction, bleeding, drowsiness, skin rash, nausea, vomiting, fever.

Pediatric Concerns: None reported in several studies, but propylthiouracil may be a preferred choice in breastfeeding women.

Drug Interactions: Use with iodinated glycerol, lithium, and potassium iodide may increase toxicity.

AHL	= 6-13 hours	M/P	= 1.0
PHL	=	PB	= 0%
PK	= 1 hr.	Oral	= 80-95%
MW	= 114	pKa	=
Vd	=		

References:

1. Cooper DS. Antithyroid drugs: to breast-feed or not to breast-feed. Am J Obstet Gynecol 157:234-235,1987.
2. Tegler L, Lindstrom B. Antithyroid drugs in milk. Lancet 2:591,1980. 3. Lamberg BA et.al. Antithyroid treatment of maternal hyperthyroidism during lactation. Clin. Endocrinol 21:81-7, 1984.
4. Azizi F. Effect of methimazole treatment of maternal thyrotoxicosis on thyroid function in breast-feeding infants. J. Pediatr. 128:855-58, 1996.

Methocarbamol   Fax #1283

Trade: Robaxisal, Robaxin
Can/Aus/UK: Robaxin
Uses: Muscle relaxant
AAP: Approved by the American Academy of Pediatrics for use in breastfeeding mothers

Methocarbamol is a centrally acting sedative and skeletal muscle relaxant. Only minimal amounts have been found in milk. Observe for sedation.

Alternatives:

Pregnancy Risk Category: C

Adult Concerns: Drowsiness, nausea, metallic taste, vertigo, blurred vision, fever, headache.

Pediatric Concerns: None reported, but studies are limited.

Drug Interactions: May see increased toxicity when used with CNS depressants.

AHL = 0.9-1.8 hours		**M/P** =	
PHL =		**PB** =	
PK = 1-2 hours		**Oral** = Complete	
MW = 241		**pKa** =	
Vd =			

References:
1.   Pharmaceutical Manufacturer's Package Insert, 1995.

Methotrexate   Fax #1284

Trade: Folex, Rheumatrex
Can/Aus/UK: Rheumatrex, Ledertrexate, Methoblastin, Arthitrex
Uses: Antimetabolite, anti-cancer, antirheumatic
AAP: Contraindicated by the American Academy of Pediatrics in breastfeeding mothers

Methotrexate is a potent and potentially dangerous folic acid antimetabolite used in arthritic and other immunologic syndromes. Methotrexate is secreted into breast milk in small levels. Following a dose of 22.5 mg to one patient two hours post-dose, the methotrexate concentration in breast milk was 2.6 µg/L of milk with a milk:plasma ratio of 0.8. The cumulative excretion of methotrexate in the first 12 hours after oral administration was only 0.32 µg in milk. These authors conclude that methotrexate therapy in breastfeeding mothers would not pose a contraindication to breastfeeding. However, methotrexate apparently accumulates in neonatal cells, particularly GI mucosa, bone marrow, and urinary bladder. Extreme caution is urged.

Methotrexate is believed to be retained in human tissues for long periods (months), and several studies have indicated a higher risk of fetal malformation in mothers who received methotrexate prior to becoming pregnant. Therefore, pregnancy should be delayed for at least 6 months to 1 year following methotrexate therapy.

Alternatives:

Pregnancy Risk Category: D

Adult Concerns: Bone marrow suppression, anemia, vasculitis, vomiting, diarrhea, GI bleeding, stomatitis, bloody diarrhea, kidney damage, seizures, etc.

Pediatric Concerns: None reported via milk, but extreme caution is recommended.

Drug Interactions: Aminoglycosides may significantly decrease absorption of methotrexate. Etretinate has produced hepatotoxicity in several patients receiving methotrexate. The use of folic acid or its derivatives may reduce the response to MTX. The use of NSAIDs with methotrexate is contraindicated, several deaths have occurred due to elevated MTX levels. Phenytoin serum levels may be decreased. Procarbazine may increase nephrotoxicity of MTX.

AHL = 7.2 hours		**M/P**	= >0.08
PHL =		**PB**	= 34-50 %
PK = 1-2 hours		**Oral**	= 33-90%
MW = 454		**pKa**	= 4.3, 5.5
Vd = 2.6			

References:
1. Johns DG, Rutherford L, Leighton PC, et.al. Secretion of methotrexate into human milk. Am J Obstet Gynecol. 112:978-980,1972. 2. Walden P and Bagshawe K. Pregnancies after chemotherapy for gestational trophoblastic tumours. Lancet 2:1241, 1979.

Methyldopa   Fax #1285

Trade: Aldomet
Can/Aus/UK: Aldomet, Apo-Methlydopa, Dopamet, Novo-Medopa, Aldopren, Hydopa, Nudopa
Uses: Antihypertensive
AAP: Approved by the American Academy of Pediatrics for use in breastfeeding mothers

Alpha-methyldopa is a centrally acting antihypertensive.   It is frequently used to treat hypertension during pregnancy.   In a study of 2 lactating women who received a dose of 500 mg, the maximum breast milk concentration of methyldopa ranged from 0.2 to 0.66 mg/L. In another patient who received 1000 mg dose,   the maximum concentration in milk was 1.14 mg/L. The milk:plasma ratios varied from 0.19 to 0.34.   The authors indicated that if the infant were to ingest 750 mL of milk daily (with a maternal dose= 1000mg),   the maximum daily ingestion would be less than 855 µg or approximately 0.02 % of the maternal dose. In another study of 7 women who received 0.750-2.0 gm/day of methyldopa, the free methyldopa concentrations in breast milk ranged from zero to 0.2 mg/L while the conjugated metabolite had concentrations of 0.1 to 0.9 mg/L. These studies generally indicate that the levels of methyldopa transferred to a breastfeeding infant would be too low to be clinically relevant. However, gynecomastia and galactorrhea has been reported in one fullterm two week old female neonate (EDM, personal communication) following seven days of maternal therapy with methyldopa, 250 mg three times daily.

Alternatives:

Pregnancy Risk Category: C

Adult Concerns: Hemolytic anemia, hepatitis, fever, rashes, dizziness, hypotension, sleep disturbances, dry mouth, depression, colitis.

Pediatric Concerns: None reported in several studies.   Gynecomastia and galactorrhea in one personal communication.

Drug Interactions: Iron supplements can interact and cause a significant increase in blood pressure. Increased toxicity with lithium has been reported.

AHL = 105 min.		M/P	= 0.19-0.34
PHL =		PB	= Low
PK = 3-6 hours		Oral	= 25-50%
MW = 211		pKa	=
Vd = 0.3			

References:
1. Jones HMR, Cummings AJ. A study of the transfer of alpha methyldopa to the human foetus and newborn infant. Br.J.Clin. Pharmacol. 6:432-4,1978.
2. White WB, Andreoli JW, Cohn RD. Alpha-methyldopa disposition in mothers with hypertension and in their breast-fed infants. Clin. Pharmacol. Ther. 37:378-90, 1985.
3. Jones HMR, Cummings AJ. A study of the transfer of alpha-methyldopa to the human foetus and newborn infant. Br J Clin Pharmacol 1978; 6:432-434.
4. EDM. Personal communication, 9/1997.

Methylergonovine   Fax #1286

Trade: Methergine
Can/Aus/UK: Methergine, Ergometrine, Methylerometrine
Uses: Vasoconstrictor, uterine stimulant
AAP: Not reviewed

Methylergonovine is an amine ergot alkaloid used to control postpartum uterine bleeding. The ergot alkaloids are powerful vasoconstrictors. In a group of 8 postpartum women receiving 0.125 mg three times daily for 5 days, the concentration of methylergonovine ranged from < 0.5 in 4 patients to 1.3 µg/L in one patient at one hour post-dose. In this study only 5 of 16 milk samples had detectible methylergonovine levels. Assuming an infant ingests 1 Liter of milk daily and taking the highest milk concentration of 1.3 ng/mL, the amount of drug ingested daily via maternal milk would only be 1.3 µg, which is 0.003% of the usual 0.375 mg daily dose. The milk:plasma ratio averaged about 0.3. Short-term (1 week), low-dose regimens of these agents do not apparently pose problems in nursing infants/mothers. Methylergonovine is preferred over ergonovine because it does not inhibit lactation, and levels in milk are minimal.

Alternatives:

Pregnancy Risk Category: C

Adult Concerns: Nausea, vomiting, diarrhea, dizziness, rapid pulse.

Pediatric Concerns: None reported, but long term exposure is not recommended. Methylergonovine is commonly recommended early postpartum for breastfeeding mothers with bleeding.

Drug Interactions: Use caution when using with other vasoconstrictor or pressor agents.

AHL = 20-30 minutes		**M/P**	= 0.3
PHL =		**PB**	= 36%
PK = 0.5-3 hours		**Oral**	= 60%
MW = 339		**pKa**	=
Vd =			

References:
1. Erkkola R, et.al. Excretion of methylergometrine (methylergonovine) into the human breast milk. Int. J. Clin. Pharmacol. 16:579-80,1978.
2. Del Pozo E, Brun del Rey R, Hinselmann M. Lack of effect of methyl-ergonovine on postpartum lactation. Am. J. Obstet. Gynecol. 123:845-6,1975.

Methylphenidate HCL
Fax #1287

Trade: Ritalin
Can/Aus/UK: Ritalin, Riphenidate, PMS-Methylphenidate
Uses: Mild CNS stimulant
AAP: Not reviewed

The pharmacologic effects of methylphenidate are similar to those of amphetamines and include CNS stimulation. It is presently used for narcolepsy and attention deficit hyperactivity syndrome. At present, there is no data available on transfer of this compound into breast milk. However, due to its small molecular weight and other kinetic data, one must assume that methylphenidate readily enters breast milk and would be absorbed by the infant. A prolonged release tablet formulation is commonly used and would extend the half-life. Risk of toxicity must be weighed against need of mother.

Alternatives:

Pregnancy Risk Category: C

Adult Concerns: Nervousness, hyperactivity, insomnia, agitation, and lack of appetite.

Pediatric Concerns: None reported, but observe for stimulation, insomnia, anorexia.

Drug Interactions: Methylphenidate may reduce the effects of guanethidine and bretylium. May increased serum levels of tricyclic antidepressants, phenytoin, warfarin, phenobarbital, and primidone. Use with MAOI may produce significant increased effects of methylphenidate.

AHL = 1-3 hours	M/P =
PHL =	PB =
PK = 1 - 3 hours	Oral = 95%
MW = 233	pKa = 8.8
Vd = 11-33	

References:
1.   Pharmaceutical Manufacturer's Package Insert, 1996.

Methylprednisolone   Fax #1585

Trade: Solu-Medrol, Depo-Medrol, Medrol
Can/Aus/UK: Medrol, Depo-Medrol, Solu-Medrol, Neo-Medrol, Advantan
Uses: Corticosteroid
AAP: Approved by the American Academy of Pediatrics for use in breastfeeding mothers

Methylprednisolone is the methyl derivative of prednisone.   Four milligrams of methylprednisolone is roughly equivalent to 5 mg of prednisone.   For a   complete description of corticosteroid use in breastfeeding mothers see the prednisone monograph.   In general, the amount of methylprednisolone and other steroids transferred into human milk is minimal as long as the dose does not exceed 80 mg per day   However, relating side effects of steroids administered via breast milk and their maternal doses is rather difficult and each situation should be evaluated individually.   Extended use of high doses could predispose the infant to steroid side effects including decreased linear growth rate,   but these require rather high doses.   Low to moderate doses are believed to have minimal effect on breastfed infants.   See prednisone.

Alternatives: Prednisone

Pregnancy Risk Category:

Adult Concerns: In pediatrics: shortened stature, GI bleeding, GI ulceration, edema, osteoporosis.

Pediatric Concerns: None reported via breast milk.   Limit dose and length of exposure if possible.   High doses and durations may inhibit epiphyseal bone growth, induce gastric ulcerations, glaucoma, etc.   Use inhaled or intranasal forms when possible to limit exposure.

Drug Interactions: Barbiturates may significantly reduce the effects of corticosteroids. Cholestyramine may reduce absorption of methylprednisolone. Oral contraceptives may reduce half-life and concentration of steroids. Ephedrine may reduce the half-life and increase clearance of certain steroids. Phenytoin may increase clearance. Corticosteroid clearance may be decreased by ketaconazole. Certain macrolide antibiotics may significantly decrease clearance of steroids. Isoniazid serum concentrations may be decreased.

AHL = 2.8 hours		**M/P** =	
PHL =		**PB** =	
PK =		**Oral** = Complete	
MW =		**pKa** =	
Vd = 1.5			

References:
1.   Anderson PO: Corticosteroid use by breast-feeding mothers. Clin Pharm 6:445, 1987.

Metoclopramide   Fax #1288

Trade: Reglan
Can/Aus/UK: Apo-Metoclop, Emex, Maxeran, Reglan Maxolon, Pramin, Gastromax, Paramid
Uses: GI stimulant, prolactin stimulant
AAP: Drugs whose effect on nursing infants is unknown but may be of concern

Metoclopramide has multiple functions, but is primarily used for increasing the lower esophageal sphincter tone in gastroesophageal reflux in patients with reduced gastric tone. In breastfeeding, it is sometimes used in lactating women to stimulate prolactin release from the pituitary and enhance breast milk production. Since 1981, at least 5 or more publications have documented major increases in breast milk production following metoclopramide use. The increase in serum prolactin and breast milk production appears dose-related up to a dose of 15 mg three times daily. Many studies show 66 to 100 % increases in milk production depending on breast milk flow of the mother prior to therapy. Doses of 15 mg/day were found ineffective, whereas doses of 30-45 mg/day were most effective. In most studies, major increases in prolactin were observed, such as 18.1 ng/mL to 121.8 ng/mL after therapy in one study. In Kauppila's study (1983), the concentration of metoclopramide in milk was consistently higher than the maternal serum levels. The peak occurred at 2-3 hours after administration of the medication. During the late puerperium, the concentration of metoclopramide in the milk varied from 20 to 125 µg/L, which was less than the 28 to 157 µg/L noted during the early puerperium. The authors estimated the daily dose to infant to vary from 6 to 24 µg/kg/day during the early puerperium, and from 1 to 13 µg/kg/day during the late phase. These doses are minimal compared to those used for therapy of reflux in pediatric patients (0.1 to 0.5 mg/kg/day). In these studies, only 1 of 5 infants studied had detectible blood levels of metoclopramide, hence no accumulation or side effects were observed. It is generally well recognized that metoclopramide will increase milk supply, but it is dose dependent, and some mothers simply do not respond. Side effects such as gastric cramping and diarrhea limit the compliance of some patients. Further, it is often found that upon discontinuing the medication, the supply of milk reduces. Tapering of the dose over several days to more than a week is generally recommended. Long-term use of this medication (>2-4 weeks) is not recommended.

Alternatives: Domperidone

Pregnancy Risk Category: B

Adult Concerns: Diarrhea, sedation, gastric upset, nausea, extrapyramidal symptoms.

Pediatric Concerns: None reported in infants via milk. Commonly used in pediatrics.

Drug Interactions: Anticholinergic drugs may reduce the effects of metoclopramide. Opiate analgesics may increased CNS depression.

AHL = 5-6 hours	**M/P** = 0.5-4.06
PHL =	**PB** = 30%.

PK = 1-2 hours (oral)   Oral = 30-100%
MW = 300   pKa =
Vd =

References:
1. Budd SC. et.al. Improved lactation with metoclopramide. Clinical Pediatrics 32:53-57, 1993.
2. Kauppila A, et.al. Metoclopramide and Breast Feeding: Transfer into milk and the newborn. Eur. J. Clin Pharmacol. 25:819-23, 1983.
3. Ertl T. et.al. The influence of metoclopramide on the composition of human breast milk. Acta Pediatr. Hung. 31:415-22, 1991.
4. Ehrenkranz RA. et.al. Metoclopramide effect on faltering milk production by mothers of premature infants. Pediatrics 78:614-620, 1986.
5. Kauppila A. et.al. A dose response relation between improved lactation and metoclopramide. The Lancet 1:1175-77, 1981.
6. Gupta AP and Gupta PK. Metoclopramide as a lactogogue. Clinical Pediatrics 24:269-72, 1985.
7. Anderson PO. Increasing breast milk supply. Clinical Pharmacy 12:479-480, 1993.

Metoprolol   Fax #1289

Trade: Toprol XL, Lopressor
Can/Aus/UK: Apo-Metoprolol, Betaloc, Lopressor, Novo-Metoprol, Minax
Uses: Antihypertensive, beta blocker
AAP: Approved by the American Academy of Pediatrics for use in breastfeeding mothers

At low doses, metoprolol is a very cardioselective Beta-1 blocker, and it is used for hypertension, angina, and tachyarrhythmias. In a study of 3 women 4-6 months postpartum who received 100 mg twice daily for 4 days, the peak concentration of metoprolol ranged from 0.38 to 2.58 umol/L, whereas the maternal plasma levels ranged from 0.1 to

0.97 umol/L. The mean milk:plasma ratio was 3.0. Assuming ingestion of 75 mL of milk at each feeding, and the maximum concentration of 2.58 umol/L, an infant would ingest approximately 0.05 mg metoprolol at the first feeding, and considerably less at subsequent feedings. Although the milk:plasma ratios for this family are in general high, the maternal plasma levels are quite small, so the absolute amount transferred to the infant are quite small. Relatively high levels could produce depression, hypotension, and hypoglycemia. Although these levels are probably too low to be clinically relevant, clinicians should use metoprolol under close supervision and with caution.

Alternatives: Propranolol

Pregnancy Risk Category: B

Adult Concerns: Hypotension, weakness, depression, bradycardia.

Pediatric Concerns: None reported in several studies, but close observation for hypotension, weakness, bradycardia is advised.

Drug Interactions: Decreased effect when used with aluminum salts, barbiturates, calcium salts, cholestyramine, NSAIDs, ampicillin, rifampin, and salicylates. Beta blockers may reduce the effect of oral sulfonylureas (hypoglycemic agents). Increased toxicity/effect when used with other antihypertensives, contraceptives, MAO inhibitors, cimetidine, and numerous other products. See drug interaction reference for complete listing.

AHL = 3-7 hours		**M/P** = 3.0	
PHL =		**PB** = 12%	
PK = 2.5-3 hours		**Oral** = 40-50%	
MW = 267		**pKa** = 9.7	
Vd = 2.5-5.6			

References:
1. Liedholm H, et. al. Accumulation of atenolol and metoprolol in human breast milk. Eur J Clin Pharmacol 20:229-31, 1981.
2. Anderson PO. Medication use while breast feeding a neonate. Neonatal Pharmacology Quarterly 2:3-12,1993.
3. Sandstrom B, Regardh CG. Metoprolol excretion into breast

milk. Br. J.Clin.Pharmacol. 9:518-9, 1980.

4.   Kulas J, et.al. Atenolol and metoprolol. A comparison of their excretion into human breast milk. Acta. Obstet. Scand. 118(Suppl):65-9, 1984.

Metrizamide   Fax #1580

Trade: Amipaque
Can/Aus/UK: Amipaque
Uses: Radiopaque agent
AAP: Not reviewed

Metrizamide is a water -soluble non-ionic, radiographic contrast medium used mainly in myelography. It contains 48% bound iodine. The iodine molecule is covalently bound, and is not available for uptake into breast milk due to minimal metabolism.   Following subarachnoid administration of 5.06 gm the peak plasma level of 32.9 µg/mL occurred at 6 hours. Cumulative excretion in milk increased with time, but was extremely small with only 1.1 mg or 0.02% of the dose being recovered in milk within 44.3 hours. The drug's high water solubility, nonionic characteristic, and its high molecular weight (789) also support minimal excretion into breast milk.   This agent is sometimes used as an oral radiopaque agent.   Only minimal oral absorption occurs (< 0.4%). The authors suggest that the very small amount of metrizamide secreted in human milk is unlikely to be hazardous to the infant.

Alternatives:

Pregnancy Risk Category: B

Adult Concerns: Nausea, vomiting, headache, bach ache, neck stiffness, seizures.

Pediatric Concerns: None reported in one study. Milk levels are too low.

Drug Interactions: Chlorpromazine, ketamine, other phenothiazines, and any medication which lowers seizure threshold,   should be discontinued 5 days prior to exposure to metrizamide. Major seizures may occur. Lactic acidosis and acute renal failure may occur when used with metformin.

AHL	= > 24 hours	M/P	=
PHL	=	PB	=
PK	= 6 hours	Oral	= < 0.4 %
MW	= 789	pKa	=
Vd	= 1.3		

References:
1.   Ilett KF, Hackett LP,Paterson JW: Excretion of metrizamide in milk. Br J Radiol 54:537-538, 1981.
2.   Johansen JG. Assessment of a Non-ionic contrast medium (Amipaque) in the gastrointestinal tract. Invest. Radiol. 13:523-527, 1978.
3.   Pharmaceutical Manufacturer's package insert, 1997.

Metrizoate   Fax #1574

Trade: Isopaque
Can/Aus/UK: Isopaque
Uses: Radiopaque agent
AAP: Not reviewed

Metrizoate an ionic radiopaque agent.   Radiopaque agents (except barium) are iodinated compounds used to visualize various organs during X-ray, CAT scans, and other radiological procedures.   These compounds are highly iodinated benzoic acid derivatives. Although under usual circumstances, iodine products are contraindicated in nursing mothers (due to ion trapping in milk), these products are unique in that they are extremely inert and are largely cleared without metabolism. In a study of 4 women who received metrizoate 0.58 g/Kg (350 mg Iodine/mL) IV, the peak level of metrizoate in milk was 14 mg/L at 3 and 6 hours post-injection.   The average milk concentration during the first 24 hours was only 11.4 mg/L. During the first 24 hours following injection, it is estimated that a total of 1.7 mg/Kg would be transferred to the infant which is only 0.3% of the maternal dose. As a group, radiopaque agents are virtually unabsorbed after oral administration (< 0.1%). Metrizoate has a brief half-life of just 2 hours and the estimated dose ingested by the infant is only 0.2 % of the radiopaque dose used clinically for various scanning procedures in infants. Although most company package inserts suggest that an infant be removed from the breast for 24 hours, no untoward effects have been reported with these products in breastfed infants. Because the amount of metrizoate transferred into milk is so small, the authors conclude that breastfeeding is acceptable after intravenously administered metrizoate.

Alternatives:

Pregnancy Risk Category:

Adult Concerns: Hypersensitivity to iodine. Arrhythmias, renal failure. Volume expansion.

Pediatric Concerns: None reported via milk in one study.

Drug Interactions: Anaphylaxis.

AHL = < 2 hours	**M/P** =	
PHL =	**PB** = < 5%	
PK =	**Oral** = Nil	
MW = 628	**pKa** =	
Vd =		

References:
1. Nielsen ST et.al. Excretion of iohexol and metrizoate in human breast milk. Acta. Radiol. 28:523-26, 1987.

Metronidazole   Fax #1290

Trade: Flagyl, Metizol, Trikacide, Protostat
Can/Aus/UK: Apo-Metronidazole, Flagyl, NeoMetric, Novo-Nidazol, Metrozine, Rozex
Uses: Antibiotic, amebicide

AAP: Drugs whose effect on nursing infants is unknown but may be of concern

Metronidazole is indicated in the treatment of vaginitis due to Trichomonas Vaginalis, and various anaerobic bacterial infections including Giardiasis, H. Pylori, B. Fragilis, and Gardnerella vaginalis. Metronidazole has become the treatment of choice for pediatric giardiasis (AAP).Metronidazole absorption is time and dose dependent and also depends on the route of administration (oral vs vaginal). Following a 2 gm oral dose milk levels were reported to peak at 50-57 mg/L at 2 to 4 hours...milk levels after 24 hours were approximately 10 mg/L. The maternal plasma level at 12 hours is approximately 20% of the peak level at 2 hours. Following a maternal dose of 200 mg three times daily, the average absorption of metronidazole by a breastfeeding infant is reported as 3 mg/kg/500 mL intake per day which is much less than the 10-20 mg/kg recommended therapeutic dose for infants. For treating trichomoniasis, many physicians now recommend 2 gm single oral dose, discontinue breastfeeding for 12-24 hours, then re-institute breastfeeding. Thus far, no reports of untoward effects in breastfed infants have been published for the 2 gm STAT dose, or the 250 mg three times daily for 10 day dosage regimen. In a group of 12 mothers who received metronidazole 400 mg three times daily, the average peak maternal plasma level was 17.46 μg/mL at 2 hours, while the average milk level was 15.52 μg/mL. In a group of 7 breastfed infants, the average maternal milk level was 12.95 μg/mL while the infant's peak plasma levels averaged only 1.62 μg/mL. The corresponding peak maternal plasma level averaged 17.46 μg/mL, or 10.7 times more than the peak plasma level in the breastfed infant. Thus the infants received only a minimal amount of metronidazole. The authors concluded that the low incidence of adverse reactions noted in their study, suggests that metronidazole may be safely administered to mothers at oral doses of 400 mg three times daily (Passmore, 1988).For intravaginal use see MetroGel. MetroGel vaginal gel produces only 2% of the mean peak serum level concentration of a 500 mg oral metronidazole tablet. The maternal plasma level following use of each dose of vaginal gel averaged only 237 μg/L, far less than orally administered tablet formulations. Milk levels following intravaginal use would probably be exceeding low. Milk:plasma ratios, although published for oral metronidazole, may be different for this route of administration. Adult dose : 250-500 mg t.i.d for 7-10 days for infections, or 2 gm STAT one dose (trichomoniasis).Pediatric dose: Term infants 15 mg/kg/day. (Not FDA cleared for infants).

Alternatives:

Pregnancy Risk Category: B

Adult Concerns: Nausea, dry mouth, vomiting, diarrhea, abdominal discomfort. Drug may turn urine brown.

Pediatric Concerns: No untoward effects have been reported in numerous studies.

Drug Interactions: Phenytoin and phenobarbital may decrease half-life of metronidazole. Alcohol may induce disulfiram-like reactions. May increase prothrombin times when used with warfarin.

AHL	= 8.5 hours	**M/P**	= 0.4-1.8
PHL	= 25-75 hours (full term)	**PB**	= 10%
PK	= 2-4 hours	**Oral**	= Complete
MW	= 171	**pKa**	=
Vd	=		

References:
1.   Heisterberg L, Branebjerg PE. Blood and milk concentration of metronidazole in mothers and infants. J Perinat Med. 11:114-120, 1983.
2.   Erickson SH, Oppenheim Gl, Smith GH. Metronidazole in breast milk. Obstet. Gynecol. 57:48-50, 1981.
3.   Passmore CM, McElnay JC, Rainey EA, D'Arcy PF. Metronidazole excretion in human milk and its effect on the suckling neonate. Br. J. Clin. Pharmac. 26:45-51, 1988.

Metronidazole Topical Gel   Fax #1562

Trade: MetroGel Topical
Can/Aus/UK: Metro-Gel, Metrogyl
Uses: Topical antibacterial
AAP: Not reviewed

Metronidazole topical gel is primarily indicated for acne, and is a gel formulation containing 0.75% metronidazole. For metronidazole kinetics and entry into human milk see Metronidazole. Following topical application of 1 gm of metronidazole gel to the face (equivalent to 7.5 mg metronidazole base), the maximum serum concentration was only 66 nanograms/mL in only one of 10 patients (In three of the ten patients, levels were undetectable). This concentration is 100 times less than the serum concentration achieved following the oral ingestion of just one 250 mg tablet. Therefore, the topical application of metronidazole gel provides only exceedingly low plasma levels in the mother and minimal to no levels in milk.

Alternatives:

Pregnancy Risk Category: B

Adult Concerns: Watery eyes if the gel is applied too close to eyes. Minor skin irritation, redness, milk dryness, burning.

Pediatric Concerns: None reported via milk. Milk levels would be exceedingly low to nil.

Drug Interactions: Although many known interactions with oral metronidazole are documented, due to minimal plasma levels of this preparation, they would be extremely remote.

AHL = 8.5 hours	M/P = 0.4-1.8
PHL =	PB = 10%
PK =	Oral = Complete
MW = 171	pKa =
Vd =	

References:
1. Drug Facts and Comparisons. 1996. ed. Facts and Comparisons, St. Louis.
2. Pharmaceutical Manufacturer's Package Insert, 1997.

Metronidazole Vaginal Gel   Fax #1291

Trade: MetroGel - Vaginal
Can/Aus/UK: MetroGel
Uses: Antibiotic
AAP: Drugs whose effect on nursing infants is unknown but may be of concern

Both topical and vaginal preparations of metronidazole contain only 0.75% metronidazole. Plasma levels following administration are exceedingly low. This metronidazole vaginal product produces only 2% of the mean peak serum level concentration of a 500 mg oral metronidazole tablet. The maternal plasma level following use of each dose of vaginal gel averaged 237 µg/L compared to 12,785 µg/L following an oral 500 mg tablet. Milk levels following intravaginal use would probably be exceeding low. Milk:plasma ratios, although published for oral metronidazole, may be different for this route of administration, primarily due to the low plasma levels attained with this product. Topical and intravaginal metronidazole gels are indicated for bacterial vaginosis.

Alternatives:

Pregnancy Risk Category: B

Adult Concerns: Mild irritation to vaginal wall.

Pediatric Concerns: None reported.

Drug Interactions: Phenytoin and phenobarbital may decrease half-life of metronidazole. Alcohol may induce disulfiram-like reactions. May increase prothrombin times when used with warfarin.

AHL = 8.5 hours		M/P	=
PHL =		PB	= 10%
PK = 6-12 hours		Oral	= Complete
MW = 171		pKa	=
Vd =			

References:
1.   Pharmaceutical Manufacturer's Package Insert, 1996.

Mexiletine HCL   Fax #1292

Trade: Mexitil
Can/Aus/UK: Mexitil, Novo-Mexiletine
Uses: Antiarrhythmic
AAP: Approved by the American Academy of Pediatrics for use in breastfeeding mothers

Mexiletine is an antiarrhythmic agent with activity similar to lidocaine. In one study on day 2-5 postpartum of a patient receiving 200 mg three times daily, the mean peak concentration of mexiletine in breast milk was 959 µg/L and while the maternal serum was 724 µg/L. Extrapolating this data, an infant ingesting 1 L of milk daily would ingest 0.95 mg of mexiletine daily, approximately 0.01 % of the daily maternal dose.   In this study the milk plasma ratio varied from 0.78 to 1.89 with an average of 1.45. It is unlikely this exposure would lead to untoward side effects in a breastfeeding infant.

Alternatives:

Pregnancy Risk Category: B

Adult Concerns: Arrhythmias, bradycardia, hypotension, tremors, dizziness.

Pediatric Concerns: None reported.

Drug Interactions: Aluminum, magnesium hydroxide, atropine, and narcotics may reduce the oral absorption of mexiletine. Cimetidine may increase or decreased mexiletine plasma levels. Hydantoins such as phenytoin may increase mexiletine clearance and reduce plasma levels. Rifampin may increase mexiletine clearance leading to lower levels. Mexiletine may reduce the clearance of caffeine by 50%. Serum theophylline levels may be increased significantly to toxic levels.

AHL	= 9.2 hours	M/P	= 1.45
PHL	=	PB	= 63%
PK	= 2-3 hours (oral)	Oral	= 90%
MW	= 179	pKa	= 8.4
Vd	= 6-12		

References:
1. Lewis AM et. al. Mexiletine in human blood and breast milk. Postgrad. Med. J. 57:546-7, 1981.
2. Timmis AD, Jackson G, Holt DW. Mexiletine for control of ventricular arrhythmias in pregnancy. Lancet 2:647-8, 1980.

Mibefradil   Fax #1567

Trade: Posicor
Can/Aus/UK: Posicor
Uses: Antihypertensive
AAP: Not reviewed

Mibrefradil is a typical calcium channel blocker used as an antihypertensive. No data are available on its transfer into human milk, although studies with rodents suggest a concentrating mechanism with a 5 fold higher concentration in milk. Oral absorption is good and half-life is rather long. Use caution with this product. See alternatives.

Alternatives: Nifedipine, Nimodipine, Verapamil.

Pregnancy Risk Category: C

Adult Concerns: Dizziness, flushing, polyuria, impotence, bradycardia, headache, palpitations, tinnitus.

Pediatric Concerns: None reported via milk, but caution is recommended.

Drug Interactions: Mibefradil may interact with astemizole, producing elevated levels of astemizole. Enhanced hypotension may occur when added to beta blockers. Elevated levels of cisapride, cyclosporin, desipramine, digoxin, imipramine, quinidine may occur with co-administered with mibefradil. Increased risk of myopathy when added to HMG CoA reductase inhibitors.

AHL = 17-25 hours	M/P = 5 (rodents)
PHL =	PB = 99.5%
PK = 1-2 hours	Oral = 70-90%
MW =	pKa =
Vd = 2.71	

References:
1. Petrie J, Glen S, MacMahon M et al: Haemodynamics, cardiac conduction and pharmacokinetics of mibefradil (Ro40-5967), a novel calcium antagonist. J Hypertension 13:1842-1846, 1995.
2. Petrie J, Glen S, MacMahon M et al: Haemodynamics, cardiac conduction and pharmacokinetics of mibefradil (Ro40-5967), a novel calcium antagonist. J Hypertens 13:1842-1846,1995.
3. Pharmaceutical Manufacturer's Package Insert, 1998.

Miconazole   Fax #1293

Trade: Monistat IV, Monistat 3, 7
Can/Aus/UK: Micatin, Monistat, Daktarin, Daktozin, Fungo
Uses: Antifungal for candidiasis
AAP: Not reviewed

Miconazole is an effective antifungal that is commonly used IV, topically, and intravaginally. After intravaginal application, approximately 1% of the dose is absorbed systemically. After topical application, there is little or no absorption (0.1%). It is unlikely that the limited absorption of miconazole from vaginal application would produce significant milk levels. Milk concentrations following oral and IV miconazole have not been reported. Oral absorption of miconazole is poor, only 25-30%. Miconazole is commonly used in pediatric patients less than 1 year of age.

Alternatives:

Pregnancy Risk Category: C

Adult Concerns: Nausea, vomiting, diarrhea, anorexia, itching, rash, local irritation.

Pediatric Concerns: None reported via milk.

Drug Interactions: May increase warfarin anticoagulant effect. May increase hypoglycemia of oral sulfonylureas. Phenytoin levels may be increased.

AHL = 20-25 hours	M/P	=	
PHL =	PB	= 91-93%	
PK = Immediate(IV)	Oral	= 25-30%	
MW = 416	pKa	=	
Vd =			

References:
1. Drug Facts and Comparisons. 1995 ed. Facts and Comparisons, St. Louis.
2. McEvoy GE(ed):AHFS Drug Information, New York, NY. 1995.

Midazolam   Fax #1294

Trade: Versed
Can/Aus/UK: Versed, Hypnovel
Uses: Short acting benzodiazepine sedative, hypnotic
AAP: Effect on nursing infants unknown but may be of concern

Midazolam is a very short acting benzodiazepine primarily used as an induction or preanesthetic medication. The onset of action of midazolam is extremely rapid, its potency is greater than diazepam, and its metabolic elimination is more rapid. With a plasma half-life of only 1.9 hours, it is preferred for rapid induction and maintenance of anesthesia. After oral administration of 15 mg for up to 6 days postnatal in 22 women, the mean milk:plasma ratio was 0.15 and the maximum level of midazolam in breast milk was 9 nanogram/mL, and occurred 1-2 hours after administration.19   Midazolam and its hydroxy-metabolite were undetectable 4 hours after administration. Therefore, the amount of midazolam transferred to an infant via early milk is minimal, particularly if the baby is breastfed more than 4 hours after administration.

Alternatives: Lorazepam

Pregnancy Risk Category: D

Adult Concerns: Sedation, respiratory depression.

Pediatric Concerns: None reported in several studies.   Wait 4 hours after dose.

Drug Interactions: Theophylline may reduce the sedative effects of midazolam.   Other CNS depressants may potentiate the depressant effects of midazolam.   Cimetidine may increase plasma levels of midazolam.

AHL = 2-5 hours		**M/P**	= 0.15
PHL = 6.5-23 hours		**PB**	= 97%.
PK = 20-50 min.(oral)		**Oral**	= 27-44%
MW = 326		**pKa**	= 6.2
Vd = 1.0-2.5			

References:
1.   Matheson I, Lunde PK, and Bredesen JE. Midazolam and nitrazepam in the maternity ward: milk concentrations and clinical effects. Brit. J. Clin. Pharmacol. 30:787-93, 1990.
2.   Spigset O. Anaesthetic agents and excretion in breast milk. Acta Anaesthesiologica Scandinavica. 38:94-103, 1994.

Minocycline   Fax #1538

Trade: Minocin, Dynacin
Can/Aus/UK: Minocin, Novo-Minocycline
Uses: Tetracycline antibiotic
AAP: Not reviewed

Minocycline is a broad spectrum tetracycline antibiotic with significant side effects in pediatric patients, including dental staining and reduced bone growth. It is probably secreted into breast milk in small but clinically insignificant levels. Because tetracyclines in general, bind to milk calcium they would have reduced absorption in the infant, but minocycline may be absorbed to a greater degree than the older tetracyclines. A dosage of tetracycline 2 gm/day for 3 days has achieved a milk:plasma ratio of 0.6 to 0.8. In another study of 5 lactating women receiving tetracycline 500 mg PO four times daily, the breast milk concentrations ranged from 0.43 mg/L to 2.58 mg/L. Levels in infants were below the limit of detection. Because we have many other antimicrobials with similar spectrums, the short-term use of tetracyclines in breastfeeding women is not generally recommended, but not necessarily contraindicated.

Alternatives: Doxycycline

Pregnancy Risk Category: D

Adult Concerns: Adverse effects include GI distress, dizziness, thyroid pigmentation, vomiting, diarrhea, nephrotoxicity, photosensitivity.

Pediatric Concerns: None via breast milk, but pediatric side effects include decreased linear bone growth and dental staining..

Drug Interactions: Absorption may be reduced or delayed when used with dairy products, calcium, magnesium, or aluminum containing antacids, oral contraceptives, iron, zinc, sodium bicarbonate, penicillins, cimetidine. Increased toxicity may result when used with methoxiflurane anesthesia. Use with warfarin anticoagulants may increase anticoagulation.

AHL	= 15-20 hours	M/P	=
PHL	=	PB	= 76%
PK	= 3 hours	Oral	= 90-100%
MW	= 457	pKa	=
Vd	=		

References:

1. Drug Facts and Comparisons. 1996. ed. Facts and Comparisons, St. Louis.
2. McEvoy GK. In: Drug Information. American Hospital Formulary Service. American Society of Health-System Pharmacists. 1995.

Minoxidil   Fax #1296

Trade: Loniten, Minodyl, Rogaine
Can/Aus/UK: Loniten, Rogaine, Apo-Gain, Minox, Loniten
Uses: Antihypertensive
AAP: Approved by the American Academy of Pediatrics for use in breastfeeding mothers

Minoxidil is a potent vasodilator and antihypertensive. It is also used for hair loss and baldness. When applied topically, only 1.4% of the dose is absorbed systemically. Minoxidil is secreted into human milk in concentrations ranging from 0.3 µg/L at 12 hours to 41.7 µg/L at 1 hour following an oral dose of 7.5 mg. Long-term exposure of breastfeeding infants in women ingesting oral minoxidil may not be advisable. However, in those using topical minoxidil, the limited absorption via skin would minimize systemic levels and significantly reduce risk of transfer to infant via breast milk. It is unlikely that the amount absorbed via topical application would produce clinically relevant concentrations in breast milk but note pediatric observations.

Alternatives:

Pregnancy Risk Category: C

Adult Concerns: Hypotension, tachycardia, headache, weight gain, skin pigmentation, rash, renal toxicity, leukopenia.

Pediatric Concerns: None reported.

Drug Interactions: Profound orthostatic hypotension when used with guanethidine. May potentiate hypotensive effect of other antihypertensives.

AHL = 3.5-4.2 hours		**M/P**	= 0.75-1.0
PHL =		**PB**	= Low
PK = 2-8 hr.		**Oral**	= 90-95%
MW = 209		**pKa**	=
Vd =			

References:
1. Valdivieso A, et. al. Minoxidil in breast milk. Ann Intern Med 102:135, 1985.

Misoprostol   Fax #1297

Trade: Cytotec
Can/Aus/UK: Cytotec
Uses: Prostaglandin hormone, gastric protector
AAP: Not reviewed

Misoprostol is a prostaglandin E1 compound that is useful in treating nonsteroidal-induced gastric ulceration. Misoprostol is absorbed orally and rapidly metabolized. Intact misoprostol is not detectible in plasma, but is rapidly metabolized to misoprostol acid which is biologically active. Secretion of misoprostol in milk is unlikely due to rapid maternal metabolism. However, secretion of its active metabolite is possible and could produce diarrhea in newborn. Misoprostol is therefore considered contraindicated by the manufacturer in nursing mothers.

Alternatives:

Pregnancy Risk Category: X

Adult Concerns: Diarrhea, abdominal cramps and pain, uterine bleeding and abortion.

Pediatric Concerns: None reported, but observe for diarrhea, abdominal cramps.

Drug Interactions: Levels are diminished when administered with food. Antacids reduce total bioavailability but this does not appear clinically significant.

AHL = 20-40 min.		**M/P** =	
PHL =		**PB** = 80-90%	
PK = 14-20 min.(oral)		**Oral** = Complete	
MW = 383		**pKa** =	
Vd =			

References:
1. Drug Facts and Comparisons. 1995 ed. Facts and Comparisons, St. Louis.
2. Pharmaceutical Manufacturer's Package Insert, 1995.

Mivacurium   Fax #1470

Trade: Mivacron
Can/Aus/UK: Mivacrom, Mivacron
Uses: Neuromuscular blocking agent
AAP: Not reviewed

Mivacurium is a short-acting neuromuscular blocking agent used to relax skeletal muscles during surgery. Its duration is very short and complete recovery generally occurs in 15-30 minutes. No data are available on its transfer to breast milk. However, it has an exceedingly short plasma half-life and probably poor to no oral absorption. It is very unlikely that it would be absorbed by a breastfeeding infant.

Alternatives:

Pregnancy Risk Category: C

Adult Concerns: Flushing, hypotension, weakness.

Pediatric Concerns: None reported.

Drug Interactions: Inhaled anesthetics, local anesthetics, calcium channel blockers, antiarrhythmic such as quinidine, and certain antibiotics such as amino glycosides, tetracyclines, vancomycin, and clindamycin may significantly prolong neuromuscular blockade with mivacurium.

AHL = < 30 minutes	M/P =
PHL =	PB =
PK =	Oral = Poor
MW =	pKa =
Vd =	

References:
1. McEvoy GE(ed):AHFS Drug Information, New York, NY. 1995.
2. Pharmaceutical Manufacturer's Package Insert, 1995.

MMR Vaccine   Fax #1298

Trade: MMR Vaccine, Measles - Mumps - Rubella
Can/Aus/UK:
Uses: Live attenuated triple virus vaccine
AAP: Not reviewed

MMR vaccine is a mixture of live, attenuated viruses from measles, mumps, and rubella strains. It is usually administered to children at 12-15 months of age. NEVER administer to a pregnant woman. Rubella, and perhaps measles and mumps virus, are undoubtedly transferred via breast milk and have been detected in throat swabs of 56% of breastfeeding infants. Infants exposed to the attenuated viruses via breast milk had only mild symptoms. If medically required, MMR vaccine can be administered early postpartum (Lawrence, 1994). See rubella.

Alternatives:

Pregnancy Risk Category:

Adult Concerns: Mild symptoms, fever, flu-like symptoms.

Pediatric Concerns: Mild symptoms of rubella have been reported in one newborn infant.

Drug Interactions:

References:
1.   Buimovici-Klein E, et. al. Isolation of rubella virus in milk after postpartum immunization. J Pediatr 91:939-41, 1977.
2.   Losonsky GA et.al. Effect of immunization against rubella on lactation products. I. Development and charcterization of specific immunologic reactivity in breast milk. J. Infect. Dis. 145:654, 1982.
3.   Losonsky GA, et.al. Effect of immunization against rubella on lactation products. II. Maternal-neonatal interactions. fJ. Infect. Dis. 145:661, 1982.
4.   Landes RD et.al. Neonatal rubella following postpartum maternal immunization. Pediatrics 97:465-467, 1980.
5.   Lawrence RA. In: Breastfeeding, A guide for the medical profession. Mosby, St.Louis, 1994.

Montelukast Sodium   Fax #1601

Trade: Singulair
Can/Aus/UK:
Uses: Antiasthmatic agent
AAP: Not reviewed

Montelukast is a leukotriene receptor inhibitor similar to Accolate and is used as an adjunct in the treatment of asthma.   The manufacturer reports that montelukast is secreted into animal milk, but no data on human milk is available.   This product is cleared for use in children aged 6 and above.   This product does not enter the CNS nor many other tissues. Although the milk levels in humans are unreported, they are probably quite low.

Alternatives: Zafirlukast

Pregnancy Risk Category: B

Adult Concerns: Abdominal pain, fever, dyspepsia, dental pain, dizziness, headache, cough and nasal congestion, some changes in liver enzymes.

Pediatric Concerns: None reported via milk.

Drug Interactions: Phenobarbital may reduce plasma levels by 40%. Although unreported, other inhibitors of Cytochrome P450 may affect plasma levels.

AHL = 2.7-5.5 hours	M/P =
PHL =	PB = 99%
PK = 2-4 hours	Oral = 64%
MW = 608	pKa =
Vd = 0.15	

References:
1.   Pharmaceutical Manufacturer's package insert, 1998.

Morphine   Fax #1299

Trade: Morphine
Can/Aus/UK: Epimorph, Morphitec, M.O.S. MS Contin, Statex, Morphalgin, Ordine, Anamorph, Kapanol, Oramorph, Sevredol
Uses: Narcotic analgesic
AAP: Approved by the American Academy of Pediatrics for use in breastfeeding mothers

Morphine is a potent narcotic analgesic. In a group of 5 lactating women, the highest morphine concentration in breast milk following two epidural doses was only 82 µg/L at 30 minutes. The highest breast milk level following 15 mg IV/IM was only 0.5 mg/L.   In another study of women receiving morphine via PCA pumps for 12-48 hours postpartum, the concentration of morphine in breast milk ranged from 50-60 µg/L. Because of the poor oral bioavailability of morphine (26%) it is unlikely these levels would be clinically relevant in a stable breastfeeding infant.

Alternatives: Codeine

Pregnancy Risk Category: B

Adult Concerns: Sedation, flushing, CNS depression, respiratory depression, bradycardia.

Pediatric Concerns: None reported via milk.

Drug Interactions: Barbiturates may significantly increase respiratory and CNS depressant effects of morphine. The admixture of cimetidine has produced CNS toxicity such as confusion, disorientation, respiratory depression, apnea, and seizures when used with narcotic analgesics. Diazepam may produce cardiovascular depression when used with opiates. Phenothiazines may antagonize the analgesic effect of morphine.

AHL = 1.5-2 hours	**M/P**	= 1.1-3.6
PHL = 13.9 hours (neonates)	**PB**	= 35%
PK = 0.5-1 hours	**Oral**	= 26%
MW = 285	**pKa**	= 8.1
Vd = 2-5		

References:
1. Feilberg VL, Rosenborg D, Broen Christensen C, et.al. Excretion of morphine in human breast milk. Acta Anaesthiol Scan. 33:426-428, 1989.
2. Wittels Bk, Scott DT, Sinatra RS. Exogenous opioids in human breast milk and acute neonatal neurobehavior: a preliminary study. Anesthesiology 73:864-869, 1990.
3. Spigset O. Anaesthetic agents and excretion in breast milk. Acta Anaesthesiologica Scandinavica. 38:94-103, 1994.

Mupirocin Ointment   Fax #1300

Trade: Bactroban
Can/Aus/UK: Bactroban
Uses: Antibacterial ointment
AAP: Not reviewed

Mupirocin is a topical antibiotic used for impetigo, Group A beta-hemolytic strep, and strep. pyogenes. Mupirocin is only minimally absorbed following topical application. In one study, less than 0.3% of a topical dose was absorbed after 24 hours. Most remained adsorbed to the corneum layer of the skin. The drug is absorbed orally, but it is so rapidly metabolized that systemic levels are not sustained.

Alternatives:

Pregnancy Risk Category: B

Adult Concerns: Rash, irritation.

Pediatric Concerns: None reported. Commonly used in pediatric patients.

Drug Interactions:

AHL = 17-36 min.	M/P	=
PHL =	PB	=
PK =	Oral	= Complete
MW = 501	pKa	=
Vd =		

References:

Nabumetone   Fax #1301

Trade: Relafen
Can/Aus/UK: Relafen, Relifex
Uses: Anti-inflammatory agent for arthritic pain
AAP: Not reviewed

Nabumetone is a non-steroidal anti-inflammatory agent for arthritic pain. Immediately upon absorption, nabumetone is metabolized to the active metabolite. The parent drug is not detectible in plasma. It is not known if the nabumetone metabolite (6MNA) is secreted in human milk. It is known to be secreted into animal milk and has a very long half-life. NSAIDS are not generally recommended in nursing mothers, with the exception of ibuprofen. See ibuprofen as alternative.

Alternatives: Ibuprofen

Pregnancy Risk Category: C

Adult Concerns: GI distress, nausea, vomiting, diarrhea.

Pediatric Concerns: None reported via milk. Observe for GI distress.

Drug Interactions: May prolong prothrombin time when used with warfarin. Antihypertensive effects of ACEi family may be blunted or completely abolished by NSAIDs. Some NSAIDs may block antihypertensive effect of beta blockers, diuretics. Used with cyclosporin, may dramatically increase renal toxicity. May increase digoxin, phenytoin, lithium levels. May increase toxicity of methotrexate. May increase bioavailability of penicillamine. Probenecid may increase NSAID levels.

AHL = 22-30 hours		**M/P** =	
PHL =		**PB** = 99%	
PK = 2.5 - 4 hours		**Oral** = 38%	
MW = 228		**pKa** =	
Vd =			

References:
1.   Pharmaceutical Manufacturer's Package Insert, 1996.

Nadolol   Fax #1302

Trade: Corgard, Nadolol
Can/Aus/UK: Corgard, Syn-Nadolol, Novo-Nadolol, Corgard
Uses: Antihypertensive, anti-angina, beta blocker

AAP: Approved by the American Academy of Pediatrics for use in breastfeeding mothers

Nadolol is a long-acting beta adrenergic blocker used as an antihypertensive. It is secreted into breast milk in moderately high concentrations. Following a maternal dose of 20 mg/day, breast milk obtained 38 hours postpartum had a concentration of nadolol of 146 µg/L. In another study of 12 women receiving 80 mg daily the mean steady-state concentrations in milk were 357 µg/L. The milk:serum ratio was reported to be 4.6. A five kg infant would receive from 2-7% of the maternal dose. The authors recommended against the use of this beta blocker in breastfeeding patients. Due to its long half-life and high milk:plasma ratio, this would not be a preferred beta blocker.

Alternatives: Propranolol, Metoprolol

Pregnancy Risk Category: C

Adult Concerns: Hypotension, nausea, diarrhea, bradycardia, apnea, depression.

Pediatric Concerns: None reported, but due to the high M:P ratio of 4.6, this product is not recommended.

Drug Interactions: Decreased effect when used with aluminum salts, barbiturates, calcium salts, cholestyramine, NSAIDs, ampicillin, rifampin, and salicylates. Beta blockers may reduce the effect of oral sulfonylureas (hypoglycemic agents). Increased toxicity/effect when used with other antihypertensives, contraceptives, MAO inhibitors, cimetidine, and numerous other products. See drug interaction reference for complete listing.

AHL = 20-24 hours		**M/P**	**= 4.6**
PHL =		**PB**	**= 30%**
PK = 2-4 hours		**Oral**	**= 20-40%**
MW = 309		**pKa**	**= 9.7**
Vd = 1.5-3.6			

References:
1.   Fox RE, et. al. Neonatal effects of maternal nadolol therapy. Am J Obstet Gynecol 152:1045-6, 1985.

2.   Devlin RT, Duchin KL, et.al. Nadolol in human serum and breast milk. Br. J. Clin. Pharmacol. 12:393-6, 1981.

Nafcillin   Fax #1303

Trade: Unipen, Nafcil
Can/Aus/UK: Unipen
Uses: Penicillin antibiotic
AAP: Not reviewed

Nafcillin is a penicillin antibiotic that is poorly and erratically absorbed orally. The only formulations are IV and IM. No data are available on concentration in milk, but it is likely small. Oral absorption in the infant would be minimal. See other penicillins.

Alternatives:

Pregnancy Risk Category: B

Adult Concerns: Neutropenia, hypokalemia, pseudomembranous colitis, allergic rash.

Pediatric Concerns: None reported. Observe for GI symptoms such as diarrhea. Nafcillin is frequently used in infants.

Drug Interactions: Chloramphenicol may decreased nafcillin levels. Nafcillin may inhibit efficacy of oral contraceptives. Probenecid may increase nafcillin levels. May increase anticoagulant effect of warfarin and heparin.

AHL = 0.5-1.5 hours	M/P	=
PHL = 2.2-5.5 hours (neonates).	PB	= 70-90%
PK = 30-60 min(IM).	Oral	= 50%
MW = 436	pKa	=
Vd =		

References:
1.   McEvoy GE(ed):AFHS Drug Information, New York, NY. 1995.

Nalbuphine   Fax #1304

Trade: Nubain
Can/Aus/UK: Nubain
Uses: Analgesic
AAP: Not reviewed

Nalbuphine is a potent narcotic analgesic similar in potency to morphine. In a group of 20 postpartum mothers who received 20 mg IM nalbuphine, the total amount of nalbuphine excreted into human milk during a 24 hour period averaged 2.3 micrograms, which is equivalent to 0.012% of the maternal dosage[1]. The mean milk:plasma ratio using the AUC was 1.2. According to the authors, an oral intake of 2.3 micrograms nalbuphine would not show any measurable plasma concentrations in the neonate. Nalbuphine is both an antagonist and agonist of opiate receptors, and should not be mixed with other opiates due to interference with analgesia.

Alternatives:

Pregnancy Risk Category: B

Adult Concerns: Hypotension, sedation, withdrawal syndrome, respiratory depression.

Pediatric Concerns: None reported via milk.

Drug Interactions: May reduce efficacy of other opioid analgesics. Barbiturates may increase CNS sedation.

AHL = 5 hours		**M/P**	= 1,2
PHL = 0.86 hours		**PB**	=
PK = 2-15 min.(IV,IM)		**Oral**	= 16%
MW = 357		**pKa**	=
Vd = 2.4-7.3			

References:
1.   Wischnik A. Wetzelsberger N. Lucker PW. Elimination of nalbuphine in human milk. Arzneimittel-Forschung 38(10):1496-8, 1988.

2.   Jaillon P. et.al. Pharmacokinetics of nalbuphine in infants, young healthy volunteers, and elderly patients. Clin. Pharmacol. Ther. 46:226-233, 1989.

Nalidixic Acid   Fax #1305

Trade: NegGram
Can/Aus/UK: NegGram
Uses: Urinary anti-infective
AAP: Approved by the American Academy of Pediatrics for use in breastfeeding mothers

Nalidixic is an old urinary antiseptic and belongs to the fluoroquinolone family.   In a group of 4 women receiving 1000 mg orally/day the concentration in breast milk was approximately 5 mg/L. Hemolytic anemia has been reported in one infant whose mother received 1 gm nalidixic acid 4 times daily. Use with extreme caution. A number of new and less toxic choices should preclude the use of this compound.

Alternatives: Norfloxacin, Ofloxacin, Trovafloxacin

Pregnancy Risk Category: B

Adult Concerns: Hemolytic anemia, headache, drowsiness, blurred vision, nausea, vomiting.

Pediatric Concerns: Hemolytic anemia in one infant. This is an old product that should not be used currently.

Drug Interactions: Decreased efficacy/oral bioavailability when used with antacids. Increased anticoagulation with warfarin.

AHL = 1-2.5 hours		**M/P**	**= 0.08-0.13**
PHL =		**PB**	**= 93%**
PK = 1-2 hours		**Oral**	**= 60%**
MW = 232		**pKa**	**=**
Vd =			

References:
1.   Belton EM, Jones RV. Hemolytic anemia due to nalidixic acid. Lancet 2:691, 1965.
2.   Drug Facts and Comparisons. 1994 ed. Facts and Comparisons, St. Louis.

Naltrexone   Fax #1487

Trade: ReVia
Can/Aus/UK: ReVia Nalorex
Uses: Narcotic antagonist
AAP: Not reviewed

Naltrexone is a long acting narcotic antagonist similar in structure to Naloxone. Orally absorbed, it has been clinically used in addicts to prevent the action of injected heroin. It occupies and competes with all opioid medications for the opiate receptor. When used in addicts, it can induce rapid and long lasting withdrawal symptoms. Although the half-life appears brief, the duration of antagonism is long lasting (24-72 hours). Naltrexone appears relatively lipid soluble and transfers into the brain easily (brain:plasma ratio = 0.81). Breast milk levels have not been reported.

Alternatives:

Pregnancy Risk Category: C

Adult Concerns: Rapid opiate withdrawal symptoms. Dizziness, anorexia, rash, nausea, vomiting, and hepatocellular toxicity. Liver toxicity is common at doses approximately 5 times normal or less. A Narcan challenge test should be initiated in patients prior to therapy with naltrexone.

Pediatric Concerns: None reported, but not cleared for infants.

Drug Interactions: Suppresses narcotic analgesia and sedation.

AHL = 4-13 hours	**M/P** =
PHL =	**PB** = 21%

PK = 1 hour
MW = 341
Vd = 19 L/kg

Oral = Complete
pKa =

References:

1. Bullingham RES, McQuay HJ, Moore RA: Clinical pharmacokinetics of narcotic agonist-antagonist drugs. Clin Pharmacokinet 8:332-343, 1983.
2. Crabtree BL: Review of naltrexone, a long-acting opiate antagonist. Clin Pharm 3:273-280, 1984.
3. Ludden TM, Malspeis L, Baggott JD: Tritiated naltrexone binding in plasma from several species and tissue distribution in mice. J Pharm Sci 65:712-716, 1976.
4. Verebey K, Volavka J, Mule SJ et al: Naltrexone disposition, metabolism, and effects after acute and chronic dosing. Clin Pharmacol Ther 20:315-328, 1976.
5. Wall ME, Brine DR, Perez-Reyes M: Metabolism and disposition of naltrexone in man after oral and intravenous administration. Drug Metab Dispos 9:369-375, 1981.

Naproxen   Fax #1306

Trade: Anaprox, Naprosyn, Naproxen, Aleve
Can/Aus/UK: Anaprox, Apo-Naproxen, Naprosyn, Naxen, Inza, Proxen SR, Synflex
Uses: NSAID, analgesic for arthritis
AAP: Approved by the American Academy of Pediatrics for use in breastfeeding mothers

Naproxen is a popular NSAID analgesic. In a study done at steady state in one mother consuming 375 mg twice daily, milk levels ranged from 176-237 µg/100 mL at 4 hours (1.76-2.37 mg/L). Total naproxen excretion in the infant's urine was only 0.26% of the maternal dose. Although the amount of naproxen transferred via milk is minimal, one should use with caution in nursing mothers because of its long half-life and its effect on infant cardiovascular system, kidneys, and GI tract.

One reported case of prolonged bleeding, hemorrhage, and acute anemia in a seven-day-old infant.

Alternatives: Ibuprofen

Pregnancy Risk Category: B

Adult Concerns: GI distress, gastric bleeding, hemorrhage.

Pediatric Concerns: One reported case of prolonged bleeding, hemorrhage, and acute anemia in a seven-day-old infant.

Drug Interactions: May prolong prothrombin time when used with warfarin. Antihypertensive effects of ACEi family may be blunted or completely abolished by NSAIDs. Some NSAIDs may block antihypertensive effect of beta blockers, diuretics. Used with cyclosporin, may dramatically increase renal toxicity. May increase digoxin, phenytoin, lithium levels. May increase toxicity of methotrexate. May increase bioavailability of penicillamine. Probenecid may increase NSAID levels.

AHL = 12-15 hours	**M/P = 0.01**
PHL = 12-15 hours	**PB = 99.7%**
PK = 2-4 hours	**Oral = 74-99%**
MW = 230	**pKa = 5.0**
Vd = 0.09	

References:
1. Jamali F, Stevens DR. Naproxen excretion in milk and its uptake by the infant. Drug Intell Clin Pharm. 17:910-911, 1983.
2. Jamali F, et. al. Naproxen excretion in breast milk and its uptake by sucking infant. Drug Intell Clin Pharm 16:475 (Abstr),1982.
3. Figalgo I, et.al. Anemia aguda, rectaorragia y hematuria asociadas a la ingestion de naproxen. Anales Espanoles de Pediatrica 30:317-9, 1989.

Nedocromil Sodium   Fax #1307

Trade: Tilade
Can/Aus/UK: Tilade, Mireze
Uses: Inhaled anti-inflammatory for asthmatics
AAP: Not reviewed

Nedocromil is believed to stabilize mast cells and prevent release of bronchoconstrictors in the lung following exposure to allergens. The systemic effects are minimal due to reduced plasma levels. Systemic absorption averages less than 8-17% of the total dose even after continued dosing, which is quite low. The poor oral bioavailability of this product, and the reduced side effect profile of this family of drugs suggest that it is unlikely to produce untoward effects in a nursing infant. See cromolyn as comparison.

Alternatives:

Pregnancy Risk Category: B

Adult Concerns: Poor taste. Dizziness, headache, nausea and vomiting, sore throat, and cough.

Pediatric Concerns: None reported via milk.

Drug Interactions:

AHL	= 3.3 hours	M/P	=
PHL	=	PB	= 89%
PK	= 28 min.	Oral	= 8-17%
MW	= 371	pKa	=
Vd	=		

References:
1. Pharmaceutical Manufacturer's Package Insert, 1996.
2. Drug Facts and Comparisons. 1995. ed. Facts and Comparisons, St. Louis.

Nefazodone HCL   Fax #1308

Trade: Serzone
Can/Aus/UK: Serzone, Dutonin
Uses: Antidepressant
AAP: Not reviewed

Nefazodone is an antidepressant similar to trazodone but structurally dissimilar from the other serotonin reuptake inhibitors. It is rapidly metabolized to three active metabolites that have significantly longer half-lives (1.5 to 18 hours). No data are available on its transfer into human milk, although it should be expected. See sertraline or trazodone as alternative.

Alternatives: Sertraline, Paroxetine

Pregnancy Risk Category: C

Adult Concerns: Sedation, dry mouth, constipation, nausea, headache.

Pediatric Concerns: None reported but caution is recommended.

Drug Interactions: Sometimes fatal reactions may occur with MAOI. Plasma levels of astemizole and terfenadine may be increased. Clinically important increases in plasma concentrations of alprazolam and triazolam have been reported. Serum concentrations of digoxin have been increased by nefazodone by 29%. Haloperidol clearance decreased by 35%. Nefazodone may decrease propranolol plasma levels by as much as 30%.

AHL = 1.5-18 hours	M/P =
PHL =	PB = > 99%
PK = 1 hr.	Oral = 20%
MW =	pKa =
Vd =	

References:
1. Pharmaceutical Manufacturer's Package Insert, 1996.

Netilmicin   Fax #1309

Trade: Netromycin
Can/Aus/UK: Netromycin, Nettilin
Uses: Aminoglycoside antibiotic
AAP: Not reviewed

Netilmicin is a typical aminoglycoside antibiotic (see gentamicin). Poor oral absorption limits its use to IM and IV administration although some studies suggest significant oral absorption in infancy. Only small levels are believed to be secreted into human milk, although no reports exist. See gentamicin.

Alternatives:

Pregnancy Risk Category: D

Adult Concerns: Kidney damage, hearing loss, changes in GI flora.

Pediatric Concerns: None reported, but observe for GI symptoms such as diarrhea.

Drug Interactions: Risk of nephrotoxicity may be increased when used with cephalosporins, enflurane, methoxiflurane, and vancomycin. Auditory toxicity may increase when used with loop diuretics. The neuromuscular blocking effects of neuromuscular blocking agents may be increased when used with aminoglycosides.

AHL = 2-2.5 hours	M/P	=
PHL = 4.5-8 hours (neonates)	PB	= < 10%
PK = 30-60 min.(IM)	Oral	= Negligible
MW = 476	pKa	=
Vd =		

References:
1.   Pharmaceutical Manufacturer's Package Insert, 1995.
2.   McEvoy GE(ed):AHFS Drug Information, New York, NY. 1995.

Nicardipine   Fax #1310

Trade: Cardene
Can/Aus/UK: Cardene
Uses: Antihypertensive, calcium channel blocker
AAP: Not reviewed

Nicardipine is a typical calcium channel blocker structurally related to nifedipine. Animal studies indicate that it is secreted to some degree in breast milk. No specific data on breast milk levels are available. See verapamil, nifedipine.

Alternatives: Nifedipine, Nimodipine, Verapamil

Pregnancy Risk Category: C

Adult Concerns: Headache, peripheral edema, flushing, hypotension, bradycardia, gingival hyperplasia.

Pediatric Concerns: None reported, but no studies available. See nifedipine as alternative.

Drug Interactions: Barbiturates may reduce bioavailability of calcium channel blockers (CCB). Calcium salts may reduce hypotensive effect. Dantrolene may increase risk of hyperkalemia and myocardial depression. H2 blockers may increase bioavailability of certain CCBs. Hydantoins may reduce plasma levels. Quinidine increases risk of hypotension, bradycardia, tachycardia. Rifampin may reduce effects of CCBs. Vitamin D may reduce efficacy of CCBs. CCBs may increase carbamazepine, cyclosporin, encainide, prazosin levels.

AHL = 2-4 hours		**M/P** =	
PHL =		**PB** = > 95%	
PK = 0.5-2 hours		**Oral** = 35%	
MW = 480		**pKa** =	
Vd =			

References:
1. Pharmaceutical Manufacturer's Package Insert, 1996.

Nicotine Patches   Fax #1311

Trade: Habitrol, NicoDerm, Nicotrol, ProStep
Can/Aus/UK: Habitrol, NicoDerm, ProStep, Nicorette, Nicotinell TTS
Uses: Transdermal nicotine, nicotine withdrawal
AAP: Not reviewed

Nicotine readily passes into breast milk and has the potential for producing serious adverse effects in nursing infants. Although highly variable, the blood level of nicotine in smokers approaches 44 ng/mL, whereas levels in patch users approximate 17 ng/mL, depending on dose in patch. Therefore, nicotine levels in milk can be expected to be less in patch users than those found in smokers, assuming the patch is used correctly and the mother abstains from smoking. Individuals who both smoke and use the patch would have extremely high blood nicotine levels and could endanger the nursing infant. One study clearly suggests that cigarette smoking significantly reduces breast milk production at two weeks postpartum from 514 mL/day in non-smokers to 406 mL/day in smoking mothers per day. High nicotine levels in infants could produce shock, vomiting, diarrhea, rapid heart beat, and restlessness.

Alternatives:

Pregnancy Risk Category: X/D

Adult Concerns: Tachycardia, GI distress, vomiting, diarrhea, rapid heart beat, and restlessness.

Pediatric Concerns: None reported, but observe for shock, vomiting, diarrhea, rapid heart beat, and restlessness.

Drug Interactions: Cessation of smoking may alter response to a number of medications in ex-smokers. Including are acetaminophen, caffeine, imipramine, oxazepam, pentazocine, propranolol, and theophylline. Smoking may reduce diuretic effect of furosemide. Smoking while continuing to use patches may dramatically elevate nicotine plasma levels.

AHL = 2.0 hours (non-patch)   M/P = 2.9
PHL =   PB = 4.9%
PK = 2-4 hours   Oral = 30%
MW = 162   pKa =
Vd =

References:
1.   American Academy of Pediatrics, Committee on Drugs. Transfer of drugs and other chemicals into human milk. Pediatrics 93(1):137-150, 1994.
2.   Drug Facts and Comparisons. 1995 ed. Facts and Comparisons, St. Louis.
3.   Pharmaceutical Manufacturer's Package Insert, 1995.

Nicotinic Acid   Fax #1510

Trade: Nicobid, Nicolar, Niacels
Can/Aus/UK:
Uses: Vitamin B-3
AAP: Not reviewed

Nicotinic acid, commonly called niacin, is a component of two coenzymes which function in oxidation-reduction reactions essential for tissue respiration. It is converted to nicotinamide in vivo. Although considered a vitamin, large doses(2-6 gm/day) are effective in reducing serum LDL cholesterol and triglyceride, and increasing serum HDL. Niacin is transferred into milk in concentrations of 147 µg/100 cc. RDA for females is 15 mg/day. The concentration transferred into milk following high maternal doses has not been reported, but it is presumed that elevated maternal plasma levels may significantly elevate milk levels of niacin as well. Because niacin is known to be hepatotoxic in higher doses, breastfeeding mothers should not significantly exceed the RDA.

Alternatives:

Pregnancy Risk Category: A   if used in doses = RDA
                               C   if used in doses > RDA

Adult Concerns: Flushing, peripheral dilation, itching, nausea, bloating, flatulence, vomiting. In high doses, some abnormal liver function tests.

Pediatric Concerns: None reported via milk, but do not exceed RDA.

Drug Interactions: Niacin may produce fluctuations in blood glucose levels and interfere with oral hypoglycemics. May inhibit uricosuric effects of sulfinpyrazone and probenecid. Increased toxicity(myopathy) when used with lovastatin and other cholesterol-lowering drugs.

AHL = 45 minutes	M/P =
PHL =	PB =
PK = 45 minutes	Oral = Complete
MW = 123	pKa = 4.85
Vd =	

References:
1. Lacy C. et.al. Drug information handbook. Lexi-Comp, Hudson(Cleveland), Oh. 1996.
2. Drug Facts and Comparisons. 1996. ed. Facts and Comparisons, St. Louis.
3. Lawrence RA. Breastfeeding. A guide for the medical profession. Mosby, St.Louis, Fourth Edition, p.132. 1994.

Nifedipine   Fax #1312

Trade: Adalat, Procardia
Can/Aus/UK: Adalat, Apo-Nifed, Novo-Nifedin, Nu-Nifed, Nifecard, Nyefax, Adalat, Nefensar XL
Uses: Antihypertensive calcium channel blocker
AAP: Approved by the American Academy of Pediatrics for use in breastfeeding mothers

Nifedipine is an effective antihypertensive. It belongs to the calcium channel blocker family of drugs. Two studies indicate that nifedipine is transferred to breast milk in varying but generally low levels. In one study (Ehrenkranz 1989) in which the dose was varied from 10-30 mg three times daily, the highest concentration (53.35 µg/L) was measured at 1 hour after a 30 mg dose. Other levels reported were 16.35 µg/L 60 minutes after a 20 mg dose and 12.89 µg/L 30 minutes after a 10 mg dose. The milk levels fell linearly with the milk half-lives estimated to be 1.4 hours for the 10 mg dose, 3.1 hours for the 20 dose, and 2.4 hours for the 30 mg dose. The milk concentration measured 8 hours following a 30 mg dose was 4.93 µg/L. In this study, using the highest concentration found and a daily intake of 150 ml/kg of human milk, the amount of nifedipine intake would only be 7.4 µg/kg/day(less than 5% of the therapeutic pediatric dose). The authors conclude that the amount ingested via breast milk poses little risk to an infant. In another study (Manninen 1991), concentrations of nifedipine in human milk 1 to 8 hours after 10 mg doses varied from <1 to 10.3 µg/L (median 3.5 µg/L) in six of eleven patients. In this study, milk levels three days after discontinuing medication ranged from < 1 to 9.4 µg/L. The authors concluded the exposure to nifedipine through breast milk is not significant. In a study by Penny and Lewis (1989), following a maternal dose of 20 mg nifedipine daily for 10 days, peak breast milk levels at 1 hour were 46 µg/L. The corresponding maternal serum level was 43 µg/L. From this data the authors suggest a daily intake for an infant would be approximately 6.45 mcg/kg/day (assuming the infant ingests 150 mL of milk/kg/day).

Alternatives: Nimodipine

Pregnancy Risk Category: C

Adult Concerns: Headache, peripheral edema, gingival hyperplasia, hypotension. Distortion of smell and taste.

Pediatric Concerns: None reported via milk.

Drug Interactions: Barbiturates may reduce bioavailability of calcium channel blockers (CCB). Calcium salts may reduce hypotensive effect. Dantrolene may increase risk of hyperkalemia and myocardial depression. H2 blockers may increase bioavailability of certain CCBs. Hydantoins may reduce plasma levels. Quinidine increases risk of hypotension, bradycardia, tachycardia. Rifampin may reduce effects of CCBs. Vitamin D may reduce efficacy of CCBs. CCBs may increase carbamazepine, cyclosporin, encainide, prazosin levels.

AHL = 1.8-7 hours		M/P	= 1.0
PHL = 26.5(neonatal)		PB	= 92-98%
PK = 45 min-4 hours.		Oral	= 50%
MW = 346		pKa	=
Vd =			

References:
1. Ehrenkranz RA, et. al. Nifedipine transfer into human milk. J Pediatr 114: 478-80, 1989.
2. Manninen AK, Juhakoski A. Nifedipine concentrations in maternal and umbilical serum, amniotic fluid, breast milk and urine of mothers and offspring. Int. J. Clin. Pharmacol. Res. 11(5):231-6, 1991.
3. Penny WJ, Lewis MJ: Nifedipine is excreted in human milk. Eur J Clin Pharmacol 1989; 36:427-428.
4. Ferguson JE, Schutz T, Pershe R et al: Nifedipine pharmacokinetics during preterm labor tocolysis. Obstet Gynecol 1989; 161:485-490.

Nimodipine   Fax #1527

Trade: Nimotop
Can/Aus/UK: Nimotop, Nemotop
Uses: Antihypertensive, calcium channel
AAP: Not reviewed

Nimodipine is a calcium channel blocker, although it is primarily used in preventing cerebral artery spasm and improving cerebral blood flow. Nimodipine is effective in reducing neurologic deficits following subarachnoid hemorrhage, acute stroke and severe head trauma. It is also useful in prophylaxis of migraine. In one study of a patient 3 days postpartum who received 60 mg every 4 hours for one week, breast milk levels paralleled maternal serum levels with a milk:plasma ratio of approximately 0.33 (1). The highest milk concentration reported was approximately 3.5 µg/L while the maternal plasma was approximately 16 µg/L. In another study (2), a 36 year old mother received a total dose of 46 mg IV over 24 hours. Nimodipine concentration in milk was much lower than in maternal serum, with a milk:serum ratio of 0.06 to 0.15. During IV infusion, nimodipine concentrations in milk raised initially to 2.2 µg/L and stabilized at concentrations between 0.87 and 1.6 µg/L of milk. Assuming a daily milk intake of 150 mg/kg, an infant would ingest approximately 0.063 to 0.705 µg/kg/day, or 0.008 to 0.092% of the weight-adjusted dose administered to the mother.

Alternatives: Verapamil, Nifedipine.

Pregnancy Risk Category: C

Adult Concerns: Hypotension, diarrhea, nausea, cramps.

Pediatric Concerns: None reported via milk in two studies.

Drug Interactions: When used with adenosine, prolonged bradycardia may result. Use with amiodarone may lead to sinus arrest and AV block. H2 blockers may increase bioavailability of nimodipine. Beta blockers may increase cardiac depression. May increase carbamazepine levels with admixed. May increase cyclosporine, digoxin, quinidine plasma levels. May increase theophylline effects. Used with fentanyl, it may increase hypotension.

AHL = 9 hours		**M/P**	**= 0.06 to 0.33**
PHL =		**PB**	**= 95%**
PK = 1 hour		**Oral**	**= 13%**
MW = 418		**pKa**	**=**
Vd = 0.94			

References:
1. Tonks AM: Nimodipine levels in breast milk. NZ J Surg 65:693-694, 1995.
2. Carcas AJ. Abad-Santos F. de Rosendo JM. Frias J. Nimodipine transfer into human breast milk and cerebrospinal

fluid. Annals of Pharmacotherapy. 30(2):148-50, 1996.

Nisoldipine   Fax #1554

Trade: Sular
Can/Aus/UK: Syscor
Uses: Antihypertensive
AAP: Not reviewed

Nisoldipine is a typical calcium channel blocker antihypertensive. No data are available on its transfer into human milk. For alternatives see nifedipine, and verapamil. Due to its poor oral bioavailability, presence of lipids which reduce its absorption, and high protein binding, it is unlikely to penetrate milk and be absorbed by the infant (undocumented).

Alternatives: Nifedipine, Verapamil, Nimodipine

Pregnancy Risk Category: C

Adult Concerns: Hypotension, bradycardia, peripheral edema.

Pediatric Concerns: None reported via milk. Observe for hypotension, sedation although unlikely.

Drug Interactions: Barbiturates may reduce bioavailability of calcium channel blockers (CCB). Calcium salts may reduce hypotensive effect. Dantrolene may increase risk of hyperkalemia and myocardial depression. H2 blockers may increase bioavailability of certain CCBs. Hydantoins may reduce plasma levels. Quinidine increases risk of hypotension, bradycardia, tachycardia. Rifampin may reduce effects of CCBs. Vitamin D may reduce efficacy of CCBs. CCBs may increase carbamazepine, cyclosporin, encainide, prazosin levels.

AHL = 7-12 hours		M/P	=
PHL =		PB	= 99%
PK = 6-12 hours		Oral	= 5%
MW = 388		pKa	=
Vd = 4			

References:
1.   Pharmaceutical Manufacturer's package insert, 1998.

Nitrazepam   Fax #1313

Trade: Mogadon
Can/Aus/UK: Mogadon, Nitrazadon Alodorm, Atempol,
Nitrodos
Uses: Sedative, hypnotic
AAP: Not reviewed

Nitrazepam is a typical benzodiazepine (Valium family) used as a
sedative. Nitrazepam is secreted into breast milk and increases from
day one to at least day 5 of therapy. Oral bioavailability is good.
Milk:plasma ratio 7 hours post-dose is low (0.27) . Estimated dose to
infant is 10-15 µg/L milk. No side-effects were reported in infants.

Alternatives: Alprazolam, Lorazepam

Pregnancy Risk Category:

Adult Concerns: Sedation, disorientation.

Pediatric Concerns: None reported, but observe for sedation.

Drug Interactions:

AHL = 30 hours	M/P = 0.27
PHL =	PB = 90%
PK = 0.5 - 5 hours	Oral = 53-94%
MW = 281	pKa = 3.2,10.8
Vd = 2-5	

References:
1.   Matheson I, Lunde PK, and Bredesen JE. Midazolam and
      nitrazepam in the maternity ward: milk concentrations and
      clinical effects. Brit. J. Clin. Pharmacol. 30:787-93, 1990.

Nitrendipine   Fax #1314

Trade: Baypress
Can/Aus/UK:
Uses: Calcium channel blocker, antihypertensive
AAP: Not reviewed

Nitrendipine is a typical calcium channel antihypertensive. It is secreted into breast milk at peak concentrations ranging from 4.3 to 6.5 µg/L one to two hours after acute dosing of 10 mg. After 5 days of continuous maternal dosing (20mg/day) the milk levels were approximately the same. Based on a maternal dose of 20mg/day, a newborn infant would ingest an average of 1.7 µg of nitrendipine per day (0.095% of maternal dose).

Alternatives: Nifedipine, Nimodipine

Pregnancy Risk Category:

Adult Concerns: Headache, hypotension, peripheral edema, cardiac arrhythmias, fatigue.

Pediatric Concerns: None reported via milk.

Drug Interactions: Barbiturates may reduce bioavailability of calcium channel blockers (CCB). Calcium salts may reduce hypotensive effect. Dantrolene may increase risk of hyperkalemia and myocardial depression. H2 blockers may increase bioavailability of certain CCBs. Hydantoins may reduce plasma levels. Quinidine increases risk of hypotension, bradycardia, tachycardia. Rifampin may reduce effects of CCBs. Vitamin D may reduce efficacy of CCBs. CCBs may increase carbamazepine, cyclosporin, encainide, prazosin levels.

AHL = 8-11 hours		**M/P**	= 0.5-1.4
PHL =		**PB**	= 98%
PK = 1-2 hours		**Oral**	= 16-20%
MW = 360		**pKa**	=
Vd =			

References:
1.   White WB, Yeh SC, and Krol GJ. Nitrendipine in human plasma and breast milk. Eur. J. Clin. Pharmacol. 36(5):531-4,1989.

Nitrofurantoin   Fax #1315

Trade: Furadantin, Macrodantin, Furan, Macrobid
Can/Aus/UK: Apo-Nitrofurantoin, Macrodantin, Nephronex, Furadantin
Uses: Urinary antibiotic
AAP: Approved by the American Academy of Pediatrics for use in breastfeeding mothers

Nitrofurantoin is an old urinary tract antimicrobial. It is secreted in breast milk but in very small amounts. In one group of nine nursing women who received 100-200 mg every 6 hours, nitrofurantoin was undetectable in the milk of those treated with 100 mg and only trace amounts were found in those treated with 200 mg (0.3-0.5 mg/L milk). In these two patients the milk:plasma ratio ranged from 0.27 to 0.31. Do not use in infants with G6PD or in infants less than 1 month of age.

Alternatives:

Pregnancy Risk Category: B

Adult Concerns: Nausea, vomiting, brown urine, hemolytic anemia, hepatotoxicity.

Pediatric Concerns: None reported via milk, however, do not use in infants with G6PD or in infants less than 1 month of age.

Drug Interactions: Anticholinergics increase nitrofurantoin bioavailability by delaying gastric emptying and increasing absorption. Magnesium salts may delay or decrease absorption. Uricosurics may increase nitrofurantoin levels by decreasing renal clearance.

AHL = 20-58 minutes	M/P = 0.27-0.31
PHL =	PB = 20-60%

PK	= Variable	Oral	= 94%
MW	= 238	pKa	=
Vd	=		

References:

1. Hosbach RE, Foster RB. Absence of nitrofurantoin from human milk. JAMA 202:1057, 1967.
2. Varsano I, et. al. The excretion of orally ingested nitrofurantoin in human milk. J Pediatr 82:886-7, 1973.

Nitroglycerine   Fax #1555

Trade: Nitrostat, Nitrolingual
Can/Aus/UK: Nitrong SR, Nitrol, Transderm-Nitro, Nitro-Dur, Anginine, Nitrolingual Spray, Nitradisc, Deponit
Uses: Vasodilator
AAP: Not reviewed

Nitroglycerine is a rapid and short acting vasodilator used in angina and other cardiovascular problems including congestive heart failure. Nitroglycerine, as well as numerous other formulations (amyl nitrate, isosorbide dinitrate, etc) all work by release of the nitrite and nitrate molecule. Nitrates come in numerous formulations, some for acute use (sublingual), others are more sustained (Nitro-Dur). The duration of action and plasma levels are dependent on the formulation. Plasma nitrate levels are exceedingly low in most cases, averaging 50-500 nanogram/mL. At present, there are no data on the transfer of nitrates into human milk but due to their powerful hypotensive effect, and small molecular weight, some probably enters milk. With the use of short acting formulations and a brief waiting period (1-2 hours), breastfeeding may be possible with close observation of the infant. But caution is advised.

Alternatives:

Pregnancy Risk Category: C

Adult Concerns: Postural hypotension, flushing, headache, weakness, drug rash, exfoliative dermatitis, bradycardia, nausea, vomiting, methemoglobinemia (overdose), sweating.

Pediatric Concerns: None are reported via milk, but nitrates are likely to penetrate if breastfeeding occurs soon after administration. Caution is advised.

Drug Interactions: IV nitroglycerin may counteract the effects of heparin. Increased toxicity when used with alcohol, beta-blockers. Calcium channel blockers may increase hypotensive effect of nitrates.

AHL	= 1-4 minutes	M/P	=
PHL	=	PB	= 60%
PK	= 2-20 minutes	Oral	= Complete
MW	= 227	pKa	=
Vd	=		

References:
1. Drug Facts and Comparisons. 1997. ed. Facts and Comparisons, St. Louis.
2. Pharmaceutical Manufacturer's Package Insert, 1998.
3. McEvoy GE(ed):AHFS Drug Information, New York, NY. 1995.

Nitroprusside   Fax #1519

Trade: Nitropress
Can/Aus/UK: Nipride
Uses: Hypotensive agent
AAP: Not reviewed

Nitroprusside is a rapid acting hypotensive agent of short duration (1-10 minutes). Besides rapid hypotension, nitroprusside is converted metabolically to cyanogen (cyanide radical) which is potentially toxic. Although rare, significant thiocyanate toxicity can occur at higher doses (> 2 μg/kg/min.) and longer durations of exposure (> 1-2 days). When administered orally, nitroprusside is reported to not be active, although one report suggests a modest hypotensive effect. No data are available on transfer of nitroprusside nor thiocyanate into human milk. The half-life of the thiocyanate metabolite is approximately 3 days. Because the thiocyanate metabolite is orally bioavailable, some caution is advised if the mother has received nitroprusside for more than 24 hours.

Alternatives:

Pregnancy Risk Category: C

Adult Concerns: Hypotension, methemoglobinemia, headache, drowsiness, cyanide toxicity, hypothyroidism, nausea, vomiting.

Pediatric Concerns: None reported but caution is urged due to thiocyanate metabolite.

Drug Interactions: Clonidine may potentiate the hypotensive effect of nitroprusside. May reduce Iodine-131 uptake and induce hypothyroidism.

AHL	= 3-4 minutes	**M/P**	=
PHL	=	**PB**	=
PK	= 1-2 minutes	**Oral**	= Poor
MW	=	**pKa**	=
Vd	=		

References:
1. Page IH, Corcoran AC et.al. : Cardiovascular actions of sodium nitroprusside in animals and hypertensive patients. Circulation 1:188-198, 1955.
2. Benitz WE, Malachowski N, et al: Use of sodium nitroprusside in neonates: efficacy and safety. J Pediatr 106:102-110, 1985.

Nitrous Oxide   Fax #1316

Trade:
Can/Aus/UK: Entonox
Uses: Anesthetic gas
AAP: Not reviewed

Nitrous oxide is a weak anesthetic gas. It provides good analgesia and a weak anesthesia. It is rapidly eliminated from the body due to rapid exchange with nitrogen via the pulmonary alveoli (within minutes). A rapid recovery generally occurs in 3-5 minutes. Due to poor lipid solubility, uptake by adipose tissue is relatively poor, and only insignificant traces of nitrous oxide circulate in blood after discontinuing inhalation of the gas. No data exists on the entry of nitrous oxide into human milk. Ingestion of nitrous oxide orally via milk is unlikely. Chronic exposure may lead to elevated risks of fetal malformations, abortions, and bone marrow toxicity (particular in dental care workers).

Alternatives:

Pregnancy Risk Category:

Adult Concerns: Chronic exposure can produce bone marrow suppression, headaches, hypotension and bradycardia.

Pediatric Concerns: None reported via milk.

Drug Interactions:

AHL = < 3 minutes	**M/P** =
PHL =	**PB** =
PK = 15 min.	**Oral** = Poor
MW = 44	**pKa** =
Vd =	

References:
1. General Anesthetics. In: Drug Evaluations Annual 1995. American Medical Association, 1995.
2. Adriani J. General Anesthetics. In: Clinical Management of Poisoning and Drug Overdose. pp. 762-3, W.B.Saunders & Co.1983.

Nizatidine   Fax #1317

Trade: Axid
Can/Aus/UK: Axid, Apo-Nizatidine, Tazac
Uses: Reduces gastric acid secretion
AAP: Not reviewed

Nizatidine is an antisecretory, histamine-2 antagonist that reduces stomach acid secretion. In one study of 5 lactating women using a dose of 150 mg, milk levels of nizatidine were directly proportional to circulating maternal serum levels, yet were very low. Over a 12 hour period 96 μg (less than 0.1% of dose) was secreted into the milk. No effects on infant have been reported.

Alternatives: Famotidine

Pregnancy Risk Category: C

Adult Concerns: Headache, GI distress.

Pediatric Concerns: None reported.

Drug Interactions: Elevated salicylate levels may occur when nizatidine is used with high doses of salicylates.

AHL = 1.5 hours		M/P	=
PHL =		PB	= 35%
PK = 0.5-3 hours		Oral	= 94%
MW = 331		pKa	=
Vd =			

References:
1. Obermeyer BD, Bergstrom RF, Callaghan JT, et.al. Secretion of nizatidine into human breast milk after single and multiple doses. Clin.Pharmacol.Ther. 47:724-30,1990.

Norethindrone   Fax #1318

Trade: Aygestin, Norlutate, Micronor, Nor-QD.
Can/Aus/UK: Micronor, Norlutate, Norethisterone, Brevinor
Uses: Progestin for oral contraceptives
AAP: Not reviewed

Norethindrone is a typical synthetic progestational agent that is used for oral contraception and other endocrine functions. It is believed to be secreted into breast milk in small amounts. It produces a dose-dependent suppression of lactation at higher doses, although somewhat minimal. It may reduce lactose content and reduce overall milk volume and nitrogen/protein content, resulting in lower infant weight gain, although these effects are unlikely if doses are kept low. Use lowest possible dose.

Alternatives:

Pregnancy Risk Category: X

Adult Concerns: Changes in menstruation, breakthrough bleeding, nausea, abdominal pain, edema, breast tenderness.

Pediatric Concerns: None reported via milk.

Drug Interactions: Rifampin may reduce the plasma level of norethindrone possibly decreasing its effect.

AHL = 4-13 hours.	M/P =
PHL =	PB = 97%
PK = 1-2 hours.	Oral = 60%
MW = 298	pKa =
Vd =	

References:
1. Kora SJ. Effect of oral contraceptives on lactation. Fertil Steril 20:419-23, 1969.
2. Miller GH & Hughes LR: Lactation and genital involution effects of a new low-dose oral contraceptive on breast-feeding mothers and their infants. Obstet Gynecol 35:44-50, 1970.

3.   Karim M, Ammarr R, El-Mahgoubh S et al: Injected progestogen and lactation. Br Med J 1:200-203, 1971.
4.   Lonnerdal B, Forsum E & Hambraeus L: Effect of oral contraceptives on composition and volume of breast milk. Am. J. Clin. Nutr 33:816-824, 1980.
5.   Laukaran VH. The effects of contraceptive use on the initiation and duration of lactation. Int J Gynecol Obstet. 25(suppl)129-142, 1987.

Norethynodrel   Fax #1319

Trade: Enovid
Can/Aus/UK:
Uses: Progestational agent
AAP: Approved by the American Academy of Pediatrics for use in breastfeeding mothers

Norethynodrel is a synthetic progestational agent used in oral contraceptives. Limited or no effects on infant. May decrease volume of breast milk to some degree if therapy initiated too soon after birth and if dose is too high.   See norethindrone, medroxyprogesterone.

Alternatives:

Pregnancy Risk Category: X

Adult Concerns: Changes in menstruation, breakthrough bleeding, nausea, abdominal pain, edema, breast tenderness.

Pediatric Concerns: None reported. May suppress lactation.

Drug Interactions:

References:
1.   Booker DE, Pahyl IR. Control of postpartum breast engorgement with oral contraceptives. Am J Obstet Gynecol 98:1099-1101, 1967.
2.   Laukaran VH. The effects of contraceptive use on the initiation and duration of lactation. Int J Gynecol Obstet. 25(suppl)129-

142, 1987.

3.   Kora SJ. Effect of oral contraceptives on lactation. Fertil Steril 20:419-23, 1969.

Norfloxacin   Fax #1320

Trade: Noroxin
Can/Aus/UK: Noroxin
Uses: Fluoroquinolone antibiotic
AAP: Not reviewed

Norfloxacin is a second-generation fluoroquinolone antimicrobial. The fluoroquinolone family is known to produce arthropathy in neonatal animals, and has been reported to do so in at least three children with cystic fibrosis who received oral dosing.   Pseudomembranous colitis has been reported in one breastfed infant whose mother consumed ciprofloxacin. Although other members in the fluoroquinolone family are secreted into breast milk (see ciprofloxacin, ofloxacin), only limited data are available on this drug.   Wise (1984) has suggested that norfloxacin is not present in breast milk. The manufacturer's product information states that doses of 200 mg do not produce detectible concentrations in milk.   Of the fluoroquinolone family, this product and perhaps ofloxacin, may be preferred over others for use in a breastfeeding mother.

Alternatives: Ofloxacin, Trovafloxacin

Pregnancy Risk Category: C

Adult Concerns: Nausea, vomiting, GI dyspepsia, depression, dizziness, pseudomembranous colitis in pediatric patients.

Pediatric Concerns: None reported via milk. Observe for diarrhea.

Drug Interactions: Decreased absorption with antacids. Quinolones cause increased levels of caffeine, warfarin, cyclosporine, theophylline. Cimetidine, probenecid,   azlocillin increase norfloxacin levels. Increased risk of seizures when used with foscarnet.

AHL	= 3.3 hours	M/P	=
PHL	=	PB	= 20%
PK	= 1-2 hours	Oral	= 30-40%
MW	= 319	pKa	=
Vd	=		

References:

1. Drug Facts and Comparisons. 1994 ed. Facts and Comparisons, St. Louis.
2. Wise R: Norfloxacin - a review of pharmacology and tissue penetration. J Antimicrob Chemother 13:59-64, 1984.
3. Harmon T, Burkhart G, and Applebaum H. Perforated pseudomembranous colitis in the breast-fed infant. J. Ped. Surg. 27:744-6,1992.

Nortriptyline   Fax #1321

Trade: Aventyl, Pamelor
Can/Aus/UK: Aventyl, Norventyl, Apo-Nortriptyline, Allegron
Uses: Tricyclic antidepressant
AAP: Not reviewed

Nortriptyline (NT) is a tricyclic antidepressant and is the active metabolite of amitriptyline (Elavil). In one patient receiving 125 mg or nortriptyline at bedtime, milk concentrations of NT averaged 180 μg/L after 6-7 days of administration. Based on these concentrations, the average daily infant exposure would be 27 μg/Kg. The relative dose in milk would be 2.3% of the maternal dose. Several other authors have been unable to detect NT in neither maternal milk nor the serum of infants. So far no untoward effects have been noted.

Alternatives: Imipramine

Pregnancy Risk Category: D

Adult Concerns: Sedation, dry mouth, constipation, urinary retention, blurred vision.

Pediatric Concerns: None reported in several studies.

Drug Interactions: Phenobarbital may reduce effect of nortriptyline. Nortriptyline blocks the hypotensive effect of guanethidine.   May increase toxicity of nortriptyline when used with clonidine. Dangerous when used with MAO inhibitors, other CNS depressants. May increase anticoagulant effect of coumadin, warfarin. SSRIs (Prozac, Zoloft, etc) should not be used with or soon after nortriptyline or other TCAs due to serotonergic crisis.

AHL = 16-90 hours		M/P	= 0.87-3.71
PHL =		PB	= 92%
PK = 7-8.5 hours		Oral	= 51%
MW = 263		pKa	=
Vd =			

References:
1. Matheson I, Skjaeraasen J. Milk concentrations of flupenthixol, nortriptyline, and zuclopenthixol and between-breast differences in two patients. Eur. J. Clin. Pharmacol. 35:217-20,1988.
2. Wisner KS and Perel J. Serum nortriptyline levels in nursing mothers and their infants.
3. Brixen-Rasmussen L, Halgrener J, Jergensen A. Amitriptyline and nortriptyline excretion in human breast milk. Psychopharmacology 76:94-95, 1982.

Nystatin   Fax #1322

Trade: Mycostatin, Nilstat
Can/Aus/UK: Mycostatin, Nadostine, Nilstat, Candistatin, Nilstat, Nystan
Uses: Antifungal
AAP: Not reviewed

Nystatin is an antifungal primarily used for candidiasis topically and orally. The oral absorption of nystatin is extremely poor, and plasma levels are undetectable after oral administration.   The likelihood of secretion into milk is remote due to poor maternal absorption. It is frequently administered directly to neonates in neonatal units for candidiasis. In addition, absorption into infant circulation equally unlikely. Dose: neonates= 100,000 units; children=200,000 units, 400,000-600,000 units in older children, administered four times daily. Clinical cures of oral candidiasis with fluconazole are approximately twice that of nystatin.

Alternatives: Fluconazole

Pregnancy Risk Category: B

Adult Concerns: Bad taste, diarrhea, nausea, vomiting.

Pediatric Concerns: None reported. Nystatin is commonly used in infants.

Drug Interactions:

References:
1. Rothermel P, Faber M. Drugs in breast milk: a consumer's guide. Birth and Family J 2:76-78, 1975.

Ofloxacin   Fax #1323

Trade: Floxin
Can/Aus/UK: Floxin, Ocuflox, Tarivid
Uses: Fluoroquinolone antibiotic
AAP: Not reviewed

Ofloxacin is a typical fluoroquinolone antimicrobial. Breast milk concentrations are reported equal to maternal plasma levels. In one study in lactating women who received 400 mg oral doses twice daily, drug concentrations in breast milk averaged 0.05-2.41 mg/L in milk (24 hours and 2 hours post-dose respectively). The drug was still detectible in milk 24 hours after a dose. The fluoroquinolone family is known to produce arthropathy in neonatal animals, and has been reported to do so in at least three children with cystic fibrosis who received oral dosing. Ofloxacin levels in breast milk are consistently lower (37%) than ciprofloxacin. If required, ofloxacin and norfloxacin are probably the better choices for breastfeeding mothers.

Alternatives: Norfloxacin, Trovafloxacin

Pregnancy Risk Category: C

Adult Concerns: Nausea, vomiting, diarrhea, abdominal cramps, GI bleeding.

Pediatric Concerns: None reported, but caution recommended. Observe for diarrhea.

Drug Interactions: Decreased absorption with antacids. Quinolones cause increased levels of caffeine, warfarin, cyclosporine, theophylline. Cimetidine, probenecid, azlocillin may increase ofloxacin levels. Increased risk of seizures when used with foscarnet.

AHL = 5-7 hours	**M/P** = 0.98-1.66
PHL =	**PB** = 32%
PK = 0.5-2 hours	**Oral** = 98 %
MW = 361	**pKa** =
Vd = 1.4	

References:
1. Pharmaceutical Manufacturer's Package Insert, 1995.
2. McEvoy GE(ed):AHFS Drug Information, New York, NY. 1995.
3. Giamarellou H, Kolokythas E, Petrikkos G, et.al. Pharmacokinetics of three newer quinolones in pregnant and lactating women. Amer. Jour. of Med. 87:5A-49S-51S, 1989.

Olanzapine   Fax #1482

Trade: Zyprexa
Can/Aus/UK: Zyprexa
Uses: Antipsychotic
AAP: Not Reviewed

Olanzapine is a typical antipsychotic agent structurally similar to clozapine and may be used for treating schizophrenia. It is not known if it is secreted into human milk, but animal studies suggest that it may be. Olanzapine may tend to elevate prolactin levels moderately like other neuroleptic drugs in this class. Use caution.

Alternatives:

Pregnancy Risk Category: C

Adult Concerns: Agitation, dizziness, somnolence, constipation, dry mouth, weight gain, elevated liver enzymes.

Pediatric Concerns: None reported. Use extreme caution.

Drug Interactions: Ethanol may potentiate the effects of olanzapine. Fluvoxamine may inhibit olanzapine metabolism. Carbamazepine may increase clearance of olanzapine by 50%. Levodopa may antagonize the effect of olanzapine.

AHL = 21-54 hours		**M/P** =	
PHL =		**PB** = 93%	
PK = 5-8 hours		**Oral** = >57%	
MW =		**pKa** =	
Vd = 14.3			

References:
1. Pharmaceutical Manufacturer's Package Insert, 1997.

Olsalazine   Fax #1324

Trade: Dipentum
Can/Aus/UK: Dipentum
Uses: Anti-inflammatory
AAP: Should be given with caution

Olsalazine is converted to 5-aminosalicylic acid (mesalamine:5-ASA) in the gut which has anti-inflammatory activity in ulcerative colitis. After oral administration, only 2.4% is systemically absorbed, while the majority is metabolized in the GI tract to 5-ASA. 5-ASA is slowly and poorly absorbed. Plasma levels are exceedingly small (1.6-6.2 mmol/L), the half-life very short, and protein binding is very high. In rodents fed up to 20 times the normal dose, olsalazine produced growth retardation in pups. In one study, neither 5-ASA or its metabolite Acetyl-5-ASA were detected in maternal milk after a single sulfasalazine 500 mg dose. However, because minimal levels of olsalazine may be secreted into human milk, infants should be closely monitored for watery diarrhea.

Alternatives:

Pregnancy Risk Category: C

Adult Concerns: Watery diarrhea, dyspepsia, diarrhea, nausea, pain/cramping, headache,

Pediatric Concerns: None specifically reported with this product, but observe for diarrhea and cramping if used for longer periods.

Drug Interactions:

AHL = 0.9 hours		M/P	=
PHL =		PB	= > 99%
PK = 1-2 hours		Oral	= 2.4% (olsalazine)
MW = 302		pKa	=
Vd =			

References:
1. Drug Facts and Comparisons. 1995 ed. Facts and Comparisons, St. Louis.
2. Miller LG, Hopkinson JM, Motil KJ et al: Disposition of olsalazine and metabolites in breast milk. J Clin Pharmacol 33(8):703-706, 1993.

Omeprazole   Fax #1325

Trade: Prilosec
Can/Aus/UK: Prilosec, Losec
Uses: Reduces gastric acid secretion
AAP: Not reviewed

Omeprazole is a potent inhibitor of gastric acid secretion. The secretion of omeprazole into human milk is unreported but it is likely to be minimal.   In rodent studies, high doses (35X) produced decreased weight gain in pups, however comparison to humans is unknown. This drug is not generally recommended in nursing mothers, but the drug is considered very safe and has few side effects. Capsules are delayed release and enteric coated due to omeprazole's sensitivity to acids in the GI tract. Omeprazole is extremely acid-labile. Most would probably be destroyed in the stomach of the infant prior to absorption in the upper intestine.

Alternatives: Famotidine, Nizatidine

Pregnancy Risk Category: C

Adult Concerns: Headache, diarrhea, elevated liver enzymes.

Pediatric Concerns: None reported via milk.

Drug Interactions: Administration of Omeprazole and clarithromycin may result in increased plasma levels of omeprazole. Omeprazole produced a 130% increase in the half-life of diazepam, reduced the plasma clearance of phenytoin by 15%, and increased phenytoin half-life by 27%. May prolong the elimination of warfarin.

AHL = 1 hr.		**M/P** =	
PHL =		**PB** = 95%	
PK = 0.5-3.5 hours		**Oral** = 30-40%	
MW = 345		**pKa** =	
Vd =			

References:
1.   Pharmaceutical Manufacturer's Package Insert, 1996.
2.   Drug Facts and Comparisons. 1995 ed. Facts and Comparisons, St. Louis.

Ondansetron   Fax #1446

Trade: Zofran
Can/Aus/UK: Zofran
Uses: Antiemetic
AAP: Not reviewed

Ondansetron is used clinically for reducing the nausea and vomiting associated with chemotherapy. It has occasionally been used during pregnancy without effect on the fetus. It is available for oral and IV administration. Ondansetron is secreted in animal milk, but no data on humans are available. Four studies of ondansetron use in pediatric patients 4-18 years of age are available.

Alternatives:

Pregnancy Risk Category: B

Adult Concerns: Headache, drowsiness, malaise, clonic-tonic seizures, and constipation.

Pediatric Concerns: None reported via milk.

Drug Interactions: The clearance and half-life of ondansetron may be changed when used with barbiturates, carbamazepine, rifampin, phenytoin.

AHL = 3.6 hours.	**M/P** =
PHL = 2.7 hours.	**PB** = 70-76%
PK = 1.7 ,3.1 (IV, PO)	**Oral** = 56-66%
MW = 293	**pKa** =
Vd =	

References:
1. Pharmaceutical Manufacturer's Package Insert, 1996.
2. Spratto GR, Woods AL. In: Nurse's Drug Reference. Delmar Publishers Inc. Albany, NY, 1995.

Oral Contraceptives   Fax #1326

Trade: Norinyl, Norlestin, Ortho-Novum, Ovral
Can/Aus/UK: Nornyl, Cilest
Uses: Contraceptive
AAP: Approved by the American Academy of Pediatrics for use in breastfeeding mothers

Oral contraceptives, particularly those containing estrogens, tend to reduce lactose production, hence reducing volume of milk produced. Quality (fat content) may similarly be reduced, although one recent study of the fat, energy, protein, and lactose concentration in milk of mothers using oral contraceptives showed no effect of contraceptives. The earlier oral contraceptives are started, the greater the negative effect on lactation. Suppression of breast milk production with estrogen-progestin contraceptives is well known, and common. Although it was previously believed that waiting for 6 weeks would preclude breastfeeding problems, this is apparently not accurate. Numerous examples of supply problems have occurred months postpartum in some patients. Suggest that the mother establish a good flow (60-90 days) prior to beginning oral contraceptives. If necessary, use only LOW DOSE combination oral contraceptives with 35-50 mcg of estrogen or better, progestin-only mini pills. Suggest alternates such as progestin-only oral contraceptives so that if a supply problem occurs, the patient can easily withdraw from the medication. Use Depo-Provera in those patients who have used it previously and have not experienced breast milk supply problems, or in those who have used progestin-only mini pills without problems. The progestins and estrogens present in breast milk are quite low, and numerous studies confirm that they have minimal or no effect on sexual development in infants.

Alternatives: Norethindrone

Pregnancy Risk Category: X

Adult Concerns: Reduced milk production, particularly with estrogen containing preparations, but also rarely with progestin only products.

Pediatric Concerns: None reported via milk. May suppress lactation, reducing weight gain of infant.

Drug Interactions: Barbiturates, hydantoins, and rifampin, may increase the clearance of oral contraceptives resulting in decreased effectiveness of the OC. Co-administration of griseofulvin, penicillin, or tetracyclines with OCs may decrease the efficacy of oral contraceptives possibly due to altered gut metabolism. May increase or decrease anticoagulant efficacy. Co-administration with cyclosporine, or carbamazepine may result in decreased OC efficacy.

References:
1.   Booker DE, Pahyl IR. Control of postpartum breast engorgement with oral contraceptives. Am J Obstet Gynecol 98:1099-1101, 1967.
2.   Laukaran VH. The effects of contraceptive use on the initiation and duration of lactation. Int J Gynecol Obstet. 25(suppl)129-142, 1987.
3.   Kora SJ. Effect of oral contraceptives on lactation. Fertil Steril 20:419-23, 1969.
4.   Costa TH and Dorea JG. Concentration of fat, protein, lactose and energy in milk of mothers using hormonal contraceptives. Annals of Tropical Paediatrics 12:203-9, 1992.

Oral Polio Vaccine   Fax #1327

Trade: Vaccine - Live Oral Trivalent Polio
Can/Aus/UK:
Uses: Vaccine
AAP: Not reviewed

Oral polio vaccine is a mixture of three, live, attenuated oral polio viruses. Human milk contains oral polio antibodies consistent with that of the maternal circulation. Early exposure of the infant may reduce production of antibodies in the infant later on. Immunization of infant prior to 6 weeks of age is not recommended due to reduced antibody production. At this age, the effect of breast milk antibodies on the infant's development of antibodies is believed minimal. Wait until infant is 6 weeks of age before immunizing mother.

Alternatives:

Pregnancy Risk Category: C

Adult Concerns: Rash, fever.

Pediatric Concerns: None reported via milk.

Drug Interactions: May have inadequate response when used with immunosuppressants. Cholera vaccine may reduce seroconversion rate when co-administered, wait at least 30 days.

References:
1. Pharmaceutical Manufacturer's Package Insert, 1996.
2. Adcock E, Greene H. Poliovirus antibodies in breast-fed infants. The Lancet 1:662-663, 1971.

Orphenadrine Citrate   Fax #1328

Trade: Norflex, Banflex, Norgesic, Myotrol
Can/Aus/UK: Disipal, Norflex, Orfenace, Norgesic
Uses: Muscle relaxant
AAP: Not reviewed

Orphenadrine is an analog of Benadryl. It is primarily used as a muscle relaxant, although its primary effects are anticholinergic. No data are available on its secretion into breast milk.

Alternatives:

Pregnancy Risk Category: C

Adult Concerns: Agitation, aplastic anemia, dizziness, tremor, dry mouth, nausea, constipation.

Pediatric Concerns: None reported due to limited studies.

Drug Interactions: Increased anticholinergic side effects may be noted when used with amantadine. Orphenadrine may reduce therapeutic efficacy of phenothiazine family.

AHL = 14 hours.		**M/P** =	
PHL =		**PB** =	
PK = 2-4 hours		**Oral** = 95%	
MW = 269		**pKa** =	
Vd =			

References:
1. McEvoy GE(ed):AHFS Drug Information, New York, NY. 1995.

Osmotic Laxatives   Fax #1582

Trade: Milk Of Magnesia, Fleet Phospho-soda, Citrate Of Magnesia, Epsom Salt
Can/Aus/UK: Acilac, Citromag, Fleet Phosph-Soda, Sorbilax, Duphalac
Uses: Laxatives
AAP: Not reviewed

Osmotic or Saline laxatives comprise a large number of magnesium and phosphate compounds, but all work similarly in that they osmotically pull and retain water in the GI tract, thus functioning as laxatives. Because they are poorly absorbed, they largely stay in the GI tract and are eliminated without significant systemic absorption. The small amount of magnesium and phosphate salts absorbed are rapidly cleared by the kidneys. Products considered osmotic laxatives include: Milk of Magnesia, Epsom Salts, Citrate of Magnesia, Fleets Phospho-soda, and other sodium phosphate compounds. Because milk electrolytes and ion concentrations are tightly controlled by the maternal alveolar cell, the secretion of higher than normal levels into milk is rare and unlikely. It is not known for certainty if these products enter milk in higher levels than are normally present, but it is very unlikely.

Alternatives:

Pregnancy Risk Category: C

Adult Concerns: Diarrhea, nausea, vomiting, hypocalcemia, hypermagnesemia.

Pediatric Concerns: None reported via milk.

Drug Interactions: May reduce absorption of anticoagulants such as coumarin, and dicoumarol.

References:
1.   Drug Facts and Comparisons. 1997. ed. Facts and Comparisons, St. Louis.
2.   Pharmaceutical Manufacturer's package insert, 1997.

Oxaprozin   Fax #1329

Trade: Daypro
Can/Aus/UK: Daypro
Uses: Nonsteroidal analgesic
AAP: Not reviewed

Oxaprozin belongs to the NSAID family of analgesics and is reputed to have lesser GI side effects than certain others. Although its long half-life could prove troublesome in breastfed infants, it is probably poorly transferred to human milk.   There are no data on transfer into human milk, although it is known to transfer into animal milk.

Alternatives: Ibuprofen

Pregnancy Risk Category: C

Adult Concerns: Headache, nausea, abdominal pain, gastric bleeding, diarrhea, vomiting, bleeding, constipation.

Pediatric Concerns: None reported,   but ibuprofen preferred in absence of data.

Drug Interactions: May prolong prothrombin time when used with warfarin. Antihypertensive effects of ACEi family may be blunted or completely abolished by NSAIDs. Some NSAIDs may block antihypertensive effect of beta blockers, diuretics. Used with cyclosporin, may dramatically increase renal toxicity. May increase digoxin, phenytoin, lithium levels. May increase toxicity of methotrexate. May increase bioavailability of penicillamine. Probenecid may increase NSAID levels.

AHL = 42-50 hours		M/P	=
PHL =		PB	= 99%
PK = 3-5 hours		Oral	= 95%
MW = 293		pKa	=
Vd =			

References:
1.   Pharmaceutical Manufacturer's Package Insert, 1996.

Oxazepam   Fax #1330

Trade: Serax
Can/Aus/UK: Apo-Oxazepam, Novoxapam, Serax, Zapex, Alepam, Murelax, Serepax, Oxanid
Uses: Benzodiazepine antianxiety drug
AAP: Not reviewed

Oxazepam is a typical benzodiazepine (See Valium) and is used in anxiety disorders. Of the benzodiazepines, oxazepam is the least lipid soluble, which accounts for its low levels in milk. In one study of a patient receiving 10 mg three times daily for 3 days, the concentration of oxazepam in breast milk was relatively constant between 24 and 30 µg/L from the evening of the first day. The milk:plasma ratio ranged from 0.1 to 0.33. Thus a breastfeeding infant would be exposed to less than 1/1000th of the maternal dose.

Alternatives:

Pregnancy Risk Category: D

Adult Concerns: Sedation.

Pediatric Concerns: None reported in one study.

Drug Interactions: May increase sedation when used with CNS depressants such as alcohol, barbiturates, opioids. Cimetidine may decrease metabolism and clearance of oxazepam. Cisapride can dramatically increase plasma levels of diazepam. SSRIs (fluoxetine, sertraline, paroxetine) can dramatically increase benzodiazepine levels by altering clearance, thus leading to sedation . Digoxin plasma levels may be increased.

AHL	= 12 hours	M/P	= 0.1-0.33
PHL	= 22 hours	PB	= 97%
PK	= 1-2 hours	Oral	= 97%
MW	= 287	pKa	= 1.7,11.6
Vd	= 0.7-1.6		

References:
1. Wretlind M. Excretion of oxazepam in breast milk. Eur. J. Clin. Pharmacol. 33:209-210, 1987.

Oxybutynin   Fax #1512

Trade: Ditropan
Can/Aus/UK: Ditropan, Apo-Oxybutynin, Oxybutyn Ditropan
Uses: Anticholinergic, antispasmodic
AAP: Not reviewed

Oxybutynin is an anticholinergic agent used to provide antispasmodic effects for conditions characterized by involuntary bladder spasms, and reduces urinary urgency and frequency. It has been used in children down to 5 years of age at doses of 15 mg daily. No data on transfer of this product into human milk is available. But oxybutynin is a tertiary amine which is poorly absorbed orally (only 6%). Further, the maximum plasma levels (Cmax) generally attained are less than 31.7

nanogram/mL. If one were to assume a theoretical M:P ratio of 1.0 (which is probably unreasonably high) and a daily ingestion of 1 Liter of milk, then the theoretical dose to the infant would be < 2 micrograms/day, a dose that would be clinically irrelevant to even a neonate.

Alternatives:

Pregnancy Risk Category: B

Adult Concerns: Nausea, dry mouth, constipation, esophagitis, urinary hesitancy, flushing and urticaria. Palpitations, somnolence, hallucinations infrequently occur.

Pediatric Concerns: Suppression of lactation has been reported by the manufacturer.

Drug Interactions: May potentiate the anticholinergic effect of biperiden and other anticholinergics such as the tricylic antidepressants. May counteract the effects of cisapride and metoclopramide.

AHL = 1-2 hours		**M/P** =	
PHL =		**PB** =	
PK = 3-6 hours		**Oral** = 6%	
MW = 393		**pKa** = 6.96	
Vd =			

References:
1. Pharmaceutical Manufacturer's Package Insert, 1997.
2. Douchamps J, Derene F, et.al. The pharmacokinetics of oxybutynin in man. Eur. J. Clin. Pharmacol. 35(5):515-20, 1988.

Oxycodone   Fax #1331

Trade: Tylox, Percodan
Can/Aus/UK: Supeudol, Endone, Proladone
Uses: Narcotic analgesic
AAP: Not reviewed

Oxycodone is similar to hydrocodone and is a mild analgesic. Small amounts are secreted in breast milk. Following a dose of 5-10 mg every 4-7 hours, maternal levels peaked at 1-2 hours, and analgesia persisted for up to 4 hours. Reported milk levels range from <5 to 226 μg/L. Maternal plasma levels were 14-35 μg/L. At the highest concentration, an infant ingesting 1 L per day would receive less than 2% of the maternal dose. No reports of untoward effects in infants have been found.

Alternatives: Codeine

Pregnancy Risk Category: B

Adult Concerns: Drowsiness, sedation, nausea, vomiting, constipation.

Pediatric Concerns: None reported via milk.

Drug Interactions: Cigarette smoking increases effect of codeine. Increased toxicity/sedation when used with CNS depressants, phenothiazines, tricyclic antidepressants, other opiates, guanabenz, MAO inhibitors, neuromuscular blockers.

AHL = 3-6 hours		**M/P** = 3.4	
PHL =		**PB** =	
PK = 1-2 hours		**Oral** = 50%	
MW = 315		**pKa** = 8.5	
Vd = 1.8-3.7			

References:
1. Marx CM, Pucin F, Carlson JD, et.al. Oxycodone excretion in human milk in the puerperium. Drug Intel Clin Pharm. 20:474, 1986.

Oxytocin   Fax #1603

Trade: Pitocin
Can/Aus/UK: Syntocinon
Uses: Labor induction
AAP: Not reviewed

Oxytocin is an endogenous nonapeptide hormone produced by the posterior pituitary, and has uterine and myoepithelial muscle cell stimulant properties, as well as vasopressive and antidiuretic effects. Prepared synthetically it is bioavailable via IV and intranasal applications. It is destroyed orally by chymotrypsin in the stomach of adults, and systemically by the liver. It is known to be secreted in small amounts into human milk. Takeda (1986) reported that mean oxytocin concentrations in human milk at postpartum day 1 to 5 were 4.5, 4.7, 4.0, 3.2, and 3.3 microunits/mL respectively. The oral absorption in neonates is unknown, but probably not extensive. Intranasal sprays (Syntocinon), contained 40 IU/mL with a recommended typical dose being one spray (3 drops) in each nostril to induce letdown. This is roughly equivalent to 2 IU per drop or a total dose of approximately 12 IU per letdown dose. Although oxytocin is secreted in small amounts in breast milk, no untoward effects have been noted. However, chronic use of intranasal oxytocin may lead to dependence and should be limited to the first week postpartum.

Alternatives:

Pregnancy Risk Category:

Adult Concerns: Hypotension, hypertension, water intoxication and excessive uterine contractions, uterine hypertonicity, spasm, etc. May induce bradycardia, arrhythmias, intracranial hemorrhage, neonatal jaundice.

Pediatric Concerns: None via breast milk.

Drug Interactions: When used within 3-4 hours of cyclopropane,

AHL = 3-5 minutes	**M/P** =	
PHL =	**PB** =	
PK =	**Oral** = Nil	
MW = >1000	**pKa** =	
Vd =		

References:
1.   Drug Facts and Comparisons. 1997. ed. Facts and Comparisons, St. Louis.

2.   Pharmaceutical Manufacturer's Package Insert, 1997.
3.   American Hospital Formulary Service, Drug Information, 1995.

Paregoric   Fax #1332

Trade: Paregoric
Can/Aus/UK:
Uses: Opiate analgesic used for diarrhea
AAP: Not reviewed

Paregoric is camphorated tincture of opium, and contains approximately 2 mg morphine per 5cc (teaspoonful) in 45% alcohol. It is frequently used for diarrhea and in the past for withdrawal symptoms in neonates (Tincture of Opium is now preferred). Because the active ingredient is morphine, see morphine for breastfeeding indications. Due to its camphor content, the pediatric use of paregoric is discouraged.

Alternatives:

Pregnancy Risk Category: B

Adult Concerns: Sedation, constipation, apnea, nausea, vomiting.

Pediatric Concerns: None reported. See morphine.

Drug Interactions: See morphine.

AHL = 1.5-2 hours	M/P	= 1.1-3.6
PHL = 13.9 hours (neonatal)	PB	= 35%
PK = 0.5-1 hours	Oral	= 26%
MW =	pKa	=
Vd =		

References:
1.   Drug Facts and Comparisons. 1995 ed. Facts and Comparisons, St. Louis.

Paroxetine   Fax #1333

Trade: Paxil
Can/Aus/UK: Paxil Aropax 20 Seroxat
Uses: Antidepressant, serotonin reuptake inhibitor
AAP: Not reviewed

Paroxetine is a typical serotonin reuptake inhibitor. Although it undergoes hepatic metabolism, the metabolites are not active. Paroxetine is exceedingly lipophilic and distributes throughout the body with only 1% remaining in plasma. In one case report of a mother receiving 20 mg/day paroxetine at steady state, the breast milk level at peak (4 hours) was 7.6 μg/L. While the maternal paroxetine dose was 333 μg/Kg, the maximum daily dose to the infant was estimated at 1.14 μg/Kg or 0.34% of the maternal dose.

Alternatives: Sertraline

Pregnancy Risk Category: B

Adult Concerns: Sedation, headache, dry mouth, dizziness, nausea, insomnia, constipation, seizures.

Pediatric Concerns: Although this product has been occasionally used in breastfeeding and pregnant women, no reports of untoward effects have been found.

Drug Interactions: Decreased effect with phenobarbital and phenytoin. Increased toxicity with alcohol, cimetidine, MAO inhibitors (serotonergic syndrome). Increased effect with fluoxetine, tricyclic antidepressants, sertraline, phenothiazines, warfarin.

AHL = 21 hours.	**M/P = 0.09**
PHL =	**PB = 95%**
PK = 5-8 hours	**Oral = Complete**
MW = 329	**pKa =**
Vd = 3-28	

References:
1. Pharmaceutical Manufacturer's Package Insert, 1996.

2.   Kaye CM, Haddock RE, Langley PF et al. A review of the metabolism and pharmacokinetics of paroxetine in man. Acta Psychiatr Scand 80(Suppl 350):60-75, 1989.
3.   Spigset O. Paroxetine level in breast milk. J. Clin Psy. 57(1):39, 1996.

Pemoline   Fax #1335

Trade: Cylert
Can/Aus/UK: Cylert, Kethamed, Ronyl
Uses: CNS stimulant for attention deficit disorder
AAP: Not reviewed

Pemoline is a specialized CNS stimulate qualitatively similar to amphetamine and Ritalin. At present there are no data available on its transfer into human milk,   but it is likely due to its low molecular weight. Maternal peak level occurs 2-4 hours after dose. Serum half-life in children (5-12 yrs) is less than that of adults.

Alternatives:

Pregnancy Risk Category: C

Adult Concerns: Agitation, excitement, elevated liver enzymes, weight loss, insomnia, tachycardia.

Pediatric Concerns: None reported,   but observe for agitation, excitement, insomnia.

Drug Interactions: May reduce effect of insulin. Increased toxicity when used with other CNS depressants, CNS stimulants.

AHL = 12 hours		M/P	=
PHL = 7-8.6 hours		PB	= 50%.
PK = 2-4 hours		Oral	= Complete
MW = 176		pKa	= 10.5
Vd = 0.22-0.59			

References:
1.   Drug Facts and Comparisons. 1995 ed. Facts and Comparisons, St. Louis.

Penciclovir   Fax #1547

Trade: Denavir
Can/Aus/UK: Vectavir
Uses: Antiviral agent
AAP: Not reviewed

Penciclovir is an antiviral agent for the treatment of cold sores (herpes simplex labialis) of the lips and face, and occasionally for herpes zoster(Shingles). Following topical administration, plasma levels are undetectable. Because oral bioavailability is nil, and maternal plasma levels are undetectable following topical therapy, it is extremely unlikely that detectible amounts would transfer into human milk or be absorbable by an infant.

Alternatives:

Pregnancy Risk Category: B

Adult Concerns: Following topical application only mild erythema was occasionally observed.

Pediatric Concerns: None reported.

Drug Interactions: None reported.

AHL = 2.3 hours		**M/P** =	
PHL =		**PB** = < 20%	
PK =		**Oral** = 1.5%	
MW =		**pKa** =	
Vd =			

References:
1.   Vere Hodge RA & Perkins RM: Mode of action of 9-(4-hydroxy-3-hydroxymethylbut-1-yl)guanine (BRL 39123) against herpes simplex virus in MRC-5 cells. Antimicrob Agents Chemother

33:223-229, 1989.
2.   Pharmaceutical Manufacturer's Package Insert, 1998.

Penicillamine   Fax #1336

Trade: Cuprimine, Depen
Can/Aus/UK: Cuprimine, Depen D-Penamine, Distamine, Pendramine
Uses: Used in arthritis, autoimmune syndromes
AAP: Not reviewed

Penicillamine is a potent chelating agent used to chelate copper, iron, mercury, lead and other metals. It is also used to suppress the immune response in rheumatoid arthritis and other immunologic syndromes. It is extremely dangerous during pregnancy.   Safety has not been established during lactation. Penicillamine is a potent drug that requires constant observation and care by attending physicians. Recommend discontinuing lactation if this drug is mandatory.

Alternatives:

Pregnancy Risk Category: D

Adult Concerns: Anorexia, nausea, vomiting, diarrhea, alteration of taste, elevated liver enzymes, kidney damage.

Pediatric Concerns: None reported, but caution is recommended.

Drug Interactions: An increased risk of serious hematologic and renal reactions may occur if used with gold therapy, antimalarial, or other cytotoxic drugs. The absorption of penicillamine is decreased by 35% when used with iron salts. The absorption of penicillamine is decreased by 66% when used with antacids.   Digoxin plasma levels may be reduced.

AHL = 1.7-3.2 hours	**M/P** =
PHL =	**PB** =
PK = 1 hr.	**Oral** = Complete

MW = 149   pKa =
Vd =

References:
1.   Ostensen M, Husby G. Antirheumatic drug treatment during pregnancy and lactation. Scand J Rheumatol 14:1-7, 1985.

Penicillin G   Fax #1337

Trade: Pfizerpen
Can/Aus/UK: Crystapen, Megacillin, Bicillin L-A, Ayercillin, Crystapen
Uses: Antibiotic
AAP: Approved by the American Academy of Pediatrics for use in breastfeeding mothers

Penicillins generally penetrate into breast milk in small concentrations which is largely determined by class. Following IM doses of 100,000 units, the milk:plasma ratios varied between 0.03 - 0.13. Milk levels varied from 7 units to 60 units/L. Possible side effects in infants would include alterations in GI flora or allergic responses in a hypersensitive infant. Compatible with breastfeeding in non-hypersensitive infants.

Alternatives:

Pregnancy Risk Category: B

Adult Concerns: Changes in GI flora, allergic rashes.

Pediatric Concerns: None reported via milk, but observe for changes in GI flora, diarrhea.

Drug Interactions: Probenecid may increase penicillin levels. Tetracyclines may decrease penicillin effectiveness.

AHL = <1.5 hours	M/P = 0.03-0.13
PHL =	PB = 60-80%
PK = 1-2 hours	Oral = 15-30%
MW = 372	pKa =

Vd =

References:
1.   Matsuda S. Transfer of antibiotics into maternal milk. Biol Res Pregnancy Perinatol 5:57-60, 1984.
2.   Greene H, Burkhart B, Hobby G. Excretion of penicillin human milk following parturition. Am. J. Obstet. Gynecol. 51:732, 1946.

Pentazocine   Fax #1338

Trade: Talwin, Talacen
Can/Aus/UK: Talwin, Fortral
Uses: Analgesic
AAP: Not reviewed

Pentazocine is a synthetic opiate and is also an opiate antagonist. Once absorbed it undergoes extensive hepatic metabolism and only small amounts achieve plasma levels. It is primarily used as a mild analgesic. No data are available on transfer into breast milk.

Alternatives:

Pregnancy Risk Category: B

Adult Concerns: Sedation, respiratory depression, nausea, vomiting, dry mouth, taste alteration.

Pediatric Concerns: None reported due to limited studies.

Drug Interactions: May reduce the analgesic effect of other opiate agonists such as morphine. Increased toxicity when used with tripelennamine can be lethal. Increased toxicity when used with CNS depressants such as phenothiazines, sedatives, hypnotics, or alcohol.

AHL = 2-3 hours	M/P	=
PHL =	PB	= 60%
PK = 1-3 hours	Oral	= 18%
MW = 285	pKa	= 9.0
Vd = 4.4-7.8		

References:
1.   McEvoy GE(ed):AHFS Drug Information, New York, NY. 1995.

Pentobarbital   Fax #1339

Trade: Nembutal
Can/Aus/UK: Nembutal, Nova Rectal, Novo-Pentobarb, Lethobarb
Uses: Sedative, hypnotic
AAP: Not reviewed

Pentobarbital is a short acting barbiturate primarily used at a sedative. Following a dose of 100 mg for 3 days,   the concentration of pentobarbital 19 hours after the last dose was 0.17 mg/L.   The effect of short acting barbiturates on the breastfed infant is unknown but significant tolerance and addiction can occur.   Use caution if used in large amounts. No harmful effects have been reported in breastfeeding infants.

Alternatives:

Pregnancy Risk Category: D

Adult Concerns: Sedation, respiratory arrest, tachycardia, physical dependence.

Pediatric Concerns: None reported, but observe for sedation, dependence.

Drug Interactions: Barbiturates may decrease the antimicrobal activity of metronidazole. Phenobarbital may significantly reduce the serum levels and half-life of quinidine. Barbiturates decrease theophylline levels.   The clearance of verapamil may be increased and its bioavailability decreased.

AHL = 15-50 hours	**M/P** =
PHL =	**PB** = **35-45%**
PK = **30-60 min.(oral)**	**Oral** = **95%**

MW = 248   pKa = 7.9
Vd   = 0.5-1.0

References:
1.   Tyson RM, Shrader EA, Perlman HH. Drugs transmitted through breast milk. II Barbiturates. J Pediatr. 14:86-90, 1938.
2.   Kaneko S, Sato T, Suzuki K. The levels of anticonvulsants in breast milk. Br J Clin Pharmacol. 7:624-627,1979.
3.   Horning, MG et.al. Identification and quantification of drugs and drug metabolites in human breast milk using GC-MS-COM methods. Milk and Lactation Mod. Probl. Paediat. 15:73-79, 1975.

Pentosan Polysulfate   Fax #1546

Trade: Elmiron
Can/Aus/UK: Elmiron
Uses: Urinary tract analgesic
AAP: Not reviewed

Pentosan polysulfate is a negatively-charged synthetic sulfated polysaccharide with Heparin-like properties although it is used as a urinary tract analgesic. It is structurally related to dextran sulfate with a molecular weight of 4000-6000 daltons.   Pentosan adheres to the bladder wall mucosa and may act as a buffer to control cell permeability preventing irritating solutes in the urine from reaching the cell membrane.   Although no data are available on its transfer into human milk, its large molecular weight and its poor oral bioavailability would largely preclude the transfer and absorption of clinically relevant amounts in breastfed infants.

Alternatives:

Pregnancy Risk Category: B

Adult Concerns: Alopecia areata. Weak anticoagulant (1/15th activity of heparin). Mildly hepatotoxic. Headache, depression, insomnia, pruritus, urticaria, diarrhea, nausea, vomiting, etc. have been reported.

Pediatric Concerns: None reported via milk.

Drug Interactions: May increase bleeding time when used with cisapride.

AHL = < 5 hours		M/P	=
PHL =		PB	=
PK = 3 hours		Oral	= 3%
MW = 6000		pKa	=
Vd =			

References:
1. Wagner WH: Hoe/Bay 946 - a new compound with activity against the AIDS virus Arzneimittelforschung 39:112-113, 1989.
2. Asmal AC, Leary WP, Carboni J et al: The effects of sodium pentosan polysulfate on peripheral metabolism. S Afr Med J 49:1091-1094, 1975.

Pentoxifylline   Fax #1505

Trade: Trental
Can/Aus/UK: Trental, Apo-Pentoxifylline Trental
Uses: Reduces blood viscosity
AAP: Not reviewed

Pentoxifylline and its metabolites improve the flow properties of blood by decreasing its viscosity. It is a methylzanthine derivative similar in structure to caffeine and is extensively metabolized, although the metabolites do not have long half-lives. In a group of 5 breastfeeding women who received a single 400 mg dose, the mean milk:plasma ratio was 0.87 for the parent compound. The milk:plasma ratios for the metabolites were lower, 0.54, 0.76 and 1.13. Average milk concentration at 2 hours following the dose was 73.9 µg/L.

Alternatives:

Pregnancy Risk Category: C

Adult Concerns: Bleeding, dyspepsia, bloating, diarrhea, nausea, vomiting, bad taste, dyspnea.

Pediatric Concerns: None reported.

Drug Interactions: Bleeding, and prolonged prothrombin times when used with coumarins. Use with other theophylline containing products leads to increased theophylline plasma levels.

AHL = 0.4-1.6 hours		**M/P** =	
PHL =		**PB** =	
PK = 1 hour		**Oral** = Complete	
MW = 278		**pKa** =	
Vd =			

References:
1. Witter FR, Smith RV. The excretion of pentoxifylline and its metabolites into human breast milk. Am. J. Obstet. Gynecol. 151:1094-97, 1985.
2. Pharmaceutical Manufactures package insert, 1997.

Permethrin   Fax #1340

Trade: Nix, Elimite, A-200, Pyrinyl
Can/Aus/UK: Nix, Lyclear, Pyrifoam, Quellada
Uses: Insecticide, scabicide
AAP: Not reviewed

Permethrin is a synthetic pyrethroid structure of the natural ester pyrethrum, a natural insecticide, and used to treat lice, mites and fleas. Permethrin absorption through the skin following application of a 5% cream is reported to be less than 2%. Permethrin is rapidly metabolized by serum enzymes to inactive metabolites and rapidly excreted in the urine. Overt toxicity is very low. It is not known if permethrin is secreted in human milk, although it has been found in animal milk after injection of significant quantities IV. In spite of its rapid metabolism, some residuals are sequestered in fat tissue. To use, recommend that the hair be washed with detergent, then saturated with permethrin liquid for 10 minutes before rinsing with water. One treatment is all that is required. At 14 days, a second treatment may be required if live lice are seen. Elimite cream is generally recommended for scabies infestations, and should be applied head to toe for 8-12 hours. Reapplication may be needed in 7 days if live mites appear.

Alternatives:

Pregnancy Risk Category: B

Adult Concerns: Itching, rash, skin irritation. Dyspnea has been reported in one patient.

Pediatric Concerns: Pruritus, skin irritation, burning.

Drug Interactions:

References:
1. Pharmaceutical Manufacturer's Package Insert, 1996.

Phenazopyridine HCL   Fax #1341

Trade: Pyridium, Eridium, Azo-standard
Can/Aus/UK: Phenazo, Pyridium, Pyronium, Uromide
Uses: Urinary tract analgesic
AAP: Not reviewed

Phenazopyridine is an azo dye that is rapidly excreted in the urine, where it exerts a topical analgesic effect on urinary tract mucosa. Pyridium is only moderately effective and produces a reddish-orange discoloration of the urine. It may also ruin contact lenses. It is not known if phenazopyridine transfers into breast milk but it probably does to a limited degree. This product, due to limited efficacy, should probably not be used in lactating women although it is doubtful that it would be harmful to an infant. This product is highly colored and can stain clothing. Stains can be removed by soaking in a solution of 0.25% sodium dithionite.

Alternatives:

Pregnancy Risk Category: B

Adult Concerns: Anemia, nausea, vomiting, diarrhea, colored urine, methemoglobinemia, hepatitis, GI distress,

Pediatric Concerns: None reported via lactation.

Drug Interactions:

AHL =		M/P	=
PHL =		PB	=
PK =		Oral	= Complete
MW = 250		pKa	=
Vd =			

References:
1. Drug Facts and Comparisons. 1994 ed. Facts and Comparisons, St. Louis.

Phencyclidine   Fax #1342

Trade: PCP, Angel Dust
Can/Aus/UK:
Uses: Hallucinogen
AAP: Contraindicated by the American Academy of Pediatrics in breastfeeding mothers

Phencyclidine, also called Angel Dust, is a potent and extremely dangerous hallucinogen. High concentrations are secreted into breast milk (>10 times plasma level) of mice. Continued secretion into milk occurs over long period of time (perhaps months). One patient who consumed PCP 41 days prior to lactating had a milk level of 3.90 µg/L. EXTREMELY DANGEROUS TO NURSING INFANT.   PCP is stored for long periods in adipose tissue. Urine samples are positive for 14-30 days in adults and probably longer in infants. The infant could test positive for PCP long after maternal exposure, particularly if breastfeeding. Definitely contraindicated.

Alternatives:

Pregnancy Risk Category: X

Adult Concerns: Hallucinations, psychosis.

Pediatric Concerns: Significant concentrations would likely transfer to infant. Extremely dangerous.

Drug Interactions:

AHL = 24-51 hours		**M/P**	= > 10
PHL =		**PB**	= 65%
PK = Immediate		**Oral**	= Complete
MW = 243		**pKa**	= 8.5
Vd = 5.3-7.5			

References:
1. Nicholas JM, Liqshitz J, Schreiber EC, et.al. Phencyclidine. Its transfer across the placenta as well as into breast milk. Am J Obstet Gynecol 143:143-146, 1982.
2. Kaufman KR, Petrucha RA, Pitts FN, Weekes ME. PCP in amniotic fluid and breast milk: case report. J. Clin. Psychiatry 44:269, 1983.

Phenobarbital   Fax #1343

Trade: Luminal
Can/Aus/UK: Barbilixir, Phenobarbitone, Gardenal
Uses: Long acting barbiturate sedative, anticonvulsant
AAP: Drugs associated with significant side effects and should be given with caution

Phenobarbital is a long half-life barbiturate frequently used as an anticonvulsant in adults and during the neonatal period. Its long half-life in infants may lead to significant accumulation and blood levels higher than mother, although this is infrequent. During the first 3-4 weeks of life, phenobarbital is poorly absorbed by the neonatal GI tract. However, protein binding by neonatal albumin is poor, 36-43%, as compared to the adult, 51%. Thus, the volume of distribution is higher in neonates and the tissue concentrations of phenobarbital may be significantly higher. The half-life in premature infants can be extremely long (100-500 hours) and plasma levels must be closely monitored. In one study, following a dose of 30 mg four times daily, the milk concentration of phenobarbital averaged 2.74 mg/L 16 hours after the last dose. The dose an infant would receive was estimated at 2-4 mg/day. Other studies have found concentrations in breast milk to average 2.1 mg/L. Phenobarbital should be administered with caution and close observation of infant is required, including plasma drug levels.

Alternatives:

Pregnancy Risk Category: D

Adult Concerns: Drowsiness, sedation, ataxia, respiratory depression, withdrawal symptoms.

Pediatric Concerns: Phenobarbital sedation has been reported, but is infrequent. Expect infant plasma levels to approximate one-third (or lower) of maternal plasma level. Withdrawal symptoms have been reported.

Drug Interactions: Barbiturates may decrease the antimicrobal activity of metronidazole. Phenobarbital may significantly reduce the serum levels and half-life of quinidine. Barbiturates decrease theophylline levels. The clearance of verapamil may be increased and its bioavailability decreased.

AHL = 53-140 hours	M/P = 0.4-0.6
PHL = 36-144 hours	PB = 51%
PK = 8-12 hours	Oral = 80% (Adult)
MW = 232	pKa = 7.2
Vd = 0.5-0.6	

References:

1.	Tyson RM, Shrader EA, Perlman HH. Drugs transmitted through breast milk. II Barbiturates. J Pediatr. 14:86-90, 1938.

2. Kaneko S, Sato T, Suzuki K. The levels of anticonvulsants in breast milk. Br J Clin Pharmacol. 7:624-627,1979.

3. Kuhnz W, Koch S, Helge H et.al. Primidone and phenobarbital during lactation period in epileptic women: total and free drug serum levels in the nursed infants and their effects on neonatal behavior. Dev Pharmacol Ther 11:147-154,1988.

4. Nau H, et.al. Anticonvulsants during pregnancy and lactation. Clin. Pharmacokinetics 7:508-543, 1982.

Phentermine   Fax #1521

Trade: Fastin, Zantryl, Ionamin, Adipex-p
Can/Aus/UK: Ionamin, Duromine
Uses: Appetite suppressant
AAP: Not reviewed

Phentermine is an appetite suppressant structurally similar to the amphetamine family. As such it frequently produces CNS stimulation. No data are available on transfer to human milk. This product has a very small molecular weight (149) and would probably transfer into human milk in significant quantities and could product stimulation, anorexia, tremors, and other CNS side effects in the newborn. The use of this product in breastfeeding mothers would be difficult to justify and is not advised.

Alternatives:

Pregnancy Risk Category: C

Adult Concerns: Hypertension, tachycardia, palpitations, nervousness, tremulousness, insomnia, dizziness, depression, headache, cerebral infarct, paranoid psychosis, heat stroke, nausea, vomiting, physical dependence as evidenced by withdrawal syndrome.

Pediatric Concerns: Growth impairment has been reported from direct use of phentermine in children age 3-15 years.

Drug Interactions: Decreased effect of guanethidine, CNS depressants.

Increased toxicity of MAO inhibitors, other stimulants.

AHL = 7-20 hours		**M/P**	=
PHL =		**PB**	=
PK = 8 hours		**Oral**	= Complete
MW = 149		**pKa**	=
Vd =			

References:
1. Silverstone T: Appetite suppressants: a review. Drugs 43:820-836, 1992.

Phenylephrine   Fax #1604

Trade: Neo-synephrine, AK-dilate, Vicks Sinex Nasal
Can/Aus/UK: Mydfrin, Dionephrine, Fenox
Uses: Decongestant
AAP: Not reviewed

Phenylephrine is a sympathomimetic most commonly used as a nasal decongestant due to its vasoconstrictive properties, but also for treatment of ocular uveitis, inflammation and glaucoma, as a mydriatic agent to dilate the pupil during examinations, and for cardiogenic shock. Phenylephrine is a potent adrenergic stimulant and systemic effects (tachycardia, hypertension, arrhythmias), although rare, have occurred following ocular administration in some sensitive individuals. Phenylephrine is most commonly added to cold mixtures and nasal sprays for use in respiratory colds, flu and congestion. Numerous pediatric formulations are in use and it is generally considered safe in pediatric patients. No data are available on its secretion into human milk. It is likely that small amounts will probably be transferred, but due to the poor oral bioavailability (<38%), it is not likely that it would produce clinical effects in a breastfed infant unless the maternal doses were quite high.

Alternatives: Pseudoephedrine

Pregnancy Risk Category: C

Adult Concerns: Local ocular irritation, transient tachycardia, hypertension, and sympathetic stimulation.

Pediatric Concerns: None reported via milk.

Drug Interactions: Concomitant use with other sympathomimetics may exacerbate cardiovascular effects of phenylephrine. This includes albuterol, amitriptyline, other tricyclic antidepressants, MAO inhibitors, furazolidone, guanethidine, and others. Increased effect when used with oxytocic drugs.

AHL = 2-3 hours		M/P	=
PHL =		PB	=
PK = 10-60 minutes		Oral	= 38%
MW = 203		pKa	=
Vd = 0.57			

References:
1.   Pharmaceutical Manufacturer's package insert, 1997.

Phenylpropanolamine   Fax #1462

Trade: Dexatrim, Acutrim
Can/Aus/UK: Eskornade
Uses: Adrenergic, nasal decongestant, anorexiant.
AAP: Not reviewed

Phenylpropanolamine is an adrenergic compound frequently used in nasal decongestants, and also diet pills. It produces significant constriction of nasal mucosa, and is a common ingredient in cold preparations. No data are available on its secretion into human milk, but due to its low molecular weight, and its rapid entry past the blood-brain-barrier, it should be expected. It is frequently used in nasal decongestants for pediatric patients.

Alternatives:

Pregnancy Risk Category: C

Adult Concerns: Hypertension, bradycardia, AV block, arrhythmias, paranoia, seizures, psychosis, tremor, excitement, insomnia, seizures, anorexia and physical dependence.

Pediatric Concerns: None reported via milk but observe for excitement, loss of appetite, insomnia.

Drug Interactions: Hypertensive crisis when admixed with MAO inhibitors. Increased toxicity (pressor effects) with beta blockers. Decreased effect of antihypertensives.

AHL = 5.6 hours.		M/P	=
PHL =		PB	= Low
PK = 1 hour		Oral	= 100%
MW = 188		pKa	= 9.1
Vd = 4.5			

References:

1. Pharmaceutical Manufacturer's Package Insert, 1997.

Phenytoin   Fax #1344

Trade: Dilantin
Can/Aus/UK: Dilantin, Novo-Phenytoin, Epanutin
Uses: Anticonvulsant
AAP: Approved by the American Academy of Pediatrics for use in breastfeeding mothers

Phenytoin is an old and efficient anticonvulsant. It is secreted in small amounts into breast milk. The effect on infant is generally considered minimal if the levels in the maternal circulation are kept in low-normal range (10 µg/mL). Phenytoin levels peak in milk at 3.5 hours Although the actual concentration in milk varies significantly between studies, the milk:plasma ratio appears relatively similar, at 0.13 to 0.45. Breast milk concentrations varied from 0.26 to 1.5 mg/L depending on the maternal dose. The neonatal half-life of phenytoin is highly variable for the first week of life. Occasional monitoring of the infants' plasma may be useful although it is not definitely required. In one study of 6 patients, only two infants had measurable plasma levels of phenytoin. All of the current studies indicate rather low levels of phenytoin in breast milk and minimal plasma levels in breastfeeding infants.

Alternatives:

Pregnancy Risk Category: D

Adult Concerns: Sedation, hypertrophied gums, ataxia, liver toxicity.

Pediatric Concerns: Only one case of methemoglobinemia, drowsiness, and poor sucking has been reported. Most other studies suggest no problems.

Drug Interactions: Increased effects of phenytoin may occur when used with: amiodarone, benzodiazepines, chloramphenicol, cimetidine, disulfiram, ethanol, fluconazole(azoles), isoniazid, metronidazole, omeprazole, sulfonamides, valproic acid, TCAs, ibuprofen. Decreased effects of phenytoin may occur when used with: barbiturates, carbamazepine, rifampin, antacids, charcoal, sucralfate, folic acid, loxapine, nitrofurantoin, pyridoxine. Many others have been reported, please consult more complete reference.

AHL = 6-24 hours	M/P = 0.18-0.45
PHL = 20-160 hours (premature)	PB = 89%
PK = 4-12 hours	Oral = 70-100%
MW = 252	pKa = 8.3
Vd = 0.5-0.8	

References:
1. Brodie MJ. Management of epilepsy during pregnancy and lactation. Lancet 336:426-427, 1990.
2. Kaneko S, Sato T, Suzuki K. The levels of anticonvulsants in breast milk. Br J Clin Pharmacol. 7:624-627,1979.
3. Steen B, Rane A. Lonnerholm G, et.al. Phenytoin excretion in human breast milk and plasma levels in nursed infants. Ther Drug Monit 4:331-334, 1982.
4. Nau H, et.al. Anticonvulsants during pregnancy and lactation.

Clin. Pharmacokinetics 7:508-543, 1982.

Phytonadione   Fax #1500

Trade: Phytonadione, Aquamephyton, Konakion, Mephyton, Vitamin K1
Can/Aus/UK: Konakion
Uses: Vitamin K1
AAP: Approved by the American Academy of Pediatrics for use in breastfeeding mothers

Vitamin K1 is often used to reverse the effects of oral anticoagulants and to prevent hemorrhagic disease of the newborn (HDN). The use of vitamin K has long been accepted primarily because it reduces the decline of the vitamin K dependent coagulation factors II, VII, IX, and X. A single IM injection of 0.5 to 1 mg or an oral dose of 1-2 mg during the neonatal period is recommended by the AAP. Although controversial, it is generally recognized that exclusive breastfeeding may not provide sufficient vitamin K1 to provide normal clotting factors, particularly in the premature infant, or those with malabsorptive disorders. Vitamin K concentration in breast milk is normally low (<5-20 ng/mL), and most infants are born with low coagulation factors (30-60%) of normal. Although vitamin K is transferred to human milk, the amount may not be sufficient to prevent hemorrhagic disease of the newborn. Vitamin K requires the presence of bile and other factors for absorption, and neonatal absorption may be slow or delayed due to the lack of requisite gut factors.

Alternatives:

Pregnancy Risk Category: C

Adult Concerns: Adverse effects include hemolytic anemia, thrombocytopenia, thrombosis, hypotension, prothrombin abnormalities, pruritus, and cutaneous reactions. Anaphylaxis.

Pediatric Concerns: Vitamin K transfer to milk is low.

Drug Interactions: Decreased effect when used with coumarin/warfarin anticoagulants.

AHL =		M/P	=
PHL = 26-193 hours		PB	=
PK = 12 hours		Oral	= Complete
MW = 450		pKa	=
Vd =			

References:
1. Olsen JA: Recommended dietary intakes of vitamin K in humans. Am J Clin Nutr 45:687-692, 1987.
2. Lane PA, Hathaway WE. Vitamin K in infancy. J. Pediatr. 106:351-359, 1985.
3. Committee on Nutrition, American Academy of Pediatrics. Vitamin and mineral supplement needs in normal children in the United States. Pediatrics 66:1015-21, 1980.

Pimozide   Fax #1345

Trade: Orap
Can/Aus/UK: Orap
Uses: Potent tranquilizer
AAP: Not reviewed

Pimozide is a potent neuroleptic agent primarily used for Tourette's syndrome and chronic schizophrenia which induces a low degree of sedation. No data are available on the secretion of pimozide into breast milk. Must weigh benefit to mother with possible dangers to child. Suggest extreme caution.

Alternatives:

Pregnancy Risk Category: C

Adult Concerns: Extrapyramidal symptoms, anorexia, weight loss, GI distress, seizures.

Pediatric Concerns: None reported but caution is urged. No pediatric studies are found.

Drug Interactions: Increases toxicity of alfentanil, CNS depressants, guanabenz, and MAO inhibitors. Do not use with macrolide antibiotics such as clarithromycin, erythromycin, azithromycin and dirithromycin, due to two reported deaths.

AHL = 55 hours		M/P	=
PHL = 66 hours		PB	=
PK = 6-8 hours		Oral	= >50%
MW = 462		pKa	=
Vd =			

References:
1. Pharmaceutical Manufacturer's Package Insert, 1996.
2. Drug Facts and Comparisons. 1995 ed. Facts and Comparisons, St. Louis.

Piperacillin   Fax #1346

Trade: Zosyn, Pipracil
Can/Aus/UK: Pipracil, Pipril, Tazocin
Uses: Penicillin antibiotic
AAP: Not reviewed

Piperacillin is an extended-spectrum penicillin, it is not absorbed orally, and must be given IM or IV. Piperacillin when combined with tazobactam sodium is called Zosyn. Tazobactam is a penicillin-like inhibitor of the enzyme beta lactamase and has few clinical effects. Concentrations of piperacillin secreted into milk are believed to be extremely low. Its poor oral absorption would limit its absorption.

Alternatives:

Pregnancy Risk Category: B

Adult Concerns: Allergic skin rash, blood dyscrasia, diarrhea, nausea, vomiting, kidney toxicity, changes in GI flora.

Pediatric Concerns: None reported via milk.

Drug Interactions: Tetracyclines may reduce penicillin effectiveness.
Probenecid may increase penicillin levels.

AHL = 0.6-1.3 hours	M/P =
PHL = 3.6 hours (neonate)	PB = 30 %
PK = 30 - 50 min.	Oral = Poor
MW = 518	pKa =
Vd =	

References:
1. Pharmaceutical Manufacturer's Package Insert, 1996.
2. Chaplin S, Sanders GL , Smith JM. Drug excretion in human breast milk. Adv Drug React Ac Pois Rev 1:255-287, 1982.

Pirbuterol Acetate   Fax #1347

Trade: Maxair
Can/Aus/UK: Maxair, Evirel
Uses: Bronchodilator for asthmatics
AAP: Not reviewed

Pirbuterol is a classic beta-2 drug (similar to albuterol) for dilating pulmonary bronchi in asthmatic patients. It is administered by inhalation, and occasionally orally. Plasma levels are all but undetectable with normal inhaled doses. No data exists on levels in milk, but they would probably be minimal if administered via inhalation. Oral preparations would provide much higher plasma levels and would be associated with a higher risk for breastfeeding infants.

Alternatives:

Pregnancy Risk Category:

Adult Concerns: Irritability, tremors, dry mouth, excitement, palpitations, and tachycardia.

Pediatric Concerns: None reported via milk, but observe for irritability, tremors.

Drug Interactions: Decreased effect when used with beta blockers. Increased toxicity with other beta agonists, MAOi, and TCAs.

AHL = 2-3 hours.		**M/P** =	
PHL =		**PB** =	
PK = 5 min.(Aerosol)		**Oral** = Complete	
MW = 240		**pKa** =	
Vd =			

References:
1. Pharmaceutical Manufacturer's Package Insert, 1993, 1994.

Piroxicam   Fax #1348

Trade: Feldene

Can/Aus/UK: Apo-Piroxicam, Feldene, Novo-Pirocam, Candyl, Mobilis, Pirox

Uses: Non-steroidal analgesic for arthritis

AAP: Approved by the American Academy of Pediatrics for use in breastfeeding mothers

Piroxicam is a typical nonsteroidal anti-inflammatory commonly used in arthritics. In one patient taking 40 mg/day breast milk levels were 0.22 mg/L at 2.5 hours after dose. In another study of long-term therapy in four lactating women receiving 20 mg/day, the mean piroxicam concentration in breast milk was 78 µg/L which is approximately 1-3% of the maternal dose. This report suggests its use to be safe in breastfeeding mothers. Piroxicam has a very long half-life. Other choices are probably preferred. See ibuprofen.

Alternatives: Ibuprofen

Pregnancy Risk Category: B

Adult Concerns: Gastric distress, GI bleeding, constipation, vomiting, edema, dizziness, liver toxicity.

Pediatric Concerns: None reported via milk in several studies.

Drug Interactions: May prolong prothrombin time when used with warfarin. Antihypertensive effects of ACEi family may be blunted or completely abolished by NSAIDs. Some NSAIDs may block antihypertensive effect of beta blockers, diuretics. Used with cyclosporin, may dramatically increase renal toxicity. May increase digoxin, phenytoin, lithium levels. May increase toxicity of methotrexate. May increase bioavailability of penicillamine. Probenecid may increase NSAID levels.

AHL = 30-86 hours		**M/P**	= 0.008-.013
PHL =		**PB**	= 99.3%.
PK = 3-5 hours		**Oral**	= Complete
MW = 331		**pKa**	= 5.1a1.8b
Vd = 0.31			

References:
1. Ostensen M. Piroxicam in human breast milk. Eur. J. Clin. Pharmacol. 25:829-30, 1983.
2. Ostensen M, Matheson I , Laufen H. Piroxicam in breast milk after long-term treatment. Eur J Clin Pharmacol 35:567-569, 1988.

Polyethylene Glycol-electrolyte Solutions   Fax #1539

Trade: GoLYTELY, Col-Lav, Colovage, CoLyte, OCL
Can/Aus/UK: PegLyte
Uses: Bowel evacuant
AAP: Not reviewed

PEG-ES is a polyethylene glycol-3350 saline laxative. It is a non-absorbable solution used as an osmotic agent to cleanse the bowel. It is completely non-absorbed from the adult GI tract and would not likely penetrate human milk. This product is often used in children and infants prior to GI surgery. Although no data are available on transfer into human milk, it is highly unlikely that enough maternal absorption would occur to produce milk levels.

Alternatives:

Pregnancy Risk Category: C

Adult Concerns: Diarrhea, bad taste, intestinal fullness. Do not use in GI obstruction, gastric retention, bowel perforation, toxic colitis, megacolon or ileus.

Pediatric Concerns: None reported via milk.

Drug Interactions: Due to intense diarrhea produced, it would dramatically reduce oral absorption of any other orally administered medicine.

References:
1.   Drug Facts and Comparisons. 1996. ed. Facts and Comparisons, St. Louis.

Potassium Iodide   Fax #1349

Trade:
Can/Aus/UK:
Uses: Antithyroid agent, Expectorant
AAP: Not reviewed

Potassium iodide is frequently used to suppress thyroxine secretion in hyperthyroid patients. Iodide salts are known to be secreted into milk in high concentrations. Milk:plasma ratios as high at 23 have been reported. Iodides are sequestered in the thyroid gland at high levels and can potentially cause severe thyroid depression in a breastfed infant. Use with extreme caution if at all. Combined with the fact that it is a poor expectorant and that it is concentrated in breast milk, it is not recommended in breastfeeding mothers.

Alternatives:

Pregnancy Risk Category: D

Adult Concerns: Thyroid depression, goiter, GI distress, rash, GI bleeding, fever, weakness.

Pediatric Concerns: Thyroid suppression may occur. Do not use doses higher than RDA.

Drug Interactions:

AHL =	M/P = 23
PHL =	PB =
PK =	Oral = Complete
MW = 166	pKa =
Vd =	

References:
1. Delange F, Chanoine JP, Abrassart C, et.al. Topical iodine, breastfeeding, and neonatal hypothyroidism. Arch Dis Child. 63: 106-107, 1988.
2. Postellon DC, Aronow R. Iodine in mother's milk. JAMA 247:463, 1982.

Povidone Iodide   Fax #1350

Trade: Betadine, Iodex, Operand, Pharmadine
Can/Aus/UK: Betadine, Proviodine, Isodine, Viodine, Minidine
Uses: Special chelated iodine antiseptic
AAP: Not reviewed

Povidone iodide is a chelated form of iodine. It is primarily used as an antiseptic and antimicrobial. When placed on the adult skin, very little is absorbed. When used intra-vaginally, significant and increased plasma levels of iodine have been documented. Topical application to infants has resulted in significant absorption through the skin. Once plasma levels are attained in the mother, iodide rapidly sequester in human milk at high milk:plasma ratios. See potassium iodide. Could potentially cause thyroid suppression. Use with extreme caution or not at all. Povidone iodide is not recommended in nursing mothers or their infants.

Alternatives:

Pregnancy Risk Category: D

Adult Concerns: Iodine toxicity, hypothyroidism, goiter, neutropenia.

Pediatric Concerns: Transfer of absorbed iodine could occur leading to neonatal thyroid suppression. Avoid if possible.

Drug Interactions:

AHL =		M/P	= >23
PHL =		PB	=
PK =		Oral	= Complete
MW =		pKa	=
Vd =			

References:
1. Delange F, Chanoine JP, Abrassart C, et.al. Topical iodine, breastfeeding, and neonatal hypothyroidism. Arch Dis Child. 63: 106-107, 1988.
2. Postellon DC, Aronow R. Iodine in mother's milk. JAMA 247:463, 1982.

Pravastatin   Fax #1351

Trade: Pravachol
Can/Aus/UK: Pravachol, Lipostat
Uses: Lowers blood cholesterol
AAP: Not reviewed

Pravastatin belongs to the HMG-CoA reductase family of cholesterol lowering drugs. Small amounts are believed to be secreted into human milk but the levels were unreported. The effect on an infant is unknown, but it could reduce cholesterol synthesis. Atherosclerosis is a chronic process and discontinuation of lipid-lowering drugs during pregnancy and lactation should have little to no impact on the outcome of long-term therapy of primary hypercholesterolemia. Cholesterol and other products of cholesterol biosynthesis are essential components for fetal and neonatal development and the use of cholesterol-lowering drugs would not be advisable under any circumstances.

Alternatives:

Pregnancy Risk Category: X

Adult Concerns: Leukopenia, elevated liver enzymes, depression, neuropathy, etc.

Pediatric Concerns: None reported via milk but studies are limited.

Drug Interactions: The anticoagulant effect of warfarin may be increased. Use with bile acid sequestrants may reduce pravastatin bioavailability by 50%. May increased toxicities of cyclosporine. Concurrent use of niacin may increase risk of severe myopathy.

AHL = 77 hours		M/P	=
PHL =		PB	= 50%
PK = 1-1.5 hours		Oral	= 17%
MW = 446		pKa	=
Vd =			

References:
1. Pharmaceutical Manufacturer's Package Insert, 1996.

Prazepam — Fax #1352

Trade: Centrax
Can/Aus/UK:
Uses: Antianxiety agent
AAP: Drugs whose effect on nursing infants is unknown but may be of concern

Prazepam is a typical benzodiazepine that belongs to Valium family. It has a long half-life in adults. Peak plasma level occurs 6 hours post-dose. An active metabolite with a longer half-life is produced. No data are available on transfer into human milk. Most benzodiazepines have high milk:plasma ratios and transfer into milk readily. Observe infant closely for sedation. See diazepam.

Alternatives: Lorazepam, Alprazolam

Pregnancy Risk Category: D

Adult Concerns: Sedation, hypotension, depression.

Pediatric Concerns: None reported via milk, but benzodiazepines may induce sedation in breastfed infants.

Drug Interactions: May decrease effect of levodopa. May produce increased toxicity when used with other CNS depressants, disulfiram, cimetidine, anticoagulants, and digoxin.

AHL	= 30-100 hours		M/P	=
PHL	=		PB	= >70%
PK	= 6 hours		Oral	= Complete
MW	= 325		pKa	= 2.7
Vd	= 12-14			

References:
1. Drug Facts and Comparisons. 1995 ed. Facts and Comparisons, St. Louis.

Prazosin   Fax #1353

Trade: Prazosin, Minipress
Can/Aus/UK: Minipress, Apo-Prazo, Novo-Prazin, Minipress, Pressin
Uses: Strong antihypertensive
AAP: Not reviewed

Prazosin is a selective alpha-1-adrenergic antagonist used to control hypertension. It is structurally similar to doxazosin and terazosin. Antihypertensives may reduce breast milk production and prazosin may do likewise. Others in this family (doxazosin) are known to concentrate in milk. Exercise extreme caution when administering to nursing mothers.

Alternatives:

Pregnancy Risk Category: C

Adult Concerns: Leukopenia, tachycardia, hypotension, dizziness, fainting, headache, edema, diarrhea, urinary frequency.

Pediatric Concerns: None reported via milk, but some in this family are concentrated in milk. Observe extreme caution.

Drug Interactions: Beta blockers may enhance acute postural hypotensive reaction. The antihypertensive action of prazosin may be decreased by NSAIDs. Verapamil appears to increase serum prazosin levels. The antihypertensive effect of clonidine may be decreased when used with Prazosin.

AHL = 2-3 hours		M/P	=
PHL =		PB	= 97%
PK = 2-3 hours		Oral	=
MW = 383		pKa	= 6.5
Vd = 0.6			

References:
1. Drug Facts and Comparisons. 1994 ed. Facts and Comparisons, St. Louis.
2. Pharmaceutical Manufacturer's Package Insert, 1993, 1994.

Prednicarbate   Fax #1483

Trade: Dermatop
Can/Aus/UK:
Uses: High potency steroid ointment
AAP: Not reviewed

Prednicarbate is a high potency steroid ointment. Its absorption via skin surfaces is exceedingly low, even in infants. Its oral absorption is not reported, but would probably be equivalent to prednisolone, or high. If recommended for topical application on the nipple, other less potent steroids should be suggested, including hydrocortisone or triamcinolone. If applied to the nipple, only extremely small amounts should be applied.

Alternatives:

Pregnancy Risk Category:

Adult Concerns: Symptoms of adrenal steroid suppression, fluid retention, gastric erosions.

Pediatric Concerns: None reported via milk.

Drug Interactions:

AHL =		M/P =	
PHL =		PB =	
PK =		Oral =	
MW = 488		pKa =	
Vd =			

References:

Prednisone   Fax #1449

Trade: Deltasone, Meticorten, Orasone
Can/Aus/UK: Apo-Prednisone, Deltasone, Novo-Prednisone, Sone, Panafcort, Decortisyl, Econosone
Uses: Corticosteroid
AAP: Approved by the American Academy of Pediatrics for use in breastfeeding mothers

Prednisone is rapidly absorbed and metabolized to the active form, prednisolone. It is known to be secreted into human milk in generally small amounts. Two hours after a 10 mg oral dose of prednisone, the concentration of prednisolone and prednisone were 1.6 µg/L and 26.7 µg/L respectively. Using this data, an infant consuming 1 liter of milk daily would ingest 28.3 µg of the two steroids, an amount that would be clinically insignificant. In a mother receiving a high dose of 120 mg/day of prednisone, breast milk levels of steroid ranged from 54.1 to 627 µg/L at 30 min. and 2 hours respectively. Assuming the infant nursed 120 cc every 4 hours, total possible ingestion would be 47 µg, an amount that would not be hazardous (Berlin, 1979). Doses of 80 mg/day in mothers produce insignificant absorption in infant (< 0.1% of dose). In small doses, steroids are not contraindicated in nursing mothers. Whenever possible use low-dose alternatives such as aerosols or inhalers. Following administration, wait at least 4 hours if possible prior to feeding infant to reduce exposure.

Alternatives:

Pregnancy Risk Category: B

Adult Concerns: In pediatrics: shortened stature, GI bleeding, GI ulceration, edema, osteoporosis.

Pediatric Concerns: None reported via breast milk. Limit dose and length of exposure if possible. High doses and durations may inhibit epiphyseal bone growth, induce gastric ulcerations, glaucoma, etc. Use inhaled or intranasal forms when possible to limit exposure.

Drug Interactions: Barbiturates may significantly reduce the effects of corticosteroids. Cholestyramine may reduce absorption of prednisone. Oral contraceptives may reduce half-life and concentration of steroids. Ephedrine may reduce the half-life and increase clearance of certain steroids. Phenytoin may increase clearance. Corticosteroid clearance may be decreased by ketaconazole. Certain macrolide antibiotics may significantly decrease clearance of steroids. Isoniazid serum concentrations may be decreased.

AHL = 3 hours		M/P	=
PHL =		PB	= 70%
PK = 1-2 hours		Oral	= 92%
MW = 358		pKa	=

Vd =

References:

1. Katz FH, Duncan BR. Entry of prednisone in human milk. N. Eng. J. Med. 293:1154, 1975.
2. Berlin CM. Kaiser DG, Demers L. Excretion of prednisone and prednisolone in human milk. Pharmacologist 21:264, 1979.
3. Ost L et.al. Prednisolone excretion in human milk. J. Pediatr. 106(6):1008-11, 1985.

Primaquine Phosphate   Fax #1516

Trade:

Can/Aus/UK: Primaquine phosphate

Uses: Antimalarial

AAP: Not reviewed

Primaquine is a typical antimalarial medication that is primarily used as chemoprophylaxis after the patient has returned from the region of exposure with the intention of preventing relapses of plasmodium vivax, and or ovale. It is used in pediatric patients at a dose of 0.3 mg/Kg/day for 14 days.   No data are available on its transfer into human milk. Maternal plasma levels are rather low, only 53-107 nanogram/mL, suggesting that milk levels might be rather low as well.

Alternatives:

Pregnancy Risk Category: C

Adult Concerns: Blood dyscrasia,   including granulocytopenia, anemia, leukocytosis, methemoglobinemia. Arrhythmia, hypertension, abdominal pain, cramps, visual (ocular) disturbances.

Pediatric Concerns: None reported from milk.

Drug Interactions: Elevated risk of blood dyscrasia with aurothioglucose. May reduce plasma levels of oral contraceptives.

AHL	= 4-7 hours	M/P	=
PHL	=	PB	=
PK	= 1-2 hours	Oral	= 96%
MW	= 259	pKa	=
Vd	=		

References:
1. Mihaly GW, Ward SA, Edwards G et al: Pharmacokinetics of primaquine in man: identification of the carboxylic acid derivative as a major plasma metabolite. Br J Clin Pharmacol 17:441-446, 1984.
2. Mihaly GW, Ward SA, Edwards G et al: Pharmacokinetics of primaquine in man. I. Studies of the absolute bioavailability and effects of dose size. Br J Clin Pharmacol 19:745-750, 1985.
3. Bhatia SC, Saraph YS, Revankar SN et al: Pharmacokinetics of primaquine in patients with p vivax malaria. Eur J Clin Pharmacol 31:205-210, 1986.

Primidone   Fax #1354

Trade: Myidone, Mysoline
Can/Aus/UK: Apo-Primidone, Sertan, Mysoline, Misolyne
Uses: Anticonvulsant
AAP: Drugs associated with significant side effects and should be given with caution

Primidone is metabolized in adults to several derivatives including phenobarbital. After chronic therapy, levels of phenobarbital rise to a therapeutic range. Hence, problems for the infant would not only include primidone, but subsequently, phenobarbital. In one study of 2 women receiving primidone, the steady-state concentrations of primidone in neonatal serum via ingestion of breast milk were 0.7 and 2.5 μg/mL. The steady-state phenobarbital levels in neonatal serum were between 2.0 to 13.0 μg/mL. The calculated dose of phenobarbital per day received by each infant ranged from 1.8 to 8.9 mg/day. Some sedation has been reported, particularly during the neonatal period.

Alternatives: Phenobarbital

Pregnancy Risk Category: D

Adult Concerns: Sedation, apnea, reduced suckling.

Pediatric Concerns: Some sedation, during neonatal period.

Drug Interactions: Acetazolamide may decrease primidone plasma levels. Co-administration of carbamazepine may lower primidone and phenobarbital concentrations and elevate carbamazepine concentrations. Use of phenytoin may reduce primidone concentrations. Primidone concentrations may be increased when used with isoniazid. The clearance of primidone may be decreased with nicotinamide.

AHL = 10-21 hours (primidone)	M/P	= 0.72
PHL =	PB	= <20%
PK = 0.5-5 hours.	Oral	= 90%
MW = 218	pKa	=
Vd = 0.5-1.0		

References:
1. Kuhnz W, Koch S, Helge H et.al. Primidone and phenobarbital during lactation period in epileptic women: total and free drug serum levels in the nursed infants and their effects on neonatal behavior. Dev Pharmacol Ther 11:147-154,1988.

Procainamide   Fax #1355

Trade: Pronestyl, Procan
Can/Aus/UK: Pronestryl, Procan SR, Apo-Procainamide, Pronestyl
Uses: Antiarrhythmic
AAP: Approved by the American Academy of Pediatrics for use in breastfeeding mothers

Procainamide is an antiarrhythmic agent. Procainamide and its active metabolite are secreted into breast milk in moderate concentrations. In one patient receiving 500 mg four times daily, the breast milk levels of procainamide at 0, 3, 6, 9, and 12 hours were 5.3, 3.9, 10.2, 4.8, and 2.6 mg/L respectively. The milk:serum ratio varied from 1.0 at 12 hours to 7.3 at 6 hours post-dose (mean = 4.3). The milk levels averaged 5.4 mg/L for parent drug and 3.5 mg/L for metabolite. Hypothetical dose per day to infant would be approximately 65 mg (includes metabolite). Although levels in milk are still too small to provide significant blood levels in an infant, one should use with caution. Only 1-2% of the maternal dose appeared in milk daily.

Alternatives:

Pregnancy Risk Category: C

Adult Concerns: Nausea, vomiting, liver toxicity, blood dyscrasia, hypotension,

Pediatric Concerns: None reported via milk. Observe for liver toxicity, hypotension, but very unlikely.

Drug Interactions: Propranolol may increase procainamide serum levels. Cimetidine and ranitidine appear to increase bioavailability of procainamide. Use with lidocaine may increase cardiodepressant action of procainamide.

AHL = 3.0 hours	**M/P** = 1-7.3
PHL = 13.5 hours (neonate)	**PB** = 16%
PK = 0.75-2.5 hours	**Oral** = 75-90%
MW = 271	**pKa** = 9.2
Vd = 3.3-4.8	

References:
1. Pittard WB III, Glazier H. Procainamide excretion in human milk. J. Pediatr. 102:631-3, 1983.

Prochlorperazine   Fax #1356

Trade: Compazine
Can/Aus/UK: Prorazin, Stemetil, Nu-Prochlor, Stemetil, Buccastem
Uses: Antiemetic, tranquilizer-sedative
AAP: Not reviewed

Prochlorperazine is a phenothiazine primarily used as an antiemetic. There are no reports as of yet concerning breast milk levels. Because most phenothiazines are transferred into human milk, it is likely prochlorperazine is likewise. If used in mother, recommend removing infant for 12 hours after last dose. There are controversial suggestions that phenothiazines may increase the risk of SIDS. Because infants are extremely hypersensitive to these compounds, suggest caution. This product may also increase prolactin levels.

Alternatives:

Pregnancy Risk Category: C

Adult Concerns: Sedation, extrapyramidal effects, seizures, weight gain, liver toxicity.

Pediatric Concerns: None reported via milk, but caution is recommended.

Drug Interactions: May have increased toxicity when used with other CNS depressants, anticonvulsants. Epinephrine may cause hypotension.

AHL = 10-20 hours	**M/P**	=
PHL =	**PB**	= 90%
PK = 3.4-9.9(oral)	**Oral**	= Complete
MW = 374	**pKa**	=
Vd =		

References:
1.   Drug Facts and Comparisons. 1995 ed. Facts and Comparisons,

St. Louis.
2. McEvoy GE(ed):AHFS Drug Information, New York, NY. 1995.

Promethazine   Fax #1357

Trade: Phenergan
Can/Aus/UK: Histanil, Phenergan, PMS Promethazine, Avomine
Uses: Phenothiazine used as antihistamine
AAP: Not reviewed

Promethazine is a phenothiazine that is primarily used for sedation, nausea and motion sickness. It has been used safely for many years in pediatric patients for vomiting and in adult patients for vomiting, particularly associated with pregnancy. Phenothiazines pass into breast milk in low to moderate levels. Infants appear slightly hypersensitive to this class of compounds and may exhibit jerking (extrapyramidal) symptoms, although they have not been reported. There are controversial suggestions that phenothiazines may increase the risk of SIDS. Long term follow up (6 years) has found no untoward effects on development.

Alternatives:

Pregnancy Risk Category: C

Adult Concerns: Sedation, apnea, extrapyramidal symptoms.

Pediatric Concerns: None reported via breast milk.

Drug Interactions: Epinephrine may cause significant decrease in blood pressure.

AHL = 12.7 hours	M/P =
PHL =	PB = 76-80%
PK = 2.7	Oral = Poor
MW = 284	pKa = 9.1
Vd = 9-19	

References:

1. Kris EB. Children born to mothers maintained on pharmacotherapy during pregnancy and postpartum. Recent Adv. Biol. Psychiatry 4:180-7,1962.
2. Ayd FJ. Children born of mothers treated with chlorpromazine during pregnancy. Clin. Med. 71:1758-63,1964.

Propofol   Fax #1358

Trade: Diprivan
Can/Aus/UK: Diprivan
Uses: Preanesthetic sedative
AAP: Not reviewed

Propofol is an IV sedative hypnotic agent for induction and maintenance of anesthesia. It is particularly popular in various pediatric procedures. Although the terminal half-life is long, it is rapidly distributed out of the plasma compartment to other peripheral compartments (adipose) so that anesthesia is short (3-10 minutes). Propofol is incredibly lipid soluble. However, only very low concentrations of propofol have been found in breast milk. In one study of 3 women who received propofol 2.5 mg/kg IV followed by a continuous infusion, the breast milk levels ranged from 0.04 to 0.74 mg/L. The second breast milk level obtained 24 hours after delivery contained only 6% of the 4-hour sample. Similar levels (0.12-0.97 mg/L) were noted by Schmitt (1987) in colostrum samples obtained 4-8 hours after induction with propofol. From these data it is apparent that only minimal levels of propofol is transferred to human milk. No data are available on the oral absorption of propofol. Propofol is rapidly cleared from the neonatal circulation (Dailland, 1989).

Alternatives: Midazolam

Pregnancy Risk Category: B

Adult Concerns: Sedation, apnea.

Pediatric Concerns: None reported in several studies.

Drug Interactions: Anaphylactoid reactions when used with atracurium. May potentiate the neuromuscular blockade of vecuronium. May be additive with other CNS depressants. Theophylline may antagonize the effect of propofol.

AHL = 1-3 days.	M/P	=
PHL =	PB	= 99%
PK = Instant(IV)	Oral	=
MW = 178	pKa	= 11.0
Vd = 60		

References:
1. Dailland P, Cockshott ID, et al: Intravenous propofol during cesarean section: placental transfer, concentrations in breast milk, and neonatal effects. A preliminary study. Anesthesiology 71:827-834, 1989.
2. Schmitt JP, Schwoerer D, et.al. Passage of propofol in the colostrum. Preliminary data. Ann. Fr. Anesth. Reanim 6:267-268, 1987.

Propoxyphene   Fax #1359

Trade: Darvocet-N, Propacet, Darvon
Can/Aus/UK: Darvon-N, Novo-Propoxyn, Capadex, Paradex, Di-Gesic, Doloxene, Progesic
Uses: Mild narcotic analgesic
AAP: Approved by the American Academy of Pediatrics for use in breastfeeding mothers

Propoxyphene is a mild narcotic analgesic similar in efficacy to aspirin. The amount secreted into milk is extremely low and is generally too low to produce effects in infant (< 1 mg/day). Maternal plasma levels peak at 2 hours Propoxyphene is metabolized to norpropoxyphene (which has weaker CNS effects). AHL= 6-12 hours (propoxyphene), 30-36 hours (norpropoxyphene). Thus far, no reports of untoward effects in infants have been reported.

Alternatives: Ibuprofen, Acetaminophen

Pregnancy Risk Category: C

Adult Concerns: Nausea, respiratory depression, sedation, agitation, seizures, anemia, liver toxicity, withdrawal symptoms.

Pediatric Concerns: None reported but observe for sedation.

Drug Interactions: Additive sedation may occur when used with CNS depressants such as barbiturates. Carbamazepine levels may be increased. Use with cimetidine may produce CNS toxicity such as confusion, disorientation, apnea, seizures.

AHL = 6-12 hours (propoxyphene)		M/P	=
PHL =		PB	= 78%
PK = 2 hours		Oral	= Complete
MW = 339		pKa	= 6.3
Vd = 12-26			

References:
1.   Catz C, Gulacoia G. Drugs and breast milk. Pediatr Clin North Am 19:151-66, 1972.

Propranolol   Fax #1360

Trade: Inderal
Can/Aus/UK: Detensol, Inderal, Novo-Pranol, Deralin, Cardinol
Uses: Beta-blocker, antihypertensive
AAP: Approved by the American Academy of Pediatrics for use in breastfeeding mothers

Propranolol is a popular beta blocker used in treating hypertension, cardiac arrhythmia, migraine headache, and numerous other syndromes. In general, the maternal plasma levels are exceedingly low, hence the milk levels are low as well. In one study of 3 patients, the average milk concentration was only 35.4 µg/L after multiple dosing intervals. The milk:plasma ratio varied from 0.33 to 1.65. Using this data, the authors suggest that an infant would receive only 70 µg/Liter of milk per day, which is < 0.1% of the maternal dose. This amount would be clinically insignificant. Long term exposure has not been studied, and caution is urged. Of the beta blocker family, propranolol is probably preferred in lactating women.

Alternatives: Metoprolol

Pregnancy Risk Category: C

Adult Concerns: Bradycardia, asthmatic symptoms, hypotension, sedation, weakness, hypoglycemia.

Pediatric Concerns: None reported via breast milk in numerous studies.

Drug Interactions: Decreased effect when used with aluminum salts, barbiturates, calcium salts, cholestyramine, NSAIDs, ampicillin, rifampin, and salicylates. Beta blockers may reduce the effect of oral sulfonylureas (hypoglycemic agents). Increased toxicity/effect when used with other antihypertensives, contraceptives, MAO inhibitors, cimetidine, and numerous other products. See drug interaction reference for complete listing.

AHL = 3-5 hours	**M/P** = 0.5
PHL =	**PB** = 90%
PK = 60-90 min.	**Oral** = 30%
MW = 259	**pKa** = 9.5
Vd = 3-5	

References:
1. Thorley KJ, McAninsh J. Levels of beta-blockers atenolol and propranolol in the breast milk of women treated for hypertension in pregnancy. Biopharm Drug Dispos. 4:299-301,1983.
2. Bauer JH, Pape B, Zajicek J et.al. Propranolol in human plasma and breast milk. Am J Cardiol. 43:860-863,1979.
3. Smith MT, et.al. Propranolol, propranolol glucoronide, and naphthoxylacetic acid in breast milk and plasma. Ther Drug Monit. 5:87-93,1983.

4.   Taylor EA, Turner P. Anti-hypertensive therapy with propranolol during pregnancy and lactation. Postgrad Med J. 57:427-430, 1981.

Propylthiouracil   Fax #1361

Trade: PTU
Can/Aus/UK: Propyl-Thyracil
Uses: Antithyroid
AAP: Approved by the American Academy of Pediatrics for use in breastfeeding mothers

Propylthiouracil reduces the production and secretion of thyroxine by the thyroid gland. Only small amounts are secreted into breast milk. Reports thus far suggest that levels absorbed by infant are too low to produce side effects. In one study of nine patients given 400 mg doses, mean serum and milk levels were 7.7 mg/L and 0.7 mg/L respectively. No changes in infant thyroid have been reported. PTU is the best of antithyroid medications for use in lactating mothers. Monitor infant thyroid function (T4, TSH) carefully during therapy.

Alternatives:

Pregnancy Risk Category: D

Adult Concerns: Hypothyroidism, liver toxicity, aplastic anemia, anemia.

Pediatric Concerns: None reported, but observe closely for thyroid function.

Drug Interactions: Activity of oral anticoagulants may be potentiated by PTU associated anti-vitamin K activity.

AHL = 1-2 hours	**M/P** = 0.1
PHL =	**PB** = 80%
PK = 1-1.5 hours	**Oral** = 50-95%
MW = 170	**pKa** =
Vd =	

References:

1.   Cooper DS. Antithyroid drugs: to breast-feed or not to breast-feed. Am J Obstet Gynecol 157:234-235,1987.
2.   Kampmann JP, et.al. Propylthiouracil in human milk. Lancet 1:736-8, 1980.

Pseudoephedrine   Fax #1362

Trade: Sudafed, Halofed, Novafed, Actifed
Can/Aus/UK: Eltor, Pseudofrin, Sudafed, Balminil, Contac
Uses: Decongestant
AAP: Approved by the American Academy of Pediatrics for use in breastfeeding mothers

Pseudoephedrine is an adrenergic compound primarily used as a nasal decongestant. It is secreted into breast milk but in low levels. In a study of 3 lactating mothers who received 60 mg of pseudoephedrine, the milk:plasma ratio was as high as 2.6-3.9. The calculated dose that would be absorbed by the infant was still very low (0.4 to 0.6% of the maternal dose). The antihistamine triprolidine is commonly used with pseudoephedrine in the formulation called Actifed. The fractional absorption of triprolidine was exceptionally small as well and was 0.06-0.2% of the maternal dose. One case of infant irritability has been reported.

Alternatives:

Pregnancy Risk Category: C

Adult Concerns: Irritability, agitation, anorexia, stimulation, insomnia, hypertension, tachycardia.

Pediatric Concerns: One case of irritability via milk. This product is commonly used in infants with minimal problems.

Drug Interactions: May have increased toxicity when used with MAOI.

AHL	= < 4 hours	M/P	= 2.6-3.3
PHL	=	PB	=
PK	= 0.5-1 hours	Oral	= 90%
MW	= 165	pKa	= 9.7
Vd	=		

References:

1. Findlay JWA, et. al. Pseudoephedrine and triprolidine in plasma and breast milk of nursing mothers. Br J Clin Pharmacol 18:901-6, 1984.

Pyrantel Pamoate   Fax #1606

Trade: Pin-Rid, Antiminth, Pin-X, Reese's Pinworm
Can/Aus/UK: Combantrin
Uses: Anthelmintic
AAP: Not reviewed

Pyrantel is an anthelmintic used to treat pinworm, hookworm, and round worm infestations. It is only minimally absorbed orally, with the majority being eliminated in feces. Peak plasma levels are generally less than 0.05 to 0.13 µg/mL and occur prior to 3 hours. Reported side effects are few and minimal. No data on transfer of pyrantel in human milk are available, but due to minimal oral absorption, and low plasma levels, it is unlikely that breast milk levels would be clinically relevant. Generally it is administered as a single dose.

Alternatives:

Pregnancy Risk Category: C

Adult Concerns: Side effects are generally minimal and include headache, dizziness, somnolence, insomnia, nausea, vomiting, abdominal cramps, diarrhea and pain. Only moderate changes in liver enzymes have been noted, without serious hepatotoxicity.

Pediatric Concerns: None reported via milk.

Drug Interactions: Pyrantel and piperazine should not be mixed because they are antagonistic. Pyrantel increases theophylline plasma levels.

AHL =		M/P =	
PHL =		PB =	
PK = < 3 hours		Oral = < 50%	
MW = 206		pKa =	
Vd =			

References:
1.   McEvoy GE(ed):AHFS Drug Information, New York, NY. 1995.

Pyridostigmine   Fax #1484

Trade: Mestinon, Regonol
Can/Aus/UK: Mestinon, Regonol
Uses: Anticholinesterase muscle stimulant
AAP: Approved by the American Academy of Pediatrics for use in breastfeeding mothers

Pyridostigmine is a potent cholinesterase inhibitor used in myasthenia gravis to stimulate muscle strength. In a group of 2 mothers receiving from 120-300 mg/day, breast milk concentrations varied from 5 to 25 µg/Liter. The calculated milk:plasma ratios varied from 0.36 to 1.13. No cholinergic side effects were noted and no pyridostigmine was found in the infant's plasma. Because the oral bioavailability is so poor (10-20%), the actual dose received by the breastfed infant would be significantly less than the above concentrations. Please note the dosage is highly variable and may be as high as 600 mg/day in divided doses. The authors estimated total daily intake at 0.1% or less of the maternal dose.

Alternatives:

Pregnancy Risk Category: C

Adult Concerns: Nausea, vomiting, salivation, sweating, weakness, asthmatic symptoms, muscle cramps, fasciculations, constricted pupils.

Pediatric Concerns: None reported in one study of two infants.

Drug Interactions: Increased effect of neuromuscular blockers such as succinylcholine. Increased toxicity with edrophonium.

AHL	= 3.3 hours	M/P	= 0.36-1.13
PHL	=	PB	= 0%
PK	= 1-2 hours	Oral	= 10-20%
MW	= 261	pKa	=
Vd	=		

References:
1.   Hardell LI, et.al. Pyridostigmine in human breast milk. Br. J. Clin. Pharmacol. 14:565-7, 1982.

Pyridoxine   Fax #1363

Trade: Vitamin B-6, Hexa-Betalin
Can/Aus/UK: Hexa-Betalin, Pyroxin, Comploment, Continus
Uses: Vitamin B-6
AAP: Approved by the American Academy of Pediatrics for use in breastfeeding mothers

Pyridoxine is vitamin B-6. The recommended daily allowance for non-pregnant women is 1.6 mg/day. Pyridoxine is secreted in milk in direct proportion to the maternal intake and concentrations in milk vary from 123 to 314 ng/ml depending on the study. Pyridoxine is required in slight excess during pregnancy and lactation and most prenatal vitamin supplements contain from 12-25 mg/day. Very high doses (600 mg/day) suppress prolactin secretion and therefore production of breast milk. Do not use in excess of 25 mg/day. One study clearly indicates that pyridoxine readily transfers into breast milk and that B-6 levels in milk correlate closely with maternal intake. Breastfeeding mothers who are deficient in pyridoxine should be supplemented with modest amounts (< 25 mg/day).

Alternatives:

Pregnancy Risk Category: A

Adult Concerns: Reduced milk production, sensory neuropathy, GI distress, sedation.

Pediatric Concerns: Excessive oral doses have been reported to produce sedation, hypotonia and respiratory distress in infants, although none have been reported via breast milk.

Drug Interactions: Decreased serum levels with levodopa, phenobarbital, and phenytoin.

AHL = 15-20 days.		**M/P** =	
PHL =		**PB** =	
PK = 1-2 hr.		**Oral** = Complete	
MW = 205		**pKa** =	
Vd =			

References:
1. Kang-Yoon SA, et.al. Vitamin B-6 status of breast-fed neonates: influence of pyridoxine supplementation on mothers and neonates. Amer. J. Clin. Nutr. 56:548-58,1992.
2. Marcus RG. Suppression of lactation with high doses of pyridoxine. S Afr Med J. 49:2155-2156, 1975.
3. Foukas MD. An antilactogenic effect of pyridoxine. J Obstet Gynaecol Br Commonw 80:718-20, 1973.

Pyrimethamine   Fax #1364

Trade: Daraprim
Can/Aus/UK: Daraprim, Fansidar, Maloprim
Uses: Antimalarial, folic acid antagonist
AAP: Approved by the American Academy of Pediatrics for use in breastfeeding mothers

Pyrimethamine is a folic acid antagonist that has been used for prophylaxis of malaria. Maternal peak plasma levels occur 2-6 hours post-dose. Pyrimethamine is secreted into human milk. In a group of mothers receiving 25, 50, and 75 mg/day of pyrimethamine for 10 days, the peak concentration was 3.3 mg/L. An infant would receive an estimated dose of 3-4 mg in a 48 hr period (following 75 mg maternal dose). A number of reports of carcinogenesis in adults are available and indicate that infants should not be exposed to this medication.

Alternatives:

Pregnancy Risk Category: C

Adult Concerns: Anemia, blood dyscrasia, folate deficiency states, carcinogenesis, insomnia, headache, anorexia, vomiting, megaloblastic anemia, leukopenia.

Pediatric Concerns: None reported, but possible carcinogenesis may preclude its use in breastfed infants.

Drug Interactions: Use of pyrimethamine with other anti-folate drugs(methotrexate, sulfonamides, TMP-SMZ) may increase the risk of bone marrow suppression and folate deficiency states.

AHL = 96 hours		M/P	= 0.2-0.43
PHL =		PB	= 87%
PK = 2-6 hours		Oral	= Complete
MW = 249		pKa	=
Vd =			

References:
1. Pharmaceutical Manufacturer's Package Insert, 1996.
2. Clyde DF, Shute GT. Transfer of pyrimethamine in human milk. J. Trop. Med. and Hyg. 59:277-284, 1956.

Quazepam   Fax #1365

Trade: Doral
Can/Aus/UK:
Uses: Sedative, hypnotic
AAP: Drugs whose effect on nursing infants is unknown but may be

of concern

Quazepam is a long half-life benzodiazepine (Valium-like) medication used as a sedative and hypnotic. It is selectively metabolized to several metabolites that have even longer half-lives. Following a 15 mg dose, only 0.11% of the maternal dose was excreted into breast milk.

Alternatives: Lorazepam, Alprazolam

Pregnancy Risk Category: X

Adult Concerns: Drowsiness, sedation.

Pediatric Concerns: None reported via breast milk. Observe for sedation.

Drug Interactions: May increase sedation when used with CNS depressants such as alcohol, barbiturates, opioids. Cimetidine may decrease metabolism and clearance of benzodiazepines. Valproic may displace benzodiazepines from binding sites, thus increasing sedative effects. SSRIs (fluoxetine, sertraline, paroxetine) can dramatically increase benzodiazepine levels by altering clearance, thus leading to sedation.

AHL = 39 hours	**M/P**	**= 4.19**
PHL =	**PB**	**= >95%.**
PK = 2 hours	**Oral**	**= Complete**
MW = 387	**pKa**	**=**
Vd =		

References:
1. Hilbert JM, Symchowicz S,Zampaglione N. Excretion of quazepam into human breast milk. J Clin Pharmacol 24:457-462, 1984b.

Quinacrine   Fax #1366

Trade: Atabrine
Can/Aus/UK:
Uses: Antimalarial, giardiasis
AAP: Not reviewed

Quinacrine was once used for malaria, but has been replaced by other preparations. It is primarily used for giardiasis. Small to trace amounts are secreted into milk. No known harmful effects except in infants with G6PD deficiencies. However, quinacrine is excreted very slowly, requiring up to 2 months for complete elimination. Quinacrine levels in liver are extremely high. Accumulation in infant is likely due to slow rate of excretion. Extreme caution is urged.

Alternatives:

Pregnancy Risk Category: C

Adult Concerns: GI distress, liver toxicity, seizures, aplastic anemia, retinopathy.

Pediatric Concerns: None reported via milk, but accumulation may occur after prolonged exposure. Use with caution.

Drug Interactions: Primaquine toxicity is increased by quinacrine. Concomitant use is contraindicated.

AHL	= >5 days	M/P	=
PHL	=	PB	= High
PK	= 1-3 hours	Oral	= Complete
MW	= 400	pKa	=
Vd	=		

References:
1. Drug Facts and Comparisons. 1994 ed. Facts and Comparisons, St. Louis.
2. McEvoy GE(ed):AHFS Drug Information, New York, NY. 1992, pp 417-26.

Quinapril   Fax #1367

Trade: Accupril
Can/Aus/UK: Accupril, Asig, Accupro
Uses: ACE inhibitor, antihypertensive
AAP: Not reviewed

Quinapril is an angiotensin converting enzyme inhibitor (ACE) used as an antihypertensive. Once in the plasma compartment, it is rapidly converted to quinaprilat, the active metabolite. ACE inhibitors are generally contraindicated during pregnancy due to increased fetal morbidity with ACE inhibitors. Small amounts are secreted in animal milk (< 5%). Secretion into human milk is suspected but unreported. Newborns are especially susceptible to ACE inhibitors.

Alternatives: Captopril, Enalapril

Pregnancy Risk Category: D

Adult Concerns: Cough, hypotension, nausea, vomiting.

Pediatric Concerns: None reported but observe for hypotension, sedation, poor suckling.

Drug Interactions: Probenecid increases plasma levels of ACEi. ACEi and diuretics have additive hypotensive effects. Antacids reduce bioavailability of ACE inhibitors. NSAIDS reduce hypotension of ACE inhibitors. Phenothiazines increase effects of ACEi. ACEi increase digoxin and lithium plasma levels. May elevate potassium levels when potassium supplementation is added.

AHL	= 2 hours	M/P	=
PHL	=	PB	= 97%
PK	= 2 hours	Oral	= Complete
MW	=	pKa	=
Vd	=		

References:
1. Pharmaceutical Manufacturer's Package Insert, 1996.

Quinidine   Fax #1368

Trade: Quinaglute, Quinidex
Can/Aus/UK: Apo-Quinidine, Cardioquin, Novo-Quinidin, Kinidin, Durules, Kiditard
Uses: Antiarrhythmic agent
AAP: Approved by the American Academy of Pediatrics for use in breastfeeding mothers

Quinidine is used to treat cardiac arrhythmias. Three hours following a dose of 600 mg, the level of quinidine in the maternal serum was 9.0 mg/L and the concentration in her breast milk was 6.4 mg/L. Subsequently, a level of 8.2 mg/L was noted in breast milk. An infant ingesting 1 Liter of milk daily, would receive approximately 1% of the total maternal dose which is below the normal therapeutic dosage used in infants. Quinidine is selectively stored in the liver, long-term use could expose an infant to liver toxicity. Monitor liver enzymes.

Alternatives:

Pregnancy Risk Category: C

Adult Concerns: Blood dyscrasia, hypotension, thrombocytopenia, depression, fever.

Pediatric Concerns: None reported, but observe for changes in liver function.

Drug Interactions: Quinidine levels may be elevated with amiodarone, certain antacids, cimetidine, verapamil. Digoxin plasma levels may be increased with quinidine. Quinidine may increase anticoagulant levels with used with warfarin. Quinidine levels or effect may be reduced when used with barbiturates, nifedipine, rifampin, sucralfate, or phenytoin. Effects of procainamide may be dangerously increased when used with quinidine. Clearance of TCAs may be decreased by quinidine.

AHL = 6-8 hours	M/P	= 0.71
PHL =	PB	= 87%

PK = 1-2 hours	**Oral** = 80%
MW = 324	**pKa** = 4.2,8.3
Vd = 1.8-3.0	

References:
1. Hill LM, Malkasian GD Jr. The use of quinidine sulfate throughout pregnancy. Obstet Gynecol 54:366-8, 1979.

Quinine   Fax #1369

Trade: Quinamm
Can/Aus/UK: Novo-Quinine, Biquinate, Myoquin, Quinbisul, Quinate
Uses: Antimalarial
AAP: Approved by the American Academy of Pediatrics for use in breastfeeding mothers

Quinine is a cinchona alkaloid primarily used in malaria prophylaxis and treatment. Small to trace amounts are secreted into milk. No reported harmful effects have been reported except in infants with G6PD deficiencies. In a study of 6 women receiving 600-1300 mg/day, the concentration of quinine in breast milk ranged from 0.4 to 1.6 mg/L at 1.5 to 6 hours post-dose. The authors suggest these levels are clinically insignificant. In another study, with maternal plasma concentrations of 0.5 to 8 mg/L, the milk:plasma ratio ranged from 0.11 to 0.53. The total daily consumption by a breastfed infant was estimated to be 1-3 mg/day.

Alternatives:

Pregnancy Risk Category: D

Adult Concerns: Blood dyscrasia, thrombocytopenia, retinal toxicity, tongue discoloration, kidney damage.

Pediatric Concerns: None reported via breast milk in several studies.

Drug Interactions: Aluminum containing antacid may delay or decrease absorption. Quinine may depress vitamin K dependant clotting factors. Therefore increasing warfarin effects. Cimetidine may reduce quinine clearance. Digoxin serum levels may be increased. Do not use with mefloquine.

AHL = 11 hours		**M/P**	= 0.11-0.53
PHL =		**PB**	= 93%
PK = 1-3 hours		**Oral**	= 76%
MW = 324		**pKa**	= 4.3,8.4
Vd = 1.8-3.0			

References:
1. Terwillinger WG, Hatcher RA. The elimination of morphine and quinine in human milk. Surg. Gynecol. Obstet. 58:823, 1934.
2. Phillips RE, Looareesuwan S, White NJ et.al. Quinine pharmacokinetics and toxicity in pregnant and lactating women with falciparum malaria. Br J Clin Pharmacol 21:677-683, 1986.

Rabies Vaccine   Fax #1468

Trade: Imovax Rabies Vaccine
Can/Aus/UK:
Uses: Vaccination for rabies
AAP: Not reviewed

Rabies vaccine is prepared from inactivated rabies virus. No data are available on transmission to breast milk. Even if transferred to breast milk, it is unlikely to produce untoward effects.

Alternatives:

Pregnancy Risk Category:

Adult Concerns: Rash, anaphylactoid reactions, nausea, vomiting, diarrhea, etc.

Pediatric Concerns:

Drug Interactions:

References:
1.   Pharmaceutical Manufacturer's Package Insert, 1995.

Radioactive Sodium   Fax #1371

Trade: Radioactive Sodium
Can/Aus/UK:
Uses: Radioactive tracer
AAP: Radioactive compound that requires temporary cessation of breastfeeding

Radioactivity in milk is present for up to 96 hours. It reaches a peak at 2 hours. Pump and discard milk until radioactivity is depleted, approximately 16 days.

Alternatives:

Pregnancy Risk Category:

Adult Concerns:

Pediatric Concerns: None reported via milk, but radiation exposure is possible.

Drug Interactions:

References:
1.   American Academy of Pediatrics, Committee on Drugs. Transfer of drugs and other chemicals into human milk.   Pediatrics 93(1):137-150, 1994.
2.   Pommerenke WT, and Hahn PF. Secretion of radioactive sodium in human milk. Proc. Soc. Exp. Biol. Med. 52:223, 1943.

Radiopaque Agents   Fax #1372

Trade: Omnipaque, Conray, Cholebrine, Telepaque, Oragrafin, Bilivist, Hypaque, Gastrografin, Renovue-Dip, Angiovist, Optiray
Can/Aus/UK:
Uses: Radiopaque agents
AAP: Not Reviewed

Agents include: Omnipaque, Conray, Cholebrine, Telepaque, Oragrafin, Bilivist, Hypaque, Gastrografin, Renovue-Dip, Angiovist, Optiray , etc.   Radiopaque agents (except barium) are iodinated compounds used to visualize various organs during X-ray, CAT scans, and other radiological procedures.   These compounds are highly iodinated benzoic acid   derivatives.   Although under usual circumstances, iodine products are contraindicated in nursing mothers (due to ion trapping in milk), these products are unique in that they are extremely inert. In one study, the amount of iohexol and metrizoate secreted in breast milk was less than 0.5% of the maternal dose. According to several Manufacturer's, less than 0.005% of the iodine is free. These contrast agents are in essence pharmacologically inert, not metabolized, and are rapidly excreted by the kidney (80-90% with 24 hours). They are known to pass unchanged into human milk after IV administration.   They are virtually unabsorbed after oral administration(< 0.1% absorption). Most are cleared for pediatric use. Although most company package inserts suggest that an infant be removed from the breast for 24 hours, no untoward effects have been reported with these products, nor any indication of oral absorption by an infant.

Alternatives:

Pregnancy Risk Category:

Adult Concerns: GI distress, rash.

Pediatric Concerns: None reported via milk. Commonly used in pediatric patients for diagnostic purposes.

Drug Interactions:

AHL = 20-90 min.		M/P	=
PHL =		PB	= 0-10%
PK = < 1 hr		Oral	= Minimal
MW =		pKa	=
Vd =			

References:

1. Pharmaceutical Manufacturer's Package Insert, 1993, 1994.
2. Nielsen ST et.al. Excretion of iohexol and metrizoate in human breast milk. Acta. Radiol. 28:523-26, 1987.
3. Fitz-John TP, et.al. Intravenous urography during lactation. Br. J. Radiol 55:603-5, 1982.

Ramipril   Fax #1373

Trade: Altace
Can/Aus/UK: Altace, Ramace, Tritace
Uses: ACE inhibitor, antihypertensive
AAP: Not reviewed

Ramipril is rapidly metabolized to ramiprilat which is a potent ACE inhibitor with a long half-life. It is used in hypertension. ACE inhibitors can cause increased fetal and neonatal morbidity and should not be used in pregnant women. Ingestion of a single 10 mg oral dose produced an undetectable level in breast milk. However, animal studies have indicated that ramiprilat is transferred into milk in concentrations about one-third of those found in serum. Only 0.25% of the total dose is estimated to penetrate into milk. However, caution should be exercised in using ACE inhibitors in lactating women, because neonates are very sensitive to these compounds.

Alternatives: Captopril, Enalapril

Pregnancy Risk Category: D

Adult Concerns: Hypotension, cough, nausea, vomiting, dizziness.

Pediatric Concerns: None reported via milk. Observe for hypotension.

Drug Interactions: Probenecid increases plasma levels of ACEi. ACEi and diuretics have additive hypotensive effects. Antacids reduce bioavailability of ACE inhibitors. NSAIDS reduce hypotension of ACE inhibitors. Phenothiazines increase effects of ACEi. ACEi increase digoxin and lithium plasma levels. May elevate potassium levels when potassium supplementation is added.

AHL = 13-17 hours		**M/P** =	
PHL =		**PB** = 56%	
PK = 2-4 hours		**Oral** = 60%	
MW = 417		**pKa** =	
Vd =			

References:
1. Pharmaceutical Manufacturer's Package Insert, 1996.
2. Ball SG, Robertson JIS. Clinical pharmacology of ramipril. Am J Cardiol 59:23D-27D, 1987.

Ranitidine   Fax #1374

Trade: Zantac
Can/Aus/UK: Apo-Ranitidine, Novo-Ranidine, Nu-Ranit
Uses: Reduces gastric acid secretion
AAP: Not reviewed

Ranitidine is a prototypical histamine-2 blocker used to reduce acid secretion in the stomach. It has been widely used in pediatrics without significant side effects primarily for gastroesophageal reflux (GER). Following a dose of 150 mg for four doses, concentrations in breast milk were 0.72, 2.6, and 1.5 mg/L at 1.5, 5.5 and 12 hours respectively. The milk:serum ratios varied from 6.81, 8.44 to 23.77 at 1.5, 5.5 and 12 hours respectively. Although the milk:plasma ratios are quite high, using this data an infant consuming 1 L of milk daily would ingest less than 2.6 mg/24 hours. This amount is quite small considering the pediatric dose currently recommended is 2-4 mg/kg/24 hours.

Alternatives: Famotidine, Nizatidine

Pregnancy Risk Category: B

Adult Concerns: Side effects are generally minimal and include headache, GI distress, dizziness.

Pediatric Concerns: None reported via milk. Although ranitidine is concentrated in milk, the overall dose is less than therapeutic.

Drug Interactions: Ranitidine may decrease the renal clearance of procainamide. May decrease oral absorption of diazepam. Ranitidine may increase the hypoglycemic effect of glipizide or glyburide. Ranitidine may reduce warfarin clearance, thus increasing anticoagulation.

AHL = 2-3 hours	**M/P** = 1.9-6.7
PHL =	**PB** = 15%
PK = 1-3 hours	**Oral** = 50%
MW = 314	**pKa** = 2.3,8.2
Vd = 1.6-2.4	

References:

1.   Kearns GL, McConnell RF, Trang JM, et.al. Appearance of ranitidine in breast milk following multiple dosing. Clin Pharm 4:322-324, 1985.

Remifentanil   Fax #1576

Trade: Ultiva
Can/Aus/UK: Ultiva
Uses: Opioid analgesic
AAP: Not reviewed

Remifentanil is a new opioid analgesic similar in potency and use as fentanyl. It is primarily metabolized by plasma and tissue esterases (in adults and neonates) and has an incredibly short elimination half-life of only 10-20 minutes, with an effective biological half-life of only 3 to

10 minutes. Unlike other fentanyl analogs, the half-life of remifentanil does not increase with prolonged administration. Although remifentanil has been found in rodent milk, no data are available on its transfer into human milk. It is cleared for use in children > 2 years of age. As an analog of fentanyl, breast milk levels should be similar and probably exceedingly low. In addition, remifentanil metabolism is not dependent on liver function, and should be exceedingly short even in neonates. Due to its kinetics and brief half-life, and its poor oral bioavailability, it is unlikely this product will produce clinically relevant levels in human breast milk.

Alternatives:

Pregnancy Risk Category: C

Adult Concerns: Nausea, hypotension, sedation, vomiting, bradycardia.

Pediatric Concerns: None reported via milk. Not orally bioavailable.

Drug Interactions: May potentiate the effects of other opioids.

AHL = 10-20 minutes		M/P	=
PHL =		PB	= 70%
PK =		Oral	= Poor
MW = 412		pKa	= 7.07
Vd = 0.1			

References:
1. Pharmaceutical Manufacturer's package insert, 1997.

Reserpine   Fax #1375

Trade: Raudixin, Serpasil
Can/Aus/UK: Serpasil
Uses: Antihypertensive
AAP: Not reviewed

Reserpine is an old and seldom used antihypertensive. Reserpine is known to be secreted into human milk, although the levels are unreported. Increased respiratory tract secretions, severe nasal congestion, cyanosis, and loss of appetite can occur. Some reports suggest no observable effect but should use with extreme caution if at all. Because safer, more effective products are available, reserpine should be avoided in lactating patients.

Alternatives:

Pregnancy Risk Category: C

Adult Concerns: Hypotonia, sedation, hypotension, nasal congestion, diarrhea, nausea, vomiting.

Pediatric Concerns: None reported via milk, but observe for nasal stuffiness, sedation, hypotonia. Use with caution.

Drug Interactions: Reserpine may decrease the effect of other sympathomimetics. May increased effect of MAOI and tricyclic antidepressants.

AHL = 50-100 hours.		**M/P** =	
PHL =		**PB** = 96%	
PK = 2 hours		**Oral** = 40%	
MW = 609		**pKa** =	
Vd =			

References:
1. O'Brien, T. Excretion of drugs in human milk. Am.J. Hosp. Pharm. 31:844-854, 1974.
2. Vorherr, H. Drug excretion in breast milk. Postgrad. Med. 56:97-104, 1974.
3. Anderson PO: Drugs and breast feeding - A review. Intell Clin Pharm 11:208, 1977.

Rho (d) Immune Globulin   Fax #1469

Trade: RhoGAM, Gamulin Rh, HypRho-D, Mini-Gamulin Rh
Can/Aus/UK:
Uses: Immune globulin
AAP: Not reviewed

RHO(D) immune globulin is an immune globulin prepared from human plasma containing high concentrations of Rh antibodies. Only trace amounts of anti-Rh are present in colostrum and none in mature milk in women receiving large doses of Rh immune globulin. No untoward effects have been reported. Most immunoglobulins are destroyed in the gastric acidity of the newborn infant. Rh immune globulins are not contraindicated in breastfeeding mothers.

Alternatives:

Pregnancy Risk Category:

Adult Concerns: Infrequent allergies, discomfort at injection site.

Pediatric Concerns: None reported via milk.

Drug Interactions:

AHL = 24 days.	M/P =
PHL =	PB =
PK =	Oral = None
MW =	pKa =
Vd =	

References:
1. Lawrence RA. Breastfeeding, A guide for the medical profession. Mosby, St. Louis, 1994.

Riboflavin   Fax #1376

Trade: Vitamin B-2
Can/Aus/UK:
Uses: Vitamin B-2
AAP: Approved by the American Academy of Pediatrics for use in breastfeeding mothers

Riboflavin is a B complex vitamin, also called Vitamin B-2. Riboflavin is absorbed by the small intestine by a well established transport mechanism. It is easily saturable, so excessive levels are not absorbed. Riboflavin is transported into human milk in concentrations proportional to dietary intake, but generally averaged 400 ng/mL. Maternal supplementation is permitted if dose is small (2 mg/day). No untoward effects have been reported.

Alternatives:

Pregnancy Risk Category: A

Adult Concerns: Yellow colored urine.

Pediatric Concerns: None reported via milk.

Drug Interactions:

AHL = 14 hours.	**M/P** =	
PHL =	**PB** =	
PK = Rapid	**Oral** = Complete	
MW = 376	**pKa** =	
Vd =		

References:
1. Deodhar AD. Studies on human lactation. Part III. Effect of dietary vitamin supplementation on vitamin contents of breast milk. Acta Paediatr Scand 53:42-6, 1964.
2. Baker SJ. Vitamin-B12 deficiency in pregnancy and the puerperium. Br Med J 1:1658-61, 1962.

Rifampin   Fax #1377

Trade: Rifadin, Rimactane
Can/Aus/UK: Rifadin, Rimactane, Rofact, Rifampicin, Rimycin
Uses: Anti-tubercular drug
AAP: Approved by the American Academy of Pediatrics for use in breastfeeding mothers

Rifampin is a broad spectrum antibiotic, with particular activity against tuberculosis. It is secreted into breast milk in very small levels. One report indicates that following a single 450 mg oral dose, maternal plasma levels averaged 21.3 mg/L and milk levels averaged 3.4 - 4.9 mg/L. Vorherr reported that after a 600 mg dose of rifampin, peak plasma levels were 50 mg/L while milk levels were 10-30 mg/L. Only 0.05% of the maternal dose appeared in breast milk.

Alternatives:

Pregnancy Risk Category: C

Adult Concerns: Hepatitis, anemia, headache, diarrhea, pseudomembranous colitis.

Pediatric Concerns: None reported via milk.

Drug Interactions: Rifampin is known to reduce the plasma level of a large number of drugs including: acetaminophen, anticoagulants, barbiturates, benzodiazepines, beta blockers, contraceptives, corticosteroids, cyclosporine, digitoxin, phenytoin, methadone, quinidine, sulfonylureas, theophylline, verapamil, and a large number of others.

AHL = 3.5 hours	**M/P**	= 0.16-0.23
PHL = 2.9 hours	**PB**	= 80%
PK = 2-4 hours	**Oral**	= 90-95%
MW = 823	**pKa**	=
Vd =		

References:

1. Lenzi E, Santuari S: Preliminary observations on the use of a new semi-synthetic rifamycin derivative in gynecology and obstetrics. Atti Accad Lancisiana Roma 13:(suppl 1): 87-94,1969.
2. Vorherr H. Drug excretion in breast milk. Postgrad Med 56:97-104, 1974.

Rimantadine HCL   Fax #1378

Trade: Flumadine
Can/Aus/UK:
Uses: Antiviral, anti-influenza A
AAP: Not reviewed

Rimantadine is an antiviral agent primarily used for influenza A infections. It is concentrated in rodent milk. Levels in animal milk 2-3 hours after administration were approximately twice those of the maternal serum, suggesting a milk:plasma ratio of about 2. Manufacturer alludes to toxic side effects but fails to state them. No side effects yet reported in breastfeeding infants. Rimantadine is, however, indicated for prophylaxis of influenza A in pediatric patients > 1 year of age.

Alternatives:

Pregnancy Risk Category: C

Adult Concerns: Gastrointestinal distress, nervousness, fatigue, and sleep disturbances.

Pediatric Concerns: None reported via milk.

Drug Interactions: The use of acetaminophen significantly reduces rimantadine plasma levels by 11%. Peak plasma levels of rimantadine were reduce 10% by aspirin. Rimantadine clearance was reduced by 16% when used with cimetidine.

AHL = 25.4 hours	M/P = 2
PHL =	PB = 40%
PK = 6 hours	Oral = 92%

MW = 179   **pKa** =
Vd =

References:
1.   Pharmaceutical Manufacturer's Package Insert, 1996.

Risperidone   Fax #1503

Trade: Risperdal
Can/Aus/UK: Risperdal
Uses: Antipsychotic
AAP: Not reviewed

Risperidone is a potent antipsychotic agent belonging to a new chemical class and is a dopamine and serotonin antagonist.   Because it is metabolized by a specific liver enzyme, it is known to interact with other medications, and some individuals have poor ability to metabolize this product.   It has been reported to transfer into animal milk, but its concentrations in human milk have not been reported. Use caution in breastfeeding mothers.

Alternatives:

Pregnancy Risk Category: C

Adult Concerns: Risks include neuroleptic malignant syndrome, tardive dyskinesia, myocardial arrhythmias, orthostatic hypotension, seizures, hyperprolactinemia, somnolence.

Pediatric Concerns: None reported via milk.

Drug Interactions: Do not use with alcohol.   May enhance the hypotensive response of other antihypertensives. May antagonize the effect of levodopa. Carbamazepine or clozapine may increase clearance of risperidone.

AHL = 3-20 hours   **M/P** =
PHL =   **PB**   = 90%
PK   = 3-17 hours   **Oral** = 70-94%

MW = 410   pKa   =
Vd   =

References:
1.   Pharmaceutical Manufacturer's Package Insert, 1997.

Ritodrine   Fax #1509

Trade: Pre-par, Yutopar
Can/Aus/UK: Yutopar
Uses: Adrenergic agent
AAP: Not reviewed

Ritodrine is primarily used to reduce uterine contractions in premature labor due to its beta-2 adrenergic effect on uterine receptors.   No data are available on its transfer to human milk.

Alternatives:

Pregnancy Risk Category: B

Adult Concerns: Fetal and maternal   tachycardia, hypertension, lethargy, sleepiness, ketoacidosis, pulmonary edema.

Pediatric Concerns: None reported via milk.

Drug Interactions: Use cautiously with steroids due to pulmonary edema. Acebutolol and other beta blockers would block efficacy of ritodrine.   Use with atropine may lead to systemic exaggerated. hypertension. Use with bupivacaine has induced extreme hypotension. Numerous other interactions are listed, please review.

AHL = 15 hours	M/P =
PHL =	PB = 32%
PK = 40-60 minutes	Oral = 30%
MW = 287	pKa = 9
Vd = 0.7	

References:

1. Gandar R et al. Serum level of ritodrine in man. Eur J Clin Pharmacol 17:117-122, 1980.

Rubella Virus Vaccine, Live   Fax #1496

Trade: Meruvax, Rubella Vaccine, Measles Vaccine
Can/Aus/UK:
Uses: Live attenuated (measles) vaccine
AAP: Not reviewed

Rubella virus vaccine contains a live attenuated virus. The American College of Obstetricians and Gynecologists and the CDC currently recommend the early postpartum immunization of women who show no or low antibody titer to rubella. At least four studies have found rubella virus to be transferred via milk although presence of clinical symptoms was not evident. Rubella virus has been cultured from the throat of one infant, while another infant was clinically ill with minor symptoms and serologic evidence of rubella infection. In general, the use of rubella virus vaccine in mothers of full-term, normal infants has not been associated with untoward effects and is generally recommended. However, use in mothers of premature, weakened infants may be associated with some risk, and a suitable risk-assessment must be done for mothers of premature or immunodeficient infants.

Alternatives:

Pregnancy Risk Category:

Adult Concerns: Burning, stinging, lymphadenopathy, rash, malaise, sore throat, etc.

Pediatric Concerns: One case report of rash, vomiting, and mild rubella infection.

Drug Interactions: Immunosuppressants and immune globulins may reduce immunogenicity. Concurrent use of interferon may reduce antibody response.

References:

1.   Buimovici-Klein E, et. al. Isolation of rubella virus in milk after postpartum immunization. J Pediatr 91:939-41, 1977.
2.   Losonsky GA et.al. Effect of immunization against rubella on lactation products. I. Development and characterization of specific immunologic reactivity in breast milk. J. Infect. Dis. 145:654, 1982.
3.   Losonsky GA, et.al. Effect of immunization against rubella on lactation products. II. Maternal-neonatal interactions. fJ. Infect. Dis. 145:661, 1982.
4.   Landes RD et.al. Neonatal rubella following postpartum maternal immunization. Pediatrics 97:465-467, 1980.
5.   Lawrence RA. In: Breastfeeding, A guide for the medical profession. Mosby, St.Louis, 1994.

Saccharin   Fax #1379

Trade: Saccharin
Can/Aus/UK:
Uses: Sweetener
AAP: Not reviewed

In one group of 6 women who received 126 mg (per 12 oz drink) every 6 hours for 9 doses, milk levels varied greatly from < 200 µg/L after 1dose to 1.765 mg/L after 9 doses. Under these dosing conditions, saccharin levels appear to accumulate over time. Half-life in serum and milk were 4.84 hours and 17.9 hours respectively after 3 days. Even after such doses, these milk levels are considered minimal. Moderate intake should be compatible with nursing.

Alternatives:

Pregnancy Risk Category: C

Adult Concerns:

Pediatric Concerns: None reported via milk.

Drug Interactions:

AHL = 4.84 hours		M/P	=
PHL =		PB	=
PK =		Oral	= Complete
MW = 183		pKa	=
Vd =			

References:

1. Egan PC, Marx CM, et.al. Saccharin excretion in mature human milk. Drug Intell. Clin. Pharm. 18:511, 1984.

Sage   Fax #1526

Trade: Sage, Dalmatian, Sage, Spanish
Can/Aus/UK:
Uses: Herbal product
AAP: Not reviewed

Salvia officinalis L.(Dalmatian sage) and Salvia lavandulaefolia Vahl (Spanish sage) are most common of the species. Extracts and teas have been used to treat digestive disorders (antispasmodic), as an antiseptic and astringent, for treating diarrhea, gastritis, sore throat and other maladies. The dried and smoked leaves have been used for treating asthma symptoms. These uses are largely unsubstantiated in the literature. Sage extracts have been found to be strong antioxidants and with some antimicrobial properties (staph. aureus) due to the phenolic acid salvin content. Sage oil has antispasmodic effects in animals and this may account for its moderating effects on the GI tract. For the most part, Sage is relatively nontoxic, and nonirritating. Ingestion of significant quantities may lead to cheilitis, stomatitis, dry mouth or local irritation. Due to drying properties and pediatric hypersensitivity to anticholinergics, sage should be used with some caution in breastfeeding mothers.

Alternatives:

Pregnancy Risk Category:

Adult Concerns: Observe for typical anticholinergic effects such as cheilitis, stomatitis, dry mouth or local irritation.

Pediatric Concerns: None reported but observe for dry mouth, stomatitis, cheilitis.

Drug Interactions:

References:
1. Leung AY. Encyclopedia of Common Natural Ingredients used in food, drugs, and cosmetics. New York, NY: J. Wiley and Sons, 1980.
2. Bissett NG. In: Herbal Drugs and Phytopharmaceuticals. Medpharm Scientific Publishers, CRC Press, Boca Raton, 1994.

Salmeterol Xinafoate   Fax #1380

Trade: Serevent
Can/Aus/UK: Serevent
Uses: Long acting beta adrenergic bronchodilator
AAP: Not reviewed

Salmeterol is a long acting beta-2 adrenergic stimulant used as a bronchodilator in asthmatics. Maternal plasma levels of salmeterol after inhaled administration are very low (85-200 pg/mL), or undetectable. Studies in animals have shown that plasma and breast milk levels are very similar. Oral absorption of both salmeterol and the xinafoate moiety are good. The terminal half-life of salmeterol is 5.5 hours, xinafoate is 11 days. No reports of use in lactating women are available.

Alternatives:

Pregnancy Risk Category: C

Adult Concerns: Tremor, dizziness, hypertension.

Pediatric Concerns: None reported via milk, but studies are limited.

Drug Interactions: Use with MAOI may result in severe hypertension, severe headache, and hypertensive crisis. Tricyclic antidepressants may potentiate the pressure response. The pressor response of salmeterol may be reduced by lithium.

AHL = 5.5 hours		**M/P**	= 1.0
PHL =		**PB**	= 98%
PK = 10 - 45 min.		**Oral**	= Complete
MW =		**pKa**	=
Vd =			

References:
1.   Pharmaceutical Manufacturer's Package Insert, 1996.

Scopolamine   Fax #1508

Trade: Transderm Scope
Can/Aus/UK: Transderm-V, Buscopan, Scopoderm TTS
Uses: Anticholinergic
AAP: Approved by the American Academy of Pediatrics for use in breastfeeding mothers

Scopolamine is a typical anticholinergic used primarily for motion sickness, and preoperatively to produce amnesia and decrease salivation. Scopolamine is structurally similar to atropine, but is known for its prominent CNS effects including reducing motion sickness. There are no reports on its transfer into human milk, but due to its poor oral bioavailability, it is generally believed to be minimal.

Alternatives:

Pregnancy Risk Category: C

Adult Concerns: Blurred vision, dry mouth, drowsiness, constipation, confusion, drowsiness, bradycardia, hypotension, dermatitis.

Pediatric Concerns: None via milk. Observe for anticholinergic symptoms such as drowsiness, dry mouth.

Drug Interactions: Decreased effect of acetaminophen, levodopa, ketoconazole, digoxin. GI absorption of the following drugs may be altered: ketoconazole, digoxin, potassium supplements, acetaminophen, levodopa.

AHL = 2.9 hours		**M/P** =	
PHL =		**PB** =	
PK = 1 hour		**Oral** = 27%	
MW = 303		**pKa** = 7.55	
Vd = 1.4			

References:
1. Lacy C. et.al. Drug information handbook. Lexi-Comp, Hudson(Cleveland), Oh. 1996.
2. Drug Facts and Comparisons. 1996. ed. Facts and Comparisons, St. Louis.
3. Pharmaceutical Manufacturer's Package Insert, 1997.

Secobarbital   Fax #1381

Trade: Seconal
Can/Aus/UK: Novo-Secobarb, Seconal
Uses: Short acting barbiturate sedative
AAP: Approved by the American Academy of Pediatrics for use in breastfeeding mothers

Secobarbital is a sedative, hypnotic barbiturate. It is probably secreted into breast milk, although levels are unknown, and may be detectible in milk for 24 hours or longer. Recommend mothers delay breastfeeding for 3-4 hours to reduce possible transfer to infant if exposure to this barbiturate is required.

Alternatives:

Pregnancy Risk Category: D

Adult Concerns: Respiratory depression, sedation, addiction.

Pediatric Concerns: None reported via milk, but observe for sedation.

Drug Interactions:

AHL	= 15-40 hours	M/P	=
PHL	=	PB	= 30-45%
PK	= 2-4 hours	Oral	= 90%
MW	= 260	pKa	= 7.9
Vd	= 1.6-1.9		

References:

1. Tyson RM, Shrader EA, Perlman HH. Drugs transmitted through breast milk. II Barbiturates. J Pediatr. 14:86-90, 1938.
2. Kaneko S, Sato T, Suzuki K. The levels of anticonvulsants in breast milk. Br J Clin Pharmacol. 7:624-627,1979.
3. Wilson JT. Drug excretion in human breast milk: principles, pharmacokinetics and projected consequences. Clin Pharmacokinet 5:1-66, 1980.

Sertraline   Fax #1382

Trade: Zoloft
Can/Aus/UK: Zoloft, Lustral
Uses: Antidepressant
AAP: Not reviewed

Sertraline is a typical serotonin reuptake inhibitor similar to Prozac and Paxil, but unlike Prozac, the longer half-life metabolite of sertraline is only marginally active. In one study of a single patient taking 100 mg of sertraline daily for 3 weeks postpartum, the concentration of sertraline in milk was 24, 43, 40, and 19 µg/Liter of milk at 1, 5, 9, and 23 hours respectively following the dose. The maternal plasma levels of sertraline after 12 hours was 48 ng/mL. Sertraline plasma levels in the infant at three weeks were below the limit of detection (< 0.5 ng/mL) at 12 hours post-dose. Routine pediatric evaluation after 3 months revealed a neonate of normal weight who had achieved the appropriate developmental milestones. In another study of 3 breastfeeding patients who received 50-100 mg sertraline daily, the maternal plasma levels ranged from 18.4 to 95.8 ng/mL, whereas the plasma levels of sertraline and its metabolite, desmethylsertraline, in the three breastfed infants was below the limit of detection (< 2 ng/mL). Milk levels were not measured. Desmethylsertraline is poorly active, less than 10% of the parent sertraline. Another recent publication reviewed the changes in platelet serotonin levels in breastfeeding mothers and their infants who received up to 100 mg of sertraline daily. Mothers treated with sertraline had significant decreases in their platelet serotonin levels, which is expected. However, there was no change in platelet serotonin levels in breastfed infants of mothers consuming sertraline, suggesting that only minimal amounts of sertraline are actually transferred to the infant. This confirms other studies. Studies by Stowe et.al. (1997) of eleven mother/infant pairs (maternal dose = 25-150 mg/day) further suggest minimal transfer of sertraline into human milk. From this superb study, the concentration of sertraline peaked in the milk at 7-8 hours, and the metabolite (desmethylsertraline) at 5-11 hours. The reported concentrations of sertraline and desmethylsertraline in breast milk were 17-173 ng/mL, and 22-294 ng/mL, respectively. The reported dose of sertraline to the infant via milk varied from undetectable (5 of 11) to 0.124 mg/day in one infant. The infant's serum concentration of sertraline varied from undetectable to 3.0 ng/mL, but was undetectable in 7 of 11 patients. No developmental abnormalities were noted in any of the infants studied. These studies generally confirm that the transfer of sertraline and its metabolite to the infant is minimal, and that attaining clinically relevant plasma levels in infants is remote at maternal doses less than 150 mg/day.

Alternatives: Paroxetine

Pregnancy Risk Category: B

Adult Concerns: Diarrhea, nausea, tremor, and increased sweating.

Pediatric Concerns: Of the cases reported in the literature, only one infant developed benign neonatal sleep at age 4 months which spontaneous resolved at 6 months. Its relationship, if any, to sertraline is unknown.

Drug Interactions: All SSRIs inhibit Cytochrome P450 enzymes and may inhibit metabolism of desipramine, dextromethorphan, encainide, haloperidol, metoprolol, etc. May induce serotonergic hyperstimulation when added too soon after MAO inhibitors, tricyclic antidepressants, and lithium. May displace warfarin from binding sites increasing anticoagulation.

AHL = 26-65 hours		**M/P**	**= 0.89**
PHL =		**PB**	**= 98%**
PK = 7-8 hours		**Oral**	**= Complete**
MW = 306		**pKa**	**=**
Vd = 20			

References:
1.   Altshuler LL.   Breastfeeding and Sertraline: A 24 hours Analysis. J. Clin Psychiatry 56(6):243-245, 1995.
2.   Wisner KL, Perel JM, Findling RL: Antidepressant treatment during breast-feeding. Am J Psychiatry 153(9): 1132-1137, 1996.
3.   Mammen OK, Perel JM et.al: Sertraline and norsertraline levels in three breastfed infants. J. Clin. Psychiatry 58(3): 100-103, 1997.
4.   Epperson, CN et.al. Sertraline and Breastfeeding. NEJM 336(16):1189-90, 1997.
5.   Stowe, ZN, Owens, MJ, Landry,JC. et.al. Sertraline and desmethylsertraline in human breast milk and nursing infants. Am.J.Psychiatry 154(9):1255-1260, 1997.

Sibutramine   Fax #1571

Trade: Meridia
Can/Aus/UK:
Uses: Appetite suppressant
AAP: Not reviewed

Sibutramine is a non-amphetamine appetite suppressant. Due to its effect on serotonin and norepinephrine reuptake, it is considered an antidepressant as well. Sibutramine is rather small in molecular weight, active in the CNS, extremely lipid soluble, and has two 'active' metabolites with long half-lives (14-16 hours). Although no data are available on its transfer into human milk, the pharmacokinetics of this drug theoretically suggest that it might have a rather high milk:plasma ratio and could enter milk in significant levels. Until we know more, a risk assessment may not support the use of this product in breastfeeding mothers.

Alternatives:

Pregnancy Risk Category: C

Adult Concerns: Adult side effects include headache, insomnia, back pain, flu-like syndrome, abdominal pain, seizures (rarely), and elevated liver enzymes. Cardiovascular events include tachycardia, hypertension.

Pediatric Concerns: None reported via milk. Caution is recommended.

Drug Interactions: Use of Sibutramine with drugs that may increase blood pressure (decongestants, cough and cold remedies) could be hazardous. Do not use with MAO inhibitors. Do not admix with drugs that inhibit cytochrome P450 enzymes in the liver (ketoconazole, cimetidine, erythromycin (minor effect).

AHL = 12.5-21.8 hours		M/P	=
PHL =		PB	= 94%
PK = 3-4 hours		Oral	= 77%
MW = 334		pKa	=
Vd =			

References:
1. Lean MEJ: Sibutramine--a review of clinical efficacy. Int J Obesity 21(suppl 1):S30-S36, 1997.
2. Stock MJ: Sibutramine: a review of the pharmacology of a novel anti-obesity agent. Int J Obesity 21(1):S25-S29, 1997.
3. Pharmaceutical Manufacturer's package insert, 1998.

Silicone Breast Implants   Fax #1383

Trade:
Can/Aus/UK:
Uses: Silicone mammoplasty
AAP: Not reviewed

Augmentation mammoplasty with silicone implants is no longer available in the USA. In general, placement of the implant behind the breast seldom produces interruption of vital ducts, nerve supply, or blood supply. Most women have been able to breastfeed. Breast reduction surgery, on the other hand, has been found to produce significant interruption of the nervous supply (particularly the ductile tissue), leading to a reduced ability to lactate. It is not known for certain if ingestion of leaking silicone by a nursing infant is dangerous. Although one article has been published showing esophageal strictures, it has subsequently been recalled by the author. Silicone by nature is extremely inert and is unlikely to be absorbed in the GI tract by a nursing infant although good studies are lacking. Testing for silicone is extremely difficult. Silicone is a ubiquitous substance, found in all foods, liquids, etc., and methods for testing for silicone as derived from silicone implants are not readily available, nor accurate.

Alternatives:

Pregnancy Risk Category:

Adult Concerns:

Pediatric Concerns: None reported via milk.

Drug Interactions:

References:
1.   Lawrence R. Breastfeeding, A guide for the medical profession. 4th ed. Mosby, St. Louis, Mo., 1995.

Silver Sulfadiazine   Fax #1475

Trade: Silvadene, SSD Cream, Thermazene
Can/Aus/UK: Flamazine, Dermazin, SSD Silvazine
Uses: Topical antimicrobial cream
AAP: Not reviewed

Silver sulfadiazine is a topical antimicrobial cream primarily used for reducing sepsis in burn patients. The silver component is not absorbed from the skin. Sulfadiazine is partially absorbed. After prolonged therapy of large areas, sulfadiazine levels in plasma may approach therapeutic levels. Although sulfonamides are known to be secreted into human milk, they are not particularly problematic except in the newborn period when they may produce kernicterus.

Alternatives:

Pregnancy Risk Category: B

Adult Concerns: Allergic rash, renal failure, crystalluria.

Pediatric Concerns: None reported, but studies are limited. Observe caution during the neonatal period.

Drug Interactions:

AHL = 10 hours(sulfa)	M/P	=
PHL =	PB	=
PK =	Oral	= Complete
MW =	pKa	=
Vd =		

References:
1. McEvoy GE(ed):AHFS Drug Information, New York, NY. 1995.

Simvastatin   Fax #1384

Trade: Zocor
Can/Aus/UK: Zocor, Lipex
Uses: Reduces cholesterol
AAP: Not reviewed

Simvastatin is an HMG-CoA reductase inhibitor that reduces the production of cholesterol in the liver. Like lovastatin, simvastatin reduces blood cholesterol levels. Others in this family are known to be secreted into human and rodent milk, but no data are available on simvastatin. It is likely that milk levels will be low, since less than 5% of simvastatin reaches the plasma, most being removed first-pass by the liver. Atherosclerosis is a chronic process and discontinuation of lipid-lowering drugs during pregnancy and lactation should have little or no impact on the outcome of long-term therapy of primary hypercholesterolemia. Cholesterol and other products of cholesterol biosynthesis are essential components for fetal and neonatal development and the use of cholesterol-lowering drugs would not be advisable under any circumstances.

Alternatives:

Pregnancy Risk Category: X

Adult Concerns: GI distress, headache, hypotension, elevated liver enzymes.

Pediatric Concerns: None reported.

Drug Interactions: Increased toxicity when added to gemfibrozil (myopathy, myalgia, etc), clofibrate, niacin (myopathy), erythromycin, cyclosporine, oral anticoagulants (elevated bleeding time).

AHL = Long		**M/P**	**=**
PHL =		**PB**	**= 95%**
PK = 1.3-2.4 hours		**Oral**	**= Poor**
MW = 419		**pKa**	**=**
Vd =			

References:
1.   Drug Facts and Comparisons. 1995 ed. Facts and Comparisons, St. Louis.

Somatrem, Somatropin   Fax #1385

Trade: Human Growth Hormone, Nutropin, Humatrope, Growth Hormone, Saizen
Can/Aus/UK: Protropin, Genotropin, Humatrope, Norditropin, Somatropin
Uses: Human growth hormone
AAP: Not reviewed

Somatrem and somatropin are purified polypeptide hormones of recombinant DNA origin. It is a large protein. They are structurally similar or identical to human growth hormone (hGH). One study in 16 women indicates that hGH treatment for 7 days stimulated breast milk production by 18.5% (verses 11.6% in controls) in a group of normal lactating women. No adverse effects were noted. Leukemia has occurred in a small number of children receiving hGH, but the relationship is uncertain. Because it is a peptide of 191 amino acids and its molecular weight is so large, its transfer into milk is very unlikely. Further, its oral absorption would be minimal to nil.

Alternatives:

Pregnancy Risk Category: C

Adult Concerns:

Pediatric Concerns: None reported via milk. Absorption is very unlikely.

Drug Interactions:

AHL =	M/P =
PHL =	PB =
PK = 7.5 hours	Oral = Poor

MW = 22,124   pKa =
Vd =

References:
1.   Milsom SR, et.al. Growth hormone stimulates galactopoiesis in healthy lactating women. Acta Endocrinologica 127:337-43, 1992.

Sotalol   Fax #1386

Trade: Betapace
Can/Aus/UK: Sotacor, Apo-Sotalol, Rylosol, Cardol
Uses: Antihypertensive, beta-blocker
AAP: Approved by the American Academy of Pediatrics for use in breastfeeding mothers

Sotalol is a typical beta blocker antihypertensive with low lipid solubility.   It is secreted into milk in high levels.   Sotalol concentrations in milk ranged from 4.8 to 20.2 mg/L (mean= 10.5 mg/L) in 5 mothers.   The mean maternal dose was 433 mg/day. Although these milk levels appear high, no evidence of toxicity was noted in 12 infants.

Alternatives: Propranolol, Metoprolol

Pregnancy Risk Category: B

Adult Concerns: Bradycardia, hypotension, sedation, poor sucking.

Pediatric Concerns: None reported via milk, but observe for sedation, bradycardia, hypotension, weakness.

Drug Interactions: Decreased effect when used with aluminum salts, barbiturates, calcium salts, cholestyramine, NSAIDs, ampicillin, rifampin, and salicylates. Beta blockers may reduce the effect of oral sulfonylureas (hypoglycemic agents). Increased toxicity/effect when used with other antihypertensives, contraceptives, MAO inhibitors, cimetidine, and numerous other products. See   drug interaction reference for complete listing.

AHL = 12 hours	**M/P** = 5.4
PHL =	**PB** = 0%
PK = 2.5 - 4 hours	**Oral** = 90-100%
MW = 272	**pKa** = 8.3,9.8
Vd = 1.6-2.4	

References:
1. O'Hare MF, Murnaghan GA, et.al. Sotalol asa hypotensive agent in pregnancy. Br. J. Obstet. Gynaecol. 87:814-20, 1980.

Spironolactone   Fax #1387

Trade: Aldactone
Can/Aus/UK: Aldactone, Novospiroton, Spiractin, Adactone
Uses: Potassium sparing diuretic
AAP: Approved by the American Academy of Pediatrics for use in breastfeeding mothers

Spironolactone is metabolized to canrenone, which is known to be secreted into breast milk. In one mother receiving 25 mg of spironolactone, at 2 hours post-dose the maternal serum and milk concentrations of canrenone were 144 and 104 µg/L respectively. At 14.5 hours, the corresponding values for serum and milk were 92 and 47 µg/L respectively. Milk:plasma ratios varied from 0.51 at 14.5 hours, to 0.72 at 2 hours. The estimated dose an infant would ingest was 0.2% of maternal dose/day. As with most diuretics, a decrease in milk production is possible but unlikely.

Alternatives:

Pregnancy Risk Category: D

Adult Concerns: Nausea, vomiting, elevated serum potassium, hepatitis.

Pediatric Concerns: None reported via milk, but suppression of milk supply is possible but unlikely.

Drug Interactions: Use with anticoagulants may reduce the anticoagulant effect. Use with potassium preparations may increase potassium levels in plasma. Use with ACE inhibitors may elevate serum potassium levels. The diuretic effect of spironolactone may be decreased by use with salicylates.

AHL = 10-35 hours		**M/P**	= 0.51-0.72
PHL =		**PB**	= >90%
PK = 1-2 hours		**Oral**	= 70%
MW = 417		**pKa**	=
Vd =			

References:
1. Phelps DL, Karim A. Spironolactone: relationship between concentrations of dethioacetylated metabolite in human serum and milk. J. Pharm. Sci. 66:1203, 1977.

St. John's Wort   Fax #1552

Trade: St. John's Wort
Can/Aus/UK:
Uses: Antidepressant
AAP: Not reviewed

St. John's Wort (hypericum perforatum L.) consists of the whole fresh or dried plant or its components containing not less than 0.04% naphthodianthrones of the hypericin group. Hypericum contains many biologically active compounds and most researchers consider its effect due to a combination of constituents rather than any single component. However, the naphthodianthrones hypericin and pseudohypericin, and numerous flavonoids have stimulated the most interest as antidepressants and antivirals. Following doses of (3 x 300 mg/day), peak steady state concentrations of hypericin and pseudohypericin were 8.5 ng/mL and 5.8 ng/mL respectively. Concentrations in brain appear to be the least of all compartments. Hypericum has become increasingly popular for the treatment of depression following results from numerous studies showing efficacy. However, large well-controlled studies are currently underway and the efficacy of SJW will be further tested in the coming year. In vitro studies have indicated that hypericin inhibits monoamine oxidase (MAO) and catechol-o-methyltransferase (COMT), the enzymes responsible for the breakdown of neurotransmitters. MAO inhibitors have in the past been subject to severe restrictions due to their dangers. Thus far, the amount of hypericin present in human tissues, does not appear to inhibit MAO in adults, although no data are available on MAO inhibition in infants. Hypericin is presently in Phase I clinical trials as an antiviral agent as well, with potential use in herpes, HIV, and other viral infections. Although there is great interest in this phytomedicine, a number of deficiencies in the clinical trails have been pointed out. They include poorly characterized depressed patient populations, heterogeneity of diagnoses, etc, but a number of current studies underway should clarify these deficiencies. At present there are no data on the transfer of hypericum compounds into human milk. Its poor penetration into the CNS could be used to suggest that it penetrates milk poorly as well, since these compartments are similar. Due to the long half-life, some would be expected to transfer into milk and subsequently the infant. At this time, due to the availability of better studied products such as sertraline (Zoloft) and paroxetine (Paxil) which do not apparently pose a great significant risk to the breastfed infant, these products should be preferentially used in postpartum depression. Caution, because of uterotonic effects, hypericum should not be used in pregnant patients.

Alternatives: Sertraline, Paroxetine

Pregnancy Risk Category:

Adult Concerns: Caution, because of uterotonic effects, hypericum should not be used in pregnant patients. Dry mouth, dizziness, constipation, and confusion have been infrequently reported. Overt toxicity is generally considered quite low. Photosensitization in fair-skinned people has been noted. No teratogenic effects have been documented.

Pediatric Concerns: None reported. Caution is urged.

Drug Interactions: May prolong narcotic-induced sedation and sleeping times. May reduce barbiturate-induced sleeping times.

AHL = 26.5 hours		M/P	=
PHL =		PB	=
PK = 5.9 hours		Oral	=
MW = 504		pKa	=
Vd =			

References:
1. St. John's Wort. In Upton, R, editor:American Herbal Pharmacopoeia and Therapeutic Compendium, 1997.
2. Stock S, Holzl J. Pharmacokinetic tests of [14C]-labeled hypericin and pseudohypericin from Hypericum perforatum and serum kinetics of hypericin in man. Planta Medica 57(suppl 2):A61, 1991.
3. Bladt S, Wagner H. Inhibition of MAO by fractions and constituents of Hypericum extract. J. Geriatric Psychiatry Neurology 7:S57-59, 1994.
4. Ernst E. St. John's Wort, an anti-depressant? A systematic, criteria-based review. Phytomedicine 2:47-71, 1995.
5. Linde K, et.al. St. John's wort for depression-an overview and meta-analysis of randomized clinical trials. British Med. J. 313:253-258, 1996.

Streptomycin   Fax #1388

Trade:
Can/Aus/UK: Streptobretin
Uses: Antibiotic
AAP: Approved by the American Academy of Pediatrics for use in breastfeeding mothers

Streptomycin is an aminoglycoside antibiotic from the same family as gentamycin. It is primarily administered IM or IV although it is seldom used today with exception of the treatment of tuberculosis. One report suggests that following a 1 g dose (IM), levels in breast milk were 0.3 to 0.6 mg/L (2-3% of plasma level). Another report suggests that only

0.5% of a 1 gm IM dose is excreted in breast milk within 24 hours. Because the oral absorption of streptomycin is very poor, absorption by infant is probably minimal (unless premature or early neonate).

Alternatives:

Pregnancy Risk Category: D

Adult Concerns: Deafness, anemia, kidney toxicity.

Pediatric Concerns: None reported via milk, but observe for changes in GI flora.

Drug Interactions: Increased toxicity when used with certain penicillins, cephalosporins, amphotericin B, loop diuretics, and neuromuscular blocking agents.

AHL = 2.6 hours	M/P = 0.12-1.0
PHL = 4-10 hours (neonates)	PB = 34%
PK = 1-2 hours (IM)	Oral = Poor
MW = 582	pKa =
Vd =	

References:
1. Wilson, J. Drugs in Breast Milk. New York: ADIS Press, 1981.
2. Snider DE, Powell KE. Should women taking antituberculosis drugs breast-feed? Arch Inter Med. 144:589-590, 1984.

Strontium-89 Chloride   Fax #1389

Trade: Metastron
Can/Aus/UK:
Uses: Radioactive product for bone pain
AAP: Not reviewed

Metastron behaves similarly to calcium. It is rapidly cleared from plasma and sequestered into bone where its radioactive emissions relieve metastatic bone pain. Radioactive half-life is 50.5 days. Transfer into milk is unreported but likely. This radioactive product is too dangerous to use in lactating mothers.

Alternatives:

Pregnancy Risk Category: D

Adult Concerns: Severe bone marrow suppression, septicemia.

Pediatric Concerns: None reported via milk. This product is probably too dangerous to use with breastfed infants.

Drug Interactions:

AHL = 50.5 days.	M/P	=
PHL =	PB	=
PK = Immediate(IV)	Oral	=
MW = 159	pKa	=
Vd =		

References:
1. Drug Facts and Comparisons. 1995 ed. Facts and Comparisons, St. Louis.

Sucralfate   Fax #1390

Trade: Carafate
Can/Aus/UK: Sulcrate, Novo-Sucralate, Nu-Sucralfate, Carafate, SCF, Ulcyte, Antepsin
Uses: For peptic ulcers
AAP: Not reviewed

Sucralfate is a sucrose aluminum complex used for stomach ulcers. When administered orally sucralfate forms a complex that physically covers stomach ulcers. Less than 5% is absorbed orally. At these plasma levels it is very unlikely to penetrate into breast milk.

Alternatives:

Pregnancy Risk Category: B

Adult Concerns: Constipation.

Pediatric Concerns: None reported via milk. Absorption is very unlikely.

Drug Interactions: The use of aluminum containing antacids and sucralfate may increase the total body burden of aluminum. Sucralfate may reduce the anticoagulant effect of warfarin. Serum digoxin levels may be reduced. Phenytoin absorption may be decreased. Ketaconazole bioavailability may be decreased. Serum quinidine levels may be reduced. Bioavailability of the fluoroquinolone family may be decreased.

AHL =		M/P	=
PHL =		PB	=
PK =		Oral	= < 5%
MW = 2087		pKa	=
Vd =			

References:
1. Drug Facts and Comparisons. 1995 ed. Facts and Comparisons, St. Louis.

Sulconazole Nitrate   Fax #1391

Trade: Exelderm
Can/Aus/UK: Exelderm
Uses: Antifungal cream
AAP: Not reviewed

Exelderm is a broad spectrum antifungal topical cream. Although no data exist on transfer into human milk, it is unlikely that the degree of transdermal absorption would be high enough to produce significant milk levels. Only 8.7% of the topically administered dose is transcutaneously absorbed.

Alternatives:

Pregnancy Risk Category: C

Adult Concerns: Rash, skin irritation, burning, stinging.

Pediatric Concerns: None reported via milk.

Drug Interactions:

References:
1.   Pharmaceutical Manufacturer's Package Insert, 1996.

Sulfamethoxazole   Fax #1392

Trade: Gantanol
Can/Aus/UK: Apo-Methoxazole, Gantanol, Resprim, Septrin
Uses: Sulfonamide antibiotic
AAP: Not reviewed

Sulfamethoxazole is a common and popular sulfonamide antimicrobial. It is secreted in breast milk in small amounts. It has a longer half-life than other sulfonamides. Use with caution in weakened infants and premature infants with hyperbilirubinemia. Gantrisin (Sulfisoxazole) is considered the best choice of sulfonamides due to reduced transfer to infant. Compatible but exercise caution.   PHL= 14.7-36.5 hours (neonate), 8-9 hours (older infants).

Alternatives:

Pregnancy Risk Category: C

Adult Concerns: Anemia, blood dyscrasia, allergies.

Pediatric Concerns: None reported via milk, but use with caution in hyperbilirubinemic neonates and in infants with G6PD.

Drug Interactions: Decreased effect with paraminobenzoic acid or PABA metabolites of drugs such as procaine and tetracaine. Increased effect of oral anticoagulants, oral hypoglycemic agents, and methotrexate.

AHL = 10.1 hours   **M/P   = 0.06**

PHL = 14.7-36.5 hours (neonate)	PB = 62%		
PK = 1-4 hours	Oral = Complete		
MW = 253	pKa =		
Vd =			

References:
1. Rasmussen F. Mammary excretion of sulfonamides. Acta Pharmacol Toxicol 15:138-148, 1958.

Sulfasalazine   Fax #1393

Trade: Azulfidine
Can/Aus/UK: PMS Sulfasalazine, Salazopyrin, SAS-500, Salazopyrin
Uses: Anti-inflammatory for ulcerative colitis
AAP: Drugs associated with significant side effects and should be given with caution

Sulfasalazine is a conjugate of sulfapyridine and 5-Aminosalicylic acid and is used as an anti-inflammatory for ulcerative colitis. Only one-third of the dose is absorbed by the mother, most stays in the GI tract. Secretion of 5-aminosalicylic acid (active compound) and its inactive metabolite (acetyl -5-ASA) is very low. Milk:plasma ratio of 5-ASA is reported to be 0.09 to 0.17. Total daily dose absorbed by infant is approximately 0.065 mg/kg. No adverse effects have been observed in most nursing infants. However, one reported case of toxicity which may have been an idiosyncratic allergic response. Use with caution.

Alternatives:

Pregnancy Risk Category: B

Adult Concerns: Watery diarrhea, GI distress, nausea, vomiting, rapid breathing.

Pediatric Concerns: Only one reported case of hypersensitivity. Most studies show minimal effects via milk. Observe for diarrhea, GI discomfort.

Drug Interactions: Decreased effect when used with iron, digoxin, and paraminobenzoic acid containing drugs. Decreased effect of oral anticoagulants, methotrexate, and oral hypoglycemic agents.

AHL = 7.6 hours		**M/P**	= 0.09-0.17
PHL =		**PB**	=
PK = Prolonged		**Oral**	= Poor
MW = 398		**pKa**	=
Vd =			

References:
1. Branski D, et. al. Bloody diarrhea-A possible complication of sulfasalazine transferred through human breast milk. J Pediatr Gastroenterol Nutr 5:316-7, 1986.
2. Jarnerot G, Into-Malmberg MB. Sulfasalazine treatment during breast feeding. Scand J Gastroenterol 14:869-71, 1979.
3. Klotz U, and Harings-Kaim A. Negligible excretion of 5-aminosalicylic acid in breast milk. Lancet 342:618-9,1993.

Sulfisoxazole   Fax #1394

Trade: Gantrisin
Can/Aus/UK: Novo-Soxazole, Sulfizole
Uses: Sulfonamide antibiotic
AAP: Approved by the American Academy of Pediatrics for use in breastfeeding mothers

Sulfisoxazole is a popular sulfonamide antimicrobial. It is secreted in breast milk in small amounts, although the actual levels are somewhat controversial. Kauffman (1980) reports less than 1% of the maternal dose is secreted into human milk, and that this is probably insufficient to produce problems in a normal newborn. Sulfisoxazole appears to be best choice with lowest milk:plasma ratio. Use with caution in weakened infants or those with hyperbilirubinemia.

Alternatives:

Pregnancy Risk Category:

Adult Concerns: Elevated bilirubin, rash.

Pediatric Concerns: None reported via milk. Use with caution in hyperbilirubinemic neonates and in infants with G6PD.

Drug Interactions: The anesthetic effects of thiopental may be enhanced with sulfisoxazole. Cyclosporine concentrations may be decreased by sulfonamides. Serum phenytoin levels may be increased. The risk of methotrexate induced bone marrow suppression may be enhanced. Increased sulfonylurea half-lives and hypoglycemia when used with sulfonamides.

AHL	= 4.6-7.8 hours	M/P	= 0.06
PHL	=	PB	= 91%
PK	= 2-4 hours	Oral	= 100%
MW	= 267	pKa	=
Vd	=		

References:

1. Rasmussen F. Mammary excretion of sulfonamides. Acta Pharmacol Toxicol 15:138-148, 1958.
2. Kauffman RE, O'Brien C, Gilford P. Sulfisoxazole secretion into human milk. J. Pediatr. 97:839-41, 1980.

Sulpiride   Fax #1579

Trade:

Can/Aus/UK: Dolmatil, Sulparex, Sulpitil

Uses: Antidepressant, antipsychotic

AAP: Not reviewed

Sulpiride is a selective dopamine antagonist used as an antidepressant and antipsychotic. Sulpiride is a strong neuroleptic antipsychotic drug, however several studies using smaller doses have found it to significantly increase prolactin levels and breast milk production in smaller doses that do not produce overt neuroleptic effects on the mother.   In a study with 14 women who received sulpiride (50 mg three times daily), and in a subsequent study with 36 breastfeeding women, Ylikorkala(1982, 1984) found major increases in prolactin levels and significant, but only moderate increases in breast milk production. In a group of 20 women who received 50 mg twice daily, breast milk samples were drawn 2 hours after the dose.   The concentration of sulpiride in breast milk ranged from 0.26 to 1.97 μg/mL. No effects on breastfed infants were noted.   The authors concluded that sulpiride, when administered early in the postpartum period, is useful in promoting initiation of lactation. Sulpiride is not available in the USA.

Alternatives: Metoclopramide, domperidone

Pregnancy Risk Category:

Adult Concerns: Tardive dyskinesia, extrapyramidal symptoms, sedation, neuroleptic malignant syndrome, cholestatic jaundice.

Pediatric Concerns: None reported via milk.

Drug Interactions: Antacids and sucralfate may reduce absorption of sulpiride. Increased risk of seizures may result from use of tramadol or zotepine with sulpiride.

AHL = 6-8 hours		**M/P** =	
PHL =		**PB** =	
PK = 2-6 hours		**Oral** = 27-34%	
MW =		**pKa** =	
Vd = 2.7			

References:
1.   Wiesel FA, Alfredsson G, Ehrnebo M et al: The pharmacokinetics of intravenous and oral sulpiride in healthy human subjects. Eur J Clin Pharmacol 17:385-391, 1980.
2.   Ylikorkala O, Kauppila A, Kivinen S et al: Sulpiride improves inadequate lactation. Br Med J 285:249-251, 1982.
3.   Ylikorkala O, Kauppila A, Kivinen S et al: Treatment of inadequate lactation with oral sulpiride and buccal oxytocin. Obstet Gynecol 63:57-60, 1984.
4.   Aono T, Shioji T, et.al. Augmentation of puerperal lactation by

oral administration of sulpiride. J. Clin. Endo. Metabol. 48(3): 478-482, 1979.

Sumatriptan Succinate   Fax #1395

Trade: Imitrex
Can/Aus/UK: Imitrex, Imigran
Uses: Anti-migraine medication
AAP: Not reviewed

Sumatriptan is a 5-HT (Serotonin) receptor agonist and a highly effective new drug for the treatment of migraine headaches. It is not an analgesic, rather it produces a rapid vasoconstriction in various regions of the brain, thus temporarily reducing the cause of migraines. In one study using 5 lactating women, each were given 6 mg subcutaneous injections and samples drawn for analysis over 8 hours. The highest breast milk levels were 87.2 µg/L at 2.6 hours post-dose and rapidly disappeared over the next 6 hours. The mean total recovery of sumatriptan in milk over the 8 hour duration was only 14.4 µg. On a weight-adjusted basis this concentration in milk corresponded to a mean infant exposure of only 3.5% of the maternal dose. Further, assuming an oral bioavailability of only 14%, the weight-adjusted dose an infant would absorb would be approximately 0.49% of the maternal dose. The authors suggest that continued breastfeeding following sumatriptan use would not pose a significant risk to the sucking infant. The maternal plasma half-life is 1.3 hours, the milk half-life is 2.22 hours. Although the milk:plasma ratio was 4.9 (indicating significant concentrating mechanisms in milk), the absolute maternal plasma levels were small, hence the absolute milk concentrations were low.

Alternatives: Zolmitriptan

Pregnancy Risk Category: C

Adult Concerns: Flushing, hot tingling sensations.

Pediatric Concerns: None reported via milk.

Drug Interactions: MAOIs can markedly increase sumatriptan systemic effect and elimination including elevated sumatriptan plasma levels. Ergot containing drugs have caused prolonged vasospastic reactions.

AHL = 1.3 hours		**M/P**	= 4.9
PHL =		**PB**	= 14-21%
PK = 12 min.(IM)		**Oral**	= 10-15%
MW = 413		**pKa**	=
Vd =			

References:
1.   Wojnar-Horton RE, Hackett LP, Yapp P, Dusci LJ, Paech M and Ilett KF. Distribution and excretion of sumatriptan in human milk. Brit. J. Clin. Pharmacol. 41:217-221, 1995.

Tamoxifen   Fax #1485

Trade: Nolvadex
Can/Aus/UK: Apo-Tamox, Nolvadex, Tamofen, Tamone Tamoxen, Genox, Eblon, Noltam
Uses: Anti-estrogen, anti-cancer
AAP: Not reviewed

Tamoxifen is an nonsteroidal antiestrogen. It attaches to the estrogen receptor and produces only minimal stimulation, thus it prevents estrogen from stimulating the receptor. Aside from this, it also produces a number of other effects within the cytoplasm of the cell and some of its anti-cancer effects may be mediated by its effects at sites other than the estrogen receptor. Tamoxifen is metabolized by the liver and has an elimination half-life of greater than 7 days(range 3-21 days). It is well absorbed orally, and the highest tissue concentrations are in the liver (60 fold). It is 99% protein bound and normally reduces plasma prolactin levels significantly (66% after 3 months). At present, there are no data on its transfer into breast milk, however it has been shown to inhibit lactation in several studies. In one study, doses of

10-30 mg twice daily early postpartum, completely inhibited postpartum engorgement and lactation(2). In a second study, tamoxifen doses of 10 mg four times daily significantly reduced serum prolactin and inhibited milk production as well (3). We do not know the effect of tamoxifen on established milk production. Tamoxifen is potentially teratogenic (category D) and should never be used in pregnant women (Note: it is useful in conjunction with clomiphene to stimulate ovulation...short term use only). It has a pKa of 8.85 which may suggest some trapping in milk compared to the maternal plasma levels. This product has a very long half-life, and the active metabolite is concentrated in the plasma (2 fold). This drug has all the characteristics that would suggest a concentrating mechanism in breastfed infants over time. Its prominent effect on reducing prolactin levels will inhibit early lactation, and may ultimately inhibit established lactation. In this instance, the significant risks to the infant from exposure to tamoxifen probably outweight the benefits of breastfeeding. Mothers receiving tamoxifen should not breastfeed until we know more about the levels transferred into milk, and the plasma/tissue levels found in breastfed infants.

Alternatives:

Pregnancy Risk Category: D

Adult Concerns: Hot flashes, nausea, vomiting, vaginal bleeding/discharge, menstrual irregularities, amenorrhea.

Pediatric Concerns: None reported but caution is urged.

Drug Interactions: Increased anticoagulant effect when used with coumarin-type anticoagulants. Tamoxifen is a potent inhibitor of drug metabolizing enzymes in the liver, observe for elevated levels of many drugs.

AHL	= > 7 days	M/P	=
PHL	=	PB	= 99%
PK	= 2-3 hours	Oral	= Complete
MW	= 371	pKa	= 8.85
Vd	=		

References:
1. Pharmaceutical Manufacturer's Package Insert, 1997.
2. Shaaban MM. Suppression of lactation by an antiestrogen, tamoxifen. Eur. J. Obstet. Gynecol. Reprod. Biol. 4:167-169, 1975.
3. Massala A, Delitala G, et.al. Inhibition of lactation and inhibition of prolactin release after mechanical breast stimulation in puerperal women given tamoxifen or placebo. Br. J. Obstet. Gynecol. 85:134-137, 1978.

Tea Tree Oil   Fax #1551

Trade: Tea Tree Oil
Can/Aus/UK:
Uses: Antibacterial, antifungal
AAP: Not reviewed

Tea tree oil, as derived from Melaleuca alternifolia, has recently gain popularity for its antiseptic properties. The essential oil, derived by steam distillation of the leaves, contains terpin-4-ol in concentrations of 40% or more. TTO is primarily noted for its antimicrobial effects without irritating sensitive tissues. It is antimicrobial when tested against Candida albicans, E. coli, S. Aureus, Staph. epidermidis, and pseudomonas aeruginosa. In several reports it is suggested to have antifungal properties equivalent to tolnaftate, and clotrimazole. Although the use of TTO in adults is mostly nontoxic, the safe use in infants is unknown. Use directly on the nipple should be minimized.

Alternatives:

Pregnancy Risk Category:

Adult Concerns: Toxic effects include allergic eczema. Petechial body rash and leukocytosis in one individual who ingested 1/2 teaspoonful orally. Ataxia and drowsiness following oral ingestion of < 10 cc by a 17 month old infant.

Pediatric Concerns: None reported via milk.

Drug Interactions:

References:
1. Review of Natural Products. Facts and Comparisons, St. Louis, Mo. 1997.

Technetium ^{99}Tc Sestamibi   Fax #1577

Trade: Cardiolite, Sestamibi
Can/Aus/UK:
Uses: Imaging agent
AAP: Radioactivity in milk present 15 hours to 3 days

Technetium-99M sestamibi is a myocardial imaging agent that is also sometimes used as an oncologic imaging agent. The radioactive technetium-99 ion is chelated to the sestamibi molecule. It is used as an alternative to Thallium-201 imaging.   Sestamibi is largely distributed to the myocardium and is a function of myocardial viability. Technetium is a weak gamma emitter with a radioactive half-life of only 6.02 hours. The biological half-life of this product is approximately 6 hours, but the effective half-life (both biological and radioactive) is only about 3 hours. Transfer of significant amounts of sestamibi into human milk is yet unreported, but is rather unlikely as sestamibi binds irreversible to myocardial tissue and does not redistribute to other tissues to a significant degree. Other forms of ^{99}TC have been reported to enter milk (Maisels 1983), but entry would be largely determined by the chemical form, not the radioactive agent. To ensure absolute safety, a mother should probably pump and dump for a minimum of 24-30 hours, before reinitiating breastfeeding.

Alternatives:

Pregnancy Risk Category: C

Adult Concerns: Dysgeusia, headache, flushing, angina, hypersensitivity, hypertension.

Pediatric Concerns: It is not known if the sestamibi chelate is transferred into human milk. But Technetium salts in general do transfer. Pump and dump for 24-30 hours or until all radioactivity is gone.

Drug Interactions:

AHL = 6 hours		M/P	=
PHL =		PB	= < 1%
PK =		Oral	= Complete
MW =		pKa	=
Vd =			

References:
1. Berman DS: Introduction - Technetium-99m myocardial perfusion imaging agents and their relation to thallium-201. Am J Cardiol 66:1E-4E, 1990.
2. Berman DS, Kiat H & Maddahi J: The new Tc-99m myocardial perfusion imaging agents: Tc-99m sestamibi and Tc-99m teboroxime. Circulation 84(suppl):7-21, 1991.
3. Maisels MJ & Gilcher RO: Excretion of technetium in human milk. Pediatrics 71:841-842, 1983.

Technetium-99m   Fax #1396

Trade: Technetium-99m
Can/Aus/UK:
Uses: Radioactive imaging
AAP: Radioactive compound that requires temporary cessation of breastfeeding

Radioactive technetium-99M (Tc-99m) is present in milk for at least 15 hours to 3 days and significant quantities have been reported in the thyroid and gastric mucosa of infants ingesting milk from treated mothers. It has a radioactive half-life of 6.02 hours. Following a dose of 15 mCi of Tc-99m for a brain scan, the concentration of Tc-99m in breast milk at 4, 8.5, 20, and 60 hours was 0.5 µCi, 0.1 µCi, 0.02 µCi, and 0.006 µCi respectively. The authors recommend pumping and dumping for a period of 48 hours following Technetium-99 treatment. Technetium-99m is used in many salt and chemical forms, but the radioactivity and decay are the same.

Alternatives:

Pregnancy Risk Category: C

Adult Concerns:

Pediatric Concerns: None reported, but may be transferred to infant thyroid. Pump and dump for a minimum of 48 hours.

Drug Interactions:

AHL = <6 hours		**M/P** =	
PHL =		**PB** =	
PK =		**Oral**	= Complete
MW =		**pKa** =	
Vd =			

References:
1. American Academy of Pediatrics, Committee on Drugs. Transfer of drugs and other chemicals into human milk. Pediatrics 93(1):137-150, 1994.
2. Evans JL, et.al. Secretion of radioactivity in breast milk following administration of 99Tcm-MAG3. Nuc. Med. Comm. 14:108, 1993.
3. Rumble WF, Aamodt RL, et.al. Accidental ingestion of Tc-99m in breast milk by a 10-week old child. J Nucl Med 19:913-915, 1978.
4. Maisels MJ, Gilcher RO. Excretion of technetium in human milk. Pediatrics 71:841-842, 1983.

Temazepam   Fax #1397

Trade: Restoril
Can/Aus/UK: Restoril, PMS-Temazepam, Euhypnos, Noctume, Temaze, Temtabs, Normison
Uses: Short acting benzodiazepine (Valium-like) hypnotic
AAP: Drugs whose effect on nursing infants is unknown but may be of concern

Temazepam is a short acting benzodiazepine that belongs to the Valium family primarily used as a nighttime sedative. In one study the milk:plasma ratio varied from <0.09 to < 0.63 (mean=0.18). Temazepam is relatively water soluble and therefore partitions poorly into breast milk. Levels of temazepam were undetectable in the infants studied, although these studies were carried out 15 hours post-dose. Although the study shows low neonatal exposure to temazepam via breast milk, the infant should be monitored carefully for sleepiness and poor feeding.

Alternatives: Lorazepam, Alprazolam

Pregnancy Risk Category: X

Adult Concerns: Sedation.

Pediatric Concerns: None reported via milk, but observe for sedation, poor feeding.

Drug Interactions: Increased effect when used with other CNS depressants.

AHL = 9.5-2.4 hours	M/P	= 0.18
PHL =	PB	= 96%
PK = 2-4 hours	Oral	= 90%
MW = 301	pKa	= 1.3
Vd = 0.8-1.0		

References:
1. Lebedevs TH, et.al. Excretion of temazepam in breast milk [letter]. Brit. J. Clin. Pharmacol. 33:204-6,1992.

Terazosin HCL   Fax #1398

Trade: Hytrin
Can/Aus/UK: Hytrin
Uses: Antihypertensive
AAP: Not reviewed

Terazosin is an antihypertensive that belongs the alpha-1 blocking family. This family is generally very powerful, produces significant orthostatic hypotension, and other side effects. As such, for the past 20 years, these drugs have always been used as the STEP II drugs used in hypertension, whereas the beta blockers, ACE inhibitors, calcium channel blockers, and thiazide diuretics have always been used first (STEP I). If the STEP I drugs don't work, then the physician employs a STEP II drug. Terazosin has rather powerful effects on the prostate and testes producing testicular atrophy in some animal studies (particularly newborn) and is therefore not preferred in pregnant or in lactating women. No data are available on transfer into human milk. Use caution.

Alternatives:

Pregnancy Risk Category: C

Adult Concerns: Hypotension, bradycardia, sedation.

Pediatric Concerns: None reported, but extreme caution is recommended.

Drug Interactions: Decreased antihypertensive effect when used with NSAIDs. Increased hypotensive effects when used with diuretics and other antihypertensive beta blockers.

AHL = 9-12 hours	M/P =
PHL =	PB = 94%
PK = 1-2 hours	Oral = 90%
MW = 423	pKa =
Vd =	

References:
1.   Pharmaceutical Manufacturer's Package Insert, 1995.

Terbinafine   Fax #1465

Trade: Lamisil
Can/Aus/UK: Lamisil
Uses: Antifungal
AAP: Not reviewed

Terbinafine is an antifungal agent primarily used for tinea species such as athlete's foot and ringworm.   Systemic absorption following topical therapy is minimal.   Following an oral dose of 500 mg in two volunteers, the total dose of terbinafine secreted in breast milk during the 72 hour post-dosing period was 0.65 mg in one mother and 0.15 mg in another. The total excretion of terbinafine in breast milk ranged from 0.13% to 0.03 % of the total maternal dose, respectively.   Topical absorption through the skin is minimal.

Alternatives: Fluconazole

Pregnancy Risk Category: B

Adult Concerns: Topical: burning, pruritus. Oral: fatigue, headache, GI distress, elevated liver enzymes, alopecia.

Pediatric Concerns: None reported via milk.

Drug Interactions: Terbinafine clearance is decreased 33% by cimetidine, and 16% by terfenadine. Terbinafine increases clearance of cyclosporin(15%).   Rifampin increases terbinafine clearance by 100%.

AHL	= 26 hours.		**M/P**	=
PHL	=		**PB**	= 99%
PK	= 1-2 hours.		**Oral**	= 80%
MW	= 291		**pKa**	=
Vd	= >28			

References:
1.   Pharmaceutical Manufacturer's Package Insert, 1996.
2.   Drug Facts and Comparisons. 1996. ed. Facts and Comparisons, St. Louis.
3.   Birnbaum JE: Pharmacology of the allylamines. J Am Acad Dermatol 23:782-785, 1990.

Terbutaline   Fax #1399

Trade: Bricanyl, Brethine
Can/Aus/UK: Bricanyl
Uses: Bronchodilator for asthma
AAP: Approved by the American Academy of Pediatrics for use in breastfeeding mothers

Terbutaline is a popular Beta-2 adrenergic used for bronchodilation in asthmatics.   It is secreted into breast milk but in low quantities. Following doses of 7.5 to 15 mg/day of terbutaline, milk levels averaged 3.37 µg/L. Assuming a daily intake of 165 mL milk, these levels would suggest a daily intake of less than 0.63 µg/kg/day which corresponds to 0.2 to 0.7% of maternal dose.   In another study of a patient receiving 5 mg three times daily, the mean milk concentrations ranged from 3.2 to 3.7 µg/L. The author calculated the daily dose to infant at 0.4-0.5 µg/kg body weight. Terbutaline was not detectible in the infant's serum.   No untoward effects have been reported in breastfeeding infants.

Alternatives:

Pregnancy Risk Category: B

Adult Concerns: Tremors, nervousness, tachycardia.

Pediatric Concerns:

Drug Interactions: Decreased effect when used with beta blockers. May increase toxicity when used with MAOI and TCAs.

AHL	= 14 hours	M/P	= < 2.9
PHL	=	PB	= 20%
PK	= 5-30 min.	Oral	= 33-50%
MW	= 225	pKa	= ?
Vd	= 1-2		

References:
1. Lindberberg C, et.al. Transfer of terbutaline into breast milk. Eur. J. Respir. Dis. 65:87, 1984.
2. Lonnerholm G, Lindstrom B. Terbutaline excretion into breast milk. Br J Clin Pharmacol. 13:729-730,1982.

Terconazole   Fax #1400

Trade: Terazol 3, Terazol 7
Can/Aus/UK: Terazol
Uses: Antifungal
AAP: Not reviewed

Terconazole is an antifungal primarily used for vaginal candidiasis. It is similar to fluconazole and itraconazole. When administered intra-vaginally, only a limited amount (5 -16%) is absorbed systemically (mean peak plasma level = 6 ng/mL). It is well absorbed orally. Even at high doses, the drug is not mutagenic, nor toxic to a fetus. At high doses, terconazole is known to enter breast milk in rodents, although no data are available on human milk. The milk levels are probably too small to be clinically relevant.

Alternatives: Fluconazole

Pregnancy Risk Category: C

Adult Concerns: Vaginal burning, itching, flu-like symptoms.

Pediatric Concerns: None reported due to minimal studies.

Drug Interactions:

AHL = 4-11.3 hours   M/P =
PHL =   PB   =
PK =   Oral = Complete
MW = 532   pKa =
Vd =

References:
1.   Pharmaceutical Manufacturer's Package Insert, 1996.
2.   McEvoy GE(ed):AHFS Drug Information, New York, NY. 1995.

Terfenadine   Fax #1401

Trade: Seldane
Can/Aus/UK: Seldane, Novo-Terfenadine, Teldane, Triludan
Uses: Long acting antihistamine
AAP: Not reviewed

Terfenadine is a second generation Histamine-1 antagonist that is significantly different from the older class antihistamines.   It has minimal sedation and a longer half-life.   Terfenadine is rapidly metabolized to an active metabolite. The half-life of the terfenadine metabolite is approximately 11.7 hours. In one study of 4 subjects, the parent terfenadine was not detectable in human milk even after reaching steady-state.   The maximum maternal plasma level of the metabolite was 309 ng/mL, whereas the milk level was only 41.02 ng/mL at maximum. Assuming a milk intake of 150 mg/kg/day for a normal infant, the highest amount of terfenadine metabolite that could be consumed by the nursing infant would be 0.009 mg/kg/day, which is only 0.45% of the maternal dose. In otherwise healthy mothers, the absence of terfenadine and the low levels of metabolite found in breast milk suggest terfenadine does not pose a significant risk to nursing infants.   Caution should be urged however, since elevated levels of terfenadine have produced significant myocardial arrhythmias in adults.

Alternatives: Loratadine, Cetirizine

Pregnancy Risk Category: C

Adult Concerns: Myocardial arrhythmias in overdose. Be cautious of multiple drug-drug interactions.

Pediatric Concerns: None reported via milk, but use with caution.

Drug Interactions: Dangerous cardiac arrhythmias have occurred with elevated terfenadine levels following use of ketoconazole, itraconazole, fluconazole, metronidazole, miconazole, erythromycin, and macrolide antibiotics, cimetidine, bepridil, probucol, astemizole, carbamazepine.

AHL	= 11.7 hours	M/P	= 0.12-0.28
PHL	=	PB	= 97%
PK	= 3.88 hours	Oral	= Complete
MW	= 472	pKa	=
Vd	=		

References:
1. Lucas Jr BD, Purdy CY, Scarim SK, et.al. Terfenadine pharmacokinetics in breast milk in lactating women. Clin. Pharm. & Ther. 57:398-402, 1995.
2. Paton DM, Webster DR. Clinical pharmacokinetics of H1-receptor antagonists (the antihistamines). Clin. Pharm. 10:477-497, 1985.

Tetracycline   Fax #1402

Trade: Achromycin, Sumycin, Terramycin
Can/Aus/UK: Achromycin, Aureomycin, Tetracyn, Achromycin, Mysteclin, Tetrex, Tetrachel
Uses: Antibiotic
AAP: Approved by the American Academy of Pediatrics for use in breastfeeding mothers

Tetracycline is a broad spectrum antibiotic with significant side effects in pediatric patients, including dental staining and reduced bone growth. It is secreted into breast milk in small levels. Because tetracyclines bind to milk calcium they would have reduced absorption in the infant.   A dosage of 2 gm/day for 3 days has achieved a milk:plasma ratio of 0.6 to 0.8. Compatible with nursing for short terms.   In another study of 5 lactating women receiving 500 mg PO four times daily, the breast milk concentrations ranged from 0.43 mg/L to 2.58 mg/L. Levels in infants were below the limit of detection.

Alternatives:

Pregnancy Risk Category: D

Adult Concerns: Pediatric: dental staining, decreased bone growth, altered GI flora.

Pediatric Concerns: None reported via milk. Poor oral absorption of tetracyclines generally limits effects.

Drug Interactions: Absorption may be reduced or delayed when used with dairy products, calcium, magnesium, or aluminum containing antacids, oral contraceptives, iron, zinc, sodium bicarbonate, penicillins, cimetidine.   Increased toxicity may result when used with methoxiflurane anesthesia. Use with warfarin anticoagulants may increase anticoagulation.

AHL = 6-12 hours	M/P = 0.6-0.8
PHL =	PB = 25%
PK = 1.5-4 hours	Oral = 75%
MW = 444	pKa =
Vd =	

References:
1. Knowles JA, Drugs in milk. Pediatr Curr 21:28-32,1972.
2. Posner AC, Prigot A & Konicoff NG: Further observations on the use of tetracycline hydrochloride in prophylaxis and treatment of obstetric infections. Antibiotics Annual 1954-1955. In: Medical Encyclopedia, New York 594-598, 1955.

Thallium-201   Fax #1600

Trade: Thallium-201
Can/Aus/UK:
Uses: Radioactive tracer
AAP: Not reviewed

Thallium-201 in the form of thallous chloride is used extensively for myocardial perfusion imaging to delineate ischemic myocardium. Following infusion, almost 85% of the administered dose is extracted into the heart on the first pass. Less than 5% of the dose remains free in the plasma in as little as 5 minutes after administration. Whereas Thallium-201 has a radioactive half-life of only 73 hours, the whole-body half-life of the Thallium ion is about 10 days. Most all radiation will be decayed in 5-6 half-lives (15 days). In a study of one breastfeeding patient who received 111MBq (3 mCi) for a brain scan, the amount of Thallium-201 in breast milk at 4 hours was 326 Bq/mL, and subsequently dropped to 87 Bq/mL after 72 hours. Even without interrupting breastfeeding, the infant would have received less than the NCRP radiation safety guideline dose for infrequent exposure for a 1 year old infant. However, a brief interruption of breastfeeding was nevertheless recommended. The length of interrupted breastfeeding is dependent on age of infant and dose of Thallium. With an interruption time varying from 2, 24, 48, to 96 hours, the respective Thallium dose to the infant would be 0.442, 0.283, 0.197, and 0.101 MBq compared to the maternal dose of 111 MBq. In another study (Murphy, 1989) of a breastfeeding mother who received 111 MBq (3 mCi), the calculated dose an infant (without any interruption of breastfeeding and assuming the consumption of 1000 mL of milk daily) would receive is approximately 0.81 MBq which is presently less than the maximal allowed radiation dose (NCRP) for an infant. The authors therefore recommend that breastfeeding be discontinued for at least 24-48 hours following the administration of 111 MBq of Thallium-201. This would dramatically reduce overall exposure of the infant.

Alternatives:

Pregnancy Risk Category:

Adult Concerns:

Pediatric Concerns: None reported in one case, but a brief interruption (depending on dose) is advised.

Drug Interactions:

AHL = 73 hours		M/P =
PHL =		PB =
PK = < 60 minutes		Oral =
MW =		pKa =
Vd =		

References:
1. Johnston RE, Mukherji SK, et.al. Radiation dose from breastfeeding following administration of Thallium-201. J. Nucl. Med. 12:2079-2082, 1996.
2. Murphy PH, Beasley CW, et.al. Thallium-201 in human milk: Observations and radiological consequences. Health Physics 56(4):539-541, 1989.

Theophylline   Fax #1403

Trade: Aminophylline, Quibron, Theo-Dur
Can/Aus/UK: Theo-Dur, Pulmophylline, Quibron-T/SR, Austyn, Nuelin
Uses: Bronchodilator
AAP: Approved by the American Academy of Pediatrics for use in breastfeeding mothers

Theophylline is a methylzanthine bronchodilator. It has a prolonged half-life in neonates which may cause retention. Milk concentrations are approximately equal to the maternal plasma levels. If a mother is maintained at 10-20 µg/mL, the milk concentrations are closely equivalent. Estimates generally indicate that less than 1% of dose is absorbed by infant. Older infants (> 6 months) have drug kinetics similar to mother, which would reduce infant serum levels. Use of prolonged release forms by mother may alter adult half-life. Generally considered compatible with breastfeeding.

Alternatives:

Pregnancy Risk Category: C

Adult Concerns: Irritability, nausea, vomiting, tachycardia, seizures.

Pediatric Concerns: None reported via milk. Observe for nausea, vomiting, irritability.

Drug Interactions: Numerous drug interactions exist. Agents that decrease theophylline levels include barbiturates, phenytoin, ketoconazole, rifampin, cigarette smoking, carbamazepine, isoniazid, loop diuretics, and others. Agents that increase theophylline levels include allopurinol, beta blockers, calcium channel blockers, cimetidine, oral contraceptives, corticosteroids, disulfiram, ephedrine, influenza virus vaccine, interferon, macrolides, mexiletine, quinolones, thiabendazole, thyroid hormones, carbamazepine, isoniazid, and loop diuretics.

AHL = 3-12.8 hours		**M/P**	= 0.67
PHL = 30 hours		**PB**	= 56%
PK = 1-2 hours (oral)		**Oral**	= 76%
MW = 180		**pKa**	= 8.6
Vd = 0.3-0.7			

References:
1. Stec GP, Grenberger P, Ruo TI, et.al. Kinetics of theophylline transfer to breast milk. Clin Pharmacol Ther. 28:404-408, 1980.

Thiabendazole   Fax #1492

Trade: Mintezol
Can/Aus/UK: Mintezol
Uses: Anthelmintic, antiparasitic
AAP: Not reviewed

Thiabendazole is an antiparasitic agent for the treatment of roundworm, pinworm, hookworm, whipworm, and other parasitic infections. After absorption it is completely eliminated from the plasma by 48 hours, although most is excreted within 24 hours. Can be used in children. Although it is effective in pinworms, other agents with less side effects are preferred. No reports on its transfer to breast milk have been found.

Alternatives: Pyrantel

Pregnancy Risk Category: C

Adult Concerns: Hypotension, nausea, vomiting, psychotic reactions (seizures, hallucinations, delirium), rash, pruritus, intrahepatic cholestasis. Transient milk hepatitis.

Pediatric Concerns: None reported.

Drug Interactions: May increase theophylline and other xanthines levels by 50%.

AHL =		M/P =	
PHL =		PB =	
PK = 1-2 hours		Oral = Complete	
MW = 201		pKa =	
Vd =			

References:

Thiopental Sodium   Fax #1520

Trade: Pentothal
Can/Aus/UK: Pentothal, Intraval
Uses: Barbiturate anesthetic agent
AAP: Approved by the American Academy of Pediatrics for use in breastfeeding mothers

Thiopental is an ultra short acting barbiturate sedative. Used in the induction phase of anesthesia, it rapidly redistributes from the brain to adipose and muscle tissue, hence the plasma levels are small, and the sedative effects are virtually gone in 20 minutes. Thiopental sodium is secreted into milk in low levels. In a study of two groups of 8 women who received from 5.0 to 5.4 mg/Kg thiopental sodium, the maximum concentration in breast milk 0.9 mg/L in mature milk and in colostrum was 0.34 mg/L. The milk:plasma ratio was 0.3 for colostrum and 0.4 for mature milk. The maximum daily dose to infant would be 0.135 mg/kg, or approximately 3% of the adult dose.

Alternatives:

Pregnancy Risk Category: C

Adult Concerns: Hemolytic anemia has been reported. Respiratory depression, renal failure, delirium, nausea, vomiting, pruritus.

Pediatric Concerns: None reported in a study of 16 women receiving induction doses.

Drug Interactions: Increased depression when used with CNS depressants (especially opiates and phenothiazines), and with salicylates or sulfisoxazole.

AHL = 3-8 hours		**M/P** = 0.3-0.4	
PHL = 15 hours		**PB** = 60-96%	
PK = 1-2 minutes		**Oral** = Variable	
MW = 264		**pKa** =	
Vd = 1.4			

References:

1. Anderson LW, Qvist T, et al: Concentrations of thiopentone in mature breast milk and colostrum following an induction dose. Acta Anaesth Scand. 31(1):30-2, 1987.

Thioridazine   Fax #1404

Trade: Mellaril
Can/Aus/UK: Apo-Thioridazine, Mellaril, Novo-Ridazine, Aldazine
Uses: Antipsychotic
AAP: Not reviewed

Thioridazine is a potent phenothiazine tranquilizer. It has a high volume of distribution, and long half-life. No data are available on its secretion into human milk, but it should be expected. Pediatric indications (2-12 years of age) are available.

Alternatives:

Pregnancy Risk Category: C

Adult Concerns: Blood dyscrasia, arrhythmias, sedation, gynecomastia, nausea, vomiting, constipation, dry mouth, retinopathy.

Pediatric Concerns: None reported due to limited studies.

Drug Interactions: Alcohol may enhance CNS depression. Aluminum salts may reduce GI absorption. Other anticholinergics may reduce the therapeutic actions the phenothiazines. Barbiturates may reduce phenothiazine plasma levels. Bromocriptine effectiveness may be inhibited by phenothiazines. Propranolol and phenothiazines may result in increased plasma levels of both drugs. Tricyclic antidepressant concentrations, serum concentrations may be increased the phenothiazines. Valproic acid clearance may be decreased.

AHL = 21-24 hours	M/P	=
PHL =	PB	=
PK =	Oral	= Complete
MW = 371	pKa	= 9.5
Vd = 18		

References:
1. O'Brien, T. Excretion of drugs in human milk. Am.J. Hosp. Pharm. 31:844-854, 1974.

Thyroid Scan   Fax #1441

Trade: Thyroid Scan
Can/Aus/UK:
Uses: Radiographic scan of thyroid gland
AAP: Not reviewed

Thyroid scanning with radioiodine (^{131}I) or technetium 99m is useful in delineating structural abnormalities of the thyroid, e.g., to distinguish Grave's disease from multinodular goiter and a single toxic adenoma or to determine the functional state of a single nodule ("hot" vs "cold").In one procedure, the radiologist uses radioactive Technetium-99m pertechnate which has a short half-life of 6.7 hours. At least 97% of the radioactivity would be decayed in 5 half-lives (33.5 hours), after which it would be presumably safe to breastfeed. In the second procedure (an uptake scan), radioactive Iodine-131 is used. The radioactive half-life of ^{131}I is 8.1 days. Five half-lives in this situation is 40.5 days. Although the biologic half-life of iodine would be less than the 40.5 days, it is not known with certainty how long is required before breast milk samples are at background levels. For safety in this case, breast milk samples should be counted by a gamma counter prior to restarting breastfeeding. ^{131}I is sequestered in high concentrations in breast milk, and breast milk levels could be exceedingly high. Excessive exposure of the infants thyroid to ^{131}I is exceedingly dangerous.

Alternatives:

Pregnancy Risk Category:

Adult Concerns: High milk radioactive levels.

Pediatric Concerns: Possible thyroid suppression is possible if high levels of ^{131}I are used.   Count breast milk samples to determine radiation levels.

Drug Interactions:

References:
1.   American Academy of Pediatrics, Committee on Drugs. Transfer

of drugs and other chemicals into human milk. Pediatrics 93(1):137-150, 1994.

2. Palmer, KE. Excretion of 125-I in breast milk following administration of labelled fibrinogen. Br. J. Radiol. 52:672, 1979.
3. Karjalainen, P, et.al. The amount and form of radioactivity in human milk after lung scanning, renography and placental localization by 131-I labelled tracers. Acta Obstet Gynecol Scand 50:357, 1971.
4. Hedrick WR. et.al. Radiation dosimetry from breast milk excretion of radioiodine and pertechnetate. J. Nucl. Med. 27:1569, 1986.
5. Romney B, Nickoloff EL, Esser PD. Excretion of radioiodine in breast milk. J. Nucl. Med. 30:124-6,1989.
6. Robinson PS, Barker P, Campbell A, et.al. Iodine-131 in breast milk following therapy for thyroid carcinoma. J. Nuci. Med. 35:1797-1801, 1994.

Thyrotropin   Fax #1405

Trade: Thyrotropin, TSH
Can/Aus/UK:
Uses: Excess TSH, Thyrotropin, hypothyroidism
AAP: Not reviewed

Thyroid stimulating hormone (Thyrotropin, TSH) is known to be secreted into breast milk. TSH is extremely elevated in hypothyroid mothers and could presumably cause a hyperthyroid condition in the breastfeeding infant. The level of TSH secreted into milk was determined in a hyperthyroid mother (Plasma TSH=110 mU/L). The breast milk TSH was low (Milk TSH= 1.4 mU/L) suggesting that human breast milk does not contain excessive amounts of TSH in the presence of severe maternal hypothyroidism, and that breastfeeding is permissible in hypothyroid mothers.

Alternatives:

Pregnancy Risk Category: C

Adult Concerns: Elevated thyroxine levels in breastfeeding infant.

Pediatric Concerns: None reported via milk. Breastfeeding by hyperthyroid mother is permissible.

Drug Interactions:

AHL =		M/P	=
PHL =		PB	=
PK =		Oral	= Poor
MW =		pKa	=
Vd =			

References:
1. Robinson P, Hoad K. Thyrotropin in human breast milk. Aust. NZ. J. Med. 24:68, 1994.

Ticarcillin   Fax #1407

Trade: Ticarcillin, Ticar, Timentin
Can/Aus/UK: Ticar, Tarcil, Ticillin
Uses: Penicillin antibiotic
AAP: Approved by the American Academy of Pediatrics for use in breastfeeding mothers

Ticarcillin is an extended-spectrum penicillin, used only IM or IV, and is not appreciably absorbed via oral ingestion. As with penicillins only minimal levels are secreted into milk. Poor oral absorption would limit exposure of breastfeeding infant. May cause changes in GI flora and possibly fungal overgrowth. Timentin is ticarcillin with clavulanate added (See Augmentin).

Alternatives:

Pregnancy Risk Category: B

Adult Concerns: Neutropenia, anemia, kidney toxicity. Changes in GI flora, diarrhea, candida overgrowth.

Pediatric Concerns: None reported via milk. Observe for changes in GI flora, diarrhea.

Drug Interactions: Probenecid may increase penicillin levels. Tetracyclines may decrease penicillin effectiveness.

AHL = 0.9-1.3 hours		M/P	=
PHL = 3.5 - 5.6 hours (neonate)		PB	= 54%
PK = 0.5 - 1.25 hours (IM)		Oral	= Poor
MW = 384		pKa	=
Vd =			

References:
1. Drug Facts and Comparisons. 1995 ed. Facts and Comparisons, St. Louis.
2. Pharmaceutical Manufacturer's Package Insert, 1995.

Ticlopidine   Fax #1464

Trade: Ticlid
Can/Aus/UK: Ticlid
Uses: Inhibits platelet aggregation
AAP: Not reviewed

Ticlopidine is useful in preventing thromboembolic disorders, increased cardiovascular mortality, stroke, infarcts, and other clotting disorders. Ticlopidine is reported to be excreted into rodent milk. No data are available on penetration into human breast milk. However it is highly protein bound, and the levels of ticlopidine in plasma are quite low. The manufacturer recommends against use in breastfeeding mothers.

Alternatives:

Pregnancy Risk Category: B

Adult Concerns: Bleeding, neutropenia, maculopapular rash.

Pediatric Concerns: None reported via milk, but caution is recommended.

Drug Interactions: Antacids may reduce absorption of ticlopidine. Chronic cimetidine administration has reduced the clearance of ticlopidine by 50%. Use of aspirin may alter platelet aggregation. Digoxin plasma levels may be slightly decreased by 15%. Theophylline elimination half-life was significantly increased from 8-10 hours.

AHL = 12.6 hours		**M/P** =	
PHL =		**PB** = 98%	
PK = 2 hours		**Oral** = 80%	
MW = 264		**pKa** =	
Vd =			

References:
1. Pharmaceutical Manufacturer's Package Insert, 1996.

Timolol   Fax #1408

Trade: Blocadren
Can/Aus/UK: Apo-Timol, Blocadren, Timoptic, Novo-Timol Tenopt, Timpilo, Betim, Timoptol
Uses: Beta blocker for hypertension and glaucoma
AAP: Approved by the American Academy of Pediatrics for use in breastfeeding mothers

Timolol is a beta blocker used for treating hypertension and glaucoma. It is secreted into milk. Following a dose of 5 mg three times daily, milk levels averaged 15.9 µg/L. Both oral and ophthalmic drops produce modest levels in milk. Breast milk levels following ophthalmic use of 0.5% timolol drops was 5.6 µg/L at 1.5 hours after the dose. Untoward effects on infant have not been reported. These levels are probably too small to be clinically relevant.

Alternatives: Propranolol, Metoprolol

Pregnancy Risk Category: C

Adult Concerns: Hypotension, bradycardia, depression, sedation.

Pediatric Concerns: None reported via milk, but observe for hypotension, weakness, hypoglycemia, sedation, depression.

Drug Interactions: Decreased effect when used with aluminum salts, barbiturates, calcium salts, cholestyramine, NSAIDs, ampicillin, rifampin, and salicylates. Beta blockers may reduce the effect of oral sulfonylureas (hypoglycemic agents). Increased toxicity/effect when used with other antihypertensives, contraceptives, MAO inhibitors, cimetidine, and numerous other products. See drug interaction reference for complete listing.

AHL = 4 hours	M/P = 0.8
PHL =	PB = 10%
PK = 1-2 hours	Oral = 50%
MW = 316	pKa = 8.8
Vd = 1-3	

References:
1. Fidler J, et. al. Excretion of oxprenolol and timolol in breast milk. Br J Obstet Gynaecol 90:961-5, 1983.
2. Lustgarten JS, Podos SM. Topical timolol and the nursing mother. Arch Ophthalmol 101:1381-2, 1983.

Tobramycin   Fax #1409

Trade: Nebcin, Tobrex
Can/Aus/UK: Nebcin, Tobrex, Tobralex
Uses: Ophthalmic antibiotic
AAP: Not reviewed

Tobramycin is an aminoglycoside antibiotic similar to gentamicin. Although small levels of tobramycin are known to transfer into milk, they probably pose few problems. In one study of 5 patients, following an 80 mg IM dose, tobramycin levels in milk ranged from undetectable to 0.5 µg/mL. Tobramycin is poorly absorbed orally and would be unlikely to produce significant levels in an infant.

Alternatives:

Pregnancy Risk Category: C

Adult Concerns: Changes in GI flora.

Pediatric Concerns:

Drug Interactions: Increased toxicity when used with certain penicillins, cephalosporins, amphotericin B, loop diuretics, and neuromuscular blocking agents.

AHL = 2-3 hours		M/P =	
PHL = 4.6 hours (neonates)		PB = <5%	
PK = 30-90 min.(IM)		Oral =	
MW = 468		pKa = ?	
Vd = 0.22-0.31			

References:
1. Pharmaceutical Manufacturer's Package Insert, 1996.
2. Takase Z. Laboratory and clinical studies on tobramycin in the field of obstetrics and gynecology. Chemotherapy(Tokyo) 23:1402, 1975.
3. McEvoy GE(ed):AHFS Drug Information, New York, NY. 1995.

Tolbutamide   Fax #1410

Trade: Oramide, Orinase
Can/Aus/UK: Apo-Tolbutamide, Mobenol, Novo-Butamide, Orinase, Rastinon, Glyconon
Uses: Antidiabetic
AAP: Approved by the American Academy of Pediatrics for use in breastfeeding mothers

Tolbutamide is a short-acting sulfonylurea used to stimulate insulin secretion in type II diabetics. Only low levels are secreted into breast milk. Following a dose of 500 mg twice daily, milk levels in two patients were 3 and 18 mg/L respectively. Maternal serum levels averaged 35 and 45 µg/L. An infant consuming 1 L of milk daily would only ingest 1.8% of the maternal dose daily. Observe infant closely for jaundice and hypoglycemia. Use only with close observation and caution. See chlorpropamide.

Alternatives:

Pregnancy Risk Category: D

Adult Concerns: Hypoglycemia, nausea, dyspepsia.

Pediatric Concerns: None reported via milk.

Drug Interactions: The hypoglycemic effect may be enhanced by : anticoagulants, chloramphenicol, clofibrate, fenfluramine, fluconazole, H2 antagonists, magnesium salts, methyldopa, MAO inhibitors, probenecid, salicylcates, TCAs, sulfonamides. The hypoglycemic effect may be reduced by: beta blockers, cholestyramine, diazoxide, phenytoin, rifampin, thiazide diuretics.

AHL = 4.5-6.5 hours		**M/P**	= 0.09-0.4
PHL =		**PB**	= 93%
PK = 3.5 hours		**Oral**	= Complete
MW = 270		**pKa**	= 5.3
Vd = 0.10-0.15			

References:
1. Moiel RH, Ryan JR. Tolbutamide (Orinase) in human breast milk. Clin Pediatr 6:480, 1967.

Tolmetin Sodium   Fax #1411

Trade: Tolectin
Can/Aus/UK: Tolectin
Uses: Non-steroidal analgesic, used for arthritis, etc.
AAP: Approved by the American Academy of Pediatrics for use in breastfeeding mothers

Tolmetin is a standard non-steroidal analgesic. Tolmetin is known to be distributed into milk but in small amounts. In one patient given 400 mg, the milk level at 0.67 hours was 0.18 mg/L. The estimate of dose per day an infant would receive is 115 µg/Liter of milk. Tolmetin is sometimes used in pediatric rheumatoid patients (>2 yrs).

Alternatives: Ibuprofen

Pregnancy Risk Category: C

Adult Concerns: GI distress, bleeding, vomiting, nausea, edema.

Pediatric Concerns: None reported via milk.

Drug Interactions: May prolong prothrombin time when used with warfarin. Antihypertensive effects of ACEi family may be blunted or completely abolished by NSAIDs. Some NSAIDs may block antihypertensive effect of beta blockers, diuretics. Used with cyclosporin, may dramatically increase renal toxicity. May increase digoxin, phenytoin, lithium levels. May increase toxicity of methotrexate. May increase bioavailability of penicillamine. Probenecid may increase NSAID levels.

AHL = 1-1.5 hours	M/P	= 0.0055
PHL =	PB	= 99%
PK = 0.5-1 hr.	Oral	= Complete
MW = 257	pKa	= 3.5
Vd =		

References:
1. Sagraves R, Waller ES, Goehrs HR. Tolmetin in breast milk. Drug Intell. Clin. Pharm. 19:55-6, 1985.

Topiramate   Fax #1502

Trade: Topamax
Can/Aus/UK: Topamax
Uses: Anticonvulsant
AAP: Not reviewed

Topiramate is a new anticonvulsant used in controlling refractory partial seizures. Very little is known about this new product. Its ability to penetrate the CNS, its rather long half-life, and its effect on reducing cognition would not make this a preferred product for breastfeeding mothers nor their infants. Use caution until more is known.

Alternatives:

Pregnancy Risk Category:

Adult Concerns: Topiramate induces a significant Cognitive dysfunction, particularly in older patients. Paresthesias, sedation, weight loss(7%), diarrhea.

Pediatric Concerns: None reported but use with caution. No studies are available.

Drug Interactions:

AHL = 18-24 hours	M/P	=
PHL =	PB	= 15%
PK = 1.5-4 hours	Oral	= 75%
MW =	pKa	=
Vd = 0.7		

References:
1. Patsalos PN and Sander J: Newer antiepileptic drugs: towards an improved risk-benefit ratio. Drug Safety 11:37-67,1994.
2. Bialer M: Comparative pharmacokinetics of the newer antiepileptic drugs. Clin Pharmacokinet 24:441-452, 1993.
3. Britton JW and So EL: New antiepileptic drugs: prospects for the future. J Epilepsy 8:267-281, 1995.

Torsemide   Fax #1412

Trade: Demadex
Can/Aus/UK: Demadex, Torem
Uses: Potent Loop diuretic
AAP: Not reviewed

Torsemide is a potent loop diuretic generally used in congestive heart failure and other conditions which require a strong diuretic. There are no reports of its transfer into human milk. Its extraordinary high protein binding would likely limit its transfer into human milk. As with many diuretics, reduction of plasma volume and hypotension may adversely reduce milk production although this is rare. See furosemide.

Alternatives: Furosemide

Pregnancy Risk Category: B

Adult Concerns: Hypotension, hypokalemia, volume depletion, headache, excessive urination, dizziness.

Pediatric Concerns: None reported. Renal calcification has been reported with other loop diuretics in premature infants, but not via milk supply.

Drug Interactions: When used with salicylates, elevated plasma salicylate levels may occur. Co-administration with other NSAIDS may increase the risk of renal dysfunction. Cholestyramine administration reduces bioavailability of torsemide. Use caution in using with lithium.

AHL = 3.5 hours		**M/P** =	
PHL =		**PB** = >99%	
PK = 1 hour		**Oral** = 80%	
MW = 348		**pKa** =	
Vd = 0.21			

References:
1. Pharmaceutical Manufacturer's Package Insert, 1997.

Tramadol HCL   Fax #1413

Trade: Ultram
Can/Aus/UK: Tramake, Zydol
Uses: Analgesic
AAP: Not reviewed

Tramadol is a new class analgesic that most closely resembles the opiates, although it is not a controlled substance and appears to have reduced addictive potential. It appears to be slightly more potent than codeine. After oral use, its onset of analgesia is within 1 hour and reaches a peak in 2-3 hours. Following a single IV 100 mg dose of tramadol, the cumulative excretion in breast milk within 16 hours was 100 μg of tramadol (0.1% of the maternal dose) and 27 μg of the M1 metabolite.

Alternatives: Codeine, Hydrocodone

Pregnancy Risk Category: C

Adult Concerns: Sedation, respiratory depression, nausea, vomiting, constipation.

Pediatric Concerns: None reported via milk. Observe for sedation.

Drug Interactions: Use with carbamazepine dramatically increases tramadol metabolism and reduces plasma levels. Use with MAOI may increase toxicity.

AHL = 7 hours	**M/P** = 0.1
PHL =	**PB** = 20%
PK = 2 hours	**Oral** = 60%
MW = 263	**pKa** =
Vd =	

References:
1. Pharmaceutical Manufacturer's Package Insert, 1996.

Trazodone   Fax #1414

Trade: Desyrel
Can/Aus/UK: Desyrel, Trazorel, Apo-Trazodone, Novo-Trazodone, Molipaxin
Uses: Antidepressant, serotonin reuptake inhibitor
AAP: Drugs whose effect on nursing infants is unknown but may be of concern

Trazodone is an antidepressant whose structure is dissimilar to the tricyclics and to the other antidepressants.   In six mothers who received a single 50 mg dose, the milk:plasma ratio averaged 0.14. Peak milk concentrations occurred at 2 hours.   On a weight basis, an adult would receive 0.77 mg/kg whereas a breastfeeding infant, using this data, would consume only 0.005 mg/kg.   About 0.6 % of the maternal dose was ingested by the infant.

Alternatives:

Pregnancy Risk Category: C

Adult Concerns: Dry mouth, sedation, hypotension, blurred vision.

Pediatric Concerns: None reported via milk.

Drug Interactions: May enhance the CNS depressant effect of alcohol, barbiturates, and other CNS depressants. Digoxin serum levels may be increased. Use caution when administering with MAOI. Phenytoin serum levels may be increased.   Use with warfarin may increase anticoagulant effect.

AHL = 4-9 hours		M/P	= 0.142
PHL =		PB	= 85-95%
PK = 1-2 hours		Oral	= 65%
MW = 372		pKa	=
Vd = 0.9-1.5			

References:
1.   Verbeeck RK, Ross SG, and McKenna EA. Excretion of

trazodone in breast milk. Br.J.Clin.Pharmacol. 22:367-370,1986.

Tretinoin   Fax #1415

Trade: Retin - A
Can/Aus/UK: Retin-A, Stieva-A, Vitamin A Acid, Renova Vesanoid
Uses: Topically for acne
AAP: Not reviewed

Tretinoin is a retinoid derivative similar to Vitamin A. It is primarily used topically for acne and wrinkling, and sometimes administered orally for leukemias and psoriasis. Used topically, tretinoin stimulates epithelial turnover and reduces cell cohesiveness. Blood concentrations are essentially zero. Absorption of Retin-A via topical sources is reported to be minimal, and breast milk would likely be minimal to none. However, if it is used orally, transfer into milk is likely and should be used with great caution in a breastfeeding mother.

Alternatives:

Pregnancy Risk Category: B topically
                            D orally

Adult Concerns: Leukocytosis, dry skin, skin irritation, blistering, scaling, pigmentary changes, nausea, vomiting. Side effects of oral use are similar to hypervitaminosis A, and include headache, increased CSF pressure, anorexia, nausea. scaling of skin, fatigue, hepatosplenomegaly.

Pediatric Concerns: None reported via milk.

Drug Interactions: Use other topical medications such as sulfur, resorcinol ,benzoyl peroxide or salicylic acid with caution due to accelerated skin irritation.

AHL = 2 hours	**M/P**	**=**
PHL =	**PB**	**=**

PK =	**Oral** = 70%
MW = 300	**pKa** =
Vd = 0.44	

References:
1.   Zbinden G. Investigation on the toxicity of tretinoin administered systemically to animals. Acta Derm Verereol Suppl(Stockh) 74:36-40,1975.
2.   Lucek RW, Colburn WA: Clinical pharmacokinetics of the retinoids. Clin Pharmacokinet 10:38-62, 1985.

Triamcinolone Acetonide   Fax #1473

Trade: Nasacort, Azmacort
Can/Aus/UK: Aristocort, Azmacort, Kenalog, Triaderm, Nasacort, Kenalone, Adcortyl
Uses: Corticosteroid
AAP: Not reviewed

Triamcinolone is a typical corticosteroid (see prednisone) that is available for topical, intranasal, injection, inhalation, and oral use. When applied topically to the nose (Nasacort) or to the lungs (Azmacort) only minimal doses are used and plasma levels are exceedingly low to undetectable. Although no data are available on triamcinolone secretion into human milk, it is likely that the milk levels would be exceedingly low and not clinically relevant when administered via inhalation or intra-nasally.   Whereas the oral adult dose is 4-48 mg/day, the inhaled dose is 200 mcg three times daily, and the intranasal dose is 220 mcg/day.

Alternatives:

Pregnancy Risk Category: C

Adult Concerns: Intranasal and inhaled: nasal irritation, dry mucous membranes, sneezing, throat irritation, hoarseness, candida overgrowth.

Pediatric Concerns: None reported via milk.   Observe growth rate.

Drug Interactions:

AHL	= 88 minutes	M/P	=
PHL	=	PB	=
PK	=	Oral	= Complete
MW	= 434	pKa	=
Vd	=		

References:
1.   Pharmaceutical Manufacturer's Package Insert, 1996.

Triamterene   Fax #1592

Trade: Dyazide
Can/Aus/UK: Dyrenium, Hydrene, Dyazide
Uses: Diuretic
AAP: Not reviewed

Triamterene is a potassium-sparing diuretic, commonly used in combination with thiazide diuretics such as hydrochlorothiazide (Dyazide). Plasma levels average 26-30 nanograms/mL. No data are available on the transfer of triamterene into human milk, but it is known to transfer into animal milk. Because of the availability of other less dangerous diuretics, triamterene should be used as a last resort in breastfeeding mothers.

Alternatives: Hydrochlorothiazide

Pregnancy Risk Category: B

Adult Concerns: Leukopenia, hyperkalemia, diarrhea, nausea, vomiting, hepatitis.

Pediatric Concerns: None reported via milk.

Drug Interactions: Hyperkalemia when administered with potassium supplements. Triamterene may reduce clearance of amantadine. May increase plasma potassium levels when administered with amiloride, or

ACE inhibitors, cyclosporine. May reduce clearance of lithium. Enhanced bone marrow suppression when administered with methotrexate. Use with spironolactone may result in hyperkalemia.

AHL	= 1.5-2.5 hours	M/P	=
PHL	= 4.3 hours	PB	= 55%
PK	= 1.5-3 hours	Oral	= 30-70%
MW	= 253	pKa	=
Vd	=		

References:
1. Mutschler E, Gilfrich HJ, Knauf H et al: Pharmacokinetics of triamterene. Clin Exper Hyper-theory Pract A5:249-269, 1983.
2. Pharmaceutical Manufacturer's package insert, 1995.

Triazolam   Fax #1416

Trade: Halcion
Can/Aus/UK: Apo-Triazo, Halcion, Novo-Triolam
Uses: Benzodiazepine (Valium-like) hypnotic
AAP: Not reviewed

Triazolam is a typical benzodiazepine used as a nighttime sedative. Animal studies indicate that triazolam is secreted into milk, although levels in human milk have not been reported. As with all the benzodiazepines, significant penetration into breast milk is likely.

Alternatives: Lorazepam, Alprazolam

Pregnancy Risk Category: X

Adult Concerns: Sedation, addiction.

Pediatric Concerns: None reported for triazolam, but side effects for benzodiazepines include sedation, depression.

Drug Interactions: See diazepam.

AHL = 1.5-5.5 hours   M/P =

PHL =	**PB** = 89%
PK = 0.5-2 hours	**Oral** = 85%
MW = 343	**pKa** =
Vd = 1.1-2.7	

References:
1. Drug Facts and Comparisons. 1995 ed. Facts and Comparisons, St. Louis.

Trimeprazine   Fax #1417

Trade: Temaril
Can/Aus/UK: Panectyl, Vallergan
Uses: Antihistamine, antipruritic.
AAP: Not reviewed

Trimeprazine is an antihistamine from the phenothiazine family used for itching. It is secreted into human milk, but in very low levels. Exact data are not available.

Alternatives:

Pregnancy Risk Category: C

Adult Concerns: Sedation, hypotension, bradycardia.

Pediatric Concerns: None reported, but as with other antihistamines, observe for sedation.

Drug Interactions:

AHL = 5 hours.	**M/P** =
PHL =	**PB** =
PK = 3.5 hours.	**Oral** = 70%
MW = 298	**pKa** =
Vd =	

References:
1. O'Brien, T. Excretion of drugs in human milk. Am.J. Hosp.

Pharm. 31:844-854, 1974.

Trimethoprim   Fax #1418

Trade: Proloprim, Trimpex
Can/Aus/UK: Proloprim, Alprim, Triprim, Ipral, Monotrim, Tiempe
Uses: Antibiotic
AAP: Approved by the American Academy of Pediatrics for use in breastfeeding mothers

Trimethoprim is an inhibitor of folic acid production in bacteria. In one study of 50 patients, average milk levels were 2.0 mg/L. Milk:plasma ratio was 1.25. In another group of mothers receiving 160 mg 2-4 times daily, concentrations of 1.2 to 5.5 mg/L were reported in milk. Because it may interfere with folate metabolism, use with caution. However, trimethoprim apparently poses few problems in full term or older infants. PHL= 14.7-40 hours (neonate), 5-6 hours (older infants).

Alternatives:

Pregnancy Risk Category: C

Adult Concerns: Rash, pruritus nausea, vomiting, anorexia, altered taste sensation.

Pediatric Concerns:

Drug Interactions: May increase phenytoin plasma levels.

AHL = 8-10 hours		**M/P**	= 1.25
PHL = 14.7-40 hours (neonate)		**PB**	= 44%
PK = 1-4 hours		**Oral**	= Complete
MW = 290		**pKa**	=
Vd =			

References:
1.   Miller RD, Salter AJ.   The passage of trimethoprim/

sulphamethoxazole into breast milk and its significance. In Daikos GK, ed. Progress in Chemotherapy, Proceedings of the Eighth International Congress of Chemotherapy, Athens, 1973. Athens:Hellenic Society for Chemotherapy, 687-91, 1974.
2.   Pagliaro and Levin (Eds): Problems in Pediatric Drug Therapy. Drug Intelligence Publications, Hamilton, IL, 1979.

Tripelennamine   Fax #1420

Trade: PBZ
Can/Aus/UK: Pyrabenzamine
Uses: Antihistamine
AAP: Not reviewed

Tripelennamine is an older class of antihistamine. This product is generally not recommended in pediatric patients, particularly neonates due to increased sleep apnea. The drug has been shown to be secreted into milk of animals. No human data exists.

Alternatives:

Pregnancy Risk Category: B

Adult Concerns: Sleep apnea in children, peptic ulcer, sedation, dry mouth, GI distress.

Pediatric Concerns: None reported, but observe for sedation, sleep apnea.

Drug Interactions: Increased sedation when used with CNS depressants, other antihistamines, alcohol, MAO inhibitors.

AHL = 2-3 hours	M/P =
PHL =	PB =
PK = 2 - 3 hours	Oral = Complete
MW = 255	pKa = 4.2,8.7
Vd = 9-12	

References:

1. O'Brien, T. Excretion of drugs in human milk. Am.J. Hosp. Pharm. 31:844-854, 1974.
2. Pharmaceutical Manufacturer's Package Insert, 1996.

Triprolidine   Fax #1421

Trade: Actidil
Can/Aus/UK: Actifed, Codral, Pro-Actidil
Uses: Antihistamine
AAP: Approved by the American Academy of Pediatrics for use in breastfeeding mothers

Triprolidine is an antihistamine. It is secreted into milk but in very small levels and is marketed with pseudoephedrine as Actifed. The average concentration in milk ranged from 1.2 to 4.4 µg/L over 24 hours. The estimated dose an infant would receive was 0.001-0.004 mg/24 hours which is 0.06 to 0.2% of the maternal dose. These doses are far too low to be clinically relevant.

Alternatives:

Pregnancy Risk Category: C

Adult Concerns: Sedation, dry mouth, anticholinergic side effects.

Pediatric Concerns: None reported. Observe for sedation.

Drug Interactions: Increased sedation when used with CNS depressants, other antihistamines, alcohol, MAO inhibitors.

AHL = 5 hours	M/P = 0.5-1.2
PHL =	PB =
PK = 2 hours	Oral = Complete
MW = 278	pKa =
Vd =	

References:
1. Findlay JWA, et.al. Pseudoephedrine and triprolidine in plasma and breast milk of nursing mothers. Br J Clin Pharmac 18:901-6,1984.

Troglitazone   Fax #1518

Trade: Rezulin
Can/Aus/UK: Rezulin
Uses: Hypoglycemic agent
AAP: Not reviewed

Troglitazone is a new compound with hypoglycemic properties. This product apparently reduces insulin resistance and is being investigated for the oral treatment of non-insulin-dependent diabetes. This medication is not chemically or functionally related to the oral sulfonylureas. Studies seem to suggest that troglitazone lowers blood glucose by improving target cell response to insulin. It requires the presence of insulin to work. It does not increase insulin secretion by the islet cells. Troglitazone decreases hepatic glucose output and increases insulin-dependent glucose disposal in skeletal muscle. Troglitazone is secreted in the milk of animals, although the levels have not been reported. Transfer into human milk has not yet been reported, but due to the high protein binding and large molecular weight, the amounts are likely to be small.

Alternatives:

Pregnancy Risk Category: B

Adult Concerns: Untoward effects have included vomiting, nausea, diarrhea, and skin rash. Decreases in red blood cell count, hemoglobin, and hematocrit have been reported. Abdominal fullness, elevated kidney toxicity (BUN) have been reported.

Pediatric Concerns: None reported.

Drug Interactions: Cholestyramine reduces the oral absorption of troglitazone by 70%. Co-administration of terfenadine with troglitazone reduces the plasma level of terfenadine by 50-70%. Co-administration with oral contraceptives reduces plasma levels of estradiol and norethindrone by 30% which could result in loss of contraception.

AHL = 16-34	M/P	=
PHL =	PB	= >99%
PK = 2-3 hours	Oral	= 50%
MW = 441	pKa	=
Vd = 10.5-26.5		

References:
1.   Pharmaceutical Manufacturer's Package Insert, 1997.

Trovafloxacin Mesylate   Fax #1596

Trade: Trovan, Alatrofloxacin
Can/Aus/UK:
Uses: Antibiotic
AAP: Not reviewed

Trovafloxacin mesylate is a synthetic broad-spectrum antibiotic for oral use.   The IV formula is called alatrofloxacin mesylate which is metabolized to trovafloxacin in vivo.   Trovafloxacin is a fluoroquinolone antibiotic similar to ciprofloxacin, norfloxacin and others.   Trovafloxacin was found in measurable but low concentrations in breast milk of three breastfeeding mothers. Following an IV dose of 300 mg trovafloxacin equivalent, and repeated oral 200 mg doses of trovafloxacin mg daily, breast milk levels averaged 0.8 mg/L and ranged from 0.3 to 2.1 mg per liter of milk.   This would average less than 0.4% of the maternal dose.

Alternatives: Norfloxacin, Ofloxacin

Pregnancy Risk Category: C

Adult Concerns: Dizziness, nausea, headache, vomiting, diarrhea have been reported.

Pediatric Concerns: None reported via milk. Only small amounts are secreted in milk.

Drug Interactions: Antacids, Morphine, Sucralfate, and iron significantly reduce oral absorption.

AHL	= 12,2 hours	M/P	=
PHL	=	PB	= 76%
PK	= 1,2 hours	Oral	= 88%
MW	= 512	pKa	=
Vd	= 1.3		

References:
1.   Pharmaceutical Manufacturer's package insert, 1998.

Typhoid Vaccine   Fax #1515

Trade: Vivotif, Berna, Typhim VI
Can/Aus/UK: Vivotif, Berna
Uses: Vaccination
AAP:

Typhoid vaccine promotes active immunity to typhoid fever.   It is available in an oral form (Ty21a) which is a live attenuated vaccine for oral administration.   The parenteral (injectable) form is derived from acetone-treated killed and dried bacteria, phenol-inactivated bacteria, or a special capsular polysaccharide vaccine extracted from killed S. typhi Ty21a strains. Due to a limited lipopolysaccharide coating, the Ty21a strains are limited in their ability to produce infection. No data are available on its transfer into human milk.   If immunization is required, a killed species would be preferred,   as infection of the neonate would be possible.

Alternatives:

Pregnancy Risk Category: C

Adult Concerns: Following oral administration, nausea, abdominal cramps, vomiting, urticaria. IM preparations may produce soreness at injection site, tenderness, malaise, headache, myalgia, fever.

Pediatric Concerns: None reported, but killed species suggested.

Drug Interactions: Use cautiously in patients receiving anticoagulants.

Do not co-administer with plague vaccine. Do not administer the live-attenuated varieties to immunocompromised patients. Phenytoin may reduce antibody response to this product. Do not use with sulfonamides.

References:

Urofollitropin   Fax #1528

Trade: Metrodin
Can/Aus/UK: Fertinorm HP, Metrodin
Uses: FSH, follicle stimulating hormone
AAP: Not reviewed

Urofollitropin is a preparation of gonadotropin (FSH) extracted from the urine of postmenopausal women. FSH is a large molecular weight peptide (34,000 daltons). Urofollitropin differs only slightly from pituitary FSH. In the female, FSH induces growth of the Graafian follicle in the ovary preparatory to the release of the ovum. Approximately 15 µg is secreted daily by the pituitary in normal individuals. It is not known if urofollitropin is secreted into human milk, but it is extremely unlikely due to its large molecular weight. Further, it would be largely destroyed in the infant's stomach and oral absorption by the infant would be extremely unlikely.

Alternatives:

Pregnancy Risk Category: X

Adult Concerns: Pulmonary and vascular complications, ovarian hyperstimulation, abdominal pain, fever and chills, abdominal pain, nausea, vomiting, diarrhea, pain at injection site, bruising. Ovarian hyperstimulation.

Pediatric Concerns: None reported via milk.

Drug Interactions: Urofollitropin does not effect prolactin levels.

AHL = 3.9 and 70.4 hours
PHL =
PK = 6-18 hours
MW = 34,000
Vd = 0.06, 1.08

M/P =
PB =
Oral = None
pKa =

References:

1. Sharma V, Riddle A, et al: Studies on folliculogenesis and in vitro fertilization outcome after the administration of follicle-stimulating hormone at different times during the menstrual cycle. Fertil Steril 51:298-303, 1989.
2. Kjeld JM, Harsoulis P, et al: Infusions of hFSH and hLH in normal men: kinetics of human follicle stimulating hormone. Acta Endocrinologica 81:225-233, 1976.
3. Yen SSC, Llerena LA, Pearson OH et al: Disappearance rates of endogenous follicle-stimulating hormone in serum following surgical hypophysectomy in man. J Clin Endocrinol 30:325-329, 1970.

Valacyclovir   Fax #1448

Trade: Valtrex
Can/Aus/UK: Valtrex Valaciclovir
Uses: Antiviral, for herpes simplex
AAP: Not reviewed See acyclovir.

Valacyclovir is a pro-drug that is rapidly metabolized in the plasma to acyclovir. Acyclovir is the active drug that is primarily used as an antiviral for herpes simplex and other viral infections. Valacyclovir has much better oral absorption that the parent drug, acyclovir. See acyclovir.

Alternatives: Acyclovir

Pregnancy Risk Category: B

Adult Concerns: Nausea, vomiting, diarrhea, sore throat, edema, and skin rashes.

Pediatric Concerns: None reported via milk.

Drug Interactions:

AHL = 2.5-3 hours		**M/P**	= 0.6-4.1
PHL = 3.2 hours (neonates)		**PB**	= 9-33%
PK = 1.5 hours		**Oral**	= 54%
MW =		**pKa**	=
Vd =			

References:
1. Pharmaceutical Manufacturer's Package Insert, 1995.

Valerian Officinalis   Fax #1594

Trade: Valerian Root
Can/Aus/UK:
Uses: Herbal sedative
AAP: Not reviewed

Valerian root is most commonly used as a sedative/hypnotic. Of the numerous chemicals present in the root, the most important chemical group appears to be the valepotriates. This family consists of at least a dozen or more related compounds, and is believed responsible for the sedative potential of this plant, although it is controversial. The combination of numerous components may inevitability account for the sedative response. Controlled studies in man have indicated a sedative/hypnotic effect with fewer night awakenings and significant somnolence. The toxicity of valerian root appears to be low, with only minor side effects reported. However, the valepotriates have been found to be cytotoxic, with alkylating activity similar to other nitrogen mustard-like anti-cancer agents. Should this prove to be so in vivo, it may preclude the use of this product in humans. No data are available on the transfer of valerian root compounds into human milk. However, the use of sedatives in breastfeeding mothers is generally discouraged, due to a possible increased risk of SIDS.

Alternatives:

Pregnancy Risk Category:

Adult Concerns: Ataxia, hypothermia, muscle relaxation. Headaches, excitability, cardiac disturbances.

Pediatric Concerns: None reported via human milk.

Drug Interactions:

References:
1. Leathwood PD, et.al. Aqueous extract of valerian root improves sleep quality in man. Pharmacal. Biochem. Behav. 17:65, 1982.
2. Von Eickstedt KW, et.al. Psychopharmacologic effects of valepotriates. Arzneimittelforschung 19:316, 1969.
3. Leathwood PD, Chaufard F. Aqueous extract of valerian reduces sleep latency to fall asleep in man. Planta Med 51:144, 1985.

Valproic Acid   Fax #1422

Trade: Depakene, Depakote
Can/Aus/UK: Depakene, Novo-Valproic, Deproic, Epilim, Valpro, Convulex
Uses: Anticonvulsant
AAP: Approved by the American Academy of Pediatrics for use in breastfeeding mothers

Valproic acid is a popular anticonvulsant used in grand mal, petit mal, myoclonic, and temporal lobe seizures. Valproic acid transfers into human milk at very low levels, generally less than 3% of the maternal dose. Average concentrations in breast milk range from 0.17 to 0.47 mg/L of milk. Valproic acid is frequently used in neonates for seizures. It is considered compatible with breastfeeding. PHL=10-67 hours (neonate), 7-13 hours (older).

Alternatives:

Pregnancy Risk Category: D

Adult Concerns: Sedation, thrombocytopenia, tremor, nausea, diarrhea, liver toxicity.

Pediatric Concerns: None reported via milk.

Drug Interactions: Valproic acid levels may be reduced by charcoal, rifampin, carbamazepine, clonazepam, lamotrigine, phenytoin. Valproic acid levels may be increased when used with chlorpromazine, cimetidine, felbamate, salicylates, alcohol. Valproic acid use may increase levels or the effect of barbiturates, warfarin, benzodiazepines, clozapine.

AHL	= 14 hours	M/P	= 0.42
PHL	= 10-67 hours (neonate)	PB	= 94%
PK	= 1-4 hours	Oral	= Complete
MW	= 144	pKa	= 4.8
Vd	= 0.1-0.4		

References:
1. Nau H, Rating D, Koch S, et.al. Valproic acid and its metabolites: placental transfer, neonatal pharmacokinetics, transfer via mother's milk and clinical status in neonates of epileptic mothers. J. Pharmacol Exp Ther. 219:768-777,1981.
2. Johannessen SI. Pharmacokinetics of valproate in pregnancy: mother-foetus-newborn. Pharmaceutisch Weekblad 14(3A):114-7, 1992.

Vancomycin   Fax #1423

Trade: Vancocin
Can/Aus/UK: Vancocin, Vancoled
Uses: Antibiotic
AAP: Not reviewed

Vancomycin is an antimicrobial agent. Only low levels are secreted into human milk. Milk levels were 12.7 mg/L four hours after infusion in one woman receiving 1 gm every 12 hours for 7 days. Its poor absorption from the infants GI tract would limit its systemic absorption. Low levels in infant could provide alterations of GI flora. PHL= 5.9-9.8 hours (neonates), 4.1 hours (older).

Alternatives:

Pregnancy Risk Category: C

Adult Concerns: Alteration of GI flora, neutropenia, hypotension, kidney and hearing damage.

Pediatric Concerns: None reported via milk.

Drug Interactions: When used with aminoglycosides, risk of nephrotoxicity may be increased. Use with anesthetics may produce erythema and histamine-like flushing in children. May increase risk of neuromuscular blockade when used with neuromuscular blocking agents.

AHL = 5.6 hours	M/P =
PHL = 5.9-9.8 hours (neonates)	PB = 10-30%
PK =	Oral = Minimal
MW = 1449	pKa =
Vd = 0.3-0.7	

References:
1.   Reyes MP, et. al. Vancomycin during pregnancy: does it cause hearing loss or nephrotoxicity in the infant? Am J Obstet Gynecol 161:977-81, 1989.

Varicella Virus Vaccine   Fax #1442

Trade: Varivax
Can/Aus/UK:
Uses: Vaccination for Varicella(Chickenpox)
AAP: Not reviewed

A live attenuated varicella vaccine (Varivax - Merck) was recently approved for marketing by the US Food and Drug Administration. Although effective, it does not apparently provide the immunity attained from infection with the parent virus. The Oka/Merck strain used in the vaccine is attenuated by passage in human and embryonic guinea pig cell cultures. It is not known if vaccine-acquired VZV is secreted in human milk, or if it is infectious in infants. Varicella vaccine may be considered for a susceptible nursing mother, if risk of exposure to natural VZV is high (AAP).Mothers of immunodeficient infants should not breastfeed following use of this vaccine. In general, it would not be wise to use varicella vaccine in a mother of a breastfed infant, as minimal transfer of virus to the infant could (theoretical) blunt subsequent antibody titer in exposed infants (as seen with oral polio virus vaccine).Recommendations for Use: Varicella vaccine is only recommended for children > 1 year of age up to 12 years of age with no history of varicella infection.

Alternatives:

Pregnancy Risk Category: C

Adult Concerns: Tenderness and erythema at the injection site in about 25% of vaccinees and a sparse generalized maculopapular rash occurring within one month after immunization in about 5%. Spread of the vaccine virus to others has been reported. Susceptible, immunodeficient individuals should be protected from exposure.

Pediatric Concerns: None reported via milk, but no studies are available. Immunocompromised infants should not be exposed to this product.

Drug Interactions:

References:
1. Tsolia M, Gershon AA, et.al. Live attenuated varicella vaccine: evidence that the virus is attenuated and the importance of skin lesions in transmission of varicella-zoster virus. J Pediatr, 116:184, 1990.
2. Hughes P, LaRussa P. et.al. Transmission of varicella-zoster virus froma a vaccinee with leukemia, demonstrated by polymerase chain reaction. J Pediatr, 124:932, 1994.

3.   American Academy of Pediatrics.   Committee on Infectious
      Diseases. Red Book 1997.

Varicella-Zoster Virus   Fax #1424

Trade: Chickenpox
Can/Aus/UK:
Uses: Chickenpox
AAP: Not reviewed

Chickenpox virus has been reported to be transferred via breast milk in
one 27 year old mother who developed chickenpox postpartum. Her 2
month old son also developed the disease 16 days after the mother.
Chickenpox virus was detected in the mother's milk and may suggest
that transmission can occur via breast milk. According to the AAP,
neonates born to mothers with active varicella should be placed in
isolation at birth and, if still hospitalized, until 21 or 28 days of age,
depending on whether they received VZIG (Varicella Zoster Immune
Globulin).   Candidates for VZIG include: immunocompromised
children, pregnant women, newborn infant whose mother has onset of
VZV within 5 days before or 48 hours after delivery.

Alternatives:

Pregnancy Risk Category:

Adult Concerns:

Pediatric Concerns: Varicella-zoster virus transfers into human milk.
Infants should not breastfeed unless protected with VZIG.

Drug Interactions:

References:
1.   Yoshida M, et.al. Case report: detection of varicella-zoster virus
      DNA in maternal breast milk. J. Med. Virol. 38:108, 1992.
2.   Report of the Committee on Infectious Diseases.   American
      Academy of Pediatrics Red Book. 1994.

Vasopressin   Fax #1435

Trade: Pitressin
Can/Aus/UK: Pitressin, Pressyn
Uses: Antidiuretic hormone
AAP: Not reviewed

Vasopressin, also known as the antidiuretic hormone, is a small peptide (8 amino acids) that is normally secreted by the posterior pituitary. It reduces urine production by the kidney. Although it probably passes to some degree into human milk, it is rapidly destroyed in the GI tract by trypsin, and must be administered by injection or intra-nasally. Hence, oral absorption by a nursing infant is very unlikely. See desmopressin for comparison.

Alternatives:

Pregnancy Risk Category: B

Adult Concerns: Increased blood pressure, water retention and edema, sweating, tremor, and bradycardia.

Pediatric Concerns: None reported via milk.

Drug Interactions:

AHL = 10-20 minutes.	**M/P**	=
PHL =	**PB**	=
PK = 1 hour.	**Oral**	= None
MW =	**pKa**	=
Vd =		

References:
1.   McEvoy GE(ed):AHFS Drug Information, New York, NY. 1995.

Venlafaxine   Fax #1425

Trade: Effexor
Can/Aus/UK: Effexor, Efexor
Uses: Antidepressant, SSRI
AAP: Not reviewed

Venlafaxine is a new serotonin reuptake inhibitor antidepressant. It inhibits both serotonin reuptake and norepinephrine reuptake. Somewhat similar in mechanism to other antidepressants such as Prozac. Fewer anticholinergic side-effects. No data available on penetration into breast milk, but due to high volume of distribution would expect significant secretion into milk. One positive feature is that this drug has a relatively short plasma half-life and limited toxicity in overdose. It is well absorbed orally (92%). Effect on infant is unreported but observe for anxiety, nervousness, and insomnia. Long term effects on neurodevelopment in nursing infants are unknown, but caution is urged. AHL= 5 hours (venlafaxine), 11 hours (active metabolite).

Alternatives: Sertraline, Paroxetine

Pregnancy Risk Category: C

Adult Concerns: Nausea/vomiting, somnolence, dry mouth, dizziness, headache, weakness.

Pediatric Concerns: None reported via milk, but no studies are available.

Drug Interactions: Serious, sometimes fatal reactions when used with MAO inhibitors, or if used within 7-14 days of their use.

AHL = 5 hours (venlafaxine)		**M/P** =	
PHL =		**PB** = 27%	
PK =		**Oral** = 92%	
MW =		**pKa** =	
Vd = 4-12			

References:
1.   Pharmaceutical Manufacturer's Package Insert, 1993, 1994.

Verapamil   Fax #1426

Trade: Calan, Isoptin, Covera-HS
Can/Aus/UK: Apo-Verap, Novo-Veramil, Anpec, Cordilox, Isoptin, Veracaps SR, Berkatens, Cordilox, Univer
Uses: Calcium channel blocker for hypertension
AAP: Approved by the American Academy of Pediatrics for use in breastfeeding mothers

Verapamil is a typical calcium channel blocker used as an antihypertensive. It is secreted into milk but in very low levels, which are highly controversial.   Anderson (1987) reports that in one patient receiving 80 mg three times daily the average steady-state concentrations of verapamil and norverapamil in milk were 25.8 and 8.8 µg/L respectively. The respective maternal plasma level was 42.9 µg/L. The milk:plasma ratio for verapamil was 0.60.   No verapamil was detected in the infant's plasma.   Inoue (1984) reports that in one patient receiving 80 mg four times daily, the milk level peaked at 300 µg/L at approximately 14 hours. These levels are considerably higher than the aforementioned.   In another study of a mother receiving 240 mg daily, the concentrations in milk were never higher than 40 µg/L.

Alternatives: Bepridil, Nifedipine, Nimodipine

Pregnancy Risk Category: C

Adult Concerns: Hypotension, bradycardia, peripheral edema.

Pediatric Concerns: None reported via milk. Observe for hypotension, bradycardia, weakness.

Drug Interactions: Barbiturates may reduce bioavailability of calcium channel blockers (CCB). Calcium salts may reduce hypotensive effect. Dantrolene may increase risk of hyperkalemia and myocardial depression. H2 blockers may increase bioavailability of certain CCBs. Hydantoins may reduce plasma levels. Quinidine increases risk of hypotension, bradycardia, tachycardia. Rifampin may reduce effects of CCBs. Vitamin D may reduce efficacy of CCBs. CCBs may increase carbamazepine, cyclosporin, encainide, prazosin levels.

AHL	= 3-7 hours	**M/P**	= 0.94
PHL	=	**PB**	= 83-92%
PK	= 1-2.2	**Oral**	= 90%
MW	= 455	**pKa**	=
Vd	= 2.5-6.5		

References:
1.   Anderson, P. et. al. Verapamil and norverapamil in plasma and breast milk during breast feeding. Eur J. Clin Pharmacol. 31:625-7, 1987.
2.   Inoue H, et.al. Level of verapamil in human milk. Eur. J. Clin. Pharmacol. 26:657,1984.
3.   Andersen HJ. Excretion of verapamil in human milk, Eur. J. Clin. Pharm. 25:279, 1983.

Vitamin A   Fax #1427

Trade: Aquasol A, Del-vi-a, Vitamin A, Retinol
Can/Aus/UK: Aquasol A, Avoleum
Uses: Vitamin supplement
AAP: Not reviewed

Vitamin A (retinol) is a typical retinoid. It is a fat soluble vitamin that is secreted into human milk and primarily sequestered in high concentrations in the liver (90%). Retinol is absorbed in the small intestine by a selective carrier-mediated uptake process. Levels in infants are generally unknown. The overdose of Vitamin A is extremely dangerous and adults should never exceed 5000 units/day. Use normal doses. DO NOT use maternal doses > 5000 units /day. Mature human milk is rich in retinol and contains 750 µg/Liter (2800 units). Infants do not generally require vitamin A supplementation.

Alternatives:

Pregnancy Risk Category: A

Adult Concerns: Liver toxicity in overdose.

Pediatric Concerns: None reported via milk, but do not use vitamin A in excess of 5000 IU/day.

Drug Interactions:

AHL =		M/P	=
PHL =		PB	=
PK =		Oral	= Complete
MW = 286		pKa	=
Vd =			

References:
1. Lawrence RA. Breastfeeding, A guide for the medical profession. Mosby, St. Louis, 1994.

Vitamin B-12   Fax #1428

Trade: Cyanocobalamin
Can/Aus/UK: Rubramin, Anacobin, Cytacon
Uses: Vitamin supplement
AAP: Approved by the American Academy of Pediatrics for use in breastfeeding mothers

Vitamin B-12 is also called cyanocobalamin and is used for the treatment of pernicious anemia. It is an essential vitamin that is secreted in human milk at concentrations of 0.1 µg/100 mL. B-12 deficiency is very dangerous to an infant. Milk levels vary in proportion to maternal serum levels. Vegetarian mothers may have low levels unless supplemented. Supplementation of nursing mothers is generally recommended.

Alternatives:

Pregnancy Risk Category: A

Adult Concerns: Itching, skin rash, mild diarrhea, megaloblastic anemia in vegetarian mothers.

Pediatric Concerns: None reported with exception of B-12 deficiency states.

Drug Interactions:

AHL =		**M/P** =	
PHL =		**PB** =	
PK = 2 hours.		**Oral** = Variable	
MW = 1355		**pKa** =	
Vd =			

References:
1. Lawrence RA. Breastfeeding, A guide for the medical profession. Mosby, St. Louis, 1994.

Vitamin D   Fax #1430

Trade: Calciferol, Delta-d, Vitamin D
Can/Aus/UK: Calciferol, Calcijex, Drisdol, Hytakerol, Radiostol
Uses: Vitamin D supplement
AAP: Approved by the American Academy of Pediatrics for use in breastfeeding mothers

Vitamin D is secreted into milk in limited concentrations and is proportional to maternal serum levels. Excessive doses can produce elevated calcium levels in the infant. Use with extreme caution and in low doses if absolutely required in undernourished mothers. RDA is 200-600 IU/day. One study shows rather poor transfer of antirachitic activity in human milk, even in supplemented mothers.

Alternatives:

Pregnancy Risk Category: A

Adult Concerns: Elevated calcium levels in breastfed infants.

Pediatric Concerns: None reported via milk, but do not overdose. Significant renal toxicity can occur in infants.

Drug Interactions:

AHL =	M/P	=
PHL =	PB	=
PK =	Oral	= Variable
MW = 396	pKa	=
Vd =		

References:

1. Rothberg AD, et. al. Maternal-infant vitamin D relationships during breast-feeding. J Pediatr 101:500-3, 1982.
2. Goldberg LD. Transmission of a vitamin-D metabolite in breast milk. Lancet 2:1258-9, 1972.
3. Takeuchi A. et.al. Effects of ergocalciferol supplementation on the concentration of vitamin D and it metabolites in human milk. J. of Nutrition 119:1639, 1989.

Vitamin E   Fax #1431

Trade: Alpha Tocopherol, Aquasol E
Can/Aus/UK: Aquasol E Bio E
Uses: Vitamin E supplement
AAP: Not reviewed

Vitamin E (alpha tocopherol) is secreted in milk in higher concentrations than in the maternal serum. Following topical administration to nipples (400 IU/feeding), Vitamin E plasma levels in breastfeeding infants was 40% higher than controls in just 6 days. Studies clearly indicate that high levels of Vitamin E are stored in the liver and tend to accumulate over time. In 1984, over 36 neonates receiving vitamin E in neonatal intensive care units died following the

IV administration of just 25-50 IU/day for several weeks. The maternal RDA during lactation is approximately 16 IU/day. Do not overdose. Do not apply to nipples unless concentrations are low (< 50-100 IU), and then only infrequently. The application of pure vitamin E oil (1000 IU/gm) to nipples should be discouraged.

Alternatives:

Pregnancy Risk Category: A

Adult Concerns:

Pediatric Concerns: None reported via milk, but caution is recommended. Do not use highly concentrated vitamin E oils directly on nipple.

Drug Interactions:

AHL = 282 hours(IV)		M/P	=
PHL =		PB	=
PK =		Oral	= Variable
MW = 431		pKa	=
Vd =			

References:
1. Marx CM, Izquierdo A, Discoll JW, et.al. Vitamin E concentrations in serum of newborn infants after topical use of vitamin E by nursing mothers. AM. J. Obstet. Gynecol. 152:668-70, 1985.
2. Hale TW, Rais-Bahrami R, et.al. Vitamin E toxicity in neonatal animals. Pediatric Res. 27(2):59A, 1990.
3. Lawrence RA. Breastfeeding, A guide for the medical profession. Mosby, St. Louis, 1994.

Warfarin   Fax #1432

Trade: Coumadin, Panwarfin
Can/Aus/UK: Coumadin, Warfilone, Marevan
Uses: Anticoagulant
AAP: Approved by the American Academy of Pediatrics for use in

breastfeeding mothers

Warfarin is a potent anticoagulant. Warfarin is highly protein bound in the maternal circulation and therefore very little is secreted into human milk. Very small and insignificant amounts are secreted into milk but it depends to some degree on the dose administered. In one study of two patients who were anti-coagulated with warfarin, no warfarin was detected in the infant's serum, nor were changes in coagulation detectable. In another study of 13 mothers, less than 0.08 umol per liter (25 ng/mL) was detected in milk, and no warfarin was detected in the infants' plasma. According to these authors, maternal warfarin apparently poses little risk to a nursing infant and thus far has not produced bleeding anomalies in breastfed infants. Use with caution. Other anticoagulants, such as phenindione, should be avoided. Observe infant for bleeding, such as excessive bruising or reddish petechia (spots).

Alternatives:

Pregnancy Risk Category: D

Adult Concerns: Bleeding, bruising.

Pediatric Concerns: None reported via milk, but observe for bleeding, bruising.

Drug Interactions: The drug interactions of warfarin are numerous. Agents that may increase the anticoagulant effect and the risk of bleeding include: acetaminophen, androgens, beta blockers, clofibrate, corticosteroids, disulfiram, erythromycin, fluconazole, hydantoins, ketaconazole, miconazole, sulfonamides, thyroid hormones, and numerous others. Agents that may decrease the anticoagulant effect of warfarin include: ascorbic acid, dicloxacillin, ethanol, griseofulvin, nafcillin, sucralfate, trazodone, barbiturates, carbamazepine, etretinate, rifampin. Due to numerous drug interactions, please consult additional references.

AHL = 1-2.5 days	**M/P** =
PHL =	**PB** = 99%
PK = 0.5-3 days	**Oral** = Complete
MW = 308	**pKa** = 5.1

Vd   = 0.1-0.2

References:
1.   McKenna Rk, Cole ER, Vasan U. Is warfarin contraindicated in the lactating mother? J Pediatrics 103:325-327, 1983.
2.   Brambel, C. and Hunter, R. Effect of dicumarol on the nursing infant. Am. J. Obstet. Gynecol. 59:1153-1159, 1950.
3.   L'E Orme M, et. al. May mothers given warfarin breast-feed their infants? Br Med J 1:1564-5, 1977.

Zafirlukast   Fax #1517

Trade: Accolate
Can/Aus/UK: Accolate
Uses: Leukotriene inhibitor for Asthma
AAP: Not reviewed

Zafirlukast is a new competitive receptor antagonist of leukotriene D4 and other components of slow-reacting substance of anaphylaxis which are mediators of bronchoconstriction in asthmatic patients. Zafirlukast is not a bronchodilator and should not be used for acute asthma attacks. Zafirlukast is excreted into milk in low concentrations. Following repeated 40 mg doses twice daily (please note: average adult dose is 20 mg twice daily), the average steady-state concentration in breast milk was 50 ng/mL (50 µg/L) compared to 255 ng/mL in maternal plasma. Zafirlukast is poorly absorbed when administered with food. It is likely the oral absorption via ingestion of breast milk would be low.   The manufacturer recommends against using in breastfeeding mothers.

Alternatives:

Pregnancy Risk Category: B

Adult Concerns: Pharyngitis, aggravation reaction, headache, nausea, diarrhea have been reported.

Pediatric Concerns: None reported.

Drug Interactions: Erythromycin reduces oral bioavailability of zafirlukast by 40%. Aspirin increase zafirlukast plasma levels by 45%. Theophylline reduces zafirlukast plasma levels by 30%. Zafirlukast increase warfarin anticoagulation by 35%. Terfenadine reduces zafirlukast plasma levels by 54%.

AHL	= 10-13 hours	M/P	= 0.15
PHL	=	PB	= >99%
PK	= 3 hours	Oral	= Poor
MW	= 575	pKa	=
Vd	=		

References:
1. Pharmaceutical Manufacturer's Package Insert, 1997.

Zinc Salts   Fax #1570

Trade: Zinc
Can/Aus/UK:
Uses: Zinc supplements
AAP: Not reviewed

Zinc is an essential element that is required for enzymatic function within the cell. Zinc deficiencies have been documented in newborns and premature infants, with symptoms such as anorexia nervosa, arthritis, diarrheas, eczema, recurrent infections, and recalcitrant skin problems. The Recommended Daily Allowance for adults is 12-15 mg/day. The average oral dose of supplements is 25-50 mg/day, higher doses may lead to gastritis. Doses used for treatment of cold symptoms averaged 13.3 mg (lozenges) every 2 hours while awake for the duration of cold symptoms. The acetate or gluconate salts are preferred due to reduced gastric irritation and higher absorption. Zinc sulfate should not be used. Excessive intake is detrimental. Eleven healthy males who ingested 150 mg twice daily for 6 weeks showed significant impairment of lymphocyte and polymorphonuclear leukocyte function and a significant reduction of HDL cholesterol. Interestingly, absorption of dietary zinc is nearly twice as high during lactation as before conception.   In 13 women studied, zinc absorption at preconception averaged 14%, and during lactation, 25%. There was no difference in serum zinc values between women who took iron supplements and those who did not (Fung et al, 1997), although iron supplementation may reduce oral zinc absorption.   Zinc absorption from human milk is high, averaging 41% which is significantly higher than from soy or cow formulas (14% and 31% respectively). Minimum daily requirements of zinc in full term infants varies from 0.3 to 0.5 mg/Kg/day.   Daily ingestion of zinc from breast milk has been estimated to be 0.35 mg/Kg/day, and declines over the first 17 weeks of life, as older neonates require less zinc due to slower growth rate. Supplementation with 25-50 mg/day is probably safe, but excessive doses are strongly discouraged. Others have shown, that zinc levels in breast milk are independent of plasma zinc concentrations or dietary zinc intake (Krebs,1995). Other body pools of zinc (i.e., liver and bone) are perhaps the source of zinc in breast milk. Therefore, higher levels of oral zinc intake probably have minimal effect on zinc concentrations in milk.

Alternatives:

Pregnancy Risk Category:

Adult Concerns: Oral Zinc salts may cause gastritis, GI upset. Gluconate salts, and lower doses are preferred.

Pediatric Concerns: None reported via milk.

Drug Interactions: Zinc may reduce absorption of ciprofloxacin, tetracyclines, norfloxacin, ofloxacin. Iron salts may reduce absorption of zinc. Foods containing high concentrations of phosphorus, calcium (diary foods), or phytates (bran, brown bread) may reduce oral zinc absorption. Coffee reduces zinc absorption by 50%.

AHL =		**M/P** =	
PHL =		**PB** =	
PK =		**Oral** = 41%	
MW =		**pKa** =	
Vd =			

References:
1. Fung EB, Ritchie LD, Woodhouse LR et al: Zinc absorption in women during pregnancy and lactation: a longitudinal study. Am J Clin Nutr 66:80-88, 1997.
2. Drug Facts and Comparisons. 1997. ed. Facts and Comparisons, St. Louis.
3. Krebs NF, et.al. Zinc supplementation during lactation: effects on maternal status and milk zinc concentrations. Am. J. Clin. Nutr. 61:1030-6, 1995.

Zolmitriptan   Fax #1572

Trade: Zomig
Can/Aus/UK: Zomig
Uses: Migraine analgesic
AAP: Not reviewed

Zolmitriptan is a selective serotonin-1D receptor antagonist that is specifically indicated for treating acute migraine headaches. Peak plasma levels of zolmitriptan during migraine attacks are generally 8-14 nanograms/mL and occur before 4 hours. Zolmitriptan is structurally similar to sumatriptan, but has better oral bioavailability, higher penetration into the CNS, and may have dual mechanisms of action. No data are available on its penetration into human milk.

Alternatives: Sumatriptan

Pregnancy Risk Category: C

Adult Concerns: Asthenia, dizziness, paresthesias, drowsiness, nausea, throat tightness, tight chest. Tachycardia and palpitations have been reported.

Pediatric Concerns: None reported via milk. See sumatriptan as alternative.

Drug Interactions:

AHL	= 3 hours	M/P	=
PHL	=	PB	=
PK	= 2-4 hours	Oral	= 48%
MW	=	pKa	=
Vd	=		

References:
1. Seaber E. et.al. The absolute bioavailability and metabolic disposition of the novel anti-migraine compound zolmitriptan. Br. J. Clin. Pharmacol. 43:570-587, 1997
2. Palmer KJ, Spencer CM. Zolmitriptan (Adis new drug profile). CNS Drugs Jun 7(6): 468-478, 1997.

Zolpidem Tartrate   Fax #1433

Trade: Ambien
Can/Aus/UK:
Uses: Sedative, sleep aid
AAP: Approved by the American Academy of Pediatrics for use in breastfeeding mothers

Zolpidem, although not a benzodiazepine, interacts with the same GABA-benzodiazepine receptor site and shares some of the same pharmacologic effects of the benzodiazepine family. In a study of 5 lactating mothers receiving 20 mg daily, the maximum breast milk concentration occurred between 1.75 and 3.75 hours and ranged from 90 to 364 µg/L. The amount of zolpidem recovered in breast milk 3 hours after administration ranged between 0.76 and 3.88 µg, or 0.004 to 0.019% of the total dose administered. Breast milk clearance of zolpidem is very rapid and none was detectible (below 0.5 ng/mL) by 4-5 hours post-dose. In one animal study, zolpidem inhibited the secretion of milk.

Alternatives:

Pregnancy Risk Category: B

Adult Concerns: Sedation, anxiety, fatigue, irritability.

Pediatric Concerns: None reported via milk.   Observe for reduced milk supply.

Drug Interactions: Use with food may significantly decrease plasma levels by 25%.

AHL = 2.5-5 hours	**M/P**	= 0.13-0.18
PHL =	**PB**	= 92.5%
PK = 1.6 hours	**Oral**	= 70%
MW = 307	**pKa**	=

References:
1. Pharmaceutical Manufacturer's Package Insert, 1996.
2. Pons G. Francoual C. et.al. Zolpidem excretion in breast milk. Eur. J. Clin. Pharmacol. 37:245, 1989.

Appendix

Glossary

adipose	the fat tissue in the body
analgesic	drugs used to treat pain
androgen	drug that mimics the action of the male hormone testosterone
anti-angina	drug used to treat the pain associated with reduced coronary flow in the heart
antidepressant	drugs that elevate or treat mental depression
antiemetic	compound used to treat nausea and vomiting.
antihypertensive	drug used to treat high blood pressure
antimetabolite	drug generally used to inhibit the immune response, such as in arthritis or cancer
antineoplastic	drug used to treat neoplasms, or cancers
antivertigo	compound used to treat dizziness bradycardia slow heart rate
anxiolytic	reduces anxiety. sedative drug
arthropathy	painful inflammation of joints
bronchodilator	drug that dilates the bronchi in the lungs
CCB	calcium channel blocker
candidiasis	fungal infection, candida, yeast, thrush
cholinergic	nerve transmitter, acetylcholine
diuretic	drug that induces excretion of water by kidneys
dL	deciliter, 100ml
DNA	deoxyribonucleic acid, chromosome, genetic components of human cells
estrogen	drugs that mimic the action of estrogens, or female hormones.
flora	bacteria normally residing within the intestine.
GI	gastrointestinal
half-life	the time required for the concentration of a drug to diminish by one-half in the specified compartment (blood).
hepatotoxic	drug that produces liver damage
hyperglycemia	elevated blood sugar (dextrose)
hypoglycemia	low blood sugar (dextrose)
hypotension	low blood pressure
immune	antibody system which fights infection, foreign protein, etc.
immunosuppressive	drugs that diminish or reduce the immune (antibody) response.
L	liter, 1000 ml, 1000 cc, approximately 1 quart

688

lipid	fat
maternal	mother
mg	milligram, one thousandth of gram
mg/L	milligram per Liter
milk-plasma ratio	ratio of drug in milk to plasma. Higher ratios indicate more drug penetration into milk. A ratio of 1 means that the amount of drug in milk is identical to that in plasma.
ng	nanogram, 1×10^{-9} gm
NICU	Neonatal intensive care unit
NSAID	Nonsteroidal anti-inflammatory
perineal	area between the anus and scrotum.
progestational	drug that mimics the action of progesterone, a female hormone.
prolactin	hormone that promotes breast milk production.
pseudomembranous colitis	severe, sometimes bloody diarrhea caused by overgrowth of offending colonic bacteria.
RNA	ribonucleic acid, genetic component of human cell.
tachycardia	rapid heart rate
teratogenic	drugs or conditions that produce birth defects in pregnant women.
μg	microgram, one millionth of a gram
μg/L	microgram per liter

Normal Growth During Development

BOYS	Weight (lb).	Length (in.)	Head Circumference (in.)
Birth	7.5	19.9	13.9
3 months	12.6	23.8	16.1
6 months	16.7	26.1	17.3
9 months	20.0	28	18.1
12 months	22.2	29.6	18.6
15 months	23.7	30.9	18.9
18 months	25.2	32.2	19.2
24 months	27.7	34.4	19.6

Please note, these data were not derived from exclusively breastfed infants.

Normal Growth During Development

GIRLS	Weight (lb).	Length (in.)	Head Circumference (in.)
Birth	7.2	19.7	13.5
3 months	11.8	23.5	15.6
6 months	15.9	25.8	16.7
9 months	18.8	27.7	17.4
12 months	21.0	29.3	17.9
15 months	22.5	30.6	18.4
18 months	23.9	31.9	18.6
24 months	26.3	34.0	18.8

Please note, these data were not derived from exclusively breastfed infants.

ANTIBIOTIC AGENTS

Drug	AHL	PB	M:P	Milk Level
Acyclovir	2.4hr	9-33%	0.6-4.1	4.16-5.81 mg/L
Amantadine	16hr	67%		
Amikacin	2.3hr	4%		
Aminosalicylic	1hr	50-73%		1.1 mg/L
Amoxicillin	1.7hr	18%	0.043	0.68-1.3 mg/L
Ampicillin	1.3hr	8-20%	0.2	1 mg/L
Azithromycin	68 hrs	7-51%		0.64-2.8 mg/L
Aztreonam	1.7hr	60%	0.005	0.18-0.22 mg/L
Bacampicillin	1.3hr	8-20%	0.2	
Carbenicillin	1hr	26-60%	0.02	0.26 mg/L
Cefaclor	0.5-1hr	25%		0.16-.21 mg/L
Cefadroxil	1.5hr	20%	0.019	0.10-1.24 mg/L
Cefazolin	1.2-2.2hr	89%	0.02	1.16-1.51 mg/L
Cefepime	2 hrs	19%	0.8	0.5 mg/L
Cefixime	7hr	70%		
Cefoperazone	2hrs.	82-93%		0.4-0.9 mg/L
Cefotaxime	<0.68hr	40%	0.17	0.26-0.32 mg/L
Cefotetan	3-4.6hr	76-91%		0.22-0.34 mg/L
Cefoxitin	0.7-1.1hr	85-99%		0.9 mg/L
Cefpodoxime	2.84 hrs	22-33%	0.16	
Cefprozil	78min	36%	0.05-5.67	0.7-3.4 mg/L
Ceftazidime	1.4-2 hrs	5-24%		5.2 mg/L

Drug	AHL	PB	M:P	Milk Level
Ceftibuten	2.4 hrs	65%		
Ceftriaxone	7.3hr	95%	0.03	0.6-7.89 mg/L
Cefuroxime	1.4 hrs	33-50%		
Cephalexin	50-80min	10%	0.008-0.14	0.20-0.50 mg/L
Cephalothin	30-50min	70%	0.06-0.51	0.27-0.47 mg/L
Cephapirin	24-36min	54%	0.068-0.48	0.26-0.43 mg/L
Cephradine	0.7-2hrs.	8-17%	0.2	0.6 mg/L
Chloramphenicol	4 hrs.	53%	0.5-0.6	1.7-6.1 mg/L
Chloroquine	72-120 hrs	61%	0.358	0.227 mg/L
Ciclopirox	1.7 hrs	98%		
Ciprofloxacin	4.1hr	40%	>1	2.26-3.79 mg/L
Clarithromycin	5-7hr	40-70%	>1	
Clindamycin	2.9hr	94%		1.0-1.7 mg/L
Clofazimine	70 days		1.7	0.9-1.33 mg/L
Cloxacillin	0.7-3 hrs	90-96%		0.2-0.4 mg/L
Cycloserine	12+hr		0.72	6-19 mg/L
Dicloxacillin	0.6-0.8hr	96%		0.1-0.3 mg/L
Dirithromycin	20-50 hrs	15-30%		
Doxycycline	15-25hr	90%	0.3-0.4	0.77 mg/L
Enoxacin	3-6 hrs	40%		
Erythromycin	1.5-2hr	84%		0.4-1.5 mg/L
Ethambutol	3.1hr	8-22%	1.0	1.4 mg/L

Drug	AHL	PB	M:P	Milk Level
Famciclovir	2-3 hrs	20%	> 1	
Foscarnet	3 hrs	14-17%	3.0	
Fosfomycin	4-8 hrs	< 3%	0.1	
Fluconazole	30hr	90%	0.46-0.85	0.98-2.93 mg/L
Gentamicin	2-3hr	<10%	0.11-0.44	0.41-0.49 mg/L
Grepafloxacin	15.7 hrs	50%		
Griseofulvin	9-24hr			
Hydroxychloro-quine	40 days	63%	5.5	1.1 mg/L
Imipenem-Cilistatin	1.3 hrs	20-35%		
Isoniazid	1.1-3.1hr	10-15%		6-16.6 mg/L
Itraconazole	64 hrs	99.8%		
Kanamycin	2.1hr	0%	<0.4	12-18.4 mg/L
Ketoconazole	2-8hr	99%		
Lincomycin	4.4-6.4hr	72%	0.9	0.5-2.4 mg/L
Lomefloxacin	8 hrs.	20.6%		
Loracarbef	1 hrs	25%		
Methacycline	7-15hr	75-90%		
Methicillin	1-2hr	40%		
Metronidazole	8.5hr	10%	0.4-1.8	15.5 mg /L
Miconazole	20-25hr	91-93%		
Minocycline	11-26hr	80%		
Nafcillin	0.5-1.5hr	70-90%		

Drug	AHL	PB	M:P	Milk Level
Nalidixic	1-2.5hr	93%	0.08-0.13	5 mg/L
Netilmicin	2-2.5 hrs	< 10%		
Nitrofurantoin	20-58min	20-60%	0.27-0.31	0.3-0.5 mg/L
Norfloxacin	5hr	20%		undetectable
Ofloxacin	5-7hr	32%	0.98-1.66	0.05-2.4 mg/L
Penciclovir	2.3 hrs	< 20%		
Penicillin G	<1.5hr	60-80%	0.03-0.13	7-60 units/L
Piperacillin	0.6-1.3hr	30%		
Pyrimethamine	96hr	87%	0.2-0.43	3.3 mg/L
Quinacrine	> 5 days	High		
Quinine	11hr	93%	0.11-0.53	0.4-1.6 mg/L
Rifampin	3.5hr	80%	0.16-0.23	3.4-4.9 mg/L
Rimantadine	25.4 hrs	40%	2.0	
Streptomycin	2.6hr	34%	0.12-1.0	0.3-0.6 mg/L
Sulfamethoxazole	10.1hr	62%	0.06	
Sulfasalazine	7.6 hr		0.09-0.17	
Sulfisoxazole	4.6-7.8 hr	91%	0.06	
Terbinafine	26 hrs	99%		0.65 mg/72 hrs
Terconazole	4-11.3hr			
Tetracycline	6-12hr	25%	0.6-0.8	0.43-2.58 mg/L
Ticarcillin	0.9-1.3hr	54%		
Tobramycin	2-3hr	<5%		0.5 µg/mL
Trimethoprim	8-10hr	44%	1.25	2.0 mg/L

Drug	AHL	PB	M:P	Milk Level
Trovafloxacin	12.2 hrs	76%		1.2-5.5 mg/L
Valacyclovir	2.5-3 hrs	9-33%	0.6-4.1	
Vancomycin	5.6hr	10-30%		12.7 mg/L

ANTICONVULSANTS AND SEDATIVES

Drug	AHL	PB	M:P	Milk Level
Carbamazepine	18-54hr	74%	0.69	1.3-3.6 mg/L
Clonazepam	18-60hr	50-86%	0.33	11-13 µg/L
Ethosuximide	31-60hr	0%	1.0	55 mg/L
Ethotoin	3-9 hrs	< 41%		
Felbamate	20-23 hrs	25%		
Gabapentin	5-7 hrs	< 3%		
Lamotrigine	24 hrs	55%		
Magnesium	<3hr	0%	1.9	
Pentobarbital	15-50hr	35-45%		0.17 mg/L
Phenobarbital	53-140hr	51%	0.4-0.6	2.1 mg/L
Phenytoin	6-24hr	89%	<0.45	0.26-1.5 mg/L
Primidone	10-21 hr	<20%	0.72	2-13 mg/L
Topiramate	18-24 hrs	15%		
Valproic	14hr	94%	0.42	0.17-0.47 mg/L

ANTIDEPRESSANTS - MISCELLANEOUS

Drug	AHL	PB	M:P	Milk Level
Amitriptyline	31-46hr	94.8%	1.0	0.151 mg/L
Amoxapine	8 hr	15-25%	0.21	<20 µg/L
Bupropion	8-24 hr	75-88%	2.51-8.58	0.189 mg/L
Buspirone	2-11hr	95%		
Clomipramine	19-37 hrs	96%	1.62	211 ug/L
Desipramine	7-60 hr	82%	0.4-0.9	17-35 µg/L
Dothiepin	14-23.9hr		0.3	11 µg/L
Doxepin	8-24hr	80-85%	1.08-1.66	27-29 µg/L
Fluvoxamine	15.6 hrs	80%	0.29	0.09 mg/L
Imipramine	8-16hr	90%	0.5-1.5	12-29 ug/L
Nefazodone	1.5-18 hrs	> 99%		
Nortriptyline	16-90hr	92%	0.87-3.71	180 µg/L
Trazodone	4-9 hrs	85-95%	0.142	

ANTIDEPRESSANTS-SSRIs

Drug	AHL	PB	M:P	Milk Level
Fluoxetine	2-3 days	94.5%	0.286	28.8 µg/L
Nefazodone	1.5-18 hr	>99%		
Paroxetine	21 hrs	95%	0.09	7.6 ug/L
Sertraline	26-65 hr	98%		19-43 ug/L
Trazodone	4-9 hr	85-95%	0.142	
Venlafaxine	5hr	27%		

ANTIHISTAMINES
H-1 BLOCKERS

Drug	AHL	PB	M:P	Milk Level
Astemizole	20hr	96.7%		
Brompheniramine	24.9hr			
Cetirizine	8.3 hrs	93%		
Chlorpheniramine	12-43hr	70%		
Clemastine	10-12hr		0.25-0.5	5-10 µg/L
Doxylamine	10.1 hrs			
Diphenhydramine	4.3hr	78%		
Fexofenadine	14.4 hrs	70%		
Hydroxyzine	3-7 hrs			
Levocabastine	33-40hr			
Loratadine	8.4-28hr	97%	1.17	

Drug	AHL	PB	M:P	Milk Level
Meclizine	6hr			
Promethazine	12.7hr	76-80%		
Terfenadine	11.7hr	97%	0.12-0.28	41.02 ng/ml
Trimeprazine	5hr			
Tripelennamine	2-3hr			
Triprolidine	5hr		0.5-1.2	1.2-4.4 ug/L

ANTIHYPERTENSIVES
ACE INHIBITORS

Drug	AHL	PB	M:P	Milk Level
Benazepril	10-11 hr	96.7%		
Bepridil	42 hrs	> 99%	0.33	
Captopril	2.2 hr	30%	0.012	4.7 µg/L
Enalapril	35 hr	60%		5.9 ug/L
Fosinopril	11-35 hrs	95%		
Lisinopril	12 hrs	Low		
Losartan	4-9 hrs	99.8%		
Quinapril	2 hr	97%		
Ramipril	13-17 hr	56%		

ANTIHYPERTENSIVES
BETA BLOCKERS

Drug	AHL	PB	M:P	Milk Level
Acebutolol	3-4 hr	26%	7.1-12.2	
Atenolol	6.1 hr	5%	1.3-6.8	0.66-1.7 mg/L
Betaxolol	14-22 hr	50%	2.5-3.0	
Bisoprolol	9-12 hr	30%		
Carteolol	6 hr	23-30%		
Esmolol	9 min.	55%		
Labetalol	6-8 hr	50%	0.8-2.6	129-662 µg/L
Levobunolol	6.1 hrs			
Metoprolol	3-7 hr	12%	3.0	0.38-2.58 umol/L
Nadolol	20-24hr	30%	4.6	146 µg/L
Propranolol	3-5hr	90%	0.5	35.4 ug/L
Sotalol	12hr	0%	5.4	4.8-20.2 mg/L
Timolol	4hr	10%	0.8	15.9 µg/L

ANTIHYPERTENSIVES
CALCIUM CHANNEL BLOCKERS

Drug	AHL	PB	M:P	Milk Level
Amlodipine	30-50hr	93%		
Bepridil	24hr	>99%	0.33	
Diltiazem	3.5-6hr	78%	1.0	200 µg/L
Felodipine	11-16hr	>99%		

Drug	AHL	PB	M:P	Milk Level
Flunarizine	19 days	99%		
Isradipine	8hr	95%		
Mibefradil	17-25 hrs	99.5%	5	
Nicardipine	2-4 hrs	> 95%		
Nifedipine	1.8-7hr	92-98%	1.0	<46 ug/L
Nimodipine	9 hrs	95%	0.06-0.3	<3.5 ug/L
Nisoldipine	7-12 hrs	99%		
Nitrendipine	8-11hr	98%	0.5-1.4	4.3-6.5 µg/L
Verapamil	3-7hr	83-92%	0.94	25.8 µg/L

ANTINEOPLASTICS - ANTIMETABOLITES

Drug	AHL	PB	M:P	Milk Level
Allopurinol	1-3hr	0%	0.9-1.4	0.9-1.4 ug/ml
Azathioprine	0.6hr	30%		
Busulfan	2.6hr			
Chlorambucil	1.3hr	99%		
Cisplatin	0.53hr	90%	>1	0.9 mg/L
Cyclophosphamide	7.5hr	13%		
Cytarabine	1-3hr	13%		
Doxorubicin	30hr	85%	4.43	128 µg/L
Fluorouracil	11 min	8-12%		
Gallium	78.3hr			0.01-0.045uCi/mL
Mercaptopurine	0.9hr	19%		

Drug	AHL	PB	M:P	Milk Level
Methotrexate	7.2hr	34-50%	>0.08	2.6 ug/L

ANTISECRETORY DRUGS

Drug	AHL	PB	M:P	Milk Level
Cimetidine	2 hr	19%	4.6-11.76	6 mg/L
Famotidine	2.5-3.5 hr	17%	0.41-1.78	72 µg/L
Lansoprazole	1.5 hrs	97%		
Nizatidine	1.5 hr	35%		nil
Omeprazole	1 hr	95%		
Ranitidine	2-3 hr	15%	1.9-6.7	0.72-2.6 mg/L

BRONCHODILATORS - B2 AGONISTS

Drug	AHL	PB	M:P	Milk Level
Albuterol	1.7-7.1hr			
Isoetharine	1-3hr			
Isoproterenol	1-2hr			
Pirbuterol	2-3hr			
Salmeterol	5.5hr	98%	1.0	
Terbutaline	14hr	20%	<2.9	3.2-3.8 ng/ml

Diuretics

Drug	AHL	PB	M:P	Milk Level
Acetazolamide	2.4-5.8 hrs	95%	0.25	2.1 mg/L
Bendroflumethiazide	3-3.9 hr	94%		
Bumetanide	1.5 hrs	95%		
Chlorothiazide	1.5 hr	95%	0.05	<1 mg/L
Chlorthalidone	54 hr	75%		
Dyphylline	3-12.8 hr	56%	2.08	
Ethacrynic	2-4 hr	90%		
Furosemide	92 min	95%		
Hydrochlorothiazide	5.6-14.8 hr	58%	0.25	
Indapamide	14 hrs	71%		
Spironolactone	10-35 hr	90%	0.72	47-104 ug/L
Torsemide	3.5 hr	99%		
Triamterene	1.5-2.5 hrs	55%		

GASTROINTESTINAL AGENTS

Drug	AHL	PB	M:P	Milk Level
Cisapride	7-10hr	98%	0.045	6.2 µg/L
Diphenoxylate	2.5hr			
Loperamide	10.8hr		0.37	0.27 µg/L
Metoclopramide	5-6hr	30%	0.5-4.06	20-125 ug/L
Prochlorperazine	10-20hr	90%		

NARCOTIC ANALGESICS

Drug	AHL	PB	M:P	Milk Level
Alfentanil	1-2 hrs	92%		0.21-1.56 ug/L
Buprenorphine	3 hrs	96%		3.28 ug/day
Butorphanol	3-4hr	80%		4 µg/L
Codeine	2.9hr	7%	1.3-2.5	140-455 ug/L
Fentanyl	2-4hr	80-86%		< 0.05 ug/L
Hydrocodone	3.8hr			
Meperidine	3.2hr	65-80%	0.84-1.59	0.13-0.275 mg/L
Methadone	13-55hr	89%	1.5	0.05-0.57 mg/L
Morphine	1.5-2hr	35%	1.1-3.6	< 0.5 mg/L
Nalbuphine	5 hrs		1.2	
Oxycodone	3-6hr		3.4	<5-226 µg/L
Pentazocine	2-3 hrs	60%		
Remifentanil	<20min.	70%		
Tramadol	7 hrs	20%		100 ug/16 hrs

ANALGESIC AND ANTI-INFLAMMATORY (NONNARCOTIC)

Drug	AHL	PB	M:P	Milk Level
Acetaminophen	2hr	25%	0.91-1.42	10-15 mg/L
Antipyrine		<1%	1.0	
Aspirin	0.25hr	49%	0.03-0.08	1.12-1.69 mg/L
Butorphanol	3-4hr	80%		4 µg/L

Drug	AHL	PB	M:P	Milk Level
Diclofenac	1.1hr	99.7%		< 19 ug/L
Diflunisal	8-12hr	99%		
Etodolac	7.3hr	95-99%		
Fenoprofen	2.5hr	99%	0.017	
Flunisolide	1.8hr			
Flurbiprofen	3.8-5.7hr	99%	0.013	0.05-0.07 mg/L
Ibuprofen	1.8-2.5hr	>99%		< 0.5 mg/L
Indomethacin	4.5hr	>90%	0.37	
Ketoprofen	2-4hr	>99%		
Ketorolac	2.4-8.6hr	99%	0.015-0.037	5.2-7.3 ug/L
Nabumetone	22-30hr	99%		
Naproxen	12-15hr	99.7%	0.01	1.76-2.37 mg/L
Olsalazine	0.9hr	99%		
Oxaprozin	50 hrs	99%		
Piroxicam	30-86hr	99%	0.008-.013	0.22 mg/L
Propoxyphene	6-12hr	78%		
Tolmetin	1-1.5hr	99%	0.0055	0.18 mg/L

PSYCHOTROPIC DRUGS

Drug	AHL	PB	M:P	Milk Level
Alprazolam	12-15hr	71%		
Butabarbital	100 hrs			
Butalbitol	40 hrs	26%		
Buspirone	2-3 hrs	95%		
Caffeine	4.9hr	36%	0.52-0.76	
Chloral Hydrate	7-10hr	35-41%		3.2 mg/L
Chlordiazepoxide	5-30hr	90-98%		
Chlorpromazine	30hr	95%	<0.5	0.29 mg/L
Chlorprothixene			1.2-2.6	19 ug/L
Clomipramine	19-37hr	96%	0.84-1.6	<342.7 µg/L
Clonazepam	18-50 hrs	50-86%	0.33	11-13 ug/L
Clobazam	17-31 hrs	90%		
Clozapine	8-12hr	95%		
Dextroamphetamine	6-8hr	16-20%	2.8-7.5	55-138 µg/L
Diazepam	43hr	99%	0.2-2.7	51-78 ng/ml
Doxepin	8-24hr	80-85%	1.08-1.6	27-29 µg/L
Estazolam	10-24 hrs	93%		
Flunitrazepam	20-30 hrs	80%		
Fluphenazine	10-20hr	91-99%		
Flurazepam	47 hrs	97%		
Halazepam	14 hrs	High		
Haloperidol	12-38hr	92%	0.58-0.81	5 µg/L
Hydroxyzine	3-7hr			

Drug	AHL	PB	M:P	Milk Level
Lithium	17-24hr	0%	0.24-0.66	0.3 mmol/L
Lorazepam	12hr	85%	0.15-0.26	8.5 µg/L
Meprobamate	6-17hr	15%	2-4	
Midazolam	1.9 hrs	97%	0.15	9 ug/L
Nicotine	2hr	4.9%	2.9	
Nitrazepam	30hr	90%	0.27	10-15 µg/L
Oxazepam	12hr	97%	0.1-0.33	24-30 ug/L
Pentobarbial	15-50 hrs	35-40%		0.17 mg/L
Prazepam	30-100hr	>70%		
Quazepam	39 hrs	> 95%	4.19	
Secobarbital	15-40 hrs	30-45%		
Temazepam	9.5 hrs	60-96%		
Thiopental Sodium	3-8 hrs	60-96%	0.4	0.9 mg/L
Triazolam	5.5 hrs	89%		
Zolpidem	2.5-5 hrs	92.5%		90-364 ug/L

THYROID FUNCTION TESTS

T_4(thyroxine)	1-7 days	10.1-20.9 μg/dL
	8-14 days	9.8-16.6 μg/dL
	1 month-1year	5.5-16 μg/dL
	>1 year	4-12 μg/dL
FTI	1-3 days	9.3-26.6
	1-4 weeks	7.6-20.8
	1-4 months	7.4-17.9
	4-12 months	5.1-14.5
	1-6 years	5.7-13.3
	>6 years	4.8-14
T_3 by RIA	Newborns	100-470 ng/dL
	1-5 years	100-260 ng/dL
	5-10 years	90-240 ng/dL
	10 years-adult	70-210 ng/dL
T_3 uptake		35-45%
TSH	Cord	3-22 μIU/mL
	1-3 days	<40 μIU/mL
	3-7 days	<25 μIU/mL
	>7 days	0-10 μIU/mL

Therapeutic Drug Levels

Reference (Normal) Values

Drug	Therapeutic Range	
Acetaminophen	10-20	μg/ml
Theophylline	10-20	μg/ml
Carbamazepine	4-10	μg/ml
Ethosuximide	40-100	μg/ml
Phenobarbitol	15-40	μg/ml
Phenytoin		
Neonates	6-14	μg/ml
Children, adults	10-20	μg/ml
Primidone	5-15	μg/ml
Valproic Acid	5-15	μg/ml
Gentamicin		
Peak	5-12	μg/ml
Trough	< 2.0	μg/ml
Vancomycin		
Peak	20-40	μg/ml
Trough	5-10	μg/ml
Digoxin	0.9-2.2	μg/ml
Lithium	0.3-1.3	mmol/L
Salicylates	20-25	mg/dL

From Therapeutic Drug Monitoring Guide, WE Evan, Editor, Abbott Laboratories, 1988.

Pediatric Laboratory Values

Test	Age	Range	Units
pH	< 1 mo.	7.3-7.46	
pCO_2	2-5d	4.1-6.3	kPa(mmHg)
pCO_2	2-5d	5.6-7.7	kPa(mmHg)
Total CO_2	< 1 yr.	15-35	mmol/L
Albumin, Serum	< 1 yr.	3-4.9	gm/dL
Phenylalamine	Newborn	0.7-3.5	umol/L
Ammonia	< 1 yr.	68	umol/L
Total Bilirubin	< 2 w	< 11.7	mg/dL
	< 10 yr.	< 0.9	mg/dL
Calcium	< 1 yr.	7.8-11.2	mg/dL
Chloride	< 2 yr.	100-110	mmol/dL
Cholesteral Total	< 1 yr.	93-260	mg/dL
Copper, Serum	1-5 yr.	80-150	µg/dL
Copper, Wiring	< 6 yr.	8-17	µg/dL
Creatine Kinose	1-3 yr.	50-305	IU/L
Creatine, Serum	< 10 yr.	0.2-1.02	mg/dL
Ferritin	1-4 yr.	6-24	µg/L
Fructosamine	5-17 yr.	1.4-2.2	mmol/L
Glucose	1-6 yr.	74-127	mg/dL
Hemoglobin A_{1C}	2-12 yr.	5.1	%HbA_{1C}
Cholesterol (HDL)	1-9 yr.	35-82	mg/dL
Iron	< 2 yr.	11-150	µg/dL
Magnesium	< 1 yr.	1.6-2.6	mg/dL
Osmolality	28d	274-305	mmol/dL
Phosphatose, alkaline	2-9 yr.	100-400	IU/L
Phosphorus, Serum	< 2 yr.	2.5-7.1	mg/dL
Potassium	< 2 mo.	3-7.0	mmol/dL
Prolactin	0-18 yr.	20 or less	ng/mL
Protein, Total	< 1 yr.	5-7.5	mg/dL
Protein, Urine	< 1 yr.	130-145	mmol/dL
Sodium, Urinary	1-6 mo.		
breast-fed		6.1	mmol/L
formula-fed		13.2	mmol/L

Common Radiopaque Agents

Generic Name (Iodine Content)	Trade Name
Iocetamic Acid (62% Iodine)	Cholebrine
Iopanoic Acid (66.68% Iodine)	Telepaque
Ipodate Calcium (61.7% Iodine)	Oragrafin Calcium
Ipodate Sodium (61.4% Iodine)	Bilivist,Oragrafin Sodium
Tyropanoate Sodium (57.4% Iodine)	Bilopaque
Diatrizoate Sodium 41.66% (24.9% Iodine)	Hypaque Sodium
Diatrizoate Meglumine 66% and Diatrizoate Sodium 10% (37% Iodine)	Gastrografin, MD-Gastroview
Diatrizoate Meglumine 30% (14.1% Iodine)	Hypaque Meglumine 30%, Reno-M-Dip, Urovist Meglumine DIU/CT
Gadopentetate Dimeglumine 46.9%	Magnevist
Iodamide Meglumine 24% (11.1% Iodine)	Renovue-Dip
Iohexol (46.36% Iodine)	Omnipaque
Iopamidol 26% (12.8% Iodine)	Isovue-128
Iothalamate Meglumine 30% (14.1 % Iodine)	Conray 30
Ioversol 34% (16% Iodine)	Optiray 160
Metrizamide (48.25% Iodine)	Amipaque

Generic Name (Iodine Content)	Trade Name
Diatrizoate Meglumine 28.5% and Diatrizoate Sodium 29.1% (31% Iodine)	Renovist II
Diatrizoate Meglumine 50% and Diatrizoate Sodium 25% (38.5% Iodine)	Hypaque-M, 75%
Diatrizoate Meglumine 52% and Diatrizoate Sodium 8% (29.3% Iodine)	Angiovist 292, MD-60, Renografin-60
Diatrizoate Meglumine 60% and Diatrizoate Sodium 30% (46.2% Iodine)	Hypaque-M, 90%
Diatrizoate Meglumine 66% and Diatrizoate Sodium 10% (37% Iodine)	Angiovist 370, Hypaque-76, MD-76, Renografin-76
Iothalamate Meglumine 52% and Iothalamate Sodium 26% (40% Iodine)	Vascoray
Ioxaglate Meglumine 39.3% and Ioxaglate Sodium 19.6% (32% Iodine)	Hexabrix
Diatrizoate Meglumine 18% (8.5% Iodine)	Cystografin Dilute
Diatrizoate Meglumine 30% (14.1% Iodine)	Cystografin, Hypaque-Cysto, Reno-M-30, Urovist Cysto
Diatrizoate Sodium 20% (12% Iodine)	Hypaque Sodium 20%

Recommended Childhood Immunization
Schedule --- United States, 1997

Age ► / Vaccine ▼	Birth	1 mo	2 mos	4 mos	6 mos	12 mos	15 mos	18 mos	4-6 yrs	11-12 yrs	14-16 yrs
Hepatitis B	HB1	HB2			HB3					HB	
Diphtheria, Tetanus, Pertussis (DTP)			DtaP or DTP	DTaP	DTP		DtaP or	DTP	DTaP or DTP	Td	
H. influenzae			Hib	Hib	Hib	Hib					
Polio			Polio	Polio			Polio		Polio		
Measles, Mumps, Rubella						MMR			MMR	or MMR	
Varicella							Var			Var	

713

Typical Radioactive Half-Lives

Radioactive Element	Half-Life
Mo-99	2.75 Days
TI-201	3.05 Days
TI-201	73.1 Hours
Ga-67	3.26 Days
Ga-67	78.3 Hours
I-131	8.02 Days
Xe-133	5.24 Days
In-111	2.80 Days
Cr-51	27.7 Days
I-125	60.1 Days
Sr-89	50.5 Days
Tc-99m	6.02 Hours
I-123	13.2 Hours
Sm-153	47.0 Hours

Lactation Fax Hotline

The Lactation Fax Hotline is a new service offered to our readers to provide 24 hour FAX-ON-DEMAND services. It is a computerized FAX service in which the user calls into the network and requests a selected set of documents. Each drug or entry is specially formatted in a professional and comprehensive format, so that users can FAX the document to any FAX number they wish, particularly to their doctor's office.

Each drug in this handbook is provided a Fax document number which is a unique number used by the Lactation Hotline. The Lactation Hotline is under constant revision, and users can request a new listing of drugs and other documents by requesting Fax Document # 100. This is a 3-4 page listing of all the drugs and other items that may be provided in the future.

The system requires a password, so users must first register for a small fee, and pay a small charge for each document sent. Users will be periodically billed for use thereafter. **For a complete registration form, call 806-356-9556 and enter ONE as your password, and the system will automatically FAX a registration form** to your FAX machine.

This service is provided so that readers can get the most current, relevant, and complete information available, and provide it to clients or physicians. Users may not copy or distribute this information, as it is intended for one user only. Presently, this service primarily contains drug information. Future changes can include almost anything relevant to users, including treatments, syndromes, meeting announcement, etc, as long as they are relevant to breastfeeding, and provide a public service.

To Register: Call 806-356-9556   Enter 1 as your password.

For Information: Call 806-358-8138.

Ordering Information

Pharmasoft Medical Publishing
21 Tascocita Circle
Amarillo, Tx 79124-7301
8:00 AM to 5:00 PM CST

Call......	**806-358-8138**
Sales....	**800-378-1317**
FAX....	**806-356-9480**

Single Copies	19.95
Shipping	3.00
Total (USA)	22.95

(Texas Residents add 8.25% sales tax)
Prices effective until April 1, 1999

Multiple Copies

1-9	Copies............19.95
10-19	Copies............18.95
20-100	Copies............17.95
> 100	Call